THE STORY OF WARWICKSHIRE CRICKET

THE STORY OF
WARWICKSHIRE
CRICKET

A HISTORY OF THE WARWICKSHIRE
COUNTY CRICKET CLUB AND GROUND
1882–1972

Leslie Duckworth

STANLEY PAUL, LONDON

Stanley Paul & Co Ltd
3 Fitzroy Square London W1

An imprint of the Hutchinson Publishing Group

London Melbourne Sydney Aucklaud
Wellington Johannesburg Cape Town
and agencies throughout the world

Set in Monotype Bell
Printed in Great Britain by
Ebenezer Baylis & Son Limited
The Trinity Press, Worcester, and London
and bound by Wm Brendon & Son Ltd
Tiptree, Essex

ISBN 0 09 119790 2

Contents

CONTENTS

Dedication

R. V. RYDER, Warwickshire's secretary for over forty years, once began to write a book about cricket, but got no further than this dedication:

To those regular spectators whose consistent support is beyond computation, and can never be repaid; whose pertinacity and ingenuity are beyond compare; whose courage laughs at locks, bolts and bars and even spikes – they who climb over the fence.

As an ardent fence-climber in my day, this dedication will do very well for me, too, for it embraces lovers of cricket the world over.

Leslie Duckworth

Dedication

❖ ❖ ❖

R. V. Ryder, Warwickshire's secretary for over forty years, once began to write a book about cricket, but got no further than this dedication:

To those regular spectators whose continuous support is beyond computation, and can never be repaid; whose pertinacity and ingenuity are beyond computation, whose tongue laughs at locks, bolts and bars and even spikes – they who climb over the fences.

As an ardent fence-climber in my day, this dedication will do very well for me, too, for it embraces lovers of cricket the world over.

Leslie Duckworth

Prologue

CRICKET ALL THEIR LIVES

'Last Munday youre Father was at Mr Payns
and plaid at Cricket and came home please anuf,
for he struck the best Ball in the Game and
whishd he had not anny thing else to do he ould
play at Cricket all his Life' – *Mary Turner, of
East Hoathly, Sussex, in a letter to her son,
September, 1739.*

Author's Preface

WILLIAM ANSELL, first secretary of The Warwickshire County Cricket Club, began his Introduction to Sydney Santall's history by saying that he did not know what an Introduction was and rarely read one. 'The Preface,' he conceded, 'sometimes gets a glance or two if I wish to know the object and purport of the writer', but as a rule he relegated both Introduction and Preface 'to that convenient category, "portions to be skipped" '.

He did, however, except historical and other serious works and as this is a history, and a serious one – though not, I hope, devoid of humour – I trust it will not be skipped if only because I feel the Warwickshire reader is entitled to an explanation of why the task of writing it should have been entrusted to a dyed-in-the-wool Yorkshireman.

The most knowledgeable man on the subject of Warwickshire cricket is unquestionably the general secretary of the Club, Leslie Deakins, who has dedicated nearly fifty years of his life to trying to make Warwickshire the finest cricket club in the land and Edgbaston the finest ground. For all that time he has been the confidant of every officer, official, player, almost every member and a goodly proportion of the general spectators, and is the repository of hundreds of stories about them. Mention a date or a name to him and you are almost certain to hear some reminiscence of the kind that ought to be in any history of the Club. He has told me a great many of them and put his encyclopaedic knowledge at my disposal, yet I know that every time he opens this book his eye will light on something that will inspire yet another recollection.

Why, then, has he not written this history? Well, time – and time alone – imposes limits on the amount of work even Leslie Deakins can do for Warwickshire, so the task has fallen to me and I can only hope that I have not left out anything which he would regard as essential to the story of his beloved Warwickshire and Edgbaston.

There are very good precedents for an association between Warwickshire and Yorkshiremen. As long ago as 1886 a meeting of the committee of the newly formed Warwickshire County Cricket Club, searching for 'ground' bowlers as they were known in those days, instructed 'that the terms be ascertained for some of the best Yorkshire bowlers for their engagement at the commencement of the season'. One of the county's first professionals, J. E. Shilton, came from Yorkshire and he has been followed by several others. Did not Yorkshire provide in R. V. Ryder, Warwickshire's secretary for many years, one of the staunchest and hardest working officials the Club has ever had, and in Ted Leyland, father of Maurice, one of the best groundsmen? It was another Yorkshireman in Edgar Hiley, chairman of The Warwickshire County Cricket Club Supporters' Association, who commissioned this book on their behalf.

Again for some reason matches between the two counties have been among the most memorable that either county has played and finally I can plead that since 1927 when I first came to live and work in the Midlands, Warwickshire and Worcestershire, especially the former in recent years, have been my adopted cricketing counties and I have spent many happy hours on their grounds.

I have not attempted a ball-by-ball account of the Club's history – though, of course, I have described the most important matches – nor will anything like all the answers to every question about the Club and its players be found here, though I hope many will be. Such a history would require not one, but many, volumes. As it is, I am very conscious that I have done nothing approaching justice to the second eleven, the Club and Ground side and the various youth teams, all sources of playing material without which any first-class club would find it impossible to survive for long, or to the men, administrators and former players, who for many years have chosen this way of giving back to the game something of what it gave to them. This, too, deserves a whole book to itself.

No one could have had greater co-operation from officers, staff and players than I have had in telling anew the story of Warwickshire cricket, which falls naturally into the eras of its three secretaries, and bringing it up to date to the end of 1972, twenty-seven years since the last history appeared.

All the information I have sought from them has been as freely given as my innumerable questions have been answered. I am most grateful for the many suggestions that have been made even when, for a variety of reasons, I have not been able to act on some of them.

Apart from them, I have been indebted to many other people for their help and for information – to the Editor of *Wisden* (without recourse to which few cricket histories would be written) for permission to make use of much material in those indispensably precious volumes; the Editors of *The Birmingham Post* and *The Birmingham Mail* for similar concessions regarding matter which has appeared in their columns, and their authors, W. E. Hall, John Solan and Michael Blair, cricket correspondents of the *Post*; W. G. Wanklyn, cricket correspondent of the *Mail*, Geoffrey Beane, also of the *Mail*, for his earlier historical researches; Mr Peter Handford, the Warwickshire Club's librarian; Mr G. M. Adams, chief librarian of The Birmingham Post and Mail, Ltd, and his colleagues, for ever-courteous help with files, cuttings and photographs; Miss Dorothy L. Richards, sister of George Egdell, a former cricket correspondent of the *Post* and co-author of the second history of the Club, for placing some of his records at my disposal; Mr Alec Hastilow and Lieut-Col. R. I. Scorer, M.C., for giving me access to their papers, cuttings and letters and other records of war-time cricket at Edgbaston; Claude Westell, former Midland cricket correspondent and dramatic critic, for his interview with Len Bates and many other recollections of Warwickshire cricket; and lovers of the game everywhere.

Finally, may I say that I have approached the task with, I hope, the sense of humility that even a guest of long standing – and especially one who has derived as much pleasure as I have from Warwickshire cricket – should still observe. It has been said that the outsider not only sees most of the game, but sees it more objectively, perhaps, than one whose county loyalties are involved. Whether that is true or not, I can only say that I have tried to be fair to every point of view and to hold the balance.

Foreword

By *Lieut-General Sir Oliver Leese Bart,*
K.C.B., C.B.E., D.S.O.

President, The Warwickshire County Cricket Club

EVERY British institution of any standing has its history prepared and published periodically. The first history of The Warwickshire County Cricket Club, after formation in 1882, was prepared by a former eminent county player, Sydney Santall, and covered the years up to 1910. Since the Club won the Championship for the first time the following year, it was rather suggested that the preparation of the history was perhaps a happy preamble to success on the field, and this was pleasantly emphasised (although the delay was a little longer) when G. W. Egdell and M. F. K. Fraser, eminent Midland sporting journalists, published their official history in 1946, for the Championship was won again for the second time in 1951.

In 1972, however, a new manuscript goes to the publishers just *after* the Club's third Championship victory. The 1972 season was probably the most successful in the Club's 90-year history to date, since the team, apart from winning the County Championship, also reached the final of the Gillette Cup and the semi-final of the Benson and Hedges Trophy.

The book will, in consequence, be of particular and immediate interest to those who follow the Club's fortunes at this time, enabling them to read of this third Championship success; but in addition it will prove a fascinating period in the history as a whole for those who, in the years to come, read the book as a comprehensive history of one of the country's leading County Cricket Clubs.

It has been felt desirable, for several years past, that the whole history of the Club from the earliest days should be reviewed, brought right up to date, embracing the works of both Sydney Santall and his successors, George Egdell and Michie Fraser, and published as one volume. In consequence, the Supporters' Association undertook the responsibility and they were fortunate in finding another Midland journalist with an innate love of cricket to undertake the task, in Mr Leslie Duckworth, formerly Assistant to the Editor and News Editor of *The Birmingham Post*, and author of several books on the game.

I, myself, have quietly contemplated the prospects that faced him and I feel there is the material here for a rather wonderful story based not only on the growth of the Club and its progress, but also in the development of its fine ground known the world over as 'Edgbaston'. I can realise from a brief assessment of the constantly changing scene in the period I have followed the Club's fortunes that there has been a splendid array of talented and characterful players, a small but dedicated body of sound administrators, regular background support from a staunch and loyal membership, as well as 'an interested public' within the County as a whole, but mainly of necessity drawn from its two great cities – and finally and more recently a powerful, and, indeed, unique, backing from the greatest Supporters' Association identified with any County Club in this country.

All this has meant development and progress down the years to the privileged position the Club now holds in the game of today, and it is therefore very much to the point that Mr Duckworth should come at this very time to record the history of the past, and that which is even now in the making, with the team finishing at the top of the County Championship Table by a wide margin in 1972. Indeed, past, present and future, it is a story well worth the writing and, if I am any judge, it will be well worth the reading.

May I, therefore, conclude this introduction by wishing the author all success in his endeavours and the Club all happiness and success in its progressive future.

Worfield
Shropshire

BOOK ONE

WILLIAM ANSELL

1882–1902

Five Men of Warwickshire

In the mad March days of 1882 Queen Victoria, as she returned to London from Windsor, survived an attempt on her life at the hands of 'a miserable looking man' (as one of the newspapers of the day described him) who pleaded hunger; a famous poet, Longfellow, died; there was talk of electric tram cars; Joachim played in Birmingham Town Hall and Vesta Tilley was in *Beauty and the Beast* at the Theatre Royal in New Street; Henry Irving revived Romeo at the Lyceum with Ellen Terry as Juliet; one of Anthony Trollope's new works, *Fixed Period*, was being serialised in *Blackwood's Magazine* ('those who admire him most will be sorry he ever began it', wrote the literary critic of *The Birmingham Daily Post*); extensions costing £500 000 were under way at New Street Station, Birmingham; and the newspapers devoted an inordinate amount of space to the departure from these shores for America of the one and only Jumbo, the great African elephant from the London Zoological Gardens, at the instigation of a showman whose name was Barnum.

It was in this month also that five men met in Leamington Spa and formed the present Warwickshire County Cricket Club. The exact date, time and place have so far defied discovery, but at least we know the names of the *dramatis personae* who took the stage in the first act which led to the creation of the county's first truly representative cricket club.

They were David Buchanan, one of the leading amateur players of the day, who on this occasion represented the Rugby Cricket Club; M. P. Lucas, representing Leamington C.C.; the Rev. G. Cuffe, Rector of St John the Baptist Church, Coventry; Col. W. Swynfen Jervis, later to be joint honorary secretary of the new club with the fifth person present, William Ansell, a Birmingham schoolmaster and then honorary secretary of the Birmingham and District Cricket Association.

To find out what brought them to this meeting, probably held at the

Regent Hotel, it is necessary to go back a little in time. Sir Neville Cardus, in one of his many delectable accounts of the game of cricket, laid it down that everything must be seen against its background, which is why, it seems to me, the first duty of the historian is to record the facts, the second to describe the circumstances in which those facts emerged and then, if possible, to interpret them in order that they may be better understood.

In other words, the history of such a body as The Warwickshire County Cricket Club cannot solely be the record of the Club viewed in isolation. It must be seen first in relation to the game of cricket as a whole and then against the general background in which it is played, for it is a living entity, made up of, and concerned with, many people over many years, and that makes it part of the social fabric. All are affected and influenced by a wider world conditioned by the changing times, so that factors which in themselves have nothing to do with cricket can affect their attitude to the game.

The prime examples of this in modern times are the motor-car – which can either make it easier for its owner to reach the ground where cricket is being played, or be the means of whisking him far away from it – and the television set which may persuade him to watch a Test at home, or look at some other programme altogether. Thus the history of the Club must also, to some extent, be a history of the times in which it exists; for the economic circumstances, the habits, customs, interests and pastimes of their day, affect it just as much as, and sometimes more than, the runs, wickets or catches the players make on the field, or the decisions reached in committee rooms.

When the Hon. H. R. Lyttelton, at the annual meeting of the Club in 1887, deplored the introduction of lawn tennis to the Edgbaston ground lest it lure strong, healthy young cricketers to play tennis instead of cricket, he was a true ancestor of the official who worries today about counter-attractions such as television, motoring, golf, sailing, or even – dare one say it? – Bingo. And the member who wrote in 1897 asking if the Club could provide accommodation for horses for those who had to travel long distances, was, in essence, posing the same kind of problem as the man who today seeks to know where he can park his car.

Perhaps it is just as well that neither of these early stalwarts lived to see the leisurely pace of the Victorian way of life so speeded up that, in the space of the three days which they and their friends would take as a matter of course to spend watching the county side at play, their descendants, less than a hundred years later, would travel to the moon and play, not cricket on that dustiest of all wickets, but a few strokes of pseudo-golf.

Probably no one can be certain just when cricket was played for the

4

very first time in Warwickshire. Rowland Bowen, the cricket historian, says* the first reference to the game in the county was in 1771, but does not give details. Even earlier, however, is a reference for which I am indebted to Dr Percy Young, the musical scholar and writer, who, researching his own subject in the newspaper files at the Birmingham Reference Library, came across the following in *Aris's Gazette* for Monday, 15 July, 1751:

> At Holte Bridgman's Cricket Ground, at the Apollo at Aston, near Birmingham, this day, the 15th Instant, will be play'd a
>
> ### MATCH AT CRICKET
>
> between Eleven of the Gentlemen of the said Holte Bridgman's Club, and Eleven of the Gentlemen of Mr Thomas Bellamy's Club, the most of three Innings, for Twenty-two Guineas: The wickets to be pitch'd exactly at Two o'Clock. The Ground will be roped out, and no Persons but the Players to be admitted within the lines. Each person to pay Two-pence for Admittance.

There were certainly matches at Rugby School for nearly a century before Santall wrote in 1910; and a game famous in literary, if not, perhaps, cricket circles, was played there in 1841. It was the first visit of the Marylebone Cricket Club to the School which, at that time, was captained by no less a person than Thomas Hughes, author of *Tom Brown's Schooldays*. He opened the School innings and scored 29 and 0. The original of Tom Brown, who rejoiced in, or regretted, the name of Augustus Orlebar, went in at No. 3, but, alas, did not improve on his captain's performance, making only 12 and 1 – run out.

Two years later, on 7 and 8 August 1843 – says Robert Brooke, of The Association of Cricket Statisticians – Warwickshire's first recorded match, against Leicestershire, was played at Coventry. According to Rowland Bowen (in an article in *Wisden* for 1963), the Wellbourne (the old name for Wellesbourne) Club in south Warwickshire, in 1826 called itself the Warwickshire Cricket Club, but later reverted to its original club name.

In November 1863, however, it changed its name to Warwickshire County Cricket Club. It was a predominantly amateur side, and not at all representative of the county as a whole, and it was dissolved after the new, more widely-based county club was established in 1882.

Undoubtedly, the best cricket to be seen not only in Warwickshire but in the Midlands at this time was played on the ground of the Leamington Club, where Victoria Park now is. The club was formed in 1848 and was taken over in the following winter by two of the best-

*In *Cricket: A History of Its Growth and Development*, Eyre and Spottiswoode.

5

known cricketers in the land: the great George Parr, of Nottingham, and John Wisden, who afterwards gave his name to cricket's Bible. They were two of the leading professionals in England and, Santall tells us, they had the ground levelled and became the sole proprietors of what was known as Parr and Wisden's Ground.

Here came all the leading amateur and professional players of the day, and teams which represented the club were as strong as any to be found in England. For instance, in the eleven which appeared for the South against the North in August 1849, were resounding names like those of Fuller Pilch, Alfred Mynn and William Lillywhite. Even so, they scored only 40 and 87, whereas the North – who included both Parr and Wisden, as well as William Clarke, the Nottingham lob bowler – made 110 and 18 for one wicket. Clarke was 51 years of age at this time and Pilch 46, but both were still formidable players. Lillywhite, when he came again the following year to play for M.C.C. was 58, but he was still capable of bowling 276 balls – they reckoned them individually then, not in overs – and taking five wickets for 80 runs.

A team playing under the name of Warwickshire, probably the Wellbourne side, met the famous I Zingari Club, which meant virtually the Gentlemen of England, at Leamington in September 1852, and scored a notable victory. True, Warwickshire had the services of Parr and Wisden, as well as Col. Swynfen Jervis, whom we have already met. They made 145 and 172, and dismissed their distinguished opponents for 84 and 69.

It would be almost true to say that in those days cricket-lovers in the county could see a better class of play – occasionally at any rate – before a true county club was established and the Edgbaston ground opened, than they could for some time afterwards. In August 1856, for instance, there was a match at Leamington between Fifteen Gentlemen and the Players, for whom appeared that curiously named cricketer, Julius Caesar, as well as Parr and Wisden, the last of whom had a great match at the Gentlemen's expense, taking eight wickets for 63 in the first innings and seven for 50 in the second. One Gentleman who distinguished himself was Mr A. Payne, whose name appears frequently in the cricket annals of these times. He was private secretary to the Earl of Stamford, at Enville Hall, near Stourbridge, and he took five for 57 and eight for 38, which, since the Gentlemen won, probably endeared him more to his master than did his secretarial services, however admirably he carried them out.

There were club grounds in the Birmingham area also, of course, but none had matches of this calibre. However, in 1861 a ground was laid in Aston Park, facing Trinity Road, and there in September was staged what has come to be regarded as a famous North v. South match. No doubt they left the turf to knit as long as they could before playing on it.

Even so, it was described by a chronicler of the time as 'terribly rough, quite unfit for cricket'. Practically all the best known professionals of the day played for one side or the other – Julius Caesar, William Caffyn, John Wisden and John Lillywhite for the North, and for the South, Richard Daft, Tom Hayward (uncle of that other famous player of the same name still to appear on the cricket scene), George Parr and J. Grundy, a well-known M.C.C. bowler of the day, whose son was later to play for Warwickshire. The South, scoring 86 and 122 to the North's 100 and 65, gained a narrow victory; but what made the game of particular interest was that when it ended the first team ever to go to Australia was chosen, for that winter. Several of the players invited declined the terms offered, however.

There was also a match between two sides calling themselves the Gentlemen and the Players of Warwickshire at Rugby School in September 1863. Among the Gentlemen was David Buchanan, who had begun as a fast bowler, left-hand, but changed his style in the sixties with such success that he became one of the best slow bowlers in the country. He captained the Warwickshire side in some of its earliest matches, and when he died in his 71st year in 1900, *Wisden* wrote of him that 'he bowled to be hit and depended for his wickets on pitched-up balls with plenty of spin on them . . . he caused far more trouble to Daft, Jupp and the rest of the players than any amateur bowler of his time.' He played for the Gentlemen at Lord's and The Oval in ten matches, and in nineteen innings he took eighty-seven wickets at a cost of fewer than 15 runs each, a low average for that class of cricket, one would have said, even on the wickets of those days.

The Professionals, who had the worst of the argument in this match, included A. Diver, coach at the School and uncle of E. J. Diver, who later played for Warwickshire. It was just after this that the Wellbourne Club changed its name to Warwickshire County Cricket Club, with the Earl of Warwick, most appropriately, as President, and Lord Willoughby de Broke, the Earl of Aylesford, Lord Leigh, Sir Charles Mordaunt and Messrs H. C. Wise and C. M. Caldicott as vice-presidents. The honorary secretary was J. M. Mordaunt and the honorary treasurer J. Greenway. The committee consisted of ten gentlemen; a ground opposite Warwick racecourse was chosen and a pavilion erected on it at a cost of £400.

Santall, who thought it a pity that the Leamington ground had not been selected, had to admit that, although the side included some very fine players, it was not representative of Warwickshire cricket as a whole. It was drawn chiefly from amateurs living in the neighbourhood of Warwick, Leamington and Rugby, with Buchanan as 'the shining light'. Supporting him as bowlers were two clerics – the clergy in those days seemed to find much more time to play cricket than they do today.

They were Canon F. R. Evans, Rector of Bedworth, near Coventry, the uncle of George Eliot, the novelist, and the first bowler to win fame at Oxford University; and the Rev. Osbert Mordaunt, curate of Handsworth and later Rector of Hampton Lucy, where he was also, strangely enough, licensee of the local tavern. He was also reputed to bowl lobs as good as, if not better than, Simpson Hayward or Walter Humphries, the reigning experts of that art. The professionals included Morley, of the King's Heath Club, described as 'the finest cricketer in the district', Lapworth, Elkington and Arnold.

The scores of county games first began to appear in the second issue of *Wisden* in 1865, in the summer of which year a club referred to as the Gentlemen of Warwickshire played matches against the Gentlemen of other counties such as Hampshire (Buchanan took fourteen wickets against them in the return match at Warwick, though we do not know for how many runs), Staffordshire, Buckinghamshire, and against teams like I Zingari, some of the games being played at Walton Hall, the home of Sir Oliver Mordaunt.

The first century scored for this club was made by Beaumont Featherstone, who lived at Maxstoke Castle, and was connected with the Dilke family. He got 104 against the Hampshire Gentlemen, playing on a neutral ground, The Oval, for what sounds the rather strange reason that there was difficulty in getting a strong Gentlemen's side to go so far away from home as Hampshire.

It is in this same season of 1865 that one meets for the first time the name of the man who is the real founder of Warwickshire cricket: one William Ansell, a schoolmaster in Birmingham, who was born near Dorking in Surrey, and whose name and most notable contribution to the Club is commemorated in the fine William Ansell stand on the Edgbaston ground.

In Aston Park, Birmingham, on 31 July and 1 and 2 August 1865, what was called the United XI – one of what in those days were known as The Two Elevens, the other calling itself All England, which gives some indication of their stature as probably the two best teams of the day – met Twenty-Two of Aston Park. The United XI had one innings in which they scored 187, and the Aston Park team were out for 92, only two men reaching double figures. Ansell was bowled by J. Grundy for 0, a very small beginning to the very great contribution he was to make to Warwickshire cricket.

The so-called County side did not make its debut at Lord's until July 1867, in a match, spoiled by weather, against the M.C.C. (for whom the Earl of Coventry somewhat unpatriotically turned out). This was also Lord Willoughby de Broke's first game for Warwickshire. Despite the fact that the M.C.C. in those days played almost every club in England – eighty-eight matches a season was not uncommon –

Warwickshire Gentlemen seemed to have some difficulty in securing other fixtures with them, though Birmingham and District Cricket Association sent a team to play them in June 1875.

It was a new fixture, but although a gentleman named W. G. Grace played, making 24 and 83, attendances were small. Nevertheless, the Birmingham side put out the lordly M.C.C. for 86, John Platts, a fast bowler, taking six for 40, and another humble journeyman, named Price, four for 45. Birmingham, who for some reason were a man short in their first innings, managed 73, of which Slack, going in first with a young professional, M. Wyre, who had already played at Lord's, scored 31. 'W.G.' had half the wickets for 45. M.C.C. were not so easily disposed of in their second innings, running up a total of 269, despite another fine performance by Platts who secured eight for 119. In their second innings – against the wiles of 'W.G.', seven for 51 – Birmingham could do no better than 82, of which Wyre made no fewer than 38.

Two years earlier, incidentally, in 1873 – and this will interest advocates of cup cricket – the Marylebone Club had offered a champion county cup for competition, all matches to be played at Lord's. It came to nothing because some acceptances of the invitations to play were withdrawn and only Kent and Sussex played in this first of all county cricket cup ties. No one seems to know what happened to the cup, but since Kent won the match by 52 runs perhaps someone should ask them to look among their souvenirs.

Little was heard of the Warwickshire side for the next few years. Sometimes they had very few fixtures, but there was still representative cricket to be seen in the Midlands. The first teams from Australia were arriving and invariably they played at least one match in the area. For instance, at Bournbrook in 1878, an Australian team led by D. Gregory, and including Boyle and Spofforth, met twenty-two of Birmingham and District and got a shock, the Rev. Osbert Mordaunt returning this analysis against them:

O	M	R	W
22	20	3	4

The veteran Birmingham sports journalist, the late W. Unite Jones, saw this match and for the benefit of possible unbelievers, commented: 'It is true there were twenty-two men in the field.' No doubt they helped to keep the Australians' scores down to 105 and 106 for 6, while Birmingham and District made 123, the match being unfinished.

Six years later, on Aston Lower Grounds in a match which finished in one day, Australia beat England by four wickets, Spofforth having even more remarkable figures than Mordaunt – seven wickets for 3 runs. The England XI included two Warwickshire players, Hugh Rotherham, member of a well-known Coventry family and one of four brothers who played for the county round about this time, and Ludford Docker, one of a trio of brothers of an equally well-known Birmingham family associated with the County Club for many years.

That winter a Warwickshire player, H. C. Maul, who was to be the first man ever to score a double century for the county, went to Australia with Lord Harris's team, but played mostly in minor matches and did little. The Australians were in the city again in 1880 and this time beat Eighteen of Birmingham and District by an innings and 9 runs.

By 1880 – and this was a particularly disastrous season from a playing point of view for the Warwickshire side, Santall tells us – a faction in Birmingham and district cricket circles was far from happy about the way cricket was developing, or, rather, not developing, in the county. Their leader and spokesman was Ansell, secretary of the Birmingham Association, formed some years previously and now consisting of some thirty-six clubs. He saw, or thought he saw, the situation very clearly and did not hesitate to speak his mind about it. In an article he contributed to Santall's history, he wrote that for many years before 'the real history' of Warwickshire cricket began in 1882 the county 'was represented by scratch teams, sometimes good, sometimes bad', but 'the old idea of a few gentlemen, with their personal friends and acquaintances, calling themselves the county was being superseded by representative committees chosen from the great cities and urban districts'. Warwickshire, in Ansell's opinion, was 'still plodding along in the old style. The huge population in and around Birmingham [it was about 400 000 then] with its young cricketers, was completely ignored as far as county cricket was concerned.'

This dissatisfaction after the 1880 season led to what Ansell called 'remonstrance' on the part of the Birmingham Association which, in fact, meant that he suggested to Col. Swynfen Jervis, then honorary secretary of the Warwickshire Gentlemen's Cricket Club, that if Warwickshire was ever to occupy a leading position in the cricket world, Birmingham's co-operation was necessary. Talent rather than titles was what Ansell was after. The offer, according to Santall, was 'gladly accepted'. It is not certain exactly when it was made, but we know that it was not until March 1882 that the historic meeting at Leamington took place.

It must have been a private gathering, perhaps over lunch, or a drink; for I have not been able to find a report in any of the newspapers, nor, apparently, were any minutes kept, or, if they were, they have long since disappeared. It was obviously a preliminary get-together to see what, if anything, could be done to improve Warwickshire cricket, and the only official reference to it that I have been able to trace is in the first of the many Club minutes so meticulously preserved at Edgbaston. This concerns a committee meeting held at the Queen's Hotel, Coventry, on Saturday, 8 April 1882, at which David Buchanan presided, and at which were also present Hugh Rotherham, of Coventry, the best amateur fast bowler of the day, who was also the originator of bogey at golf; Edward Clements, a Birmingham lawyer; A. H. Albut, about whom nothing seems to be known; Col. Swynfen Jervis and William Ansell.

At this meeting Buchanan gave an account of the Leamington gathering at which it was decided formally to start a Warwickshire County Cricket Team, as he called it. The joint honorary secretaries, Col. Jervis and Ansell, were instructed to issue circulars to the various clubs in the county asking for their co-operation, and it was resolved that a Warwickshire County Cricket Club Committee should be formed constituted as follows:

Birmingham and District Cricket Association	*4 representatives*
Warwickshire Gentlemen C.C.	*3 representatives*
Coventry	*2 representatives*
Rugby	*1 representative*

and the Committee was given power to add to their number.

It was decided that the circulars – and it is a pity there is not one extant, so far as I know – should give an account of the suggested scheme and solicit subscriptions or donations: a £10 donation to constitute life membership, and an annual subscription of not more than one guinea, which would give free admission to matches played by the county team. Lord Willoughby de Broke was invited to become the first President of the Club and various other county notabilities vice-presidents.

'Thus', wrote Ansell, 'the amalgamation of the county element and the democratic Birmingham association was completed and the Club started on its new career.' One would dearly have loved to know what Ansell said at those two meetings. It may not have been a shotgun wedding, but he was certainly the midwife of Warwickshire cricket and he was to 'boss' it for another twenty years.

The Proving Years
(1882-1893)

THEORETICALLY, Ansell thought, the plan of choosing the best teams irrespective of the station or position of the players, or the expense, and to play matches in turn on the best local grounds, was a good one; but in practice, the results, in his opinion, were bad. The first season of 1882 opened with what was really a practice match between Warwick County and Eighteen Colts of Warwickshire, played at Aston Lower Grounds, Birmingham, now the site of the Aston Villa Football Club ground, where all kinds of entertainments were held in those days. Rain delayed the start for three hours so, not surprisingly, the attendance was small, 'scarcely more than 100 people being present', according to *The Birmingham Daily Post*. The Eighteen batted first and made 95, to which G. Peyton, of the Star of Hope Club, contributed 34. In reply the Eleven scored 61 for nine wickets, of which Col. Jervis scored 15 not out and G. H. Cartland, a name destined to figure for many years in the annals of the Club, 11.

George Cartland, who was born on 30 January 1853, was a member of a well known King's Heath, Birmingham, family and by all accounts was a gifted and lovable man for whom cricket came first among recreations, though he was also fond of fishing, racing, his garden and his dogs.

His daughter, Mrs Dorothy Hamilton-Cox, who lives at Longdon, Tewkesbury, recalls fathers versus sons matches in which the former had to play with narrow bats and suffer other handicaps. Even so, Cartland overcame them so well that she remembers one occasion when her mother advanced on the field calling: 'George, *come out*. You are making too many runs.' Santall described him as 'a good batsman with a nice style'.

12

Cartland went to school at Colwall in Worcestershire and later to Exeter College, Oxford. He studied law and was called to the Bar, but did not practise long before going into business and becoming chairman of various companies, experience which stood him in good stead during his long career on the administrative side of the game.

The first match proper was against Staffordshire in the fourth annual cricket week at Lichfield in July when rain again 'somewhat disturbed the ground', as a contemporary report put it, at least on the day before the match. 'The home side went first to the wickets', the account goes on, 'and had, as a whole, to face good bowling and fielding, although a little more attention on the part of the latter, might have prevented Heath's score passing the half-century.'

Heath was A. H. Heath, one of the early stalwarts of Staffordshire both on and off the field, who had been responsible for sending down one of cricket's most remarkable overs while playing for the M.C.C. against Surrey in 1876. The first ball was a wide; the second jumped over long stop's head and went for four byes; the third knocked the batsman's middle stump out of the ground; the fourth nearly bowled the newcomer; the fifth was a wide for which two were run; and the sixth was played.

On this occasion he was Staffordshire's top scorer with 52 and thanks also to Captain Powis, 35; E. D. Crane, 27, and H. Fishwick, 25; they totalled 173 in the first innings. Warwickshire could do no better than 120, of which C. R. Durban, long associated with the Aston Unity Club and later a member for over thirty years of the County Committee, made 32. The other members of the Warwickshire side – it is not clear who led it – were H. Godson, C. Allen, A. E. Ansell, Preston, J. E. Williams, Colonel Jervis, W. H. Graham, E. A. Clark, J. Parnell and Woodward, who took six of the Staffordshire wickets, though it is not recorded how many runs were scored off him. In the second innings Staffordshire scored 132, which gave them a lead of 185, and Warwickshire had scored 10 for the loss of one wicket when rain came and left Staffordshire having the best of a drawn game.

But then came the first victory at Worcester where the home county was beaten by an innings thanks to some fine bowling by Buchanan and Rotherham, of which Santall does not give any details; and then on what should have been the second day of the return match in Birmingham a curious letter appeared in the correspondence columns of the *Birmingham Daily Post*. It was from G. Reeves Smith and Son, Aston Lower Grounds Co. (Ltd), Holte Hotel, Aston, and it was headed 'The County Cricket Match Disappointment'. The letter said that the dates for the match – the teams were not named – were fixed by letter on 19 June and then subsequently confirmed by the secretary of the Warwickshire team as recently as the 7th, luncheon having been

13

ordered for the teams in his letter of that date. Posters, the letter went on, had been put out by the clubs, but 'not having received any communication whatever from anyone connected with the teams, nor seen anyone connected with them but a scorer, we are not in a position to offer any satisfactory explanation to the public. Perhaps the secretary can give the necessary explanation.'

If he could, he did not deign to do so, at least so far as I can trace, in the columns of the *Post*, though it transpired later that Worcestershire, like Hertfordshire with whom a fixture had also been arranged, had been unable to raise a team. Indeed, from reading the newspapers no one would even have known that the Warwickshire Club had been re-formed, which argues either that the officials were very lax in publicising the new venture, or that the sports reporters of those days were a good deal less enterprising than they are today.

The *Post* cricket correspondent on 10 April had an article which ran to one and a half columns in which he speculated on the coming season – he lamented, incidentally, that there were no batsmen in his day like Hayward, Daft and Pearson, or bowlers like Wilsher, Griffith, Caffyn, Sewell and Bennett, which has a familiar ring – and devoted most of the rest of his generous space to an assessment of the visiting Australian side and dealt with the prospects of Gloucestershire and Middlesex. But not a word did his article contain about the newly formed Warwickshire side.

The county's only remaining match in 1882 was the return game with Staffordshire, played at Coventry on 21 and 22 August. Warwickshire were without their captain, Hugh Rotherham, who, for some reason not stated, was playing with Uppingham Rovers, an odd thing to be doing when there was a county side to lead, so Colonel Jervis took over the captaincy. Lord Willoughby de Broke was also included in the team, but he was recorded in the score as 'absent'!

In the circumstances, Warwickshire were fortunate to escape with even the worst of a draw, having to follow on after Staffordshire had scored 284, thanks largely to a brilliant century by A. E. Allcock and despite the fact that J. E. Williams, one of the Warwickshire bowlers, returned the following remarkable figures:

O	M	R	W
78	35	75	7

Even allowing for the fact that they were four-ball overs in those days, that represents a fair stint of bowling. Williams was also the top scorer with 29 in Warwickshire's very poor first innings of 77, and they had barely begun their second when rain began to fall and kindly drew a veil over it all.

No wonder Ansell was depressed at the end of a first season which had aroused so little interest that the Club's income amounted to only £25 16s 3d, with expenditure of £25 7s 0d – hardly the sort of surplus on which to found a county cricket club. Perhaps he felt envious of the success that attended a match between a United All England XI, captained by W. G. Grace, and Twenty-Two of Salters Cricket Club and District on their ground in Roebuck Lane, West Bromwich, at the August Bank Holiday. The weather was delightful and there was a very large attendance.

All England won the toss and scored 215, 'W.G.' being 67 not out and E. M. Grace 44. The newspaper report put it delightfully: 'The next to handle the willow was Mr W. G. Grace, whose advent into the field was greeted with cheering from all parts. The third ball from Reeves was driven by the veteran cricketer beyond the boundary for four.' The Twenty-Two side made only 98, but they improved on this in the second innings which produced 118. All England, however, won easily by ten wickets. Between them the two Graces accounted for thirty-one of their opponents' wickets.

English cricket had much more to weep about than Warwickshire's dismal beginning. The Australian tour of that year went on until late in September. At the end of August they met England at The Oval and inflicted one of the most crushing defeats in Test history, though it was not so much the margin between the two sides as the manner in which the victory was accomplished that rankled so much. When England got Australia out for 63 and led them on the first innings with 101 and then dismissed them again for 122, it looked odds on an English victory. But what a fall there was, my countrymen. This was how the *Post* of next day described it:

Amid intense excitement, at Kennington Oval yesterday, the greatest event in the cricket world that has ever happened – the match between Australia and England – ended in a well-earned victory for the colonists [*sic*] by seven runs. Little description of the details of the game is needed. The Englishmen had the match in their hands, but by timid, half-hearted batting, threw the match away . . . The chief honours went to Spofforth. The demon bowler, as he has been called, was at his best and took full advantage of the weakness of the Englishmen . . . Such a game cannot be spoken of in the usual way. It is a turning event in the cricket world and will need many defeats of the Australians before we can hold our heads up, or talk with authority of the national game.

What had happened, when the writer at last got around to telling us about it, was that Spofforth, who had taken seven wickets for 46 in England's first innings, repeated the performance, only at a cost of two runs fewer, in England's second innings, which produced no more than 77, of which Grace, with 32, scored almost half. Fourteen wickets for 90 – the demon bowler indeed.

15

No doubt William Ansell shed a tear with all the rest for English cricket, but he was not one for crying unduly over spilt milk and he had more immediately pressing things on his mind. That November the Committee met again at Leamington and discussed fixtures for the following season. It was decided to arrange matches if possible with M.C.C. and Ground, Leicestershire – whom the Birmingham Association had had the temerity to beat in a one-day match in August – and Staffordshire 'out and home', as away and home games were called then, plus a Colts' match, and games with Harrow Wanderers and Uppingham Rovers.

A list of players from whom it was proposed to choose the county eleven for the season was drawn up:

1. D. Buchanan	11. G. Mills
2. H. Rotherham	12. H. Godson
3. W. S. Jervis	13. G. Udall
4. Parnell or Packer	14. J. Williams
5. C. Allen	15. Rev. Porter
6. F. Breeden	16. L. C. Docker
7. G. Cartland	17. D. Docker
8. Rev. O. Mordaunt	18. R. Docker
9. G. Peyton	19. W. Ansell ⎱ Available only in
10. S. Talboys	20. E. W. Hopewell ⎰ August

In the spring of 1883 Buchanan was unanimously elected captain – in the early matches it seems to have alternated between him and Hugh Rotherham – and he also took on the joint secretaryship with Ansell. Colonel Jervis had resigned this position, but he was persuaded to become honorary treasurer in place of Ansell and later Buchanan assumed the treasurer's job also.

The fixture list had boiled down to five matches, M.C.C. and Ground and Cheshire being met twice each and Staffordshire once. Two games were won, two lost and one drawn, the sort of moderate success which dogged Warwickshire cricket, with occasional exceptions, for many years. The M.C.C. were soundly thrashed by 144 runs at Coventry on the Butts ground where Hugh Rotherham scored 36 and took twelve wickets for 34 runs; but the new county side's first visit to Lord's, which was not then quite the cricket holy of holies it later became, resulted in a defeat by ten wickets.

Lord Willoughby de Broke played in three matches, but scored only 14 runs, and altogether twenty-six players took part in the five games. They included Ansell, who played five innings, and Pallett, of the Aston Unity Club, who was to be one of Warwickshire's opening bowlers for several seasons.

This mediocre record and the continued lack of public support – the subscription list amounted to no more than seventy guineas – was not good enough for Ansell, but he realised that more members and spectators would not be attracted unless Birmingham, where the bulk of the county's population lived and worked, became the centre of the Club's activities. The other members of the Committee took the same view and that autumn, when the Birmingham and District Cricket Association held its annual dinner and prize distribution and unanimously resolved that a ground should be secured in the city, the case was put so strongly by Ansell that the Mayor, Sir Thomas Martineau, who presided, promised the movement his official support.

Obvious though such a step seems now, it was then by no means so simple a matter as it appeared. At the first public meeting called by the Club – the old one had been dissolved in December 1883 – at the Regent Hotel, Leamington, on 19 January 1884, when there were only thirty-one people present in addition to the honorary secretary, they were requested to 'discuss fully its prospects and the means to be adopted for the promotion of its interests'. After 'animated discussion' it was proposed that the Club should play its matches on different grounds, but an amendment was moved that in the interests of Warwickshire cricket it was desirable to establish a central county ground.

The voting was 18 to 10 for the amendment and a committee of 13 members was appointed to make inquiries and to report within two months. A subscription list was opened and the amount promised at the meeting was £48, not a figure calculated to send Ansell home rejoicing. Meanwhile the provisional committee met and decided to urge on another public meeting at Leamington on 8 March that no opportunity should be lost to secure a permanent county ground at Birmingham and that in the meantime county matches should be played, as hitherto, on those grounds in the county considered most convenient and – perhaps even more important – where most gate money could be taken.

Two reports were presented to the meeting, one of them from the provisional committee arguing that Birmingham was the right locality for a central ground because of its large population; that in all cases where county cricket had been successful it had been in such areas; that the professionals would ultimately come from Birmingham; and that a ground in the city would be in use for the greater part of the winter – the report did not say what for – thus providing a constant source of revenue. They did not call it multi-purpose use in those days, but they had the same idea.

Rugby shared the committee's view, but the Leamington-Warwick axis had its way. They argued that four-fifths of the subscriptions promised so far had come from Leamington and district and, despite the fact that Ansell pointed out that this was because all the meetings so far had been held in Leamington, and Birmingham had not had the same chance to subscribe, the words 'at Birmingham' were deleted from the resolution finally passed, which left Warwickshire as a wandering club, so to speak.

But Ansell was not a man to give up so easily and his hand was strengthened by the fact that so little interest was taken in the first three home matches of 1884 at Coventry and Rugby that the gate receipts amounted to no more than £11 3s 6d. Moreover, of the seven matches played only two were won and four were lost. Ansell would probably have been secretly pleased if his Birmingham Association team had been able to show the county side a thing or two, but the Association was beaten by 41 runs. Northamptonshire, Leicestershire and Hertfordshire were all played twice and a feature of the home game with Herts on the Coventry ground was that Buchanan and Rotherham bowled unchanged in both innings, the former taking eleven wickets for 63, a very reasonable performance for a man aged 54, and the latter nine for 27.

The hunt for a ground went on. Many sites were inspected, but usually the terms were too high. For one at Camp Hill, the site of the old Pickwick Club ground, Ansell said £20 000 was asked. They looked at the Aston Lower Grounds, but there had already been complaints about the wicket; and the side-shows, in Ansell's view, would have been insufferable. In any case, it was then in Worcestershire; ten years later Aston Villa Football Club acquired the site. Sir Thomas Martineau's choice would have been the ground then held by the Y.M.C.A. at the corner of Eastern Road and Bristol Road, but it was ruled out because of dampness and general inaccessibility. Ansell would have preferred the Wycliffe Ground in Pershore Road, with the present site of St Ambrose's Church adjoining, for football, but the ground landlord, Lord Calthorpe, declined to negotiate and instead offered a meadow of rough grazing land in Edgbaston.

In June, 1885, the Committee went to inspect it and then resolved 'that it is desirable to secure the piece of land offered by Lord Calthorpe upon a lease of 21 years for use as a county cricket ground'. After some discussion about the probable cost (estimated at £1250) of laying out, draining and fencing the ground, it was decided to adjourn and ask the Mayor to call a public meeting to arouse interest and raise the money. The Committee's view was that a 'Cricket Ground Company' should be formed to raise the necessary capital and let the ground to the Club to manage at a reasonable rental.

The meeting was duly held at the Council House, Birmingham, on 16 July 1885, among those present being Alderman Sir Thomas Martineau, Lord Willoughby de Broke and Messrs Buchanan, J. Cartland, G. H. Cartland, R. Sale, E. O. Smith and many other gentlemen who, according to *The Birmingham Gazette* report, 'were occasioned much amusement' by the suggestion of a Mr William Evans that the proposed county ground should be established at Kenilworth.

The Mayor disclosed that 'the whole of the one side of Birmingham was occupied by the estate of Lord Calthorpe, which they had first understood was closed against them because there was a feeling on the part of his lordship's agent that no ground should be let for purposes at which money should be taken'. However, they had seen Lord Calthorpe's agent, Mr Edwards, and they were able to mention a piece of land which he hoped would satisfy all requirements.

The Mayor described the land, which was in the Edgbaston Road, which led out of Bristol Road, crossing Pershore Road and running out towards Moseley. It was 12 acres in extent, which was perhaps more than was needed for cricket, but a portion of it might be made available for tennis and other recreation, and he did not believe they could procure such a large and suitable piece of land elsewhere near the town. It was about twenty minutes' walk from New Street Station and fifteen minutes' from the Moseley Station of the Midland Railway.

Lord Calthorpe, it appeared, was prepared to let this land on a lease for 21 years at a rental of £5 an acre, or a total of £60 per annum, which did not seem to the Mayor too large a sum when they considered the amount they might fairly expect to take when the ground was open. The cost for enclosing it would be £300, for draining £450, a pavilion £400 and its furniture £100, a total outlay of £1250. The Mayor thought that the gentlemen who advanced this capital were entitled to expect a fair return for their money, *but the main object should be not to make dividends but to advance the interests and position of the cricket club.*

The italics are mine because I think it is fair to stress that, whoever has been in office, this has continued to be the object of those who have guided the destinies of Warwickshire cricket, whether in the years of success or failure. As for these initial costs, how fantastically they now compare with the valuation of £712 128 placed on Edgbaston in October 1972.

Nevertheless, there were financial worries in those days just as there are now. David Buchanan pointed out that there were only sixty-seven members on the list of the County Cricket Association, now in its third year, and a deficiency at the beginning of the year of £24 had been increased to £54 with two matches still to play, figures which will no doubt bring a wry smile to the face of the present honorary treasurer who had to include in the 1971 balance sheet the record deficiency of £29 097.

Back at the 1885 meeting, a member from Leamington withdrew his proposal that his town should have the ground at a site which would have cost £140 a year, and eventually the following resolution was proposed by Lord Willoughby de Broke, seconded by C. G. Beale, and carried unanimously: 'That in the opinion of this meeting a county cricket ground should be formed for Warwickshire on the lines indicated by the Mayor'. Next a resolution was carried that a limited liability company be formed to raise the necessary funds, and a provisional committee was appointed to make the necessary arrangements.

How truly rural was the setting of the new ground is shown by the fact that it was laid down that the lessees should have power to make a temporary roadway from Constance Road to a lane shown on a map in such a manner as not to prevent cattle from the other lands gaining access to the water in the river. Assuming there were cattle there now, it seems highly unlikely that they would want to quench their thirst in the waters of the river today.

According to *The Birmingham Daily Post* of 17 July 1885, Lord Willoughby de Broke had 'expressed apprehension that the land would prove damp, as it lies low and is liable to flooding at certain seasons'. The *Post*, however, commented that 'in other respects the situation seems to be an eligible one, large enough for all requirements and easy of access to both town and country. It will be their own fault if the cricketers of Birmingham and the neighbourhood do not soon achieve for themselves a leading position in the national cricket field.'

The lessees of the new company were Lord Willoughby, G. H. Cartland and William Ansell and they were also appointed the first directors, with the Mayor and Messrs D. Buchanan, R. Williams, C. G. Beale and E. O. Smith. The Cricket Ground Company was duly registered with a capital of £3000 in £10 shares; it was decided that matches should be played under the title of Warwickshire Club and Ground; the subscription was fixed at one guinea; and the secretary was instructed to advertise for a professional bowler and groundsman and local practice bowlers.

Whether acquiring a ground, even though it could not be played on yet, provided a stimulus or not, the Warwickshire team in the 1885 season took on a new lease of life which enabled it to win twice as many matches as it lost. One of the victories, over Staffordshire at Smethwick, was particularly exciting. Warwickshire, left to get only 45 to win, lost six wickets for 15 runs, but then Lord Willoughby and Hugh Rotherham stopped the rot, as they used to say, and Warwickshire won by three wickets. Other highlights were the first century for the Club, 115 against Hertfordshire at St Albans by H. C. Maul, and the bowling of John Edward Shilton, first of the many Yorkshiremen to throw in their lot with the Club, who proved to be a fine bowler and a considerable character to boot. Against the Birmingham Association he took nine wickets for 54, which largely helped the county to win by six wickets, and he finished the season with forty-eight wickets, twice as many as any other bowler, and for only 8 runs each. The bowling generally was so good that only one team made more than 150 runs against them.

The surprising thing about the season, however, was that no fewer than thirty-six players were called on for only seven matches. Three reasons were given for this – the inability of amateurs to spare the time; the limited income of the Club, which precluded the employment of the best professionals; and – more novel – inadequate knowledge possessed by the Committee of the men's form. 'There appears to be a dearth of good run-getting batsmen,' wrote the author of the annual report for 1885, no doubt William Ansell. 'In this department of the game the county seems sadly deficient.' Nevertheless, Warwickshire, from being at the foot of the list of second-class counties, 'had sprung up to a position of second to none in the minor shires and if this form is maintained its rank as a first-class county is only a question of time'.

It was, in fact, still nine years off, but no one knew that as preparations went ahead to get the new ground ready for the 1886 season. A groundsman and caretaker had been appointed, the first man to hold the position being Frank Breeden, professional from Elstree School, Wellingborough, Northamptonshire, who was engaged at a salary of £100 a year, with the proviso that he should find his own help. From the list of his duties it sounded as if he would need it:

1. Responsibility for preparation of match and practice wickets.
2. To be generally responsible for the custody of the ground, track, buildings and plant, etc.
3. Cleaning and keeping in good order necessary washing materials, urinals, lavatories, etc., and the pavilion generally.
4. To be in constant attendance at the ground.
5. So to arrange ground work as to be able to bowl when required.
6. Wife to prepare lunches if considered necessary by the committee.

He was also asked to find his own accommodation until the pavilion was ready and for this he was allowed five or six shillings a week.

It was in the spring of 1885 that the emblem of the Bear and Ragged Staff first climbed into the Club records in a design for the county cap – dark blue with the bear and staff worked on the front in white silk. Originally the badge – not the crest or coat of arms of the Beauchamp family, the Earls of Warwick – represented a dancing bear, or a bear chained to a tree trunk for baiting, a common sight in the towns and at fairs in medieval days, according to Mr Henry Phythian-Adams, M.A., the Warwickshire heraldic expert. The device subsequently appeared in the arms granted to the county of Warwick and in those granted to the Borough of Warwick, where a demi-bear holding a ragged staff occurred as a crest. The use of the device by The Warwickshire County Cricket Club is not, strictly speaking, heraldic, Mr Phythian-Adams said, but it is a symbol expressing at once loyalty to the county and a nice sense of continuity from the past.

Sixty-three new members were elected at the annual meeting in 1886 towards the target of 300–400 it was felt would be needed in the first year of the new ground, the opening of which – on 7 June, with a two-day match against the M.C.C. – was, of course, the event of the year. Three thousand people were there to see it. Warwickshire on this auspicious occasion were captained by G. H. Cartland, later to be chairman of the Club for forty-six years, who had the honour of making the first half-century, 55, to be scored on the ground. The team included Dudley Docker, Collishaw, Bird (the only man from whom the great S. F. Barnes had any coaching), Allen, E. C. Wheeler, Shilton, Morgan, Mason, Richards and Harborne. The previous August Collishaw had made a memorable début at Lord's where, going in first wicket down for the Edgbaston Club, he had scored 77 and 39, being not out at the close of each innings so that he was batting while eighteen wickets fell.

Warwickshire won the toss and batted first, but managed only the modest total of 127, Dudley Docker being top scorer with 31, but it was sufficient to give them a lead of 17 on the first innings against a team which, although described by Santall as weak, could still boast players of the calibre of W. Barnes, Scotton and Flowers. Collishaw took four of their wickets for 10 runs. But for Cartland's 55 Warwickshire would have been in a sorry plight in the second innings when only one other player, Collishaw again, reached double figures against the bowling of Flowers, who followed his five for 32 in the first innings with seven for 34 in the second. Warwickshire were all out for 109 and the M.C.C. had made 70 for three wickets when stumps had to be drawn to enable them to catch a train. The full scores of the match have been given before, but no history of the Club would be complete without them, so here they are, this time with the complete bowling analyses, parts of which were omitted in the earlier histories:

WARWICKSHIRE

FIRST INNINGS		SECOND INNINGS	
E. C. Wheeler b Scotton	24	b Flowers	2
Shilton c Scotton b Flowers	20	b Flowers	2
Collishaw b Barnes	1	c Scotton b Flowers	18
D. Docker c Scotton b Rylott	31	c and b Flowers	8
Richards run out	1	b Flowers	0
Allen c Sherwin b Flowers	26	b Flowers	6
G. H. Cartland c Sherwin b Flowers	1	c and b Barnes	55
Mason b Rylott	1	lbw b Barnes	6
Morgan b Flowers	3	b Scotton	9
Harborne b Flowers	8	b Flowers	0
Bird (W.) not out	2	not out	0
Extras	9	Extras	3
	127		109

M.C.C.

FIRST INNINGS		SECOND INNINGS	
Barnes b Shilton	15	c Harborne b Shilton	3
Scotton b Bird	42	b Bird	5
A. E. Leathem b Harborne	3	b Mason	21
W. R. Collins c Cartland b Shilton	4		
Flowers b Collishaw	24	not out	37
F. T. Cox lbw b Collishaw	4		
Sherwin c Morgan b Bird	2		
G. H. Chandler b Collishaw	1		
L. J. Saville b Collishaw	0		
Rylott b Bird	9		
T. Bird not out	0		
Extras	6	Extras	4
	110	(for three wickets)	70

WARWICKSHIRE

	FIRST INNINGS				SECOND INNINGS			
	O	M	R	W	O	M	R	W
Flowers	42·1	25	32	5	29·2	15	34	7
Barnes	25	11	25	1	21	14	19	2
Rylott	33	17	32	2	16	6	33	0
Scotton	10	5	16	1	5	3	8	1
Leathem					2	0	10	0

M.C.C.

First Innings	O	M	R	W		Second Innings	O	M	R	W
Shilton	33	19	31	2			11	5	22	1
Harborne	22	8	32	1			2	0	10	0
Bird	19·1	7	31	3			9	2	28	1
Collishaw	10·7	6	10	4			1	0	6	0
						Mason	0·1	0	0	1

Warwickshire's membership went up to 651 during the season, partly due, of course, to the opening of the ground and partly to the first visit of the Australians to oppose the county on 9 and 10 August. The Club had spent £300 on a grandstand and seating, but unfortunately rain permitted play on only one day. Even so, 6000 people came to see the tourists. The match marked the début for Warwickshire of H. W. Bainbridge, the third we have met so far of the county's small band of long-serving members, who, as player, official and administrator was to be associated with the Club for the greater part of his life. He was top scorer with 30 out of 70, but the Australians could make only 107 and 35 for three, Shilton taking eight wickets for 55 runs in the match.

Bainbridge had been captain of cricket at Eton in 1882 and in the F.A. Cup Final of the following year he had had the distinction of representing the Old Etonians against Blackburn Olympic, the first provincial club to win the trophy. He got his cricket Blue at Cambridge in 1884 and in the 1885 Varsity match he made 101, helping to put on 152 for the first wicket, then the best opening stand for either university. Altogether he played against Oxford three times, totalling 262 runs for an average of 43, and in all he scored 449 runs for Cambridge. That same summer he also made 82 against C. I. Thornton's XI, 63 against Yorkshire (the bowlers were no less lights than Peel, Bates, Peate, Ulyett, and Tom Emmett) and 42 against an All-England XI.

So he was a batsman Warwickshire were very glad to have, though before he joined them in 1886 he played several times for Surrey. Soon they were also to have the services of the forceful Ludford Docker, who had previously played for Derbyshire, and was later to become President of the Warwickshire Club.

There was one other county match of note in 1886 when Warwickshire played Somerset for the first time. They won at Bath, thanks to some fine bowling by Shilton, and in the return game at Edgbaston they were beaten by 83 runs largely because of the bowling of a boy of 18 named S. M. J. Woods, who took twelve wickets in the match for only 57 runs. The Australians made a second appearance at Edgbaston late in September against an England XI captained by W. G. Grace. They scored 186 and 56 for two, to which England countered with 208, of which Walter Read made 97. The England side included Ludford Docker.

The 1887 issue of *Wisden* at last deigned to notice Warwickshire's existence, for they figured for the first time in 'The Counties' section:

Of the counties which are not reckoned first-class not one has brighter prospects than Warwickshire, cricket in the county having received a great impetus through the opening of the new ground at Edgbaston, Birmingham. In 1886 Warwickshire played in all eleven matches, winning four, losing three and leaving four unfinished . . . In bowling the county is particularly strong, including as it does Shilton, Pallett, Mr C. W. Rock, Mr Whitby and Mr H. Rotherham.

Rock was a native of Tasmania who was at Cambridge, and H. O. Whitby, who came from Leamington, was also at Cambridge. *Wisden* also published line scores of all the matches and the Club averages. The batting was headed by Collishaw, with 445 runs for 24·13 and the bowling by Pallett, who took thirty-nine wickets for 8·6 runs each, though Shilton took most – eighty-two for 9·15. Only twice were scores of over 150 made against the county.

Pallett, who learned his cricket with the Aston Unity Club in Birmingham, was for a number of years reckoned by some judges to be the best slow-to-medium right-arm bowler in England. Ansell thought that if he had been playing for a first-class county just before Warwickshire were promoted he would have been regarded as the finest bowler of his type in the country. Dick Lilley, later Warwickshire's and England's wicketkeeper for many years, said Pallett could make the ball turn even on a hard wicket and when it was sticky he was practically unplayable. Lilley said he never saw a right-hand bowler who could bowl both the off- and the leg-breaks with such accuracy as Pallett. When he beat the bat he usually hit the wicket.

Pallett, who began life as a teacher and for a time did secretarial work for the Club, and Shilton, a fine left-hand bowler, made as good an opening pair as any in the country. Indeed, R. V. Ryder was later to write of them that 'it is scarcely an exaggeration to say that [they] bowled Warwickshire out of second-class cricket into first-class cricket'. In all matches Pallett took nearly 1000 wickets for the county – 958 for 15·87 runs each – and Shilton 735 for an average of 14·68.

When the annual meeting came round in 1887 Lord Willoughby de Broke ventured to think they might safely say that Warwickshire were on the high road to success both financially and in a cricket sense. The accounts showed a surplus of £188 and membership had gone up from 51 in 1885 to 782. They contributed £710 in subscriptions, while £869 was taken at the gates. No less a figure than Dr Grace had said the new county ground promised to be one of the best in the country, and it was decided to give every club of any note in Warwickshire the opportunity of playing on it. As only five to seven acres out of the twelve were needed for cricket, the remainder was being put to many uses – tennis, bowls, football (a county football team was formed that summer), a county lacrosse match and even baseball.

Bainbridge, who, with Hugh Rotherham, had been on a tour of America with an amateur side which won eight out of nine matches, was both elected to the Committee and invited to captain the side in a number of matches in 1887. He had already acquired the name of 'Bags' from his sailor-like habit of hitching up his flannels while batting. Yorkshire were met for the first time this season and dismissed Warwickshire twice in one day – between 11.54 a.m. and 4.15 p.m. to be exact – for 128 and 96 in one match and for 95 and 35 for seven in the other, but otherwise they put up some notable performances.

Wisden was particularly flattering about their rout of Somerset at Edgbaston in July. After Warwickshire had scored 244 in their first innings, they dismissed Somerset for 160 and then topped their first innings score with 404, of which H. C. Maul made 141 to add to his 24 not out in the first innings. Somerset were then put out for 87, Pallett returning these remarkable figures:

O	M	R	W
11·3	6	8	6

'This,' commented *Wisden*, 'was perhaps the most directly encouraging thing for the game in Warwickshire that has ever occurred.'

Against Notts Ludford Docker batted so well, scoring 70 and 56 not out, that Arthur Shrewsbury, at this time the leading professional in England, invited him to join the team he was taking to Australia that winter. In this extraordinary game no fewer than 185 of the 370 overs bowled were maidens, and that prince of accuracy, Attewell, bowled 38 out of 61 in the first innings and 23 out of 27 in the second.

Surrey were met for the first time this season. The game, at The Oval, was spoiled by rain, but it provided one of those often remarkable instances, in which cricket abounds, in which a man emerges from obscurity, enjoys one crowded hour of glorious life and then disappears whence he came. Only one man achieved any distinction in this game – C. G. Lawton, who was making his début for Warwickshire. He went in first wicket down before a run had been scored, was missed from a hard chance when he was 42 and scored 97 of the first 117 runs made from the bat, the total having reached 120 when he was dismissed. In seventeen other innings that season Lawton scored only 207 runs, average 16·6 and then was heard of no more, at least in county cricket.

Both Docker and Maul averaged over 30 this season and three other members of the side over 20, while Shilton, Pallett and Bird all did well with the ball, Pallett taking fifty-one wickets for 12·29 each and Shilton forty-five for 19·17.

All this time Ansell had been working strenuously behind the scenes trying to persuade the cricketing powers of the day that they had a first-class county in the Midlands if only they would open their eyes. In July 1887, he took part in forming the County Cricket Council, though, not surprisingly, he opposed a motion that it should be left to the first-class counties to frame what should be the qualifications. He argued that when the rules were framed the first-class counties were the only ones in existence, but times had changed and it was now absurd to shut out the more recently formed county clubs.

Whether it was because of Ansell's campaign we shall never know, but the Editor of *Wisden*, in the 1888 edition, was constrained to comment on distinctions between first- and second-class counties. 'To embrace all these counties' – there were nineteen of them – 'in one competition would be impracticable,' he wrote. 'No summer would be long enough to play through the necessary games and the younger clubs would be altogether unequal to the financial strain.'

'Let us continue to have the meeting of first-class with second-class counties,' he went on, 'but let them be understood to mean practice for the stronger and experience for the weaker clubs. Let us retain, as now, the competition among the leading counties; and let us, if we can, encourage the weaker counties to systematize their programmes of matches among themselves . . . what I want to see done, and what I believe would be an admirable thing for cricket, would be the frank acceptance of the position by second-class counties who play a regular series of matches among themselves and who, by the common consent of those who have to compile cricket statistics, are yet below the first rank.'

In other words, the second-class counties should be good boys, content with the station to which the first-class counties had been pleased to call them, because the record-keepers did not want to have to bother doing any more statistical work. It was decidedly not an attitude to commend itself to Ansell.

It was easy, [the Editor of *Wisden* admitted], to understand the feeling of dislike with which the term second-class was regarded when that was meant to include all the teams which were not considered first-class, but as soon as it is a creditable thing for a young cricket county to be reckoned the equal of other aspiring teams that are undoubtedly good, the reproach, if it ever really existed, will pass away and people will see that while everyone cannot be first-class, the division into first- and second-class, and the systematising of the less important county matches, will bring credit and, indeed, profit, to the teams which are behind leading rank.

'Derbyshire,' the Editor went so far as to advise, 'should not in their own interests fly at such high game.' As for Warwickshire – for the first time there was a section devoted to the doings of the Minor Counties – *Wisden* said it had been a season of fluctuations, 'but there seems every prospect of the popularity of the game increasing in Birmingham. The team have only to show that they can play good cricket to get people to go and see them.' (Ah, if that were all, as Warwickshire were to find out.) 'Energetic management, a good ground and some degree of assertiveness' (an obvious tilt at Ansell) 'are no doubt excellent levers by which to advance the estimation in which a club is held, but the only real means of reaching a good position in the cricket world is to display skill in the game itself. Everyone will be glad to see the Metropolis of the Midlands taking a more important part than heretofore in the national game.'

Any reader who wants a good question for a cricket quiz might try asking 'Was there ever a winter in which two English teams went to Australia?' The answer is, 'Yes, in the winter of 1887–8.' One was led by Arthur Shrewsbury, and the other by G. F. Vernon, of Middlesex, which sustained a heavy loss despite the fact that it included such notabilities as W. W. Read, A. E. Stoddart, T. C. O'Brien, the Hon. M. B. Hawke (later Lord Hawke), Bates, Peel, Attewell and Bobby Abel. 'Such a piece of folly', was *Wisden*'s comment.

Shrewsbury's team, which included Ludford Docker, lost only two matches, though Docker himself did not have a very successful tour. In 11-a-side matches he played eleven innings, but scored only 138 runs, and in all matches, twenty-seven, he made 414 for an average of only 16·14. His scores in the one match he played against Australia were 21 and 4. The two touring teams joined forces for one match against Combined Australia, but Docker did not play in it.

There were several remarkable performances, corporate and individual, in 1888, when eight matches were played against other second-class counties, three being won and only one lost, the other four being drawn; and *Wisden* was able to refer to 'evident improvement in form shown by Warwickshire and other second-class counties'. Warwickshire finished third in the table, and *The Birmingham Daily Mail* commented that in Bainbridge, Docker and Maul the county 'possessed three batsmen of the first water' and attributed the Club's success to three causes – 'improvement in batting, unity of the eleven (at least eight players turned out regularly) and a rainy season suitable to our slow bowling.'

One of these three batsmen, H. C. Maul, distinguished himself by making the first double century credited to the county – 267 against Staffordshire, which included 40 fours, 7 threes and 48 singles. Warwickshire's total of 569 long remained a record for the county ground. Another personal record was set up by Collishaw, who became the first Warwickshire professional to make a century for the Club – 145 against Leicestershire at Edgbaston. Shilton had twelve wickets for 65 runs in this match, the last four in the second innings falling to consecutive balls, but Pallett exceeded even this against Somerset, who were dismissed at Bath for 47 and 41, leaving Pallett with these figures:

	O	M	R	W
First innings	23	16	20	8
Second innings	20	7	26	7

Against Yorkshire at Halifax, where twenty-eight wickets fell in the only day's play possible, eighteen of them Yorkshire's – they were shot out for 66 and 88 – Pallett had a match record of nine for 51, and against the M.C.C. nine for 35, though Shilton took the prize in this match for a freak first innings analysis of 22 overs, 20 maidens, 3 runs and 1 wicket. Warwickshire, thanks also to 112 from Ludford Docker, won handsomely by an innings and 187 runs. Docker's century was the middle one of three hundreds he made in consecutive innings, the others being 132 and 110 in cup matches for Smethwick.

The rain may have been good for bowlers, but not for the gates, the receipts of £432 being considerably below the match expenses of £575. Early in February the Committee had been warned that there was a deficit on the previous year of £504 and an overdraft at the bank of £453. These must have seemed as large sums in those days as the figures of today seem to us, and the chairman was duly deputed to interview Mr Howard Lloyd, of Lloyds Bank, on the matter.

The report of a committee appointed to inquire into the first of the financial crises which have dogged the Club at intervals throughout its history found that one of the heaviest items of expenditure, naturally, was for ground expenses and wages, so they immediately set about what now seem cheese-paring economies. First they recommended that Shilton should be given three months' notice, but that an engagement be found for him at Lord's if possible, thereby saving nearly £100 – or getting the M.C.C. to pay it for them – 'subject, of course, to the engagement of another professor'.* Happily someone had second thoughts about this and Shilton stayed.

Next they proposed saving £12 10s 0d on Breeden by engaging another groundsman at 25s a week, plus house, coal and gas and a lad to assist for thirty weeks at 5s a week; saving £25 on horses, which cost £47, proposing that one horse should be bought and another borrowed; and that lunches for 'professors' at county matches should be withdrawn, thereby saving £9 10s 0d.

*This was the name by which the professionals were sometimes known in the early days. They are the subject of a separate chapter beginning on p. 43.

The Club may have seemed parsimonious to its own employees, but it agreed to find six bottles of champagne for a luncheon for the Australians who appeared at Edgbaston in May, though it refused double fees to the professionals for this match and eventually decided that the financial result of the game did not justify any increased payment. It relented, however, to the extent of paying for the professionals' lunches and later agreed that a bottle of beer and a sandwich should be allowed to each gatekeeper and policeman at county matches. (There was an echo of this last decision many years later.) But the account of the caterer for refreshments to the Australians was very closely scrutinised and he was warned that in future nothing would be paid for unless it had been expressly ordered by the honorary secretary.

The match itself – two shillings admission was charged to the enclosure and a shilling for the centre stand – was a disappointment from Warwickshire's point of view, for the county were beaten by an innings and 150 runs. The Australians opened with a first innings total of 346, of which Blackham, 'prince of wicketkeepers', made 96 and Trott 83, but Warwickshire were all out in 46 overs for only 67 runs – Turner, 'the terror', and Ferris, each taking five wickets – and for 129, Ferris getting another five, which made his match record ten for 84. In the first innings only Shilton, 23, and Richards, 15, reached double figures, but in the second Maul batted well for 40, Law 37 and Bainbridge 23. Lilley made his first-class début in this match and Blackham, it seems, was greatly impressed with him after he had stumped Trott and Bonnor.

The Committee's recommendations for economies were adopted and after one North Country club had refused to release their groundsman, John Bates, of Werneth, was appointed, a decision which not only gave Edgbaston some of the finest wickets in the country, at least for batsmen, but one of the best batsmen the Club ever had in his son Len, born in the groundsman's flat which was merged into the new Committee Room during the reconstruction of the old pavilion in 1971, the year he died.

By June, thanks to economies and generous donations, notably from Mr C. B. Holinsworth, of Edgbaston, and his brother, A. B., who were two of the Club's earliest benefactors, and now offered to be one of fourteen contributors of £25, or one of seven of £50, the treasurer was able to announce a credit balance of £316. And the Committee was sufficiently emboldened to go ahead and spend £20 on the clock that was to adorn the pavilion for many years to come, a decision no doubt made easier for them by Cartland agreeing to undertake the expense.

Nothing succeeds like success. Warwickshire, more ambitious now, arranged no fewer than sixteen matches for the 1889 season, six of them with first-class counties. An indication of the varying valuations placed on opponents is shown by the fact that in May the Committee decided that talent money should be offered for the season at the rate of £1 extra per man for games with Gloucestershire, Yorkshire, Lancashire and Leicestershire, but only 10s for matches with Somerset, Hampshire, Staffordshire and the M.C.C., who were not rated so formidable opponents.

The Club had something to pay out at the end of the season, too, for they won eight of the sixteen games and finished at the head of the Second-Class Counties. They beat Yorkshire and Gloucestershire – despite the fact that there were the two Graces, W.G. and E.M., to open the innings against them – lost twice to Lancashire and once each to Yorkshire and Gloucestershire. Three batsmen, Docker, Law and Richards, each scored over 500 runs and ten members of the team had double-figure averages, with five between 28 and 20; Docker heading them all with 48·8. Of the 139 wickets taken by Warwickshire bowlers in county games, Pallett and Shilton had 103 between them and 191 in all matches, Shilton being the first Warwickshire bowler to take 100 wickets – and that was the number exactly – in a season, for 13 runs each. Pallett had 91 for even fewer runs – 11·9.

Without Bainbridge, Docker and Pallett, Warwickshire were easily beaten at Sheffield, but in the return game they had sweet revenge. At one point in their first innings they actually had eight Yorkshire wickets down for 36 – Pallett and Shilton were in very good form – but thanks to a ninth-wicket stand by Moorhouse and Whitehead Yorkshire totalled 101. Even this was too many for Warwickshire who were all out for 89, and when Yorkshire had recovered and made 199 in their second innings another defeat seemed likely; but Richards, going in first, hit a fine 120 not out, which earned him a collection of £20, plus £5 offered by a Birmingham gentleman for any professional scoring 100.

Lilley really distinguished himself in this match. Dick – how did they arrive at that diminutive from such Olympian names as Arthur Augustus unless, as A. A. Thomson said, his friends had to call him something? – had been noted by Shilton when he was coaching one evening at the Bournville Club, for whom Lilley, as an employee of Cadbury Bros, was playing. He had volunteered to keep wicket in the absence of the Bournville club's regular wicketkeeper and kept for the rest of the season. The following season, on Shilton's recommendation, he was invited to play in a Club and Ground match against Smethwick and from that modest encounter he had gone straight into the county's game with the Australians.

Now against Yorkshire he stumped four men, caught three and did not allow a single extra in Yorkshire's first innings. This was the real beginning of a career which lasted twenty-three years and twice took him to Australia, as well as to play with Indian princes, one of whom, Ranjitsinhji, gave him a gold pencil, now in the possession of the Warwickshire Club.

Warwickshire had two hard tussles, also, with Lancashire who, at Old Trafford, made 404, Sugg 91 and Johnny Briggs 78 – the latter then putting them out twice for 99 and 161, taking eleven wickets in the match for 10 runs each. At Edgbaston, however, Lancashire were got rid of for 62, the same as Warwickshire's first innings total, and although they did little better in their second innings with 85, they might well have won the match but for some brilliant hitting by Briggs again.

Financially, things were better, too. There had been considerable profit from the Australian match, as well as 100 new members with an increase of £119 in subscriptions, and for the first time the gate receipts topped £1000 – £1069 to be exact. There was also a saving in working expenses of £221. Even so, with expenses and payments amounting to £1189 there was a deficiency of £119 on county matches alone, but special donations of £473 put the accounts on the right side again and eventually there was a surplus of £120.

The football club, which had been given the name of Warwick County Football Club, was not so fortunate. It had a deficit of £100 in the 1888–9 season, but the guarantors were willing that it should be carried forward provided that the cricket committee recognised it as a liability to be paid by them if necessary.

For the first time in 1889 the Club published a printed report, listing the officers, rules, results of matches, a financial statement, fixtures and names of subscribers. It was the first Year Book, though hardly comparable with those to come later.

It was unfortunate for Ansell, still fighting the battle for first-class status, that in 1890 there was 'a sad falling off' in form by Warwickshire, as *Wisden* put it. True, Yorkshire were beaten twice, but they had a much weakened side out each time, and Warwickshire dropped to sixth place among the eight clubs which constituted the Second-Class Championship.

Curiously enough, Warwickshire did better against the first-class counties than they did against those of lower ranking, but they were put out for two of their lowest-ever totals – 27 in the first innings at Taunton against Somerset, the ultimate champions, and for 29 by Lancashire at Edgbaston.

Yorkshire were without Lord Hawke, Peel, Ulyett and Hunter in the first match at Halifax, where Pallett took seven wickets for 42 and Warwickshire won by 46 runs, and the first three of those players were also absent at Edgbaston where Warwickshire won by an even bigger margin, eight wickets.

They also put up 'a creditable fight' – *Wisden*'s phrase – against the

Australians, who were routed for 89 by Pallett (seven for 38) and Shilton, but against Turner and Ferris again, Warwickshire could manage no more than 38. Although Pallett again bowled well – he had eleven wickets in the match for 92 – Australia made 132 and then got Warwickshire out a second time for 51, so that they won by exactly their second innings total. Only five bowlers were needed in the entire match, the fifth being Cresswell, formerly of Derbyshire, who took three for 21 in Australia's second innings.

Obviously it was the batting which let the side down. Only Docker had an average of over 20, but Pallett and Shilton each took over 100 wickets. Pallett, who sent down 1065 overs and 3 balls – the Hollies of his day, obviously – had 125, and Shilton 106. Between them they took 231 of the 280 wickets which fell to the county's bowling during the summer. Shilton bowled 870 overs, so it was virtually a two-man attack.

It was a stormy season on the domestic front despite the fact that at the annual meeting Cartland had been able to report that the Club was growing stronger year by year. In 1887 subscriptions had been £678, in 1888 £797 and in 1889 £870, but they would not be satisfied, he said, until they had subscriptions of £2000 a year – Birmingham ought to furnish at least 1000 members – and until the ground was one of the best in the country for accommodation.

How dependent the counties were on the extra receipts they could obtain from matches with the Australians is shown by the fact that the first four visits by the tourists to Edgbaston brought the Club £1372, of which, however, considerably more than half had to be paid to 'the strangers', as the honorary treasurer quaintly called the visitors.

In his Introduction to Santall's book, Ansell left an account of his efforts to persuade the powers-that-be to accept Warwickshire as a first-class county. 'What constituted a first-class county', he wrote, 'no one knew. How a second-class county might rise to first-class rank, none could tell. The M.C.C., which poses as the Jockey Club of cricket, shirked the question, as it always does when the question is difficult, and so matters drifted.'

Ansell recalled how Warwickshire appealed to the County Cricket Council, which had been formed a few years earlier by Lord Harris, who, in November 1885, had called a meeting of representatives of second-class counties at Lord's, largely, one imagines, at the behest of Ansell, who first put forward the idea of promotion and relegation between first- and second-class counties. Not even the latter, eager though they were to improve their status, would go all the way with that, but they did agree to a rather pious resolution that the older counties should 'encourage the growth of cricket of the younger counties by playing home and away matches with at least one of them every year.'

Only Yorkshire, Surrey and Lancashire acted on this and it was a very poor substitute for what Ansell wanted, but eventually, following a further meeting of the Cricket Council in December 1889, a sub-committee was formed 'to classify counties and to provide means of promotion from one class to another.' Ansell was a member of it and it can be accepted, I think, that he was the principal architect of a scheme eventually adopted for recommendation to the Cricket Council which laid it down that 'the two weakest first-class counties should, in each year, play the strongest two second-class counties for right of place'.

Later, Ansell told us, this recommendation was altered by deleting the word 'two', so that only one county was involved in promotion or relegation each year. Not surprisingly, the second-class counties objected to this watering down of the original scheme and Ansell was given a brief to advocate a return to it when it came before the Cricket Council again in December 1890.

'Stormy' is Ansell's description of that meeting and even *Wisden*, noted for its use of moderate language, says it came 'to a startling conclusion'. Ansell, putting his case, said he saw no reason why the number of first-class counties might not be increased to ten or a dozen, provided a county was entitled by merit to advancement. There was a debate in which it was made very clear that the first-class counties were fighting hard for their ancient privileges, and after a long discussion Warwickshire's original scheme was rejected by 11 votes to 4.

Ansell says that the chairman, Mr M. J. Ellison, of Yorkshire, was 'ineffective' and eventually he gave his casting vote for an amendment that the Council should adjourn *sine die*. This was 'a smash-up', in Ansell's words, of the Cricket Council itself and 'a most disastrous finale', for in his view it was serving a most useful purpose and 'might, indeed probably would, have legislated much more effectively than the M.C.C. for most of the evils which have crept into the game.'

The story goes that as he came out of the meeting Ansell was inter-viewed by a reporter who asked him: 'How did you get on, sir?' Ansell, who had kept the door ajar with his heel, replied in a voice loud enough to be overheard: 'No better than you can imagine with a nincompoop in the chair and a set of idiots sat round him,' a remark which symbolised his forthright manner of speaking, but did not always endear him to those with whom he had to deal.

So that, at least for the time being, was that. It did not, of course, mean that Ansell ceased from his labours, but he would no doubt have been more encouraged if the players had strengthened his case by showing better form in the field. The season of 1891 was disastrous in more senses than one. To begin with it was a wet summer, only two matches out of seventeen were won and Warwickshire finished at the foot of the second-class counties table, which had been reduced to seven clubs through the promotion of Somerset to first-class status.

Again it was the batting which let them down, the side being put out for 31 by Cheshire, 57 by Durham and 54 by Surrey, for whom Lockwood did the hat trick at Edgbaston and took four wickets in four balls at The Oval. C. B. Fry made his début in this match, but it was not a very auspicious one, his scores being three and none not out. Altogether, it was just as well that Pallett and Shilton kept up their form with the ball, though this time neither took 100 wickets.

During July, Lilley was taken ill and did not play again that season, at the end of which the Club sent him south for his health. It was indirectly as a result of this that the name Quaife first came into the Warwickshire records, in which it was to figure prominently for over a quarter of a century. Quaife told in an article he wrote for *The Birmingham Post* in January 1951, how it all came about.

He was born on 17 March 1872, at Newhaven, Sussex, for whom he played in one match after being coached by Alfred Shaw. His first encounter with the Warwickshire players of his day was at Newhaven, where he was working in a solicitor's office, in a match against a Handsworth Wood touring team, for whom J. Ernest Hill, who had recently made his début for Warwickshire, and his brother, H. G. Hill, were playing. H.G., a slow left-arm bowler, hit his off stump but without disturbing a bail.

Quaife then recalled how he first came to Birmingham over fifty years ago. 'It was pouring with rain,' he wrote, 'and I took a cab to lodgings in the Pershore Road district . . . and I wondered whether I had made a mistake. I had come to play in a match for the benefit of Dick Lilley, who had been very ill. I was one of several young players who had been invited to play with the object of an engagement, but they engaged someone of a sturdier type, evidently forgetting that good things are often found in small parcels.'

Subsequently both he and his elder brother Walter, who had scored over 3000 runs for Sussex between 1884 and 1901, decided to throw in their lot with Warwickshire, Willie adding 'G' to his initials to prevent confusion with his brother, though, in fact, Walter was four inches taller. Although frequent reference was made throughout Willie's career to his lack of inches, nowhere had I seen it stated what his exact height was, so I sought clarification from his son Bernard, living in the delightful depths of Dorset, who also was not precise, but put it at five feet three or four inches.

The poor results of the 1891 season undoubtedly did not help Warwickshire's chances of being elevated to first-class status, one newspaper, not identifiable, commenting on 'lamentations loud and long' and adding pointedly that 'a little more modesty in pushing her claims would not have been out of place. To claim equality with Surrey, Lancashire, Nottinghamshire and Yorkshire . . . is the height of folly.'

The writer of this article said the batting had deteriorated, largely because of want of practice at the start of the season, that the fielding had been less reliable and that two matches had been lost through inability to hold catches. He suggested that, in future, April should be devoted entirely to practice at the start of the season, and that each professional, and amateur, too, where possible, should be expected to spend a certain number of hours per day in the nets. He also suggested that the engagement of one of the leading batsmen in the land as coach 'would be an expenditure wisely incurred'.

Whether the Committee read the article or not, they engaged no less a player than Arthur Shrewsbury to act as coach at the beginning of 1892, Mr C. B. Holinsworth nobly footing the bill of £50 which covered the period from 18 April until 13 May. One player at least admitted benefiting from Shrewsbury's instruction. Lilley, in his now little-known book,* wrote that,

it was an education in itself to closely observe his movements. After he had coached us at the wickets and told us how to play the various strokes, he would himself have half an hour with the bat, and so practically demonstrate what he had told us. He gave us every inducement to bowl him, and on one occasion placed half a sovereign on each of the stumps, but try all we knew, there were none of us all through the month he was with us, who were able once to disturb his wickets.

Lilley says Shrewsbury greatly improved their play and completely altered his own style. His help, he said, was most valuable in showing him how to move his feet in order to play back or forward and he found he was able to play the ball easily without any suggestion of a cramped attitude. Some of the findings of the leading professional batsmen of the day on Warwickshire's players are not without interest even at this distant date:

MR J. F. BYRNE: Should be a welcome member of your county team when he gets thoroughly into practice.

MR J. E. HILL: As a batsman well worth a place in your county team, as he hits well all round the wicket, with a good defence. Should have a fine average at the end of the seaon.

And of the professionals:

LILLEY: Only saw him take wicket once – North v. South at Birmingham last season and from that should judge him to be thoroughly efficient. Likely to obtain runs when going in late.

SHILTON: Bowled well in practice and should be useful in matches. He is not likely materially to alter his style of batting.

DIVER: It is a great pity he is not able to play for you this summer. He is a

*Twenty-Four Years of Cricket, Mills and Boon, Ltd.

very dangerous batsman, but should show a little more judgment in his batting when playing against first-class teams.

SANTALL: Should make a really first-class bowler. He has a fine delivery to puzzle batsmen, with all the break that is requisite from the off. Should he improve as I anticipate he will, he should make one of the best bowlers in England.

The Committee had already anticipated Shrewsbury at least about Santall for they had put it on record that they thought he was one of the best of the ground bowlers, and in November 1891, he was offered an engagement on the ground for twenty weeks beginning the following May. Thus began another long association with the county not to be broken for nearly half a century.

In its comments on the dismal results of 1891 *Wisden* had been optimistic enough to forecast that Warwickshire would make amends the following season and they duly did so in the most spectacular fashion possible, rising from the foot to the head of the second-class table. They won seven of the fourteen games they played, though they did not beat one of the first-class counties. Surrey, indeed, on a soft and difficult pitch at The Oval, dismissed them for only 23 in their second innings. There were four 'ducks' and no one got double figures. Lohmann, who had taken six wickets for 64 in the first innings, got another six, this time for only 17, while Lockwood had four wickets for 5 runs.

Warwickshire also lost twice to Lancashire and once to Notts, but, generally speaking, there was an all-round improvement in the batting, both Bainbridge and Lilley making centuries. Lilley and Ludford Docker played in the North v. South match in June, the latter making 24 and 43 not out.

The improvement in play was not, alas, matched by correspondingly healthier finances. At the lively annual meeting David Buchanan presented a balance sheet which showed debts of £925, with only £84 to meet them, as well as a notice from the bank that the £500 overdraft must be liquidated by the end of the month. Fortunately, at a previous committee meeting it had been decided by ten votes to three that as long as Ansell was willing to act as honorary secretary the question of a paid secretary should be deferred until the adverse balance had been paid off and income sufficiently increased to meet the proposed extra annual expenditure.

Nevertheless, when Ansell was unanimously elected secretary at the annual meeting he wanted to know if he was being elected for a period, or only until the next annual meeting, depending on whether a resolution standing in the name of Ludford Docker was passed. If this affected his position in any way, he said, then he was not at the disposal of the Club. If the Club had confidence in him, then he would accept.

Docker's resolution was to the effect that, having regard to the fact that the annual income of the Club was about £1200 and that the turn-over was some £3000 a year, its interests could best be served by the appointment of a paid secretary who would devote his whole time and attention to the business.

When as much as £700 was being paid to 'ground bowlers' someone, it was felt, should be on hand to see that they did their job properly – one member said that when he went to the ground he never saw such mis-management in any other club, but if he gave any details he was not reported – and the Club ought to be able to save £150 out of £700. The former figure was what, presumably, it was thought they would have to pay a full-time secretary.

Docker repudiated any suggestion that he was making complaints against Ansell, though he said it was no use denying that Warwickshire were unpopular with other counties. They had been accused of adopting a dictatorial attitude and trying to teach other counties the way they should conduct their affairs, and the result had been that they had been quietly snubbed. This was a theme to which other speakers addressed themselves, even Bainbridge saying there was no doubt about Warwick-shire being unpopular. He thought their mistakes had been in encour-aging outside professionals and pressing the county classification scheme. If it were possible for Mr Ansell to retire, he would do so full of honour. A left-handed compliment if ever there was one.

But it took more than this to daunt Ansell. He saw no reason for resigning and when it was charged against him that the county's unpopu-larity had been brought about through his action, his reply was that, if so, he had done his duty fearlessly. He maintained that the unpopularity arose through the acquistion of Davidson and Quaife.*

The suggestion of paying £150 for a secretary is a vivid sidelight on the salaries of those days. One speaker even thought they could get a man with a university degree for that sum, but Bainbridge doubted if they would get a good man for under £250.

The committee meeting which followed the annual general meeting had before it a letter from Ansell saying that, while anxious to be relieved of the responsibilities of office, he thought he had a duty to the large number of members who attended the annual meeting 'during what promises to be a trying time'. He placed himself entirely in the hands of the Committee and put forward a variety of recommendations about procedure at meetings of sub-committees, the appointment of a

---

*Davidson was a fast bowler who spent two years qualifying for Warwickshire and then suddenly left to return to Derbyshire, 'the act of a dishonest man', in Cartland's opinion. Ansell's reference to Quaife must have been to Walter Quaife, who had informed Warwick-shire that he had been dismissed by Sussex who had denied him the use of ground and buildings. He was asked to come to Birmingham to discuss the matter and was immediately engaged to play until the end of August 1891.

pavilion attendant, a scorer, and a chief ground bowler to be responsible for practice arrangements.

Ansell left the room while his letter was considered and when he returned Cartland expressed to him the unanimous desire of the Committee that he should continue as honorary secretary, his recommendations being referred to various sub-committees. The dispute brought another letter, this one from Dudley Docker, Ludford's brother, tendering his resignation, but the chairman was asked to interview him with a view to getting him to withdraw it and continue on the Committee. There is no indication whether he did so, but in May came two more letters, one from Dudley Docker saying that it was pressure of business which caused his resignation, and the other from Ludford, also resigning and giving as his reason his disapproval of the Committee's policy.

The chairman was asked to find out what policy it was he disapproved of and there came a further letter from Ludford Docker saying he had made this clear at the annual general meeting, but that he was willing to talk it over with the chairman, if necessary. The resignation was accepted, but happily this did not lead to a permanent breach with the Club, which he was later to serve as a very forthright president for many years.

Arrangements had been made for Shrewsbury to attend net practice daily from 12 noon until 2 p.m. and from 3 p.m. until 5 p.m. each player being asked to practise at least three days a week; but before the period of his engagement expired on 13 May there was a complaint to the Committee by both professionals and amateurs that attendance at the practice net was not satisfactory, which was hardly surprising in view of the fact that at the annual meeting the captain himself had joined issue with the chairman about the necessity for much practice. Bainbridge said he believed in it for a fortnight or so before the season began but not while it was in progress.

By September 1892, it had become apparent that at the end of the year the overdraft would reach £750 and the bank had intimated that no further cheques should be drawn unless it could be guaranteed. It was decided that there should be an immediate appeal for help to members of the public – the first of several that were to be launched during succeeding years. A sub-committee was appointed to canvass leading citizens for subscriptions and it was decided that, of all things (among others, of course), a bazaar should be held. The ever-willing Mr Holinsworth, more practical, offered to lend £250 to meet 'pressing liabilities' on condition that it was guaranteed by members of the Committee.

The appeal circular attributed the heavy loss during the season to wet weather for the Surrey match, in which not a ball was bowled – and

39

one abandoned match meant a much greater loss in those days than it does now because there were fewer games played and, therefore, fewer chances to recoup losses; an early end to the North v. South game; and cold, unseasonable weather during the matches against Notts and other counties.

There was a deficiency on the year eventually of £400, which, when added to the previous adverse balance, made an urgent appeal absolutely necessary, £1150 being needed to meet present liabilities and enable the Club to start 1893 clear of all debt. In the end the appeal realised £1167 – just enough. I have not been able, alas, to find out how much the bazaar made, but a special match Aston Villa F.C. arranged with Notts County during the winter produced £150, and at the annual meeting in March 1893, Cartland, acting chairman in Lord Willoughby de Broke's absence, was able to announce that the appeal had then realised £940.

This prompted him to remark that the Club seemed to be playing a game of see-saw, for if they had a good cricketing year they seemed to do badly financially and *vice versa*. Regretfully, Ansell observed that they had not yet arrived at the point when the general public looked upon the county Club as the representative body; if gentlemen subscribed to local clubs they thought they had done their duty to the game. Alas, he would probably have no reason to revise that opinion if he were alive today.

When asked why matches were not played in other centres than Birmingham, Cartland replied that the experiment of playing games in various parts of the county had proved 'very unsuccessful'. County matches cost £50 a day and Birmingham was the only place in which any money could be obtained; they could not get even small guarantees from Leamington or Coventry.

Despite the financial stringencies, the secretary was empowered to engage Lockwood, Briggs, J. T. Hearne, or Attewell, in that order, as coach for a month from 10 April to 6 May at terms not exceeding £25. No one could accuse Warwickshire of not going for the best. Eventually Attewell was engaged at £20 for three weeks from 12 April, compared with the £50 paid to Shrewsbury the year before, so they were spending £30 less. The Committee's generosity, however, did not extend to granting all the points of a memorial signed by most of the professionals asking for better terms in certain matches, which would have cost no more than £47, or double payment against the Australians, though they did grant permission to play a match for the benefit of the ground staff.

Whatever their dissatisfactions, no one could have complained that the players did not give of their best in the 1893 season. For the second year in succession they headed the Second-Class Counties Championship – they tied with Derbyshire with exactly the same record – *Played 8,*

Won 7, *Lost* 1, *Points* 6. It was a pity they did not meet each other for a decider.

They had a handsome win at Edgbaston over Yorkshire, the Champions, admittedly without Peel, Wainwright and Hunter, though it is doubtful if even they would have made much difference against a Whitehead in such form that in the first innings he took eight wickets for 49. All of them came in the last eleven overs for 19 runs, a feat which earned him a collection of £10.

On a bumpy wicket at The Oval, where Tom Hayward made his début, Lilley hit brilliantly for 124 out of 260. He did not go in until No. eight and batted only two hours and five minutes. Although Surrey almost had to follow-on, they won by seven wickets, Warwickshire collapsing in the second innings for 92. Surrey also beat them heavily at Birmingham where the Australians, led by Blackham, appeared twice.

The first occasion was in May against the county, who made 159 (Docker 40) and 153 (Walter Quaife, who had now qualified, 56). In all, George Giffen took thirteen wickets for 141, but the Australians, scoring 286, won by ten wickets. The second visit was in August. *Wisden* thought it 'quite a happy idea to try the Australians against a team selected from the second-class counties, but the game did not attract the public in very large numbers and unfortunately the weather was far from favourable'. The Second-Class Counties XI consisted largely of Warwickshire players – Bainbridge, Walter Quaife, Diver (who had just qualified), Lilley, Pallett and Shilton, and there were four from Derbyshire. Giffen, who was again too much for them, though Quaife made 47 and 34, took seven for 53 and the Australians won by four wickets.

There were three other particularly interesting matches in the 1893 season, in which, incidentally, not one match was drawn, which must be some kind of a record. The match against Cheshire at Birkenhead was all over in a day, Pallett and Whitehead getting them out for 67 and 39. Then W. G. Quaife made his début against Durham and began his career for Warwickshire, as he was to end it thirty-five years later, with a not-out century, in this case 102, which must be unique. Brother Walter made one also; only three Warwickshire players needed to bat in the match which was won by an innings. Finally Leicestershire were beaten by one run at Leicester in what was to prove Warwickshire's last match as a second-class county. Two batsmen, Walter Quaife and Diver, each scored over 700 runs this season and averaged 31, but no bowler took 100 wickets, though Pallett and Shilton had good support from Whitehead.

Before the end of the year Frederic Messiter, who had been honorary treasurer since the early days, intimated his intention of resigning on the grounds of ill-health, and this action, perhaps, prompted a letter from Ansell suggesting that this was a suitable opportunity for the Committee to consider anew the question of paid officials because increasing demands on his time were beginning to tell on him.

The question was referred to various committee chairmen to confer with both Messiter and Ansell, but before any action was taken Ansell and Bainbridge were appointed to represent the county at a meeting at Lord's and to support a proposal from Yorkshire that, for the purposes of classification, there should not be any distinction between counties which played home and away games with no fewer than six other counties.

Meeting followed meeting and eventually Warwickshire, Derbyshire, Essex, Leicestershire and, later, Hampshire, were admitted to first-class status and Ansell's dream had come true. It was, he wrote afterwards, 'a simple act of justice which took many years to bring about, and today [1910] a recognised system of promotion is as far off as ever. Such is the inherent conservatism of the game and such the ineptitude of its governing body.' What, one wonders, would he have said eighty years later when a system of relegation and promotion, which might have done as much to stimulate interest in cricket as it did in football, seems even more unlikely?

The change came too late, however, for Warwickshire to take part in the County Championship in 1894 when it was decided that it would consist of thirteen counties in all. *Wisden* for 1895 still referred to 'The Leading Counties in 1894' and did not mention the County Championship until the following year. The reason, they said, was that 'inasmuch as all the fixtures for the year had, as usual, been made in the previous December, it was tacitly agreed that the promotion of Derbyshire, Warwickshire, Leicestershire and Essex should not, last season [1894] interfere with the competition for the County Championship which was accordingly carried out in exactly the same manner as in 1893, each of the leading counties [Surrey, Yorkshire, Middlesex, Kent, Lancashire, Somerset, Notts, Sussex and Gloucestershire] playing out and home matches with all the others.'

In Ansell's view the inclusion of the new counties 'gave fresh life to the County Championship all over the country and public interest in the game was much wider and more keen than it had been for years'.

'The Professors'

It is perhaps opportune to take a closer look at 'the professors', as the old-time professionals sometimes used to be called. The term probably originated with the University players they coached, by whom they were doubtless regarded as another kind of 'professor' who knew far more about the game than they did. The players did not object; indeed, according to 'Tiger' Smith, they rather welcomed the description since they felt it gave them a status over and above that of merely paid servants of the Club.

When I was a schoolboy, classroom-bound during long summer days, I used to think – and still do when I have to stay indoors and work when the sun is shining – that there could be no lovelier life than that of a professional cricketer, being able to bat, bowl or field the day long in the fresh air.

The old 'pros' certainly did that, but while being referred to as 'professors' may have made them feel better, it hardly helped to fill their pockets. The early records of the Warwickshire Club – and I have no doubt those of many others – are crammed with items about their pay and conditions. Even allowing for the change in money values, a fact of which it is often necessary to remind oneself in going through these old records, it is hard to escape the conclusion that professional cricketers then were pretty poorly paid even by the standards of those days – especially when one remembers there was no pay at all for most of them in the winter months, so that one comes across request after request to be found work. It sometimes happens even today.

Winter pay was a perpetual problem even sometimes with senior professionals. Ansell once had occasion to write to Lilley warning him against playing football in the winter because of the risks of injury. To which Lilley replied: 'I can assure you I don't play because I like the game. I play because it helps me to get a living in the winter, for what I can get by playing cricket would not keep me in the winter as well. I wrote to the Committee last year to ask if they could do anything for me and they wrote to say they could not, so what am I to do? I am obliged to do the best I can for myself.'

There was something approaching alarm and despondency among many clubs in 1896 when Yorkshire, even then one of the wealthier clubs, proposed to pay their ten regular players £2 a week from September to April inclusive. The Editor of *Wisden* for 1897 wrote that the proposal 'excited a feeling of anxiety, not to say alarm. It is clear that only clubs with a large amount of money – Yorkshire's experiment will cost roughly £600 – will be able to act with such liberality, and there is a fear that young players will drift away from their own counties to Yorkshire in the hope of participating in the benefit . . . The earnings of the players have certainly not risen in proportion to the immensely increased popularity of cricket during the last twenty years, but to represent the average professional as an ill-treated, or down-trodden, individual is, I think, a gross exaggeration.'

Some players might have taken a different view. It should be remembered that these men, such as Pallett, Shilton, Collishaw, Richards, Santall, Whitehead, Quaife and Lilley, were the backbone of the sides for which they played and the clubs could hardly have kept going without them. Yet even the best of them sometimes lived a hand-to-mouth existence and not always because of their own follies and indulgences.

We have already read some of the economies Warwickshire made when faced with financial difficulties. In 1886 Shilton, opener of the attack with Pallett and a head ground bowler as they were called then, was engaged at £3 10s 0d a week for twenty-two weeks in the summer and at £1 10s 0d for thirty weeks in the winter, which, however, was reduced if he got other employment as well. For every match won he received another £1, so by comparison with some of his colleagues he was doing well. His less fortunate brother, Talbot, was engaged to assist him in laying the ground at 15s a week.

Shilton was, perhaps, the first of Warwickshire's cricket 'characters'. He had, rightly, a very good opinion of his own prowess and, indeed, it is said that he fancied himself to be irresistible, a good fault in any bowler. Asked once, 'Who is the best bowler in England?' he replied. 'Well, it isn't for me to say, is it?' His questioner then asked him who were the two best bowlers in England, to which he answered: 'Well, me and "Knack" Pallett want a bit o' beating.' He is also reported to have said: 'I reckon that me and George Lohmann could get any side out for 50.' And once when he was coaching at Warwick School and he had bowled a young cricketer named Page with a beautiful ball, the boy asked him diffidently: 'How should I have played that, Mr Shilton?' Shilton's far from modest reply was: 'Well, now . . . you should have

44

. . . you might have . . . well, to tell the truth, Mr Page, that ball was unplayable.'

Not recorded, alas, is his comment on the member who, after he had bowled his fastest and best at him in the nets, rewarded him with two-pence. One of the best stories about him was told by Unite Jones, the old Birmingham sporting journalist. Warwickshire were having a very tight match with Yorkshire. Defeat was staring them in the face, eight wickets being down for 53. But Shilton was not down-hearted. 'Well, there's no one out of any importance,' he told Bainbridge. 'There's me and Knack [Pallett] here and here we're going to stop.'

And stop they did. Shilton's excessive patting of the pitch annoyed Lord Hawke, who naturally regarded it as time-wasting – how the wheel was to come full circle at Edgbaston years later! – and said: 'Come on, Shilton, get on with the game.'

But Shilton was a Yorkshireman, too, and was relishing the situation more than most. 'It's all right, my lord,' he said coolly. 'This isn't Warwickshire versus Yorkshire, it's Yorkshire versus Yorkshire and I know all the Sheffield tricks.'

'And the pair', Unite Jones reported, 'were still scratching about at half past six.'

Shilton used to be known as 'Lord Warwick' because he was often seen driving round in a hansom cab. There were three things he loved – batting, bowling and talking.

On occasions the old 'pros' were treated almost as lesser breeds with-out the law. Lilley, who was not exactly the office boy, was once rebuked by the secretary, on the Committee's orders, for writing an 'impertinent' letter declining to accept the terms offered to him, and tell-ing him that his request would not be considered. When a number of the players dared to engage a solicitor to act for them in their financial negotiations with the Club, they were told that the circumstances of the case 'do not justify the interposition of a legal firm between themselves and the professionals of the Club in negotiations for engagements' and the Committee declined to discuss the points raised except directly with the players themselves.

This was during what might be called 'the Edgbaston mutiny of 1890'. It first came officially to the notice of the Committee at their April meeting when Ansell reported the receipt of the letter from the solicitors who wrote that they had been consulted by Shilton, Law, Richards and Collishaw about the terms offered them by the Club, of which no details were given. The players, the letter went on, were unable to agree to them 'and they are all determined to hold together in this matter and demand from the Committee an engagement for the whole of the season at first-class county terms, namely £5 a match with £1 extra for a win and £1 additional for each innings of 50 runs and each hat trick performance; and £1 extra in out matches where the team travels over 100 miles'.

The players contended that although they formed the backbone of the county team they were worse off than the Club and Ground professionals of other counties. 'Some of our clients', the solicitors' letter went on, 'are in good situations and unless they receive better pay the remuneration from the county does not recompense them sufficiently for the loss of business and wages which they sustain in playing for the county.' The letter added that their terms for the match with the Australians would be £8 each, as all other counties paid their professionals extra for matches versus the tourists.

After the Committee had declined to deal with the solicitors, a sub-committee was appointed to see the professionals, and eventually the recommendations of the Finance Committee that the first-class pay in first-class matches should be £5 a match with £1 extra for a win, £1 for 50 runs, £1 for a hat trick, £1 for a win in Leicestershire, Somerset and Essex matches and 10s versus Cheshire and the M.C.C., were adopted. One shudders to think what the headquarters of cricket would have thought about being rated so low, though doubtless it took just as much effort on the part of the players to defeat them as it did any other team. It was also agreed that the players who took part in the match against the Australians would be given £10 each and that they should be invited to the annual dinner, 'the understanding being that the professionals pay for their own drinks'. No reckless pushing of the boat out here.

In 1887 it had been agreed that the pay for professionals for 'every night out' – and that did not mean what it sounds like – should be increased from 7s 6d to 10s, but they would not get far on that even in those days and six years elapsed before there was even a slight improvement. Then in 1893 most of the professionals signed a memorial on pay in County, Club and Ground matches and a benefit match for the staff which suggested, first, that in Worcestershire, Shropshire, Dublin University and North and East Riding matches, they should receive 10s 6d a day and all expenses paid to professionals engaged on the ground, and in the case of men not on the staff £1 1s 0d a day and expenses; second, that in county matches away from home fees should be paid on the second day of the match and in home matches immediately they ended; third, that all professionals playing for Warwickshire against the Australians should receive double pay; and fourth, that the players should have the use of the ground for two days before the end of August to play a match for the benefit of the ground staff.

The Committee went into a huddle to consider this and emerged from it the following month having worked out that Point One would cost the Club £47 5s 0d and that funds did not permit them to agree to it;

Point Two was granted as far as was practicable; on Point Three it was agreed only that professionals should be paid first-class pay and that if the match was a financial success there was a promise of a bonus. The following season the Committee conceded that professionals' pay in all matches should be £5 for three-day games and £4 for two days with 'the usual extras'.

There were other occasions when the Committee seemed to be treating its professionals rather like naughty children. For instance, in May 1889, some articles appeared in one of the newspapers which alleged that there was discontent among the Warwickshire professionals about the terms on which they were engaged and the amount of their fees. One by one, Pallett, Lilley, the two Birds, Cresswell, Whitehead, Law and Shilton were called in and asked if they were dissatisfied, or had spoken to the Press, and all denied having done so, or that they were unhappy.

It must be admitted that sometimes players did, indeed, behave rather like wayward infants and then the Committee saw fit to lay down rules and regulations for them. This happened in 1887 after Grundy had been brought before the Committee for some unspecified misdemeanour, and was told that he would not be required again that season and that unless he reformed he would not be engaged for county matches the next season.

This led to further action against the professional staff following the complaints of slackness already mentioned. Breeden was given three months' notice and then re-engaged at the same salary, but on weekly notice only, and his duties were clearly set down in writing (one would have thought this would have been done when he was first engaged at the same time as his more domestic chores); a printed notice stating the hours that he and all the other ground bowlers were expected to bowl was placed in the pavilion and the professionals' room for the guidance both of them and the members.

Breeden himself was expected to play or umpire in Club and Ground matches whenever required to do so, with the alternative of dismissal if he refused, and he had also to arrange his ground work so as to be able to bowl from 2 p.m. to 4 p.m. daily (but not, presumably, on Sundays – that heresy was not to come until many years later) and he was to have charge of the nets during that time. Shilton was also to bowl from 4 p.m. until 6 p.m. and from 6.30 p.m. until dusk, during which time he would be in charge.

Professionals were not to be allowed in the pavilion at all except during the lunch time, when partaking of lunch, or when specially sent for; the evening bowlers were expected to play in at least six Club and Ground matches if required and a bowlers' time book was to be kept by the gatekeeper. All this may well have been justified, but there were other occasions, no doubt forced on the Committee by the need for economy, when they seemed to be taking advantage of a player.

For instance, in August 1901, Hargreave declined the Committee's offer of an engagement for the following season at £92 and asked for a renewal of the old terms – £3 10s 0d a week in the summer and £1 10s 0d in the winter. It was pointed out to the Committee that the terms of his first engagement were higher than those now offered because, during the period he was qualifying, he was not in a position to earn match money and, moreover, because the £1 10s 0d in winter was in lieu of employment the Club had not been able to find for him.

The Committee, however, would not increase its offer and later in the year Hargreave asked to be engaged at £92 a year and employment at £1 5s 0d a week, or £105 without employment. The Committee merely renewed their original offer of £92, provided he kept his qualification intact. That was on 4 December and in the meantime Hargreave asked permission to offer his services elsewhere if he failed to get increased terms. He did not get them. On 1 January 1901, the Committee decided to keep the offer open for only another seven days and at their next meeting on 5 February it was reported that Hargreave had accepted the offer. Compelled to do so might have been a more accurate way of putting it.

At other times, however, the Committee could show impulsively warm-hearted generosity. I have already mentioned that when Lilley fell ill he was sent away to the south of England; when John Bates, the respected groundsman, became dangerously ill in February 1897, the honorary treasurer engaged a night nurse for him, and when his doctor pointed out that several alterations should be carried out to make his flat more free from damp and cold, the Committee, their consciences pricked, perhaps, decided that every assistance should be given and spent £24 12s 0d on various alterations.

The plight of an individual player could move the Committee to sympathy, but it was usually a different matter altogether when general principles were involved. At the annual general meeting in 1892, the chairman, George Cartland, condemned a player who had left to go to Derbyshire when for two years Warwickshire had been paying him while he qualified, but said nevertheless that there must be 'a sort of free trade in professionals' and that a man must have the right to take his labour to the best market.

This provoked Lord Willoughby to interject 'No, No'. Cartland then remarking that their noble President said not, but he was afraid he was a very ultra Tory if he thought so, a remark greeted with laughter.

It was not altogether surprising, perhaps, that some players ended their days in straitened circumstances, not to say penury. In a few instances, this was undoubtedly due to their own failings, among which an addiction to what used to be known as 'the demon drink' ranked high. Not that they were able to imbibe all that much on the wages they were paid, even though beer was cheap in those days; it was their admirers who were often the danger, so much so that in 1890 Ansell thought it necessary to appeal to the public not to treat professionals to drinks.

Warwickshire, said Ansell, had as steady a lot of young fellows as ever stepped on to a cricket field. They were not of the loafer class, but worked hard at one trade or another when not playing cricket. People fancied that when they bought players a drink they were doing a kindness; in reality they were doing a grave injury. One of the best bowlers had said to him not long ago: 'Drink, sir, why I could swim in drink! I wish they wouldn't give me drink. I wish they'd give me the money.' It was a remark almost paralleled years later by S. F. Barnes, who said he could have drowned in drink.

'I wish they'd given me the money.' It was a sentiment most of his fellow professionals would have agreed with. There was what seems to have been an unnecessarily complicated system of payments in those days – it is not always simplicity itself even today. Sometimes players were paid for a summer season, usually of twenty weeks, or a winter season as well if they were lucky enough to be on the ground staff. This was a basic wage in case they were not selected to play. If they were chosen, they were also paid match fees, but for every match they played they had to make a return payment to the Club to compensate for what they had already been paid in basic salary.

Players were also sometimes engaged on a match fee basis only but guaranteed, though not always, a certain number of matches. These depended very much on a man's form, as, indeed, did all engagements, and very often, too, his behaviour on and off the field was taken into account. Here, for instance, is a Match Committee report on professionals' pay from the minutes of 1893:

Name	Terms	Winter pay	To act as coach in schools	County pay
DIVER	£3 10s per week for season	None	Yes	1st Class
QUAIFE	£4 per week for season	£1 a week	Yes	1st Class
MAJOR	Agreement lapsed – engaged verbally at £2 10s a week for season	None	Yes	Same as our own men
BATES	£1 12s 6d a week, house rent, coal, gas	Same as summer	—	—
PALLETT	£90 per annum	Same all year	—	—

Cresswell, Lilley and Santall, with whom there were no agreements at this time, were all paid £2 10s 0d per week, per season, but no winter pay. This entry was followed by a note on Shilton to the effect that he was engaged for all matches until the end of 1894. If he failed to keep

E

up his form, a vote of three-quarters of the members of the Committee was required before he could be dropped and Shilton had to attend to give an explanation.

Coaching, of course, was a very useful way for professionals to augment their incomes, as it still is, and there was also talent money which varied according to the financial fortunes of the Club and was allotted at the end of the season. This, too, was often a matter of dispute between Club and players, and there was one year, 1898, when a new system was introduced with the aim of improving on the existing system, as it was thought, 'and especially of stimulating professors to win matches', when the Quaife brothers, Pallett and Whitehead all complained that it had been forced on them contrary to their wishes. They suggested equal division according to the number of matches they had played, instead of a sliding scale of £2 a man for first-class matches won, 10s for second-class matches won and the rest to be apportioned by the Committee on the recommendation of the captain at the end of the season.

The total amount involved at this time was only £10 – it grew considerably in later years – but the Committee would not yield and temporarily withheld the money. Even small amounts were of considerable value to the players in those days, but it was not always a desire for more money which actuated them. Professional pride also entered into it, as W. G. Quaife, by then one of the Club's best players, demonstrated in 1903. Under the win and talent money scheme then in operation he gained £10 for win money, but only another £1 7s 6d for talent money – perhaps a reflection of his slow play – which he asked to be allowed to return. He said he had no desire to be disrespectful to the Committee, but he did not care to acknowledge so small a sum as a recognition of his performance in 1903 – he had scored 807 runs with an average of 38·56, but had bowled only forty overs and taken two wickets for 159. Hargreave, too, joined in the complaint.

The Committee's view was that the new system was acceptable to the majority of the players, but some men suffered a loss compared with the old system and this year the losers were two of the most deserving players – which one would have thought was a very good reason for not adopting it, but for devising a scheme under which the most deserving were most rewarded. Instead, a small sub-committee was appointed to look into the matter and to try to work out a better system. In the meantime, the secretary was instructed to pay Quaife's cheque into the Club account. One hopes he got the money – and a little bit more – eventually.

It was Quaife, incidentally, who first broke the one-year engagement barrier which up till then had existed in the Warwickshire Club. One can understand the reason for its existence – the fear that a player might lose his form, or his health, and that the Club would be saddled with responsibility for him; the instability of their financial situation with no large reserves to draw upon. Even so, one marvels at the risks they sometimes ran of losing a key player by refusing the terms he wanted, though it has to be remembered that first-class clubs were few in those days, that it took three years to qualify by residence for another club and that there were no lucrative jobs to go to in the few leagues that existed. It took Quaife several years, even when he was a senior professional and a player of England rank, to get an engagement for more than one year at a time from Warwickshire and eventually he asked for, and got, one for five years, a revolutionary departure from practice for Warwickshire. Quaife was a man not easily put down and, like Barnes, he stood firm for better conditions and for the dignity of the profession. He was usually behind any move for better pay and conditions made by the Warwickshire players. Today, he and Barnes would have been the shop stewards of cricket, or at least leading lights of the Cricketers' Association.

In the circumstances, it is not to be wondered at that players set great store by their benefits, though not a few of them showed they could not be trusted to handle considerable sums of money in ways from which they would derive the greatest good. Conscientious clubs, of which Warwickshire can fairly be said to have been one, were concerned about the future of their players. As long ago as 1898, Cartland, presiding at an annual meeting, said he would like to see the proceeds of benefit matches devoted to the permanent benefit of the player instead of them being given to him in a lump sum.

He had no doubt been influenced by the unhappy outcome of the very first benefit Warwickshire ever granted – at the end of June 1895 – to Shilton, the man, Ansell said, who had, perhaps more than any other, done something for Warwickshire cricket. He had been allocated the plum match of the season, against Yorkshire, and Ansell said they intended to make a big effort, 'if not to place him exactly in a position of competence, at any rate to enable him to live comfortably for the rest of his life'. How sadly mistaken he was.

When Shilton submitted the names of some players he hoped would play in the Warwickshire team, the Committee, lacking previous experience in organising a benefit, asked Ansell to ascertain the practice of other counties with regard to financial arrangements. Unfortunately Shilton was not in the best of health at this time – he suffered from asthma and bronchitis – and on 21 May the Committee decided that he should be presented with £7 10s 0d on condition that he spent it on a visit to Torquay, half to be paid in advance and half on completion of the visit. Subscriptions were invited for the benefit fund.

By 19 June, however, the Committee was forced to have a discussion about Shilton's position 'he being in prison for debt'. Fortunately he was freed in time for the match, though it must be doubted whether he was really fit to play. Much rain fell before the game and Bainbridge took the bold course of putting Yorkshire in to bat, though he doubtless felt that a worse fate might be to face their bowlers on a wet wicket. His courage and wisdom were rewarded, for Yorkshire were dismissed for 163, Pallett and Santall taking nine wickets between them. Shilton, put on last, no doubt for sentimental reasons, bowled only four overs, one a maiden, for 10 runs and no wickets. He did not bowl in the second innings and when Warwickshire batted he went in last and made none not out. Warwickshire, with 253, got a useful first innings lead, but then Yorkshire recovered to 378 for four and Warwickshire had made 130 when the match was drawn.

This was Ludford Docker's last match for the county and it turned out to be Shilton's also. Soon afterwards he applied to the Committee for funds to enable him to revisit Torquay 'to recruit his health', but in view of the many charges on his benefit fund no decision was reached. The whole matter was referred to a special committee, which took counsel's opinion because of legal complications arising from the fact that Shilton, it seemed, had been made bankrupt in 1886, had not obtained his discharge and was in debt to various people to the extent of £600 to £700. It appeared that he had induced some of his creditors to postpone proceedings against him on the grounds that the money he got from his benefit would enable him to meet their claims. Shilton himself had also collected considerable sums and the total amount in the honorary treasurer's hands was only about £230.

It was not until February 1896 that the situation was at last clarified. A statement then showed receipts of £515 and payments of £99 for match expenses, £190 to creditors and £224 to Shilton. However, the Club's official list gives his benefit total as £500, so, presumably, the Club made up the amount. When he wrote thanking the Club, Bainbridge said of him that though he might have made mistakes in his time he was a thoroughly keen and enthusiastic cricketer and a good trier to the last. When he died three years later at the age of only 42, *Wisden* commented that he 'will always be remembered as one of the players who did most to bring the Warwickshire eleven to the front'. He was not the only Warwickshire player to die at a comparatively early age. Cricket was not, on the whole, a long-lived profession at that time.

What happened to Shilton may also have influenced Lord Hawke, for in November 1899, he wrote to other counties suggesting a meeting to discuss investing benefit money by the management committees of the clubs. After divided opinions had been expressed in the Warwickshire Committee, Bainbridge was appointed the Club's delegate to the meeting. Some members were in favour of benefits being granted only if the county authorities had power to invest the proceeds, a viewpoint of which others strongly disapproved on the grounds that the proceeds of a benefit should become the absolute property of the player. The meeting took place in December and a resolution was passed strongly expressing the view that counties should reserve direct control over the investment and disposal of all benefit matches.

When Pallett had his benefit in 1897 there was even a proposal that as 'he had not satisfied the Committee that the money would be put to judicious use', they should decline to make any grant to the fund. This was defeated, but only by six votes to four. Nevertheless many of the players did agree to let the Club invest their benefit money. Even for the best of them there were so few of what are now called fringe benefits that cricket was an extremely precarious profession. And even such 'perks' as there were cost the player money. When Pallett went to coach the boys of Malvern College, 5s a day was docked from his ground wages, as was usually the case with outside engagements. It cost Lilley and Hargreave, both senior professionals, £15 each to secure their release from having to bowl at the nets.

There was another revolt about pay and talent money in 1906 which got a mention even in *Wisden*, which did not usually concern itself with such matters. The Committee decided that in future when a player was engaged in a county match his ground staff wages should be stopped and that £100 should be the maximum for a ground staff retaining fee, subject to reductions at the rate of £1 a match. The players were then asked to agree to rates of payment of 25s a week in winter (32 weeks) and 40s in summer (20 weeks), £1 per man per match to be deducted when playing a home county match.

Santall, Baker, Charlesworth, Moorhouse, Kinneir and Weldrick were all offered engagements on these terms, but it was decided that Field, Smith – 'Tiger' Smith – and Whittle should not be engaged on the ground staff, but that engagements should be found for them if possible, either at Lord's, or with local clubs 'at no cost to the county club'. All sorts of what now seems undignified haggling went on over terms for 'Tiger', largely, so far as one can tell, so that Warwickshire would not have to pay overmuch for his services, although they needed them. There is an entry in the minutes for 23 August 1907, which reads:

Smith, E. J. £1 weekly during winter if willing to work (or 10s weekly if no employment found): £2 weekly during summer and farm out at Leamington if possible, or elsewhere, failing which on ground staff.

Even allowing for the dry secretarial jargon – especially 'farm out' – this reads like a very inhuman entry, though it should, of course, be remembered that for two-thirds of the year the Club had no income and made no demands on the player who was free to earn another living if he could find one. At one time Smith wrote asking Warwickshire for a letter stating that they had dispensed with his services so that he would have been free to apply elsewhere, as well he might, but the Committee refused on the ground that they were willing to help him in obtaining a club engagement. Happily 'Tiger' had many happier memories of his treatment by Warwickshire than that.

There must have been some publicity about all these proposals for at the September meeting of the Committee the Press were rebuked for inaccuracies. All the same, all six players interviewed declined the terms – £80 less £1 per home match. They asked for £90 and the Committee agreed to this 'if necessary'. Finally a compromise of £85 was reached and it was agreed that Field should be given a trial in the spring and, if fit to bowl, should be engaged on similar terms.

These increases, it was stated, would cost the Club £90 in 1906 and £30 in 1907. Perhaps if the Committee could have brought itself to have been a little more generous, the players might have reacted to the incentive by trying harder, the county might have won more matches and that in its turn might have meant more members in particular and more spectators generally. Always the emphasis seemed to be on not giving the players incentives to do better, or even rewarding them when they did, except grudgingly. At the end of this particular season there was no talent money to be distributed because the accounts were likely to show a deficit of £800. Quaife and Santall protested, of course, but to no avail. The Club always argued that its rates of pay were as high as, or higher than, those of the majority of first-class counties, which was the reply the players once got when they applied for increased pay for away matches; but I doubt if they got any comfort from that, or from the rather tactless statement Cartland made at one annual meeting when he said that both men and ladies would rather see a strong amateur team like Worcestershire than a side composed almost entirely of professionals such as Warwickshire unfortunately was now. 'The presence of amateurs', he said, 'kept the professionals together, prevented friction and tended to produce better performances.'

Slowly but surely the professionals struggled to better themselves, but it was hard going. As early as 1857 there had been formed The Cricketers' Fund Friendly Society. It was reorganised in 1864, with Lord Harris, who did much to improve the lot of the professional, a leading figure. Even his name, however, could not soften some of the hard heads and hard hearts which ruled at Edgbaston in those days. When the Society wrote asking for support, the Committee at first proposed that it should send three guineas – but this was later reduced to two.

No doubt if William Ansell were alive today, he would say that if the Warwickshire Committee of those days had not most carefully watched the pennies the Club might not have survived and he would have been right. It must also be stated that the over-riding impression left after reading about the old 'professors' is that, despite their financial worries, most of them were happy men who played cricket primarily because they loved the game and not for what they could get out of it. What a pity they cannot come back and see the Edgbaston of today, with its ample dressing-room accommodation, the playing equipment, the television set, the physiotherapy unit to minister to their aches and pains, the Indoor School for practice and coaching, the parking spaces for the players' cars. The old-timers had only bicycles to ride on.

First-Class Company
(1894–1899)

WARWICKSHIRE began their first-class career as if they had deliberately set out to show the powers-that-be how utterly wrong they had been in denying them their rightful status, and the counties they had not had the opportunity of meeting what worthy opponents they had been missing. In the very first fortnight of the 1894 season they trounced Notts at Trent Bridge by six wickets, Surrey at The Oval by seven wickets and Kent at Edgbaston by eight wickets. This was splendid form which they were able largely to maintain so that they lost only two of the fifteen first-class matches they played and only three of the twenty-two games they undertook in all, the most ambitious programme of fixtures they had ever arranged.

Their success 'set all the cricket world talking', commented *Wisden*, which added that it 'had been achieved by thoroughly good all-round cricket, the batting being wonderfully consistent, and the bowling of Pallett, Whitehead and Shilton being often most destructive and the fielding on nearly all occasions being smart and accurate'.

No fewer than seven of the batsmen averaged over 20 and Ludford Docker, with 37·20, had the best average of any amateur in first-class cricket. Pallett had a brilliant season, with seventy-nine wickets for only 11·69 runs each, and he finished sixth in the first-class averages, only Pougher and Tom Richardson of regular bowlers being above him. In all matches he took ninety-nine wickets for 13·19, and Whitehead ninety-one for 15·86.

It was Whitehead, a leg-spin bowler, who could also turn them from the off, and had been a schoolboy prodigy with Kings Heath, who was largely responsible for those first three wins in the merry month of May. His part in those early games has been rather overlooked because

56

in the very first match of all against Notts (during which, incidentally, there was a snowstorm), J. Ernest Hill, who happily survived many years to become the county's oldest cricketer and died only in 1963, scored the Club's first century in the first-class game. Despite Warwickshire's success, it was the only century made for them during the season.

Warwickshire batted first, with Walter Quaife opening the innings with Bainbridge and brother Willie at No. four, but they could give only a moderate start. Hill came in sixth and stayed for four hours and a half in making his 139 not out, Warwickshire totalling 351. Notts could not cope with Whitehead, from whom they found it extremely difficult to score at all. No fewer than 24 of the 41·4 overs he bowled in the first innings were maidens and only 47 runs were scored off the other overs while he was taking eight wickets. Notts were all out for 149 and followed on, but they did better in their second innings with 275. Whitehead's two wickets this time cost 98 runs, 20 of his 53 overs being maidens. Diver's six for 58, according to Santall, represented more wickets than all the rest of his career in county cricket put together. Warwickshire hit off the runs they needed for the loss of four wickets.

Against a full-strength Surrey side at The Oval, including seven England players – Abel, Hayward, Maurice and Walter Read, Lockwood, Brockwell and Richardson – Whitehead took another eleven wickets, eight for 39 in the first innings and three for 89 in the second. He opened the bowling – there was no bowing down to the twin gods of shine and seam in those days – and Surrey were got out for 98 and 207. Warwickshire's 242 in the first innings made their eventual victory an easy one. It was the first time Warwickshire had beaten them and it was Surrey's only defeat that season. The match also marked the début of 'a promising colt' from Peterborough who had been playing for Northants as an amateur, one Sydney Santall. He scored 18 runs and took one wicket for 30 and five for 51, a very encouraging start to one of the longest careers in the county's history.

Willie Quaife has put it on record that as he went in to bat, brother Walter was coming out, dismissed by Tom Richardson. 'This chap's very fast', said Walter as they passed, 'don't lift your bat high at the start.'

'Fortunately', said Willie afterwards, 'I took his advice. His first ball was a yorker which I stopped dead in the crease. I went on to make 92, which gained me a permanent place in the team. It was a glorious start [to the season] and newspaper reporters hinted "The Champions are coming".' They were rather a long time about it, but Willie remembered his brother's advice about back-lift so well that in later years Neville Cardus, after referring to him as 'the formidable W. G. Quaife, most notorious of stone-wallers', said it was 'almost beyond the powers of science to get him out on a hard wicket under six hours'.

Against Kent it was Pallett who took the honours – seven for 13 and six for 65 – and before the month was out he had fourteen Essex wickets for 100 runs. Warwickshire had another first win against Derbyshire at Edgbaston, again very largely as a result of some devastating bowling by Whitehead – seven for 41 and five for 17 this time – and Lilley stumping Derbyshire's last man with two minutes to spare. Although it was a draw, there was also a fine match with Yorkshire at Sheffield. Bainbridge had two half-centuries in this game and Ludford Docker 38 and 85 not out.

The South Africans were here on a tour which proved a financial disaster. Perhaps because Warwickshire had attained first-class, though not yet Test, status, Edgbaston was allotted two matches with them. One was abandoned after the county had had the best of matters and the second drawn.

On the administrative side, the M.C.C. got round to defining the first-class counties – 'those whose matches with one another, with M.C.C. and Ground, with the Universities, with the Australians and such other elevens as shall be adjudged "first-class matches" by the M.C.C. Committee. There shall be no limit to the number . . .' Hitherto the sporting papers of the day had usually decided which of the 'big six' – Yorkshire, Notts, Lancashire, Surrey, Middlesex and Kent – should be awarded first place, but now that there were thirteen clubs to choose from it was decreed that at the close of each season the Committee of the M.C.C. would decide who were champions. No county was eligible unless it had played six home and away matches, one point being awarded for each win, one deducted for each defeat and unfinished games being disregarded. The county which, in finished matches, obtained the greatest proportionate number of points would be reckoned Champion County. Simplicity itself. How much more needlessly complicated has cricket – and much else besides – become.

Warwickshire wanted Hampshire included, thus giving eight home and eight away matches, and they were admitted the following season, 1895, in which Warwickshire arranged ten home and ten away games. They took an even more important decision – to advertise for an assistant secretary at a salary of £100 a year, as well as a scorer 'to make himself generally useful'. The assistant secretary would devote his whole time during the summer to the work of the Club under the supervision of the honorary secretary and the honorary treasurer.

In due course the Committee interviewed six candidates – Messrs Newey, Ryder, Bishop, Dowler, Ellis and Grigg – and after some discussion it was unanimously resolved that Mr H. A. Newey, of Station Road, Gravelly Hill, Birmingham, be appointed at the salary announced, subject to one month's notice on either side, but the notice from Mr Newey not to terminate during May, June, July or August – for obvious reasons.

The 'Mr Ryder' was of course, R. V. Ryder, later to serve Warwickshire for fifty years, but this time rejected, he told us in an article he wrote for the Egdell-Fraser history, because at 22 he was considered too young. One year later, when Mr Newey left, he was back again and this time he stayed.

Reading through the old minute books from 'the towers of Ilium' that are the Edgbaston of today, one can easily get the wrong impression that these early times were the dowdy, fuddy-duddy days of the ground's history, but then, as now, there was always something, some improvement, under way, just as there is today, even if not on the same scale. Warwickshire's great misfortune has been that neither then, nor now, was there the public worthy of it and that, in the post-war years especially, the enterprise of the administrators has not always been matched by the performers in the middle, home side and visitors – but especially the latter – alike.

The first pavilion, as we know, had been erected in 1885–6 at a cost of approximately £400; now a sub-committee was appointed to consider enlargements and alterations to it. The Committee considered it was essential to provide further accommodation for Bates as well as the members – it was considerate of them to put the groundsman first – and in due course produced a scheme for proper accommodation for him either in the pavilion, or by building a cottage adjoining. They also provided for a large Committee room and offices; a dining-room; a bar; accommodation for ladies; extensions to the professionals' quarters – all at a cost of a mere £750, plus furniture and fittings at £250, total £1000. Just by way of comparison, the alterations to the centre pavilion carried out in 1971 have so far cost £40 000 and it was estimated that a complete new building, which had to be deferred, would have cost £500 000. Times and the value of money change.

One other decision, possibly of even greater importance to the future of the Club, was taken this season. A small sub-committee was appointed to look out for young cricketers and with the power to engage 'an old professor' whose duty it would be to visit the park and club grounds in search of likely lads. It was the beginning of the never-ending search for talented youth without which no club can continue to exist.

It was a pity that 1894 did not rank as a year in the County Championship, for Warwickshire had a better record then than in their first year proper in 1895. In 1894 they had won six and lost only two Championship games and at the annual meeting they were rather strangely reported as having finished third in the list of second-class counties; since they could not take part in the County Championship proper, as they were entitled to do, the second-class competition was the only one in which they could be placed.

In the Championship in 1895 they won the same number of games, but lost four more than they did in 1894, yet finished joint sixth with Middlesex and Essex. On that basis they would have been very near the head of the table had they been able to compete in higher company in 1894. With the exception of 1901, sixth was to be the highest position they would occupy for sixteen years until they won the Championship for the first time in 1911.

After 1895 came the years the Egdell-Fraser history described, rightly, I fear, of 'undistinguished mediocrity' as far as performances on the field went. In 1896 they dropped to 12th place and then it was 7th, 9th, 7th again, 6th, 5th, 6th, 7th for three years in succession, 6th and 9th. Then for three seasons they plumbed the depths, 12th, 12th and 14th, before rising to the heights of 1911.

These years were roughly what might be described as the Ryder–Quaife régime – the former in administration and the latter on the field. They were two of the dozen or so key figures there have been in the history of the Club. On the administrative side have been William Ansell, George Cartland, as chairman, with Ryder as secretary, followed by H. W. Bainbridge, Dr Harold Thwaite, C. A. F. Hastilow and Edmund H. King, with, of course, Leslie Deakins as general secretary. They were, perhaps, matched on the field by Quaife, Lilley, Santall, 'Tiger' Smith, Foster, Wyatt, Hollies, Dollery and M. J. K. Smith.

Quaife's name has been one to conjure with in Warwickshire cricket, as Ryder's was, from the turn of the century until nearly the thirties. For twenty-two out of the thirty-two seasons he played for the Club he scored over 1000 runs, averaging 50 or over seven times, and if he never set the Rea on fire with the speed at which he made his runs, he was consistency itself. He was the anchor man of Warwickshire's batting for a quarter of a century and more, just as Wyatt was between the wars, and sometimes it was not altogether their fault if this crushing responsibility did not always sit lightly on their shoulders. What Warwickshire's batting would have been like without them on many occasions is too depressing to contemplate.

These were also the years of what came to be known as 'the beautiful Edgbaston wickets', laid down with loving care by John Bates, the groundsman, to whom in this spring of 1895 – 20 March – was born a son in the bedroom under the bell-tower of the old pavilion, later to become a committee room and converted only in 1971, though the bell still remains. He was christened Leonard Thomas Ashton, but was to be known to all and sundry thereafter as Len, and he was to become one of the loveliest batsmen who ever graced any ground.

There are two Warwickshire players I particularly regret never having seen. One is Frank Foster and the other is Len Bates. Bates was sometimes criticised for lack of concentration (which one might well expect to find in a man addicted to reading the classics at odd moments, even, it is said, on the field) and for inconsistency, and there was, perhaps, a will-of-the-wisp quality about his play, to judge from all accounts, but anyone whose batting could rouse Maurice Leyland to such an expression as ' 'E played too pretty' must have been very well worth seeing.

But his career is to come – it is his father with whom we are concerned at the moment and the wickets he created. What bowlers, who watered them with their sweat and tears, thought of his handiwork is a subject for painful conjecture. In Bates's time bowlers had to be content with the wickets that God and the groundsmen sent them, though it is true that if they had hearts as big and flesh as willing as, say Tom Richardson – and later Frank Field and Harry Howell – they could still be overcome, as the Surrey man showed, for instance, in the return game in 1897 when he took six for 80 and five for 74 and Warwickshire were dismissed for 163 and 211. This was after Surrey had piled up 568. Warwickshire had no Richardson and, indeed, their great need at this time was a fast bowler.

One unfortunate result of these perfect batting wickets was the large number of drawn games they tended to produce. For instance, of the first seven games in 1895 four were drawn, all through heavy scoring. The other three were lost and Warwickshire did not win a game until the middle of June. In the opening match of the season against Essex no fewer than 1013 runs were scored for the loss of only twenty-five wickets.

The batting was certainly strong enough – Warwickshire were the only county side not dismissed for under 100 – and they had three players who scored over 1000 runs in county games alone: Quaife, Bainbridge and Lilley, the last named showing so much improvement that *Wisden* began to write once more about great wicketkeeper-batsmen.

Even at 47, W. G. Grace was a great draw at Edgbaston in June for he had completed his 1000 runs in May and it was 23 July before anyone got him out for less than double figures. It is said that those who saw it long remembered A. C. S. Glover's leap in the air for joy when he got 'W.G.' out. Glover's leg-spin bowling was not regarded very seriously, but he took some useful wickets. (One of them was J. T. Brown's who, on his return to the dressing-room, was asked by one of his team mates, 'What were it, Jack?' And Jack replied: 'She were a fair rainbow'.) Incidentally, Glover is believed to have been the first player to have used a towel for wiping the wet ball. The match receipts were £559 – and what club would not be pleased to have that amount from

61

a county match today? Warwickshire did well to contain Grace to 43 and 11.

Against Lancashire they could not prevent Johnny Tyldesley, in only his second match, from making 152 not out, the first of the many big scores he, as well as other members of his family, were to make off the Warwickshire bowling down the years. Jack Hobbs, Percy Holmes, Herbert Sutcliffe and, in recent years, Roy Virgin, of Somerset, were other batsmen who developed a pronounced partiality for it.

Nevertheless, Santall bowled so well in the return match with Lancashire at Liverpool, where Warwickshire beat them for the first time in the matches between the clubs, that his captain recommended the Committee to grant him £2 as extra talent money. Santall took one for 26 in the first innings, but in the second his figures were:

O	M	R	W
30·2	14	36	5

which one would have thought would have been worth £2 of any-body's money, but opinion in Committee was divided, the majority tak-ing the view that 'it would create a dangerous precedent', something they had a horror of doing in those days.

Astonishingly enough, I have not been able to find any minute which says in so many words that in 1895 Rowland Vint Ryder was engaged as assistant secretary of the Club, though we know from his own writings that this was so. Ansell had been re-elected honorary secretary, although he said he now regarded his work as ended, but from now on Ryder was increasingly to be the administrative power in the land. Cer-tainly after 1902, when Ansell finally retired, Ryder *was* The Warwick-shire County Cricket Club. Committees might take decisions, but he was the man who largely influenced them and carried them out.

He was born at Wetherby in the East Riding of Yorkshire on 1 March 1873, but he spent most of his early life in Staffordshire assisting his father in a printing and newspaper publishing business. As a young man, he played a good deal of cricket and twice turned out for Stafford-shire. When he came to Edgbaston there was no other clerical staff, no telephone and not even a typewriter, though he did have some assis-tance later, first from H. A. Mason and then before the First World War from Walter Round. Even so, one would have thought that Ryder would have been overwhelmed with work, but he still found time to play a great deal of Club and Ground cricket, also appearing once or twice for the county side, though not in Championship matches, as well as supervising the net practice on occasions.

'Unhurried leisure', he has told us, 'was the keynote of the game and, for most of the time, of its organisation in my early days. Cricket had fewer rivals; there were plenty of interested people to enjoy this popular pastime . . . Fixture-making culminated in a visit to Lord's in December where the silk hat and the frock coat were *de rigueur*. Most matches started on Mondays and I may say that many of my Sundays were far from days of rest . . . I often spent Sunday in a hansom cab trying to find someone to complete the team. The telephone then had no place in team collection. I imagine my Committee regarded it as a luxury. We even worked the first Test Match without the help of "this sometimes blessed invention".'

Ryder later recalled an occasion in 1896 when one Warwickshire player, T. S. Fishwick, made his début largely because his name caught the secretary's eye as he was reading the morning paper just after having been informed that J. E. Hill could not play against Derbyshire. It was a happy chance – Fishwick, belatedly invited to fill the gap, made top score of 55.

Two years later Warwickshire were so hard pressed to find a team because so many of the amateurs were away shooting that the secretary was commanded to proceed to The Oval in the highly unusual role for him of captain, but he persuaded a friend to take it on and Charlesworth, though he would not qualify until the following May, was pressed into service. Wrote Ryder many years later: 'Murder will out, you see, even after thirty years.'

There was much work to be done before that eventful Test in 1902. When Ryder arrived the Club had negotiated another 21-year lease with the Edgbaston Estates on the same terms as before; the Committee were haggling about what they regarded as the excessively high tenders for the new pavilion – the lowest was £1027 and ultimately they had to settle for £1374, £120 in excess of the estimate; and there was Shilton's benefit to arrange and, eventually, sort out. But there was one good omen – a profit on the year's working, though it was only £60.

If for nothing else, the season of 1896 would have been memorable for just one match in May – that against Yorkshire at Edgbaston, which produced a record, which still stands, of the highest innings, 887, ever played in county cricket. In modern conditions it is almost certain that it will never be exceeded. Until I began the research for this book it had long been a mystery to me – and to other Yorkshiremen of my acquaintance – why the county, for which winning at cricket was the be-all and end-all of the game, should go on batting for so long that they did not leave themselves sufficient time to be certain, as far as one can be certain of anything in cricket, of getting Warwickshire out twice and gaining a victory which could have made all the difference to their chances of winning the County Championship. As it happened, it did not do so, otherwise even such a powerfully influential and dominating figure as Lord Hawke might well have heard a few strong words from the Yorkshire committee.

One says this even allowing for the fact that, at the time, a declaration could be made only on the third day of a three-day match, or in a one-day game. Yorkshire could always have thrown their wickets away as soon as they thought they had enough runs and, on the face of it, it looked as if they over-estimated the strength of their own bowling rather than under-estimated that of the Warwickshire batting. But was it as simple as that?

Yorkshire batted for nearly the whole of the first two days of the match, their innings not finishing until 6.20 p.m. on the second day. Every Warwickshire supporter has that score printed indelibly on his memory and I apologise for reproducing it again, but it is part of the Club's history, albeit a painful one, and cannot very well be omitted:

YORKSHIRE – First Innings

The Hon. F. S. Jackson c Law b Ward	117
Tunnicliffe c Pallett b Glover	28
Brown c Hill b Pallett	23
Denton c W. G. Quaife b Santall	6
Moorhouse b Ward	72
Wainwright run out	126
Peel not out	210
F. W. Milligan b Pallett	34
Lord Hawke b Pallett	166
Hirst c Glover b Santall	85
Hunter b Pallett	5
Extras	15
Total	887

The bowling analysis makes even sadder reading for Warwickshire eyes:

	O	M	R	W
Santall	65	9	223	2
Ward	62	11	175	2
Glover	30	1	154	1
Pallett	75·3	14	184	4
Quaife, W. G.	8	1	33	0
Bainbridge	6	1	17	0
Hill	3	0	14	0
Lilley	6	1	13	0
Quaife, W.	9	1	18	0
Diver	10	1	41	0

Only Law of the Warwickshire team did not bowl and Pallett's four for 184 in such an innings must represent his finest sustained performance. And do not forget they had only one ball throughout the

The President: Lieut-General Sir Oliver Leese, Bt, K.C.B., C.B.E., D.S.O.

Top left: H. C. Maul, one of the leading amateurs during the formative years of the Club. He toured Australia and was the first Warwickshire player to make a double century, though not in a first-class match.

Top right: David Buchanan, one of the founding members of the Club – he was at the original meeting in Leamington – and a leading player in the earliest days. He was the first captain and also acted in the first year as joint honorary secretary with William Ansell.

Bottom left: G. H. Cartland, scorer of the first half-century ever made on the Edgbaston ground, in the match against M.C.C. to mark its opening, and chairman of the Club for nearly fifty years from 1885 to 1931.

Bottom right: Hugh Rotherham, the Club's second captain from 1884 to 1886, and a noted fast bowler.

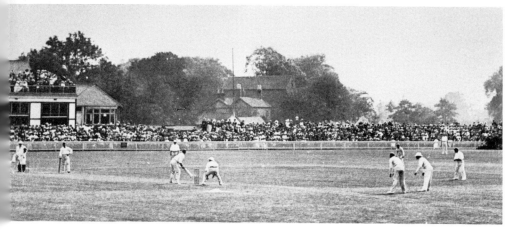

Top left: Ludford C. Docker, President 1915–30, and noted for his outspoken comments on the game.

Top right: Lord Calthorpe, President 1907–08. The Club's association with his family dates back to the earliest days.

Bottom: One of the earliest photographs taken of the Warwickshire ground at Edgbaston during the match with the Australians in 1899. The pavilion still occupies the same site.

H Pallett (seated) and J. E. Shilton, Warwickshire's first regular pair of opening bowlers who, R. V. Ryder said, 'bowled the county into first-class cricket.'

Opposite top left: A. A. Lilley, an impression by A. Chevallier Tayler, of Warwickshire's and England's wicket-keeper of the 1890's and early 1900's.

Opposite top right: The date this photograph of A. A. Lilley was taken by H. W. Thomas and the publication in which it appeared are not known, but it was probably about the turn of the century. 'As a wicket-keeper,' said the caption, 'he has certainly few if any superiors at the present time.'

Above: Hanging in the pavilion at Edgbaston is this photograph of the England team which met Australia in 1902 in the first Test Match ever played on the ground. It has been said that this was the finest team which has ever represented England on the cricket field. Back row (left to right): Hirst, Lilley, Lockwood, Braund, Rhodes and Tyldesley (J.T.). Front row: C. B. Fry, F. S. Jackson, A. C. McLaren, K. S. Ranjitsinhji and G. L. Jessop.

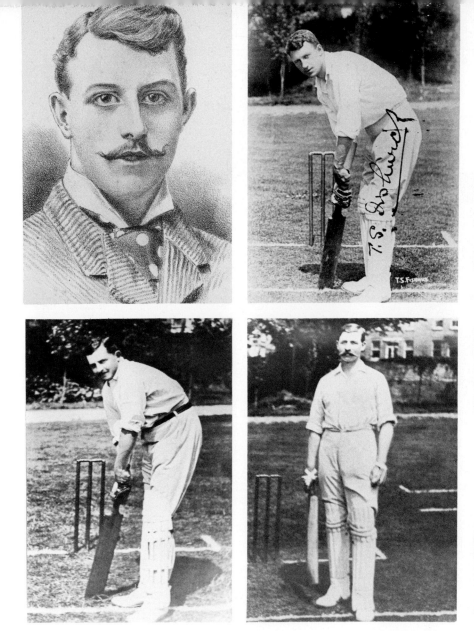

Top left: An artist's impression of J. Ernest Hill, who scored the first century for Warwickshire in 1894 after the county had been admitted to first-class company that year – 139 not out at Trent Bridge. He died in 1963 at the age of 96.

Top right: T. S. Fishwick, who shared the captaincy with H. W. Bainbridge in 1902 and again with J. F. Byrne in 1907.

Bottom left: A. C. S. Glover, captain in 1908 and 1909.

Bottom right: J. F. Byrne, captain from 1903 to 1906. He then shared it for another year with T. S. Fishwick.

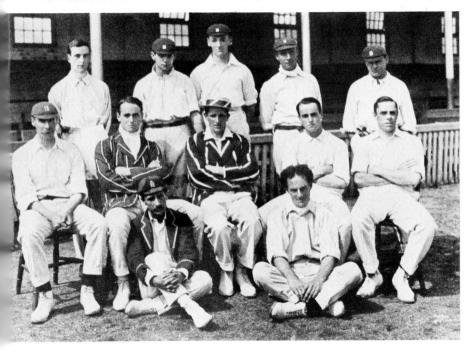

Top left: Percy Jeeves, whose death during the First World War after he had shown great promise as an all-rounder, was a great loss to Warwickshire cricket.

Top right: Sydney Santall, all rounder, coach and first historian of the Club.

Bottom: The County Champions 1911. Back row (left to right): W. C. Hands, E. J. ('Tiger') Smith, J. H. Parsons, C. Charlesworth, S. P. Kinneir. Front row: S. Santall, F. G. Stephens, F. R. Foster (captain), G. W. Stephens, F. Field. Seated on the ground: W. G. Quaife, C. S. Baker.

Above: William Ansell who played the leading part in founding the Warwickshire Club and was its first honorary secretary.

Opposite top left: F. R. Foster who captained the Club from 1911 to 1914 and led the team to its first County Championship in the first of those years. In the opinion of many unquestionably the most brilliant all-rounder the Club has ever had.

Opposite top right: Going out to bat for Warwickshire, W. G. Quaife, whose name in the early part of the century was synonymous with that of the county for whom he scored nearly 34000 runs.

Opposite bottom: Three Warwickshire players – F. R. Foster, Smith and Kinneir – were in the M.C.C. team which went to Australia in 1911–12. Back row: Kinneir, Smith, Woolley, Barnes (S. F.), Iremonger, the scorer, Vine and Strudwick. Middle row: Rhodes, J. W. H. T. Douglas, P. F. Warner (captain), F. R. Foster, T. Pawley (manager), Hobbs and George Gunn. Front row: Hearne (J. W.) and Hitch.

Opposite top left: Curly-haired C. Shaw Baker as he was in 1905 and a selection of his drawings and newspaper cartoons above which speak for themselves.

Opposite top right: G. W. Stephens, captain in 1919, the very difficult year after the First World War.

Opposite bottom left: Frank Field, a great-hearted fast bowler.

Opposite bottom right: A 'tiger' behind the stumps – E. J. Smith in his heyday as a player.

Above: R. V. Ryder, William Ansell's successor in the office of secretary, but the first to be a paid official of the Club. For nearly fifty years, from the first season after it achieved first-class status, until almost the end of the Second World War, his was the principal guiding hand in Club affairs.

Opposite: Championship Celebration Dinners. Dinners to celebrate the winning of the County Championship in 1911 (above) and 1951 (below). Both were held in the former Grosvenor Room of the Grand Hotel, Birmingham.

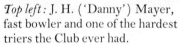

Top left: J. H. ('Danny') Mayer,
fast bowler and one of the hardest
triers the Club ever had.

Above: The Recorder. George C.
('Chicko') Austin, scorer for the
First XI from 1911 to 1963 and
associated with the Club in all for
nearly sixty years.

Left: Canon J. H. Parsons, M. C.,
Hon. C. F., who celebrated his
seventieth birthday in 1960 with a
spell in the nets at Edgbaston to
keep his eye in so that he could
coach the boys of his parish.

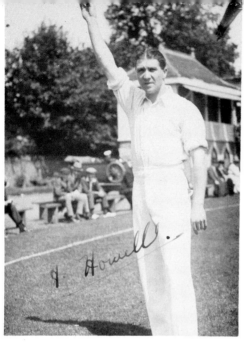

Top left: Harry Howell, a fine fast bowler, who took over 100 wickets in six consecutive seasons from 1920 to 1925. He was a native of Birmingham.

Top right: Norman Kilner, one of the many Yorkshiremen who have found cricketing homes outside the borders of their native county. He did Warwickshire much good service.

Bottom left: No more graceful batsman ever stepped on to Edgbaston's turf than L. T. A. (Len) Bates, who was born in the old pavilion, – his father was groundsman for many years. Maurice Leyland, whose father was also groundsman at Edgbaston, said of him once: ''E'd 'ave played for England, yer know, but 'e played too pretty.'

Bottom right: George Paine in his heyday as a slow left-arm bowler.

Sir Charles Hyde, Bart., President from 1931 to 1942.

innings – 274·3 overs. According to Ryder, 'it was still in excellent shape and condition at the end of the innings' (it was made by Duke and Son), a good deal more than can be said for most modern cricket balls to which bowlers seem to draw the umpires' attention every few minutes. Lord Hawke later had the ball cut in half and mounted on an inkstand.

It is said that at the end of the second day when he bowled F. W. Milligan, Pallett turned to his nearest colleague and said that was the first ball he had made turn in the match. Commented Ryder: 'The mind of John Bates, our groundsman, had indeed triumphed over matter.'

Only five byes in an innings of such magnitude tells more plainly than anything else could who was the best wicketkeeper in the land. No doubt Lilley found the pieces of wet sponge he wore inside his gloves, which he considered a purer and better protection than the raw beef favoured by some other wicketkeepers, a particular boon and a blessing in this match which he does not even mention in his book. It was form which earned Lilley a place in all three Tests against Australia and an illuminated address from the Club.

The Yorkshire amateurs – Lord Hawke, F. S. Jackson and F. W. Milligan – were staying with Cartland and legend has it, and I hope it is true, that after the first night there was no champagne with their dinner (though his daughter doubts it), and probably the Committee regretted the £10 9s 6d they had voted earlier for the expenses of a dinner to the Yorkshire team.

I doubt very much whether George Hirst approved of such goings-on, but he did his best to make up for Yorkshire's use of so much time by taking eight wickets for 59 when Warwickshire batted. W. G. Quaife, going in first wicket down, carried his bat for 92, but Warwickshire were all out for 203. They followed on a mere 684 runs behind, but they had lost only one wicket when stumps had to be drawn. It was the first important game in which four separate hundreds had been made in an innings and almost certainly the first in which four bowlers each had more than 100 runs scored off them.

Not surprisingly, Lord Hawke was widely criticised for having allowed the Yorkshire innings to continue for so long, though I think *Wisden* let him off lightly by this comment: 'No doubt Yorkshire did not need so many runs to win the game and as a general rule any action which tends to lessen the prospects of a game being brought to a definite issue is to be deplored. In this particular instance, however, an exception may be made inasmuch as the Yorkshiremen had not only the opportunity to make history, but the additional spur of trying to beat a record held by their Lancashire neighbours.'

And there, one imagines, lies the clue to the mystery. There had been a dispute between the Yorkshire and Lancashire executives because

Yorkshire, instead of arranging their home fixture with Lancashire for the Bank Holiday as usual, preferred to meet the Australians at Sheffield, and dates for the annual games between the two counties were not agreed upon until so late in the afternoon of the secretaries' meeting at Lord's that there remained no suitable vacant dates for the first match of the season between them. As a result one of the most important matches for both of them had to be decided on what were, practically speaking, the very first three days of the season. Yorkshire won – as eventually they did the Championship, with Lancashire second – but no doubt it left some ruffled feelings.

The season before, Lancashire had run up the previous record innings total of 801 against Somerset, the match in which MacLaren made his then individual record score of 424. So I have no doubt that when Lord Hawke saw how well the Yorkshire innings had begun at Edgbaston he decided to carry on and see if Yorkshire could do their traditional enemy one in the eye. Thus Warwickshire, if this theory is correct, were innocent victims of an old feud, but, as a Yorkshireman, one still blushes to think of that ridiculously protracted innings. It would have been poetic justice if that draw, which could so easily have been a win, had cost them the Championship.

Yorkshire's new record total also beat the 843 made by the Australians against the Past and Present team of Oxford and Cambridge at Portsmouth in 1893, which had ranked as the highest score ever made in a first-class match. All three totals have been beaten several times since, the record, for those who like to wallow in statistics, now standing at over 1000–1107 by Victoria against New South Wales at Melbourne in 1926–7.

By way of a footnote, one of the last survivors of that match, William Ward, a left-handed bowler from Smethwick, who opened Warwickshire's attack with Santall and who continued to visit Edgbaston until the early sixties, died in Birmingham in January 1962. The following year J. Ernest Hill, the last survivor of all, also died.

The Yorkshire match was not the only cause of depression in the Warwickshire camp in 1896. It was a poor playing season altogether and they finished twelfth out of fourteen counties. Their bowling, said *Wisden*, was too much of the same character and lacking pace, 'a particular handicap in view of the fact that they are possessed of one of the best and truest grounds in England'. Shilton had played his last match and Whitehead had unfortunately dropped out of the side. No batsman, not even Quaife, made 1000 runs and Lilley's form fell away badly, though not behind the stumps – he took eight catches against the M.C.C. at Lord's and he also had five against Yorkshire, though not in the match in which they would have been of most value.

It was doubtless his performance at Lord's which earned him his selection against Australia and it was in the second Test at Old Trafford that he did something else for England besides keeping wicket and batting. He also bowled – and took a wicket. The story goes that, as usual, Australia's batting was posing problems, so W. G. Grace, the captain, called on Lilley to take off his pads. His first over included one wide, and it cost 14 runs. In the fifth he bowled a long hop to Harry Trott, who, as it was pitched well to the off, tried to cut it, but only succeeded in touching the ball to J. T. Brown, the Yorkshire opening batsman, who had taken Lilley's place behind the stumps. Grace then took Lilley off with the remark: 'Put the gloves on, Dick, I shall not want you to bowl again – you must have been bowling with your wrong arm.' Wrong arm or no, Lilley was often called upon to turn it over when all else failed, though never again in a Test. Infuriatingly, the records are silent on what sort of a bowler he was.

It was in this same Test – also the game in which 'Ranji' played a miraculous innings of 154 and Tom Richardson bowled himself to a standstill – that Lilley was accidentally responsible for a vital missed catch, one of *the* vital missed catches of cricket history, in fact. Australia wanted 9 runs with three wickets to fall when Kelly gave a chance behind the wicket. Lilley took the ball cleanly enough, but as he did so pulled his arm back so sharply that the ball was jolted out of his hands and it was ruled that the catch had not been made.

Ryder, whose salary had already been increased to the princely sum of £125 a year on condition he signed a three-year agreement at the same figure, had some pre-Test experience of handling the sort of crowd the Australians could draw, for Edgbaston entertained them twice. The first time was in June when the Australians met a Midland Counties XI, which included Quaife, Lilley and Bainbridge, and which beat them, thanks to a 68 by Quaife, by four wickets. In August they played the county side who, despite a five for 62 performance by Quaife, were beaten by an innings and 60 runs. Over 10 000 people paid for admission, very nearly the largest crowd Ryder saw on the ground in fifty years, and largely because of the tourists' visit gate receipts this season were a record at £2601, and 350 new members joined.

There was one other incident in 1896 that should not go unrecorded. At a general Committee meeting on 10 August 'Barnes's application for extra expenses in connection with the Essex match at Leyton was declined'. It was the only match played that season by the one and only 'S.F.' and that refusal may well have played a part in influencing his decision to go to the Lancashire League, though he had not given Warwickshire any particular grounds for thinking that his services would be worth retaining. Indeed, in the two seasons, 1895–6, in which he played in three matches he took only three wickets at a cost of just over 66 runs each.

I have heard it said, obviously in exaggeration, that at one time or another Warwickshire have expressed interest in, if not actually approached, practically every cricketer of any note in England (and a good many from overseas) and there is always curiosity about those a county let go. Barnes was the first, though not even a crystal ball would have enabled the Committee to see what was in store for him, any more than it would have helped much in the case of Wilfred Rhodes, who followed in his footsteps soon afterwards.

Before the end of the year, because Leicestershire had been able to arrange fixtures with only seven counties (which might have meant their disqualification, as well as that of others), Derbyshire proposed that the number required to qualify should be reduced from sixteen to fourteen, a move which would be looked on with much favour at Edgbaston later if it was not then. And then – oh heresy of heresies – Mr Ellison, of Yorkshire, whose casting vote it will be remembered had wiped the County Cricket Council out of existence, was 'understood to remark that perhaps the sooner the County Championship was abolished the better', a sentiment to which even Warwickshire is not yet prepared to subscribe. Fortunately neither proposal came to anything.

Willie Quaife was not the only one of the brothers who occasionally gave the Warwickshire Committee a headache. The secretary had an acrimonious correspondence this year with Walter over the brothers' delay in moving back into the county from Acock's Green, then in Worcestershire, so as not to jeopardise their qualification. Willie, meanwhile, was granted an increase in pay, but was told by the Committee that they could entertain none but yearly agreements, a penny-wise, pound-foolish policy surely in the case of the only batsman in the side rated to be England class.

The following August – 1897 – he renewed his application, asking for a five-year engagement and to be allowed £1 a week during the winter as a retainer; but again the Committee turned him down, though for 1898 they offered him increased terms of £80, the highest grade of payment for ground engagements then in force, though it was not stated whether this was for Warwickshire or for the country as a whole. Next month Quaife told them he had received a better offer from a county not named and again he asked for a five-year agreement at his present terms, with the addition of £1 a week in winter.

The Committee had a long discussion about this. It was proposed that the terms should be £70 for the summer, £1 a week in the winter and a five-year agreement, but there was an amendment that Quaife be offered £80, plus £1 a week in winter, but still only for a year and that this should be made an ultimatum. The resolution was defeated by six votes to four and in October Quaife accepted these terms and signed an agreement binding him to continue his qualification for the county, with a clause giving the Club the option of renewing the agreement for a further period of one, two or three years. It was agreed to offer the same terms to Lilley, who also accepted, so it could be said that in fighting his own battles Quaife had helped his fellow players also, as Barnes did so often. Whether it was intentional or not does not matter.

I have no doubt that Warwickshire wish they could have bound Rhodes as well. His name occurs three times among the 1896 records, first when on 6 August he applied with a number of others for a post on the ground staff. When the secretary was instructed to make inquiries about the applicants' abilities, Rhodes was a professional with Galashiels, the Scottish club. One of the applications was declined and the others, including that of Rhodes, deferred for further consideration. Later he was invited to qualify and accepted, but there was a change of mind and the last item in the minutes for the meeting of 4 October 1897, reads as follows:

It was decided that, on account of heavy expenses already incurred in connection with next year's ground staff, an engagement could not be offered to W. Rhodes, of Huddersfield.

Rhodes never attended the Edgbaston ground for a trial, but at least Warwickshire did not turn him down because they could not discern genius when they saw it, even if it was incipient. They had not long to wait, however, before they realised that what looked like becoming a really big fish had slipped through their net. In *Wisden* for 1898, only a year later, Rhodes was one of the Five Cricketers of the Year, having emerged at the age of 21 as the natural successor to Bobby Peel and taken 126 wickets for his beloved Yorkshire for only 13·84 runs apiece. He also scored 472 runs, averaging 21·45, and in Yorkshire's opening match of the season against Warwickshire at Leeds he gently rubbed it in by taking five of their wickets for 69 runs in the first innings. He met with less success, however, at Edgbaston in August, Warwickshire tanking the Yorkshire bowling to the tune of 406; Quaife made 157 not out, and Rhodes's one wicket cost him 55 runs.

But Warwickshire's great need at this time was not slow but fast bowlers and the previous June they had offered a temporary engagement on the ground staff, with a view to testing him, to one Frank Field, of Pershore. They had also taken on a promising young batsman from Wiltshire named Kinneir, who bore the splendidly Roman name of Septimus.

It was a wonderfully dry summer in 1897 and Warwickshire's batsmen revelled in it on the Edgbaston wickets, no fewer than eight of them having averages between 46 and 22. The bowling, though, fell off badly – in eighteen matches fifteen men were tried. The county did not win one of their first six matches and the first three at Edgbaston did not produce a result, the wickets being so good. What *did* the bowlers think about it? One would give much to know, especially those off whom Jessop took 126 in 95 minutes and almost changed a match Gloucestershire were losing into a win. One of them was Pallett, whose one wicket in this innings cost him 70 runs, but he had a much worse experience, in his benefit match of all games, against Lancashire. He had to bowl 29 overs in the first innings and 34 in the second for three wickets in all for 144. At least the fact that Tyldesley got a century in each innings, 106 and 100 not out (a feat which, until then, had been performed only by Grace, Stoddart, Brann, Storer, 'Ranji' and MacLaren), ensured that the match lasted three full days and brought him a round £500.

In the same month Edgbaston had the chance of seeing a noted fast bowler from, of all places, America – J. B. King, who came over with the Philadelphians, who beat the county by five wickets. King, who had bowled 'Ranji' with the first ball he ever sent down to him, took five wickets for 95 in Warwickshire's first innings and seven for 72 in the second, clean bowling six batsmen in succession. In view of their desperate need for a fast bowler it is a wonder Warwickshire did not invite him to stay over here and qualify for them. Sixty years later they would probably have done just that. Field, incidentally, had made his début in the Lancashire match, not the ideal occasion with Tyldesley in such form.

Warwickshire had their moments, however, an opening partnership of 288 between Bainbridge, 162, and Quaife, 178 not out, at Southampton against Hampshire, who retaliated with one of 222 by Andrew and Hill; but Surrey went even one better – a then record first-wicket stand of 379 by Abel, 173, and Brockwell, 225.

How varied were the problems with which a county cricket club secretary has to deal was illustrated by the fact that in April a member wrote to Ryder suggesting that accommodation should be provided for horses, as many members had to travel long distances. The Committee did consider the request, which was not so frivolous as it may sound, for Ryder once recalled that of all the people who made their way to Edgbaston for the first Test in 1902, by coach and horse, by hansoms, carriages and pairs, on bicycles and on foot, not one came in any kind of motor vehicle.

The two Quaifes were soon in the news again. Bainbridge badly hurt his wrist while fielding against Lancashire at Edgbaston in June and was unable to play again for the rest of the season. A. C. S. Glover, who had previously captained Staffordshire, took over. He and Walter had words during the match with Gloucestershire at Cheltenham. Walter, according to his captain, told him on the field to speak up; and said, on being asked to bowl, 'I don't intend to bowl again as I do no good to the side'; and when told to go in to bat with three-quarters of an hour left for play on the evening of the second day was alleged to have remarked: 'No one but a man who had captained the side but a few times would have done anything but send his last man in.'

Quaife denied having been insolent, but after being told he would be suspended until he had apologised – there was a proposal that his services be dispensed with forthwith – he wrote to Glover, saying no offence had been intended and gave an undertaking that nothing unpleasant would occur in future.

Brother William achieved distinction in a happier way. He headed both the county and the national batting averages with these figures:

INNS	N.O.	RUNS	HIGHEST	AVE
28	8	1219	157 n.o.	60·95

All too often, however, he took an inordinate time about getting his runs, so much so that *Wisden* commented that 'more than once in his anxiety to keep up his end and secure a not-out innings he prejudiced his side's prospects of success. Against Essex he took three and a half hours in scoring 61 when time was more of an object than runs to his county. He was striving for a sixth consecutive not out innings, it is true, but a little unselfishness would have been more sportsmanlike and Warwickshire were sadly in need of another victory.'

In the six innings referred to he scored 60, 117, 157, 24, 52 and 61 – a total of 471 runs. Another innings, 44 against Kent, took him two hours and a half. It is worth noting, incidentally, that of Quaife's total of 1142 innings for Warwickshire, 181 of them, well over one-sixth, were not out. He was certainly the uncrowned not-out king of cricket.

Quaife's painstaking methods had been adopted despite some criticism at the annual meeting that spring. Cartland, commenting on the record of unfinished matches at Edgbaston ('they wanted to go on', he said, 'until they had made their ground the most convenient and most comfortable ground in the kingdom'), had remarked that some of the matches which had been drawn ought to have been wins if players had sacrificed themselves for the benefit of the side. Playing for one's average, he added, was a curse to the eleven.

Santall took the trouble to work out that in eleven matches at Edgbaston in 1899, 8955 runs were scored for the loss of 201 wickets, an average of nearly 31 runs a wicket. An average of 813 runs were scored in each match. Strangely enough, however, Quaife found Cartland defending him at the annual meeting which followed further criticism in *Wisden* for playing for his own success rather than the team's. Alluding to Quaife's success in heading the averages, Cartland said that 'although some of them would like to see more lively play on the batsman's part, they must bear in mind that, being a little man, he had to bat his own way. It he had been a few inches taller he might possibly have been the most brilliant instead of the safest batsman in the country.'

Perhaps it is all a matter of seeing things in perspective. 'Tiger' Smith once told me that if Willie Quaife came back today he would be regarded as one of the fastest players in the game. 'Jim', Quaife told 'Tiger' once, 'if you're here at six o'clock you won't be running so fast then.' And Willie Quaife was often there at six o'clock.

Despite the fact that Warwickshire won only two Championship matches in 1898, they improved their position in the table to joint ninth with Derbyshire and Sussex, but although it was a wet summer – one match was abandoned without a ball being bowled – the bowling still showed, in *Wisden*'s phrase 'the same mediocrity . . . which has been their bane for years'. Warwickshire scored an average of only 23·05 runs per wicket, opponents being slightly better at 24·63 – the game's chroniclers were beginning to get statistically minded. Santall took twice as many wickets as anyone else – and this time twenty bowlers were tried – but even he could manage no more than sixty-eight. Young Field got thirty. The other newcomer, Kinneir, showed more than usual promise by averaging over 40, and the second of Warwickshire's great 'characters', Crowther Charlesworth, from Swinton in Lancashire, qualified.

Someone tried to tempt Ryder away with an offer of a business partnership, which prompted him to ask what were his prospects with Warwickshire. He got the answer in the form of a four-year agreement with increases of £25 each year. Quaife was less successful. He made his, by now, annual request for a five-year engagement, but still he did not get it, nor the increase he sought in pay from £112 a year to £156. The following year, though, he achieved his ambition. In January he informed the Committee that he had had another offer of 'considerably better' terms than Warwickshire had offered him – a ten-year engagement at slightly over £200 a year from a club, again not named, and he said he was not inclined to accept less than £3 a week from Warwickshire.

There was a long discussion in Committee, some members feeling that they could not depart from their previous decision, others that the Club could not afford to lose Quaife's services and that, in the circumstances, it would be wise to retain him. The trouble was that they did not know whether he was bluffing or not. Eventually it was moved, seconded and agreed by twelve votes to five that Quaife's application for a five-year agreement at £3 a week be granted, subject to his good conduct and keeping up his form. It was also agreed that Lilley should be offered the same terms and, he, too, accepted. One is tempted to wonder whether or not they were working together with Quaife, being tougher, the negotiator.

It was perhaps just as well that Warwickshire did retain him for in 1899 Quaife became the second Warwickshire player to be asked to play for England. He was one of five changes made for the third Test against Australia at Leeds and he justified his inclusion for, when England had four wickets down for 69, he and Fry put on 50 runs without being separated at the end of the first day. 'Quaife', *Wisden* reported, 'maintained a wonderful defence for an hour and three-quarters.' Next morning, without adding to his score of 20 not out, he was bowled, but he had done enough, though he did not bowl, to be picked for the fourth Test. Lilley made 55 in England's first innings and stumped one and caught four. In the Old Trafford game Quaife opened the innings with Fry, but was dismissed for 8 and 13 and was dropped for the last Test.

Worcestershire, now a first-class county, came into the Championship this season. The first match between them at Edgbaston was washed out and Warwickshire won the return at Worcester by 204 runs with half an hour to spare. This was largely due to another not out hundred by Quaife, following 58 in the first innings. At one point in the game Santall's bowling figures were:

O	M	R	W
12	11	1	4

In fact, Warwickshire did not win a match until 2 August and four of their five wins were in the last month of the season. Nevertheless they finished seventh in the table. *Wisden* once more drew attention to the weakness of the bowling which, it was suggested, often made Warwickshire play better to draw games than to win them and the result was 'a lack of dash and brilliancy that do so much to make a team popular with the cricket-loving public'.

There was a match of fantastic scoring with Hampshire whose total of 425 was nevertheless easily beaten by Warwickshire's 657 for six declared, still the highest total ever made by the county. Quaife 207 not out, T. S. Fishwick 109 and Glover 119 not out were its architects. There were three more Warwickshire centuries in the match at Leicester, this time by Kinneir and both Quaifes, but the Australians crushed the county by nine wickets.

Glover had an extraordinary experience in the match against Gloucestershire at Edgbaston, which must be without parallel for a county, or, indeed, any kind of captain. The Warwickshire fielding, it seems, was loose, to say the least, and a section of the crowd jeered the offending players.

Late in the afternoon, [according to the account in *The Birmingham Post*] Glover ran to field a ball which had been hit to the corner of the ground near the covered stand. He stopped the ball from reaching the boundary, but was then seen to throw it in the direction of the ring of spectators – an action which provoked a roar of disapprobation and cries of 'Turn him off' and 'Summon him'.

It subsequently transpired that the ball had struck an old gentleman, fortunately not very violently, on the thigh and it then cannoned against the ankle of an elderly lady. At the close of the game the Warwickshire captain tendered an apology to both the spectators who had been hit by the ball and explained that his act was prompted by a very insulting remark from one of the crowd. Whatever the provocation, however, the act was foolish and undignified, as Glover himself will doubtless freely admit.

He did – in a letter to the Committee in which he also apologised, and could have used the excuse that he slipped when fielding the ball, but refrained, adding:

Some people are hasty and I fear I am one of them – but I consider I was deeply insulted and perhaps I am a little ready to rise at insult. (The last time I played football a rough spat in my face and, of course, closed my career.) This element we hope never to see at cricket and I hope the counties will try and prevent as far as possible coarse insults being hurled at players who are doing their best if not successfully . . . I may say I don't fancy myself as captain and would rather be relieved of the duties. It would honestly be better for the county, though I hope an amateur may always hold that post if Mr Bainbridge's wrist fails again.

The Committee accepted his explanation and expressed regret that he had been insulted, but one wonders what its attitude would have been had the player concerned been a professional. Quaife was in trouble again for ignoring a ruling on the Essex ground at Leyton that the professionals should not use the centre gate of the pavilion. Quaife considered this insulting to the professionals and when a member of the ground staff was sent to tell him to move from in front of the pavilion Quaife told him to tell the Essex secretary that if he wished to see him he should come himself. The Warwickshire Committee, on this occasion, expressed strong disapproval of Quaife's action.

By the end of the year, thanks to the Birmingham Corporation having provided an additional embankment, for which the members supplied seats, and to other alterations, Cartland estimated that something like 20 000 people could now see the game in comfort at Edgbaston, an important consideration when the Committee put forward the claims of the ground to stage a Test Match. That day was not far distant.

Into the 1900s
(1900–1902)

THE first half-dozen seasons after the turn of the century conformed pretty much to the same pattern – strong Warwickshire batting, with Quaife the predominant, if not always the swiftest-moving, figure; and bowling which, though it improved with the full flowering of Sam Hargreave – who took over 100 wickets in five seasons out of six between 1901 and 1906 – was still not decisive enough to make the figures in the 'Wins' column of the County Championship table exceed those in the 'Draws'.

Unquestionably the greatest event in Warwickshire cricket between 1900 and the winning of the first Championship in 1911 was not any of the doings of the county side, but the staging of the first Test Match at Edgbaston in 1902. That was an objective for which the Committee, led by Ansell, had worked from the earliest days, and it was one which ever since has been in the forefront of the plans of their administrative successors, so much so at times that over half a century later the Committee was criticised for giving more thought to Test Matches than to building up a successful county team.

Perhaps the critic overlooked the fact that, in improving the ground so that it met the requirements of the Board of Control, the Committee was not only enabling the highest class of cricket to be seen in the Midlands and providing a source of income from the Test Match Pool which it would have been difficult, if not impossible, to do without, but was also improving amenities for its own members and for the general public on whose support the Club depends. In fact, that first Test, far from making a fortune for Warwickshire, put the Club in the red to the tune of over £3000, but it was in financial difficulties before then, at the end of 1900 to be exact.

The season had barely begun before news came of the death at the age of 70 of one of the Club's pioneer founders, David Buchanan, though the obituary in *Wisden* did not deign to mention any club for which he played other than the Gentlemen. It did, however, describe him as 'one of the very best slow bowlers of the last generation', though, in fact, he had begun as a fast bowler, changing his style in the sixties with great success. He played for Warwickshire from 1864 until 1885 and besides sometimes captaining the side he acted as honorary treasurer from 1884 to 1891.

Wisden's summing up of the county's performances in 1900 was that 'the batting was never stronger and the bowling scarcely ever poorer' the latter being partly due to the fact that early in the season Santall contracted scarlet fever and did not play in the first seven games, though it was hardly fair to Field, who took eighty-eight wickets for the county. There were fourteen draws, seven matches being ruined by poor weather and Cartland made yet another reference to the fact that 'there was no ground in the country so heart-breaking for bowlers', though the Committee, so far as one can discover, took no action to change this state of affairs.

Warwickshire lost only two games, but they also won only two and none after 5 June. The annual report showed that they averaged 28·07 runs per wicket to their opponents' 25·64. Somebody also worked out that between 1894 and 1900 inclusive the county side scored 48 047 runs, average 24·43 per wicket, and their opponents 48 861 runs, average 26·21, so they were slightly on the debit side.

For the fourth successive season Quaife headed the batting averages – where would they have been without him, slow or not slow? – scored another double century, 223 not out against Essex, while Walter made 115, the second time they had done this fraternal double. Quaife and Kinneir, now spoken of as the best left-hand batsman in the kingdom, occupied eighth and ninth position in the national averages in company with 'Ranji', Fry, Abel, Hayward, J. R. Mason and R. E. Foster, and that betokened their class beyond any doubt.

Ernest Hill played his last match for the county and finished as he began with a century – 145 against the West Indies who were here for the first time because the South African tour had been cancelled owing to the Boer War. The M.C.C. ruled that matches against them should not rank as first class. Warwickshire beat them by an innings and 111 runs.

Quaife was not the only double century-maker this season. Devey hit a brilliant 246 against Derbyshire, Warwickshire scoring 522 for three wickets in five and a half hours on the first day, a rate of scoring which would cause coronary thromboses all over the ground today. Devey also distinguished himself on the football field – and in the Aston Villa board room for over thirty years.

Against Leicestershire at Edgbaston, Santall showed that there was nothing wrong with the bowling for once – he took eight for 23 and the visitors were all out before lunch for 47, up to then the lowest score for which Warwickshire had dismissed any county. Fifty-one years later they also dismissed Glamorgan before lunch.

At this time the ground staff consisted of eight men, seven of whom were qualified for county cricket, and Moorhouse, who qualified in 1901. Engagements were also entered into with Diver and Dickens to play when required in county matches, and with Whittle to complete his qualification. These engagements which, it was stated, entailed an expenditure of £1000, provided only one man for Club and Ground matches and net practice, and the secretary was instructed to advertise for extra men on the ground staff and for evening bowlers, as well as a second wicketkeeper.

The Committee probably regretted their action when bad weather in August Bank Holiday week spoiled the Worcestershire and Yorkshire matches and led to another financial crisis. They were informed that between then and next May £1950 would have to be paid in players' wages, clearing off accounts and other charges, and the honorary treasurer could see only £950 in assets during the period. Eventually the bank was persuaded to agree to an overdraft of £1000 provided it was doubly guaranteed. So a millstone was acquired which has hung round the Club's neck ever since. Legend has it that at a later Committee meeting Cartland noticed a stranger present. 'Who', he asked Ryder, 'is that gentleman?' Ryder replied in a whisper that the visitor was a representative of the bank who was there to deal with the question of security for the Club's overdraft.

'Then', said Cartland, 'we had better take that matter first' and, turning to the banker, he added courteously: 'Your security, sir, is sitting round this table. You may leave.'

One effect of the economy 'squeeze' was that when a public appeal was made on behalf of Santall, whose illness, of course, meant a considerable loss to him, the Club felt that beyond paying his wages in full, funds could not be drawn upon in view of the disastrous season. The appeal, without the Club's official help, eventually raised £40.

Financial worries persisted throughout 1901 and finally led to an increase in subscriptions, but there were more cheerful things to report. W. G. Quaife was chosen as one of the Five Cricketers of the Year in *Wisden*, which paid a glowing tribute to him – 'he stands in the very front rank of contemporary batsmen' – and also referred to the way in which he had overcome his physical limitations:

His success may be described as a triumph of natural ability and hard work over physical disadvantages. One of the shortest men who ever took a leading position in the cricket field, he has by careful study of the art of batting almost

77

neutralised his lack of height and reach. Debarred by physical limitations from forcing play in front of the wicket, he has mastered practically every way of scoring behind the stumps and . . . he is so exceptionally quick on his feet that he can make nearly any ball look easy to play. The only reproach that can be urged against him is that he keeps his average a little too much before his mind and is apt to play a slow game when caution is the last thing needed by his side.

A shrewd summing-up, one is tempted to say, but in another context it is surprising to find Quaife listed among a number of bowlers whose actions came under suspicion about this time. They included one or two very well-known names – Mold, the Lancashire fast bowler, and even Surrey's Lockwood, for instance. Quaife, 'whose old delivery', *Wisden* commented, 'had been very properly condemned by the county captains as unfair, taught himself during the winter [of 1899–1900] to bowl the now fashionable leg-breaks and so well did he get on that he took thirty-seven wickets in county matches.' They cost him 22·51 runs each.

The county captains had agreed that in future they would not bowl certain players, of whom Quaife was one, and that some should be warned by the committees, but no drastic measures were taken for the time being, it being left to the captains to 'name' anyone and recommend his suspension to the M.C.C.

Quaife, in fact, headed both batting and bowling averages in a season in which Warwickshire played fewer Championship matches, sixteen, than any other county. Ansell thought this had something to do with the slow play of the season before last – 1899. Many counties were in financial difficulties, he told the annual meeting of 1901, and because Warwickshire were not such an attractive side as some others they were dropped from fixture lists, though later he said it was purely for financial reasons.

The meeting was crowded, no doubt in anticipation of a proposal, firstly to increase the subscription to not less than a guinea and a half and secondly, that after 1 January 1902, an entrance fee of 10s 6d should be charged – but this was withdrawn and postponed for a season on condition that the Committee would support it if 1901 was also an unsuccessful season from a playing point of view.

There was less to worry about in this sphere. At their best, Santall thought, the team 'was the strongest that has ever entered the field in the history of the Club' and they finished fifth in the Championship. Both Quaife, who had four hundreds in five consecutive innings, and Kinneir again averaged over 50; Charlesworth showed great improvement; and the bowling was much stronger thanks to Hargreave, who became the first Warwickshire bowler to take over 100 wickets, in all matches, in first-class cricket. Field suffered a good deal from strains and the pain of rheumatism, but still contrived some fine performances.

Warwickshire also had the distinction of gaining their first success over a first-class touring side. The South Africans, paying only their second visit to this country, were at Edgbaston in May; they were beaten by an innings on, for once, a bowlers' wicket, Santall, Hargreave and Field dismissing them for 74 and 185.

Lilley took his benefit against Yorkshire and despite interference by rain ultimately did very nicely out of it – £849, the highest for the county yet. In Yorkshire's second innings of 401 for five he had to bowl as well as stump for his supper – and had George Hirst caught. When Warwickshire batted and made 320 in reply, Lilley scored 29 of them before he was bowled by Schofield Haigh.

Early in the year Messiter, who had been honorary treasurer for nine years, resigned owing to ill-health and Ryder took over this office as well, with J. C. Lane acting in an honorary capacity. There was also some concern about the health of the President, Lord Willoughby de Broke. It was reported at a Committee meeting in February that he had not replied to a letter asking if he wished to be considered for re-election, and an approach had been made to Earl Howe, a Warwickshire man, a large property owner in Birmingham and first on the list of vice-presidents, who had expressed his willingness to consider the offer.

Later, however, Lord Willoughby de Broke intimated that he would continue as his health had greatly improved and at the annual meeting he was duly re-elected. In October, however, there came a letter from Charles Harding, of Edgbaston, donor of the Club's scoreboard, and signed by fourteen other 'influential members', including the Holinsworths, supporters of the Club in a variety of practical ways, pointing out the great disadvantage year after year of electing as president one who was unable to come to the ground, to attend annual general meetings, or show any active interest in the affairs of the Club. But at least he paid an annual subscription of £5 5s 0d, which was more than could be said for four of the vice-presidents, who, it had been stated in reply to a question at the annual meeting, were non-subscribers.

The letter-writers suggested instead the names of Mr Alfred Lyttelton and Lord Howe. The present state of things, they concluded, impeded the progress of Warwickshire county cricket and it was felt that, without any disloyalty to Lord Willoughby de Broke, a change should be made. This put the Committee in a difficulty and finally it was left to George Cartland, as chairman, to write telling him of the letter 'as they [the Committee] cannot contemplate any division of opinion or discussion on the subject at the annual meeting which could alike be most distasteful to you, distasteful to them and injurious to the interests of the Club.'

The following February, however, there was correspondence 'from which it appeared the President had no wish to resign his office, as it was thought probable, on account of ill health'. It was therefore agreed to submit his name once more to the annual meeting where he was re-elected and it was stated that his health was so much better that he hoped to be at the Test Match. But at the end of the year, alas, members of the Committee were expressing deep regret at his death while on a sea voyage for the benefit of his health. He was, said Cartland, 'a staunch and good friend of cricket. He took it up when hardly anybody was willing to do so and he was always asking in what way he could help them.'

At the end of the 1901 season, in which he played only six innings, Walter Quaife, who had been with the Club nine years, applied for a benefit in 1902. Quaife had not always endeared himself to the Committee by his ways and this request caused them some concern. Twice they put off making a decision and eventually the matter was deferred *sine die* and it was resolved that Quaife should not be re-engaged for 1902. It was a sad ending to a career which had begun with Sussex in 1884 and had seen two appearance for the Players in 1889 and 1895, in which season he scored 1294 runs for the county.

It was probably not so much an indication of the Club's financial difficulties – indeed, there was a small working surplus at the time – as of the infinite resource of its officials that in December, while Lilley was away touring in Australia, and the proceeds of his benefit were lying idle in the bank (apart from earning interest, of course), the honorary treasurer borrowed from them to avert the necessity for an overdraft. It was intended, he said, that Lilley should have the benefit of interest on the moneys used and the action was approved; but one wonders what might have happened had something gone wrong, or what if Lilley would have wished to invest it in something he thought more profitable to himself? Ultimately there was a loss of £100 on the season, and the Committee decided to increase the subscription.

There were other examples of financial ingenuity about this time. When they could not agree an 'extras' item on the account of one of the builders of the new covered stand erected for the Test Match, the Committee finally agreed to pay, but the chairman undertook to obtain a donation from him if possible. He got one, too – for five guineas. There was also an argument with an architect about his fee, which he was asked to reduce to a nominal one. He was paid, but he, too, was 'touched' for a five-guinea 'donation'.

Quaife, like Lilley, had been selected to go out to Australia in the winter with MacLaren's team. Both played in all five Tests in which they performed creditably but without distinction, Lilley being fourth in the averages with 211 runs for 23·44 and Quaife fifth with 184 runs for an average of 20·44. In all matches, Quaife, with one century against a district side, scored 975 runs and Lilley 479.

First Test at Edgbaston (1902)

THE year 1902 provided two landmarks in the history of Warwickshire cricket – the first Test Match at Edgbaston, which realised one of William Ansell's great ambitions for the Club, though it brought many problems in its train, and later his own resignation. Weather-wise, it was a dismal season and Warwickshire suffered more than any other county, with the result that the finances were 'grievously affected', as were those of the Test itself.

Probably few people at that time had any idea of the work entailed in staging a Test. But Ryder had. He has told feelingly of the thirty-six general committee meetings held that year, not to mention the sub-committees; of one permanent and two temporary stands, providing accommodation for another 3500 people, being built at a cost of £1500; of providing a catering staff of 200; of making accommodation for ninety Pressmen even in those days; of sixty gatemen and sixty policemen having to be hired; of arrangements to be made for cheap rail fares within a radius of sixty miles of Birmingham (at a fare and a quarter, one shilling return) and of a thousand and one other tasks that had to be done. 'It was an anxious time as the day drew near,' Ryder wrote in an article he contributed to *Wisden*. 'Had we thought of everything? Events were to prove that we hadn't.'

And no one knew how many people would come – 10 000, 20 000 – or what the weather would be like. Cartland, at the annual meeting which preceded the game, said they were not gambling in any way on the Test Match, but, in fact, the whole thing was a gamble from Warwickshire's point of view and if no one else knew it Ryder certainly did, as he worked on with no clerical help, no telephone, no type-writer . . .

A lively picture of the scene in the city that opening day was drawn by a reporter in *The Birmingham Post*: 'At the corner of the road it was amusing to come across the imposing, but obviously excited, coachman (with a pair of restive horses) trying to ascertain from a humble pedestrian the whereabouts of the county cricket ground, the while a lady, cool, composed and statuesque, reclined in a tandem. Every minute a hansom dashed up. Carriages and pairs were as common as blackberries in autumn, hansoms were ubiquitous, bicycles crept in and out everywhere.' 'Where, indeed, was the automobile?' Ryder asked. 'At the Test Match here last June [1924] we parked 1200 of them and so far as I know not a single equine enthusiast saw the match.'

This 1902 Test falls into the category, for me at least, of 'Great Games I Would Like to Have Seen', perhaps even more so than the other two in the same season. The first was at Old Trafford where Tate was put on the rack while it rained, and the second at The Oval, where we won by one wicket after a marvellous century by Jessop, and Hirst and Rhodes got the last 13 runs wanted in singles, while everybody has forgotten Lilley's precious 16.

The Australians arrived at Edgbaston – where Bates had prepared one of his most beautiful wickets – unbeaten, and having won three of their seven matches by handsome margins. England had assembled to meet them what P. F. Warner thought – and many still think – was the finest team which has ever represented England on a cricket field. Archie MacLaren was their captain and with him were C. B. Fry, K. S. Ranjitsihnji, the Hon. F. S. Jackson, J. T. Tyldesley, G. H. Hirst, G. L. Jessop, L. C. Braund, W. H. Lockwood, W. Rhodes and A. A. Lilley. Their photograph adorns – and that is the word – the wall of the Pavilion at Edgbaston and I never pause and gaze at it, as I do every time I visit the ground, without a pricking of the eyes at the glory that was English cricket in those golden days. Go and look at it some time – and marvel. In all, fourteen players had been selected and it says much for the plethora of talent there was to choose from at that time that the three players omitted were Tom Hayward, J. R. Mason and C. B. Llewellyn.

It was a cloudy day and there was rain about, but when MacLaren won the toss he decided to bat, for the wicket looked easy. But we were soon in for shocks. MacLaren was run out for 9, Fry was caught without scoring, 'Ranji' went for unlucky 13 and England were 35 for three wickets. That brought Jackson and Tyldesley together, but the struggle was by no means over. Jackson got a half-century; Tyldesley was missed three times when he was 41, but he made 138 in four hours and twenty minutes and, with the help of Hirst, pulled the innings round to respectability.

There were 7000 people present on the second day when MacLaren, acting, it is said, on Lilley's local knowledge, let England go on batting so that his bowlers would not have to contend with slippery footholds, eventually declaring at 376 for nine wickets. The stage was set for one of cricket's greatest performances.

Trumper and Duff opened Australia's innings against Yorkshire's famous pair, Hirst and Rhodes, and the score was only 7 when Braund missed Duff at slip off Hirst. Braund bowled an over to allow the Yorkshiremen to change ends and then the fun really began. Duff was caught by Jessop at point off Rhodes, Braund made amends by marvellously catching Clem Hill for 1 and the score was 10 for two, then 14 for three and 17 for four.

The wicket, it has been said, was never really difficult, though it did not get any easier and Rhodes was spinning the ball viciously. The score became 25 for five, then 25 for six. Trumper, batting as only he could, made 18, but was at last bowled by Hirst . . . 31 for seven, 35 for eight, 35 for nine and 36 all out. A more remarkable bowling analysis has rarely, if ever, been seen in any match let alone a Test:

	O	M	R	W
HIRST	11	4	15	3
RHODES	11	3	17	7
BRAUND	1	0	1	0

Lilley's contribution, apt to be overlooked, was not to allow a bye, to stump Noble and catch Armstrong and Hopkins.

Australia, of course, followed on and had scored 8 without loss when rain stopped play at 6 p.m., the day ending in semi-darkness. It then rained for the next twelve hours and by 9 a.m. next day the ground was a lake with not a square yard of turf visible. Any further cricket seemed so remote as to be hardly worth considering, especially when at 11.30 a.m. it began to rain again. Naturally the gates were not even opened and half the gatemen and half the policemen, who had been specially engaged to control the expected crowds, were allowed to go.

Then just after noon the weather improved considerably. At 2 p.m. the sun shone and by 2.30 p.m. there were people waiting hopefully outside the ground. The umpires made periodic inspections, but neither they nor the captains would commit themselves. Meanwhile the crowd outside grew increasingly impatient. At 3.30 p.m. the umpires looked again, decided that play might soon be possible and advised, it was reported, that the gates could be opened at 3.45 p.m. (The official Club minute says 4.30 p.m.).

The umpires took another look at 4 p.m. and decided to wait another half-hour. By this time between 2000 and 3000 people had congregated at the city end of the ground where there was only one turnstile manned and two policemen on duty. When it was decided to open this there was what is usually described as 'an ugly rush'; the crowd shouted 'Burst the gates' and pressed against some hoardings, which collapsed, many people being thrown to the ground. Others rushed over them and several were injured, while some had their clothes plastered with tar which was still wet.

It was estimated that there were between 11 000 and 12 000 people on the ground by the time play was eventually resumed on a swamp of a wicket at 5.15 p.m. There was still time for England to win, especially if they could bowl as they had done in the first innings, but the Australians, of course, had other ideas. They lost two wickets to Rhodes for 42, but that was the end. They had merely put off the evil hour, though. They went on to Headingley and suffered an even worse indignity against Yorkshire – this time they were all out for 23.

There was one other Test in the 1902 series in which Warwickshire had an interest through one of its players, Lilley, who played at Old Trafford where 'the most thrilling finish of all', in Sir Neville Cardus's view, occurred. England, with two wickets still to fall, were within 8 runs of victory when Lilley made a fine hit to square leg. It looked a certain four, but the wind got under the ball and slightly turned it in its flight, and Clem Hill, running at top speed for 30 yards along the boundary edge, took it one-handed – one of the great catches of cricket which won the match for Australia by three runs. Cardus has a purple passage about it:

The impetus of his run carried him twenty yards beyond the place where he made the catch – a catch which put incredulity into the face of every man and woman at Old Trafford that day. 'A sinful catch,' said the parson.

The hectic first Test at Edgbaston was over so far as the play was concerned, but not for Ryder. Of the first day he afterwards wrote: 'Eight hours after stumps were drawn I balanced up and as I crawled home between 2 a.m. and 3 a.m. I thanked my lucky stars I lived near the ground.' I have no doubt it was the same on the other days of the match and even after it was all over he woke up to a host of worries. Although over 25 000 people had attended the match, after all the accounting had been done and the Australians' share settled, the honorary treasurer worked out that the total deficit by 31 December 1902, would be £2000 and that a further £500 would be required before the start of the 1903 season. So it was decided that a private and public appeal for £3000 should be made.

In the meantime, as if Ryder had not enough on his hands, claims began to come in for damage to clothing suffered by the unfortunate spectators who had been caught in the rush through the gates and had got tar on themselves. But the Committee, while sympathising, were not accepting responsibility for the behaviour of the crowd outside the ground, even when one man wrote threatening proceedings unless £3 was sent to him.

The appeal, to 'all sport-loving inhabitants of the county', provided Ryder with 'a thrilling experience' and certainly the Club found many willing to help the special committee which had been set up. All kinds of events were arranged, including a match between Aston Villa and the famous Corinthians F.C., which was rained off the first time, but raised £112 on the second occasion when the team drove to Villa Park in a coach and four.

Eventually the £3000 was raised, and £561 more, and the Club's financial troubles were over for the time being. Ansell and Ryder must certainly have been pleased with *Wisden*'s comment: 'The Edgbaston ground proved well fitted for a Test Match.'

The rest of that season's cricket rather pales into insignificance by comparison. The Australians were at Edgbaston again in July and this time fared very differently. Warwick Armstrong, who was touring for the first time, took six wickets for 13 and the county were all out for 124. Then the crowd saw an admirable 48 from Trumper and 83 from S. E. Gregory before he was bowled by Sam Hargreave, now in the opinion of many, second only to Rhodes as a slow left-hander. On this occasion he took four for 81 in an innings of 316. Warwickshire showed better form at their second attempt, but only 40 minutes' play was possible on the second day and the game was drawn.

W. G. Grace, by this time aged 54, got the only century I can trace that he ever made against Warwickshire – 129 for his London County XI at the Crystal Palace. Even then he was missed before he had scored. In the County Championship Warwickshire had a good season, finishing sixth, *Wisden* commenting that 'they have seldom had a better eleven than in 1902'. At Worcester they had a taste of Simpson-Hayward's lobs, five for 38, which won for their neighbours their first County Championship match. Rhodes had another very successful visit to Edgbaston which produced four wickets for 41 and four for 16, including a spell of four for 6. There was a hair-raising finish to a low-scoring match with Hampshire at Bournemouth, where Warwickshire won by 8 runs. When the last Hampshire player came in they still needed 14, but got only 5, Lilley taking a catch off Santall.

It was during this season that there came on the scene the first of the many overseas players with whom Warwickshire have negotiated throughout much of their history. He was Dr L. S. Poidevin, the Australian, who offered to qualify to play for them. The Committee said they would very much like to have him as a member of the side, but felt there would be very considerable difficulty in making such payments as he suggested on behalf of an amateur cricketer, and at the time there was no possibility of creating an assistant post of any kind, though one would have thought that Ryder could well have done with some help. However, the doctor was told that should he decide on Birmingham for his 'medical school' and became qualified there would be no difficulty about 'a very liberal allowance for expenses'. Negotiations fell through, however, and Poidevin later played for Lancashire.

The Committee had to wait until almost the very end of the year before they knew the final details of the Test Match budget. The total receipts worked out at £1883, expenses £437, with £761 paid to the Australians and £683 to the Board of Control. Each of the five clubs on whose grounds the matches were played received 40 per cent of the net takings, amounting to £503, of which first-class counties took £195 which, with one or two other items, made Warwickshire's total share £764. One wonders if they thought it worth all the effort they had put into it. At any rate, on 30 December it was decided to make an appeal for more members.

At the annual meeting in March of that year, a clerical member, the Rev. A. A. Charlesworth, obviously one of the critics of the fixture list, had suggested that Ansell should be made a vice-president and that he should make way for a successor as honorary secretary so that the Club could be differently represented at the secretaries' meeting at Lord's at which the fixtures were arranged.

This was surely a polite way of kicking Ansell upstairs, but the proposal did not find a seconder and the chairman answered for him that Mr Ansell did not wish to be 'raised to the House of Lords'. Ansell, who was re-elected, said the reason why several counties did not play Warwickshire was purely financial and not personal.

Nevertheless, at the end of the season he intimated his intention of resigning his official connection with the Club. It was decided to ask him to talk it over, but at the October meeting of the Committee a letter from him was read which made it clear that he had not seen eye to eye with them on policy:

I think it is pretty clear from the events of the year that I am now no longer in touch with the general policy of the Committee. I refer particularly to the question of ground equipment and the curtailment of the privileges of the public in the matter of 'pass-out' checks. As the Club is worked at present, it appears doubtful whether any honorary secretary is necessary. The office is purely a nominal one, carrying responsibility with little power, and the Committee would do well, I think, to consider whether it is advisable to continue the office or not.

One can hardly imagine Ansell being content with a 'nominal' office and this was an obvious indication that Ryder had already taken over from him, as *Wisden* remarked. During his last two or three years in office, they said, Ansell delegated many of his old duties to Ryder and so 'his resignation will not mean so much to the Club as it would have done ten years ago. It must not on that account, however, be allowed to pass without fitting notice. To Mr Ansell more than anyone else Warwickshire owed promotion to the ranks of the first-class counties.'

The parting of the ways was indeed not allowed to pass. On 19 May the following year – Bainbridge, who had played his last match against the Australians, never missing a season since he first played in 1886, had been appointed honorary secretary for the time being – a complimentary dinner was given to Ansell at the Old Royal Hotel, Temple Row, Birmingham, at which the guests were all past and present members of the Committee. George Cartland presided and after giving Ansell the whole of the credit for starting the Club, of which in late years he had been chaperone, manager and 'general boss' – Leslie Deakins once pictured him, accurately, he assured me, as 'managing and controlling the Club over the breakfast table' – presented him with a combined secretaire and roll-topped desk. To Mrs Ansell was given a handsome gold and opal bracelet.

Ansell began his reply by mentioning that the gathering happily was taking place on the 28th anniversary of his wedding and he spoke of 'the splendid help' he had received from his wife. Then he went on to talk of the Edgbaston ground which, as shown by the Test Match, was a national institution, and said that the Club was one of the foremost in the country. The team, he added, was young and vigorous and it was just in that state that, when properly handled, it might be welded into a most formidable combination. Later there were further tributes to him at the annual meeting when he was elected an honorary life member and was invited to sit for his portrait.

So ended the first phase of Warwickshire's history. Without Ansell's imagination, foresight, drive and initiative, the formation of a truly representational county cricket club might have been delayed for several years. He made enemies and trod on sensitive toes, but he got things done at a time when they needed doing and though some of those in loftier places looked down their noses at his sometimes pushing ways, it was he more than anyone who won Warwickshire first-class status when, with someone less forceful at the helm, they might have languished for many more seasons in lower company. Now in 1903 began officially, if not already in practice, the Ryder régime which was to last until the outbreak of the Second World War.

BOOK TWO

ROWLAND VINT RYDER

1903–1944

Crosses To Bear
(1903–1907)

On the very same happy day in May 1903, on which The Warwickshire County Cricket Club was acknowledging its indebtedness to Ansell, Arthur Shrewsbury, the greatest professional batsman of his day, unable to face an illness he believed to be incurable and a summer in which he would not play cricket, shot himself. Thereafter, as if weeping for his loss, the skies opened on one of the wettest summers anyone could remember. Only one match at Edgbaston completely escaped interference by the weather.

With the retirement of Bainbridge from the field to the office, Warwickshire had a new captain in J. F. Byrne. Born near Birmingham, bluff, hearty, and a distinguished England full-back at Rugby, he was the first link between Moseley R.F.C. and Warwickshire cricket which has persisted to this day. He played cricket to match – a hard-hitting batsman, a fast bowler and a fine fielder. He had first played for Warwickshire in 1892, but apart from one season in 1897, when in twenty innings he scored 642 runs, little had been seen of him except for occasional matches.

He began most encouragingly with a splendid win at The Oval. During the winter Hargreave had been out to Australia and New Zealand, and as he was not expected to return in time he had been left out of the team for this game. However, the first day was washed out and the ship docked at Tilbury just in time to allow him to join the team on the second day, on which he proceeded to bowl Surrey to defeat. They were all out for 82 in the first innings and for 89 in the second, Hargreave taking six for 41 and nine for 39, a remarkable homecoming to say the least.

As Hargreave began, so he went on and at the end of the season he had taken 123 wickets for an average of 12·17 runs each, finished seventh in the first-class averages and had earned from *Wisden* the description of being 'among the great bowlers of the year'. Santall worked out that Warwickshire were the strongest bowling side in the country, dismissing their opponents for 16·84 runs per wicket, a remarkable change from immediate past seasons. Hargreave must have been particularly pleased to take eleven wickets for 68 against Lancashire on his former ground at Old Trafford.

Warwickshire had two encounters this season with S. F. Barnes, who was playing what turned out to be the last of his only two full seasons of county cricket. At Old Trafford in May he took five wickets for 58, but at Edgbaston he had to be content with three wickets in each innings for 77 and 68 respectively.

The authorities were trying to tinker with the laws even in 1903. The Warwickshire Committee opposed a proposal circulated by the M.C.C. that stumps should be widened from eight to nine inches. The Committee thought that this would tend to increase caution by slow batsmen and that raising them two inches would be more likely to help the bowlers. Cartland, at the annual meeting, thought it would be better to make the bat narrower. The comments of the batsmen were not forthcoming.

The Earl of Warwick was elected President, with the new Lord Willoughby de Broke and Ansell as vice-presidents; Bainbridge was confirmed as honorary secretary, Ansell's advice to do away with the office being politely ignored, as it was for sixty more years. Despite the Test Match, the accounts for the year showed a deficiency of £603, though the membership had gone up to 1837, plus 125 ladies. Even so, the Committee felt free to offer a new three-year contract to Ryder, as well as a special bonus of £25 for all the extra work he had done for the appeal, but it would still not subscribe to a telephone, deciding to continue sending out match results to the clubs and elsewhere by telegram.

One of Byrne's first acts was to suggest that compensation should be paid to Field when he was left out of the team because it was thought the pitch would not suit him after rain, a proposal I have never heard of before or since – though, as a minute recorded, it did seem 'rather a pity that a player should suffer a pecuniary loss through no fault of his own'. As might have been expected with such a precedent, however, the matter was deferred and the secretary was instructed to find out how often Field was kept out of the side in the previous season for this reason. If the secretary ever did so, the information is not recorded and at the next meeting of the Committee it was decided to consider his case at the end of the season. In fact, it dragged on for several seasons until at last it was agreed.

Before the end of 1903, Quaife, Lilley and Moorhouse, another

Yorkshireman and an all-rounder, were all given five-year contracts, and Charlesworth and Field three-year engagements. Santall, however, only received one for one year, as did a young wicketkeeper of 18 from the Bournville Cricket Club, one Ernest James Smith. He had been born in Benacre Street, Birmingham, about a mile from the ground, on 6 February 1886, the year it was opened, so he never had any difficulty in remembering that date. Even though he lived so near, he was in Worcestershire and when they wanted to register him Warwickshire offered him a six weeks' trial and at once asked him to go on the staff.

Wicketkeeping was his great interest then and that was why Warwickshire wanted him as a possible successor to Dick Lilley, who had also played for Bournville. Smith batted anywhere at this time, he told me.

We were coached in April by Alfred Shaw, the Notts bowler, who could reputedly pitch the ball on a sixpence. You had a lecture from him before you went in and after you came out. We were natural players then, not spoiled by coaching. The old coaches tried to encourage your natural abilities. When I was a youngster, W. G. Quaife used to say, 'If I do anything wrong, tell me.'

One man stands out for me from those days – Crowther Charlesworth, because he was such a great help to the young players. I owe to him practically all my knowledge of cricket. Although he was a rough and ready individual, he was a great fellow. He would coach you and tell you where you went wrong. Jack Parsons, Percy Jeeves and I were three who owed much to him. After a couple of pints he wanted to sing. He was always merry and bright. We also owed a lot to Sam Hargreave.

I was paid 25s a week to begin with. We were paid £5 for a home match, £6 for one over 100 miles away, £2 for a win and nothing for a draw. We had to pay our own railway fares and hotels – the return fare to London then was about 9s 7d and you could get dinner, bed, and breakfast at the Adelphi in Adam Street for 7s 6d then. We had nothing to grumble at.

It was Dick Lilley who christened me 'Tiger'. In my early days I was a bit rough and ready. It so happened one day when I came in from net practice that a game of 'Nap' was taking place in the dressing-room. One of the players, who had gone 'Nap', stooped down to pick up a card which had dropped on the floor. He got his 'Nap' and the remark was passed that anyone could get 'Nap' by picking up cards from the floor. 'Well, then, count them,' said I, and this led to an argument – I was defending a youngster from a bully – and we fell foul of each other. Just about this time a boxer named 'Tiger' Smith fought 'Iron' Hague for the British championship and Dick Lilley called me 'Tiger'. The name has stuck with me ever since. And I am proud of the title.

'Tiger' made his début against the South Africans, who won by ten wickets. He kept wicket and remembers missing J. L. Tancred and seeing J. H. Sinclair hit a ball over the pavilion and clear across the road into the courts of the Tally Ho! Lawn Tennis Club, no mean blow. He did not play his first County Championship match until the following year and, indeed, until 1909 he probably played more matches for the M.C.C., with whom Warwickshire placed him to save money, than he did for the county.

Lilley had the honour of captaining the Players in both the Lord's and Oval matches, the first Warwickshire player to do so. The Gentlemen won both games and, at The Oval especially, completely outplayed their opponents. This was largely due to B. J. T. Bosanquet, who, four years earlier, had first introduced the googly to the cricket fields of England. Lilley had often chaffed him about it and said that if he ever bowled it against him he would never get him out.

Bosanquet was fond of telling the story of what happened when finally they met in this match. 'I got a few wickets in the second innings,' he said. 'Then one of the "pros" came in and said, "Dick's in next. He's calling us a lot of rabbits – says he can see every ball you bowl. Do try and get him and we'll rag his life out." Dick came in. I bowled him two overs of leg-breaks, then changed my action but bowled another leg-break. Dick moved to play it gracefully to fine leg and it removed his off stump. I can still hear the reception he got in the dressing-room.'

In the match Bosanquet took eight wickets, six of them for 60 in the second innings, and then scored 145. Lilley said later that although he had 'kept' so much to him he was completely deceived by the ball that bowled him.

Lilley had the reputation also of being superstitious and George Austin, the Warwickshire scorer, used to tell how, at an hotel in the south of England, after he had gone to bed, a member of the side noticed that the number of his room was 31 and changed the figures round to 13. Next morning when it was pointed out to Lilley that he had slept in a room numbered 13 he was in such a state that he refused breakfast until someone took pity on him and told him of the joke.

The 1904 season was saddened by the early death of yet another Warwickshire beneficiary – Stephen James Whitehead, who died the day after the match ended. It was against Essex, which had been allotted to Whitehead and Richards jointly. He was only 41 and apparently in the best of health for he attended on the first day when Warwickshire, on that 'naturally perfect wicket', as MacLaren described it in an article he wrote for *Wisden* on the preparation of pitches, amassed a total of 614 for eight wickets, 200 of them being made by Quaife without being dismissed.

'The best of comrades and a credit to the profession to which he belonged,' was how Santall remembered him. 'A fine bowler on his day, he had few superiors in the seasons 1893 and 1894,' in which he took sixty-nine and ninety-one wickets for just over 15 runs each. Unfortunately the receipts for the match with Essex came to only £308 and with expenses at £105, there was only £203 left to be divided between the players. There were also claims against Whitehead's estate, including one by W. G. Quaife, presumably for cricket equipment – he had gone into business with Lilley and founded what became a famous firm – amounting to £34.

The Committee decided to place Richards's share on deposit at the bank and to invest all the moneys for Whitehead's estate for the benefit of his four children. Fortunately the *Sports Argus*, one of Birmingham's two Saturday evening sports editions, later to be merged, came to the rescue with a fund for Whitehead's children, which brought in £135. Even so, after payment of all the claims, Whitehead's share was only £52, plus the newspaper's cheque.

Northamptonshire were admitted to first-class company this season, which turned out a gloriously fine summer, good for batsmen at Edgbaston if nowhere else. Quaife had an average of 63. Warwickshire played only sixteen games in the Championship, the fewest of any county and, without Field owing to injury except for four games, finished joint seventh with Essex. One result probably gave them more pleasure than all the others – for the first time in the County Championship they beat Yorkshire and at Huddersfield, too, though only by 6 runs after a desperately exciting finish. In a low-scoring game Warwickshire began by losing seven wickets for 79, but Santall, with 51, and Moorhouse, with 28, took the total to 164. When Yorkshire batted Field bowled so well, taking seven for 63, that Yorkshire were all out 116. Warwickshire were put out for 82 in their second innings, which left Yorkshire needing 131 to win. They had six men out for 66, and when E. Smith and Haigh put on 48 they seemed safely home, but with eight down for 120 Hunter was foolishly run out and Hargreave finished them off, taking five for 45. Field had four for 56 and match figures of eleven for 119. Warwickshire's fielding throughout was described as 'brilliant'. The defeat virtually cost Yorkshire the Championship.

From their visit to Edgbaston emerged a good newspaper story, told by Unite Jones. With the Yorkshire team came the usual band of Press followers headed by the bearded patriarchal figure of A. W. Pullin, who for years had been cricket correspondent of *The Yorkshire Post* under the pseudonym – more favoured then than the writers' own names – of 'Old Ebor'. After lunch one day he was missing from the Press box and there was curious speculation as to where he could be. Someone recalled that during the interval he had been seen in close consultation with Lord Hawke and the worst was feared. What was Pullin up to? Had he been given some exclusive story and, if so, what was it?

Eventually Pullin returned to the Press box and, watched curiously by his colleagues, wiped his moist brow, sharpened a pencil and began to write, covering page after page of Press telegraph forms, which he 'posted' through the flap leading to the special Post Office telegraph department then next door to the Press box from which it was separated by only a thin partition. No sooner had the first folio arrived than there rang out a penetrating voice which could be heard not only all over the Press box, but outside as well. 'What do you think, Bill', it said, 'Tom Emmett's dead.' 'Old Ebor' could only splutter with indignation as every man in the box hurriedly began to write the story that was no longer a scoop.

The special appeal, the chairman said at the annual meeting, had made it possible to wipe out the losses of 1902 and 1903, and start 1904 with a balance of nearly £1500 so that the Club, according to the honorary treasurer, was in a more favourable position than it had ever been in its history. Despite this and a fine summer the Committee later in the year decided to save £16 by not engaging a coach for young players, a penny-wise pound-foolish decision surely, and also that in future the question of talent money should be deferred until the end of the season and be paid according to how the results of the season had worked out. Eventually £73 was available to be shared between thirteen players.

The Committee also decided that win money of £1 be paid for Championship matches only, and that inquiries should be made about the possibility of curtailing expenses on players' and umpires' lunches 'now usually found by the county Club at considerable cost'. Players were also warned early the following season that because of the financial position they must not look to the Club for help in cases of accident, sickness or injury, but should insure against them. It so happened that only eight of them had then done so. At the end of the season there was a loss of £659, due, according to the annual report, not to bad weather but to lack of public support: 'The fact is that there has been little or no growth in the patronage of the public during the past ten years. Unless this is to be forthcoming there is little prospect of the Club being able to pay its way.' This was the cross which Ryder had to bear during his entire secretaryship.

The slow tempo of Warwickshire's cricket in 1905 came in for some sharp criticism from *Wisden*. They did not win a match until the beginning of July and there were no fewer than thirteen draws. Although the side often made plenty of runs, 'they took so much time in doing so that their opponents, with little else left than a draw to try for, also played slow cricket. To this fact may be ascribed the apathy of the Birmingham public and the comparatively small attendance at several of the games despite the delightful weather with which most of them were favoured. A little more resolution to try and win and a little less of the dogged endeavour to avoid being beaten would, in our opinion, largely increase the local interest and strengthen the financial position of the county club.' The writer might also have mentioned that Field was often out of the side owing to injury, a fact which did not help them to get rid of their opponents any more easily.

Wisden's was not the only voice raised in protest. At the beginning of August, a member of the Committee, H. Margetts, wrote complaining of slow play by Quaife and Kinneir whom he considered should be reproved by the Committee. He did not specify in which match this was alleged to have occurred, but the Committee, though as a whole they did not agree with their fellow-member's strictures, forwarded the letter to the captain for him to act on as he thought fit.

Cartland also took up the question at the next annual meeting. He said he did not know why their team seemed to have got an exceedingly bad name for slow scoring and not winning matches, and he went on to cite figures proving that in matches on their own ground Warwickshire players scored seven runs an hour more than their opponents, so few runs, one would have thought, that spectators could be pardoned for not noticing them. The scoring, Cartland then went on to admit, was slow, but Warwickshire were not the chief offenders. He was afraid Birmingham people were only inclined to support those who were successful and that, he thought, was bad sportsmanship.

Warwickshire certainly thought they were the victims of it in what might be described as 'The Curious Case of the Bowler who Took a Rest' when Leicestershire came to Edgbaston in May. It was an even-scoring match which Warwickshire lost by a mere nine runs, but what made it remarkable was that Gill, the Leicestershire fast bowler, left the field in Warwickshire's second innings, for what both *Wisden* and Santall described as a rest, and then came back and took two of the last three wickets – something which could not happen today. As he had bowled 31·1 overs in the first innings, taking eight for 89, and 26·2 overs in the second, he perhaps felt he was entitled to a rest, but the incident caused 'some feeling', though there is no record that Warwickshire's captain took any action.

For the rest, Quaife scored more runs than ever, over 2000 in all, including 255 not out against Surrey at The Oval, up to then the highest individual score for the county. This was one of his six centuries and he averaged 63 and finished third in the first-class averages. He could be considered unfortunate not to be picked for the Players, let alone for any of the Tests against Australia, in all of which Lilley kept wicket.

Another double centurion was Byrne, who had a mammoth opening partnership with Kinneir of 333 against Lancashire, the latter scoring 158 and Byrne going on next day to 222. This partnership stood as a record for the county for over fifty years.

The Australians went away from Edgbaston victorious by an innings and 51 runs. Noble made 125, the first 100 of them in an hour, and Cotter, who made the ball kick nastily, took seven for 76, finishing off the Warwickshire innings with five for 15 in four overs.

It might be said to have been poetic justice for both counties that both the matches between Warwickshire and Worcestershire in 1906 were drawn because of heavy scoring for, as *Wisden* was at pains to point out, 'the wickets at Edgbaston are too good for the majority of bowlers, as may be gathered from the fact that only two matches were played out there. Worcestershire', *Wisden* went on, 'share with Warwickshire the doubtful distinction of having one of the most heartbreaking pitches to bowl on in England in fine weather.'

At Edgbaston 1058 runs were scored while twenty-seven wickets fell and at Worcester it was even worse – 1191 for only twenty-four wickets. The last half-dozen matches between the sides had been left unfinished, yet there was never a ghost of a suggestion that anything should be done about it. Obviously they should have dug up that wicket long before they eventually did so.

There were nine draws altogether, but despite the fact that Byrne lost the toss twelve times running Warwickshire won seven matches and finished one place higher in the table, sixth. Considering they were without Field, who broke down with elbow trouble in the second match of a dry season in which the county could ill afford to be without a really fast bowler, this was not bad. Fortunately Hargreave again took over 100 wickets, 101, twice as many as any other bowler, though Quaife did much more bowling than usual, which probably upset his batting because for once he fell just short of getting his 1000 runs. The batting honours this season went to Fishwick and Devey, both of whom played some dashing innings, the latter being the only batsman to reach a four-figure aggregate, though C. S. Baker, from Lancashire, made two centuries in only his second season.

This was the *annus mirabilis* of George Hirst – over 2000 runs and 200 wickets in the same season – and he gave a perfect demonstration at Edgbaston of how to bat on a wet wicket. He came in when there were four wickets down for 35 and made 104 out of Yorkshire's total of 190. He batted for three hours and a quarter without making a mistake and was last man out, caught in the deep.

The match – the only one he played for the county – nevertheless provided Irving Smith with two vivid memories, and he had many, including one of touching 'W.G.'s' blazer when he was taken by his mother to Edgbaston at the age of two. Smith, who lived to be 84, went in at No. six when Rhodes was bowling and 'scratched away and held up for an over or two'. The Yorkshire players, he once said, were very nice about it. David Hunter, the wicketkeeper, told him not to worry, but to treat it as a club match, and when there was some barracking from the crowd Lord Hawke told him not to bother about it – 'I'll go and quieten the beggars,' he said. Smith made only one run, but J. T. Tunnicliffe complimented him on his good-length bowling, and that, too, was something for an old man to remember.

Against Somerset at Edgbaston Warwickshire left it until the last ball of the match to win. This was the first time they had won the toss after Byrne's run of ill-luck and after brilliant hitting by Fishwick they left Somerset needing 454 to win. They nearly got them, too, but Charlesworth bowled three men within minutes. The last man had to survive only two balls, but was bowled middle stump by the second, Finally, there were curious goings-on at Hastings, where, after Sussex had tied the scores, Warwickshire had to bat again to make one run to win – and did it with a wide, first ball. This may well have been the first and only match won in this strange way.

The Earl of Warwick's three-year term as President ended and Lord Calthorpe succeeded him at the annual meeting, which found Cartland lamenting the fact that, despite the tour by the Australians, membership was not so large as in the previous season and gate receipts were again comparatively small. Somerset's share of the gate at Birmingham was exactly £8 4s 0d and Warwickshire's at Taunton £10 8s 0d, though it must be remembered that each county was meeting the other for the first time. In fact, there were losses on all the new matches, the others being with Sussex and Northants, and the treasurer pointed out that the Club had begun to lose money in 1899, that for the last five years the losses had amounted to £2500 and that they could not go on losing £500 a year. Despite a share of £315 of the Test profits, the loss on the year was £312.

All this prompted Cartland to ask if there was a lukewarmness about cricket generally. Only three county clubs had had satisfactory seasons, despite the Australians' visit, and he thought the powers-that-be ought to consider how to make the game more attractive. The year is 1906, remember, but what a familiar ring his words have. Warwickshire had suggested that all the counties should play one another and Mr Bainbridge had also expressed the opinion that in the Championship matches only wins should count. That, Cartland thought, would induce everybody to do his best to win.

Bainbridge himself thought the system of scoring was the cause of slow play – one point for each win, one deducted for each loss and unfinished games not reckoned, and the Championship being decided by the county gaining the greatest proportionate number of points in finished games. Warwickshire's scheme was eventually rejected by the Advisory County Cricket Committee, as was a suggestion from Essex for one point for a win on the first innings and two for a win on both innings.

At the end of the year, with the accounts indicating a probable deficit of £800, there was no talent money and Quaife and Santall protested. Ryder did more than that – he spent the winter months in a personal canvass in the city, knocking on doors to obtain new members, and enrolled 600 of them, an astonishing achievement.

In 1907 no one scored 1000 runs and only three hundreds were made, but at long last Santall achieved 100 wickets – and for only 16·79 each. It was the only season in his long career in which he did so. It was an exceptionally wet season and Warwickshire won one more match than they lost and ended in ninth position in the table. After being beaten by Sussex in the first match, they did not lose another one until mid-July, by which time they were fourth, but then they fell away badly, although they were the only team to beat Worcestershire, who finished joint second, at Worcester. The Committee gave trials to several young amateurs, including the Stephens twins – G.W., later captain for a season, and F.G. – from Moseley, and H. J. Goodwin, then at Cambridge University, also to be captain. The Stephens brothers, both fine athletes, endeared themselves to spectators by their brilliant fielding in the country, while Goodwin was a splendid slip field.

Kinneir distinguished himself in a very unusual way at Leicester, where he carried his bat through each innings – 70 out of 239 in the first innings and 69 out of 166 in the second. It is a rare feat. Up to that time it had been done only three times – by W. Lambert, who made 107 and 157 for Sussex v. Epsom at Lord's in 1817; by 'W.G.', with 130 and 102 for South of the Thames v. North of the Thames at Canterbury in 1868, though it is doubtful if either of these games ranked as first class; and by Harry Jupp for Surrey against Yorkshire at The Oval in 1874 for 43 and 109. Kinneir scored a quarter of all his runs for the season – 638 – in this one match, and two of the three Warwickshire centuries were also made in it, Lilley's 171, his highest score in first-class cricket, and Baker's 105. They put on 228 in only 150 minutes for the fifth wicket.

Warwickshire used only two bowlers against Leicestershire at Coventry – Hargreave five for 43 and three for 39, and Santall four for 54 and seven for 48 – Warwickshire winning by eight wickets, and they played Braund rather than Somerset at Bath. In Warwickshire's first innings he took seven for 105, then made 29, his side's highest score; he took another seven wickets for 36 in Warwickshire's second innings and then got another 13 not out. Braund won by seven wickets – and he deserved it.

Hobbs, then 24 and coming into his kingdom, also batted through the innings at Edgbaston, playing superbly and completely overshadowing everyone else for 60 out of 155; he made 150 out of 283 in the return match at The Oval. Another master, J. T. Tyldesley, hit a magnificent

209 at Edgbaston. Devey played his last innings for the county. He had been a member of the team on and off for twenty years but developed late. According to Santall, he was one of the few batsmen in England who could really master a sticky wicket. Altogether he scored 7659 runs for the county, average 25·31.

South Africa invaded us this season with a gaggle of googly experts – Schwarz, Faulkner, Vogler and White. As one veteran said afterwards, 'It was like playing Briggs through the air and Tom Richardson off the pitch.' They bamboozled Warwickshire, getting them out for 202 and 136, only Quaife and Lilley playing them with any confidence. The South Africans won by 276 runs.

The by now usual inquest on the state of the game was held at the annual meeting. The acting chairman, Alderman C. G. Beale, said it was hard to understand how the loss of £877 had arisen, but the Club must not be allowed to die for lack of nourishment and he thought an appeal should be made to the cricket patriotism of Warwickshire. He was at a loss to suggest a cause – the weather had been good, the cricket brighter, but they must admit there had been a general decline in interest in Warwickshire cricket. It was said that Birmingham was more a football than a cricket city, but he thought the two games appealed to different classes altogether. Failing increased support, though, it would be impossible to carry on the Club on first-class lines.

The honorary treasurer's view was that cycling, motoring and golf had already been contributory causes. There seemed, however, a want of appreciation of the game and he instanced how, when Somerset were trying to save the match at Edgbaston, many people left because, as they said, the play was slow. Those who left were deprived of witnessing a fine finish. Warwickshire could not possibly go down into the second class, though it was true that when they were second class they did better than they had been doing. He complained of lack of support from Coventry, Leamington, Nuneaton, Tamworth and Rugby, although special terms were offered to subscribers there. Perhaps if Warwickshire had played more games on these grounds they might have got better support.

Fewer than 100 members were at the meeting and a newspaper report of the day stated: 'It might have been the meeting of shareholders of a successful company rather than that of a county cricket club with an adverse balance of £877 on the year's working' – so soon, it might have been added, after a successful appeal for £3000. But Warwickshire members, it seems, have always been like this. Throughout the Club's history they have rarely offered comment at meetings, still less criticism, which suggests either that they have always had complete faith in their officers, or that they have been too apathetic to make a fuss.

The most serious aspect of the situation then, of course, was an unexpected decrease in subscriptions of £300, hence the canvass and an offer of various concessions, which could be said to constitute the Club's first package-deal offer. The target was 2500 members, 600 more than they had.

Warwickshire's Foster
(1908–1910)

STRICTLY speaking, Warwickshire's near neighbours, Worcestershire, are the only county which can claim the alternative title of 'Fostershire', gained when no fewer than eight members of that distinguished cricketing family – the Rev. H. Foster and his seven sons – played for them. There was a time, however, during the seasons from 1908 to 1914 when Warwickshire might fairly have borrowed the title, if only because of the shining deeds of a player of the same name, though no relation, for whom those lucky enough to have seen him claimed that he was the most brilliant all-rounder the county has ever had. It could truly be said that he shot into the cricketing sky like a rocket, blazed with brilliance for a brief spell, and then, alas, came down like a rocket also.

Frank Rowbotham Foster was born in Small Heath, Birmingham, on 31 January 1889, into a family owning a clothing firm which still has many branches over the Midlands today, and he himself was working in the trade when he was first invited to play for Warwickshire in 1908. He played his early cricket at Solihull Grammar School, as it was then, and Hall Green Cricket Club and it was his performances as a fastish left-arm bowler for the latter which first brought him to the notice of the county. In his first match for the second eleven at Worcester he went in last and scored 50; no one had said anything about his batting, but they were soon to remedy the omission.

At the time he was working for Wilkinson and Riddell, Ltd, then in Cherry Street, Birmingham (later Wilkinson, Riddell and Larkins, Ltd, Smethwick), as 'last man' in the hosiery department, as he has told us in a book* remarkable for its naïvety and unblushing confessions, and it was

Cricketing Memories, The London Publishing Co. Incorp, 1930.

his job to sweep the floor each night. It was while clearing up one evening that he threw a bundle of stockings at one of his friends and narrowly missed hitting in the face Col. Howard Wilkinson, one of the principals of the firm, who merely asked Foster if he were the cricketer and when Foster replied 'No, sir', remarked, 'Dear me, dear me, how very unfortunate,' and walked away.

It was another director of the firm, Mr C. S. Riddell, who gave Foster permission to play in five matches for Warwickshire in 1908, and when he left for his first match against Derbyshire at Derby gave him six stamped telegraph forms so that he could wire the scores back to the warehouse, one at lunch and one at tea each day. Foster discloses in his book that he was so nervous that he did not have the pluck to go near the telegraph office and that he destroyed all the forms, an act for which he belatedly begged forgiveness.

He need not have been nervous for although in his first two seasons – in 1909 he played in seventeen matches – he did nothing sensational, taking twenty-three wickets in one and forty-eight in the other and scoring 24 runs and 530 respectively, eyes long skilled in picking out youngsters of promise had been looking him over and been impressed. In an article about him which he wrote for *Wisden* in 1911, P. F. Warner remembered Dick Lilley telling him two or three years earlier that Warwickshire had found a left-hander who, if he was not over-bowled, ought to be heard of, and J. T. Tyldesley, who usually got a century against Warwickshire and hit 152 against the county at Edgbaston in 1909 (MacLaren also helping himself to 100 in 80 minutes), let it be known that, in his opinion, 'a new left-handed bowler of exceptional ability had been discovered.'

What sort of bowler was he? 'My bowling', Foster himself wrote, 'was simply a gift from God . . . and all I had to do was to use my brains and so improve that gift . . . No left-hander should ever attempt to bowl over the wicket . . . I took a short eight-yard run, holding the ball always in the left hand with "seam up" and I always delivered the ball from the very edge of the bowling crease.'

Warner has described how, 'bowling round the wicket with a high delivery, his action was the personification of ease. A few short steps, an apparently medium-paced ball through the air, but doubling its speed as it touched the ground, he kept an exceptional length on the leg stump. He swerved a little with the new ball, but the angle of delivery made the ball swing into the batsman without swerve.' Warner thought that Foster 'must possess very powerful muscles at the back of his shoulders for he is one of those bowlers who, if I may use the expression, come very suddenly on to the batsman.'

'Tiger' Smith, who 'kept' to Foster throughout his career, thought he came faster off the pitch than did even Frank Field, a genuinely fast bowler – with respect to all those who think it mathematically impossible for a ball to increase its speed after pitching, though everyone agrees that Foster, like Tate, seemed to possess this power. And for Foster there was only one wicketkeeper, his beloved 'Tiger', 'the very best leg taker I have ever seen.' He was also indebted to Sam Hargreave who, he says, taught him how to bowl the leg-spinner and let him into the mysteries of 'undercut' and how to flight the ball.

Others have filled in details of that portrait of him, bat upraised, that hangs in the pavilion at Edgbaston. He was six feet tall, strikingly handsome, very appealing to the ladies, according to Mrs Margaret Abbott, Ryder's daughter, and hero-worshipped by all the young people; 'every boy's cricket hero', in M. F. K. Fraser's phrase. 'Tiger' once wrote of him that 'in all departments of the game he was joyous to watch and he was capable of filling a ground by his presence'. 'Joyous' – how long is it since that word was used of any cricketer, and who now can fill a ground?

That 'most promising recruit', as Santall described him, in his very first county match at Derby, took two wickets for 14 in the first innings and four for 38 in the second, including two wickets in two balls. L. G. Wright was his first victim in county cricket, as he had been the first to fall to S. F. Barnes, with whom Foster, in Australia, was to form what many good judges think was the best opening attack England has ever had. Foster's visit to The Oval that season was also his first ever to London, but what he remembered about it was that he had Tom Hayward stumped by 'Tiger' and Jack Hobbs himself caught by Baker, 'not bad for a youngster of 18 in his second county match', as he put it.

Not bad at all, indeed, but he had to wait a little longer before he stamped his name indelibly on Warwickshire and England cricket. In the meantime, Santall, after fourteen years' faithful service to the county in which he had taken nearly 1000 wickets, more than any other Warwickshire bowler up to that time, had his benefit against Yorkshire, but it was spoiled by rain and eventually he received no more than £400, a scant reward indeed.

A. C. S. Glover, a useful bat, good leg-break bowler and field, took over the captaincy from Byrne, and Field, laying at last the bogey of strains and injuries, had a full season and showed what a fine fast bowler he was by taking 102 wickets for 20 runs apiece, which took him to the head of the county averages. 'His idea of a pleasant bowling spell', said the Edgell-Fraser history, 'was an hour under a grilling sun; his idea of a rest to be put on at the other end. Not the most heart-breaking wicket ever prepared at Edgbaston, or anywhere else, could tame Field's fiery spirit. He was all heart, plus a considerable bulk of body.'

It was as well that Field struck his best form, for unhappily

Hargreave was unable to play after the end of June owing to an accident, and Warwickshire's attack had a demoralising experience – whose did not? – against Jessop who celebrated the opening of the Cheltenham Festival by hitting 72 in thirty-five minutes. There was more heavy scoring at Worcester, Warwickshire making 566, Quaife 189 not out, and Worcestershire 556, H. K. Foster 215; 1351 runs in all.

Warwickshire tried Saturday starts in three of their home matches this season and found they paid. Looking back, it seems incredible that they had not been introduced long before, but no doubt the amateurs wanted their weekend leisure, and since they largely ruled the administrative roost they had their way until the financial shoe began to pinch so much that even they could no longer resist the change, though it was seven years before it became general.

Saturday starts, Ryder told us in an article he wrote for *The Cricketer* in 1925, began with correspondence between Leicestershire and Warwickshire, and he gave credit for them to Mr S. Robson, then Leicestershire's secretary, who suggested that they should be tried during 1908, to which Warwickshire agreed. The first county match to start on a Saturday was between Leicestershire and Warwickshire on 9, 11 and 12 May at Leicester.

In 1909 Warwickshire had five games which started on Saturdays. Yorkshire and Kent were opposed to them, but in January 1913, Warwickshire supported the proposal of the Advisory County Cricket Committee that in 1914 and succeeding years all first-class matches should start on Saturdays or Wednesdays. The scheme was adopted for 1915, but, because of the war, could not start generally until 1920.

An unusually large attendance at the annual meeting in March 1909, heard the chairman comment that, despite fine weather, this was the ninth successive season that the Club had shown a deficit, a fact which led Cartland once more to remark that Birmingham was a football city and that it seemed to him 'a shocking thing' that while they were having meagre attendances last August, immediately afterwards 12 000 to 15 000 people attended Aston Lower Grounds to see a football practice match.

Fortunately there were to be more spectators at Edgbaston during the summer of 1909, which brought Edgbaston's second Test, again with Australia. Rarely can England's selectors – on this occasion C. B. Fry, A. C. MacLaren and H. D. G. Leveson Gower – have been so severely criticised. 'How these gentlemen came to make such a muddle of the business no one has ever been able to understand,' was *Wisden*'s comment, and after England's defeat at Lord's in the second Test MacLaren offered to resign, but his offer was not accepted.

At Edgbaston, however, all was well, England winning by ten

wickets after another lamentable collapse by Australia. They had already been twice beaten – by Surrey and M.C.C. – when they arrived here, again after much rain had fallen the previous day and during the night. Heavy showers shortly before 11 a.m. and 12.30 p.m. on the first day caused a delay until 5 p.m. when bad light held up play for a further 40 minutes. In the little time remaining Australia lost two wickets for 22 runs. Next day Blythe – six for 44 – and Hirst – four for 28 – finished off the innings in an hour and a half for 74.

England did not do much better, losing three wickets for 17 before lunch, but J. T. Tyldesley and A. O. Jones added 41 and Jessop hit 22 in 20 minutes, so they finished with 121. Early on the third day it seemed as if Australia would not have any trouble in drawing the match, thanks to a good stand between Sid Gregory and Ransford; but then the former, when he seemed firmly set, played an unguarded stroke, and his departure was followed by an astonishing collapse. The last five wickets fell for nine runs in half an hour, again to Blythe and Hirst who shared ten wickets between them, each conceding 58 runs. On a wicket one would have thought ideally suited to him, Rhodes was called on for only one over, off which eight runs were scored, a good point for a cricket quiz, perhaps, but think of the wealth of English cricket which could have *two* slow left-arm bowlers of such calibre in the side.

England won the match with four fours, three to Hobbs, playing in his first Test, and one to Fry, all run. Both had failed to score in the first innings, as did Lilley, who caught one batsman late in the second innings. In the second Test he had better fortune, scoring 47 and 25 not out; in the third four and two; in the fourth 26 not out; and in the fifth at The Oval two not out, which, surprisingly enough, gave him second place in the England batting averages, with 106 runs for 35·33.

Warwickshire's share of this Test series worked out at a total of £886, and one result of this was that at the end of the season it was possible to distribute £60 in talent money, which had not been paid for the four preceding years. After winning the Test at Leeds the Australians came back to Edgbaston in July and although they rested five men who had won that victory they almost polished the county side off by an innings, for Warwickshire had eight wickets down when stumps were drawn. Noble, 131, and Bardsley, 118, were the chief contributors to their total of 456, 105 of which came off Field, who nevertheless took half their wickets.

When Warwickshire went in, Edgbaston saw the unusual sight of Trumper opening the bowling. He sent down eleven overs, two of which were maidens, for 49 runs but did not take a wicket. Even without his help, Warwickshire were dismissed for 186 and they had lost eight for 185 in the second innings when the end came.

It was just as well there was some money to come from the Tests for the county side had a very poor season, not winning a match until half-way through July and finishing twelfth in the table. Glover lost the toss fifteen times. Foster, although it was suggested he sometimes tried to bowl too fast, took forty-nine wickets in this his second season, but Field's tally in a wet summer fell to fifty wickets. Perhaps it was as well for him financially that in January it had at last been agreed that, when he was left out of the team more than three times in a season because of weather considered unsuited to a fast bowler, he should be given half fees for matches at Birmingham and full fees for those at Coventry and Leamington.

Of the batsmen only Quaife made more than 1000 runs and he was not getting any younger, nor were one or two others, a fact on which Cartland was soon to remark. Warwickshire had their fill of Hobbs this season – 159 not out at The Oval, where Hayward got 204 not out as well – and centuries in each innings at Edgbaston – 160 and 100, the second time he had performed the feat. His four innings against Warwickshire came to 460 runs. Kinneir's 61 and 90 seemed very moderate by comparison, though he, too, had made a fine 133 at The Oval.

This last match was a shattering experience for Russell Everitt (at the time of his death in 1973 the Club's oldest former player, aged 92) for it was his first game for the county and suddenly he found himself captaining the side. When he arrived on the ground there was a telegram from Glover saying he was ill and unable to play and that he was to take over.

Warwickshire had the humiliating experience of being put out twice for under a hundred – 64 and 84 – by the Lancashire bowlers, Dean and Huddlestone, at Aigburth, and then just to rub it in MacLaren hit the Warwickshire bowling all over the field. One of the curiosities of cricket occurred at Northampton – nine batsmen were bowled in Warwickshire's first innings and in the second all ten were caught. For Worcestershire at Edgbaston Ted Arnold and Walter Burns put on 393, a stand which nobody anywhere has yet beaten for the fifth wicket.

The year 1910 began with the usual lamentations from the county committees over what *Wisden* called 'diminished receipts and deplorable balance sheets' and, indeed, the previous autumn Derbyshire had come near going out of existence. Cartland, at the annual meeting in March, said it was seventeen years since Warwickshire had received so little gate money, though their share of the Test Match profits had given the Club a substantial balance of £477. Those rival attractions cropped up again – 'golf as a game for younger men and, of course, motoring has done a great deal of harm. It is one of the phases of English life which seems to be changing.' He would have been vastly surprised, if not downright alarmed, to see how much it was still to change.

Foster really came into his own this season with over 100 wickets – 112 in all matches – for the first time in his career. 'All matches' included three for the Gentlemen at The Oval, Lord's and at the Scarborough Festival. In the first he took the wickets of Hayward and Rhodes for 34 and those of J. T. Tyldesley, Jack Sharp, T. Jayes and Harry Dean; at Lord's he had Tyldesley and Rhodes again, plus Hardstaff and Fielder, all clean bowled; and at Scarborough five for 83, including Hobbs, Hirst, Woolley and Smith, with Hirst and Haigh in the second innings. He was less successful for The Rest against the Champion County, Kent, though Warner thought that had it been necessary to choose an England XI this season Foster would probably have got a place.

Despite his individual success, the county had one of the worst seasons in its history and finished fourteenth out of sixteen, their lowest position up to then. Santall says that only too often they found themselves in an advantageous position, but could not drive it home. Part of the trouble, perhaps, was that Glover had given up the captaincy and his batting was badly missed. Goodwin reappeared and although he said he could play in only half the matches he officially led the side when he could; otherwise J. H. Phillips (whose grandson, Captain Mark Phillips, was to marry Princess Anne) took over.

There was one innings played this season which is still talked about by the few remaining veterans who were lucky enough to see it. It was against Derbyshire at Blackwell when 1259 runs were scored. Nearly half of them came from Warwickshire's first innings – 504 for seven declared – and nearly half of those came from Charlesworth, who made 216 in as many minutes, an astonishing rate of scoring for so long an innings. He and Kinneir added 166 in 135 minutes and in all Charlesworth hit six sixes and thirty fours. Derbyshire, not to be outdone, made 430 in their second innings, which was the fourth of the match; Warren, 123, and Chapman, 165, added 283 in two hours fifty-five minutes for the ninth wicket, a record for first-class cricket which still stands.

Champion County
(1911)

❖ ❖ ❖

IT would have been surprising if the changes in captaincy had not had their effect on the side's performances and, indeed, they had gone from bad to worse – ninth in 1907, twelfth in 1908 and 1909, and fourteenth in 1910, which was almost rock bottom – and it was obviously highly desirable for the team to have continuity in leadership. Even so, it was a bold decision on the part of the Warwickshire Committee in January 1911, to invite Foster, who was only just 22, to take over the captaincy.

The following month Santall's first history of the Club appeared and one of the contributors to it was Bainbridge, who, perhaps surprisingly in view of his earlier objections to practice sessions when they had been first suggested, made the rather belated admission that throughout the period in which Warwickshire had been a first-class county they had suffered from inefficient fielding and catching. 'If the catches missed by Warwickshire players in these years could speak,' he wrote, 'and were combined in chorus the deafening noise would make us understand why our bowlers did not always do what was expected of them, for in some of the years here recorded Warwickshire's batting and bowling were good enough to have brought the county much higher honours if only they had been in combination with equally meritorious fielding.'

Ryder, too, had many interesting things to say about the cost of running a first-class cricket club which provided not only interesting comparisons with the past but with the future. During the time Warwickshire had been a first-class county, he disclosed, the average annual expenditure was £4800 and the minimum outlay necessary to keep the Club on its 1911 footing was £4250, made up of: match expenses £1800; professionals' wages £1000; groundsman £200; rent, rates and repairs £550; postages, advertising and printing £150; cricket

109

gear, horse's keep and sundry expenses £150; office and general expenses £400. Well, at least there's no horse to worry about today.

Another contributory cause of Warwickshire's decline had been mentioned at the annual meeting in 1910 – ageing players who suffered more in a damp season than younger ones – and Cartland returned to the theme at the 1911 meeting when he suggested, apropos lack of interest in the game – jocularly, one wonders? – that batsmen should run out every boundary hit and that the grass in the outfield should be left rough so as to make boundaries more difficult to get, which, he said, 'would prevent stout and elderly gentlemen continuing so long in county cricket as they had done in the past'. On neither occasion, however, did Cartland name names.

Foster had no sooner accepted the honour of the captaincy than he confounded everyone by announcing his impending retirement from first-class cricket. The mystery of why he did so I have still not been able completely to solve. He was certainly a creature of impulse and must often have been a puzzle, not to say a trial, even to members of his own family. He says in his book that at the end of each season, when he was asked if he was going to play for Warwickshire again, his answer was always, 'No.' 'My mind', he adds, 'was forever torn between what I wanted to do and what my father wanted me to do. "You must make up your own mind, Frank," Dad said to me.'

In its issue of 2 May, however, *The Birmingham Post* published a brief announcement which gave a romantic clue to the reason for Foster's decision:

Unfortunately Mr Foster has up to the present been unable to accept the position, an engagement of a more romantic character as regards his future, it is said, causing an alteration of his immediate plans. Recognising the loss to the team, persuasion has been brought to bear upon him to alter his decision, but up to the present these efforts have been unsuccessful. It is expected, however, that something of a really definite nature will be forthcoming today or tomorrow. In the meantime, C. F. R. Cowan took over and will probably do so for the remainder of the season if Foster withdraws from county cricket.

What was said to Foster and what Foster said to the lady in the case, if, indeed, there was one, we shall never know, but it was not said in time for him to lead the team in the first match of the season on 4, 5 and 6 May. That task fell to Captain Cowan, a distinguished naval officer, who was to serve the Club in a variety of capacities for many years. He had an unhappy baptism on this occasion, however, for Warwickshire 'dispirited and obviously short of practice', as the annual review in *Wisden* put it, were hopelessly beaten in a day and a half. They were put out for 62 and 87 and lost by an innings despite the fact that they kept Surrey's score to 195. The one bright spot was that Harold Bates, Len's elder brother, making his first appearance and opening the bowling, slow left hand (though he had begun as a right-hander), with Santall, took the wickets of Hayward, Hobbs and Ducat for 56 runs.

E. H. D. Sewell, who contemptuously dismissed Warwickshire after this performance as not even a good Minor Counties side, should have been made to eat his words later in the season, for it was this team, with one change, the addition of Foster, which swept the board and won for Warwickshire their first County Championship; the first county outside the original nine, which inaugurated it.

Foster did not mention in his book anything about the 'engagement of a more romantic nature' mentioned in the newspaper report, but he heard the result of the Surrey match while still at the warehouse and when he went home his father said: 'They want you, my boy; you had better go.' So on 9 May the *Post* published at the head of the first column of the cricket news another brief announcement to the effect that 'Mr F. R. Foster has decided to place his services at the disposal of the Warwickshire Committee for the current season. He will accept the captaincy and will play in the match against Lancashire at Manchester on Thursday.'

Not even the most fervid supporter of Warwickshire cricket could have discerned here the beginning of a journey to the head of the County Championship table. The county's form in the last few seasons alone would have seemed to rule that out as the remotest of possibilities, but no one then guessed what capacity for inspired leadership lay latent in that handsome, rather devil-may-care young man, or how the team would respond to it. They were soon to see.

A new system of scoring, proposed by Somerset, who had finished at the foot of the table the previous season when Kent had won the title for the second year in succession, was in force for 1911. This time five points were awarded for a win outright; in drawn matches three points went to the side leading, and one point to the side behind, on the first innings; matches in which there was no result on the first innings not counting.

What no one could know at this stage was that it was going to be a long, hot summer, with hard, fast wickets ideally suited to the two Franks, Foster and Field, both of whom mercifully kept free of injury. As *Wisden* said, 'they bowled day after day on wickets of lightning pace and proved a great combination . . . it was as well for the county that they kept up their form as they did. The change bowling, it must be confessed, did not amount to much.' But for the first time since the days of Pallett and Shilton, Warwickshire had two bowlers each of whom took over 100 wickets.

After that doleful débâcle at The Oval, Warwickshire played like a revitalised team and won three matches in succession – the first of their double triumphs over Lancashire, this time at Old Trafford; against Leicestershire at Edgbaston; and Sussex at Coventry. At Old Trafford, J. T. Tyldesley for once failed, perhaps owing to one of those flashes of inspiration, or bluff – the Edgell-Fraser history says Foster was a bluffer; 'he gave the most outrageous orders; the events justified them' – which marked Foster's captaincy, especially this season.

He gave the ball to a young man named Parsons, who had been engaged only the season before as 'ground bowler' and had just come into the first eleven. Parsons got Tyldesley caught. It was his only wicket, but it was the one Foster wanted above all others, so the move had paid off and Lancashire were beaten by 117 runs. In Lancashire's first innings three bowlers took three wickets each and in the second, four bowlers shared them – it was the first of many real team efforts which Foster inspired.

Parsons developed into one of the most colourful and forthright cricketers who has ever played for Warwickshire. He began as a professional, went into the Church of England and once more played as an amateur, being one of the few men to have played for both Gentlemen and Players, three times for each.

He had been born in Oxford, but his father came to Birmingham and kept first The Bull's Head in Old Square and later The Ship at Camp Hill. Jack had played only works cricket – he had been apprenticed to motor engineering – until one Saturday afternoon, when he was 19, he turned out for King's Heath against a side which included Lilley and Charlesworth. He does not remember what happened in that match, but Lilley must have liked the look of him and suggested a trial at Edgbaston which he duly had and was promptly offered £3 a week during the summer and £1 10s 0d in the winter.

Sitting on the pavilion balcony one afternoon, he talked about those early days:

We all went to the nets about 2 p.m. bowling at the young amateurs – Alec Hastilow was one of them – till 4.30. Then we used to go off – we were not allowed in the pavilion – and buy a glass of tea for a penny and a penny bun or cake. At 5.30 we used to go out again and bowl until 7.30 or 8 p.m. There was no question of the youngsters on the ground being coached. There were four of us and we had to go into another net to have our practice among ourselves. I consider that did us a power of good. We used to be sent sometimes to Lichfield on Wednesday afternoons to play for Lichfield – I got a few bob and rail fare – and there were Club and Ground matches. Then suddenly I was chosen for the second eleven against Worcestershire II on an August Bank Holiday and I made 200. Frank Chester was playing and M. F. S. Jewell and then, to my amazement, I found I was in the Warwickshire side against Derbyshire at Edgbaston and I played in the first eleven for the rest of the season. The old 'pros' were grand fellows. They all, either consciously or unconsciously, played according to the principles of the game.

– and for Jack Parsons that meant an upright stance, a straight bat and driving that rattled pavilion rails and roofs.

Charlesworth, one of Parsons's heroes, had made 110 against Lancashire and he followed this with 51 not out against Leicestershire at Edgbaston, where Warwickshire lost the toss, but hit off 266 runs to win, the last 82 coming in an hour. Then at Coventry he made 116 in two hours and Foster took six for 40 in the first of his many fine individual performances during the summer.

Even if, because of this marked improvement, Warwickshire had begun to cherish any ideas of winning the Championship, which is unlikely, their hopes received a setback from their neighbours at Worcester. It was a close thing for first innings lead, Warwickshire just topping Worcestershire's 201 with 213; but then Pearson turned the tables with a fine 155, though he was let off at 25. Warwickshire were left with exactly 300 to get to win, but no one was inspired this time and they were all out for 183.

Then, returning to Edgbaston to meet Yorkshire, they had an even greater disappointment. Not only did Foster make his first century, 105, in first-class cricket – and he could not have done it at a more opportune moment, for Warwickshire had lost half their wickets for 61 – but when Yorkshire batted he bowled with superb energy and skill. He sent down twenty-nine overs and three balls, four of them maidens, for 118 runs and nine wickets. At one point he bowled five overs and three balls for 31 runs and seven wickets. This was the first time anyone had taken so many wickets in an innings on the ground.

Even so, Yorkshire scored 347 to Warwickshire's 317 and although Warwickshire made 248 in their second innings after an opening stand of 130 by Kinneir and Parsons, Yorkshire won by four wickets, Foster bowling another twenty-seven overs and taking three for 84. Ah, the prodigies of effort one is capable of at 22.

It required a little less effort to dispose of the Indian touring side for 76 and 185 and win by ten wickets, and then Warwickshire went on to Blackwell in Derbyshire and gained some more Championship points in a low-scoring match in which no one distinguished themselves except 'Tiger' Smith, who made 81 in the second innings, and Warren, who had eleven wickets for 138 in the match for Derbyshire.

Gloucestershire next took them down a peg in a game of remarkably even scoring at Gloucester – Charlesworth's 42 was the highest score on either side – and Field and Dennett each took twelve wickets in the match for 79 and 142 respectively. Then, with the return to Edgbaston for the Hampshire match on 29 June, began a remarkable run of nine wins outright and three on the first innings, fifty-four points out of a possible sixty, which took Warwickshire to the Championship.

They crushed Hampshire by an innings and 296 runs after Kinneir had made 268, the highest individual innings so far played for the county. He batted seven hours ten minutes and was missed four times, and Warwickshire delayed their declaration until he had beaten the record, luckily without paying the penalty. One wonders whether Foster would have risked it, but both he and Mead were engaged in the Test trial at Lord's. However, Field did the hat trick, so all was well.

Warwickshire had the best of a draw with Surrey and this time it was Foster's turn to make a double century exactly and 'Tiger' followed it with another hundred. Next came four victories in succession over Northants, Sussex, Gloucestershire and Yorkshire, the last named on their own midden (if lordly Harrogate will permit so crude a description) which mightily pleased everyone except Yorkshire folk. Northants at Edgbaston had to endure both a century and a half-century from Quaife, to say nothing of 98 from Foster, who, with Field, was also in his best form with the ball, and that was too much for them; at Chichester Sussex had centuries in each innings – 124 and 110 – inflicted on them by Kinneir, the first Warwickshire player to achieve such a feat.

Back in Birmingham, Quaife again, this time with two not-out innings, 104 and 57, and Foster, with 56 and 87, to say nothing of eight wickets as well, put paid to Gloucestershire by seven wickets, 12 000 people packing the ground for a Saturday start. There followed the astonishing away match with Yorkshire, which it was vital for Warwickshire to win if they were to keep their now rising Championship hopes alive.

Because of rain a fresh wicket had to be prepared and Foster decided to bat on it when he won the toss. He had no cause to regret his action when Warwickshire made 341, of which he scored 60. He took four wickets for 94 when Yorkshire batted and just failed, with 310, to get first innings points. To their lead of 31 Warwickshire added a second innings of 225, of which Foster this time contributed an even greater share than he had done in the first innings – 101.

According to his racy account, the Harrogate wicket was guarded overnight because it was feared that a few over-zealous Yorkshire supporters might take it into their heads to water the wicket and thus make it easier for their heroes to get the 257 they needed to win, and the umpires took steps next morning to see that the wicket had not been tampered with. Foster admits to spending a hectic time the previous evening with a few friends in Huddersfield and had barely tumbled into bed when Frank Field and the Warwickshire 'trainer' (unnamed) arrived in his bedroom at 7 a.m., having suspected, perhaps, that the skipper might be in need of freshening up before play started. At any rate, Foster says, they stripped him, put him into a bath and then for an hour 'pumped and pummelled' him and ordered a beef steak and a pint of beer for his breakfast.

Foster has said he 'could hardly crawl to the wicket when the day's fun began', but he caught Rhodes out in Field's first over. In this innings Field had three men caught and bowled, most unusual for a fast bowler, which suggests that the ball was kicking up and that batsmen were playing their strokes too soon. According to Foster the ball was flying about badly and George Hirst, annoyed at being hit on the legs so often, threatened in fun to throw his bat at him if he 'bruised his dear old legs any more. Luckily for me, Field caught and bowled George Hirst soon after the latter made his famous remark.'

Field must have been well-nigh unplayable. 'Tiger' Smith, in an article he wrote for *The Birmingham Post* in February 1951, said the wicket was so bad that one renowned Yorkshire player – Smith does not name him – said to a colleague: 'Get thi' pads on – *I've* a wife and two children to look after,' and that another batsman walked out without an appeal being made saying he had had enough. Yorkshire's last nine wickets went down in an hour for 44 runs and they were all out before lunch for 58, Warwickshire winning by 198 runs. As A. A. Thomson, who saw the match, put it, he watched Foster 'virtually demolish Yorkshire with both bat and ball'.

There followed draws against Hampshire at Southampton – another hundred from Kinneir and a colossal partnership of 292 in only two hours 40 minutes by Mead, 207 not out, and Johnson, 122 – and against Worcestershire at Edgbaston. Batting honours this time went to Baker, with a not out 101; Foster again with 85 and 62; and F. G. Stephens, 50 and 96. Even at this distance of time one reads with a feeling of drowsy warmth stealing over one that it was so hot that poor Field had to retire with slight sunstroke after bowling thirteen overs in the second innings. On the opening day, August Bank Holiday Monday, 19 000 people filled the ground, a record up to then and a sign that at last the Midland cricketing public, such as it was, was interested in coming to watch a winning team.

This they continued to be against Derbyshire at Edgbaston, Foster taking ten wickets for 103 in the match. Quaife thought that his innings in this match was one of the best he ever played. 'We were about 48 behind on the first innings', he wrote, 'and at lunch we had lost four wickets for about 40, myself none not out. The wicket was broken at one end. After lunch I got settled, scored 144 not out and we won the match easily.' Then it was Lancashire's turn. They had come on from Canterbury where they had done Warwickshire a good turn by beating Kent, their nearest rivals, but if they expected any thanks they were disappointed. They brought another Tyldesley, in Ernest, to plague Warwickshire, but they were got rid of for 210, Field taking half their wickets for 78; and then Warwickshire batted with such consistency that although no one got a century – Foster 98, Kinneir 80 and Quaife

67 – they totalled 422. Field bowled even better in the second innings and took six for 74, five of them clean bowled.

Warwickshire won by an innings and triumphed by the same margin over Leicestershire at Hinckley where the experiment of playing a match was so successful that 5000 people came on the Saturday and 4000 on the Monday. They saw Warwickshire rattle up 365, Charlesworth 142 of them in 150 minutes, and C. J. B. Wood, Leicestershire's renowned opener, carry his bat through an innings for the fourth time, scoring 54 out of 164; but Field claimed nine wickets and Foster seven.

Kent, after losing to Lancashire, had won their next two matches, but they went down to Surrey at The Oval by 9 runs and beat Yorkshire by ten wickets at Canterbury, just before Warwickshire went to Northampton, where they had to win to clinch the title. It is said that as the team left New Street Station, Birmingham, a supporter called out: 'Going to beat 'em, Mr Foster?' and that Foster replied: 'Beat 'em? We'll paralyse 'em.'

Whether this is true or not, it is what Warwickshire did, winning like the Champions they proved to be by an innings and 35 runs. They would have done it in two days but for interruptions due to rain. There was a perfect wicket, but the sun came out only fitfully through lowering clouds and rain seemed certain before Monday. Field groaned when his captain told him he had lost the toss. 'What good are you?' Foster says Field asked him, and then added: 'Never mind, leave it to me, skipper, I'll bowl 'em out.'

And he and Foster did. They had Northants in and out in two hours before lunch for 73, only two men getting double figures. Field had four wickets for 27 and Foster five for 18. By close of play on the first day Warwickshire, thanks to another century by Charlesworth, had scored 226 for the loss of nine wickets and they went happily back to their hotel. Sunday was wet and hopes of a win sank to zero and did not rise when Monday dawned miserable and uninviting, though the rain had stopped. When they reached the ground they found it was not fit for play so they had an early lunch. Play began eventually at three o'clock and despite a wet ball and conditions not at all suitable for him, Field, as his captain afterwards put it, 'bowled like an England fast bowler'. By the end of the day Northants had lost seven wickets and still needed 71 runs to avoid an innings defeat, G. A. T. Vials, their captain, having played a very stubborn innings, batting two hours for an invaluable 30.

'Naturally', Foster tells us in his book, 'we all spent a very pleasant evening at our hotel and, as we were very anxious about the weather, we stayed up all night to welcome the dawn. As the clock struck four o'clock I, for one, tried to snatch a few hours' sleep, but I am sorry to say I was fetched out of bed again to finish an exciting game of "Farmer's

Glory" . . . pretty useful for keeping one wide awake. The sun was shining when we left the card table for the breakfast table.'

It took only 35 minutes for Warwickshire to finish off the innings, Foster eventually taking six of the second innings wickets for 63 and Field three for 60, and Warwickshire had won their thirteenth match and become Champions by a percentage of 0·16 – 74·00 to 73·84 – and you could not have it much closer than that. Then, according to *The Sportsman*, 'the crowd surged on to the ground and gave the victorious players a splendid reception. Mr A. J. Darnell, honorary secretary of the home county, in a neat little speech, congratulated Warwickshire on winning the match and the Championship which, he said, was the culmination of a brilliant season.'

There followed a champagne reception in the dining-room of the Northamptonshire Club and the team drove back to their hotel in a four-in-hand coach. There was more champagne on the train to Birmingham, and by the time they arrived, the skipper wrote later, punning atrociously, 'there was no "sham" about the "pain" in our heads'. Next morning *The Birmingham Post* completed the story under the headlines:

Warwickshire Team's Welcome
Enthusiastic Scenes
Reception at the Grand Hotel

. . . when it became known just after 12 o'clock that the team were without a doubt champions enthusiasm among sportsmen in the city was unbounded, while no little interest was evinced by the citizens generally . . . Mr Foster found New Street Station and its precincts thronged by a crowd who cheered wildly as the saloon drew up at No 3 platform where the officials waited.

There were no formalities at the station and in Queen's Drive lines of cars awaited them and took them to the Grand. Thousands of people had assembled along the route. There was a reception in the Grosvenor Room where Mr Cartland presided and proposed heartiest congratulations, seconded by Mr Bainbridge, who declared 'that was the greatest day that had ever dawned on Warwickshire cricket'. Mr Byrne, another former captain, also spoke.

In reply, Foster made the first speech of his life on the day he, too, felt was the greatest of his life. He thanked the team who, he said, had done all that could be wished of them and he especially mentioned Field, 'whose bowling performances had been a feature of the season and had contributed greatly to the success achieved'; Quaife, 'the mainstay of the team throughout the season'; and Charlesworth, 'the finest bat in England bar none. If the team were in a hole he always went in with a smiling face and he usually came out with a more smiling face.'

The Birmingham Post's leader writer waxed eloquent: 'The triumph of Warwickshire fills us with exaltation. It is something that has been well earned, something that exalts a noble game, something that vindicates qualities of which all Englishmen are proud. The virtues of patience, determination and courage are all expressed in this victory.' The writer went on to pay a glowing tribute to Foster 'who imparted a bold and adventurous spirit to the style of play; he inspired courage, and stirred hope. He created backbone.'

Foster later reproduced in his book F. H. Townsend's cartoon in *Punch* showing Shakespeare shaking Foster by the hand over the wickets, the caption underneath reading:

TWO GENTLEMEN OF WARWICKSHIRE

Mr F. R. Foster (Captain of the Warwickshire XI who have just won the Cricket Championship): Tell Kent from me she hath lost it – 2 *Henry VI*, iv 10.

William Shakespeare: 'Warwick, thou art worthy' – 3 *Henry VI*, iv 6.

And Warwickshire surely were worthy, although there were commentators who tried to denigrate their performance by pointing out that they played six fewer matches than Kent, whom they never met, an omission from their fixture list dating back to 1899 and due, it was stated, to unpleasantness caused by some of the Warwickshire professionals during the match at Catford that year, though I have not come across it.

There were also comments that Warwickshire were lucky not to have been weakened by other calls and it is undoubtedly true that one of the reasons for their success, as was also to be the case in 1951, was that they were able to keep more or less the same team intact. They called on remarkably few players, usually in this batting order: Kinneir, F. G. Stephens, Charlesworth, Quaife, F. R. Foster, Baker, Parsons, Smith, G. W. Stephens, Santall, and Field, plus Lilley and W. C. Hands.

The Editor of *Wisden* went out of his way to point out that 'under the old methods [of scoring] Kent would have come out first', and the author of the introduction to the county's record for the season, though he agreed that it was a good thing for cricket that the Championship had gone to one of the outside counties, by which he presumably meant provincial, argued that 'probably few cricketers would contend that Warwickshire had the best eleven of the year', and that 'under all conditions Kent, no doubt, had the strongest side'.

What perhaps he should have written was that Warwickshire had the side best able to take advantage of an exceptionally fine summer, especially in Field and Foster. Kent had only one really fast bowler in Fielder and the hard, dry wickets were not suited to their normally most effective bowlers, Blythe and Woolley, although the former still managed to take well over a hundred wickets. But at least the *Wisden* commentator recognised the catalyst in all this – a young and enthusiastic captain who was able to inspire his men to deeds of which no one had previously thought them capable.

'. . . there can be no question', he wrote, 'that Warwickshire's triumph was mainly due to F. R. Foster. Not since W. G. Grace in the early days of the Gloucestershire eleven has so young a captain been such a match-winning force on a county side. Foster was always getting runs, always taking wickets and above all this he proved himself a truly inspiring leader. No longer can it be said that Warwickshire played a slow or unenterprising game. They went out on all occasions to win, their cricket being keen and energetic to a degree.'

It was a wonderful season for Foster. He led his team to the Championship, he became the first Warwickshire player to do the 'cricketers' double' and he headed both batting and bowling averages. In Championship games alone he scored 1383 runs, with a highest score of 200, one of his three centuries, for an average of 44·61, and he took 116 wickets for just under 20 runs each – 19·15. Both he and Field bowled over 700 overs and the latter took six more wickets than Foster – 122; but at slightly higher cost – 19·48.

Kinneir, who scored five centuries, was second in the county averages, with 1418 runs at 44·31 an innings, and fifth in the national averages. Two other batsmen got over 1000 runs – Charlesworth, 1298 (four hundreds) and Quaife, 1108 (three hundreds); while 'Tiger' Smith added 807 runs to his splendid work behind the stumps, especially in 'keeping' to Foster; and Parsons also topped 500. Five batsmen had averages over 35 and ten over 20 and in all, seventeen centuries were scored. *Wisden* commented that the steadiness of Kinneir and Quaife 'blended admirably with the brilliant hitting of Foster and Charlesworth . . . Foster does not play quite straight, but has a wonderful eye'.

But after the jubilation came the anti-climax. Warwickshire, as Champion County, for the first time met The Rest at The Oval and were most horribly massacred. Perhaps it was the inevitable reaction; perhaps it was because there was a fortnight's interval between the triumph at Northampton and the visit to London and the champagne had gone flat; Warwickshire were no longer on the crest of a wave. Moreover, Field, who must already have been a tired man, bowled like the hero he was for the full fortnight of the Scarborough Festival – ten wickets against the Gentlemen and nine against the M.C.C.'s team for Australia, which included three of his colleagues, Foster, Kinneir and Smith, and by the time he rejoined them in London he was hardly as fresh as he might have been. And there was a lot more bowling for him to do.

At least Warwickshire had the consolation of knowing that they went down to one of the strongest sides The Rest can ever have put into the field in this game – in Foster's opinion it was *the* best. This was the batting order and pretty formidable it was: R. H. Spooner, Hobbs, Mead, P. F. Warner, J. W. Hearne, C. B. Fry, Rhodes, Woolley, Hitch, Strudwick and Dean.

Warwickshire won the toss on a perfect wicket on which, although Kinneir was absent, they could have expected to make a reasonable score, but 'partly through over-anxiety', thought *Wisden*, 'their batting went to pieces, the match being as good as lost by lunch-time on the first day'. Warwickshire were dismissed for 129 by Hearne (five for 66) and Dean (four for 34), only Charlesworth and Baker, with 25 each, putting up much resistance.

Then the bowlers who had carried pretty well all before them all the season got the drubbing of their lives. Warner made 244, Fry 102 not out, Mead 101, Hobbs a mere 97, Hearne 52. Even so, out of The Rest's 631 for five Smith allowed only five byes. It is difficult to look at the analyses of Foster and Field without thinking there have been several misprints:

	O	M	R	W
FOSTER	34	2	155	1
FIELD	48	8	181	0

As if this were not enough Warwickshire then had to bat a second time on a wet pitch and although Quaife defended stubbornly, as only he could, for 36, they collapsed again before Woolley (four for 52) and Rhodes (four for 14) and were all out 137, beaten by an innings and 365 runs.

One hopes that neither this defeat, nor the news that Warwickshire's application for a Test in the 1912 Triangular Tournament had been unsuccessful, spoiled the taste of the victory dinner the team were given at the Grand Hotel towards the end of the month. But nothing could take away the title and there were congratulations for the three who were going to Australia. Foster, of course, was an obvious choice. Kinneir probably won his place not only for the consistency of his batting – his average in all games was almost 50 – but because of the two innings of 158 and 53 he had played against the Gentlemen at Lord's in July. The fixture had been treated as one of the Test trial games and, as the Players left out Hayward and Hirst, Kinneir took his chance with both hands. As for Smith, no one 'took' Foster as he did.

The Earl of Warwick presided at the dinner, with Foster on his right and George Cartland, the chairman of the Club, on his left. Among those present, most fittingly, was William Ansell – who must have felt a proud man that night, having seen two of his dreams for Warwickshire come true – and Gilbert Jessop; while messages came from Lord Hawke, F. E. Lacey, secretary of the M.C.C., C. B. Fry,

R. H. Spooner, P. F. Warner, H. D. G. Leveson Gower and – happy thought on someone's part in view of the long link with the county side – from a company of the Royal Warwickshire Regiment, whose Commanding Officer had always been a vice-president of the Club, then stationed in India.

Viscount Cobham who proposed the toast of the Club, said the eleven had been 'electrified into extraordinary efficiency by the presence of a new element – Mr Foster', but Cartland, replying, said he honestly [but perhaps rather tactlessly?] believed they had two elevens in their history as good as the present one, magnificent though it was, 1894 and 1901. The Warwickshire men, he said, 'had good cricket in them and merely wanted someone to bring it out. They found it in a most capable captain.'

It was G. L. Jessop who proposed the toast of the Warwickshire XI and Foster who, of course, had 'a great ovation' and Lilley, Quaife and Field all spoke in turn. There were presentations to all the players and it was announced that upwards of £300 was available for distribution from the Talent Money Fund that had been set up.

There was another presentation that evening – to Dick Lilley, Warwickshire's and England's wicketkeeper these many years, who, the previous month, had resigned his position in the team. He had more or less given up the job of wicketkeeping to Smith in 1910, but, according to Foster, it was something else which precipitated Lilley's departure now.

Lilley, wrote Foster in his book, had got into the habit of ordering men about in the field – 'he waved men here and he waved them there' – perhaps not surprising in a senior player of long experience who was the county's sole representative in the England XI. The matter came to a head in the match against Yorkshire at Harrogate where Lilley, according to Foster, gave his orders loud enough for the crowd to hear them and was promptly told by Foster to mind his own business. 'It was essential', he wrote, 'that I, as captain, had no rival or opposition.'

There was dead silence later when Foster went into the players' dressing-room to lead them out on to the field after lunch and he realised that if they were to win the Championship they must avoid internal dissension at all costs. So, Foster says, when he was asked about the team for the next match his advice was 'Drop Dick'. The Committee, he adds, 'spoke very nicely' to him and he had no further interruption from any member of the Warwickshire team.

It was the end of an honourable career of quiet, but superb, efficiency for Warwickshire and England, for whom Lilley played thirty-five times altogether. 'There have been greater wicketkeepers to fast bowling' was the verdict in *Wisden* (omitting to mention it was on W. G.'s advice he stood back) 'but season after season he was a marvel of consistency,' a quality which brought him in county cricket alone 504 catches behind the wicket and 132 stumpings, as well as 13 625 runs, with sixteen centuries and an average of over 28.

This episode apart, Warwickshire 'were the happiest family of cricketers this world will ever see', said Foster. ' "Get on or get out" was our motto. We were not really a great eleven, as real Champions should be, but we blended together in a really wonderful way and that, to my mind, was the secret of our phenomenal rise to fame.'

According to *Wisden*, from the moment the team had begun to win matches 'people flocked to the Edgbaston ground in such numbers as to relieve the Committee of all anxiety about money.* Such sudden enthusiasm suggests rather too much the spirit of Association football and is apt to cause misgivings among old-fashioned cricketers. One can only hope that the Birmingham public, having at last taken up cricket in real earnest, will support their eleven in bad seasons as well as in good ones.'

The Editor did not think 'there is much fear of Birmingham cooling down if F. R. Foster can be induced to go on playing for the next five or six years. The importance of Warwickshire having an England cricketer as captain can scarcely be over-estimated.'

Alas, neither of them knew their Brummies.

*The receipts, £2754, were a record for any season except those in which there was an Australian tour.

Fleeting Fame
(1912–1918)

As the ship taking the M.C.C. team out to Australia sailed south-wards Foster doubtless felt that after such a hard Championship-winning season he was entitled to some relaxation. In his account of the voyage we read of Saturday night 'binges', followed by Sundays in bed and a night out in Colombo 'where we all gathered round the bar in the club house and I, personally, signed so many chits that I was under the table, or near enough . . . we had dinner, we had wine, we had more wine, we had even more wine and then someone said, "What time does your boat sail, old bean?" "Boat", I spluttered, "I don't know or care." '

And he went on to tell how he and J. W. H. T. Douglas shared a rick-shaw. Foster, however, did not like it and took a flying leap out, 'chucked the native into a prickly shrub, picked up the shafts myself and pulled Johnny in great style to the waiting boat', where 'Plum' Warner, who was the captain, told him he had better go to bed, 'so off I went to bed like a naughty child.'

The rest of the voyage 'passed merrily', but then it was Australia and another bowling triumph. He and Barnes proved a deadly com-bination; indeed, 'one of the biggest things in bowling history', as A. A. Thomson put it.

Wisden's chronicler of the tour was moved to say that:

finer bowling than theirs I have never seen on hard, true wickets. In the Test Matches alone they took 66 wickets – Barnes, 34, and Foster, 32, out of the 95 that fell. In all first-class games Foster took 62 and Barnes 59, the former at a cost of 20·19 and the latter 20·86. Foster is the best bowler of his type I have ever seen. Bowling round the wicket with a high delivery, his action was the personification of ease. A few short steps, an apparently medium-paced ball through the air, but doubling its speed as it touched the ground, he kept an exceptional length on the leg stump. He swerved a little with the new ball, but the angle of the delivery made the ball swing into the batsman without swerve. Foster at times bowled at the left-hander's legs. He used this form of attack against Hill, Bardsley and Ransford and kept them on the defensive. He is not such an artist with the ball as Barnes, but he is a most dangerous bowler who, on his day, can 'go through' the best side.

'Tiger' Smith is still happily alive to testify to their skill for he 'kept' to them both; indeed, it has been said of him that he was the only wicketkeeper in the country who could 'keep' to Foster, the ball came with his arm so much and so quickly off the pitch. 'Tiger' told me that Foster's faster ball was sometimes through the batsman before he had time to get into position to play a stroke. He recalled one match in which a batsman, after being bowled by Foster, said that he was not ready and was allowed, at Foster's suggestion, to have the wickets put up again, something hardly likely to happen today. It did not matter in this case – the wickets were spreadeagled again by the next ball.

The other wicketkeeper in the side on this tour was Strudwick who remembered Foster partly for a very curious reason. In an article he wrote for *Wisden* in 1959 Strudwick recalled the first time he 'kept' to Foster in the 1911 Trial Match at Lord's.

The first ball he bowled, [he wrote], swung right across the pitch to continue outside the leg stump, turned sharply and went over the top of the off stump, leaving the batsman and me stone cold and hitting the sight screen with a bang. James Seymour, the batsman, had half turned to play the ball to leg. I said to him: 'It looks as if there will be fifty byes before lunch, but I'm not going to stand back to him.' Nor did I.

In the first match at Sydney in 1911 I gave Foster the signal to bowl one outside the leg stump for me to try and stump Duff who, I thought, might move his foot in making his shot. Instead of bowling the ball I wanted, Foster sent it very wide outside the off stump and four byes resulted. The second time I signalled I made sure he saw what I meant. This time he bowled the ball straight to Frank Woolley at first slip. Then I realised he did not intend to give me the chance he might have allowed had 'Tiger' Smith, his own county's wicketkeeper, been behind the stumps.

Foster played in all five Tests and had Smith to 'keep' for him in all but the first, but whether the way Strudwick alleged he bowled when he was 'keeping' to him had any bearing on the selectors' decision is something we shall never know now. Strudwick was Smith's senior by seven years, but the choice probably fell on Smith because he was more familiar with Foster's bowling. They used to exchange signals as well, though Foster was a little put out when an Australian tram conductor told him he had spotted one of them – a change of step as a sign to 'Tiger' that he was going to bowl a slower one, something the Australian thought he should do more often.

It was while he was in Australia that Foster first began bowling to a leg trap. Foster says he saw Barnes bowling leg theory one day and thought that he, a left-hander bringing the ball into and across the right-handed batsman, could do it better. Barnes told me that it was he who gave Foster the idea and Foster, who also talked it over with 'Tiger', later agrees in his book that it was Barnes who made him alter his mode of attack and bowl to four short legs, his 'death trap', as Foster called it. Nevertheless, Foster always claimed that he bowled at the stumps and not at the batsman, which is borne out by the fact that he hit the stumps more frequently than any bowler who had been to Australia until then, eighteen of his thirty-two Test wickets being clean bowled.

Among his performances was the one he considered the best of his career – five for 36 in twenty-six overs, nine maidens, in the third Test at Adelaide. He also made 683 runs, 226 of them in Tests, with a highest score of 71 and an average of 32·38. He hit consecutive centuries, 158 and 101, in State games.

Kinneir got to play in only one Test, the first, at Sydney where, opening with Hobbs, he made 22 and 30. 'Kinneir', I am sure, wrote *Wisden's* correspondent, 'would have made a lot of runs had he played regularly, but there was no room for him in the best eleven, his fielding being so moderate. He is a very neat left-handed bat and by no means the slow scorer he is supposed to be. He played particularly well at Brisbane against an Australian XI. Opening with Rhodes, he made 63 and 18.'

'Tiger' was more fortunate. Warner, in his comments on the tour, wrote that we were fortunate in possessing two such fine wicketkeepers as Smith and Strudwick, but he would not commit himself to saying which he thought was the better of the two. He thought Smith's work in the second Test at Melbourne – in which Barnes performed his fabulous five-wickets-for-six-runs feat, 'Tiger' taking three catches – and in the first innings of the third,

magnificent; he kept well in the fourth, but in the final game at Sydney he was distinctly below the standard of what one expects from an England wicketkeeper and let pass a greater number of byes. Smith is extremely good at taking Foster, who is a difficult bowler to keep wicket to, a thorough understanding appearing to exist between them, and he is extraordinarily clever on the leg side. He catches his catches and is, at his best, a great wicketkeeper. If he had not kept so badly at Sydney one would have formed an even higher opinion of his work. In one respect he is certainly not the equal of Strudwick and that is in getting up to the wicket when standing back to a fast bowler to take a return.

Smith had not then developed the batsmanship which was to make him a regular opener for Warwickshire for several years and did not have a very happy tour as a batsman, scoring only 47 runs in five Test innings and a mere 139 in eleven innings on the whole tour.

It was not a case of all hard work and no play making Frank a dull boy on the tour. Foster was a great gambler, inordinately so in later life, and while he was in Australia he backed more than a few horses. He went through the card at a Melbourne meeting and kept waiting the Governor-General, Lord Duncan, who had invited all the English players to be his guests at the races. 'If you must bet, dear reader', was the advice he gave in his book, 'as I suppose the majority of you do, keep your investments within the limits of what you can afford to pay in comfort.' It was unfortunate that in later years he did not heed his own advice.

Winning the Championship did not seem to make the Warwickshire Committee any the more generously disposed to the men who had achieved this distinction. It was decided to offer Quaife a retaining fee of £100 for the 1912 season and to intimate to him that the Committee felt he ought to come to the level of the other players, but as it was agreed that this would be rather a big reduction the Committee wished to meet him to the extent of offering him £100 instead of £85.

Quaife, who was not easily imposed on, objected, declined the offer in an interview and said he thought the Committee ought not to offer him less than £125, but it was some time before the Committee (who, it might have been thought, would not dare to risk losing its most consistent batsman) gave way. Quaife's benefit fund, incidentally, realised only £410, which seems a mere bagatelle by modern standards; but any reader who thinks that the players of those times were not particularly well rewarded, should spare a thought for the man who was to record every run Warwickshire scored for over fifty years.

George Austin had been appointed scorer in the spring of the Championship year. His predecessor's services had been dispensed with at the end of the 1910 season because of complaints about him borrowing money. It was hardly surprising that he had done so. George Austin was first engaged at 12s 6d a week, with expenses at the rate of 10s a day for matches over 100 miles from Birmingham, four days to be allowed. There could not have been much change out of that.

Still, the Club did give Foster, Kinneir and Smith a complimentary dinner on their return from Australia, though it was limited to officers and players, who were the guests of the Committee. Kinneir, one hopes, also had some compensation for his disappointments in Australia by figuring as one of the Five Cricketers of the Year in *Wisden* of 1912. Whoever wrote the appreciation of him, highly praised his performance in the Gentlemen v. Players game at The Oval: 'His play made a great impression. It was thought that with his strong defence and extreme steadiness he would be just the man for the Sydney and Melbourne wickets . . . but I doubt if Kinneir would have been asked if Mead had in the first half of the season obtained the big scores that he afterwards made. He [Kinneir] had been the soundest and most consistent of all left-handed batsmen, knowing no serious rival until Woolley and Mead appeared on the scene. All that one can urge against him is that he is inclined at times to carry caution to an extreme.'

It was probably inevitable that, after the success of winning the Championship and Foster's second triumph in Australia, the 1912 season would be something of an anti-climax, though this was a problem which never seemed to trouble Yorkshire or Surrey in the days when they won the title season after season. Winning the title has never become a way of life for Warwickshire as it did for those counties.

There were several factors to account for this, at least in 1912. One was the wet summer – 'one of the most appalling ever known', was how the Editor of *Wisden* described it. Certainly it put off Warwickshire's bowlers who had thrived on the hard, fast wickets of 1911. Foster's total for the county in Championship matches dropped from 116 to 85 and Field's from 122 to only 53. In Foster's case, this was partly due to the fact that he, as well as Smith, was away for all the six Tests in the Triangular Tournament.

Not that Foster was any more successful in higher company; he scored only 104 runs in the Tests and took only thirteen wickets for 234, average 18, whereas Barnes had thirty-nine. There was only one match, against South Africa at Lord's on a drying pitch, in which they reproduced their Australian form. They got South Africa out for 58 – five times Foster hit the stumps, including those of Llewellyn with what was described as a shooter – and 217. Between them, Barnes and Foster took nineteen wickets in the match, Barnes eleven for 110 and Foster eight for 70, *Wisden* commenting that Foster, 'except for the balls that took wickets, did not look so difficult as Barnes, who broke both ways and kept a perfect length'.

The fact was that Foster was a very tired young man. Even at 23 one cannot go on playing cricket continuously for months on end and living the 'high life' which he so fully enjoyed. 'There can be little doubt', the author of the Warwickshire article in *Wisden* wrote, 'that Foster was further handicapped by his hard work for the M.C.C.'s team in Australia during the winter. It was rather too much for so young a bowler to go through three seasons without a rest . . . he seldom gave one the impression of being quite fresh. It cost him more effort than before to get his pace off the pitch.'

Foster also made a tactical error and later admitted in his book that his bowling suffered because he bowled leg theory 'far in excess of what was actually required by the changed circumstances of the weather

in England that summer as compared with the climate of Australia.'
Out there the ball would not swerve after the first two or three overs, he
was rarely able to straighten it and spin was hopeless, hence his resort
to leg theory. He only once tried to bowl orthodox slow left-arm
spinners even in England. That was in the first home match of this
season against Middlesex on a very soft wicket. After lunch he found he
was turning the ball so much that he dispensed with the leg trap and
returned figures of 24 overs, 12 maidens, 29 runs, 6 wickets. He took
the last 4 wickets in 4 overs and 4 balls for only 7 runs. It is surprising
he did not resort to these tactics more often when conditions were
suitable.

In May there was certainly no need to do so for Warwickshire won
four matches off the reel, but although the batting looked strong on
paper only Quaife made over 1000 runs and his average of 37 was
rather flattered by eight not outs, while Foster and Kinneir, who had
averaged 44 apiece for the county in 1912 dropped to 19 and 17 respectively, and Charlesworth from 39 to 20. Smith scored only 57 runs in
eight innings in the Tests, but fortunately did better for his county –
839 runs for an average of 24·67.

If there is a heaven to which poor, tired fast bowlers go they will
surely not have to bowl in their benefit matches as Field had to do in his
against Lancashire – three hours of hard labour during which he sent
down 35 overs, six of them maidens, for 110 runs and only one wicket,
though it was one worth having – J. T. Tyldesley's. At one point during
the season it looked as if Warwickshire had found a splendid reinforce-
ment for him in a young, fast, right-handed bowler named Colin
Langley who, although he had few opportunities, took nineteen wickets
at just over 10 runs each, which included one notable performance of
eight for 29 against Worcestershire. His figures – 70·2 overs, 21
maidens, 197 runs, 19 wickets – put him at the head of the first-class
averages, no less; *Wisden* commenting: 'As regards the future, nothing
in Warwickshire cricket last season was so hopeful as the appearance
in the team of C. K. Langley . . . he made a strong impression, several
good judges considering him quite first rate.' Alas, he never repeated
this form and the future did not permit him to play as often as he no
doubt would have liked, but administratively he served the county with
distinction for many years.

But for the fact that they lost their last three matches, Warwickshire
might well have finished higher in the Championship table than ninth,
which, however, was a sad enough fall from grace. Possibly they
derived some consolation from holding the Australians to a draw with
some consistent batting, one of Foster's better bowling performances –
seven for 94 – and a storm which caused the game to be abandoned,
but although South Africa's team was reckoned the weakest they had

sent over so far, they disposed of Warwickshire, without Foster, by six wickets.

There had been a deficit of £434 at the end of 1910 which had been turned into a surplus of £570 – the first for some years – by the beginning of 1912, so the Club could well afford the gold watch and chain it presented to R. V. Ryder to mark seventeen years of 'devoted service to the Club' and as a memento of Warwickshire becoming Champion County; it also happened to mark his birthday. Nor could the Committee have grudged the £50 it gave to the testimonial organised by the players to John Bates, the faithful groundsman, who had produced some of the most perfect wickets in the country and now retired owing to ill-health. The testimonial in all raised £140 and the Committee also granted him a pension of £20 a year – on condition that he kept up the full contribution of 7d a week National Health Insurance. Son Len had been helping his father on the ground in winter at 10s a week; in the summer he got 20s. Ryder gave us a glimpse of a lad who 'used to roam about with a decrepit old bat in his hand knocking an old ball about and enjoying at the end of a summer's day a little parental tuition at the nets'. The head groundsman's post was then advertised at a starting wage of 30s a week, plus house, gas and coal allowance. No fewer than fifty applications were received, the job eventually going to Arthur Taylor.

Warwickshire had been well pleased with the results of its experiment in starting matches on Saturdays, and they now proposed to the Advisory County Cricket Committee that in 1914 and succeeding years, all first-class matches should be begun on Wednesdays and Saturdays and that the Committee should also consider having all fixtures arranged by a single authority, so as to ensure an equal allocation of Saturday dates to each county. Eventually the first part of Warwickshire's proposal was accepted and in the county's programme of twenty-four matches for 1915 were sixteen Saturday and eight Wednesday starts, which, of course, were never played.

Although in 1913 they won one more match than in the previous season, Warwickshire also lost more, so that although, with the help of a dry summer, four batsmen scored over 1000 runs, they dropped two places in the table to eleventh position. Kinneir unhappily was not one of those batsmen. Just when he ran into form with an innings of 152 not out at The Oval he was compelled by bad health to stop playing and it was feared that he would have to give up cricket. Fortunately he recovered and in 1914 played in every match.

The real trouble, however, was with the bowling. Foster had to have a rest early in the summer, but although he eventually took ninety-one wickets in Championship games they cost him 24·6 runs each. Field, too, was often out of action owing to injuries and strains, to which he was almost perpetually subject, and took only thirty-five wickets. Five matches were lost before the end of June and the situation would probably have been a good deal worse had it not been for the discovery by Ryder while he was on holiday of what *Wisden* described as 'an absolute prize' in the person of Percy Jeeves, another Yorkshireman who was allowed to escape. He came almost straight from village cricket in 1911, had appeared once for the first eleven against the Australians in 1912, taking two wickets for 35, and he could not have made his entrance at a more timely moment. In that first season he was almost certainly over-bowled for he sent down nearly 800 overs, over a quarter of them maidens, and took 106 wickets for 20·88 runs each, topping the county averages.

And that was not all. He also scored 765 runs, averaging 20·13, a very useful all-round contribution. His bowling was on the fast side of medium, with an easy action and plenty of life off the pitch, and his hitting seemed effortless, the hallmark of good timing. In that first season he made one of the biggest hits ever seen at Edgbaston, a magnificent drive which cleared the pavilion, carried Edgbaston Road and dropped clean into the meadow which was then opposite the main entrance to the ground. 'One of the best of the cricketers discovered in 1913 with class written all over him,' was the verdict and he and Parsons, who for the first time scored over 1000 runs, his average going up from 10 to 31, were spoken of as 'the great hopes of Warwickshire cricket'. These were not Jeeves's only claims to fame. P. G. Wodehouse, seeing him play at Cheltenham in 1913, thereupon decided to name his famous manservant character after him.

There were several outstanding performances both for and against the county this season. At The Oval in May, Quaife, for the first time in his career, made two hundreds, 124 and 109, in a match, a feat emulated by Charlesworth in the return game at Edgbaston later in the season, with 100 in the first innings (in which Quaife got a third century off the Surrey bowling, 105) and in the second 101 not out in 70 minutes. Between these two events were two Warwickshire batting débâcles – against Middlesex, 63, of which Foster, arriving late and going in last, made 27 not out, and against Kent at Tonbridge where resumption of fixtures between the two clubs was made memorable by Warwickshire's dismissal for an incredible score of 16, the lowest in the entire history of the Club.

Warwickshire batted first and scored 262 and when they had dismissed Kent, the eventual champions, for 132 largely because of Foster's six for 62, they must have thought they had the match well in hand. But Blythe and Woolley, on a treacherous pitch made to order for them, must have been very nearly unplayable and returned these incredible and almost identical analyses:

	O	M	R	W
WOOLLEY	5·2	1	8	5
BLYTHE	5·0	1	8	5

The Warwickshire innings makes unbelievable reading, but historical honesty compels its inclusion:

WARWICKSHIRE – SECOND INNINGS

Charlesworth c Seymour b Blythe	1
Parsons st Huish b Woolley	5
Foster c Hubble b Blythe	2
Quaife b Blythe	0
Baker c Humphreys b Woolley	4
Jeeves c Blythe b Woolley	0
G. Curle st Huish b Blythe	0
Hands b Woolley	0
Santall c Huish b Woolley	3
*S. H. Bates not out	0
J. Brown st Huish b Blythe	1
Extras	0
Total	**16**

And as if he had not already done enough damage, Woolley followed up with 76 not out, an innings described as 'of dazzling brilliancy'.

Despite their in-and-out form Warwickshire, whose membership by the end of 1912 had topped 2000 for the first time, continued to attract public support and from outside the city, too, thereby contradicting those who were in the habit of saying that it was a Birmingham rather than a county club. With a surplus of £600, Warwickshire were one of the few counties to be showing a balance on the right side. Even so, when the captain suggested that the talent money for distribution at the end of the season should be increased from £87 to £100, his amendment was defeated by seven votes to five. The Committee watched every penny in those days – they had to.

'Tiger' Smith spent the winter of 1913–14 in South Africa, whither he voyaged by the first available boat after D. C. Robinson, of Gloucestershire, who had gone out as second wicketkeeper to Strudwick, was invalided home almost as soon as he reached his destination. Smith played in one Test and had nine matches altogether, but was still out of form with the bat in this higher company and scored only 154 runs.

Financially there was not a cloud on the Club's horizon as it entered the 1914 season. There had been surpluses of £571, £419 and £495 in the previous three years and though the cost of running the Club had

*This was a scorer's error for L. A. Bates. See p. 221.

risen to something like £4500 a year, the Coventry and Nuneaton fixtures had proved a great success, the Club had now redeemed its debentures, and had a net balance of £2263. The Committee was confident enough to approve a recommendation of the executive committee to offer £5000 for the purchase of the ground, though the completion of the transaction had to wait until after the war, now looming so close ahead though few people were yet aware of it.

There was a blow at the start of the season when a letter was received from Foster resigning the captaincy owing to the claims of business following the death of his father. Naturally, efforts were made to retain his services and though there is no reference in the minutes to the outcome they must have been successful, for although he caught a chill in the early part of the season, he played for the rest of the summer and was something like his old self again; he was the only Warwickshire bowler to take over a hundred wickets – 117 for 18·24 runs each.

Jeeves had eighty-five and in only his second full season was picked for the Players, as was Parsons, whose driving was making fieldsmen's fingers tingle all over the country. Field, who again missed several matches, had sixty-four wickets and another young fast bowler, Harry Howell, who had come into the side the previous season, forty-one. Warwickshire's great need had once been for fast bowlers; now it was for slow ones, for Santall played in only ten matches. Still, *Wisden* thought them 'one of the best bowling teams of the year'.

But it was not for their bowling that 1914 was a memorable year in the Club's history, quite apart from other events. Foster, who was one of five batsmen to score over 1000 runs, made 1396 in Championship matches and nearly one-quarter of them were scored in one great innings of 305, which is still the highest individual score made for the county. It happened in the match against Worcestershire at Dudley, yet another of the many instances of Warwickshire players saving their best performances for away games.

Worcestershire batted first, but could make only a modest 188 and Warwickshire had already passed this total before Foster went in. Parsons, now going in first with Kinneir, made 102 and Quaife 85 by way of appetisers and then came the main course. Foster appeared on the scene when the third wicket fell with the score 197 and he remained to torment the toiling Worcestershire bowlers for four hours twenty minutes, his 305 being made out of a total of 448 put on while he was at the wicket.

It is reported that until he had made 150 he hardly ever put the ball in the air, that he did not make a poor stroke until he was passed 200 and that he never gave the ghost of a chance. Had a time and motion study expert been present he might have compiled a progress chart like this:

50 runs in one hour
100 runs in 75 minutes
150 runs in two hours 35 minutes
200 runs in three hours five minutes
300 runs in four hours ten minutes.

The statistical minded might also find it of interest that Foster had the lion's share in each of the following partnerships:

With Quaife (43) 120 in 85 minutes
With G. W. Stephens (10) 40 in ten minutes
With Baker (20) 60 in 35 minutes
With 'Tiger' Smith (42) 166 in 70 minutes
With Jeeves (16) 51 in 20 minutes.

Curiously enough, he did not hit a six, but he had one five – Dudley is a large ground – forty-four fours, fourteen threes and twenty-one twos. The 'no six' record, however, rather conflicts with a story George Austin used to tell about this innings. George said that during the lunch interval he went up to Foster and said, 'Well played, skipper.'

'George', replied Foster, 'I'll hit one down that bloody chimney,' gesturing towards the stack of Palethorpe's factory at Dudley Port and considerably further away than the record hit for the ground. 'Sure enough', George added, 'the moment he resumed his innings he hit one high over the score box, but not quite to Dudley Port.'

Warwickshire did not declare their innings until the total had reached 645 for seven wickets, which seems either like a lack of confidence in their bowlers or rubbing it in excessively. Worcestershire had to score 457 merely to avoid defeat and they soon lost four wickets for 85. Then along came Field to put them out of their misery with a bowling performance as remarkable in its way as Foster's innings. He had taken four wickets for 58 in the first innings. Now he bowled 8 overs and 2 balls, 7 of them maidens, for 2 runs and 6 wickets. The compiler of statistics in *Wisden* was obviously so incredulous of this catastrophic bowling that he got the figures wrong and the following year *Wisden* published one its rare corrections.

The correction, of the number of maiden overs from six to seven, was accompanied by a note from the Editor, S. H. Pardon, himself. He added that the only scoring stroke made off Field in these fifty balls was a lucky two from the second ball of the second over before he had taken a wicket. 'Field', wrote Pardon, 'delivered five no balls, with one of which he clean bowled M. K. Foster. In taking his six wickets he received no assistance, three batsmen being bowled, two caught and bowled [Field was particularly good at stopping hard returns off his own bowling] and one leg before wicket. The feat certainly deserves to be placed in future on the same footing as Pougher's famous five wickets for no runs for M.C.C. and Ground against the Australians at Lord's in 1896 and Peate's eight wickets for 5 runs for Yorkshire against Surrey at Holbeck in 1883.'

The margin of Warwickshire's victory was an innings and 321 runs and it is worth noting that in the next game at Edgbaston against Middlesex Foster had an even more remarkable exercise in monopolising the scoring – 51 out of 52 in fifteen minutes while he was at the wicket, including four sixes.

There were one or two outstanding bowling performances against Warwickshire as well. At The Oval in May Bill Hitch did the hat-trick – Smith, Jeeves and Hands – and later in the season at Edgbaston the Northamptonshire spin bowler, S. G. Smith, went one better, taking four wickets in four balls to finish off the Warwickshire innings. In this match A. W. Foster, F.R.'s younger brother, kept wicket in place of 'Tiger', who had been injured. An elder brother, W.H., F.R.'s bowling partner in many fine performances for the Hall Green Club, was later to become a vice-president of Warwickshire.

And in the last match of the season against Surrey at Edgbaston both Jeeves and Foster gave the crowd something to remember them by. On a hard, fast pitch, Surrey were got rid of for 126 and 130. Jeeves bowled Hayward in each innings, twice dismissed Ducat and once bowled Hobbs. He had seven for 88 and Foster nine for 72 in the match.

When on 16 March that year the Committee had decided to rent the county ground at a cost of five guineas from 31 August to 4 September inclusive for a croquet tournament, it had seemed that England stood very much where she had always done, but by the beginning of August the threat of war had begun to cast its shadows over all the cricket fields of England. Worcestershire came to Edgbaston for the return match at the beginning of August, but without both G. N. and N. J. A. Foster, both of whom had been called away on military duties.

A special meeting of the General Committee on 7 August, called to consider what should be done about the county's remaining fixtures, decided to carry them out 'as they feel that no good purpose can be served at the present moment by cancelling matches', but by the middle of the month even the croquet tournament had been cancelled. Warwickshire played five more matches during the month and lost all but one – it must have been difficult to concentrate on the game – twice to Kent and once each to Yorkshire and Hampshire. But for this run they would have finished much higher than seventh in the Championship, which had to be abandoned, with Surrey, then the leaders, remaining Champions by general consent, though not before they had been beaten at Edgbaston by 80 runs. It was only their second defeat of the season.

Meanwhile, for anyone who was still interested in cricket, the news filtered through from Cambridge that a young Warwickshire man, the

Hon. F. S. G. Calthorpe, a member of the family to whom the Club owed its ground, had taken twenty-six wickets for 16·03 runs each and had been placed fifth in the first-class averages, and that nearer still at Malvern, a schoolboy named Partridge was already thought good enough to play for the Gentlemen. They were two gleams of light on a dark horizon.

Though no one dreamt it at the time, this was Foster's last season with Warwickshire. He went into the Royal Flying Corps but in 1915 met with a motor-cycle accident near Worcester in which he severely injured his foot. He played in several games during the war, but found that his foot had not sufficiently recovered to stand the strain of first-class cricket again, though his retirement from the game was not officially announced until 1919.

Perhaps this is as good a place as any to assess the philosophy of a player to whom *Wisden* once referred as 'the greatest match-winning force since Grace'. His creed, he told us, was that 'the bat should always beat the clock'. By that he meant 'at least 61 runs per hour, a run a minute, and if both batsmen at the wicket cannot manage *that* between them it is a sorry look-out for the spectator and for the advance of Brighter Cricket.' What he, who always thought about the interests of the spectators, would have said of the funereal pace at which many modern innings are played, is an interesting point for speculation. It would have been something forceful, to be sure.

'I wonder', he wrote, 'how many present-day county captains [he was writing of the 1930 era] consider the poor spectator. I wonder how many . . . make their team "play the game" from the spectators' point of view.' He went on to add that 'his one and only intention' during the whole of his career was, at the beginning of each match in which he played as captain, to put himself in the mind of an ordinary cricket spectator – with cricket brains – and to ask himself this question: ' "What have I come here to see? A funeral, an exhibition of 'slow-motion' cricket, or cricket as it should be played?" I wonder how many present-day county captains could achieve the hard task of making their team "play the game" from a spectator's point of view? And yet the captain is chosen by the committee of each county cricket club and they, the Committee, love, simply love, to welcome a large crowd.'

Would it be *lèse-majesté* to say that there are some county captains who ought to have that passage put up in the dressing-room? Foster said he always believed in getting opponents in for at least thirty minutes' batting before the end of a day's play when they were tired and Warwickshire won a good many matches under his captaincy by doing this.

Twice he did the 'cricketers double' – in 1911 and 1914 – and although in his short career he scored over 5000 runs and took over 500 wickets, it is not these figures so much as what Ryder called 'the galvanic force-fulness of his leadership' for which he will be remembered in the annals of Warwickshire cricket, to which he gave new life. 'As a player', 'Plum' Warner once wrote of him, 'we shall seldom see his like again on the cricket field,' and for Ryder, as well as for many other people, he wrote 'an exciting chapter in the book of English cricket'.

At a meeting of the Committee on 3 September it was reported that Parsons had enlisted in the Warwickshire Yeomanry. Parsons used to tell an amusing story about this. It seems that Ryder sent for him – he was in uniform by then – and told him that Foster wanted to see him at his home in Wake Green Road, Birmingham. Parsons went there and rang the front door bell. The door was opened by a butler and then Parsons heard his captain's voice from the head of the stairs demanding: 'What the hell are you doing in that? Warwickshire won't pay you in the bloody Army.'

'What', asked Parsons, 'could I say except "Good afternoon" and walk away?'

The Committee, contrary to Foster's anticipations, decided to pay Parsons' wages in full during his absence on active service, and to sound out the other employees as to how they were willing to assist in the war effort, a special sub-committee being appointed to interview them. A week later nearly a team of players saw the Committee.

From the M.C.C. had come a communication saying that Lord Kitchener would encourage formation of a Cricketers' Corps provided that a battalion of at least 1000 men could be secured. Among those who thereupon volunteered for service in it, in the 2nd Birmingham Battalion (15th Warwicks), or other units as was most convenient, were 'Tiger' Smith, Jeeves, the two Bates (Len and Harold), Luckin, George Austin and Round, Ryder's assistant. Before the Birmingham Battalion was sent to Wensleydale in Yorkshire some matches were played in May 1915, at Edgbaston and elsewhere. Alec Hastilow was a member of the team.

It was decided that agreements with players for the 1915 season, if any, should be completed and that those players and other employees not eligible for active service should contribute to a War Fund on the following scale:

Those receiving up to 20s a week	6d a week
Those receiving between 20s and up to 30s	1s a week
Those receiving over 30s	2s a week

By the time it was known that there would be a loss on the season of £500 and in view of the uncertainty about 1915, though it had been agreed that agreements with players should be honoured, it was decided to issue a statement to members telling them the expenditure likely to be needed to keep the Club in existence – £1800 was the estimate even for a blank season – and to ask that subscriptions should be paid in the normal way because it was intended, if the ground was not required by the War Office, to whom it was offered, to arrange the usual Club and Ground matches and continue facilities for net practice. It takes a great deal to make the English forget entirely about cricket.

There is a sad footnote to be added. Pallett was reported to be ill and arrangements were made for his admission to a home for incurables at Leamington at the expense of the Club. The players made a collection for him which was paid in small weekly instalments to his wife, but later when Pallett was removed from the home at his own request it was paid to him. Later, however, he had to be admitted to Erdington Infirmary where he died in June 1915. He had played for Warwickshire from 1883 until 1898 and in all he took 958 wickets for the county, 296 of them in first-class cricket, for 21·50 runs each. A good and faithful servant.

W. G. Grace died in the second year of the war at his home in Kent and for many people both at home and abroad the world seemed a little darker. *Wisden* of 1916 was kept from being an even less bulky shadow of itself by various articles and vital statistics, among them, be it noted, a special list of players who had clean bowled the great man in first-class cricket. It included Warwickshire's own 'W.G.' and Santall, both of whom did so twice, and Field.

For the most part the minutes of the Club, which were still most meticulously kept, though at less frequent intervals, of course, make melancholy reading. No further meeting of the General Committee was held until April 1915, when the War Office notified the Club that it did not require the use of the ground. Everything had to be done on a hand-to-mouth basis because no one knew how long the war was going to last – players' wages paid up to April 1916, the secretary's agreement renewed for just a year at a salary of £300, less £25 which he wished to forgo in the circumstances.

The annual general meeting was still held in that month and a loss of £714 was reported, due almost entirely to the falling-off in gates during the previous August, normally the Club's money-making month. George Cartland, who presided, was proud to say that every man of the requisite age and capability was ready to enlist, and he recalled that he had had the pleasure of escorting eight of them to the Council House to be enrolled.

George Austin, he said, failed to pass into the Army, so he had joined the Royal Marines and 'was now enjoying himself in the Dardanelles'. (The word falls strangely on the ears now.) He had written home to Mr Ryder, saying: 'I expect you have heard we have had the first match with the Turks just over a fortnight ago. We made a good show; there was some big hitting and runs were plentiful.' That brought laughter. 'I don't think the Turks had seen such big hitting before and they must have been glad when the innings were closed.' (More laughter.)

It was not long, alas, before news came from this particular theatre of war which met with a sadly different reception, but in the meantime the chairman could go on to say that there was evidence, which it would be impossible to dispute, that cricket and English sport had great influence on the morale and courage of our soldiers. Englishmen, he went on, fought like gentlemen and this was because the sporting instinct was instilled into them by the manly games in which they participated.

So for the time being the ground – the head groundsman had been re-engaged – would be open for practice as usual, and for tennis, too; the Moseley Club would play half a dozen matches and it was hoped from time to time to arrange some regimental matches among soldiers training in the district. No less a giant than Jessop was at Lichfield and said he could turn out a good team for occasional matches, though whether he later shattered any roofs around Edgbaston I have not been able to discover. Requests were being received from men serving at the front for old bats and balls in order that games might be arranged among the troops. We had not yet appreciated that cricket was not a German game.

By the end of 1915 the secretary was able to report that £1105 had been received in subscriptions from 1155 members, some of them away on active service, and though this left the Club with a substantial balance the secretary sought other employment and was allowed to accept a post as a temporary clerk at Lloyds Bank, though the Club executive later agreed to give him a further agreement for one year from 15 April 1916, at his then salary less any earnings from outside work. Later he worked for a Birmingham firm of accountants, Tyler and Wheatcroft, at a higher salary than the bank paid him.

The feature on Leading Counties again appeared in *Wisden* in 1916 and under Warwickshire there was this entry:

Mr Ryder gives a very encouraging account of the condition of the Warwick-shire Club in war time. Subscriptions were so well kept up as to cover the expenditure for 1916 – about £750 being received. The Club's bank balance remains untouched and there is a sum of £1400 in the bank. The county has suffered a grievous loss in the death in action of Percy Jeeves. J. H. Parsons, who enlisted as a trooper, has gained a commission. He has seen fighting in the Dardanelles and at Salonika.

Percy Jeeves, Royal Warwickshire Regiment, killed on 22 July, was a grievous loss indeed, 'England losing a cricketer of whom very high hopes have been entertained,' as *Wisden* said. Warner, too, had thought very highly of him and had predicted that he would be an England player. In that briefest of brief careers, two seasons and a match against the Australians, he had scored 1169 runs and taken 193 wickets for just over 20 runs each.

The Club later received a letter from Brigadier E. A. Wiggin expressing in complimentary terms his great satisfaction with the work done by Sergeant J. Parsons in Salonika while acting as troop leader with the Warwickshire Yeomanry. Parsons had begun as a trooper and eventually went through all the non-commissioned ranks to squadron sergeant-major. Then the Yeomanry were terribly cut up at Gallipoli, Parsons' unit having only sixty-seven men left. In July 1916, he was commissioned 'on the field' to the Worcestershire Yeomanry. He served the rest of the war with them, was awarded the M.C., mentioned in despatches, and took part in what is believed to have been the last cavalry charge ever made by the British Army in one of the three battles it took to win Beersheba. Stanley Evans, later to become an M.P. and a junior Cabinet Minister, who presented the bell of the Harborne Somerville Club to Edgbaston, where it still calls the faithful to play, was in that historic affair too.

We were charging some infantry, [Parsons said], when my horse fell and shot me over his head. I sat up and started to back away and as I did so a Turk stopped and put up his rifle. I pointed my revolver at him and he dropped the rifle and made off after his retreating comrades. Then I was sent to India to train cavalry there and to the North West Frontier with the Duke of Connaught's Own Lancers. I got a little cricket in India with Lord Lloyd and Gregg, of Hampshire, among others.

Parsons, who ended the war as a captain and squadron leader, had his own sword and one he picked up from the Turks beaten by his local blacksmith, at Liskeard in Cornwall, into a ploughshare which was used in providing corn from which bread was made for a Communion service at the parish church.

A month after the news of Jeeves's death, Sergeant Harold Bates, also of The Royal Warwickshire Regiment, and one of the two sons of the groundsman, who had been born at Edgbaston, was reported killed. He was a useful all-rounder, left-hand bowler and right-hand bat, who played occasionally for the county, but was mostly on the ground staff at Lord's.

Meanwhile it was decided that while the war continued, no further agreements should be entered into with the professionals, though more cricket was played in 1917. Boxing and professional billiards had carried on, war or no war, so why not cricket, the Editor of *Wisden* asked. 'There was something illogical, not to say absurd, in placing a ban on cricket,' he wrote. Two Saturday matches played at Lord's for charity raised £1300 and there was a miscellany of minor games at Edgbaston.

The Editor also took a look at the way cricket might be carried on after the war and said it 'would not be a misfortune if the counties had to be content for a year or two with shorter programmes', a comment that would have found a sympathetic ear at Edgbaston today. The Editor thought:

Bowlers would keep fresher and every match would be more of an event. From the time that the list of first-class matches had to be so largely extended, our programme was always too heavy. The suggestion put forward by Mr Ludford Docker, the Warwickshire President [he had been elected in 1915] that county matches should be limited to two days does not appeal to me at all. Modern wickets are so good that a drastic change would, in my opinion, be doomed to certain failure. Unless there was an agreement to decide on the first innings, a two-days match in fine weather would, nine times out of ten, end in a draw.

Before the year was out three prominent members of the Club had all lost sons – Second-Lieutenant Harold J. Goodwin, R.G.A., captain for a season before Foster took over, a member of the General Committee and only son of the Club's honorary treasurer, Mr F. S. Goodwin; and the sons of the chairman, George Cartland, and of Sir Hallewell Rogers. While at Marlborough Goodwin had played an innings of 365, sharing in two double century partnerships, and sent up the remarkable total of 1200 runs with a hit for 11, though the writer of his obituary notice in *Wisden* did not tell us how this was achieved. In the same match he took fifteen wickets for 57 runs, his team winning by an innings and 421 runs. He was a hard-hitting bat, a good leg-break bowler and a fine field, but unfortunately he was able to play for the county only in 1907–8. While at Cambridge he had also got his Blue for hockey at which he played for England.

In his report for 1917 Ryder was able to announce that members had paid over £600 in subscriptions so that expenses for the year had been covered and the pre-war bank balance left untouched, a very desirable position in view of the repairs which would have to be done to the ground before first-class cricket could be played again. The first gleams of hope that this might be soon came in November 1918, when Ryder was authorised to relinquish his temporary appointment, and in the following month when it was reported that the Advisory County Cricket Committee had decided to restart cricket in 1919 and that matches would be limited to two days each – Ludford Docker's proposal.

Rifleman Arthur Taylor, head groundsman, who had been a prisoner of war in Germany, returned home to Birmingham for two months' leave and was received by the Committee, who congratulated him on his safe return and agreed that he should begin work on the ground at once. The Ground Committee was authorised to take on hand the work of repairs to the pavilion and other buildings, though only those deemed necessary to enable the ground to be opened for county cricket.

In *Wisden* for 1919, which heralded the resumption of cricket, the Editor returned to what was in store for us: 'I have a very strong opinion', he wrote, 'that a grave mistake has been made in not letting the game alone. The restriction of all county matches to two days strikes me as a sad blunder . . . By their recent action the Advisory Committee have made an absolute fetish of the Championship, risking on its behalf famous county matches that can boast a tradition of over fifty years . . . To my mind it would have been far better to have dropped the Championship for one year . . . while the game was being brought back to its old footing.'

The vote for two-day games was by eleven to five and Saturday starts were made optional. But the county had more pressing problems nearer home to solve before Warwickshire cricket could return to the even tenor of its way, though never again could it be 'as you were'.

Rebuilding a Team
(1919–1922)

❖ ❖ ❖

I⊤ is doubtful if any county was so severely handicapped as Warwick-shire in resuming cricket after a war which had so violently disrupted the promise of the 1914 side. Foster, the dashing leader, had gone because of a cruel accident; poor Percy Jeeves, Harold Bates and H. J. Goodwin had been killed in action; Colin Langley had given up the first-class game because of war wounds; Kinneir had announced his retirement during the previous autumn; Santall was now coach; Parsons, though on leave, was still a captain in the Indian Army; Quaife was 47, an age when most cricketers have long since retired; and Charlesworth was also turned 40.

The absence of Foster and Jeeves alone meant that the greater part of the bowling strength – between them they had taken 202 wickets in the last season before the war – had been wiped out, and, as it happened, Field, who was also reaching the veteran stage for a fast bowler, was still playing in the Bradford League on Saturdays and was able to turn out for the county on only a few occasions. Only five of the men who had played regularly in the 1914 side came back to Edgbaston five years later – Quaife, Charlesworth, 'Tiger' Smith, Field and C. S. Baker, who was soon to be released to become a newspaper cartoonist.

Baker had been, and was still to be, a man of many parts – musician, draughtsman, cricketer, cartoonist, music-hall artist, grower of violets – there cannot have been many more varied careers. He had been born in Manchester and after leaving grammar school worked as a draughts-man, but tired of it and applied for a trial with Warwickshire whom he joined in 1903. Curly-haired, a dashing left-hand bat who could also bowl a bit, he became a regular member of the side in 1905 and in his dozen or so full seasons scored nearly 10 000 runs.

He never lost his love of drawing and, indeed, it was not unknown for him on occasions to play county cricket by day and do a lightning black and white sketching act at a convenient music hall at night. After he left Warwickshire he became a freelance cartoonist in Fleet Street, but later moved to Cornwall where he went into the family business of nurseryman. He also had a second lease of life as a cricketer, joining Cornwall when he was 42. In his first season, as an interview with Gerald Pawle in *The Cricketer* reminded us, he scored more runs – 756 for an average of 63 – than anyone else in the whole competition, and even in his 47th year he headed both batting and bowling averages for the county. In six seasons for them he made 2500 runs and took seventy wickets. When he celebrated his 90th birthday on 5 January 1973, he and Canon Parsons, 'Tiger' and W. C. Hands were the only survivors of the 1911 Championship side.

Other professionals available in 1919 were the young Len Bates and Harry Howell, destined to step into Field's boots. The amateurs included G. W. Stephens, who, after first declining, took over the daunting job of captain; W. C. Hands, to whom it had also been offered; R. L. Holdsworth, from Oxford, and the Rev. E. F. Waddy, an Australian with no mean record out there, who had come to teach at Rugby School. Altogether no fewer than twenty-five players appeared in the principal matches in 1919.

Writing later of the first post-war meeting of the Committee in November 1918, Ryder commented: 'It was more or less groping in the dark, with a little ray of light here and there, somewhat dim and ill-defined may be, but sufficiently luminous to make possible the first few steps in the new road that must be trod.' One member asked him: 'Can you rebuild the team in five years?' 'At any rate', Ryder added, 'it sounded a note of reason. Miracles were not expected.'

Hardly had the season opened when there was news of the death of another player – Alfred Law, born in Birmingham during 1862, one of the leading professional pioneers, who between 1885 and 1899 scored 4500 runs for the county.

The public had been starved of first-class cricket for five years and on grounds all over the country there were crowds far larger than they had been before the war, even though they were now on shorter commons – two-day matches. But neither the players nor the public liked the long hours of play – until 7.30 p.m. – and unless there were prospects of a good finish few people stayed until the close. The Editor of *Wisden* pronounced the experiment 'doomed before half the season had run its course', and in August the Advisory Committee decided to revert to the three-day game, a move which Warwickshire also welcomed by then. One is tempted to wonder now whether continuing the experiment, with perhaps some modifications, would have averted, or postponed, the decline which the game later suffered.

It so happened that this was a fine summer, which proved a great handicap to Warwickshire with their weakened bowling strength. Howell, the leading bowler, took only forty-eight wickets, which cost him nearly 30 runs each, and not even their batsmen could take advantage of it, none getting 1000 runs. Bates, soon coming into his own, led them with 823 runs, while Quaife had 818. Parsons got over 500, which made everyone wish he could have played more often.

Even so it is a shock to look at the Championship table and find Warwickshire at the foot of it for the first and only time in the Club's existence. (Worcestershire did not enter the competition this year, perhaps wisely.) Warwickshire played only fourteen games, won only one of them – against Derbyshire in the Bank Holiday match – lost seven and drew six. This time both Tyldesleys, J. T. and Ernest, scored centuries against them at Old Trafford; it looked as if some old habits at least were going to be resumed.

I have one vivid personal recollection of Warwickshire, or, rather, of Calthorpe this season. I saw the match against Yorkshire at Bradford in August and still recollect the awe with which I regarded the colossal six he hit off Rhodes. He was batting at the football end and had already hit Rhodes for one six. The second one soared high over the bank at the side of the pavilion, cleared the road behind it and dropped on the far side of the bowling green which then lay beyond. Next ball but one, Rhodes dropped just a shade shorter, Calthorpe accepted the challenge and was caught by Denton in the long field. But what glory! The old maestro took eight wickets for 44 in Warwickshire's second innings – beautiful bowling.

Some indication of the keenness of the public to see cricket again came at Edgbaston when 10 000 flocked to see the first day of the match with the Imperial Forces side. They won by an innings and it was a fellow Australian, in the Rev. E. F. Waddy, who had the best score for Warwickshire, 73.

One of the first administrative matters which had to be dealt with after the war was an application from the irrepressible Frank Foster to be appointed Warwickshire's 'team manager' at a salary of £1000 a year, an idea which, like the salary, was ahead of its time and must have shaken a few committee members. The executive hastily passed it on to the general committee with a recommendation that it be not accepted and the general committee endorsed that view without recorded comment. A pity. In February came his letter saying that he would not be able to take any further active part in the game. He was warmly thanked for his services and elected to honorary life membership and to the Committee, but he rarely attended the meetings and was replaced in 1922. Thereafter his contracts with Edgbaston were intermittent.

Ludford Docker proved an outspoken President, who used the platform of the annual meeting to pronounce on a multitude of matters about the game. This year he began by saying he hoped county cricket would never be regarded either as a business, or as a profession – it was a game and there must be no return to the dull monotony of professional cricket. Bainbridge, too, returned to this theme, saying that the great need in county cricket was a succession of good amateurs in the side; it was absurd to say that a team made up of ten or eleven professionals represented the cricket strength of the county. In that at least he was surely right.

There was a surplus of £237, but with large sums needed for renewals and repairs, a call went out for an increase of 1500 members on the existing figure of 1149 who had survived the war. Many other adjustments had to be made to post-war conditions, notably terms of engagements and allowances and charges for admission, which actually went up to 1s, but only 8d after 4.30 p.m. and boys 4d, including, if you please, entertainment tax in each case. Those taking advantage of the cheaper rate, however, amounted to only 7 per cent of total admissions.

Wages problems were not so easily disposed of. In April there came a deputation from the professionals – Quaife, Baker and Smith – who urged that in view of the cost of living – it was going up, as always after wars – increased charges for rail fares and the cost of cricket materials, the terms offered by the Committee were not proportionately higher than pre-war rates. For once the Committee agreed with the players and for 1920 increased the match fees to £6 for home games, £8 10s for away matches and bonuses of from £10 to £25 to be paid at the end of the season. The Committee also agreed that the Club should pay all rail fares and that George Austin should be paid rail fares and an allowance for out-of-pocket expenses in away games.

For once Quaife found himself out on a limb on this occasion. He told the executive committee that he had agreed with Howell, Smith and Bates not to accept an engagement unless all four players were granted certain terms, so he declined the Committee's inclusive offer of £10 a match, only to find that the others, without his knowledge, had signed agreements on these terms. He therefore sought to reopen negotiations and eventually the Committee agreed to pay him £11 a match, equal to a possible maximum of £308 for the season, compared with £320 in the cases of Howell, Smith and Bates. Quaife, it should be remembered, lest it be thought strange that he was paid less than the others, had been relieved of all ground duties. A further application for an increase by him was refused.

Parsons was also engaged in a great deal of negotiating. He wanted a retaining fee of £160 a year for six years, plus all the concessions granted to the other players, plus a guaranteed benefit of £900 in

1924. The Committee played true to form and haggled. Then it was said Parsons had decided to return to his regiment in India, next that he had secured an extension of his leave. Finally he did return to India and was not available for several seasons.

Ansell died before the end of the year, but he had lived long enough to see his twin ambitions realised. Of all the people who have been associated with the Club he, perhaps, is the one it would be most interesting to have visit the ground today. One has the feeling that he would approve of most of what he saw, not least the stand which bears his name, but that there would be much about the state of cricket that would disturb him.

Stephens gave up what had not been a very satisfactory captaincy at the end of the 1919 season and the Hon. F. S. G. Calthorpe was elected to take his place. He and R. E. S. Wyatt between them captained Warwickshire for all but the first and last two years of the period between the wars, Calthorpe for ten of them and Wyatt for eight; and a greater contrast between captains, both in temperament and their approach to the game, it would be hard to imagine.

'Tiger' Smith served under more captains than any other player now associated with the Club and I once asked him who was the best. He said that when they are leading a winning side all captains are good, but otherwise he would not commit himself except to add: 'I think the happiest was Calthorpe', a view confirmed in a totally different way by Ryder who, when Calthorpe died in 1935 at the untimely age of only 43, put on the wreath sent to the funeral these words: 'In memory of happy days and unforgotten laughter', as joyful an epitaph as anyone could wish to have. Ryder's son, Rowland, remembered 'the careless aristocratic grace of his run up to the wicket', which twisted like a corkscrew.

Calthorpe may not have been the most knowledgeable or successful captain Warwickshire ever had, especially in the latter respect, towards the end of his régime, but he played cricket as if it was a game to be enjoyed and his team obviously enjoyed it with him, as did, often, the spectators. To Wyatt, who was unquestionably one of the most knowledgeable cricketers who has ever played for the county, life on the cricket field was real and earnest, something which called for the most serious study, sometimes to the point of tedium, though everything he did had a reason and, as far as he was concerned, no effort was spared to achieve it. Only recently Wyatt was reported as saying how much he enjoyed playing in Yorkshire. 'They played the type of game I liked to play myself', he said, '. . . they gave nothing away.'

It is arguable which is the most successful attitude to adopt. Only twice in the ten years Calthorpe led the side did Warwickshire finish higher than tenth in the Championship. During Wyatt's eight years there were only three times when the Club was lower than tenth and once it finished fourth. Yet the average position under Calthorpe's leadership was only two places worse than the average under Wyatt – 11·7 compared with 9·5. It should also be remembered that Calthorpe took over at a time when the team had to be rebuilt. It took four years for them to reach a single-figure position, whereas Wyatt's years, 1930 to 1937, although they had not been doing too well just before he took over, were beset by no such problems.

Calthorpe came to Edgbaston with an excellent reputation. He had been one of the best all-rounders of his time at Repton, where they produce no mean cricketers still, being described as 'the backbone of a strong side's bowling' in 1911. At Cambridge he got his Blue while still a Freshman and played for the University for two seasons before serving in the Royal Flying Corps and he would have been captain in 1919 had not the letter of invitation unhappily miscarried.

Before the war he had played a few times for Sussex, but in 1919 he threw in his lot with Warwickshire, though he might easily have been lost to cricket altogether for he was a scratch golfer, as befitted one who lived near the Worplesdon course. Fortunately he kept mostly to cricket, a game of which it can be said he enjoyed every minute. From a personal point of view, he began very well, only just missing the 'double'. He scored 872 runs in Championship matches, including his first century in county cricket, 102 against Gloucestershire, and took ninety-one wickets for 23·20 runs each and was deservedly chosen for the Gentlemen. His opening partner in bowling, Howell, had a splendid season, bowling really fast and taking 132 wickets for only 17·50 each – 'Oh, my Calthorpe and my Howell long ago', as Rowland Ryder, 'R.V.'s' son, reminisced later. But the county lacked change bowlers, and only Quaife, who also took forty-four wickets, and Bates made over 1000 runs. Howell bowled so well that during the summer he had a very attractive league offer, but fortunately the Committee had the good sense to sign him on a five-year agreement with a benefit at the end of it.

So although Foster and Jeeves were still greatly missed, Warwickshire rose one position in the table to twelfth. They tried a number of amateurs during the season, but in only one match, against Worcestershire at Edgbaston in August, did any of them rival Calthorpe. Then Holdsworth made 141, G. W. Stephens 111, Calthorpe 87, the Rev. E. F. Waddy 71 and C. A. Fiddian-Green 53, but when Cambridge (with whom matches were resumed, as they were against Oxford) came in June, Warwickshire had a glimpse of a youngster they very much wanted to play for them.

This was N. E. Partridge, who came trailing clouds of glory from his days at Malvern where he set staid schoolmasters searching for superlatives to describe his performances. He was so very, very good that, according to Wyatt, he was invited to play for the Gentlemen at The

147

Oval, but the headmaster would not allow him to accept it for fear of what effect it might have on his ego. If he had played for the Gentlemen while still at school he would have been only the second schoolboy to have done so, the first being Alfred Lowth, who had been invited as long ago as 1836. The honour later came to G. T. S. Stevens, who was picked as twelfth man for the Gentlemen at Lord's and was eventually preferred to so fine a bowler as J. C. White.

Partridge was one of the five Public School Cricketers of the Year in the 1919 edition of *Wisden,* to which E. B. Noel contributed an article in which he said that in 1918 Partridge 'accomplished the most remarkable performances of any boy last year and very few in any year have approached him'.

For several years, [Mr Noel wrote], Mr C. Toppin . . . has had the highest hopes of his possibilities and he fully justified his hopes last year, both as a batsman and a bowler – but it is, I think, his batting that is the more remarkable. It is considered by many that he is already fit to play in any company, even the highest. Mr Toppin says of him: 'As an all-round player, I have never seen Partridge's equal as a boy. It is very sad that his cricket should come in these broken times.' And let it be remembered that Mr Toppin has had such great cricketers under his care as those of some of the famous Foster family, S. H. Day, W. H. B. Evans and many others.

As a batsman he is essentially an attacking player, with the possession of almost every shot of the cricketer of potential fame; as a bowler his action is not particularly impressive, but he is sound and liable to defeat anyone at any time. His performances in school matches are so remarkable that I give them below. His average for the year was:

	INNS	N.O.	TOTAL	HIGHEST	AVE
Batting	6	1	514	229 n.o.	102·8

	O	M	R	W	AVE
Bowling	126	23	370	32	11·5

Mr Noel quoted as proof of Partridge's stamina that on the first day of the Repton match – a very hot day – he bowled thirty overs and made 160 not out. Next day he took his score to 229 not out. He also made 112 and 131 against Cheltenham. The following year Mr Noel recorded that Partridge's batting performances did not equal those of 1918, but he had 'a most marvellous record in bowling' and this on a wicket which was then a batsman's paradise:

O	M	R	W	AVE
292	39	922	71	12·98

Even though his batting fell away and he got 'a pair', he still scored 569 runs (in fifteen innings as compared with six) and averaged 43·76.

Partridge went on to Cambridge, where it was thought he would go straight into the University XI, but, commented *Wisden*, G. E. C. Wood 'to say the least was in no hurry to give him his Blue. As he had a batting average of 24 and took thirty-eight wickets, Partridge got on fairly well, but it cannot be said that he rose to anything like the height of his school reputation.'

In the match at Edgbaston Partridge showed something of his quality by scoring 68 and 94 and taking one wicket for 95 and three for 35, Cambridge winning by 159 runs. Partridge, in first-class cricket, never did quite fulfil his promise, but from time to time he showed flashes of brilliance which made one certain that had he had more time to play the first-class game than business permitted him to do, he could have been an England captain with the flair and dash that only the amateur at his best has brought to the game.

After he gave up the first-class game, he played a good deal of club cricket, chiefly for Wolverhampton, where I was once called out of the Press box to deputise for an umpire who had not arrived. During the opposing side's innings, I 'stood' at the end from which Partridge was bowling and I have never seen, not even from Constantine in his later experimental days, such a bewildering variety of deliveries. He bowled every type of ball and used the full width of the crease to get maximum variation of angle. It was a performance of extraordinary virtuosity which made one wonder how any batsmen could survive for long against him. The fact that they often did, even in club cricket, suggests that it was perhaps his own versatility that was his greatest handicap. Had he bowled more to a plan and with less tendency to experiment, he might have been more successful, but one had the feeling that that would have been too dull and boring for him. As for his batting, it was of the kind, when he was in the mood, which could change the course of a game in a few minutes. Whatever he was doing on the field, he was always a delight to watch.

If anyone should tell you that he once saw Jack Hobbs take five Warwickshire wickets for a mere 21 runs at Edgbaston and that the same season he headed the Surrey bowling averages, do not contradict him – it did happen in 1920. Warwickshire were all out for 70 and then Hobbs made his usual hundred against them, his third in successive innings. Ducat got 104 and Surrey declared at 258 for four and then put Warwickshire out a second time, for 159. This time Hobbs took only one wicket for 4 runs.

Howell, turning out for the Players at The Oval, found himself opposed to his captain and had him caught by Hobbs. He bowled at a great pace, made the ball lift and in the second innings took six for 40. He followed this in the Lord's match with four for 49 and two for 29, and it was no surprise when he was chosen to go to Australia in the winter. There, however, although he played in three Tests, he suffered badly from missed catches and took only seven wickets which cost him no fewer than 66·85 runs each, though in all matches he had 38 for 27·44 each.

During the year the Committee went ahead with the purchase of the freehold of the ground for £5000, which had had to be postponed because of the war. It was arranged to do so by raising £6000 on mortgage debentures, the money to be found by the President and friends, with the Club paying six per cent interest to the ground company. The extra £1000 was to cover stamp duty and charges. The transaction was completed by the following year.

The accounts presented at the annual meeting, where there were many complimentary things said about Ansell, showed a deficiency of £136 and subscriptions were raised, that of ordinary members from £1 1s 0d to £1 5s 0d. By December the picture looked brighter. There had been record crowds – 123 209 – and subscriptions from a record 2084 members, 612 having joined during the year, brought in £2554. Crowther Charlesworth's benefit brought him just over £1000, the first four-figure benefit in the Club's history, and he was wise enough to allow them to buy £1000-worth of War Loan for him at £835. At the end of the season when he retired in his 45th year he went as coach to the Royal Naval College, Dartmouth.

The year 1921, in the records of which the names of Gregory and McDonald are written in letters of fire, was a disastrous one in almost every way for English cricket. It was a terrible year, too, for deaths – William Gunn, Ephraim Lockwood, Arthur Mold among them. It was almost as if they could not bear to witness England's disgrace. Warwickshire were not spared their share of weeping and wailing for they dropped to sixteenth position in the Championship table, only the newly admitted Glamorgan being below them. They lost twice as many matches as they won, yet Calthorpe, although breaking a bone in his hand which kept him out of the game for two to three weeks, nearly did the 'double' again. Once more Howell, despite missing ten games because of a strained foot, took exactly 100 wickets in all matches. Among other casualties were Rotherham, who had his arm badly hurt in trying to stop a fierce return, and Charlesworth, who had his face badly cut just above the right eye.

Warwickshire, who were allotted two matches with the Australians, perhaps because the first one, with the Test immediately following it, was limited to two days, escaped Gregory and McDonald who were being rested, until the second game. In their absence at the end of June, the county achieved the respectable first innings total of 262 against Hendry, Armstrong, Mailey, Ryder and Pellew; but then they trounced the Warwickshire bowling to the tune of 506, Armstrong making 117 and Oldfield 123. Oldfield and Mailey put on 124 in 40 minutes for the last wicket, which nobody, not even the Australians, should have been allowed to do. In their second innings Warwickshire lost six wickets for 58, but Quaife made 39, and Partridge, on his first appearance for the county, 37 not out, and they saved the day. Partridge had scored 29 in the first innings and had taken three wickets for 113, which, considering the quality of the opposition, could have been worse.

On the second visit in August the county were not so lucky. This time the twin fast-bowling terrors did play and, with Armstrong, twice dismissed them, for 133 and 118. The Australians, having made 312 for seven declared, won comfortably by an innings and 61 runs. Among the spectators on this occasion were six Birmingham schoolboys, one of whom, Leslie Deakins, was destined to spend a good many more hours on the ground.

Howell, incidentally, played in one Test Match against the tourists, but did not take a wicket. While he was away because of his injury, Warwickshire lost seven matches in succession. One of them was against Cambridge, who thus beat Warwickshire twice, and if that should occasion any surprise it should be remembered that this was the year of the three brilliant Ashton brothers – Claude, Gilbert and Hubert – not to mention C. H. Gibson, C. S. Marriott and A. G. Doggart.

Calthorpe played the innings of his life, 176, against Somerset, just when it was badly needed and went even one better with 209 against Hampshire; but it was Quaife, at the age of 49, who was still the most consistent batsman, though a redheaded young man named Scorer troubled his namesakes, the recorders, to the tune of 113 and several other useful scores.

Once more Quaife found himself in conflict with the authorities. Late in August a report appeared in *The Birmingham Post*, which stated that he was thinking of ending his connection with Warwickshire at the end of the season, though not necessarily with first-class cricket. He was thereupon asked to attend a meeting of the executive committee at which he admitted that the statement had been made with his authority and gave as his reason that his son, Bernard, although given a guarantee of six matches, had been played in only four, and that he was dissatisfied with the way certain professionals had been treated by the Committee.

Quaife declined either to apologise for his action in communicating such a statement to the Press before consulting the Committee, or to withdraw the statement. He was given until 1 November to consider the matter and in the meantime the Committee called the other professionals in for an interview. They gave their views on some matter unspecified which the Committee agreed to consider, but later Howell, it was stated, 'saw his folly' and regretted that he had allowed himself to be influenced to make complaints. Quaife had further interviews, but whether he ever apologised, formally or not, I have not been able to discover. At all events, he went on playing, and it was just as well for Warwickshire that he did so.

Among the young players signed this season was a young wicket-keeper named George Duckworth from Lancashire. It is said that when he heard that an emissary from Warwickshire was coming to see him play for his local club, George got himself promoted in the batting order so that he could impress as a wicketkeeper-batsman, which is what he was engaged as. He accepted a qualifying engagement with Warwick-shire, stayed one year and then broke it to return to Lancashire, for whom, of course, he had a birth qualification, and who urgently needed a wicketkeeper. At least Warwickshire did not let him go because they could not recognise promise when they saw it, and Duckworth could hardly be blamed; it would be some nine years before 'Tiger' retired.

If nothing else had happened in 1922 one match alone would have singled it out as remarkable. It was not only the most astonishing Warwickshire have ever played, but because of the unexpectedly devastating reversal of fortunes that occurred, it must rank as one of the most extraordinary matches anywhere.

The fixture was with Hampshire at Edgbaston on 14, 15 and 16 June. It began calmly enough, though, as there had been some rain, Tennyson sent Warwickshire in. They might well have got them out fairly cheaply, but for two innings, one of 84 by Reg Santall, Sydney's son, and the other of 70 by Calthorpe. As it was, Warwickshire made 223, which was moderate enough at that stage, but assumed almost gigantic proportions in view of what was to come.

Hampshire began their innings about 4 p.m. on a wicket which, it was reported, was now so easy as to be almost perfect. Forty minutes later they were all out for 15, the lowest total for which Warwickshire have ever dismissed any side. Whether this was due to the fact that the wicket was not so easy as it appeared, or whether it was that the Warwickshire bowlers, Calthorpe and Howell, were inspired we shall now never know. The facts were that Hampshire's first three batsmen, Bowell, Kennedy and H. L. V. Day, were all dismissed without scoring, one of them by Howell, who broke Bowell's middle stump, and two by Calthorpe. Five more 'ducks' followed and only three men, Mead, who made six not out, Tennyson who got four, and Shirley one, scored at all. There were four byes.

Ryder wrote afterwards that had Smith managed to stop that ball wide on the leg side, Calthorpe and Howell would have established a world record: 'Of course, they bowled immensely well, but it is simply impossible to explain how eleven first-class players were dismissed on a good wicket for so small a score.'

Mead, too, was 'baffled by it all' to the end of his days, he told John

Arlott.* He went in at the fall of the second wicket and was not out 6 when the innings closed. 'Nobody bowled me anything that I couldn't play in the middle', he said.

According to Rowland Ryder, in an article he wrote for *Wisden* in 1965, the total should have been fewer still. He recalled discussing the match with George Brown, the Hampshire wicketkeeper-batsman, who said they should have been out for seven. 'Tiger' was unsighted when he allowed the byes and Brown contended that Tennyson was missed at mid-on,† the ball then travelling to the boundary. This was how the Hampshire wickets fell:

1	2	3	4	5	6	7	8	9	10
0	0	0	5	5	9	10	10	15	15

'Tiger' said afterwards that he had never seen Howell bowl so fast; and according to H. L. V. Day, Calthorpe was swinging the ball prodigiously. 'He bowled me one,' he said, 'which started at mid-on and finished at third slip, bowling me on the way.' Howell and Calthorpe returned the sort of analyses that no writer of fiction would have dared to invent:

	O	M	R	W
HOWELL	4·5	2	7	6
CALTHORPE	4	3	4	4

It is said that as the last Hampshire batsmen returned to the pavilion, Tennyson turned to his shocked team mates and said: 'Never mind, lads, we'll get 500 next time.' Day said Calthorpe proposed that, as the game was bound to finish early next day, the amateurs should play each other at golf. This, he added, brought a flood of good Anglo-Saxon from Tennyson, who, without batting an eyelid, said that not only would Hampshire be batting until lunch-time on the third day, but would win the match. At any rate, some bets were made at very long odds, Newman, the Hampshire bowler, saying that Tennyson bet Calthorpe £10 that Hampshire would still pull it off.

When they followed on, 208 behind, Calthorpe, according to 'Tiger', did not put Howell on immediately, saying that 'they want to see a bit of cricket up there'; up there, presumably, being the pavilion balcony where doubtless members of the Committee were ensconced. Nor at first was Howell needed. Kennedy was out for seven, bowled Calthorpe; Quaife got Bowell for 45 and Day for 15 and when Howell did go on he bowled Mead for 24. Six wickets were down for 186 and Hampshire were still well behind. Tennyson went for 45 and then came that genial giant, George Brown, who, the season before, had stood up to a

The Cricketer's Bedside Book, Batsford.
†Newman's recollection was that it was at slip.

battering from Gregory and McDonald and had then kept wicket for England as well.

Shirley, with a useful 30, helped him to add 85. Even so, McIntyre failed, but then Livsey, the wicketkeeper, came in at No. 10. He rose to the occasion so splendidly that he went on to make his first century in county cricket – and he could hardly have chosen a more appropriate moment to do it. Meanwhile Brown stayed anchored, batting for four hours and a half before Smart bowled him. Livsey was not out 110 and Hampshire had reached 521, which gave them the hardly believable lead of 313. The Calthorpe–Howell figures this time were very different:

	O	M	R	W
HOWELL	63	10	156	3
CALTHORPE	33	7	97	2

Quaife had three for 154 in 49 overs, which virtually amounted to cruelty to aged cricketers. He was the third of the seven bowlers Warwickshire tried, but it might have been a different story if Calthorpe had taken the new ball when it was available. He did not do so because Warwickshire did not want the game over too quickly! But Brown and Livsey got set and then it was too late.

Warwickshire had to get 314 to win, but it seemed as if the Hampshire come-back had knocked all the fight out of them. 'Tiger' growled back with 41, Quaife still had sufficient energy left to make 40 not out and Calthorpe 30, but they could muster no more than 158 and Hampshire had won a famous victory by 155 runs. Last memory of a memorable match – Tennyson giving a passable imitation of a Highland fling in the shower. The full scores, I think, are worth giving:

WARWICKSHIRE

First Innings		Second Innings	
Bates c Shirley b Newman	3	c Mead b Kennedy	1
Smith c Mead b Newman	24	c Shirley b Kennedy	41
F. R. Santall c McIntyre b Boyes	84	b Newman	0
Quaife b Newman	1	not out	40
Hon. F. S. G. Calthorpe c Boyes b Kennedy	70	b Newman	30
Rev. E. F. Waddy c Mead b Boyes	0	c and b Kennedy	7
Fox b Kennedy	4	b Kennedy	0
Smart (J.) b Newman	20	b Newman	3
Smart (C.) c Mead b Boyes	14	c and b Boyes	15
Howell not out	1	c Kennedy b Newman	11
Leg-byes	2	Byes 6, leg-byes 4	10
	223		158

HAMPSHIRE

FIRST INNINGS		SECOND INNINGS	
Bowell b Howell	0	c Howell b Quaife	45
Kennedy c Smith b Calthorpe	0	b Calthorpe	7
H. L. V. Day b Calthorpe	0	c Bates b Quaife	15
Mead not out	6	b Howell	24
Hon. L. H. Tennyson c Calthorpe b Howell	4	c Smart (C.) b Calthorpe	45
Brown b Howell	0	b Smart (C.)	172
Newman c Smart (C.) b Howell	0	c and b Quaife	12
W. R. Shirley c Smart (J.) b Calthorpe	1	lbw b Fox	30
A. S. McIntyre lbw b Calthorpe	0	lbw b Howell	5
Livsey b Howell	0	not out	110
Boyes lbw b Howell	0	b Howell	29
Byes	4	Byes 15, leg-byes 11, no-ball 1	27
	15		**521**

BOWLING – HAMPSHIRE

	O	M	R	W	O	M	R	W
Kennedy	24	7	74	2	26	12	47	4
Newman	12·3	0	70	4	26·3	12	53	5
Boyes	16	5	56	4	11	4	34	1
Shirley	3	0	21	0	—	—	—	—
Brown	—	—	—	—	5	0	14	0

WARWICKSHIRE

	O	M	R	W	O	M	R	W
Howell	4·5	2	7	6	63	10	156	3
Calthorpe	4	3	4	4	33	7	97	2
Quaife	—	—	—	—	49	8	154	3
Fox	—	—	—	—	7	0	30	1
Smart (J.)	—	—	—	—	13	2	37	0
Santall	—	—	—	—	5	0	15	0
Smart (C.)	—	—	—	—	1	0	5	1

Altogether June was a most depressing month for Warwickshire for they also suffered two crushing defeats by Yorkshire, Percy Holmes scoring a double century against them in each match, 209 at Edgbaston and 220 not out at Huddersfield. In the second match every Warwickshire player was called upon to bowl; Calthorpe was never averse to letting anyone try his hand in an emergency, though it was not his doing on this occasion. The defeat was partly due to absences – he and Howell

THE STORY OF WARWICKSHIRE CRICKET

were unable to play – and injuries. Smart, at slip, fractured his right thumb while trying to stop a ball cut by Holmes, and Quaife was struck on his left side by a ball from Waddington, had to be X-rayed and was ordered to rest. In Warwickshire's second innings, on a damaged pitch and in a bad light, Len Bates showed the stuff he was made of, batting through the innings for 50 out of a total of 125 and defying the Yorkshire bowlers for an hour and 55 minutes.

There was another remarkable happening this season, believed to be unique in first-class cricket. When Warwickshire went to Derby, also in June, father and son on one side opposed father and son on the other – W. and R. Bestwick and W. G. and B. W. Quaife – and at one point in the match the two Quaifes were batting against the bowling of the two Bestwicks. W.G. was bowled by R. Bestwick, but not until he had made 107, but Bernard fell to Jackson for 20. Warwickshire had only one innings, Derbyshire being twice routed by Howell for 130 and 122. In the return match at Edgbaston only one Quaife, W.G., and one Bestwick, R., played in a match that was ruined by rain.

That was almost the fate, also, of 'Tiger's' benefit match against Lancashire, not a ball being bowled on the first day. Then he went in to open the innings with Bates, but was out for nine and Warwickshire were all out for 191. Lancashire failed to get first innings lead, but Warwickshire's batting broke down badly in the second innings, Smith making 17 this time, and Lancashire won by seven wickets. The benefit, thanks to other efforts, eventually realised £700, and he, too, allowed the Club to invest the bulk of it in War Loan.

For the second time in the season every Warwickshire player bowled in the match at Edgbaston against Middlesex, but that did not prevent them from making 535 for six declared. Hearne got the third double century of the season against the Midland county. Notwithstanding all their disappointments, Warwickshire went up four places in the Championship table. Three batsmen made over 1000 runs – Quaife, still the most dependable, Smith and Bates – and at the age of 50 Quaife, very appropriately, also took fifty wickets.

For the third summer in succession Howell took over 100 wickets and Calthorpe made another fine all-round contribution – 972 runs and seventy-two wickets, but it was Partridge, playing his first full season, who headed the bowling averages with fifty-five wickets at 18·58 each. He could not, however, reproduce his Malvern batting form, scoring no more than 433 in 26 innings. As for Bates, *Wisden* remarked that he 'looks such a high-class batsman that one feels he ought to be better than he is'.

Ludford Docker had begun 1922 with one of the fulminations with which he invariably enlivened the annual meeting. This time his target was 'that curse and abomination of the game, the two-eyed stance . . .

I have never seen so many batsmen either lbw, or bowled through playing back to half-volleys as last year and I hope I shall never see the like again'.

There were others thinking along similar lines, for *Wisden*'s Editor quoted some figures given by the Hon. R. H. Lyttelton in a letter to *The Times* showing the growth in the number of lbw decisions in first-class matches – in 1870, 44 out of 1772 wickets; in 1890, 219 out of 3792 wickets; in 1910, 451 out of 6704 wickets; and in 1923, 921 out of 7919

But there were some things for the President to be cheerful about – finances much improved, though Entertainment Tax was becoming a constant worry; there was a surplus of £1106; there were record gates; and £5000 had been spent during the last three years on improvements to the ground. Docker said he put his faith in players under 30 – was this a dig at Quaife? – and Cartland said half a dozen professionals had been engaged, but Warwickshire was not producing young players of her own. Calthorpe criticised the fielding – a large number of catches were dropped.

One of the players Warwickshire badly wanted back was Parsons and this summer there began a series of protracted negotiations with him. Letters and cables flew between Edgbaston and India almost as fast and as thickly as they were to do between England and Australia in the 'bodyline' years of 1932–3. How different from modern times when the captain flies out to see the player. The impression one is left with in all this is that, as usual, Warwickshire wanted Parsons as cheaply as they could get him, and that Parsons, while trying to do the best for himself, was having great difficulty in deciding whether he wanted to stay in the Army, or play cricket.

It was not until July 1923, a month after he had cabled saying that he was going to stay in the Army, that he arrived back in England, visited the ground and almost before one could say 'Jack's back', he played in the remaining matches of that season on a match fee basis. By October terms were finally agreed with him – he was engaged for five years at £156 a year, plus match fees as in force during the term of the agreement, and a guaranteed benefit of £750 in 1926. He would be a member of the ground staff, but exempt from ground bowling duties.

An amusing footnote to all this to-ing and fro-ing was that in December 1922, a letter was received from Parsons asking that wages cheques should be made payable to Captain J. H. Parsons. The reply sent by the Committee agreed to the request, but pointed out that, as a professional cricketer, the Army rank could not be used in matters concerning his cricket position.

Nor did it avail him when Yorkshire next came to visit Edgbaston.

157

Bill Bowes tells the story of how Edgar Oldroyd, while waiting to go in to bat, went and sat in a deckchair in the pavilion enclosure, only to be informed by the attendant that he was occupying the seat of Captain Parsons.

'Oh, am I?' retorted Edgar. 'Well, you go and tell him that Private bloody Oldroyd's sitting in it now.'

I doubt whether the message, at least in those terms, was ever conveyed to Parsons, but I am sure he would have enjoyed the joke as much as anyone.

Calthorpe spent the winter of 1922–3 in Australia and New Zealand with the M.C.C. team which MacLaren took out. He played in two Tests in which he was more successful as a bowler than as a batsman, taking eleven wickets, though in all matches he scored more runs than anyone except Chapman – 1038, average 35·79, and took fifty-four wickets for 25·35, so it was a successful all-round venture. Before he went out there he got married and the players gave him a pair of wine coolers for a present. By June 1924, they were congratulating their skipper on the birth of a son.

Enter Wyatt
(1923–1926)

IN the November of 1922 a name which was to figure long and prominently in the annals of Warwickshire cricket appeared in the records of the Club for the first time in a rather curious way. The desirability was mentioned to the Committee of finding employment for R. E. S. Wyatt, as he was a promising player and was anxious to play county cricket. In April 1923, the secretary received instructions – from whom it was not stated – about an engagement for him whereby he would be able to play county cricket the whole season.

Robert Elliott Storey Wyatt was born on 2 May 1901, at Milford, Surrey. He has told us in his book* that when he was 3 years old his father taught him how to stand and hold a bat; a stance, he remarks, which was exactly the same when he was 29 years old. He first went to Milburn Lodge School, Esher, and later, when the family moved to Worcester, to King Henry VIII School, Coventry.

He played in his first match when he was 8 – a second eleven game at his preparatory school. He made 36 runs and counted every one of them, a habit he retained throughout his cricket career. He always knew exactly how many runs he had made, without looking at the scoreboard, and how many had been scored off his bowling, and it was not unknown for him to correct even the scorers. Next came village games at Meriden and the works team at the Rover Company, where he went to learn automobile engineering, followed by club cricket with the Coventry and North Warwickshire side, with whom he practised assiduously, evening after evening.

To him cricket had already become what it was to remain – the most important thing in his life, though he has said he never thought he

*Three Straight Sticks, Stanley Paul and Co. Ltd.

would ever be good enough to play first-class cricket, so much so that when towards the end of the 1921 season he was asked to play for the county second eleven he almost declined. But his father persuaded him to do so and he played at Derby, making 30 not out. Even so, it is doubtful if he would have cast in his lot with Warwickshire had it not been for the fact that Surrey, prompted by one of their members in the Coventry and North Warwickshire Club, courteously asked Warwickshire if they intended to play him, otherwise Surrey would invite him to join them.

As Wyatt comments in his book, 'nothing makes you want a thing more than the fear that somebody else is after it', and Warwickshire reacted quickly, inviting him to play in no fewer than the first twelve matches of 1923. By a curious coincidence, he made his debut for Warwickshire against Worcestershire, with whom he was to end his first-class playing career. He scored 37, but although that season he often opened the innings with Smith or Bates – Warwickshire did not seem to be able to settle on an opening pair about this time, a decided weakness – and played forty-eight innings, he scored no more than 658 runs for an average of only 16·04. He also took thirty-five wickets, but they cost him 31 runs each.

Nevertheless, George Egdell, then the cricket correspondent of *The Birmingham Post*, in his review of the season, welcomed him 'as one of the most promising all-round players discovered in Warwickshire for a long time', and added, 'he should have a highly successful career in front of him, for he is a steady, watchful batsman and as a medium-paced bowler makes use of a natural off-break.'

In his early days, however, Wyatt gave few signs of the great value he was to be to the county in the sixteen seasons he had with them – 'the happiest of my life', he once said, despite the circumstances in which he parted from the Club just after the Second World War. His comparative failure was undoubtedly partly due to the fact that Calthorpe found him more useful as a bowler than as a batsman and consequently put him low down in the order.

In 1923, though, things of greater dramatic impact were occurring, for this was Howell's great year. Whatever rests he had during the summer were well earned for he worked like the ever-willing horse Warwickshire turned him into. He was grossly over-bowled for a fast bowler – 1067 overs, nearly twice as many as anyone else – just as Hollies was in years to come, though the latter did not take as much out of himself as did Howell. Warwickshire have never had enough quality bowling throughout their history, but when they did find a good one he certainly earned his keep.

But Howell had the satisfaction of achieving his finest performance – all ten wickets and they were Yorkshire's, too. It happened at Edgbaston in May and it was all the more meritorious because it was done on a wicket which should have been more suited to a spinner than a fast bowler. No play was possible on the first day until 4.30 p.m. when Yorkshire went in and, before the close, Howell had collected five of their wickets for 37. Next morning he took the other five for only 14 and finished with these figures:

O	M	R	W
25·1	5	51	10

It was only the second time in Yorkshire's history that they had had to suffer such an indignity and the first had been as long ago as 1865. Yorkshire were all out for 113, but then, in Rowland Ryder's phrase, they 'fielded like eleven tigers', and got Warwickshire out for three runs fewer. Yorkshire declared their second innings at 162 for six, Howell taking two for 54 this time and Calthorpe four for 52; but Macaulay, Robinson and Kilner disposed of Warwickshire for only 81, of which Quaife, 22, and Jack Smart, 20, made more than half between them.

Even in an innings of 286 by Worcestershire at Worcester, Calthorpe tried nine bowlers. Perhaps it was a desperate effort on his part to take some of the burden off Howell who, for the fourth year in succession, took over 100 wickets. This year he reached his peak with 152 for the county for under 20 runs each. In successive matches at Edgbaston he took twelve wickets – for 112 against Surrey and for 197 against Kent, who were beaten twice. He also had another good match against Yorkshire at Hull – six for 80 and three for 93 – and he was selected for the Players at Lord's, but did not get a wicket against one of the strongest teams the Gentlemen can ever have turned out, G. T. S. Stevens and M. D. Lyon both making hundreds.

Quaife, 51 on 17 March, was again the only batsman to score over 1000 runs – for the twenty-second time in his extraordinary career – but Parsons, coming with his late-in-the-season run, got in nine innings which produced 302 runs, including one century, which took him to the top of the county averages with 33·55.

Ludford Docker's theme at the annual meeting had been defence, defence, defence which, he said, was the order of the day without any real effort being made to get runs. Slower and less interesting play, he said, had scarcely been witnessed at Edgbaston than on the occasion of the visiting counties last season – and he did not except even the Champion County. The absolute refusal to 'get at the bowler before he gets at you' reduced the play to 'an exasperating spectacle of over-cautious barndoor cricket, pitiable in its inexcusable timidity and utter absence of enterprise'. And we tend to think slow play a modern invention. The man in the crowd, in Docker's view, was thoroughly fed up with the dull and slow cricket being played by our best professional batsmen. If these batsmen were only to hear some of the forcible, uncomplimentary remarks frequently made by onlookers, he added, they would realise they were killing the goose that laid the golden eggs.

Docker's speech was reprinted in full in *The Cricketer* of April 1925, with the added comment: 'We feel that Mr Docker takes too pessimistic a view, but there is force in what he says.'

The batsmen had very nearly killed the goose – to the extent of a drop of nearly £5000 in income compared with 1921. Largely because of deplorable weather, gate receipts were down by half and there was a loss on the 1922 season of £622, though membership mercifully was still keeping up. At long last it was decided to provide an office and a counting room, on the ground, though not before the safe had been burgled and over £7 taken. The Club, it appeared, had not had a policy of insurance against burglary, as the proposals made for cover had been declined in 1912. Money must have been tight then as well as now, for when a gateman found £5 on the ground it was decided to retain it until the end of the season in case the owner claimed it and then, if he did not, to pay the gateman £1 and credit the Club funds with the rest!

There was another kind of insurance, the rates of which the Club found 'absolutely prohibitive' – those covering them against matches ruined by rain – and because of losses it was decided to make the annual subscription not less than £1 11s 6d for ordinary members and to increase other categories as well. There was considerable opposition, but the President said the Club must be put on a sound financial basis and there were three other clubs, though he did not name them, which had £2 and £2 2s 0d subscriptions.

When the treasurer said the resulting increase in revenue would be barely enough to cover the deficit and that they were proposing to spend another £2000 on ground improvements, it was suggested that the pavilion might be used for social gatherings in the winter. Perhaps, it was hinted, a series of whist-drives might be organised, but the meeting drew the line at whist as an aid to cricket. Later committees could not afford to be so particular.

Yet another pioneer of the game in the county died before the winter set in – Canon Osbert Mordaunt, for forty-eight years Rector of Hampton Lucy, near Stratford, who had played for Eton as long before as 1860 and was described as 'a capital hitter and good field, generally at point or slip'. He also developed into a good lob bowler – and he could deliver the ball with either hand. He played several notable innings for the Gentlemen of Warwickshire, and for 22 of Birmingham against the Australians in 1878 he had the truly astonishing analysis of

4 wickets for 3 runs. One would dearly like to know whether he was bowling lobs against them.

Not long afterwards came news of the death of the first of two Warwickshire players who achieved the rare distinction of appearing for both the Gentlemen and the Players – E. J. Diver, who had played three years for Surrey as an amateur, but turned professional when he qualified for Warwickshire by residence. He played for them between 1893 and 1901, but although he had some memorable innings – including one for the Gentlemen against the Australians in a match which he and A. G. Steel virtually won on their own – he never really fulfilled his promise, though he scored nearly 6000 runs for Warwickshire at an average of 26.

Edgbaston's third Test was against South Africa in 1924 and it gave rise, indirectly, to one of cricket's most famous utterances – Lord Hawke's 'Pray God no professional will ever captain England'. It was a remarkable match in many ways, as so many of the Tests played at Edgbaston have been. It took place in June and, as usual, lots of rain had fallen, so H. W. Taylor put England in to bat despite the fact that he was short of bowlers and had pressed into service G. M. Parker, a fellow countryman, who was then playing in the Bradford League.

This was Sutcliffe's first Test and he opened the innings with Hobbs with what was to be the first of many profitable partnerships together, though he was very nearly run out in the first over. This one produced 136 runs – Hobbs 76, Sutcliffe 64 – and it was followed by innings of 64 by Woolley, 74 by Hendren and 59 by Roy Kilner. Poor Parker, accustomed only to league cricket, bowled himself into the ground and at one point had to leave the field in a state of exhaustion. He sent down thirty-seven overs, two maidens, for 152 runs, but he took six wickets. Even so, England made 438.

South Africa's first innings produced the first of this game's sensations. The opening bowlers were the Sussex 'strikers', as they might now be described, A. E. R. Gilligan, the captain, and Maurice Tate, and they did indeed strike the South African batting as if they were lightning itself. They were routed for their lowest total in a Test – 30, of which Catterall made 12. The bowling analyses speak for themselves:

	O	M	R	W
GILLIGAN	6·3	4	7	6
TATE	6·0	1	12	4

South Africa followed on, of course – not even for gate money would England have had the sauce to bat again with a lead of over 400 – and this time there was a great improvement – a total of 390, of which Catterall made a fine 120, though it was not enough. Gilligan and Tate were still the most successful bowlers, the former having another five wickets for 83 and Tate four for 103, but Parkin, Kilner, Fender and Woolley were also tried. Parkin bowled sixteen overs, five maidens, for 38 runs, without taking a wicket and the fact that he was so little used in a fairly long innings provoked him to writing an article for a Sunday newspaper which included this passage:

I am not going to stand being treated as I was on Tuesday last. On the last morning of the match there was 105 minutes play. With Catterall hitting so finely it was necessary for the England captain to make many bowling changes. During these changes I was standing all the time at mid-off wondering what on earth I had done to be overlooked. I can say that I have never felt so humiliated in the whole course of my cricket career. I admit that on Monday I was not at my best, but why should Mr Gilligan have assumed that I would be worse than useless on Tuesday? . . . I feel I should not be fair to myself if I accepted an invitation to play in any further Test Match.

Whether because of the article or not, Parkin did not get any further invitation. *The Birmingham Post*, in its report of the match, commented that Parkin, 'although not so expensive as some of the others, was very disappointing on Monday and was not called upon to share in the attack yesterday'.

Wisden's Editor, who was not at the match, wrote that, reading the reports, he thought that Parkin should not have been passed over as a bowler on the third morning and, being at the top of his form, he had a grievance. Still that did not in anyway excuse him for rushing into print and saying he would never play for England again. As a result of his outburst he was not asked to play in any of the subsequent Test Matches and I do not think his claims to a place in the M.C.C.'s team for Australia were ever discussed.

Parkin, however, went on the tour as a correspondent and made more critical comments there. It was left to Lord Hawke, at the annual meeting of the Yorkshire Club the following January, to put the seal on the incident in a speech containing a passage which has since been quoted – and mis-quoted and taken out of context – countless times:

Pray God no professional will ever captain the England side. I love professionals, every one of them, but we have always had an amateur skipper. If the time comes when we are to have no more amateurs captaining England, well, I don't say English cricket will become exactly like league football, but it will be a thousand pities, and it will not be for the good of the game.

Lord Hawke did not live to see Hutton captain England, or receive a knighthood, two events on which it would have been stimulating, to say the least, to have had his comments.

Meanwhile, as in 1902, the Test had brought financial embarrassment to Warwickshire, the county's share of the receipts being £662, compared with £886 in 1909 and £763 in 1902 – and £2500 had been spent on ground and pavilion improvements. Moreover, it was a wet summer and once more Warwickshire found themselves harder hit than any other county. The Notts match at Edgbaston was abandoned without a ball being bowled and there were five blank Saturdays, so once more the Club found itself facing a deficiency, this time of £3175. Again an appeal was made to the public and again they responded splendidly, over £3500 being raised – 'stronger evidence of the stability of the county club could scarcely have been afforded', said *Wisden*.

The second visit of the South Africans to Edgbaston was one of the few games not affected by the weather, 1141 runs being scored and only twenty-eight wickets falling. The touring team twice topped 300 and Warwickshire 400, Reg Santall making 102 and on the other side H. W. Taylor 97 and 116. Warwickshire tried six bowlers in the first innings and no fewer than nine in the second.

Despite the weather, Warwickshire, for the first time for several seasons, managed to win more matches than they lost and moved up three places in the table to ninth. They owed it mostly to Howell, who, although it was hardly the sort of season a fast bowler would like to take around with him, took 120 wickets for only 16 runs each. Again he bowled twice as many overs as anyone else except Wyatt, who improved to sixty-one wickets for 21·44.

Howell nearly repeated his feat of taking all ten wickets, at Taunton, where he had a field day. He and Wyatt tumbled Somerset out for 99 in the first innings, with five for 36 and five for 47 respectively; and Howell followed this in the second innings with nine for 35, five clean bowled. He also virtually won the match against Glamorgan at Edgbaston by taking six for 66 in the second innings. His benefit produced a well-deserved £804.

He also played in a Test trial and eight wickets in one Players' match and three in the other got him into the final Test at The Oval, but it was spoiled by rain and he did not take a wicket. In the winter of 1924–5 he went to Australia with Gilligan's team, but this was Tate's tour and Howell did not play in any of the Tests. In all matches in which he bowled only 125·4 overs he took twenty-three wickets, so if the tour was not exactly a rest cure he was not over-worked for once, though, like several other Warwickshire players, he never seemed to be able to reproduce for others the form he showed for the county.

Of the batsmen in 1924 only Parsons made over 1000 runs, Quaife dropping to 802 for once, and Calthorpe headed the batting averages. His tally of wickets fell away still further to only twenty-four. Hearne added 101 not out at Edgbaston to his remarkable series of scores against Warwickshire since the war – 215 not out in 1920, 202 in 1921,

221 in 1922 – an aggregate of 739 runs for once out. Just to rub it in, he finished off the match, which Middlesex won by an innings, by taking five for 31.

Slow play had come in for another castigation from Ludford Docker, who said his great fear was that cricket would lose its popularity if that wretched method of play continued. He hardly liked to admit it, but he was sorry to say that it was a fact that first-class cricket was now, for good or evil, inextricably involved in finance, and its prosperity, indeed its very existence, must depend upon the support accorded it by the general public. A man of shrewd discernment was Ludford Docker, and how right he was in both these instances, for the decline of cricket surely started when it ceased primarily to be a game and instead, in the minds of some, became a business for both clubs and players.

Wisden in 1925 commented on a suggestion by Calthorpe, supported by Arthur Gilligan, that during an Australian visit the County Championship should be suspended, or largely curtailed, but it was hardly to be expected that it would find favour with the first-class counties. There was another echo at Warwickshire's annual meeting of Lord Hawke's reference to professionals when Bainbridge, referring to 'an unfortunate discussion' as to whether it would not be a good thing to have a professional captain sometimes, said there was nothing new in the idea – there had been professional captains many years ago and the only person at all unhappy was the professional.

The professional captain, Bainbridge added, was placed in an awkward position as there must occasionally be causes for complaint about the team, and if a professional had to go before the Committee and make a complaint about some of the team he would afterwards have a dog's life. If there were not an amateur good enough, he would have no hesitation in making a professional captain, but if there were, then he should be made captain.

But what if there were a professional good enough? It was not long before Warwickshire realised they had such a player.

Ryder's completion of thirty years' service to the Club was marked by taking out for him a £1000 life endowment policy and he was also given a gratuity of £50 for extra work entailed by the South Africa Test and the special appeal.

Weather-wise it was a better summer and of the twelve Championship matches played at Edgbaston nine were finished – at one point the team completed ten games in succession. Had Warwickshire begun the season in better form they might have finished near the head of the table instead of eighth, a slight improvement; but by the middle of June they had won only one match and been beaten six times. Then of the next seventeen games seven were won and only five lost. One reason for the improvement was that at long last Calthorpe found a more or less regular opening pair in Smith and Parsons, both of whom scored over 1400 runs. Quaife, too, was in the four-figure bracket again and Bates, after two bad seasons, improved to a similar total. Santall, who looked a better bat than he sometimes proved to be, was only a few runs short of four figures and Wyatt managed 729, but had still not realised his promise. Altogether sixteen centuries were scored by ten players.

Once again, Howell, who was ill in May, was called on to bear the main burden of the bowling and for the sixth season in succession he took over 100 wickets, the only Warwickshire bowler up to then to have performed such a feat of consistency for so long. It was, therefore, a severe blow to the Committee when at the end of the season he said he could not go on another year. His decision stirred *Wisden* to the comment that 'unless some bowler of real skill is discovered the prospects of Warwickshire disposing of their opponents at a reasonable cost next summer appear slight to a degree'.

Calthorpe's bowling ability declined so badly that after the home match against Lancashire he did not take a wicket in four successive games. Wyatt was bowling more now – 676 overs in 1925 – but his thirty-six wickets cost 36·26 runs each and of the thirteen bowlers listed in the averages Quaife, with fifty-nine wickets, was the best – at his age, too. But he was coming to the end of his long career. Late in the season he wrote asking for a second benefit, as he thought it might be expedient to retire from county cricket in 1926, and also wanting to know if his services would be required in that season. He was told that his engagement would be continued and he was allotted a second benefit in 1927.

There were several remarkable matches during the season, including the two against Kent, who staged almost as dramatic a recovery at Edgbaston as Hampshire had done. After Warwickshire had scored 137, they got rid of Kent for 42 in only 70 minutes. Again it was Calthorpe and Howell who did the damage – six for 17 and four for 24 respectively – only Woolley, with 10, reaching double figures. When Warwickshire had made 246 in their second innings leaving Kent to get 342 to win, victory seemed certain, but both Hardinge and Woolley made centuries, the latter driving with tremendous power, and Kent won by seven wickets. This time Calthorpe took one for 41 and Howell none for 80. Such is cricket.

In the return game at Tonbridge, Kent's first innings totalled 312, but seven men between them contributed only 19 runs to this total. Warwickshire were giving a trial to a young fast-medium bowler, R. Cooke, who, coming on first change, did the hat trick, had four wickets in five balls and finished with five for 22 to polish off the innings. It was another of those flash-in-the-pan affairs, for in the whole season he took only nine wickets, for 25 runs each, and he was not re-engaged. Freeman and Woolley got Warwickshire out for 137, and although they did a little better with 209 in the second innings, Kent needed only 33 runs to complete the double.

It was Warwickshire's turn for heavy scoring against Sussex at Edgbaston where they set up a record which may never be beaten. Sussex opened with 243, and after gaining a first innings lead of 21 they followed with 370 for eight before declaring. Warwickshire not only got the 392 they needed to win – and that in the fourth innings – but they did it for the loss of only one wicket, each of the three batsmen getting a century – Smith 139 not out, which he regards as the best innings he ever played; Parsons 124 in a first-wicket stand of 176; and Calthorpe 109 not out. They even won with three-quarters of an hour to spare against an attack consisting of Tate, Gilligan, Bowley, Wensley and George Cox.

But perhaps the most remarkable innings of the season came from Reg Santall against Yorkshire at Dewsbury. Sutcliffe took a double century off the Warwickshire bowling and Roy Kilner 124, but Santall excelled them both with an innings of 119 not out, made in 100 minutes and including no fewer than seven sixes and eight fours. Even allowing for the small ground, it was an astonishing effort against Waddington, Macaulay, Rhodes and Kilner – though Yorkshire still won by an innings and 56 runs. Although he was still going in late, Wyatt managed his first century against Worcestershire at Dudley, where he shared in a double century partnership with Croom, son of the Huntley and Palmer groundsman at Reading, who had come into the side the previous season, and also made his first hundred for the county.

Both Parsons and Howell turned out for the Players at The Oval, the former making 72 and 14, some of them off his captain's bowling. Calthorpe also played in the Lord's match, as well as in the Scarborough Festival game in which he and the Gentlemen's other bowlers were severely savaged by Hobbs and Hendren. During the winter Calthorpe took a team out to the West Indies where, however, wet weather spoiled several matches. He scored 201 runs and took seventeen wickets rather expensively at 33·94 each.

All round, 1925 was a more successful season – better weather and more attractive cricket which drew 113 020 spectators, compared with 61 423 in 1924; 89 410 in 1923; and 156 375 in 1921 when, of course, the Australians were here. There was a profit of £1636. The season was saddened, unfortunately, by the death of Frederic Messiter, the former honorary treasurer, caused by a motor vehicle as he was crossing Edgbaston Road to enter the ground. He left a permanent memorial to himself at Edgbaston in the form of impeccably written-up cash books.

There was cause for general rejoicing in 1926 for England recovered the 'Ashes' by a great victory at The Oval, but precious little to be pleased about with Warwickshire's performances in a frustrating season. No player for the county had a chance to show what he could do in the Tests, though Smith did keep wicket for the North side which faced the Australians at Edgbaston early in June. It was after this game that Root, of Worcestershire, was hailed as 'the mystery bowler', though he did not remain one for long. As a result of his seven wickets for 42 in the first innings, the Australians nearly had to follow on. Root did not bowl in the second innings, it no doubt being thought best not to let the tourists have another look at him before the first Test at Nottingham.

The Australians' second visit to Edgbaston was in August when the county emerged creditably from a heavy-scoring match in which each side completed an innings before a thunderstorm burst over the ground before lunch on the third day. Quaife, at 54, was Warwickshire's most successful bowler in an innings of 464 which gave the Australians some useful batting practice, and Parsons scored 80 of Warwickshire's 363 for nine, amassed by very consistent batting, every player reaching double figures. The receipts, alas, were negligible.

There was always keen competition among the Warwickshire players to get in the team to meet the Australians – and not merely because the match fee was higher than that for a county game. Len Morris, who played several games for the county about this time and later served as President of Warwickshire Old County Cricketers' Association and as a director of Birmingham City F.C., recalled asking Calthorpe what the team would be, only to be told that it had been chosen before the season started!

Wisden's forecast about the weakness of Warwickshire's bowling proved only too accurate. They were just incapable of getting other sides out and there were no fewer than seventeen draws. Only two matches were won and nine lost. Six totals of 400 and over and twelve of 300 were hit off them. Quaife tried nobly to make up for the departure of Howell and the absence through illness of Calthorpe for thirteen matches. He not only bowled more overs for the county, 786, than he had ever done before, he also took eighty-two wickets, more than he had taken in any season of his career. Wyatt just beat him with eighty-six, and a new fast bowler from Kingsbury Colliery, J. H. 'Danny' Mayer, playing his first full season after being in Scotland for two years, got thirty-four.

The batting was sound enough, with Parsons making four centuries, and Wyatt, improving; Norman Kilner, from Yorkshire; Bates and Quaife, yet again, all getting over 1000 runs.

Norman Kilner, Roy's brother, was one of a number of Yorkshiremen who, about this time, were unable to command a regular place in the very strong Yorkshire side of those days, and moved elsewhere. Their loss was Warwickshire's gain since for a score of years or more he was one of the main props of the county's batting.

Partridge took over from Calthorpe during the latter's absence and it was to him that Wyatt owed his chance to show what he could do as a batsman. He made a century in May against Derbyshire and thereafter he was sent in first. He showed his appreciation and his ability by making 1297 runs and very nearly accomplished the double, for in all matches he took ninety-two wickets, one of his best bowling performances being his seven for 43 against Middlesex. 'All matches' included his first appearance for the Gentlemen at both The Oval and Lord's. At The Oval he scored one and 55, but took no wickets for 38 and at Lord's he made 75 and took one for 114. After this he played for the Gentlemen for fourteen consecutive seasons until war came.

Calthorpe missed twelve matches and when he returned he lost the toss thirteen times in succession. Had he lost the next one at Taunton he would have established the sort of world record any captain would go to any lengths to avoid. The General Strike affected Warwickshire cricket to the extent that Hampshire arrived three men short at Edgbaston and replacements were specially sent; but they had a wasted journey, for rain washed out the match, though not before Boyes had done the hat trick.

Bates achieved the highest innings of his career so far with a superb 187 against Derbyshire, making 93 out of a partnership of 125 with Kilner, and Warwickshire contributed to another kind of record in the match with Sussex at Horsham where George Cox, in his 53rd year, took eight for 56 and nine for 50 – seventeen wickets in a match, a feat which had then been performed only fifteen times.

When Warwickshire went to Lord's they met for the first time a young slow left-arm bowler named Paine. He did not do much on that occasion – no wickets for 22 – but at Edgbaston in August he had five Warwickshire wickets for 77 and three for 25, and the Committee liked the look of him sufficiently to begin making inquiries about him, for they were badly in need of a slow spin bowler, especially one who could do what J. C. White did against them at Edgbaston – 56·4 overs, 30 maidens, 62 runs and seven wickets.

And that, pretty well, is the sort of thing Paine showed he could do after he had later accepted an offer to come and qualify for Warwickshire. He proved himself a bowler who thought a great deal about his craft – he used to put white tape round the ball when he was practising so that he could see how much he was spinning it. He was unlucky from the point of view of representative cricket in that he was playing at the same time as Verity, who also might have come to Warwickshire, although at that time he was largely an 'arm' bowler and did not possess the arts of length, flight and spin he afterwards acquired.

Parsons had his benefit against Lancashire in June and McDonald nearly spoiled it for him, the match finishing in two days. After

Lancashire had made 403, with the usual Tyldesley century, from Ernest, McDonald went through Warwickshire at a great pace – literally. In the first innings of 148 he had six for 96 and in the second of 175 seven for 60. Not even the beneficiary distinguished himself. He was not given even the customary single in the first innings and scored only 18 in the second. Still, he had good cause to be satisfied with the result, for it came out at a higher figure than he had originally stipulated – £881, the bulk of which he allowed the Club to invest for him. At this time Kent were making a taxation test case out of Seymour's benefit, which eventually went to the House of Lords, where it was won on appeal. Other clubs shared in the costs which in Warwickshire's case came to £6 8s 0d – cheap at the price.

At Swansea in July Warwickshire saw an England batsman-to-be, in C. F. Walters, take 116 off their bowling, and at Worcester they tried yet another opening pair in Wyatt and Kilner, successfully, too, for they put on 221, Kilner making his first hundred for the county, and with Bates against Surrey he helped in a stand of 244. 'Tiger' distinguished himself against Derbyshire by dismissing seven of their batsmen in the first innings – three stumped and four caught, a feat then unprecedented in first-class cricket and still a record for the county.

At the annual meeting in March a Dr Harold Thwaite had been elected to the Committee and thus began an official association with the Club, which he had first supported when he was a medical student at Birmingham University in 1900, and which was to take him to the highest office the Club had to offer. He was the first of a long line of distinguished medical men who have served Warwickshire cricket over the years – Sir Leonard Parsons, R. Scott Mason, Surgeon Captain A. A. Sanders, Dr Stanley Barnes, Sir Gilbert Barling, Professor William Gissane and Professor A. L. d'Abreu.

Ludford Docker returned to his favourite theme of unenterprising play, saying it was 'downright pathetic' to see a bowler of Armstrong's gentle pace sending down half-volleys at Edgbaston with one single man in the outfield and a batsman – he would not mention who was in at the time – never even trying to hit him to the boundary. He did not think he had ever spent such an unhappy half-hour looking at a cricket match before. As for the lbw law, Docker said he would like to alter it and give the batsman out if his leg, being between wicket and wicket, prevented the ball from hitting the stumps no matter where it pitched.

In August Edgbaston had a new groundsman in Ted Leyland, father of Maurice, thus establishing another link with Yorkshire, especially when Maurice was away touring and the new-fangled wireless was brought into use to keep his father in touch with what t'lad were up to for England. Leyland had succeeded Arthur Redman, who had resigned.

In the winter of 1926–7 both Wyatt and Parsons went on their first tour abroad to India, though, of course, for Parsons it was a return to the scene of much of his Army service, so he must have met many old friends and acquaintances. He very nearly did not get there. When the team boarded the boat at Tilbury none of the players had any idea of the fixture list. When they got to Port Said it was put up on the ship's notice board and he was amazed to find that all the big matches were to be played on Sundays, whereupon he told the captain, A. E. R. Gilligan, that he strongly objected to playing on that day.

I had several talks with him and other senior members of the team [Parsons said] and eventually I was informed that M.C.C. had sent a message to the ship to the effect that if I refused to play on Sundays I was to be sent home on the next boat and pay my own fare. This really put me on the spot as I had left my wife and young son at home. Finally I agreed to play on Sundays providing that if we were doing so anywhere near a church then, whatever the circumstances of the match, I should be allowed to leave the ground to attend church in the evening. This arrangement was agreed to by the M.C.C. and only twice during the tour did this occur. On both occasions we were the fielding side and I went off, a substitute taking my place while I attended church.

But what, one wonders, would have happened if the church bells had begun ringing for service while Parsons was batting?

Both scored well on the tour, Wyatt, with five centuries, making nearly 2000 runs and Parsons, with two hundreds, well over 1000. Wyatt, who also took thirty-three wickets for 29·39 runs each, had the valuable experience of opening the innings with Sandham, the only batsman who scored more runs than he did. At Colombo on the way out he had the possibly unique experience of making a century, 124, and doing the hat trick on the same day. Gilligan was much impressed with his form and prophesied he would play for England.

Howell, who did play in one match this season – his two wickets costing 119 runs – asked to renew his connection with the Club. Later, he accepted an engagement with Aston Unity which meant he was available for the county in mid-week games.

He did, in fact, reappear in a few matches in 1927, but the state to which Warwickshire's bowling had been reduced can be seen from the fact that Quaife took most wickets, fifty, only five fewer than his years. Calthorpe's quota was a mere thirty-four. Wyatt missed four matches owing to a chill; Mayer injured his elbow and could not play after June; Partridge played in only six matches; E. P. Hewetson, the Oxford fast bowler, in one; and T. W. Durnell, a lively fast bowler from Smethwick and still happily serving the Club on the Committee, suffered a strain and had many business calls, though he had a splendid seven for 29 against Northants. Many young bowlers were tried by what must have been a well-nigh desperate selection committee, but none looked like providing the answer to Warwickshire's prayer except Paine who was still qualifying.

With such handicaps, it was not surprising that no fewer than twenty-one games were drawn in a season of very wet weather, there being five games in which no result was possible because there were fewer than six hours of play in any of them. There was one sequence of fifteen drawn games after the weather had broken down in the middle of the summer. The batting, however, showed considerable improvement, especially that of Parsons, who hit five centuries and finished with an average of 52. Wyatt and Bates also averaged nearly 40.

Quaife added another 775 runs to his enormous tally for the county and took his well-deserved second benefit against Hampshire at Edgbaston in July, but rain restricted play to 90 minutes late on the Saturday afternoon when 2000 people were present. Kilner and Smith scored 72 without being separated and that was all. Even so, nearly £1000 was raised for Warwickshire's longest-playing servant. Even added to his previous £410, it still seems a very inadequate reward.

Quaife showed how fit he still was when Glamorgan came to Edgbaston at the beginning of August after Warwickshire had been without a win since May. Batting first, they lost Smith for none and Kilner for 16; but first Bates, 79, then Quaife, 155 not out, and finally Parsons, 225, on an ascending scale, beat the Glamorgan bowlers, seven of them, to a pulp and amassed 543 for eight wickets. Quaife batted six and a quarter hours – how on earth did he do it at 55? – and was still unbeaten when Calthorpe declared. Parsons reached 102 out of 145 and glorious is the only word that describes his driving.

He made another fine century, 136, against Yorkshire at Hull, where Warwickshire ended the Champions' run of seventy first-class matches without a defeat. The return match at Edgbaston was remarkable for the lowest possible score, nought, for which Danny Mayer batted 35 minutes, while Santall got the runs to give Warwickshire the first innings lead. 'It was the longest 35 minutes I've ever spent on a cricket field,' said Danny after withstanding much ragging from the Yorkshire team.

Mayer was involved in another remarkable last-wicket stand against Surrey at The Oval, but this time he showed he could get runs. His previous highest score had been 19, but now he proceeded to hit 14 fours and, with 74 not out, helped Wyatt to put on 126 in 75 minutes.

Wyatt tells a good story about the two centuries the one and only George Gunn scored at Trent Bridge off the Warwickshire bowling. Gunn had been out of form and on his way out to bat he passed Wyatt and told him the Notts Committee had said he hadn't been getting too many runs, so he was going to get a century. Wyatt laughed and said 'We'll see about that'. But it was George who saw about it. He batted five hours and his 100 included 77 singles, which must have been a record for any innings of his. On his way in the second time George confided to Wyatt that the Committee had complained that he had got his runs too slowly, so this time he was going to get a quick century. He did – 110 in an hour and three-quarters.

It was the third time this incalculable genius had performed the feat, and Wyatt has gone on record as saying that he believed George Gunn could do almost anything he wanted on a cricket field if he gave his mind to it.

It was Bates's turn to make two centuries against Kent at Coventry – 116 and 144 – the second with Smith, 132, making a second-wicket partnership of 296. Smith made his own record score of 177 against Derbyshire at Edgbaston, a match Warwickshire just missed winning by a whisker, Derbyshire's last pair being together when the extra half-hour ended.

In June came a *démarche* from the players for an increase of £1 in all away matches. This was triggered off by their refusing, on grounds of extra expense, what amounted to an instruction from the captain and the secretary that they should travel overnight for the Middlesex match at Lord's, as was customary for matches played in London. The Committee took a serious view of this action and considered that the application came with bad grace in the circumstances. They took the view, as they so often did, that the Warwickshire professionals were better paid than most and they would not, therefore, accede to the request, although they would consider sympathetically any cases of hardship involving extra hotel and travelling expenses as they arose; they also offered to reconsider the question of rail fares in 1928.

There followed a deputation consisting of Quaife, Smith, Parsons and Bates, who asked the Committee to reconsider their decision and it became clear that there was some feeling against the secretary because of the request that they should travel overnight. It was not the first time that Ryder was considered to have intervened in matters the players thought did not concern him and it led to differences later, notably during Wyatt's captaincy. On this occasion, however, the Committee declined to change their decision and the players were told that no alteration in terms could be considered until next season, though in August, as some hardships had been incurred in travelling to places like Horsham, Hull, Swansea, Taunton and Portsmouth, some extras were paid.

The New Zealanders came to Edgbaston in July and had much the best of a game spoiled by rain which robbed them of a win. C. S. Dempster, who later came to play for the county, showed his class with an innings of 180, in which he hit Quaife for five successive fours. Warwickshire saved their worst batting performance for the last match of the season, Hampshire's famous pair of opening bowlers, Kennedy and Newman, running through the side at Portsmouth for a mere 36. Only Bates, 11, got double figures. On a drying pitch Kennedy took the last six wickets in three overs for 4 runs and came out with this ridiculous-looking analysis:

O	M	R	W
10	7	8	7

At the beginning of the year Warwickshire had lost their honorary treasurer for nineteen years, F. S. Goodwin, who resigned on leaving the county. He was the father of H. J. Goodwin, the former captain, killed in the First World War. He was succeeded by Cecil Wheeler, who had played for the county in the very early days. At the annual meeting the President was absent owing to illness, so Cartland brought forward his own complaint – bowlers who had gone 'swerve mad', while Calthorpe correctly forecast the end of the percentage system of scoring.

Farewell to Quaife
(1927–1929)

IN August 1927, Bernard Quaife, who had not been able to establish a regular place for himself in the Warwickshire team, was released to play for Worcestershire who, sometimes having difficulty in raising a side because they could not afford a large staff of professionals, were glad of the services of a more than useful amateur who wanted only the usual expenses. (One of the oddities of father and son playing together, one as a professional and the other as an amateur, was that the son could have what he liked to drink for lunch, while his father could have nothing costing more than ninepence.)

Three months later, when Quaife senior was presented with his benefit cheque, there was a discussion about his future, which led to the first of the departures which caused controversy in the Club down the years. An executive committee minute for 9 November records that Quaife expressed his thanks for the kindness and courtesy always extended to him by the Committee and that he said that except for the county of his birth (Sussex), if he had his time over again, he would choose Warwickshire as the county he would prefer to any other. The minute added: 'After hearing the views of the committee [not stated] Quaife intimated his intention to retire as from the end of 1927.'

There was a further meeting of the executive on 22 November when a letter was read from Quaife in which he said that at the meeting to which he was called to receive his cheque he was

very surprised to find that you thought it was time I retired from county cricket, although I had just previously written to you that I felt I could, and should like to, play another year. However, finding that you desired otherwise, I had no option but to acquiesce. It seems to me somewhat unfair that neither the public nor myself should have had any notification before last season closed. My desire was, and still is, to play at least some part of next season and for the public to have due notice of the date of my last match. Members of the Warwickshire Club and others interested would rightly consider that I was acting very ungraciously in retiring immediately after they had contributed so generously to my benefit fund. Naturally I do not wish to lose the position I hold in their esteem and therefore I do not wish any statement to be made to them through the Press which could possibly leave them under the misapprehension that I desired to retire.

This was a googly of a distinctly awkward nature for the Committee, but Cartland said he had talked the matter over with Quaife the previous day and it was decided to send him a reply saying that the contents of his letter had caused them considerable surprise. Nothing, they said, had transpired at the 9 November meeting

to suggest that there was any mental reservation on your part when you intimated your intention to retire from county cricket. The Committee had assumed that, on receiving the proceeds of your second benefit, you would probably regard the occasion as a suitable moment for announcing your retirement, and in discussing the matter it was made clear that the Committee were favourably disposed to that view, without reflecting on you in any way, mainly because the claims of younger players could not be overlooked. You agreed, although stating that you could go on for another year if the Committee wished. Eventually, without a single discordant note, and apparently in all sincerity, you announced your retirement and took leave of the Committee individually, after expressing your appreciation of the kindness and courtesy which they had always extended to you. The executive committee's report was presented to the General Committee, who unanimously approved it and the matter is now closed.

But it was not, not by a long way. First, in December, Quaife wrote saying he would like to add to his previous letter that, having regard to the weakness of the bowling, at all events during the early part of the season, he thought his services would be of considerable value to the team. 'This', he added, 'would get rid of the difficulties with all those who contributed to my benefit fund as set forth in my previous letter. It will be a very great wrench both to myself and my friends for me to stop playing at once. If I played to the end of June, or some date in July to be fixed by the Committee, I think it would be best for all concerned.'

The Committee, however, unanimously decided that it could not accede to Quaife's request, having regard to the vital importance of the claims of younger players. They recommended that a letter to this effect should be sent to Quaife and that in making the announcement to the Press it should be made clear, as Quaife wished, that it was in deference to the wishes of the Committee that Quaife expressed his willingness to retire.

Where the 'willingness' came in it was difficult to see and one can hardly believe that one more season would have made all that difference to the young players. There were many who thought the Committee could have waited a little longer with a player of such standing and allowed him to bow out gracefully with thanks and encomiums all round, and on 28 February 1928, George Ward gave notice that at the annual meeting he would move the following resolution:

That this meeting of the members of Warwickshire County Cricket Club is not in agreement with the Committee as to the dismissal of W. G. Quaife and proposes that his services be retained for the season 1928.

There were about 400 members at the meeting at which the President began by saying that under the rules of the Club the motion could not be accepted, but he would permit a discussion on Quaife's position, with the result that he promised the Committee would consider suggestions, including one that Quaife should be invited to play in one or two matches in the coming season. Quaife, he said, had been treated 'very generously', but how generously he did not reveal.

J. P. Heaton, the deputy chairman, said it was probably not generally understood that Quaife had not for some years been on the Warwickshire staff – a technical quibble, surely – so that the question of his dismissal did not arise, but this did not satisfy George Ward. He thought the procedure was 'not cricket' and he asked why, if Quaife was not on the staff, he was asked to resign? It became obvious, as surely it should have been from the very first whisper, that he was contemplating retirement, that the feeling was that Quaife should have a farewell match.

The Birmingham Mail had a leading article deploring that the matter had been raised at the annual meeting, but criticising the Committee for closing Quaife's career in mid-season, which it considered an error of judgment. Eight days later it was decided that Quaife should be given a farewell match and he was allowed a free choice. At first he chose the Leicestershire match, but later changed his mind and asked for the Derbyshire game, at the same time denying newspaper rumours that he was unlikely to play in it. He had also inquired if he would be allowed to coach schoolboys on the county ground during the Easter holidays and to use the nets during the season for his own practice, but the Committee replied that in view of the arrangements already made this was not possible, though it is difficult to see why not. One would have thought the Committee would have been grateful for the advice of so accomplished a player, but perhaps they feared friction with Santall.

The farewell match duly took place on 4, 6 and 7 August, and what a perfect ending Quaife made it. He could hardly have chosen a more eloquent way of suggesting to the Committee that their decision to retire him was a trifle premature. As *Wisden* said, 'he could not have wished for a more fitting close to his long career than in playing an innings of 115 on his last appearance for the county. Notwithstanding his 56 years and the fact that it was his first and only county match of the season [But one can be sure he had taken very good care to keep in practice], he batted with all his old time steadiness and skill for four hours and twenty minutes, offering no chance and making his runs with a nice variety of strokes.'

So he ended his career with Warwickshire as he began it, with a century, his seventy-second, and it should never be forgotten that they were all made in an era of great bowling, fast and slow. He helped in compiling Warwickshire's highest score of the season – 564 for seven declared. Parsons made 114, completing his century with a six over the pavilion; Bates 90, Calthorpe 71 not out, Wyatt 47 and Smart 40 not out, very consistent scoring. When Derbyshire batted, Quaife also took a hand in the bowling, more than a hand, in fact, for he bowled thirty-four overs, of which nine were maidens, for 56 runs and two wickets, and in the second innings another six overs, this time without a wicket, though no doubt by this time he was feeling the strain of fielding. But he had done more than enough.

Ryder, I think, drew the best picture of Quaife.

Some there were, [he wrote in 1925], who blind to the finer points of his play, were inclined to cavil at the rate of his run-getting; but the imperturbable Quaife never deviated from the course he steadfastly set himself to pursue, year in and year out. How many times has he saved Warwickshire, now turning aside imminent defeat, now making victory possible by his dominance. Picture him at the wicket, having taken guard, preparing to receive the ball. Precise, neat, cautious, he wriggles his right foot secure, draws forward his left leg, places his bat full face to the bowler, left wrist well round the front of the handle, perfectly poised, he is ready to move quickly into the position to parry the thrust and cunning of the bowler. His footwork is an object lesson to any cricketer. He possesses all the strokes the game has evolved although he rarely attempted to out-Jessop Jessop! And his unquestioned greatness rests most surely on his many wonderful achievements when conditions have favoured the bowler and runs have been difficult to get.

Wisden for 1928 summed it all up – 'a memorable career' and that, perhaps, was rather stating the obvious. 'Quaife first appeared for Warwickshire in 1893, so his association with the county extended over a period of nearly thirty-five years. A most skilful and stylish batsman, a clever slow bowler, and a brilliant field – especially at cover point – he scored in first-class matches 35 836 runs, played seventy-one innings of a hundred or more and took 928 wickets* – truly a wonderful record for one of the shortest men who ever figured largely in important cricket.'

*These figures did not, of course, include that last innings.

179

George Egdell, in a tribute in *The Birmingham Post* to 'one of the Masters of the Art of Cricket', recalled his brilliant fielding at cover point in his prime; his bowling, which had grown more destructive as his years increased, his fitness (until two seasons before he retired he had played hockey) and his artistic and never tedious batting. Since 1896 there had been only three seasons in all matches in which he failed to reach a four-figure aggregate and his record of achieving it in 24 seasons was exceeded only by the other 'W.G.'.

Quaife's batting was not missed as much as might have been expected, largely due to Wyatt's powers coming to full flower. For the first time he reached 2000 runs for the season – 2020 for an average of 63·12. Quaife had done it in 1905, but that was in all matches. Wyatt's runs were scored for Warwickshire alone; they included six centuries. There was no doubt that going to India and South Africa in the previous winter had done him much good. His first Test in South Africa was a failure, but in the second he made 91. In the third he brought off one of the best bowling performances of his career, taking three wickets for 4 runs, and in the last Test he gave the first of many demonstrations of his pluck and determination not to be put down by mishaps which would have crippled men of less fortitude. He had a finger broken, but went on batting until the close of England's innings when he was 20 not out. In the end he finished third in the averages with 56, but he had acquired something more valuable than runs – experience and knowledge, much of it gained in talks with Ernest Tyldesley.

Back home in 1928, he faced the West Indies who were given three Tests, though none at Edgbaston where, against the county, Constantine put in one of his most fiery spells of bowling. As Wyatt went out to bat Bates was being carried off unconscious, completely knocked out by a bouncer, and both the first two balls Wyatt received hit him glancing blows on the head and went for four byes. This was a clear indication that there was pace in even the Edgbaston wicket for those who had the skill to extract it.

Despite this bombardment, Warwickshire won by seven wickets, for Parsons did a little retaliatory attacking of his own, scoring 201 in the match for once out. Driving with great power, he hit 161 at more than a run a minute, including four sixes off successive balls from Scott, the tourists' slow bowler. One of them went right into the refreshment room where a lady suddenly found herself holding only the handle of the cup from which she had just been drinking tea. Two of the sixes cleared Edgbaston Road and landed in the grounds of the Tally Ho! Tennis Club. Next ball Parsons was brilliantly caught on the boundary by Constantine, who also contributed what we later came to realise was a characteristic effort – 70 out of 77 in forty minutes. Bernard Quaife had a vivid recollection, too, of his wonderful fielding at cover. Once he fielded a ball and threw down the wicket at the batsman's end. He then ran across to the on side, picked up the ball and hit the wickets at the other end. 'Still not out', Quaife commented, 'but wonderful to watch'. The bat with which Parsons performed his doughty feat – it had been done only twice before – is now enshrined in a special showcase in the pavilion at Edgbaston.

Besides Wyatt, Parsons (five centuries), Croom, Kilner, Smith and Bates all scored over 1000 runs, so there was nothing to worry about in the batting. It was the lack of penetration in the bowling which resulted in another plethora of draws – nineteen of them this time. Mayer had had an operation on his leg and missed successive matches, though he still contrived to take seventy wickets; Durnell and Partridge were both injured; Wyatt bowled less because of muscular strains and his forty-nine wickets were obtained for 34·57 runs each.

The bowling ran into a tornado of runs at Maidstone – Hardinge, 205, Woolley 156, Ames 109 – a total of 519 for six declared. Howell had returned for this match and probably wished he had not for both he and Mayer had over 100 runs scored off them for two wickets each. Then Woolley and Freeman each collected ten wickets and that was the end of Warwickshire. Worse was to come at Coventry where the heavens really did fall. This was the Notts innings as far as it needed to go – Gunn 148, Whysall 132, Walker 146 not out, A. W. Carr 58, Barratt 139 not out, a total of 656 for three declared, one of the highest scores ever made against the county.

Who would be a bowler? D. L. Clugston, who later led the Club and Ground side for many years, will probably never forget it for he bowled twenty-six overs, not one of which was a maiden, for 137 runs and no wicket. He was one of eight bowlers tried. Still, Warwickshire had some compensations, Wyatt 134 not out, Smith 108, and the match was drawn, there being no play on the third day, so 1027 runs, including six centuries, were scored for the loss of only twelve wickets in two days. Paine recalls that at one point Carr resorted to bowling lobs.

To some extent now, and increasingly later, Wyatt found that he had inherited Quaife's role as anchor man and he played a number of rear-guard innings – 82 and 102 against Leicestershire and 91 not out against Hampshire. He loved a fight back but probably it had an inhibiting effect on his batting, a factor which his critics sometimes forgot. It did not prevent his being selected for the Test trial at Lord's where he did not, however, distinguish himself.

That summer Parsons had an experience which changed his life and there cannot, surely, have been another like it in the whole history of cricket. He was waiting to go in to bat at Edgbaston when the Vicar of St Anne's, Moseley, Birmingham, the church Parsons and his wife attended – he then lived in a house overlooking the ground – came excitedly into the dressing-room and told him that Dr J. W. Hunkin, the Archdeacon of Coventry, wanted to see him.

'I was rather annoyed', Parsons said, 'but just then a wicket fell and out I went. I got one of the quickest 70s I ever made and to my amazement, when I came off the field, I was greeted by the Archdeacon with: "Parsons, we have been talking a lot about you and think you ought to become a parson." ' I had never given it a thought – I think my wife had a lot to do with it – but I did then and eventually they persuaded me. So I went to college at Birkenhead in the winter and came back and played cricket in the summer.

'In 1929 I was ordained and began my ministry on the staff of the old Cathedral at Coventry. I remember that I had a letter from "Plum" Warner saying he was going to propose me as a member of the M.C.C. and that Peter Eckersley, of Lancashire, would second me. I was elected a member and whenever I went to Lord's and bumped into Warner he always stopped and spoke to me and once he said, "If only you'd gone to Australia in 1914 they would never have got you out. Your name was down to go, but the war stopped it."

'Later I was a curate at Rugby with Dr Hunkin and though I used to play quite a bit still I had my job to do, of course. I started a youth club which is going to this day. I used to take the P.T. classes. Then Dr Hunkin said: "We want you to go to a living." It turned out to be Hodnet in Shropshire, the home of the Heber-Percy family. On Sunday mornings the lord of the manor would come into church and all his tenants would be there and he used to come on Sunday evenings, too, and the church used to be three-quarters full – all through my Saturday activities.'

The story goes that about this time Parsons, who normally fielded at slip – and brilliantly – was noticed to be out in the deep, a fact remarked on by one of the opposing early batsmen who asked Jack Smart, the wicketkeeper, what he was doing out there.

'Oh', said Jack, 'I expect he'll be preaching the sermon next Sunday and he'll have asked the skipper if he can have a bit of peace and quiet so he can prepare it.' One can imagine Calthorpe indulging such a request, but not Wyatt.

That August it was decided to make a special gift to Wyatt to mark his achievement in scoring 2000 runs during the 1928 season. It was also decided to pay him £300 and expenses during 1929 instead of £200 and expenses, as hitherto, as assistant secretary, the first intimation in the records that he was doing such work. He had, however, made it clear from the start that unless he had some job he could never have played first-class cricket and he says that he had been led to believe that the Committee would see to it that he had a good job in engineering with reasonable time off to play cricket. That, however, would take a little time to arrange and in the meantime they offered him the post of assistant secretary. The other position never materialised, a sore point with Wyatt, and he later worked for two winters in the advertising department of the B.S.A. company in Birmingham.

In October came news of the death of Septimus Kinneir, killed while motorcycling home after playing golf. He was only 55. The following month J. F. Byrne drew attention to the plight of another old player, Crowther Charlesworth, who was out of work and in need of help. It was decided to interview him in the hope of finding him suitable employment.

'One of the most drastic reforms in cricket legislation for years', was how the annual report described the changes made in the running of the County Championship for 1929, which also brought a major change to Warwickshire in particular – in the captaincy. Every county had to play twenty-eight games, no more, no less, and there were eight points at stake in every game; these being shared when no first innings decision was reached. The stumps were one inch wider and one inch higher, a change Warwickshire had opposed, and a batsman could be out lbw even if he snicked the ball.

Whether it was due to the change in the laws or not, the number of unfinished games dropped from 122 to 89, but there were some reversals of form. Warwickshire's batting as a whole fell away, but not Wyatt's. In all matches he scored over 2000 runs for the second season in succession, 2630, with an average of 53·67, which took him to fifth place in the national statistics. He was only 60 short of the 2000 for the county alone and he scored seven centuries, a Warwickshire record.

Parsons was not now able to play so often, and Bates's batting suffered a decline, but G. D. Kemp-Welch, who had got his Blue at Cambridge while still a Freshman, came into the side later in the season. Mayer took over 100 wickets for the first time – 121 for 22·12 – and to help him was a sprightly amateur fast bowler from Sutton Coldfield, D. G. Foster, who took fifty-two wickets and showed great promise, while Paine, in his first full season, took fifty-seven, and Wyatt helped out with forty-nine.

Paine had a somewhat disillusioning introduction to the first-class game which he did not find imbued with the noble spirit of cricket he had heard so much about. Batting against Eastman at Chelmsford, he played a forward stroke and saw Hipkin scoop the ball up off the ground and throw it in the air. Paine started to walk out, whereupon Hipkin promptly ran him out – an action for which the Essex player received a sharp rebuke from Calthorpe, who was batting at the other end.

Paine found him an understanding captain, but even he could not help when, coming on once to bowl to Dai Davies, of Glamorgan, whose score was in the late nineties, he was greeted with the remark, 'Give me one, youngster, and I'll give you my wicket.' George generously obliged, but so far from giving him his wicket. Dai went on to add another 50. Cricket, too, has its deceivers.

Edgbaston had a Test with South Africa that year and I shall always remember it because I had to endure watching young Bruce Mitchell, opening the innings with Catterall, take seven hours to make 88 – they seemed like seven years. On a pitch described as easy and devoid of life, England batted first. Sutcliffe and a new partner, E. T. Killick, also to become a parson, put on 59, but by half past two six wickets were down for 128. Hammond was out for 18 and Duleepsinhji, playing in his first Test, 12. It was left to Hendren, 70, and Tate, 40, to salvage something from the wreckage.

Even with Mitchell's monumental effort, South Africa gained a lead of no more than 5 and then England, thanks to Sutcliffe's 114 and Hammond's 138 – a second-wicket partnership of 221 in only 175 minutes – were able to declare at 308 for four, leaving South Africa to get 304 to win in under three hours. They did not attempt it. This time Mitchell made 61 not out, he and Catterall, 98, putting on 171 for the first wicket in the time available. Eighteen thousand people saw the match and the receipts were £756, compared with £191 from the Tests with the West Indies. The tourists' second visit to Edgbaston was made memorable by an innings of 126 by young H. G. Owen-Smith, who was later to score an even finer hundred and, as England's full back, a try which is still talked about by those who saw it. Warwickshire got first innings lead but nothing else.

They had more satisfaction in scoring 536 for the loss of seven wickets from a Yorkshire attack consisting of Robinson, Macaulay, Bowes, Rhodes and Leyland. Smith, despite a strain, made 142 and Santall 100. Rhodes, then 52, was still able to bowl 70 overs, of which 21 were maidens, for 115 runs and two wickets. This was D. G. Foster's first game and he got three for 99, but it was in the next match with Glamorgan that he really tasted blood – he fairly ripped their second innings apart with figures of 11·5 overs, 7 maidens, 11 runs, 6 wickets, in his last spell taking five for 4 in six overs. Three times this season he got Woolley out and against Hampshire at Edgbaston he did the hat trick. His form was so impressive that he was chosen for the Gentlemen at The Oval where Wyatt got 115 and 55 and Parsons, having now changed sides, 46 and 54.

Wyatt took centuries in successive matches at Edgbaston – 150 against Glamorgan and 161 off Surrey, and a few days later he made 125 against Middlesex. In the first match he and Parsons hit 182 in 110 minutes – Wyatt could score quickly enough when he wanted to do so – and in the second game he and Kilner put on 229. He was obviously the form horse for the season – he had been unlucky not to be chosen to go to Australia with Chapman's team the previous winter – and he was in the Test trial at Lord's in June, making 22 and 25 not out, but he was not selected for a Test until the fourth at Old Trafford. There in his first Test in England he shared in a record partnership with Woolley. They came together when the second wicket fell at 36 and added 245 in two and three-quarter hours. He was overshadowed by Woolley – who would not be? – but he showed superb defence for four hours and scored 113 – the figure he had dreamed the night before he would see on the Manchester scoreboard. He was the first amateur since the war to make a century in his first Test. In the fifth Test, however, he was out for 6 in the first innings and did not get a chance to bat again.

By the beginning of August, Ryder was sounding a warning that the financial position of the Club – gate receipts had fallen by £1408 – was seriously threatened by dwindling public support, due to many counter-attractions of a kind never previously encountered, though he did not name them. They were, however, greyhound racing and speedway, then booming. Ryder wanted, without delay, a careful inquiry into the possibility of cutting expense and finding new sources of income, but the Committee deferred the matter for further consideration, as they did the terms of players' engagements for 1930.

Early in September, Calthorpe, who was moving to the south of England, resigned the captaincy. His form both as batsman and bowler had been steadily declining and the county had dropped three more places in the table to fourteenth position. It was probably time for a change. His successor would have seemed to be obvious, but the Committee first offered the appointment to Partridge, who, however, declined it for business reasons – indeed, he played in only one match in 1930. During the winter Wyatt went to the West Indies with a team captained, oddly enough, by Calthorpe, and it was not until he returned to England that he was offered the captaincy. He did not have a very successful tour, partly because early on a ball from Martindale broke a bone in his foot so that he was able to play in only the third and fourth representative matches, in which he scored 96 and took four wickets for 125. In all games he made 407, with a highest score of 81. Calthorpe, incidentally, had the services of Wilfred Rhodes, then aged 52, on this tour and made such good use of them that in one match he bowled forty overs in the first innings and fifty-one in the second. 'I were the donkey,' he said, but enjoyed every minute of it.

In October the Committee approved savings totalling £600 a year and the following month, within a day of completing his 62nd year, there died Dick Lilley, perhaps the most notable cricketer the city of Birmingham has ever produced. After retiring he had settled at Brislington, near Bristol, and had helped to re-establish the Gloucestershire side after the war. It was said that even at the end of his career his hands showed scarcely a trace of the pressures to which they had been subjected – 'a most consistent and so pronounced an artist', was *Wisden's* verdict. No wicketkeeper of his time was so sure a catcher of the ball – he took 705 of them altogether and stumped 200 batsmen, as well as scoring 15 746 runs. He was also regarded as a fine judge of the game, whose opinions were often sought by captains. He played in thirty-one Tests, all but three against Australia, caught sixty-five and stumped nineteen and scored 802 runs; but it was not generally realised that he also took thirty-eight wickets in first-class cricket as a bowler. In one season, 1897, he bowled 129·3 overs and took twelve wickets.

Lilley, A. A. Thomson wrote of him, was 'not as dazzling to the eye as George McGregor, who came before, or Godfrey Evans, who came after, but the very acme of soundness. Lilley wore England's stumping gloves for nearly twenty years, and his right to them was never questioned'.

Another old player, Sam Hargreave, though he was not old in years, only 52, died the following January at Stratford-upon-Avon. He was one of the most successful bowlers Warwickshire ever had over a short period, taking over 100 wickets five times between 1901 and 1906. Altogether he took 865 wickets for the county for 21·62 runs each.

Before the end of 1929 Cecil Wheeler resigned the honorary treasurership on the grounds of ill-health and he was invited to be a vice-president, but by the following March both he and J. P. Heaton had died and Dr Thwaite assumed office for the first time – as honorary treasurer.

Wyatt Takes Over
(1930–1931)

Two captaincies came to Wyatt in 1930, first of his county; second, very late in the season, of his country. It was, indeed, a memorable year for him, as it was, of course, for cricket generally, for this was also Year One of Bradman and it was the problems he posed which eventually led to the invitation to Wyatt who had been passed over by the selectors until the last Test.

None of these was played at Edgbaston, which was not to see another Test for nearly thirty years, largely because of the rapid development of the Trent Bridge ground with which at this time Warwickshire could not keep pace. In 1930, as it happened, the Midlands, apart from the first of those three double centuries Bradman made at Worcester at the opening of his first three tours, saw little of the Australians in 1930 because their match at Edgbaston was washed out, the only play being two hours and a half on the first day in which Warwickshire scored 102 for three wickets, Wyatt 22 not out. Bradman was not playing anyway.

When he was invited to be captain of Warwickshire Wyatt told the Committee: 'I shall make mistakes. There has not been a captain yet who didn't, but I shall always have a reason for what I do and I don't mind any member of the team asking me.' He always did have a reason and probably few captains have given as much serious thought to the game and its tactics as he did. He was a striking example, it was said, of a player who by taking thought added cubits to his stature. He claimed, for instance, that he devised the umbrella, or Carmody, field, as it came to be called, long before the Australians used it. He did it for Danny Mayer and because he knew he would be criticised for it, he kept Mayer's bowling records for before and after the change – they showed an improvement in the number of wickets he took.

187

It was hardly to be expected that Wyatt would immediately transform Warwickshire's fortunes. Far from this happening, they finished one place lower in the table, fourteenth, winning only twice, fewer than any other county, losing nine and drawing seventeen Championship games. With eight matches played, they had won two and were unbeaten, but they did not win again and they were beaten in four of their last six matches. Statistics in *Wisden* showed that of 140 Championship games in the last five seasons Warwickshire had won only fifteen matches, lost forty-one and drawn eighty-four.

Once again the bowling was the trouble, though in spite of a wet summer Mayer took 108 wickets for 20·34 each. Next best was Paine, who, with rain about, perhaps ought to have done better than seventy-five wickets, but no one else took as many as fifty. Wyatt's thirty-three were very expensive – 43·90 runs each. Derek Foster was able to play in only four games and in an early match against Surrey he showed Warwickshire what they were missing by taking seven for 42, all of them at one time while only 26 runs were hit off him. His eighteen wickets at only 16·77 runs each easily put him at the top of the county averages.

For the most part there was nothing wrong with the batting. Six players scored over 1000 runs and three times totals of 500 and over were run up, but there were also three against them so they cancelled each other out. The fielding was poor and there were so many missed catches that Bainbridge suggested that the slips should wear gloves. Of the 500-plus totals, 543 for seven were scored against Worcestershire and Bates was run out going for the single that would have given him his double century. He took his benefit against Lancashire and made 38 before being bowled by McDonald, who did the hat trick and took four wickets in six balls. Warwickshire's last five wickets fell for 27 runs. In the second innings Bates was again bowled by McDonald, but this time for none and Lancashire won by three wickets. Bates's popularity was reflected in a benefit of nearly £800.

Just as some batsmen took a liking to Warwickshire's bowling, so there were some bowlers against whom the county's batsmen were rarely successful. One of them was 'Tich' Freeman, who took fourteen of their wickets for 143 at Tonbridge and then eleven for 160 at Edgbaston. Warwickshire's four totals were 149, 160, 265 and 223, and Kent won each match by an innings despite scores of 117 and 98 by Wyatt in the second game. Another was Charlie Parker, of Gloucestershire, who at Cheltenham took fourteen Warwickshire wickets for 97. Against Derbyshire, in a fight to gain first innings lead, Wyatt batted six hours and a quarter for 145, which contained no fewer than seventy-nine singles, but Warwickshire fell just short – 419 to 448. Santall had a great match against Yorkshire at Edgbaston. He was top scorer with

57 out of 148 in reply to Yorkshire's 364 for nine declared and then, despite foot trouble which forced him to have a runner, made 105 not out in the second innings.

England chose no fewer than twenty-one players in the Test series, in which Australia were beaten only once (in the first game at Nottingham) and the only Test in which Bradman did not get a century was the fourth. Wyatt had pretty well given up hope, despite his good form, of being called upon and was very surprised to receive a letter at Cheltenham, where Warwickshire were playing Gloucestershire, from H. D. G. Leveson Gower, telling him the selectors would like him to lead the side in the final game at The Oval, and asking him to come to London to select the team, as the captain had the casting vote.

Wyatt was under no illusions as to what might happen when it was announced that he was replacing so popular a figure as Chapman, who, he thought, had not done too badly in the four Tests and had made a brilliant century in the second. Why, then, was he dropped? *Wisden* took the view that 'there existed the chance that Wyatt's watchful methods might invest England's batting with some much-needed stability and prove invaluable in a match with no time limit.' It was to be played to a finish.

Wyatt himself thought there was a feeling that Chapman's 'rather care-free dashing style of batting was too risky' and that he had not shown sufficient appreciation of the difference between three- and four-day matches. Of course, when the announcement was made the newspaper correspondents – there was no television to bother about then – had a field day. So, too, did the photographers, the telegram-senders and the letter-writers, most of whom assumed, wrongly, that there had been a row; in fact Chapman was invited into the England dressing-room for the match and during the following winter Wyatt went on a tour to South Africa under his captaincy.

Wyatt began well by winning the toss with his lucky half-sovereign, but after a reasonable start by Hobbs and Sutcliffe England were soon in trouble and when Wyatt's turn came to bat they were 197 for five. He was a little unnerved by the magnificent reception the crowd gave him and he still remembers in detail every ball of the five that remained to be faced in Grimmett's over. The last one very nearly bowled him, but he settled down and at the close he and Sutcliffe were still together, the Yorkshireman not out 138 and Wyatt 39.

Next morning they added 51 before Sutcliffe was out after a record sixth-wicket partnership for England of 170. He had made 161 and Wyatt went on to 64 after three hours' batting, the total being taken to 405. When Australia batted, Duckworth had one of his rare off-days, missing Ponsford twice as well as Woodfull and Bradman, the last of whom made 232 when he should have been out for 82.

Altogether Australia piled on 695 runs, but that was hardly Wyatt's fault.

When England batted a second time Hobbs had a wonderful ovation on going out to bat in a Test for the last time and on his home ground. England had to bat on a rain-affected pitch and were all out for 251, to which Wyatt this time contributed only 7. Australia had won by an innings and the rubber, too, was theirs. The Wyatt-for-Chapman gamble had not come off, though the blame could hardly be laid at Wyatt's door. *Wisden* commented that 'the lack of Chapman's special skill in the field was clearly felt and it cannot be said that the course taken was justified by results'.

Warwickshire nearly lost their best bowler during the season. Perhaps wanting an easier life, Mayer signed an agreement with the Accrington Club and it cost Warwickshire £300 by way of compensation to secure his release, as well as a two-year agreement with him at a guaranteed minimum of £350 and a benefit in 1933. They did lose 'Tiger' Smith, their wicketkeeper for twenty years, who, because the Committee did not offer to renew his agreement for 1930, but wanted him to play on a match fee basis, asked them to nominate him for the county umpires list, which they agreed to do. At the time it looked like the parting of the ways; who could have told then that he would be very much around for many, many more years? Up to that time he had scored 15 901 runs for the county, held 643 catches – he used to say he never missed one; they just dropped out – and stumped 139 batsmen.

His eventual successor, Jack Buckingham, another Yorkshireman, was always known as 'The Duke' because of his name and immaculate appearance both on and off the field – he always wore silk shirts – though he cannot remember who gave him the title. He had played professional soccer for Shrewsbury, Wellington and Stafford Rangers, but at the time Warwickshire became interested in him as a wicket-keeper who could also get a few runs, he was a male nurse at Erdington Hospital, Birmingham. After he had played in a few Club and Ground matches, he was invited to join the staff, and in the evening paper of the day he accepted the terms offered, he read that 'Tiger' was retiring; had he known that, he said afterwards, he would have asked for better terms.

That was in 1931 and in the meantime Jack Smart took over. He had come to the county as a batsman-bowler, but had understudied Smith and on the latter's retirement he followed him, neatly and tidily, and with a sense of humour often to be found in men who squat behind the stumps and see most of the game. It was Smart who christened Eric Hollies 'Spike' when one wet day he turned up wearing a gangster-style raincoat and with his hat pulled down over his eyes.

What must have been a very pleasant duty fell to Wyatt at the

Scarborough Festival. Wilfred Rhodes played in his last match there against the Australians and took five for 93, being unlucky not to have Bradman out first ball. Wyatt presented him with the ball and later Ryder wrote to Rhodes saying that 'at this distance in time I have no regrets [that you did not come to us in 1897]. Much as you might have done for Warwickshire cricket, everyone will feel that the fates decreed for the best.'

There was a very curious episode at the end of 1930 when Wyatt was asked to go and see the chairman, and the honorary treasurer, Dr Thwaite, at the offices of the Birmingham Chamber of Commerce where annual and Committee meetings were held. Wyatt has told* of his amazement at being asked if he would like G. D. Kemp-Welch, the Cambridge Blue, to be captain. When he had recovered from his surprise, he pointed out that the rules hardly permitted him to elect the next captain and that it was up to the Committee. He added that if they could give him a reason why, in the interests of Warwickshire cricket, they considered it would be better for Kemp-Welch to be captain, then he would not have any objection. It was then made clear to him that the Committee thought he was more interested in playing international than Warwickshire cricket and that he preferred Tests to county games.

It was hardly the most tactful suggestion that could have been made to the man who had just captained England against Australia and had declined the selectors' suggestion that he should miss two Warwickshire matches to do so – those against Somerset at Weston-super-Mare before the Test, which he was compelled to leave before it ended in order to attend the selectors' meeting in London, and against Leicestershire at Hinckley, immediately after six tiring days in the Test, when he scored 174 not out, an innings largely responsible for one of the only two wins Warwickshire had that season.

Before he left the room Wyatt pointed out, among other things, that most counties reckoned it an honour for one of the side to be chosen to play for England, especially as captain, for it often led to better gates. When he returned Bainbridge told him: 'We have had a very interesting chat. You won't hear anything more about this and please don't mention it to anyone.' And, indeed, no mention was made of it for many years.

Wyatt has since said that, of course, he loved playing in international cricket, which seemed to him to offer the highest challenge, but he added: 'I doubt if I got any more pleasure out of it than I did playing for Warwickshire against Yorkshire, or, for that matter, playing regularly for Warwickshire with players most of whom I looked on as my greatest friends, to whom, incidentally, I was later accused of giving no encouragement.'

Even forty years afterwards, Wyatt was still inclined to think that

*In *Three Straight Sticks*.

191

Ryder had something to do with this interview and that it was not so much a question of the chairman and the treasurer sounding him out about the possibility of Kemp-Welch becoming captain, as a threat that they would elect him if Wyatt did not do so, which, of course, he had no power to do. The rest of the Committee, he said, had no knowledge of the meeting until he mentioned it to them years afterwards.

Wyatt thought Ryder felt he would have more influence with Kemp-Welch than he had over Wyatt. In his book he expressed the view that Ryder was 'much too inclined to interfere with the running of the county eleven. I naturally resented this interference because the responsibility and the decisions must be those of the appointed captain.' There were several occasions, he said, on which the team was altered after it had been selected during his presence. This usually happened in away matches when he was unable to rectify it.

'Sometimes,' he wrote in his book, 'members of committees are not very experienced cricketers themselves, and they are not always right in their view of what goes on during play. There is a tremendously important job to be done by committees with regard to finance, the running of the ground and so on, but they should leave the conduct of the game itself to the captain. Otherwise they unsettle him and unsettle the side.'

Perhaps this is an opportune moment to say something on the other side by way of clarification about the position of county cricket club secretaries in general and of Ryder in particular, since he cannot speak for himself. This is especially so in regard to what was regarded as 'interference' in team selection, for it has already been seen that sometimes, had it not been for Ryder, Warwickshire might not have been able to field a side at all.

If the clubs secretaries serve own their own grounds, they are responsible for many other things in addition to secretarial duties. They have to be ground managers, involved in all that takes place thereon, in and out of season; they are responsible for watching over the existing premises and putting forward schemes for further development; they are also match managers, responsible for the administration of all county games and, possibly, Test matches as well, and that means they may also take a prominent part in finding and developing players. This would be particularly true in Ryder's case when he was the club's only official, long before the days of scouts and coaches, so it was not surprising if he acted as manager, as well as secretary, and even occasionally as team selector.

Wyatt was probably glad to get away to South Africa during the winter of 1930–1, though he did not have a wildly successful tour. He played in all five Tests, but made no more than 205 runs, with a highest score of 54, and did little bowling. He had better fortune for Warwickshire when he returned home for the 1931 season, as did the county, which rose five places in the Championship table to ninth. Perhaps that was partly due to the fact that, although the New Zealanders were here, Wyatt was not invited to play in any of the Tests against them, which meant that he was available for his county throughout the summer.

He was one of four batsmen to make over 1000 runs, the others being Croom – who with six centuries was a much improved batsman – Bates and Norman Kilner. Parsons, who had been made deputy captain, was able to play more often than expected and although he just missed reaching 1000 runs he headed the Warwickshire averages with 56·29 and was fifth in the national averages with 60·10. Kemp-Welch, who had a very successful time with the University, played in ten matches for the county, but made only 311 runs.

Warwickshire's improved form was due to a variety of factors – the batting, perhaps, first, but primarily a wider variety of bowling, though Paine was the only one who took more than 100 wickets. Mayer had seventy-five, Wyatt fifty-six and Foster, who was able to play in twenty matches, forty-seven. Because of weather the team had hardly any outdoor practice in May and lost the first three matches, but they were beaten only once after the beginning of June.

One of the games they lost in May was against Yorkshire at Headingley, where they were the victims of the best bowling performance of the season by Verity who, in the second innings, took the wickets of Smart, Foster, Tate and Paine in one over and returned this splendid analysis:

O	M	R	W
18·4	6	36	10

As if that was not enough – Warwickshire were all out for 72 – in the return match later the same month Percy Holmes hit yet another double century – his fourth – against them. He and Sutcliffe had an opening partnership of 309, their sixtieth three-figure opening stand.

Woolley played an astonishing innings, even for him, at Folkestone, where Mayer began by taking four wickets for 14. But Woolley, in first wicket down, made 51 out of 67 and 103 out of a total of only 144 in little more than two hours, batting with almost contemptuous ease while his colleagues were floundering.

But it was no more remarkable than George Gunn's 183 made in seven hours ten minutes at Edgbaston in July – at the age of 53. He was missed two or three times and these may well have been occasions when the spectators blessed the offending fieldsmen whatever the bowlers thought about them. For a large part of the time his son, G.V., was batting with him. He made exactly 100, his maiden century. This is believed to be the only occasion on record of a father and son each making a century in the same innings of a first-class game.

It was after this match, in which Warwickshire scored 511 for three declared – Croom made 159 and Bates 105 – and Notts 521 for seven, that George Gunn walked straight off the field into Ryder's office and told him: 'Another two years of pitches like that and you'll kill the bloody game.' The shaft went home – next season Warwickshire tried to get pitches which gave the bowlers some help.

Yet another new system of scoring had been introduced – fifteen points for a win, five points for first innings lead and three to the other side – and against Leicestershire at Edgbaston in August Warwickshire were involved in their first experience of the freak declarations to which the system led captains in the scramble for full points. Trying to make a match of it on the third day, each captain declared the first innings at none, but then Warwickshire could score only 85 for three in reply to Leicestershire's 179 without loss, so each side took four points for a tie on the first innings.

Parsons had a fine 190 against the New Zealanders, who were very nearly beaten after having had to follow on, and then he had an extraordinary experience at Worcester which may well be unique. He forgot his spectacles and, thinking that the Warwickshire innings would last until he got back, he went home for them. But he had miscalculated – they collapsed, eight wickets going down for 71 runs – so he missed his innings. No harm was done, however. In the second innings he made 16 and Warwickshire won by 87 runs.

A compliment to Warwickshire's strength was that no fewer than five members of the team were invited to take part in the Gentlemen v. Players match at The Oval: Wyatt, Parsons and Foster for the Gentlemen and Croom and Mayer for the Players. Wyatt, Foster and Kemp-Welch also played in the Lord's match, but neither batsmen nor bowlers distinguished themselves on either occasion.

Playing for the Rest of England against the Champion County at The Oval, Wyatt received one of those injuries with which he was plagued throughout his career and which earned him the unenviable title of England's most brittle cricketer. On this occasion a ball from Bowes hit him on the back of his hand and broke a bone in it. The doctor at the hospital to which he was taken told him that he was not to bat again in that match on any account. (Bowes was another bowler Warwickshire had approached, but turned down after a trial on a wet day and he went to Lord's.)

Wyatt went to the ground next morning and had begun packing his bag when Jupp, who had been not out with him overnight, asked: 'Aren't you going in again? You must be gutless.' This was a charge that not even Wyatt's severest critics would have brought against him, but the remark made him change his mind and disobey the doctor's orders. Although the hand must have been very painful, he managed to stay in for the rest of the afternoon with D. R. Jardine and he believes that it was the way he batted with a broken hand which convinced that man of iron that Wyatt was just the type for the dour struggle ahead in Australia. So it was an ill wind . . .

In later years almost every mishap that could befall a batsman happened to Wyatt. He fractured a jaw, two toes, two ribs, had a broken bone in his foot, a broken thumb, three fractured fingers and a broken bone in his wrist. Hammond once called him 'the most fractured man in big cricket', but none of his injuries discouraged him from playing. It was not without good reason that he was also called 'one of the greatest fighting cricketers of all time'.

Perhaps, however, he would have been hit fewer times had he been willing on occasions to agree that sometimes discretion is the better part of valour and had moved his feet more quickly.

In February 1931, the Committee had set up a Special Development Fund, which could be considered the beginning of the expansionist policy which was to transform Edgbaston into one of the country's finest cricket grounds – until the others woke up and began to follow their example. This was largely Dr Thwaite's doing. Gate receipts, he told the Committee, were the lowest since 1924 and public interest must be stimulated and a winning team built up. The comfort of the public must be considered, the players' wages had been increased, and new ones engaged, and there would be further expense in connection with the Minor Counties competition which it had been decided to enter. The fund was being created to meet these needs and so that the work on the ground improvements could begin as soon as possible.

After sixteen years as President, Ludford Docker announced his retirement at the annual meeting, but, characteristically, he did not depart without a farewell broadside. This time it was against no less a cricket authority than Lord Harris, with whose recent statement that the public must not ask for 'brighter cricket' he disagreed. Docker said he did not believe that either the public or the players had reached the stage of attaching so much importance to results that risks must not be taken. If the game was to be slowed down even to the pace of some of the Test matches, it would lose much attraction for the onlooker. A voice crying in the wilderness indeed at this time, but later proved so very right.

Docker proposed Sir Charles Hyde, then proprietor of *The Birmingham Post*, as his successor and he was duly elected, Docker becoming a vice-president. One of the candidates for a seat on the Committee was W. G. Quaife. There were nine of them for seven seats and the lowest of the seven received ninety votes to Quaife's sixty. This did not deter

Quaife from offering himself as a candidate for several years, but always without success, though one would have thought the professionals' point of view would have been both useful and welcome.

The Club lost another distinguished servant immediately after the annual meeting – George Cartland resigned as chairman of the Committee to make way for a more active man. 'My interest in the Club', he wrote in a letter announcing his resignation, 'is as great now as it was forty-six years ago when I took a leading part in its formation and I trust I shall live to see our county Champion County again.'

Unhappily he did not. That same year he fell through the open stairway of a shop in Worcester and though he appeared to make a good recovery he died in February 1934, shortly after his 81st birthday. He had played his first innings for Warwickshire the year the ground was opened. There was a kindly reference to him at a meeting of the Committee as 'their chairman and best friend for forty-six years. His services to the work of county cricket will not easily be forgotten here – they were a constant interest and delight to himself and of priceless value to Warwickshire.'

Bainbridge succeeded him as chairman and Derek Foster took his place on the Committee.

Hollies and Dollery
(1932–1933)

Two other names destined to figure long and honourably in the history of Warwickshire cricket were first mentioned at the end of the 1931 season. The bearer of one of them, William Eric Hollies, was engaged for two years at £4 a week in summer and £2 10s 0d a week in winter. In the case of the other, H. E. Dollery, it was decided to take no action, but why is something of a mystery.

Warwickshire might very easily have lost Hollies to Worcestershire, in which county his birth was registered by mistake instead of in Staffordshire where he was born, at Old Hill. It was so near a thing that he had a trial for them only the day before he came to Edgbaston for Warwickshire to take a look at him.

If ever a player could be said to have had cricket in his blood it is Eric Hollies. His grandfather had been a well-known local fast bowler; his father played for Old Hill in the Birmingham League and was one of the last of the lob bowlers; one of his sisters could bowl both leg-breaks and googlies when she was 14 and another captained the Halesowen Girls' Grammar School team. Young Eric was given his first bat – one that had been cut down in size for him – when he was 8, though he had been playing for years before that with all kinds of pieces of wood on the pit mounds near his home.

Every evening during the summer he used to go with his father to the nets on the Old Hill ground to field and – if he was lucky – to get a bat and a bowl at the end of practice. His father taught him to bowl the leg-break and the googly at a very early age – there is a story of an astonished holidaymaker on the sands at Rhyl exclaiming, 'Good heavens, do you know that boy's bowling googlies?' – and he never had any difficulty in acquiring skill at that most tricky and uncontrollable of

197

deliveries. His life in summer was made up of games of cricket on the pit mounds and on the Old Hill ground and in the winter he bowled in the family garden at home, putting down a sheet of tin where he wanted to pitch the ball – he knew by the noise when he had succeeded.

By the time he was 13 he was playing for the Old Hill third XI. He was then attending Halesowen Grammar School, walking two and a half miles there and two and a half miles back each day, an exercise he thought helped him to acquire the stamina to bowl the thousands of overs he sent down during his long career and which enabled him still, at the age of 60, to play league cricket every Saturday.

Captain of Old Hill at that time was H. W. Homer, who had had a house built next to the ground so that he could be as near as possible to the nets. He was a gentle enthusiast who later captained Staffordshire for several seasons and has been for many years now a revered and distinguished figure at Edgbaston where he has served in many capacities; Hollies owed much to his encouragement. He was soon playing in the first eleven, one of the youngest players ever to appear in the Birmingham League, so it is not surprising that word soon got round about this young spin bowler.

One evening in June 1931, he was in the nets at Old Hill when Fred Root, the Worcestershire bowler, against whom he had played in a benefit match earlier in the month, came out of the pavilion, crossed the field to the nets and told Hollies he was anxious that he should have a trial for Worcestershire. It transpired that Root had mentioned him to the Worcestershire Committee following the benefit match, but as he did not then know Hollies's name he had referred to him as 'that young, fair-haired leg-breaker at Old Hill'. So Worcestershire sent a representative to see him, but by a very curious coincidence there was another young leg-spinner, Gilbert Hackett, playing for Old Hill at the time and it was he, not Hollies, who got the invitation to go for a trial.

Root, of course, had discovered the error, so here he was again and this time Eric's father agreed to let the boy have a trial at Worcester, one Wednesday. Then the Old Hill Club received a letter from Warwickshire inviting him to go to Edgbaston the next day. So Hollies had trials on two consecutive days for two different counties. That at Worcester lasted only a few minutes because it began to rain, but Root and Major M. F. S. Jewell had already seen enough and Hollies was offered an engagement – £250 a year, plus a job of chopping wood on the estate of Worcestershire's President, then Lord Doverdale. Perhaps they thought it would help to strengthen the lad's back muscles, which it probably would have done.

Next day he went to Edgbaston with his father and Billy Edwards, the Old Hill chairman, and had half an hour in the nets bowling to Aubrey Hill while Syd Santall, the coach, looked on. Then he went into the office to talk to Ryder and Dr Thwaite, who eventually offered him terms, based on more pay in summer than in winter, but working out at slightly less on average than Worcestershire had offered. That was soon adjusted and Hollies had started on the road which was to make him the most successful bowler Warwickshire have ever had and one of the very best of his kind, certainly the most economical the game has ever known.

Few would have guessed it that first season of 1932, though he got a warm recommendation from G. W. Stephens, then playing for Moseley, who made 80 or so, many of them off Hollies in a Club and Ground game, and afterwards went straight into Ryder's office and said: 'Whatever you do, don't let that little leg-spinner get away. He's going to be a good 'un.' He bowled in five matches and took precisely four wickets, which worked out at 80·25 runs each. He was never so expensive again and his experience in one of those games, against Hammond, which was rather like letting a lamb out with a lion, nearly finished him before he had even started. It certainly caused him to change his bowling style.

He began with a pretty disheartening experience in the Sussex match at Edgbaston late in June when he bowled twenty-seven overs, only one of which was a maiden, for 150 runs and one wicket in a Sussex innings which went to 511 for seven, though he had some consolation when he survived for twenty-five minutes and scored four runs in a vain effort with Mayer to save the game – there were only five minutes to go when Hollies was out. It was the first of a number of rearguard actions for which he acquired quite a reputation down the years.

This, however, was nothing to the ordeal he had to go through at Gloucester. He was brought on, the fifth bowler tried, when Hammond was in full spate and I have heard Wyatt severely criticised for putting him on at all in the circumstances. Hollies was very much put off his stride because Beet, the former Derbyshire player, no-balled him three times in one over. Hammond hit all three of them for six, which must have been a shattering experience for a young player. He had only six overs and, when he was mercifully taken off, this was his analysis:

O	M	R	W
6	0	57	0

Nearly ten runs an over – and Hammond had made 92 in 100 minutes. Nothing like this had happened to the boy even in nightmares and he worried and worried all through the rest of the innings and the second innings when he was not asked to bowl. Although Warwickshire eventually won by four wickets, I doubt if it was much consolation to him. In those days players came home for the weekend from matches at Gloucester and during the train journey back to Birmingham Hollies was pondering where he had gone wrong and how to put it right. The first thing he did when he got back to Old Hill that Saturday evening was to go round to Bert Homer's house and talk it over with him.

On the Sunday morning they went to the nets on the Old Hill ground and there tried to work out what to do to prevent anyone collaring his bowling again, Hammond included. They finally came to the conclusion that it was because he had been giving the ball too much air and Hammond had had ample time to get down the pitch and hit him before the spin could take effect. Thereafter Hollies decided that he would bowl a little quicker through the air and push the ball through more, so that even a quick-footed batsman – and there were some about then – would not have time to get to the pitch of the ball and drive him. In future years, when he had to conserve his energies, he was to toss it up only to later-order batsmen, or to those whose footwork he knew to be poor, and if anyone did venture to drive him he then invariably bowled him a quicker and shorter ball, contrary to the tactics of the classic slow left-handers such as Rhodes, who used to give the batsman determined to hit him a little more rope still, until usually he hanged himself. Giving runs away to get catches was never a practice to which Hollies subscribed, and he has reminded us that 'there have not been many occasions when I could afford to throw the ball up and gamble . . . Circumstances have forced me to bowl economically.'* I used to think Hollies dropped short only because for years he had to keep one end going for Warwickshire and was relied on to keep almost any batsman reasonably quiet. I did not know then that he was also remembering what Hammond had done to him at Gloucester years before.

It is running a little ahead of the story, but this is perhaps the most fitting place to add a footnote which might well be subtitled 'Hollies's Revenge'. The following season, when Gloucestershire came to Edgbaston, there was some rain on the first day when they were batting and they were 178 for four when Hollies was called on a second time to bowl. He then proceeded to take their remaining six wickets for 9 runs and they were all out 187. He had Hammond caught by Croom for 55 and finished with these figures:

O	M	R	W
29·4	11	54	8

Hollies went on learning his craft, mostly from Ted Leyland, with whom he often talked about tactics, and Wyatt, and in the winter he went in for weight-lifting to build up his strength. He was going to need it.

Before the 1932 season had begun Dr Thwaite, at the annual meeting, had given a most comprehensive review of the financial position. The £2000 loss in 1931, he said, was the worst yet. In four of the first five

*I'll Spin You A Tale, Museum Press, Ltd.

years of their existence as a first-class county they made a profit and then from 1900 an annual loss was made for nine years. This was rather surprising, he said, when they recalled that at that period Warwickshire had a very good side, being fifth in the Championship in 1901 and at no time in that decade much lower. During the thirty-seven years as a first-class county there had been a profit in eighteen and a loss in nineteen seasons. Aggregate profits amounted to £9895 and losses to £12 631. In response to special appeals nearly £9000 had been contributed. These figures showed a surplus of about £6000, the actual sum raised on debentures some years ago and redeemed in connection with the purchase of the ground.

It would seem, he went on, that considering the population of the Birmingham area alone, they had never had a really satisfactory cricket public. Their great weakness was the lack of support from the country districts. So, said Dr Thwaite, they found themselves owning the ground and with a small cash balance in hand to start the 1932 season.

That summer was very wet, May being one of the worst months for cricket that anyone could recall. Warwickshire had a very even season. They did not win a match until the middle of June but then they won five and lost five, the rest being drawn. On the first innings they won eight and lost eight, twice by a single run. Once again the batting was very strong, with five players scoring over 1000 runs and Wyatt as many as 1347, more than anyone else; but in bowling, Paine – who sent down more than 1000 overs and took 109 wickets for 18·48 runs each – lacked support.

Even without the benefit of hindsight, it is difficult to understand why Warwickshire were so hesitant about engaging Dollery, but in July the 'no action' of the previous year was changed to a temporary arrangement for two years at £3 a week and the following spring sanction was given for him to be engaged on a month's trial for Smethwick as Saturday 'pro' at £3 a week, to be equally divided between the county club and the player.

So it could not have been money and it could hardly have been his previous record, which was most impressive. Dollery would be the first to deprecate the use of term 'schoolboy wonder', but that is what he was. He played for the first eleven at Reading Grammar School when he was only 13 and in 1930, while still at school, he made 101 out of 140 against an M.C.C. XI which included S. J. Pegler, the former South African Test bowler. Next season, also against the M.C.C., he scored 104 not out in a total this time of only 115, the next highest scorer being No. eleven with three. In his last two seasons he captained the school eleven.

When he was still only 15 he played for Berkshire in the Minor Counties competition – his home backed on to Huntley and Palmer's ground – and two years later he made a century in each innings for them against Monmouthshire. At the end of that season he had scored 531 runs, average 44·25; the following summer he headed the county's averages with 47·12 and was chosen to play for the Minor Counties side against the West Indies touring team, but scored only 6 and 1.

It was A. B. Croom, the groundsman, and father of Warwickshire's 'Arthur' Croom, with whose family he spent much of his time, who brought him to the notice of Warwickshire. Dollery has told how when he failed his first trial – perhaps this was the reason for the Committee's hesitations – Ryder took him into his office and with a walking-stick showed him the gap he had left between his bat and his pads. Through A. B. Croom he got a second chance and this time he was invited to qualify. He was only 17 when he came to Edgbaston for the interview with Ryder, who engaged him originally as an office boy at £2 10s 0d a week for six weeks. When he asked where he was to sleep that night – it was too late to return to Reading – he says that Ryder replied: 'Knock on every door – someone will take you in.' It must have been one of his absent-minded moments. Fortunately for Warwickshire someone did take Dollery in – at 33 Princess Road near the ground. He stayed there for many weeks, but the following season went to the Crooms.

Human nature being what it is, it could hardly be expected that any youngster would be called Horace, one of the names Dollery received at his christening, and eventually he became 'Tom' because, it seemed, that was the name which fitted best. And 'Tom' it remained.

Paine must have enjoyed returning to Lord's for the first match of the season, for after Warwickshire had collapsed against Durston and G. T. S. Stevens for a miserable 69 – the first four men were out without scoring – he routed his old colleagues for even fewer – 62 – doing the hat trick, his full analysis being: Overs 13·1, Maidens 6, Runs 14, Wickets 7. Paine also figured in an exciting finish in the return match at Edgbaston, but this time as a batsman. Again Warwickshire collapsed, this time against Durston and Peebles, but Paine stayed with Wyatt for half an hour while 46 were added for the ninth wicket, Paine's share being 1 before he was run out, and then Mayer carried on for another fifteen minutes for 1 not out. When the last over began, Wyatt, who had played a sterling innings, was 99 not out. He played four balls and then hit the fifth to the boundary, but Warwickshire were still 24 runs short – what a pity he could not have hit a few fours a little earlier. Paine then went on to Northampton and made his highest score in county cricket, 70, after being sent in as night watchman.

Freeman again took on Warwickshire almost single-handed at Folkestone, taking seventeen wickets in the match for only 92 runs, Kent winning by 74 runs. But Warwickshire had a brilliant victory at Gloucester by four wickets after a wonderful innings of 211 by Bates and some remarkable hitting by Croom. Thus once again the home crowd was deprived of a fine performance by their own players, but at least when the All India side came to Edgbaston they were able to see that lovely batsman and beautiful fieldsman, C. K. Nayudu, who made 162 and hit a ball from Jarrett, one of his six sixes, into the middle of what is now the Colts ground, finishing nearly in Cannon Hill Road. They also saw that fine opening attack of Amar Singh and Mohammed Nissar.

News came of three very promising boys with Warwickshire qualifications, one of them being Peter Cranmer, of St Edward's School, Oxford, and of the death of an old one in Harry Howell, at the very early age of 41. He had made only a few appearances in the last three seasons, but in his career, what Rowland Ryder called his 'sturdy craftsmanship', brought him getting on for nearly 1000 wickets for only just over 20 runs each; splendid figures for a fast bowler whose career extended over only ten full seasons, in six of which in succession he took over 100 wickets.

Cranmer was another schoolboy star. That season at St Edward's, where E. P. Hewetson, the Oxford fast bowler, who earlier had played for the county, first spotted him, he scored 911 runs in eighteen innings, with a highest score of 156, averaged 56·93, and took ten wickets. The following year he made 636 runs, highest innings 152, averaged 35·33 and took nineteen wickets. He proved to be the fresh breeze of which, later, Warwickshire were to be sorely in need.

There was a first mention this season of Sunday cricket, when it was ruled that no professional should be allowed to play it without permission, and for the first time also the name of Leslie Deakins appeared in the minutes when the terms of the engagement of the secretary and his 'clerk' were reviewed.

Leslie Deakins was Gloucestershire born, the son of a stonemason, who played club cricket for Tewkesbury. While he was still a boy the family moved to Birmingham and Leslie went to Grove Lane School for whom he kept wicket. He was working in a law office when he saw, in the 'Situations Vacant' columns of *The Birmingham Mail*, the Warwickshire Club's advertisement for an assistant to the secretary. He applied and on 3 December 1928, he was engaged at a salary of 45s per week. Whatever amount he earned later, he has surely been worth every penny the Warwickshire Club has ever paid him.

On this occasion, instead of an inclusive sum of £850 being paid to the secretary for his services and those of his assistant – a curious arrangement – it was decided that each should be separately employed, Ryder at £750 a year and his assistant at £156. It was agreed that there should not be any liability on Ryder's part to contribute towards the clerk's remuneration in 1932 and Leslie Deakins was also permitted to work part time for Dr Thwaite.

I had often wondered what he best remembered when he looked back on those early days of his long association with the Club and this is what he told me:

I first saw Edgbaston in 1919 at the age of 10, immediately after coming up from Gloucestershire to Birmingham, and then again two years later in the high summer of 1921 when a cricket-loving North-country schoolmaster took six of us to the ground to sit, three either side of him, to watch the county's match with the Australians, and, in the process and with the help of his most knowledgeable and enjoyable commentary, to learn what the real game was all about.

Long before play started I can recall being enthralled by the wonderful expanse of beautiful turf and captivated by the thought of earning the right, one day, to walk on it. It never occurred to me, nor, indeed, to the school-master and my five other colleagues, that it was anything other than sacrilege that such a hallowed area, rich in cricket history, should be desecrated by the feet of the multitude. The ground represented a particular heaven you earned, if you were good enough, the right to enter, and if you were not good enough, then you must admire, and, indeed, consider yourself privileged to do so, from afar.

I have never had reason or need to vary that schoolboy assessment and know that it holds good today in the minds of all boys who really love and under-stand the game. In the subsequent years I watched county cricket from time to time, and played the game when I could, until that day when feeling, I sup-pose, a little depressed by my future as a law clerk, I answered an advertise-ment and, following a satisfactory interview, came to Edgbaston as of right and literally received the keys to one of the great cricket grounds of the world.

I have rubbed my eyes many times in the intervening years and wondered whether it really was me seated here in the office at the ground, first as assistant to R. V. Ryder and subsequently as holder of the office of secretary myself, privileged to enjoy the morning's bright sunlight as the ground came to life, equally privileged to live through that day on the ground, and in the evening's mellow sunlight to sit beneath the clock in the pavilion watching the shadows lengthen and chatting about the game with Ted Leyland, then head grounds-man, with whom I shared many happy hours in the fourteen years before the Second World War.

Of all the books on the game I might have read, or all the authorities I might have consulted, none could have taught me more about cricket than that old Yorkshireman, great player in his own right and father of Yorkshire and England batsman, Maurice Leyland; his Warwickshire counterpart, 'Tiger' Smith, perhaps better known to most of us closer to him as Jim Smith, who has played in every country where the game is known, and possessor of a unique knowledge of its lore and technique; to say nothing of the man at that time acknowledged as the greatest authority on the administrative side of the game, R. V. Ryder, at whose side I was privileged to work every day.

In this same period Sydney Santall, author of the Club's first history, was head coach and ground superintendent, an upholder of the old traditions and at all times endeavouring to ensure that the game went on in the way he knew and approved, with all the cricket in the county focused on Edgbaston.

On the field itself, men like Len Bates, of the handsome countenance and elegant stroke play; Norman Kilner, the rugged, practical Yorkshireman who opened the innings; 'Danny' Mayer, splendid exponent of new ball bowling, who was moved to few words but great endeavour; George Paine, who headed the all-England averages in 1934, a talented left-arm bowler; and, leading the side following the departure of the Hon. F. S. G. Calthorpe, Bob Wyatt, of the resolute fighting spirit and unrelenting dedication to the game.

On occasions the scene was graced by the presence of men like Canon J. H. Parsons, who appeared in both the Gentlemen's and Players' sides in the years between the wars, whose philosophy and practice in batting were founded on straight driving of superb quality, and who was inclined to discount runs scored square, or by deflection, behind the wickets. These men in a practical and always delightful way reaffirmed for me the words of Lord Harris . . . 'You do well to love this game'.

It is to them all I would dedicate the results of any endeavours I have made and any success I might have enjoyed over the years which have been concentrated on developing the great Edgbaston ground, obtained in perpetuity for cricket by the efforts of the Club's founder, William Ansell, and endowed by the various playing and administrative talent of all who succeeded him.

In the winter of 1932–3 Wyatt achieved a great ambition and went out to Australia with the M.C.C. team as vice-captain to Jardine. This, of course, was the notorious 'bodyline' tour and Wyatt must bear some of the responsibility – which, to be fair to him, he has never shirked – for a policy which did more to disrupt cricket relations than anything that had happened before, or has happened since, until the recent lamentable cancellation of tours to and from South Africa and Australia.

'Bodyline' is part of this history only insofar as it affected the Warwickshire Club's leading player and the little-known connection with it of the former Warwickshire captain, F. R. Foster. Before the England team left for Australia, Jardine paid frequent visits to Foster's flat in London and got from him the placings he had used for his leg-side fields on his Australian tour when he first tried out leg theory.

'I had no hint', Foster told the Press after the bodyline controversy, 'that these would be used for bodyline bowling. I would like all my friends in Australia to know that I am sorry that my experience and my advice were put to such unworthy uses.'

The leg theory attack was, of course, evolved with the idea of curbing Bradman's phenomenal scoring, which, to some extent, it succeeded in doing, but Wyatt has told me since that his final view of it, which he expressed to Jardine at the time, was that 'a concentrated leg-side attack was not in the best interests of cricket. I took the view that any form of attack which bred ill-feeling was bad for the game. Actually, G. O. Allen was the only other member of the side who expressed the same view during the tour. The remaining members, at the time, including Hammond, were all in favour, although I believe he altered his views later.'

Bodyline apart, Wyatt did not have a very successful tour from a playing point of view. He had gone out in good heart and good form for, leading the M.C.C. Australian XI against The Rest of England at Folkestone, he had made 81 and 171 not out; but in Australia, although he played in all five Tests, a century eluded him. He made 327 runs, with a highest score of 78, and averaged 46·71, but he was not at his best. He bowled only two overs in the Tests, not surprising in view of the great wealth of talent available. On the whole tour he scored 883 runs, including 80 in the two Tests against New Zealand. *Wisden*'s verdict was that he was 'a most valuable member of the combination'.

Back home in England, Wyatt soon heard Bainbridge express the hope that he would not encourage his bowlers to exploit the leg theory too much, though he did not think it unfair. He need not have worried – Warwickshire just had not the bowlers to exploit it, but Wyatt, as well as a few other England players, had a taste of their own medicine from the West Indians. It has always been believed that it was intimated to the tourists that they might let us see for ourselves what bodyline was like. In Martindale and Constantine they certainly had the men to demonstrate it, and in the second Test at Manchester they really let the ball fly.

None of the England players who took part will easily forget it. Wyatt had what he described as 'an indifferent match' and he has recalled that 'hardly a ball passed me on the off side while I was batting'. He was out for 18 to a wonderful catch by Constantine when hooking a bouncer from Martindale. Hammond had his chin laid open and had to retire for a while – perhaps it was this experience that made him revise his ideas about fast leg theory – but Jardine stood up without flinching to everything they could fire at him, endured for five hours and made 127, his first century in a Test, which showed what courage and skill could do.

Wyatt had another dose of it at Edgbaston, but this time he retorted with 150 not out in Warwickshire's total of 367 for seven declared, and on the very same day he was chosen to lead England again owing to Jardine being injured. This time he led them to victory by an innings and 17 runs, largely due to brilliant slow bowling by C. S. Marriott, who, Wyatt said incidentally, once bowled him the best over ever sent down to him, beating him four times in the first five balls and getting him out with the sixth. Wyatt had decidedly the last word with the West Indies at the Scarborough Festival, making 108 and 83 against them.

That, with 136 not out for The Rest against the Champions, Yorkshire, was the climax to one of his best seasons; in it he made eight centuries, scored 2379 runs, 1742 for the county, and took fourth place in the national averages with 59·47. In his last seven innings he scored 584 runs at an average of over 145. It was, indeed, a remarkable summer for batsmen. Between May and the first two weeks in September no fewer than thirty-four totals of between 500 and 592 were amassed and there were only five totals under 50 all season. Warwickshire had two of over 500 against Worcestershire and Northants and one of 400 against Surrey; Santall hit a scintillating double century, Kilner just missed one with 197 and Wyatt had a 187 not out.

Despite Wyatt's success, Kilner was outstanding among the five Warwickshire batsmen who had four-figure aggregates. He made 2107 for the county alone, a Warwickshire record, including six centuries; but though he averaged nearly 48 Wyatt pipped him on the post with 51·35 in all Warwickshire matches. Parsons was able to play only three innings, in which he made 65, 130 and 3 not out, an indication of how useful his contribution could have been.

Paine was again the outstanding bowler, with 118 wickets, but Hollies, with seventy-nine, was coming on apace, and the annual report for 1933 described his bowling as 'a noteworthy feature of the attack'. Mayer was the only other bowler to take more than fifty wickets. Wyatt bowled only twenty overs in Championship matches. *Wisden* said he led the side well – they finished seventh, their best position for nineteen years – and set a fine example with his fielding which was not generally followed, but there was criticism of 'the tendency of several of the team to play "safe" cricket . . . there was never any doubt that the Warwickshire batsmen could get runs quickly when so minded; but they rarely exercised their talents in forcing the game. As the season advanced the impression grew that certain members of the eleven adopted a policy in which the avoidance of defeat was the first principle.'

There is a familiar ring about this – was not almost the same thing said about Quaife? – but even if Wyatt himself was not meant, it was certainly a reflection on his leadership. Perhaps it was taken to heart for the charge of cautious cricket could certainly not have been laid against them during the first match of the 1933 season against Worcestershire in which they had to get 280 in less than three hours. At tea they were well behind the clock, but Kilner, 102, Croom, 115, Wyatt and Paine all hit well, but with twenty minutes left 36 were still needed. Then Perks did the hat trick and it looked all over for Warwickshire, but Paine had one of those inspired rushes to the head which sometimes come off and hit Perks for 22 off one over – five fours and a two – and won the match with four minutes to spare.

Nor could anyone complain about Santall's batting at Northampton. In less than two hours before lunch he smashed his way to 173 – 50 out of 66 in forty-five minutes, 100 out of 132 in eighty minutes, 150 out of 201 in 110 minutes. Then he went on to make it 200 out of 297 in two and three-quarter hours. His 201, the highest score he ever made for the county, contained four sixes and twenty-four fours, and must rank as one of the fastest big innings ever played. He gave only one chance, a difficult one, at 173. Three of the Northants bowlers had over 100 runs hit off them, for Kilner and Croom also made centuries – they had put on 219 for the first wicket before Santall even appeared on the scene. Five centuries were made in the match, Bakewell and Timms hitting back for Northants.

Kilner's 197 was – of course – against his old county and it could not have been made at a more appropriate time for it was in reply to 205 by Sutcliffe and 124 by Barber. Despite a split finger he batted over six hours. Some more of the slow scoring *Wisden* had complained about occurred at Manchester where Warwickshire took six and three-quarter hours to make 279 – Kilner four hours for 84, Hill eighty minutes for 17 and Bates, of all people, ninety-five minutes for 27. Against Somerset Wyatt and Bates took four hours to put on 136, while against Glamorgan at Cardiff, Kilner was again the culprit with 145 in six and a half hours. Not even a hat trick by Paine could prevent the match being drawn.

'Danny' Mayer began his benefit against Sussex by bowling John Langridge for one – how pleasant it was to see the latter still umpiring in 1973 – but that was the limit of his success, Sussex scoring 457 for eight in reply to Warwickshire's 307, and he was unable to bowl in the second innings owing to an injury. A sum of just over £500 could hardly have seemed adequate recompense for all the perspiration he had poured out in Warwickshire's cause – he was always a tremendous trier.

In Wyatt's absences, Warwickshire for the first time for twenty years were led by a professional, Bates, who had charge of an all-professional side, whose success, however, was not reflected in the annual accounts, which showed a loss of £2259, though a special appeal by Sir Charles Hyde raised £1735. One result of this was that matches at Coventry, which cost £100 more to stage than those at Edgbaston, were discontinued for the time being, Dr Thwaite disclosing that the list of country members did not exceed 500 and that in certain towns they could not count on the support of more than a dozen, which caused him to fear, as well he might, that 'the sense of loyalty where Warwickshire cricket was concerned was not very strongly developed in the county'. They could only count on an income of £8000 whereas they needed £10 000 and unless further help was forthcoming the Club would have to be run on more modest lines. One form this took, unfortunately, was withdrawal from the Minor Counties competition in 1934, and the Committee even declined to go on paying the modest annual subscription of £2 10s 0d to that organisation. The services of three players were also dispensed with, though earlier in the year an attempt had been made to qualify by residence another 'schoolboy wonder', Cyril Washbrook, while he was at Bridgnorth Grammar School in Shropshire, where he was almost impossible to get out and who had also shown splendid form with Warwickshire II, making a century against Derbyshire II. At that time he was undecided as to whether he would go to Birmingham University and study chemistry, in which case he could have played for Warwickshire under a residential qualification, or take up cricket as a profession, in which case the only county for which he possessed a quali-fication was Lancashire where he was born. He finally plumped for cricket and played at once for his native county.

Warwickshire applied for a Test Match against South Africa in 1935, but it was declined and it was little consolation to be told by the Board of Control that 'the general arrangements at Birmingham left nothing to be desired'. The Board, however, felt that the financial returns would be better at Trent Bridge.

Wyatt had been invited to take a team to the West Indies during the winter of 1934–5 and was given permission to include some Warwickshire players if they were selected, but in view of what had hap-pened not long before and in the light of what was to come, it is a little strange to find the Committee providing him with an endowment policy entitling him in ten years to £1000, making, 'in view of your services to the Club, some provision for your future'. The letter to Wyatt inform-ing him of this added 'the hope that for many years there may be between yourself and them [the Committee] the friendliest possible spirit and co-operation for the beneficial working of the Club'. The letter was signed by Sir Charles Hyde, Bainbridge and Dr Thwaite.

Half-way Peak
(1934–1935)

NINETEEN THIRTY-FOUR might be described as the half-way peak between the two Championships of 1911 and 1951. It was certainly Wyatt's most successful year as captain, the county rising to fourth position in the table. Ten matches were won, more than in any other season since 1911. And this, despite the fact that he was recalled to captain England and had to miss several games because of a broken thumb; he played in only a dozen Championship matches and the side was variously led by Kemp-Welch, Partridge, Parsons and Bates. *Wisden* attributed the county's improvement to maintenance of batting strength and an improvement in bowling and fielding – 'a spirit of aiming for victory imbued the county players, a bigger appeal consequently being made to supporters'. Perhaps they had all been reading *Wisden* and taken its chidings to heart.

Did Wyatt, too, one wonders? Of his captaincy of England against the Australians – he missed the first Test because of his injured thumb, but led them to the first England victory at Lord's for thirty-eight years – the Editor of *Wisden* had this to say:

Without committing any personal blunder either in tactics or strategy, Wyatt, I am afraid, was not the ideal leader. It is difficult definitely to point out where he failed to fill the bill, but if a great trier himself, both as batsman and fielder, in what, after all was never a well-balanced eleven, he did not possess the essential attribute of a great captain in being able to inspire the men under him to a big effort.

Would it be inaccurate or unfair to add that, on the whole, this was also true of his leadership of Warwickshire?

Wyatt received his thumb injury, which must have been very painful, from a ball from Farnes in the Test trial and C. F. Walters, appearing in his first Test, took over. Wyatt played in the remaining Tests, though he must have found the thumb a handicap – he had a special shield made for it in Birmingham – but he scored only 135 runs with a highest score of 44. He will remember the series if for nothing other than the fact that he was the middle victim of O'Reilly's famous three-wickets-in-four-balls over at Old Trafford. Off the first ball after a break for refreshments Walters was caught at short leg; the second bowled Wyatt middle stump – S. J. Southerton in *Wisden* wrote that O'Reilly probably bowled no better ball the whole season than this – and Hammond glanced the next to the boundary and was clean bowled by the fourth.

The Australians scored heavily during the Tests, but when they came to Edgbaston they could manage no better total than 221, Paine taking four wickets. Warwickshire replied with 179, of which three men, Croom, Santall and young Cranmer, made 141 against Grimmett, who had five for 76. At their second attempt the Australians had got 185 for four by the close of the second day and there was no play on the third.

So far as Warwickshire were concerned, Wyatt's aggregate of runs was halved, but he still managed to head the averages with 47·75, Kemp-Welch made 123 not out against Glamorgan in the only match in which he was able to play and Cranmer, Collin, Buckingham, who took over the wicketkeeping from Smart, and Dollery all showed promising form. The annual report, indeed, waxed quite lyrical over the advent of Cranmer who was hailed as 'a new glory . . . whose prodigious hitting and activity in the field endeared him to the hearts of the regular habitués of the Edgbaston ground'.

The bowling, however, was still largely a one-man band called Paine, who, said *Wisden*, 'not only showed himself to be the most destructive left hander, but, indeed, the premier bowler of his type in the country'. He took no fewer than 156 wickets, thus beating Howell's record of 152, eleven years before, and he headed the averages for both country and county, the former an honour which eluded even Hollies. Three times he took twelve wickets in a match and he also scored 500 runs, including 51 and 39 not out against his old county, as well as eight wickets. This put him well in the all-rounder class.

There was one match especially he had cause to remember, that against Glamorgan which provided one of the most astonishing catches ever seen at Edgbaston. Hollies has described how after Paine had bowled all day without getting a wicket, T. L. Brierley, who had had to retire hurt earlier in the day, came back again as last man.

He drove a ball so hard back at Paine that he had no time to get out of the way, let alone catch it. The ball hit him on forehead and glanced off high into the air. Almost stunned, Paine fell to the ground and the other players moved to help him. But not Peter Cranmer. He had been fielding at extra cover and as the ball soared up he sprinted nearly twenty yards to mid-off, dived full length and caught it just before it touched the ground. By this time, Paine had largely lost interest in the affairs of this world, though he soon recovered to find that he had taken a wicket after all.

Mayer took eighty-eight wickets, but badly needed an opening partner of some pace, and Hollies nearly caught him up with eighty-four.

The season for Warwickshire opened with a sporting gesture of some note by A. E. R. Gilligan, the Sussex captain, who, when Warwickshire wanted only 14 to win with nearly an hour to play, led his men on to the field at Edgbaston in pouring rain until the runs had been obtained. The fifty spectators who had assembled in the hope of seeing a Warwickshire victory rose to the Sussex team as they came off the field and afterwards, in a letter referring to this match Gilligan wrote: 'I always like to think that cricket and Christianity are closely allied,' a sentiment Canon Parsons would approve even if most people would hardly see its relevance to that situation.

That same month at Edgbaston a young man named Hutton made his first appearance in a county Championship match for Yorkshire. He went in at No. five and 'showed sound form', making exactly 50 before being caught and bowled. Then he took the first three Warwickshire wickets to fall for 65 runs, but rain prevented him from having a second innings.

The return match at Scarborough provided Warwickshire with one of their finest wins. Parsons was captaining the side and shortly after they arrived several members of the team were standing on the sea front just as two holidaymakers, obviously Yorkshiremen, came by. They must have recognised some of the Warwickshire players for one of them remarked inhospitably, 'It's a pity we can't get a decent side up here instead of a poor crowd like you.'

Warwickshire, however, gave their friends from the promenade something to think about when they got Yorkshire out for 101, Paine taking eight for 62. But then Warwickshire spoiled it all by letting themselves be dismissed for their lowest score of the season, 45; only Buckingham, with 14 not out, reaching double figures. However, Paine then took another four wickets and Mayer and Hollies three each, so Yorkshire were out a second time for only 159 – and it would have been a much lower total if no fewer than five catches had not been dropped.

That left Warwickshire 216 to get on what had now become a difficult pitch. Yorkshire thought it would be a walk-over, but first Parsons and then Norman Kilner began to get some runs and soon those fieldsmen clustered round the batsman's wicket – the wicketkeeper, three slips and a fine leg – began 'nattering'. It became so bad that Parsons walked away from the wicket and told them: 'I wish you chaps would keep quiet.'

'Tak' no notice of t'bloody parson,' said one of the Yorkshire players and once again as the bowler prepared to run up to the wicket the talking broke out again. Again Parsons moved away and this time Brian Sellers, the Yorkshire captain, came up and asked him what was the matter. Parsons told him, but all Sellers said was, 'What can I do about it? You know what they are.'

'Well,' said Parsons, 'I got 94 and then had a bang and played on.' What he did not say was that his runs were made out of 121 added while he was at the wicket by superb driving – three sixes and twelve fours. Only 12 runs were needed when he was out and Warwickshire got them with one wicket still outstanding. The Yorkshire players, Parsons said, walked off the field without a word.

Two other Warwickshire players vividly remember that match. One of them was Tom Dollery, who was making his first appearance in the senior eleven. It was not an auspicious début. He made one and nought precisely and that single nearly ran out Parsons, which would have been a catastrophe indeed. The other player was Hollies, whose wicket was the one outstanding and whose young ears that afternoon heard words that he did not even know existed. Macaulay, in particular – as was his wont when things were going badly for Yorkshire – being full of oaths strange even to a Black Country lad.

Hollies says that when Mayer made the winning hit for four off Macaulay, the Yorkshire bowler, beside himself with rage, threw his cap on the ground and jumped on it. The story goes that when it was all over and the Warwickshire players were celebrating in the dressing-room, Hollies, still white and shaken, sat alone in a corner until someone noticed him and asked him how he'd liked facing Macaulay.

'It wor 'is bowlin' wot frit me,' said Eric, still the Black Country boy, 'it were 'is language. It were fearful. It's all over now, but I shor forget this day if I live to be thousands. I cor repeat wot 'e said. 'E come out wi' words I'd never 'eard at Old 'ill.'

Wyatt showed how much his stubbornness meant to Warwickshire when, against Worcestershire at Kidderminster on a wicket saturated with dew, Perks tore into their innings and took the first four wickets for 5 runs. Wyatt damaged a toe and had to retire, but with the score at 79 for seven he returned and made 68 not out, which enabled the Warwickshire total to reach 209. Then when Smart fractured a finger Wyatt kept wicket.

Before August was out Warwickshire had lost another old stalwart in Frank Field, who was probably unluckier even than Wyatt in the matter of injuries, though his were not from being hit. Had he been free of them it is certain that he would have taken many more than the 993 wickets with which he is credited for the county. He was not as consistent as Howell perhaps, but Foster, whose opening partner he was, rated him the best fast bowler in England in his day. He was certainly one of the greatest in heart.

George Paine in August had been offered a new three-year agreement with an increase of £40 a year, but he later clashed with the Committee over his choice of benefit match. Santall, Croom and Kilner were all ahead of him in the queue, so he thought he was justified in asking for the plum Bank Holiday match with Derbyshire in the fourth year of the agreement he sought, with a guarantee of £1000 and a summer wage of £9 a week instead of the £8 offered.

The Committee agreed, provided they had an option to continue the agreement for a further period of one, two or three years, but they jibbed at the Bank Holiday fixture and the guarantee. Paine replied that he did not think the proceeds from a benefit other than a Bank Holiday match would come up to his expectations and that, unless the Committee could offer him some alternative prospect of realising four figures, he would reluctantly be compelled to resign if he did not get a reply before he sailed for the West Indies tour, for which he had been chosen along with Hollies under Wyatt's leadership.

This put the Committee in some difficulty for they could not afford to lose their most effective bowler, and after considerable discussion it was agreed that the Bank Holiday match of 1938 should be set aside for the benefit. Paine got the Committee's letter agreeing to this on the morning he was due to sail.

It was not an outstandingly successful tour for any of the Warwickshire players, or for the team as a whole, for the West Indies, for the first time, won a rubber against us. *Wisden* did not think much of the team which, it said, could 'scarcely be regarded as representative of the full strength of England', though it included, besides the Warwickshire trio, E. R. T. Holmes, D. C. H. Townsend, Kenneth Farnes, W. E. Harbord, Hammond, Hendren, Leyland, Ames, Iddon, 'Big Jim' Smith and Farrimond. It was also dogged by injuries, and Wyatt made one or two controversial decisions for which he was criticised.

England won the first Test in which all three Warwickshire players took part, but lost two of the others and drew one. Wyatt and Paine were in the second and they were all in the third and fourth, but Wyatt's best score was 71, Paine's best performance was four for 168, while Hollies had seven for 50 in one innings. Nevertheless Hollies headed the Test averages with ten wickets for 21·7, Paine being fourth with seventeen for 27·47. In all matches Wyatt scored 386 runs and headed the bowling averages with eighteen wickets for 17·05, Paine took most wickets, forty for 23·92 and Hollies had thirty-six for 19·15.

The tour ended disastrously for Wyatt. Shortly after the start of England's first innings in the last Test, when he had made only a single, Wyatt, who had not been feeling well before he went in, was struck in

214

the face by a rising ball from Martindale which fractured his jaw in four places, as the X-ray revealed when he got back to England. Wyatt said afterwards that it was like being hit by a sledge-hammer and the pistol-shot noise of the bone breaking was heard even outside the ground. He was carried off the field unconscious with blood pouring from his mouth.

The next evening he should have spoken at a farewell dinner, so he sent Holmes as his deputy with a written message to Martindale saying it was a fair ball, not a bouncer, but short of a length and lifting quickly and that he attached no blame to Martindale for the mishap. The message, it is reported, brought tears to Martindale's eyes and he was there to see Wyatt off on the boat.

It was feared that Wyatt would be unable to play any serious cricket for a long time to come, but he recovered very quickly and he was soon in the thick of the battle again when he got home, this time against the South Africans. The accident had happened in mid-March; before May was out he had made a couple of centuries. The first ball of the season from Alf Gover missed his jaw by a couple of inches.

Bainbridge, at the annual meeting in March 1935, had the pleasant task, though he was a little early, of reminding members and the public that this was the Club's fiftieth year on the Edgbaston ground and it was something, he thought, to have kept the flag flying for fifty years. Cricket was not a game that was very remunerative and it seemed to him strange that a city like Birmingham, which had three magnificent football teams in its area, could not help one cricket team to be really flourishing financially. What a fine thing it would be if in this fiftieth year the city would re-equip the pavilion and stands and provide something as good as any other county possessed. What, the members might well have sighed, a hope.

Dr Thwaite revealed that the visit of the Australians had been worth £2560 to the Club – £1518 from the Test Match Pool and £1041 from the match with the county – but either expenditure must be cut by about £1000 a year, or the income must be increased by the same amount. Warwickshire's membership in a glorious summer had increased by very little. Lancashire's last year produced £9250, but never in its history had Warwickshire reached £5000. When he reflected on the size of the population of Birmingham he found it difficult to explain this difference, but it had always been the same. Only a small percentage of members had contributed to the £600, promised or paid, for the Nursery Fund.

Some notable tributes were paid to Ryder at the annual meeting and later in the year a testimonial fund was launched for him with a donation from the Club of 100 guineas. In all the appeal realised £1608.

One of cricket's most controversial changes, which is still argued about, came into effect this year – the change in the lbw law:

215

The striker is out lbw if, with any part of his person (except his hand) which is between wicket and wicket, he intercept a ball which, in the opinion of the umpire at the bowler's wicket, shall have been pitched on the off-side of the striker's wicket and would have hit it.

It was widely believed that Bradman was the instigator of the change and that it largely arose because of the discomfiture to which fast leg theory had subjected Australian batsmen, the idea being, presumably, that if bowlers were given an incentive to pitch the ball on or outside the off stump they would be less tempted to bowl it at or outside the leg stump, and also in the hope that it would tempt batsmen into playing more off-side shots, which have always been among the most attractive in the game.

There were many critics of the change, Wyatt among them, and he has not changed his view that it did untold harm to the game, particularly in this country, by making defensive bowling so much easier, and that the only way to brighten up the game is to encourage aggressive bowling which gives the good player the opportunities of making more strokes.

Oddly enough, however, both Wyatt and Sutcliffe, who was also among the critics, made more runs under the new rule than they had done in the previous season. In 1934 Wyatt made 1776 runs and finished fifteenth in the first-class averages; in 1935 he scored 2019 runs and was fifth, while Sutcliffe rose from seventeenth place to second. Many other factors, of course, affected their scoring.

Despite his failures in the West Indies, Wyatt was again chosen to captain England against South Africa, though it was the last series in which he did so. South Africa won a Test in England for the first time and it was enough to give them the rubber in a series in which four games were drawn.

Again Wyatt was unlucky with injuries to players, though he himself escaped this time, but once more he was concerned in a controversial decision when, in the final Test, which England had to win to tie the series, he sent South Africa in to bat on a perfect Oval wicket – 'probably the most daring [course of action] ever adopted in Test cricket', as *Wisden* described it. The gamble did not succeed, for South Africa made 476 and even though England topped this with 534 for six declared it did not help. *Wisden* also pertinently pointed out that in sixteen months we had lost in rapid succession the honours against Australia, the West Indies and South Africa. Wyatt was captain in ten of those games, so it is not really surprising that, justifiably or not, he gained a reputation as an unlucky captain. His own contribution in the series was 317 runs for an average of 45·28.

The South Africans also won by an innings at Edgbaston, where Warwickshire were hindered by a strain Hollies suffered late on the first

216

day, so that he was unable to take any further part in the game. The tourists made 498, and with Crisp taking five wickets in each innings for a total of only 67 runs, Warwickshire were out for 221 and 103. One of the most remarkable catches ever seen at Edgbaston was taken in this match. Vincent hit a terrific drive into the covers where Collin managed to half stop it. The ball flew into the air and Collin caught it as he fell with his hands behind his back. Vincent was half-way down the pitch for a run when the catch was completed and he stopped, put down his bat and led the applause.

For a time Warwickshire were challenging Yorkshire for the Championship, but after Croom broke a finger in the August Bank Holiday match there was a slump and they finished eighth, a drop of four places. There was no complaint this season that they played unattractive cricket. *Wisden*, in fact, went to the other extreme and commented that 'often their lack of restraint brought disaster, only the soundness of Wyatt preventing a complete collapse'. He might well have been driven to reflect that, where cricket commentators are concerned, one cannot win. He never lost his form and headed the county averages for the fourth year in succession.

But the most hopeful factor for the future was that both Hollies and Dollery 'arrived', as they say of racehorses. Dollery hit a century in the first county match of the season, won his cap and went on to an aggregate of over 1000 runs, compared with 181 the previous summer, an improvement in form which led many judges to hail him as the most promising batsman in the country. That first hundred was one of four made in the match with Gloucestershire, three of them being for Warwickshire, and one of them was another 'first' – to Collin. Together they put on 199 for the sixth wicket.

Hollies 'improved by leaps and bounds' in *Wisden*'s phrase and headed the county's averages for the first time with 127 wickets for only 18·91 runs. Paine, who, on his return from the West Indies, had suffered from rheumatic troubles and also had his tonsils removed, was far from being at his best and lost some of his spin and skill in flighting the ball, though he still got his hundred wickets. So Warwickshire had two bowlers with over that total, for the first time for many a summer.

Hollies's form was good enough to win him selection for the third Test at Leeds, but he was deprived of his chance by a curious mishap, the full story of which has not been told, except privately, to this day. Warwickshire were playing Glamorgan at Swansea and one night after Hollies had gone to bed another Warwickshire player entered his room in error and fell on his bed. The jolt shook Hollies so violently that his neck was badly ricked and he had to cry off.

Understandably, P. F. Warner, chairman of the Selection Committee, wanted to know exactly what had happened and the Warwickshire

Committee held an inquiry. 'The result of the investigations,' it was reported, to them afterwards, 'had not disclosed any reasons for any serious action and Mr Bainbridge had written suitably to Mr Warner. In sympathy with Hollies, it was decided to pay him £8, the amount of a home match fee.'

Hollies never disclosed who the other player was, or discussed the incident, and this was all he had to say about it in his book:*

I had gone to bed early after a long day of bowling. Later on one of the team, who had the room adjoining mine, mistook the door on coming up to bed and came into my room. He did not put the wall light on, obviously intending to use the bed light, and flopped down on to the bed. I was sound asleep at the time and the sudden shock of the player dropping on me made me jerk up from the pillow. In doing so I severely injured my neck, which I believe was wrenched out of place. I spent an agonising night, unable to move my neck and head from their strange position almost against one shoulder. Next morning Bob Wyatt took me to the local hospital for treatment, but it was no good. Instead of travelling to Leeds with the skipper I had to go back to Birmingham for further treatment. I was terribly disappointed at the time for I was only 23 and I felt that so much might have depended on that Test.

It might indeed. It was the first of several mishaps that kept Hollies from playing in Tests and he did not make his début in England until 1947. Wyatt, in his book, refers to 'some playful game with Santall', but it was far from a game for Hollies who felt the effects of the injury for a long time afterwards, though if he did feel any resentment he characteristically did not show it.

Wisden may have absolved Wyatt from slow play, but the Northampton crowd certainly did not do so in June. Warwickshire were in danger of collapse, but Wyatt dug his heels in as only he could, and the crowd showed its displeasure by barracking. Hollies, who was last man in as usual, says that three times Wyatt stepped away from the wicket because of the noise as Clark ran up to bowl and three times he hit the stumps, which only made matters worse.

Eventually the umpires and Northants officials pacified them and this time, when Clark resumed bowling, his first ball knocked out Wyatt's middle stump, much to the crowd's delight. By then, however, he had made 98 and had carried Warwickshire's total to 206. In terrific heat on the Monday, Paine bowled fifty-two overs and took seven for 99, a strange contrast with The Oval in May when it was so cold that beef tea was taken out to the players.

Santall had his benefit in July against Sussex, but he made only 9 and 12 and although rain cut short play on the Saturday Sussex won by eight wickets. The benefit was more productive – just over £700.

*I'll Spin You A Tale

At the end of the season Len Bates, the senior professional, retired from first-class cricket after twenty years of notable service to Warwickshire, during which he had delighted thousands by the artistry of his batting. He was appointed head coach and groundsman at Christ's Hospital, Horsham, where he spent twenty-seven happy years. In later years, however, his legs gave him trouble and he had first one leg and then the other amputated, afflictions which he bore with both courage and cheerfulness.

I had hoped to go and see him before writing this history, but it was not possible. Fortunately I found that a former colleague, Claude Westell, who had seen him play for Warwickshire, lived only a few miles away in another Sussex village. What happier arrangement than to ask him to go and see again and talk with someone he had always admired both as a man and as a cricketer? So it was arranged and this was the account he sent of their meeting:

Given two people who are really cricket-hearted, cricket, I firmly believe, can and will be talked about in any place at any time. There are, however, some places, some moments, that are obviously more favourable than others and sometimes by a rare stroke of good fortune one finds 'the time and the place and the loved one' all together.

Such was my happy experience when I set out from Storrington [the Tillingfold of Hugh de Selincourt's classic *The Cricket Match*] for Coldwaltham, some four miles distant. Our meeting was to mean the fording of near on forty years of time and more than 160 miles of country between the Midlands and West Sussex.

The afternoon was cloudless and warm, an afternoon for cricketers, redolent with memories of the graces that the game had brought. Coldwaltham is one of those villages still happily to be found which has escaped from the menace of wide-scale, wildcat, indiscriminate 'planning' and expansion. It lies at the foot of the Downs on the line of the ancient Stane Street and it remains virtually unspoiled.

The setting for this 'sweet remembrance of things past' could not have been fairer or more peaceful. We sat in the sunny lounge of the bungalow in Arun Vale where my host had greeted me from the wheel-chair in which he was fated to spend so much of the later years of his retirement. As we talked we looked out on the long line of Downland from Chanctonbury Ring to Bury Hill against a background of blue sky, the quiet broken only by the sound of our voices and the tinkle of the cups during the tea interval, which was timed with the perfection one would expect from a cricketer's wife with a long line of teacups, cakes, sandwiches and hungry men stretching back into the past.

Edmund Blunden, in his *Cricket Country*, has told us that he has heard it proposed that cricket 'the ever changeful, changeless game which some, even among the English, view as the prime English eccentricity, is a something to which, for thorough appreciation, a man must have been bred from the cradle, or about there'. If so it be, then Len Bates qualified without question, for he was born within the very gates of the Edgbaston ground in a committee room lying below the bell tower in which was hung the bell that was sounded to give due notice that play was soon to start – 'a happy sound to hear'.

That was a far different Edgbaston from today's imposing arena, with its stately pleasure domes and all mod. cons. As a gathering place for those who watched the game in 1895 the ground may have been primitive and uncomfortable by comparison with today, but the Club had every cause for satisfaction that the wickets prepared by Bates senior and his staff were of high quality.

Bates was eager to talk about those early days and I just as eager to listen. When he told me how for sixteen years he enjoyed the freedom of Edgbaston, came to love every inch of its turf and to know the Warwickshire players as friends as well as heroes, I was able to understand what an important influence Edgbaston had been in moulding his future as an accomplished performer, a devout votary and, in the mellowing years, a trusted and efficient coach at a famous public school and – like his father – an expert groundsman.

In his early days he became his father's willing helper and his first job on match days was to put on the horses' boots, those protective leather coverings which were worn by the animals to protect the turf from the metal shoes. This labour of love was carried out at four in the morning and was, in due time, combined with others on and about the ground so that he was gradually introduced to the craft of groundsmanship. On playing days the boy would, as he now put it, 'devour' the cricket which went on so near at hand. 'I never missed a ball from the start of play to the drawing of stumps,' he said.

There were further new delights for the lad as he grew older and was allowed to join the Warwickshire players at their practice and he still remembers with what glowing contentment he would turn in to bed after a session when Charlesworth, one of the earliest of his heroes, had bowled to him until darkness had begun to fall. Even at that stage he was no complete neophyte for, from the age of 6, his father had made a regular practice of bowling to him his lobs on the cinder path surrounding the playing area, or the gravelled one which led to the groundsman's living quarters.

In these salad days he was never allowed, as were his friends, to use a boy's bat. When he faced the bowling of his father, or the members of the Warwickshire staff, he defended his wicket and learned the appropriate attacking strokes, with a discarded Club bat cut down to size by the removal of six inches or so from the bottom of the blade. This doubtless had its compensations. What young batsman would not have been thrilled to the core by the thought that the bat he was holding had been in the hands of Quaife, Kinneir, Charlesworth or even the skipper, Frank Foster, and that it may have yielded runs galore in county matches?

At 16 he would be there at the nets bowling to members from two to four in the afternoon and again from six till dusk. 'It was bowl, bowl, bowl and when I wasn't bowling I was helping my father on the ground, repairing the turf or tending the wicket.' In 1913 at the age of 18, Len, having taken part the previous season in some Club and Ground fixtures, made his first-class début against Sussex and in the week following played an undistinguished part in the remarkable match at Tonbridge when Blythe and Woolley skittled

Warwickshire for 16. By some mischance it was recorded in the score book that it was 'S.H.' – the elder brother who was not playing in this game – and not 'L.A.' who was 'not out 0' in Warwickshire's unproductive innings, so that the fledgling was denied the credit of a mention even in *Wisden* where the error was perpetuated.

At the height of the following summer came the war which robbed Bates, as it did many another cricketer, of some valuable playing years. At the age of 19 he joined his county regiment with which he served throughout the war, fought in both the Somme battles and came through unscathed. During those five years he never handled a bat* and he still muses a little wistfully, but with no trace of bitterness, on how his career as a cricketer might have shaped had it not been so ruthlessly curtailed.

The spring of 1919 found him back at his green birthplace, a refreshing sight after the mud of Flanders. He was not long in giving proof that despite those barren years he was worthy of his place and the return of the native was marked that summer by two centuries. He and W. G. Quaife were the only members of the team to score their thousand runs or so, and as time moved on he developed into a proved member of the side and a stylish and often aggressive run maker.

The legend has been handed down that on a torrid afternoon at Edgbaston when the Warwickshire bowlers and fielders sweated profusely a wicket fell at last and Bates, who, as usual in those days, was fielding out in the country, lay down to rest and fell asleep. He was still recumbent and somnolent when the new batsman arrived in the middle and took guard. Calthorpe, his captain, so it is said, turned in despair to Wyatt and said, 'What can you do with a chap like that?' to which Wyatt responded: 'Why don't you put him at cover? He won't be able to fall asleep there.' So Bates was posted to cover point – and became one of the best fielders in that position Warwickshire ever had.

Bates's version is a little different. 'We were playing the South Africans,' he said. 'It is perfectly true that I was only too glad to lie down at the fall of that wicket for it was blazing hot and I had had a rare lot of running about, but I did not fall asleep though I didn't hurry to get up when the batsman came in. I was certainly not moved to cover. I was put on to bowl and in my first over I got Blanckenberg's wicket, caught by Norman Kilner in the slips. Willie Quaife invariably fielded at cover in those days and a very fine cover he was. No captain would have thought of replacing him. It wasn't until Quaife's retirement at the end of 1928 that I took over that position.'

It was during the twenties that I first began to watch and to admire Bates's batting. He was then probably at his best – cool, competent and often sparkling. I particularly remembered an innings he played against Notts at Coventry when after Warwickshire had lost four wickets for 40 in less than an hour Bates strolled out and scored 50 in thirty-five minutes, hitting Sam Staples four times for six, twice out of the ground, eventually reaching 73 in seventy minutes.

'Yes', said Bates wistfully, 'I used sometimes to do that sort of thing,' and he went on to tell me how he once got himself out playing an adventurous stroke and Patsy Hendren said to him, 'You know, Len, you have too many

*Except for a few games in 1915.

strokes,' meaning, of course, that he would have made many more runs had he been more cautious and adopted the technique of the artisan rather than the artist.

After Len's retirement as coach at Christ's Hospital, handsome tribute to his virtues as cricketer, coach and friend was paid in the school magazine *The Blue*.* This was written by D. R. W. Silk, one of the young cricketers whom he watched over and guided and who after leaving school proved the value of the coaching he had received. Silk was a Cambridge Blue and captain in 1955, played for Somerset and had charge of two M.C.C. touring sides and he was enthusiastic in his praise of his mentor and friend of his school playing days.

Dennis Silk's article contained many schoolboy memories of Len which bring home to one his complete immersion in the game he so loved: Len in his home at Horsham with half a dozen senior members of the eleven sharing one of Mrs Bates's gargantuan spreads and the host ruminatively fingering an orange and muttering, 'You know, I think I could get this to move a bit in the air if the wind was coming from Chelshams'; Len's struggle with the absurd requirements of the school as he says thoughtfully of a promising cricketer, 'You know, if I could have that boy just two hours in the morning and he could play all the afternoon every day, I could make him into a cricketer before he was twenty-two,' and then, as if a sudden thought had struck him, 'But then, of course, I suppose there's his schooling'; and there was the delicious comment he wrote to Silk after they had spent two days at Lord's: 'That place breathes cricket – I daresay the pigeons lay eggs with seams on them.'

Bates needed no coaxing – does any old timer? – to give his views on cricket then and now and the changes that had come about in his time. He was firm in his belief that there was not enough off-side cricket today and far too much faith was being placed in the seam bowlers at the sacrifice of the slow spinners. This had led to strokes being severely limited and batsmen being driven to either unimaginative and stubborn inaction, or reckless, unscientific slogging. 'How often do you see a batsman attempting a late cut nowadays?' he asked; 'yet once it was a profitable stroke, good to make and good to watch.'

A reform he believed would be for the good of the game would be to restrict bowlers to a run-up of eighteen yards, and, like so many of us, he was by no means happy about the growth of one-day restricted-over competitions. These he believed were an encouragement to the quick-runs-at-all-costs spirit and were eliminating the finer points of the game. 'Instant cricket' was proving a deterrent to the spin bowler and placing a false value on negative seam bowling.

'I think it would be a sad day for cricket if ever this one-day scramble for runs, which admittedly is drawing the crowds and bringing in much-needed money, were to replace entirely the three-day county matches which have become so essential to our cricket pattern. Maybe room can be found for the two styles, but I do so hope that the old will not be shelved.'

I asked which of the cricketers with whom he had played had most impressed

*It was reproduced in the Warwickshire Club's annual report in 1963.

him and without a second's hesitation he answered 'Willie Quaife. He was the most correct batsman I have known. He was a great influence for good during my formative years and a model for any young cricketer. Though he was small, his faultless footwork and perfect timing more than made up for his lack of inches.' When I asked him to nominate the best captain under whom he had played, he hesitated, thought for a moment and then chose Frank Foster because he was firm, knew his own mind and stood by his decisions. He had control of his team and of a situation and was never afraid to take a chance when it came to declaring. Wyatt was a sound captain, but a cautious one. He lacked Foster's spirit of adventure and was disinclined to take risks. As a batsman he was highly concentrative. After a long term in the middle he could go back over the innings some time after it had ended and give a detailed account of every stroke and every ball.

Recalling matches in which he had played, he said that in the famous Hampshire game of 1922 he was fielding at deep fine leg and just failed to cut off those four byes. When Quaife was tossing up his slows with a high trajectory Brown at the bowler's end would be calling out advice to his partner as to how he should play every ball – and the message was arriving in good time, too.

I asked him which of his innings had brought him most satisfaction and he quoted two. First, there was his highest, the 211 against Gloucestershire when he hit six sixes and twenty-four fours and the last of the sixes which took him from 196 past the 200 mark was the sweetest of all. The other innings of which he was most proud was his 50 not out on a real 'sticky dog' at Hull. When Len at a vital point in his innings audaciously tried to late cut Macaulay and sent the ball soaring high over the heads of the slips, Mac slowly walked the length of the wicket to within a yard of Bates and said: 'You know, Len, there's one thing I do like about you. You do give the lads a chance.'

Bates was 40 when his first-class career ended. In his fifteen seasons as a regular member of the county eleven he scored 19 304 runs, including eighteen centuries and he had topped the thousand in a season twelve times. Among the players who passed through his hands at Christ's Hospital and reached county standard were Jeff Smith (Kent) and Jack Bailey (Essex), but his star pupil was John Snow, for whose early training his coach must have full credit. He it was who urged Snow to bowl the ball that leaves the right-handed batsman and he also saw his possibilities as a batsman and dropped the hint to Arthur Gilligan.

Len's days as coach at Christ's Hospital came to an end in 1962 when his legs began to give him trouble. During the first two years of his retirement they became worse – he had used them well in the service of cricket, too well maybe – and he was found to be suffering from hardening of the arteries. An operation which it was hoped would clear them of the secretions was performed at Guy's Hospital. But when the patient came round from the anaesthetic he learned that amputation was deemed necessary first of one leg and then, with the danger of gangrene setting in, of the other. That was why he greeted me six years later from a wheel-chair.

He told me he was hoping soon to be ready for the artificial limbs that would free him from the chair. Before he was incapacitated he had raised from seed in his new garden a level, weed-free lawn worthy of a cricketer and an expert groundsman. 'Cabin'd, cribb'd, confin'd, bound-in' as he had been since his return from hospital, he had continued to tend it so that it evoked the admiration and envy of his neighbours. He told me, too, that he had taken up painting and had done some landscapes in water-colour, though he had had no tuition since he was a schoolboy and he joined an art class in the district.

I had had some misgivings at going to see him lest I caused him any embarrassment, but I need have had no such fear. He spoke briefly, calmly and without a trace of bitterness or self-pity of his operations and their aftermath and I knew that heavy though his burden he was proving more than equal to the challenge. He was still 'playing pretty', as he always did because he could and would do no other.

As I made my way down the path past that smooth, weedless lawn to the waiting car and turned to see Len waving a smiling farewell from his chair in the window, the feeling that rose above all others that the afternoon had brought was one of gratitude and pride that I should have been given the privilege of meeting so fine a cricketing character. And as I was borne back to Tillingfold in the softening light, though we were passing through gracious Sussex countryside, my thoughts were in the Midlands and at Edgbaston, the Edgbaston of faraway days. I thought of the infant looking out from the room beneath the bell tower on that brave new world of green which had become his heritage and I hoped, oh so dearly, that Warwickshire, the nurse who had cradled him, reared him and fitted him for the game of cricket and the game of life, would be remembering him as proudly as he remembered her.

Dropping the Pilot
(1936–1939)

ANOTHER member of the Club, long in service, became less active at the beginning of 1936: J. F. Byrne resigned from the Committee as he found it impossible to attend meetings. He was elected a vice-president and was succeeded on the Committee by Edmund H. King, who thus began a distinguished administrative association with the Club which led not only to the chairmanship but to an influential and respected position in the game at large.

In view of what had happened on the question of the captaincy, members of the Committee must have been pleased to hear Wyatt say at the annual meeting that his greatest ambition was to lead Warwickshire to the head of the Championship table and that he would rather achieve that feat than captain England again, which, in fact, he was never to do.

During July, fifty years after the opening match on the ground, the President entertained the Committee and a few friends to celebrate both that anniversary and Bainbridge's continuous service to the Club during the whole of that period. On 9 October at a lunch attended by about 150 guests, including the Lord Mayor, Alderman Harold Roberts, Lord Cobham, past and present players and active supporters, there was a presentation of antique silver to Bainbridge to mark his fifty years as player, captain, adviser, honorary secretary and chairman.

Viscount Cobham proposed the toast of the Club, the same toast his father had proposed at the dinner to celebrate the winning of the Championship, and recalled when he and his brothers used to cycle from Hagley Hall to watch matches at Edgbaston (several miles away). He also remembered a white cricket ball being tried – Warwickshire were ever willing to experiment.

Sir Charles Hyde made the presentations and, good businessman that he was, also took the opportunity to appeal 'for buns for an impoverished bear'. Later in the year the bear got them in the form of £5336 which wiped out the accumulated deficit of £3025, leaving cash assets of £2500, a much happier state to be in.

But if there were many things to celebrate on the administrative side, there were none from a playing point of view, for Warwickshire had one of their worst seasons since the war, with not a single home win. The Club slipped five places down to thirteenth in the Championship table which, for a welcome change from the ever-winning Yorkshire, was headed by a Midland county, Derbyshire, who did not lose a match. *Wisden* gave three principal reasons for Warwickshire's failings – the decline of the batting in general and in particular of Wyatt, who only just reached 1000 runs for the county, though he made three centuries and still headed the averages. He played better towards the end of the season and, somewhat luckily, made the M.C.C. team which went out to Australia.

Wisden commented that Wyatt,

went through one of those periods which come to all great batsmen at one time or another, and it was to Wyatt's credit that he did not allow his failures to upset him unduly. Indeed, with the characteristic grimness which he revealed in his batting, Wyatt fought back so well that he finished the season in fine style ... But Wyatt's decline left Warwickshire with a problem which was never solved until the captain himself regained his full powers. The other batsmen, most of them free scorers, had come to rely upon him to save them from disaster and when that occurred there was no one able to retrieve matters.

Dollery was the only other batsman to score over 1000 runs; Croom, in his benefit year, unfortunately failed for the first time since 1927 to reach that aggregate; and twelve times the side was dismissed for under 150 and only twice scored more than 300. There was also a falling-off in the bowling. Paine was absent two months owing to illness and took only thirty wickets. No bowler took one hundred, Mayer being nearest with eighty-four, and Hollies getting only seventy-nine. *Wisden* said he tried to bowl more quickly and sacrificed flight, which suggests that he had been used largely as a stock bowler with instructions to keep the runs down.

At the beginning of the season it had been announced that Warwickshire had decided for the coming year to dispense with complete covering of the wicket except in three matches – Croom's benefit and the two games of the August Bank Holiday week. The change, it seems, was prompted by the success of an absorbent roller, though Dr Thwaite, who made the announcement, had to admit that one could not overlook the fact that a match fought out on a rain-damaged wicket was much more likely to produce thrills than when the pitch was easy and full of runs.

Warwickshire, in fact, had taken a leading part in making protection of wickets permissible. As long before as 1910 the county had presented a resolution, which had been passed by the secretaries' conference to the Advisory Committee, for protection of the ends of the wicket. It was withdrawn in favour of one slightly different, which was approved and this was the practice until 1924 when, in the autumn following a very wet summer, Warwickshire submitted arguments in favour of complete covering and eventually counties were given permission to do this.

Alas, neither covering nor absorbent rollers were able to prevent Croom's benefit against Sussex being ruined by rain. The poor man had the mortification of seeing two Sussex batsman make hundreds, but not even getting a chance to bat himself. Nevertheless, thanks to other efforts, the benefit realised £679, so it could have been much worse.

Warwickshire took part in another benefit – against Leicestershire – which produced one of the most exciting matches they had played in for years. It was George Geary's and he had the benefit at Hinckley that a bowler dreams about and dreads – to do well, but not so well that the match is over too soon and is a financial failure. Geary had the best of both worlds.

Warwickshire were sent in to bat, perhaps because there was a worn patch at one end on which Geary dropped the ball so accurately that the Chinese water torture would probably have seemed a more pleasant alternative to the batsmen. Thanks, however, to Croom, who, for the fourth time in his career, batted through, this time for 69, the first innings struggled to a total of 133, Geary finishing with six for 36.

When Leicestershire batted he was top scorer with 25, Leicestershire falling 25 runs behind, but then in Warwickshire's second innings Geary returned the sort of figures which makes one convinced the printer has dropped the type and gathered it up anyhow:

O	M	R	W
13·3	8	7	7

It was, of course, the best bowling performance of the season and Warwickshire were all out for 78. Leicestershire had to get 104 to win and when their ninth wicket fell they were still 11 runs short. It would be the perfect story-book ending to say that Geary hit them off, but in fact, it was Leicestershire's New Zealander, C. S. Dempster, who drove Mayer for a noble six – and that took some doing – and then made the winning hit. Wonderful cricket – and Warwickshire's bowlers did not come too badly out of it either; Hollies had ten for 58 in the match and Mayer seven for 54.

Warwickshire and Gloucestershire met in a match at Bristol this season which was to have far-reaching consequences for the Club and its captain. Gloucestershire batted first on a very slow wicket and painstakingly made 453 for eight declared. Warwickshire, after a good start, collapsed and were all out 169. They followed on 284 behind, faced with two alternatives – to go down fighting, or to try to save the game by stubborn defiance.

To a man of Wyatt's temperament, there was only one answer. He himself batted two hours and quarter for 25 and Dollery stayed ninety minutes for seven runs. When I read these latter figures I could hardly believe them, but, as I suspected, Dollery was batting under orders – 'I was told not to hit the ball past silly mid-on, or silly mid-off,' he said. The reason, as Wyatt explained when asked about it, was that the wicket had gone to pieces and the bounce of the ball was so uneven that a forcing stroke in front of the wicket, particularly to an off-spinner such as Goddard, was likely to prove fatal. But the dour struggle was in vain. Despite the caution, Warwickshire were all out for 167, beaten by an innings and 117 runs and one is left asking, as members of the Committee asked, whether it would not have been better to have gone out in a do-or-die blaze of glory.

What, one wonders in the light of subsequent events, would have been the Committee's reaction to such a finish, or to a hardly-won draw? It certainly did not like what happened, and in July Wyatt received a letter signed by Bainbridge, which he described in his book as 'one of the strangest ever sent by a county Committee to a captain of a county side'.

'The Committee', he wrote, 'seemed to put our failure down to my management of the team both on and off the field, apparently ignoring the fact that under my captaincy Warwickshire had risen from nearly bottom in the table to the highest they had been since before the 1914 war. The Committee said I hadn't given enough encouragement to the younger players, nor taken an interest in their development.'

The Committee, Wyatt felt, seemed to think that somehow he should be able to inspire the team to be better players than they were, and it was particularly discouraging to him to get such a letter at a time when he was more than usually off form himself and needed a bit of bucking up, though it was his first bad run since he had been in first-class cricket.

Wyatt immediately wrote to the chairman saying that it seemed clear the Committee had been misinformed about his attitude and asking to see them at once so as to discuss the matter thoroughly. He was very surprised to receive a reply saying there was no point in his meeting the Committee, as there would be no use in discussing the matter at all. Further, the chairman bluntly suggested that he should think less of his personal success and more of the county, a comment which Wyatt thought, to put it mildly, was 'insulting'.

To write so critical a letter and then refuse to hear what the captain might have to say may at first sight seem to argue both closed minds and high-handedness on the part of the Committee, though by this time, surely, Wyatt must have had many opportunities of making his views and his playing policy clear to them. On the question of young players, it must always be difficult for a captain, playing in matches all the season, many of them away from home, to keep an eye on any not playing in the first eleven, or to see second-eleven matches, though Wyatt says he usually made a point of watching players in the nets when he went to practise himself before the day's play. On the other hand, it was unfortunate, from Wyatt's point of view, that young players were often engaged in the winter months when he was usually touring abroad, or at trials when he was engaged in match play.

The leading young players in the county side at the time were Hollies, Dollery and Wilmot, 'all of them loyal friends of mine and very appreciative of help and advice', he said. Hollies has gone on record in his book as saying that Wyatt 'was ready to help any young player who was keen and eager and willing to help himself, but he had no time for the easy-going, lackadaisical type of player'. Hollies wrote that he would always count himself fortunate that when he was trying to win a place in county cricket Wyatt should have been his captain. He added that he played under four captains with Warwickshire and Wyatt was 'without doubt the finest'.

Writing of Wyatt's remarkable cricket knowledge, Hollies says he 'knew the strength and weakness of every batsman, all the shots he was capable of playing and his natural strokes. I have seen him place the field for an incoming batsman almost before he reached the wicket. Wyatt', he added, 'simply lived cricket.' And when Wyatt eventually relinquished the captaincy Hollies's father wrote thanking him for the help and advice he had given to his son 'which, I am sure, has been the chief cause of any success he has achieved in the cricket world'.

Wyatt says that during the whole of his career with Warwickshire he was asked to look at only two players with a view to them being taken on the staff 'My knowledge of the game', he added, 'was apparently of no value to the county Club, so it must have been a surprise that I was appointed at a later date Chairman of the Selectors!' There is, of course, a considerable difference in Test Match selection and finding new material.

He was not in favour with the selectors, however, as a captain in 1936. India were here and G. O. Allen was appointed captain for the first time. Wyatt got 55 against them for the M.C.C. at Lord's in May, but in the first Test he was out for nought in the only innings he had and he was left out of the side for the second and third Tests. The match against the tourists at Edgbaston was spoiled by rain, but he made a further 57 against them. He was out of luck in Australia. In the third match of the tour, which he had opened with a century, a bone in his left wrist was fractured by a ball from MacKay and he missed the first three Tests. He played in the fourth and fifth and scored 100 runs. In all three-day matches he scored 785 runs – Hammond and Barnett each topped 1000 – and he was third in the averages.

There were many losses by death this year. They included Calthorpe, at the tragically early age of 43; John Bates, the former head grounds-man; and Fred Collishaw, who played in the first match at Edgbaston. Calthorpe had been one of the best amateur all-rounders of the day, good enough to lead an M.C.C. team on a tour abroad and to take over 500 wickets for Warwickshire and score 8311 runs. Though he was not one of the most dynamic or successful of captains, he left many happy memories of his days at Edgbaston. So, too, did Bates, head groundsman from 1888 until until 1912 and creator of some of the finest batting wickets in England, whose advice was sought by many other counties.

And 1937 had barely begun before there was news of the death of a colourful athletic figure in Howard Vaughton. Elected to the Commit-tee in 1899, he served continuously until 1933 when he was elected a vice-president. He was a member of the executive and chairman of the ground committee for many years and in his younger days had been a very versatile athlete. He played cricket against the Australians in 1880, in 1882 he represented England at Association Football and in 1887 he helped Aston Villa to win the F.A. Cup for the first time. He was also a cyclist, sprinter, skater and hockey player.

The opening of 1937 – the 150th anniversary of the M.C.C. – was marked by the first of the many munificent gifts which Dr Thwaite was to lavish on the Club – a new scoreboard, which was accepted, to quote Bainbridge, 'with enormous gratification', and opened the following season. Not to be outdone by her husband, Mrs Thwaite presented the clock and weathervane for it and later some new seating for the ladies' enclosure.

Unhappily there were some financial clouds about. Despite the special appeal, Warwickshire's accounts showed a loss on the previous year of nearly £2000. The Leicestershire Club was reported to be in a parlous condition, but fortunately an appeal made it possible for them to carry on. Again Warwickshire took the lead in a matter which affected every county – a proposal that the whole question of county cricket finance should be examined by a non-partisan commission with the object of preparing a scheme for acceptance by all the counties; that the M.C.C. be invited to appoint three commissioners to undertake a thorough investigation of the counties' problems with the special aim of assisting the weaker ones; and that funds up to £500 be provided to cover the expenses of the inquiry, this to be a first charge on the Test Match account. The proposal was unanimously adopted, led to the first of many inquiries made during the years to follow into the state of cricket, and ultimately to the Findlay Report.

The President, Sir Charles Hyde, followed this up at the annual meeting with a solemn warning that unless play in the first-class game was brightened up the future of the county clubs would be endangered.

Let all those guilty of slow cricket be forgiven [he said], but not after this season. The weather and the Test Matches will never keep cricket clubs going if they do not give the public attractive cricket. The public is sick of watching some of the deadly dull performances of last season. They must have good sporting cricket, otherwise we shall have no right to appeal for support. The display of the Warwickshire team at Bristol last season was a blot on cricket. That sort of thing must stop. The selection committee, the captain and the players must bear that in mind. Today people like jazz, not funeral dirges. I do not blame them if they stop away from dull cricket.

Incidentally the average rate of scoring in first-class cricket in 1936 was 60 runs an hour, hardly what would be called dull in later years.

After those comments and bearing in mind the Committee's letter to Wyatt, though there was no reference to it at the meeting, it is ironic to read that a hearty vote of thanks was accorded to Wyatt – who was still in Australia – for his services as captain, and to the other amateurs who had assisted; and that the following month a recommendation from the executive committee that Wyatt be re-elected captain was approved by the general committee. C. A. F. Hastilow, who was now on that committee, took over the leadership of the second eleven from Captain Cowan.

For Wyatt the 1937 season which followed his return home was one of undiluted success. It was almost as if he had determined to show the Committee how wrong they had been about him, though *Wisden* still found it necessary to criticise the batting generally for being too cautious, especially as the players showed they could get runs quickly when they had to do so. Nevertheless, although they won fewer matches than they lost and Derbyshire dismissed them for 28, the lowest score of the season, they slightly improved their position in the table to eleventh.

Wyatt made no fewer than eight centuries, a record for the county, with two double centuries in one month, July. For the sixth season in succession he headed the county averages and was sixth in the national averages with an aggregate of 2625 runs and an average of 53·27. Four other batsmen got their 1000 runs, but Dollery, who hit four hundreds, including 152 against Glamorgan, full of glorious driving and cutting, was rather inconsistent. He played well enough, however, to get national recognition for the first time, playing for both the North against the South and for the M.C.C., but his highest score was 41. Aubrey Hill, a Coventry product, although he played in only nine matches, got two hundreds and finished fourth in the averages. One has the feeling – and it is shared by other people I have talked to – that this young man, in and out of the side, was never given the chance he should have had to realise his considerable potential, and for that the selection committees and captains must bear some responsibility.

Ord, who when he first came from Northumberland for whom he had played with his brother, J.D., had sent a photograph showing the perfect stance he had throughout his career, now made his first century, though he had not come on as well as had been hoped. Buckingham improved both as batsman and wicketkeeper in his first full season. In the match with Leicestershire, who scored a total of 620 runs, he did not concede one extra. Meanwhile, his predecessors, 'Tiger' and Jack Smart, with the Club's blessing, had become first-class umpires.

Of the bowlers Hollies came out best with 104 wickets, Mayer's total again being in the 80s, but Paine, although he bowled in thirty-five innings, was far from recovering his old form, largely because of a rheumatic condition which limited his movements. He took sixty-five wickets but they cost him 30·04 runs each. The county badly needed a stock bowler and it is to be feared that Hollies suffered as an attacking bowler largely through having to keep one end going more or less continuously. Against Hampshire at Bournemouth, for instance, he performed the mammoth feat of bowling 49·5 overs, with nine maidens, for 205 runs and four wickets. When he reached his hotel he flopped into a chair and stayed there, not even getting up for dinner. It was in this match that R. H. Moore played the highest individual innings, 316, ever made against Warwickshire. He went in first and was last out after batting six hours and twenty minutes, hitting three sixes – one of which gave him his first century of the season – and forty-three fours. And not one single chance did he give to Warwickshire's perspiring bowlers.

The first of Wyatt's double centuries was made in Kilner's benefit against Derbyshire and Wyatt was criticised for allowing the Warwickshire innings, and his own, to go on so long that the bowlers did not have enough time to get Derbyshire out twice. What were the facts? On the first day on an easy wicket Warwickshire scored 334 for three, Wyatt being 155 not out and Dollery 86 not out. It was not ultra-rapid scoring in those days, though one doubts if anyone would complain if Warwickshire did this regularly today. Wyatt took an hour and three-quarters over his first 50 and an hour and a half over his second, and at the close of play he had been batting five hours and five minutes for his 155 – roughly a run every two minutes. 'The rate of scoring was not as quick as the conditions invited,' according to the cricket correspondent of *The Birmingham Post*.

Next day Warwickshire took their total to 523 for eight, their highest for twenty-three years, before Wyatt declared at 3 p.m. after eight and three-quarter hours of batting. He had made 232. In the first twenty-five minutes of the day Dollery did not score, but Wyatt was aggressive from the start. Nevertheless, as *The Birmingham Post* account of the match

recorded, 'there was some surprise that Wyatt was not sufficiently satisfied with Warwickshire's position to close the innings at the interval
(the score was then 461 for four, Wyatt 225 not out). Apparently he
regarded the wicket as too favourable to batsmen at that point and preferred to keep Derbyshire in the field for a further three-quarters of an
hour.'

But during that time only seven runs were added, so what was the
point? In all, Wyatt batted seven and one-quarter hours. At the close of
the second day, on which 1737 people paid £95 for admission,
Derbyshire had scored 99 for one wicket. On the third day Derbyshire
took their total to 218, had to follow on and had scored 153 without loss
before rain prevented any more play after two 40-minute breaks. So
whether, if Wyatt had declared earlier, Warwickshire would have had
time to get Derbyshire out twice is a matter for conjecture.

Kilner's benefit eventually brought him £778, but although he had
scored over 1000 runs he was not re-engaged. Ryder had the unenviable
job of telling him that openings must be made for younger players.
Kilner was then 41 and he had been one of the county's most consistent batsmen, for in every one of his twelve seasons he scored over
1000 runs and in 1933 over 2000.

It was one of the ironies of the game that it was the Derbyshire attack
off which Warwickshire had scored all those runs which should be the
one that in the return match put them out for 28. On the first occasion,
true, Derbyshire were without Copson and Mitchell and it was the
former, who, returning to the side after a month's absence through
injury and bowling at great speed, moving the ball late both ways,
wrecked their innings at Derby with these figures:

O	M	R	W
8·2	2	11	8

Of the total of 28, Buckingham, with 9, was top scorer, Kilner and
Dollery each made 7, Cranmer 2 and Wyatt and Ord one each. Copson
took the last four wickets, of Dollery, Mayer, Fantham and Hollies, in
four balls.

Derbyshire put together 227 and when Warwickshire batted a
second time it looked as if it was going to be the story of the first
innings all over again. Copson bowled Kilner for nought and Santall for
one in his first and second overs, but he had to wait a long time for this
third wicket, for Hill, 105, and Dollery, 98, put on 231 and Copson this
time finished with two for 82. Such are the ups and downs of a bowler's
life. It was Mitchell who finished off the innings. Even so Derbyshire
lost five wickets in hitting off the 93 runs they needed.

Wyatt's other double century, 201 not out, was made against
Lancashire at Edgbaston. After Lancashire had been dismissed for 261,

an innings notable for a piece of what used to be called hurricane hitting – 51 in twenty-four minutes with one six and six fours – by Sibbles, Warwickshire made 457 for eight; Wyatt and Dollery, who began cautiously but then attacked the bowling vigorously, putting on 319 for the fourth wicket, a new Club record. In this instance Wyatt could hardly be criticised for building up a lead of 196. In their second innings Lancashire had made 226 for eight when the end came after Warwickshire had claimed the extra half-hour. If anything, one would say that it was a lack of penetration in the bowling rather than a prolongation of the batting which cost Warwickshire this match, but there were other views.

Following the match with Sussex at Edgbaston, in which six centuries were scored, three by each side – Kilner and Hill made 220 for Warwickshire's first wicket – the Committee, worried about all the heavy scoring, gave instructions to restrict the rolling of the wicket. The effect was seen in the match against Gloucestershire when, rather than wait for the prepared pitch to recover from the rain, the captains agreed to play on one which had not received any attention until the morning of the match. They got more than they bargained for. The pitch was described in *Wisden* as soft on top and hard underneath and Mayer, making the ball lift nastily, baffled everyone except Charlie Barnett, who, characteristically, hit 52 of the first 57 runs in a Gloucestershire first innings which realised 107, Mayer seven for 46.

Gloucestershire did not have a fast bowler who could exploit the conditions and Warwickshire made 222. With Mayer almost repeating his feat in the second innings, Gloucestershire were all out for 83. This time Mayer came out with six for 24 and his figures for the match – thirteen wickets for 70 runs – were the best of his career.

The New Zealanders were here that summer and played three Tests, though no Warwickshire players were called on for them, which was surprising in view of the form of Wyatt and Dollery. At least, however, they provided Warwickshire with the first sight of a batsman they liked the look of so much that they later persuaded him to play for them, largely through the good offices of Alec Hastilow. This, of course, was Martin Donnelly, who, at Edgbaston, hit 94, including thirteen fours, of the tourists' first innings total of 280. Wyatt reached exactly the same score as Donnelly, but by methods rather more dour.

Some time during the season someone, whose name was not stated, had the bright idea of suggesting sound-amplifying equipment for the ground, but it was not approved; it had to wait until the war years when Lieut. Col. R. I. Scorer introduced it to keep the public informed about what was happening on the field in the charity games he organised. If it had been installed and had been used to broadcast the dropping of Wyatt from the captaincy the news could hardly have created a greater sensation than it did among the general public, though Wyatt himself could not have been unprepared for it. Throughout the season, he has said, he was subjected to adverse criticisms by the Committee, one of them being that he played for himself and not for the team. Another was that they felt that against Lancashire he should not have waited to declare until he had completed his double century, whereas Wyatt contended that an earlier declaration would not have made it any easier for Warwickshire to win.

Wyatt felt that generally he had not been getting the support a captain was entitled to expect from the Committee. 'The then secretary, R. V. Ryder, and I', he says 'had for a long time not seen eye to eye about the running of the county XI. I thought he wanted to influence, if not make, decisions which properly belonged to the captain of the side.'

In his book Wyatt more or less absolves Bainbridge ('I don't think he was responsible for any of the trouble that occurred') and Dr Thwaite ('he was not an expert on the finer points of the game') from responsibility for his dismissal, although they had to pass sentence, so it is obvious that, for him, Ryder was the *éminence grise* in the affair. Even if he were, however, he had overwhelming support, as subsequent voting by the Committee showed.

Whatever else may have transpired behind the scenes, the first official move must have come at the executive committee meeting on 26 August. There is a pencilled note in the margin of the minutes of the meeting on that day which reads: '1st meeting re. R.E.S.W. and captaincy'. There is no indication of who made it and there is no reference to the captaincy in the minutes. This is explained, however, in the minutes of the meeting on 21 October when it is stated that the question of the captaincy was discussed *for the second time* (my italics). Sir Charles Hyde, who presided, explained that after the previous discussion on 26 August, obviously not recorded for some reason, steps were taken to interview Mr Wyatt, when the views of the Committee were explained to him.

According to Wyatt – and again the meeting was at the Chamber of Commerce offices where he saw Bainbridge and Dr Thwaite – he was told that they were going to make a change in the captaincy and appoint Peter Cranmer. Wyatt said that he could not undertand why they had refused to see him when he had asked to meet them the previous year, pointing out that 'even a murderer has some sort of trial'. He added that if he had been able to see them many misunderstandings would have been cleared up and that in any case, as captain of the side, he ought to have attended all the meetings of the executive committee, but as he was not invited to half of them, he seldom had an opportunity of discussing anything with them.

The charges that had been made against him in the letter, which he has never published, though he allowed me to see it, were repeated to him. He was told, he wrote in his book, that he had not given enough encouragement to the young players – which surprised him then as much as it did when it was first said – that he had thrown away the Lancashire match; that under his captaincy the side had been getting into a rut and that it was felt a change was necessary.

He would have been less than human if he had not been 'very hurt and distressed', to use his own words and his feelings were not assuaged by various stories which were put about, by, he alleged, some members of the Committee, as the reasons for his departure. Whether this is so or not, the fact remains that, rightly or wrongly, he was regarded by some of his colleagues and members as a selfish player; indeed, one of his contemporaries in the side expressed the view to me that had he been an unselfish man he 'would have been the best captain ever'. As it was, this player felt that because of his anxiety to do well himself, Wyatt did not give his bowlers time enough to get the other side out, and this man was not the only critic in the team.

To complete the official side of the story, the executive made the following recommendation to a full meeting of the General Committee on 25 October:

That whilst appreciating the services of Mr R. E. S. Wyatt as captain of the Club for eight years, the Executive Committee, after careful consideration, have unanimously decided to recommend that – in the best interests of the Club – a change be made in the captaincy and that Mr Peter Cranmer be invited to accept the position for 1938.

Dr Thwaite and Bainbridge explained the views of the executive, but then Mr A. Turnell moved an amendment to the effect that the matter of the captaincy be left in abeyance until the annual meeting in March and this was seconded by Norman Partridge. The amendment was defeated, though no figures of the voting were minuted. After this the President asked other members of the Committee to express their views. Messrs. A. L. Murray, C. K. Langley, C. A. F. Hastilow, C. F. R. Cowan, L. G. Parsons and Guy Heaton all supported the recommendation, while Messrs. A. C. Griffiths and N. E. Partridge were against it. Mr Griffiths then asked that the resolution should be presented in two parts. The President agreed and a vote was taken on the following motions:

Part 1. That a change be made in the captaincy. [This was carried by eighteen votes to two.]

Part 2. That Mr Cranmer be invited to accept the position for 1938. [This was carried by sixteen votes to three.]

And that was that, though it was not the end of the affair. When the terms of the resolution were given to the Press Sir Charles Hyde added the comment that 'there has never been any friction between the late captain and the Committee' – a statement with which the former captain would hardly have agreed – 'but it was felt that the team had got into a groove and a change was thought necessary'.

He added that, of course, it was somewhat in the nature of an experiment to appoint Mr Cranmer captain, but he was a most popular figure on the football and cricket fields and had captained the English Rugby team with success. 'He has a breezy personality', the President added, 'and should "ginger up" Warwickshire county cricket.'

In the absence of any detailed reasons being given for Wyatt's dismissal, *The Birmingham Post* was understandably restrained in its comments 'pending a full explanation at the next general meeting. All that can be done today is to emphasise appreciatively the great services Mr Wyatt has rendered to Warwickshire cricket.' The paper went on to describe him as 'by far the best all-round amateur England has produced since the war', and said he 'was never a lucky captain', but they all hoped, as did the President, that Wyatt would continue to play for Warwickshire. Then, however, a cautionary note was sounded: 'There are dangers in a city whose cricket thrives only on success in a "brightness first" movement. Mr Wyatt as a player and adviser could still render Warwickshire service of immense value.'

As was only to be expected, there was a good deal of outside comment, much of it sympathetic to Wyatt, and one remark, by Lancashire's former captain, P. T. Eckersley, then an M.P., that there were 'surely cricket brains in the south able to profit by the extraordinary lapse of that most intelligent city whence come celebrated politicians', gave rise to rumours that Wyatt might be leaving Warwickshire to join Surrey, the county of his birth. He never thought seriously about it and it says much for his sense of loyalty to the Club, despite what had happened, that he thought it would show a poor spirit to leave the team simply because he was no longer captain.

The fact that Wyatt was dismissed at the end of one of the most successful seasons he ever had, surely makes it clear that the move had been decided on regardless of his personal performances and this was confirmed at the annual meeting the following March. One of the largest attendances at an annual meeting up to that time, about 320 members, heard the President begin by explaining the circumstances in which the Committee had decided on a change in captaincy – no hurried decision, as it had been in the minds of the Committee for over twelve months.

'It is a great responsibility to drop our pilot', said Sir Charles, 'but the Club has been sailing in troubled waters for some time and I hope we have not committed any injustice to one who has served us for so long. I have had several talks with Mr Wyatt and on Sunday last he told me that the resolution had not been inspired by him.'

This was a reference to a resolution before the meeting in the name of Mr L. Palmer Grice strongly disapproving of the action of the Committee and calling upon them to rescind the decision and to invite Wyatt to continue as captain. There had been some discussion as to whether it should be accepted as it did not comply with the rules as to the date of its delivery, but it was eventually allowed though the Committee had decided that if it were carried the Committee and their President would resign forthwith.

The meeting was informed of this decision by Sir Charles, who added that Wyatt was still engaged in business negotiations, but thought he would still be able to play for Warwickshire, although this depended on other circumstances. Dr Thwaite added that throughout Mr Wyatt had been given to understand that the Committee hoped he would continue to play for Warwickshire, though not as captain. There was no reflection on him and never had been in any sense except that it was felt there must be a change of policy.

J. F. Byrne appealed for the resolution to be withdrawn on the ground that the change had been decided by the right and proper authority, the Committee, which would be placed in an untenable position if the resolution were passed. Mr Grice, however, declined to withdraw. He did not question the legality of the Committee's action, but said they should act in accordance with the wishes of the majority of the members and some felt that they had not done so. He had received a shoal of correspondence supporting this action. The treatment Mr Wyatt had received was shabby.

After the resolution had been seconded, there was a general discussion in which Sir Gilbert Barling, the Birmingham surgeon, pointed out that although there was scarcely a better cricketer in England than Wyatt he had two functions – as a cricketer in the Warwickshire team and as a captain. The Committee was not turning Mr Wyatt down as a cricketer, but it was felt that a change of captaincy was desirable and from what he had seen he fully agreed.

When an amendment had been moved and seconded to the effect that the meeting had full confidence in the Committee and all its actions, the chairman took a vote on it by a show of hands and declared it carried by 'an overwhelmingly majority' and it was then confirmed as a substantive motion. The hearty vote of thanks to Mr Wyatt for his services as captain, which was then carried unanimously, must have read rather ironically to one pair of eyes at least.

The Wyatt upheaval was not the only thing Ryder had to concern himself with about this time. Once again the financial position of the Club was serious.

Such is the expenditure and such the probable support that your Committee faces each season [he wrote in the annual report for 1937], the possibility of a loss approaching £2000. Efforts are constantly being made to reduce expenditure. The danger is that in doing so efficiency may be threatened. An increase in public support appears to be the only solution. Subscriptions in 1937 at £4133 show a decrease of £153. That is most serious. Gate receipts of under £3000 in 1937 can only be described as poor. To some extent weather is a deciding factor. It is quite clear, however, that the game is not attracting the Saturday afternoon public it used to do. This is the most disappointing feature of county cricket finance in Warwickshire.

Ryder was so concerned about the position that in December he had taken the unheard-of initiative of asking that his salary should be reduced by £100, an offer that was accepted. Entertainment Tax was one of the biggest financial bugbears the counties had to contend with and it had been stated at the annual meeting that the previous year the county clubs had paid out £75 000 worth of it, £5000 more than the total of their losses. As for public support, even the benign Dr Thwaite was moved to say with unusual bitterness that if Warwickshire were as consistent in their cricket as in their losses they would win the Championship. During three days of the Yorkshire match they had taken the trivial sum of £150 – but at least there was something else to blame this time as a rival attraction: the Coronation festivities.

There was an indication of how much the big personalities of the game meant at the turnstiles when it was decided to make inquiries about the possibility of insuring against Bradman *not* taking part in the Australians' match for a sum of (*a*) £250 and (*b*) £500, but the reply from the insurance broker the Club consulted was that he had had Lloyd's market thoroughly searched, but it was impossible to obtain a quotation to cover the risk of Bradman not playing.

Sydney Santall had at last retired as coach after forty-seven years' service with the Club and it was decided to elect him an honorary life member and to invite donations to a testimonial fund limited to vice-presidents and members of the Committee. This eventually realised £152. The post was offered to Norman Kilner for the 1939 season.

The Committee's first gesture to their new captain was to congratulate him on his selection as captain of the England Rugby team to meet Wales at Cardiff. Although he was young – barely 21 – and inexperienced and had done little so far to justify his place in the side – his 576 runs in thirty innings in 1937 was his best season so far – there is no doubt that Cranmer was a popular choice as captain with the public. What Ron Maudsley, later to succeed him, once referred to as his 'wonderful cheerfulness', kept breaking out and he never lost heart even when things seemed at their worst. He brought a dash of the Cavalier spirit to a side which, perhaps, had been suffering from too much of the Roundhead outlook.

Hollies neatly summed up the difference in their approach to their bowlers. 'When Bob Wyatt gave me the ball', he wrote, 'the conversation of encouragement would go something like this: "So-and-So's a weak leg-side player; make the most of that, and remember that you're a better bowler than he is a batsman. Now work on him." Peter Cranmer would say: "Have a bowl, Eric, and get the beggars out." ' And Eric would go on and bowl and bowl and bowl.

In view of the fact that Kilner had gone, it was just as well that Cranmer still had the help of the Roundhead for all except five matches in 1938. Wyatt's business negotiations had been with the *Daily Mail*, which had engaged him to report the Tests against Australia. The Committee raised no objections provided he did not write about any Warwickshire matches in which he was engaged, or criticise any Warwickshire player unless he were appearing in a Test. They also stipulated that if he played for the county it would be as any other amateur and that no alteration would be made in the present financial arrangements.

Even with Wyatt's help, however – and he must have permitted himself a quiet smile when he once again headed the averages – it was hardly to be expected that Cranmer would transform the team's performances overnight. *Wisden's* verdict was that Warwickshire showed plenty of keenness and a happy spirit, but that the batting lacked stability and the bowling was weak. Santall, who took Kilner's place as opener, rarely came off and just failed to get 1000 runs; Croom became over-cautious, did not make one century and only just reached four figures; Hill might well have been given more opportunities, playing only fourteen innings, though it has to be admitted that he scored only 171 runs; Dollery made no more than 1272, but Cranmer increased his aggregate to 962 and hit bravely on occasions – 98 in eighty minutes at Hove and 80 in the same number of minutes at The Oval. The bowling, frankly, was rather feeble and no one took 100 wickets.

Nevertheless, there were some cheerful moments. The team began well, winning four out of five matches in June though they did not keep that up; by the end of the season they had won one more match and lost one fewer than in 1937 – seven all – yet they dropped two places down the table to thirteenth. One of the June victories over Derbyshire saw yet another record stand for sixth wicket, of 220, between Dollery and Buckingham. It could not have come at a more timely moment for five wickets were down for 39. Dollery made 134 not out and he still regards this as the outstanding innings of his career; Buckingham's share was 124, his first century for the Club, and it won the match and well earned the silver cigarette cases with which an anonymous vice-

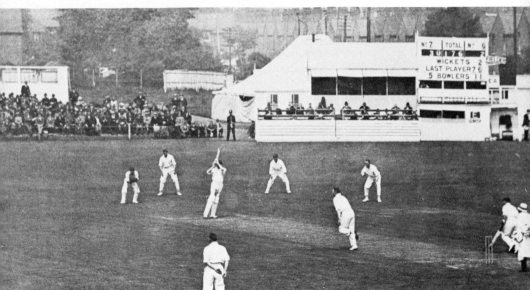

Top left: Three Warwickshire century makers and only one wicket down – a scoreboard record of a famous win over Sussex in 1925. The three players – the Hon. F. S. G. Calthorpe, J. H. Parsons and 'Tiger' Smith – between them hit off the 392 runs needed to win for the loss of only one wicket.

Top right: Warwick Armstrong, the Australian captain, and the Hon. F. S. G. Calthorpe come out to toss during the tourists' visit to Edgbaston in 1921.

Bottom: When South Africa played a Test Match at Edgbaston in June 1924, the ground still had a rather rural appearance. The batsman is Frank Woolley.

Left: R. E. S. Wyatt, captain of England, captain of Warwickshire and many other sides, one of the world's most travelled and experienced cricketers, a doughty opponent and a batsman of great stubbornness.

Right: Jack Buckingham, known as 'The Duke' because of his surname and his always immaculate appearance.

Top left: N. E. Partridge, school-boy prodigy and one of the most brilliant amateur all-rounders who ever played for the county, though not often enough.

Top right: The Hon. F. S. G. Calthorpe, captain from 1920 to 1929.

Right: M. P. Donnelly, the New Zealander, one of the first overseas players to appear in the Warwickshire side. Unfortunately he rarely reproduced for them the form which made him one of the world's outstanding batsmen.

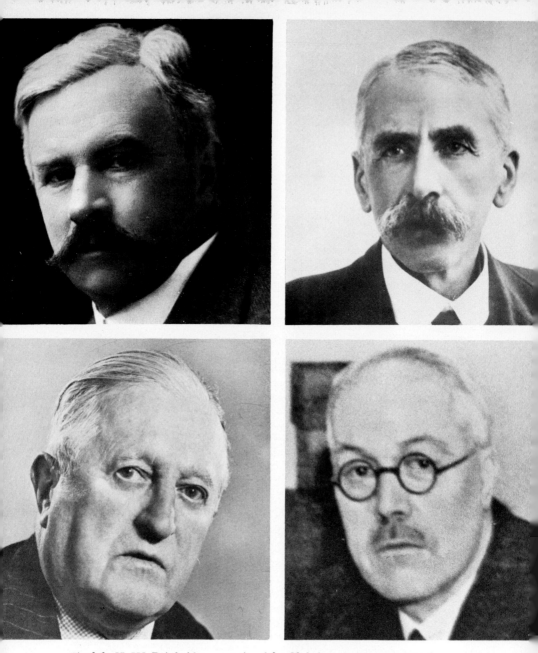

Top left: H. W. Bainbridge, captain of the Club from 1887 to 1901 and again, jointly with T. S. Fishwick in 1902, and honorary secretary from 1903 to 1940.

Top right: F. Sidney Goodwin, honorary treasurer 1909–26.

Bottom left: Captain C. F. R. Cowan, R.N., honorary treasurer 1943–57 and captain of the 2nd XI.

Bottom right: Colin K. Langley, chairman and honorary secretary from 1943–48.

Top left: Peter Cranmer. England rugby international and dashing cricketer who took over the captaincy from R. E. S. Wyatt in 1938 and held it until 1947, apart from the war years, 1940–45 inclusive, when he served with the Armed Forces.

Top right: R. H. Maudsley who shared the captaincy with H. E. Dollery in 1948.

Bottom: Wartime cricketers. One of the happy groups of players and officials who helped to keep cricket going at Edgbaston during the Second World War. Left to right they are: P. King, G. E. A. Paine, F. Moore, C. W. Grove, E. R. King, J. Buckingham, D. J. Kenyon, R. T. D. Perks, N. E. Partridge, E. Cooper, 'Tiger' Smith (umpire), Eric Perry, 'Roly' Jenkins, Lieut-Colonel R. I. Scorer, Billy Lee, H. H. I. ('Doc') Gibbons, J. Smart and A. F. ('Spinney') Lane.

Top: A typical left-hander's stroke during Hitchcock's maiden century for the county against Leicestershire at Hinckley in 1955.

Bottom: May chops a ball from Ramadhin into the gully and he and Cowdrey equal the world record partnership for the fourth wicket, 388, in the Test at Edgbaston in 1957. Kanhai was keeping wicket for the West Indies.

Top: Warwickshire in 1946. Back row: W. E. Hollies, W. E. Fantham,
H. E. Dollery, E. J. Smith (coach), M. Barker, K. A. Taylor, N. A.
Shortland and J. S. Ord. Front row: R. Mead-Briggs, C. S. Dempster,
P. Cranmer (capt), C. C. Goodway and C. H. Adderley.

Bottom: The 1951 Champions. Back row: E. J. ('Tiger') Smith (senior
coach), Wolton, Gardner, Townsend, Weeks, Thompson, Spooner,
Hitchcock, Taylor and George Austin (scorer). Seated: Grove, L. T.
Deakins (general secretary), Hollies, Dr Harold Thwaite (President),
Dollery (captain), C. A. F. Hastilow (chairman), Ord, Capt. C. F. Cowan,
R.N. (hon. treasurer), and Pritchard.

Top left: Dr Harold Thwaite, one of the many great servants of the Warwickshire Club and instigator of its great period of development after the Second World War.

Top right: Dr Stanley Barnes, one of the Club's most generous benefactors, who died in his first year as President, 1955.

Bottom: The opening of The Thwaite Gates in 1952 in honour of one of Warwickshire's most distinguished servants. In the group are (left to right) Capt. C. F. R. Cowan (Hon. Treasurer), Alderman R. C. Yates (Lord Mayor of Birmingham), C. A. F. Hastilow (Chairman), Mr William Findlay (President of the MCC), Guy Heaton (Chairman of the House and Ground Committee), Dr Harold Thwaite (at the microphone) and H. E. Dollery (Warwickshire's captain).

Top: The famous 'Three Ws' of the West Indies at Edgbaston – Walcott (behind the stumps), Weekes and Worrell – with Grove cutting a ball between them.

Bottom: Protest Meeting. So crowded was the special meeting called in 1953 to discuss the decision of the Committee not to re-engage C. W. Grove that some members had to sit on the floor. Standing on the right is Denis Howell, later to become Minister for Sport, one of the leaders of the 'critics'.

Left: The crowd invades the pitch as the 1950 West Indies tourists are beaten on the third day.

Below left: Edgbaston in 1951 when county cricket really drew the crowds – a then record attendance of over 28 000 to see the match with Lancashire which had an important bearing on the Championship.

Opposite top left: Batsman, change bowler who broke up many partnerships and a brilliant fielder, Alan Townsend was one of the best all-rounders who ever played for Warwickshire. Here he is hitting a ball from Jack Young, of Middlesex, for six.

Opposite far right: All Yorkshire-men who have left their native county like to do well against their former colleagues when they meet and no doubt Norman Horner enjoyed making this sweep off Wardle.

Opposite bottom left: Bert Wolton lays about him – this was a boundary off Broderick – in making a match-winning century on the last day against Northants in 1954.

Opposite bottom right: Smiter of sixes. W. J. Stewart, who holds the six hitting record for Warwickshire, took 17 of them off the Lancashire attack at Blackpool in 1959, scoring a century in each innings of the match.

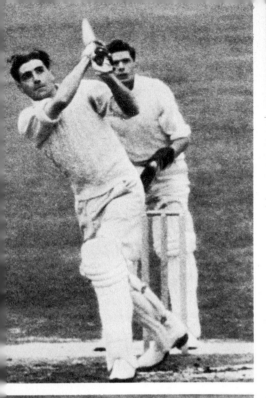

Top left: When Wilf Wooller, Glamorgan's captain, completed the 'cricketer's double' during the match at Edgbaston in 1954, C. A. F. Hastilow, Warwickshire's chairman, went out on the field and drank a congratulatory glass of champagne with him.

Top right: The Australians survive – but only just. Only a great defensive, farming-the-bowling innings by Lindsay Hassett, their captain, saved the Australians from defeat at Edgbaston in 1953. He batted 170 minutes for 21 not out, Hassett and Benaud had a mixed reception when they returned, with 'Tom' Dollery, to the pavilion when stumps were drawn after the tourists had saved the game.

Bottom: Fred Gardner played the innings of his life against the 1953 Australians, making a century. Here he is placing a ball between Hole and Benaud.

Right: Taker of all ten wickets. Congratulations from his captain, M. J. K. Smith, and other team mates for J. D. Bannister after he had taken all ten wickets of the Combined Services in May, 1959.

Below: Spooner as wicket-keeper. No doubt about this one for Leicestershire's Australian, Vic Jackson, has both feet off the ground, as Spooner whips away the bails. Gardner is at slip. The bowler was Hollies. Jackson was one of Spooner's 73 victims during Championship year in 1951.

Top left: Eric Hollies, past master of the art of leg spin bowling.

Top right: Eric Hollies' 2000th victim in first-class cricket was Dews, of Worcestershire, whose wicket was taken at Dudley in 1955. Congratulations from colleagues all round, including a handshake from Jack Bannister.

Bottom: Farewell to Edgbaston. There were only a few faithful spectators to see Eric Hollies play his last match at Edgbaston against Surrey in 1957, but his team mates and the Surrey batsmen gave him a farewell round of applause. From left to right there are: A. Townsend, R. C. E. Pratt, E. B. Lewis, W. J. Stewart, N. F. Horner, T. H. Clark, Elliott and Buller (umpires), C. W. Leach, F. C. Gardner, Swaranjit Singh, S. S. Griffith, O. S. Wheatley and M. J. K. Smith.

There was no batsman more attractive to watch than 'Tom' Dollery when he was in his prime. This shot to leg was played during his match-saving century against Lancashire in 1951, the second Championship year. Dollery was also a very capable wicket-keeper as this stumping of his rival captain E. D. R. Eagar, of Hampshire, off Hollies, shows. He lost the ball only after he had removed the bails. (Below)

Left: Starkie, the Northants bowler, came in for some punishment in the match at Coventry in 1951 – J. S. Ord cover drives him, a model stroke.

Below: Warwickshire have had few, if any, finer fielders than Alan Townsend seen here catching D. Slade (Worcestershire) off Cartwright at Dudley.

president presented them. When they got back to New Street Station they found Ryder there to meet them. They went into the first-class refreshment room – there were such things then – where whatever drinks they fancied were on him. It was a very human gesture.

Buckingham had another fine match at Northampton in August, this time both behind and in front of the stumps. In Northamptonshire's first innings he stumped two and caught three, then made 137 not out and stumped one and caught one. With Hollies taking six for 66 in both innings, Warwickshire won by eight wickets. It was unfortunate, though, that a Warwickshire player did not win the prize the President had said he would give to the player – it was intended to limit the awards to Warwickshire players, but the stipulation was omitted – who made the first century to be recorded on the new scoreboard, now in action. That honour, however, fell to Herbert Sutcliffe, who made 142 out of a Yorkshire total of 415 which they scored in June. This time there was no one to stop the rot when Warwickshire batted against Bowes, Smailes and Wilkinson, and they were all out 41. In the circumstances they did well to make 232 in their second innings; this time Emmott Robinson helped himself to four wickets for 10 runs.

Hollies had the first of his historic encounters with Bradman at Edgbaston in July. The great man had begun with his third double century in successive tours at Worcester and though he was not per-haps quite the run-glutton of old, he did more than his share of getting them during what was generally a season of heavy scoring. At Edg-baston he made 135, the last 85 coming in an hour. Hollies did not get his wicket on this occasion, but he bowled extremely well, particularly after Bradman was out, and he took five wickets for 130. It would be too much to say that the writing was on the wall, for the Australians made 390 for eight declared, but there were hints of it. That could not be said for the batting, which foundered against O'Reilly, for 179 and 118, the Australians winning by an innings.

At long last Paine had his disputed benefit against Derbyshire over the August Bank Holiday weekend, but from a playing point of view it was an unhappy match for him. He got 'a pair' and his twenty-five overs yielded 102 runs for only one wicket. Dollery did his best for him with 113, but Warwickshire were all out 187 and 162 and Derbyshire won by an innings and 28 runs. But there were compensations for Paine – not the four figures for which he had hoped, but a matter of £876.

At the end of the season in October, Paine declined the terms offered to him 'unless he was granted minimum earnings of £250', but the executive committee recommended that his proposal should not be accepted and that no further offer should be made to him. Perhaps the Committee were influenced not only by his loss of form and doubts about his physical fitness, but by the fact that they had engaged in May one

C. W. Grove, who came with a splendid record from the Birmingham League.

Paine played only once for Warwickshire after this, but whatever doubts there may have been about his physical fitness – he suffered from a prolapsed disc leading to osteo-arthritis – it did not prevent him from playing league cricket for a number of years, nor from coaching. In later years he served the Club through the Supporters Association and in a variety of other ways, particularly in connection with non-turf pitches.

The Committee were also somewhat discouraging to Cyril Goodway, an amateur batsman-wicketkeeper with Smethwick and Staffordshire, who had not raised any objection to Warwickshire availing themselves of his services when they wished to do so. He now wrote saying that he had been offered the captaincy of Staffordshire, but preferred to play for Warwickshire if some guarantee could be given him of opportunities of first-class cricket. The executive committee decided that they could not give such a guarantee, though he was invited to play against the West Indies and Cambridge the following season. His opportunity to serve the Club more fully was to come.

Before the war clouds gathered over Edgbaston for the second time in 1939, the Club's supporters were given a few memories to cherish during the dark days until first-class cricket could be resumed. They saw Dollery fulfilling his promise and perhaps later they reflected on the glories of which those lost five years had deprived them; if they ventured as far as Dudley they saw Cranmer score 50 of his 68 in ten strokes – five sixes and five fours; and they read about a fantastic match at Llanelly in which there were three declarations, one of which it was ruled was illegal and brought a letter from the M.C.C.

The year began with more administrative difficulties and the resignation from the Committee of A. C. Griffiths, who had opposed Wyatt's dismissal and now disagreed with the methods of engaging players, their selection and the management of coaching, which brought out the information that in the previous season invitations for boys to play in trial games had been sent to forty-one public schools and thirty-one grammar schools; eighty-two names were sent in and seventy boys attended. Mr Griffiths was also critical about finance and resigned from both the general and finance committees.

After the furore of Wyatt's departure, the most notable feature of the annual meeting was that for the first time in fifty years Bainbridge was absent through indisposition. The following month Sir Charles had to announce that Bainbridge wished to retire from the chair, which he had held for eight years, for reasons of health, and Dr Thwaite succeeded him but without relinquishing the office of honorary treasurer. The Club suffered a loss the same month through the death of F. S. Goodwin, who had been honorary treasurer from 1909 to 1926; other deaths during the year were those of Hugh Rotherham, one of the best of the early fast bowlers, and the Rev. Edward Pereira, who had played occasionally in the 1880s and 1890s.

Dollery was undoubtedly Warwickshire's player of the year; it was almost as if he sensed what was coming and had decided to make hay while the sun still shone. He scored most runs – 1362 in Championship matches – headed the averages with 42·56, played the highest innings, 177, made three other centuries, and was chosen for the Players at Lord's. Hill, back to form, was the only other player to reach a four-figure aggregate, though Wyatt, who had been on a private tour to South America during the winter, made 990 and Santall 913.

Hollies was the only bowler to take 100 wickets (110 for 22·00), Mayer had eighty-four and Grove was coming along with thirty-four; but no one was found to replace Paine, and the burden Hollies had to bear was all the heavier. Buckingham had the satisfaction of setting up a new county record. Against Sussex at Edgbaston he was concerned in the dismissal of their first six batsmen – one stumped and five caught, and he would have had another one, the last wicket, if Hollies, whom he had asked to 'drop one outside his leg stump', had not clean bowled the batsman instead.

Although their playing record was slightly worse than in the previous season, Warwickshire went up two places in the table to eleventh and would probably have been better placed but for four defeats in August. Dollery's 177 turned what at one time seemed like a defeat by Derbyshire into a victory by an innings; and he played a match-saving innings of 170 against Hampshire, he and Ord (105 not out), adding 215 for the fourth wicket in only 140 minutes.

But the greatest reversal of fortunes came at Edgbaston against Leicestershire when Wyatt gave a masterly demonstration of what technique and experience could achieve. After Leicestershire had been disposed of for 146, Hollies taking six for 55, Warwickshire's innings was shattered by a 17-year-old medium-paced swing bowler named Drake, who had not previously taken a wicket in the County Championship. Now in forty-two balls he sent back four men for two runs, half the side being out for 14. But Wyatt, who had gone in at No. 4, pulled the innings round to such an extent that although no one who batted with him got more than 8 the total reached 105, of which Wyatt made 74 not out. This was batsmanship of the highest order. Drake's eventual figures were five for 21.

Warwickshire were thus 41 behind, but Mayer, Wilmot and Hollies then tumbled Leicestershire out for 86, Mayer bowling the last three men in one over. He hit the middle stump every time and was later presented with it mounted and inscribed, a change from having the ball. He deserved it for he was the sort of bowler who would go on until he could stand no longer. In this strangely fluctuating game, which Warwickshire won by nine wickets, Santall was out for none in the first innings and hit a dashing 71 in the second; while Drake did not take a wicket in Warwickshire's second innings and had 42 runs hit off him.

Hollies became the fifth bowler to take nine wickets in an innings – this was against Glamorgan at Edgbaston. He had nine for 93 in the first innings, the last seven for 29 runs in only seven overs, but on the same ground later in the season, Watts, of Surrey, swinging the ball in a heavy atmosphere, took all ten:

O	M	R	W
24·1	8	67	10

Oddly enough, not a single Warwickshire player was clean bowled in either innings. At one point Watts had taken four for 6.

It was in the return match with Glamorgan at Llanelly that both captains had a fit of the declarations. There was no play because of rain on the Saturday and a start was not possible until 4 p.m. on the Monday. During an early tea M. J. Turnbull and Cranmer agreed that each should declare with their first innings scores equal. Warwickshire batted first and when Croom and Hill had made 48 Cranmer called them in. Glamorgan also scored 48, but lost one wicket in the process. However, Turnbull's declaration came when only fifty minutes remained for play, instead of not later than an hour and forty minutes from the close, the rule in a two-day match in accordance with Law 54; though, as *Wisden* remarked afterwards, it was a moot point whether this stipulation applied to a first declaration only.

Warwickshire then batted a second time and this time declared with their score at 197 for six wickets. Glamorgan, left with two hours and a half to get the runs, did so with a quarter of an hour to spare. Improper perhaps, even illegal, to quote the annual report, but a little enterprise had made an enjoyable game out of what seemed a hopeless situation and no one was any the worse off – except Warwickshire.

Dollery was top scorer with 70 in the only innings he had for the Players at Lord's where Wyatt was in the wars again. Against Sussex at Horsham he had been hit over the heart by a ball from Nye, but went on batting until he had made 25. When he got back to the pavilion he was told he must not take any further part in the match, but did so when Warwickshire were doing badly and this time another ball from Nye broke his thumb and burst the nail. Two doctors disagreed about the treatment and the injury kept him out of the game for several matches. When he returned at Lord's he had to bat on a fiery wicket against Bowes and Copson. He was hit all over the body, but then got another one on the thumb, which burst a blood vessel and this time he did not take any further part in the match.

The first whisper of what was to come was heard in June when there were hints to the players about joining the Territorials. 'Every facility', they were told, 'will be given to members of the staff who desire to join the Territorial services.' The West Indies were here, but had to sail for home with several matches unplayed, though not, fortunately, that at Edgbaston where in rainy weather they had the better of a draw.

Several county matches were also cancelled. Warwickshire were at Lord's when the end came, getting, what Eric Hollies in his earlier days would have described as some 'ommer – Middlesex 525 for seven declared, Robertson 154 and Edrich 101. The three wickets Hollies took cost him 145 runs. Warwickshire's last efforts before the curtain fell were 194 and 131. Hollies and Dollery should have gone on to Folkestone for the Festival there, but they returned to Birmingham and when they parted at the station that evening it was the last time they were to see each other until they reassembled at Edgbaston at the start of the 1946 season.

Cricket in Wartime
(1939–1945)

ONE difference between the two world wars was that much more cricket of various kinds was played in the Second than in the First, though, as no one quite knew what to expect, it took a little time to get going. Then, as the so-called 'phoney war' went peaceably on, most people began to lead something like more normal lives.

In the meantime many things had happened to many people. Dollery and Wyatt should have been on a tour of India with a team captained by E. R. T. Holmes. Instead Dollery followed Cranmer into the Army; Captain Cowan was back in the Navy and they were soon to be followed into the Services by several other players, while others went to work in various wartime jobs.

By 11 September the executive committee was already considering the position of the Club 'in view of the possibility of a long war', and it was decided forthwith to cancel all agreements with the players, though the head groundsman was to be paid in full until the end of the year when his engagement was to terminate. Ryder formally resigned his position, but it was decided to re-engage him at half pay. Leslie Deakins was retained at full pay until the end of October, when the salary paid to Wyatt as assistant secretary also ceased and he was empowered to take over the endowment policy which had been taken out for him.

It was also decided to give up the tenancy of the town office and the executive committee was appointed as a special committee to carry on the affairs of the Club during the war. Already the Birmingham Watch Committee had offered to rent the pavilion and the practice shed for the Auxiliary Fire Service at £208 a year to cover all rates and water rate, the Club accepting the offer with some provisos. As it happened 'the shed', known to all county cricketers as the luncheon room, was soon a casualty to a high explosive bomb – 150 incendiaries also fell on the ground – and a claim for £1167 damage was made. It took a long time to settle it.

On the outbreak of war the Committee had communicated to the members in the following terms:

The Committee has carefully considered the position of The Warwickshire County Cricket Club during the war. Cricket will not be played, but it has been unanimously decided that the Club must be kept in being and the grounds in something like reasonable condition. Owing to the wet season our finances are in a bad way. Most drastic economies are being effected, but to carry on we must have money so as to lessen a bank overdraft which may be necessary. The Committee appeals to subscribers to help the Club by paying their subscriptions for 1940 in advance.

By the end of the year £707 had been received from 384 subscribers and it was estimated that about £1500 would be needed in 1940 to meet payments due to players on the agreements in force at the outbreak of the war, and for management expenses and rates. The circular, however, had been wrong in stating that no cricket would be played, though it is true that in 1940 it was confined to local clubs like Sparkhill and Lloyds Bank to whom the ground was let for Saturday matches; though an eleven representing the county visited Worcester at the August Bank Holiday.

The Warwickshire team included Wyatt, Hill, Santall, Ord, Buckingham, R. I. Scorer, Paine, Hollies, Grove and A. K. Jackson, several of whom were playing in league and club cricket. Hollies, for instance, back with his old club, Old Hill, kept his hand in to the extent of beating Freeman's 1937 record by taking ninety-nine wickets for 9·92 runs each; and Wyatt, playing for Moseley, had a batting average of 64·5. He had gone into the insurance business and later joined the R.A.F. C. F. Walters reappeared for Worcestershire in this match which, despite the fact that Grove did the hat trick, they won by 91 runs. Perks, for the third time in three days, took seven wickets, this time for 40.

The annual meeting was held as usual in March when the accounts showed a loss of £997 and the President, Sir Charles Hyde, said Entertainment Tax was slowly killing cricket, Dr Thwaite adding that during the first sixteen years after the last war the Club paid £18 000. He also protested against the extension of the football season, though it seemed an odd time to do so.

The President also had a dig at 'freak declarations' and said that under the present system of scoring points a club now appeared to need the services of a skilled mathematician to advise whether an innings should be declared or not, or whether a side should bat at all. What would he have said had he lived until the so-called computer age?

Members had begun the meeting by standing in silence out of respect for H. W. Bainbridge, one of three distinguished members of the Club who died during the year, the others being Ludford Docker and H. C. Maul. By the end of the year John Devey, former player and director of Aston Villa F.C. and Frank Breeden, the first groundsman, had also died. Bainbridge had given a lifetime of service to the Club as player and administrator, which can hardly have been paralleled anywhere; Docker, over six feet in height, brought the same bluff heartiness to his speech-making as he had done to his batting and fast bowling; and Maul was outstanding among the early amateurs, his splendid off-drive being spoken of long after he had retired. A quartet impossible to replace.

Before the end of the year, too, Ryder had obtained other employment and the chairman had announced that he would take over the business management of the Club, which Leslie Deakins carried on in an honorary capacity from Dr Thwaite's home until he was called up into the Navy, and even afterwards. After that Dr Thwaite's own accountant, C. W. Cotterill, of Sherrey, Garland & Co. of Birmingham, took over, the expense being met by Dr Thwaite.

There was still only club cricket in 1941 at Edgbaston, from which nearly 700 seats had been taken to be used in Birmingham's air raid shelters, but again a team was sent to Worcester for a Bank Holiday game, despite the fact that so many players were now in the armed forces – Cranmer, Kemp-Welch, Dick Sale, the Rev. J. H. Parsons, Norman Shortland, Dollery, J. R. Thompson, Santall, Fantham and H. J. Roberts among them. Again Worcestershire won, this time by 32 runs. Hollies – he and Mayer held two of the first three places in the Birmingham League averages – took four for 36 and was hit by his fellow leg-spinner, Roly Jenkins, for a six and a five.

The most interesting game played in the Midlands that year, however, was the Tom Brown Centenary Match at Rugby School. This celebrated the first visit of an M.C.C. team in 1841. R. I. Scorer, opening the innings for the M.C.C., was top scorer with 38 out of 149 for nine declared. One of the M.C.C. players, L. G. H. Hingley, who had been captain of Rugby the year before, had been on a bombing raid over Germany the previous night and arrived on the ground only just in time to take part in the match. Sad to say, he was later killed in action. The bowling of 'Big Jim' Smith, of Middlesex, and Wyatt was too much for the School, who were all out 31, Smith doing the hat trick and Wyatt taking four for 14.

The British Empire XI was formed this year and Wyatt headed their averages with 412 scored in six innings – average 82·40. With Scorer also in the side, they played a match at Coventry against a Coventry and District XI, for which several Warwickshire players turned out, while for Coventry and District against London Counties, Wyatt made 140. R. C. Robertson-Glasgow, reviewing the 1942 season in *Wisden*, commented: 'Pilot Officer R. E. S. Wyatt showed little, if any, decline in batting skill and none at all in keenness.'

Warwickshire drew what had by this time become the annual match with Worcestershire at Worcester; and then Edgbaston on a Sunday – 15 July – staged a match between C. C. Goodway's XI, made up mostly of Warwickshire players, including Wyatt, and a British Empire XI, who beat them easily by five wickets.

Midway in 1942, Mr Ernest Bevin, the Minister of Labour, wrote to civic heads asking if they could do something to provide some entertainment for workers in munition plants who, because of the black-out, rarely saw the daylight in winter, and for those who had obeyed the call to have their holidays at home. Alderman Norman Tiptaft was Lord Mayor of Birmingham at the time and among the people he sent for to help him carry out the Minister's wishes was Lieut-Col. Scorer.

'Rusty', as everyone knew him – he had got the name because of the colour of his hair – was Middlesbrough-born, but left there in 1894 and had been a 'Brummie' ever since. As a boy, he remembered seeing Willie Quaife bowling to 'W.G.' and he watched the famous Edgbaston Test of 1902. He went to King Edward's Grammar School, Five Ways, played for Handsworth Wood Cricket Club in 1912 and later for Moseley, whom he captained for twenty years and whose President he was for so long that their new ground was named after him. He played for Warwickshire's second eleven before the war and made his first appearance in the senior side in June, 1921, against Surrey. He recalled that when he got one off the edge off Bill Hitch, Jack Hobbs remarked: 'Good show, sir, we call that the Surrey cut.' But he survived to play several useful innings in the twenties, including his first and only century for the county against Hampshire.

When the Lord Mayor's request came he was already helping to entertain Servicemen by running the Queensberry All-Services Club in Hurst Street, Birmingham – it went on for seven years and 80 000 servicemen visited it – was in charge of a battalion of the Home Guard, and also had his own business. Nevertheless, he also took on the job of trying to organise some cricket.

Naturally the first thing he did was to visit Edgbaston to see what the possibilities were there, but his heart must have sunk when he saw the state of the ground. Ted Leyland's engagement as head groundsman had come to an end on 31 December 1939 and Norman Kilner had taken charge, but without help. At the end of 1941 he went to work in munitions and although the wartime executive of the Club had decided to advertise for a successor, none had been appointed at that time. In the meantime, the green grass grew all round.

This was how Scorer saw it in a broadcast he made towards the end of the war: 'Those of you who knew the ground in peacetime would have received the same shock as I did when I saw it . . . The grass was eighteen inches high and you couldn't see a seat on the banks for four-foot thistles. A bomb had knocked askew the small scorebox near the pavilion and the whole scene presented a picture of complete desolation. It seemed impossible to get the ground ready for a festival in six weeks' time. We hadn't even got a fixture.'

But he saw Colin Langley and told him what he hoped to do. 'You must be a bloody fool,' Langley told him bluntly. 'You'll lose all your money.'

'Can I have the ground for a week?' asked 'Rusty', and was given a reluctant 'Yes'. That was enough for him. He had a ground. How to get it fit for cricket? It was impossible to get labour at this time, so he rang Sir Charles Hyde and asked if he could help. Sir Charles immediately lent the mower from the sports ground of The Birmingham Post and Mail, Ltd, and his own gardener; city officials and members of the Parks Department came along; petrol coupons were wheedled out of reluctant officials who asked, 'Don't you know there's a war on?' and somehow or other the ground was got fit for play, though not all at once, of course. The Warwickshire Club let him have it free of charge and Dr Thwaite and George Payne, chairman of the ground committee, helped all they could. At the annual meeting the following year Dr Thwaite admitted that 'matters had got very much out of hand' and referred to Lieut-Col. Scorer's 'hard work'.

Scorer wrote to all the players he could think of who might be available, and at first he did not get a very good response, though as the Festival became known much stronger sides became available. Eventually a programme of five games was arranged for the week of 3 to 8 August – Warwickshire v. Worcestershire, the Birmingham League v. Coventry and District, Warwickshire v. a National Civil Defence XI, the Birmingham League v. a United Services XI and the Birmingham Combined Civil Defence v. The Home Guard and the Air Training Corps.

The Festival was announced as by invitation of the Lord Mayor in connection with the 'Spend Your Holidays at Home' scheme, and the prices of admission were 1s (or a party of 150 for £5), schoolboys 6d (110 for £2 10s 0d). An appeal was made for offers of help to work the scoreboard, man the turnstiles and act as attendants; and for hospitality for the players who were paid third-class rail fares and hotel expenses, but no fees. It was all conducted in a 'Hit-over-the-pavilion' spirit. This the players were particularly encouraged to do by a local manu-facturer, Mr A. W. Heath, who, in 1934, had offered the Warwickshire professionals £1 for every six hit in a season in excess of three. For the Festival games he gave £1 for the best six hit each day and the best batting and bowling performances.

'Tiger' Smith and Jack Smart reappeared as umpires, the band of the 30th Warwickshire Home Guard played and all was merry and bright except the weather. Despite this there was some good cricket. In the first match Reg. Perks hurt his left hand, but that did not stop him hitting a couple of sixes with his right and Wyatt, too, came out of his shell and hit three sixes, a four and a two off one over in an innings of 171 not out for Warwickshire against the Civil Defence XI, which included Gimblett and the Langridge brothers.

From that first Festival in 1942 nearly £450 was handed over to the Lord Mayor's War Relief Fund and before August was out 'Rusty' was delighted to get a card from Sir Charles Hyde telling him: 'You did a really great job.' The President added a vignette of 'W.G.' – Grace not Quaife: 'I wonder if you listened to the story of W. G. Grace on the wireless last night? He was my "hero" forty-six years ago when I was at Clifton College. He was detested at home, and was a super bully and a bad sportsman and damned fine cricketer!'

Unfortunately for Warwickshire cricket (and a good many other institutions as well) Sir Charles Hyde died early in 1943 and Warwickshire cricket lost a good friend as well as a President. The annual report of the Club, which was now being written by Dr Thwaite, commented that 'Councillor Lieut-Col. Scorer's organisation of the arrangements left nothing to be desired.' In September 1942, Warwickshire appointed as groundsman Fred Pope, father of the Derbyshire players, and he was authorised to get help from Auxiliary Fire Service personnel stationed on the ground, when they were off duty, at 1s 6d per hour, so that solved one problem for the Festival organisers.

When the annual meeting was held there was a surplus of £357 and Dr Thwaite said that the Committee would like to build up as large a reserve as possible to provide funds for reconditioning the ground after the war. By November the Committee were already looking ahead to the resumption of cricket and agreed to support two-day matches, though they were opposed to any suggestion of time-limit cricket. Warwickshire wanted two-day cricket to start on Wednesdays – half-day closing – and Saturdays, and advocated that one point should be awarded for a win, and half a point for a tie, the county winning most matches to be champions. How beautifully simple. Dr Thwaite was also authorised to take some soundings on the possibility of Sunday play.

In 1943 Scorer and his fellow organisers were more ambitious. A subscription list was opened in order to cover expenses and defeat the weather, which was a little kinder, though there was some rain on four out of the five days of Festival week. However, the teams were much stronger and 20 000 spectators entered the ground. As a result at the end of the week nearly £1300 went to charity.

A Royal Australian Air Force XI appeared this time. Hollies saved up one of his best performances for them – seven for 18 – and they were all out 115. Wyatt hit 101 in an hour for the Festival XI, who made 246 for three wickets. Against the National Civil Defence XI the Festival XI scored even more heavily, 279, Wyatt 76 this time, while Jenkins had six for 91 and Hollies four for 72. Then Sergeant Washbrook made 107 of the R.A.F. XI's total of 350 against the Festival XI, for whom Gimblett made 81 and Lieut Maurice Leyland 51 in a stand of 102.

By the end of the week the general consensus of opinion was that the Festival should become an annual feature of the Edgbaston year. In a leading article *The Birmingham Post* pointed out that there were exceptional circumstances – lack of rival attractions, propaganda, holidays-at-home and absence of first class cricket throughout the season, although to serious students Festival cricket might be synonymous with the frivolous. But the paper praised the lightheartedness of the play and added: 'If county cricket is to survive, it will have to appeal to other than serious students and the diminishing band of wealthy patrons.'

One of Scorer's many correspondents, signing himself 'Ginger', had the same idea: 'If some of the cricket wasn't up to Hobbs–Bradman standards, most of it was grand festival cricket and with my knowledge of the game I am afraid that is what I am out to see.' He need not have been afraid; it was what everyone wanted to see, but did not always get. In a letter of congratulation 'on the splendid result', P. F. Warner commented: 'Like you, I do not agree with Warwickshire's proposals for two-day cricket. Two-day cricket was tried in 1919 and was a complete failure. Why anyone should wish to resuscitate a failure I cannot think. However, I have a feeling that as time passes and the matter is more clearly gone into, Warwickshire may change their mind. At any rate they seem to be very much in the minority.'

R. C. Robertson-Glasgow had a wise comment on three-day matches in an article he wrote for *Wisden* in 1944. He quoted the famous Warwick-shire-Hampshire match of 1922 in support of his argument in favour of three-day games and added: 'The three-day match is a thing of hope. It gives time for recovery and surprise.'

Scorer received many letters about the Festivals, for by now the results of the games were being widely broadcast. Many of them came from men serving overseas who said how wonderful it had been to be taken back to Edgbaston again.

Even during the war years those responsible for the administration of the game were far from idle. Flying Officer Wyatt, as he then was, served on a Select Committee to consider the post-war game and Colin Langley was among those who gave evidence. The Committee's report, running to 6000 words, said that no recommendations could be effective unless the game was played in the best possible manner and spirit. (This was to be heard many times but little except lip service was paid to it.)

The Committee thought that no radical changes in the game were called for, but attacking play was stressed:

Before each season counties should make it clear to their captains and players that it remains the policy of the Committee that the team shall aim for victory from the first ball of the match; players shall adopt a dynamic attitude towards the game.

It was unanimously decided that Sunday county cricket should not be introduced, time-limit cricket was rejected and knock-out cricket would be examined later. A sub-committee was set up to investigate this the following summer and plans were put forward for a Cricket Cup, but again it was shelved, yet another report being asked for at the end of 1946.

The Select Committee took the view that 'two-innings matches give the fullest scope for captaincy to reap its reward', otherwise the value to the all-rounder would be lessened and skilled specialisation increased. A new ball after fifty-five overs was suggested as an experiment, fast wickets were thought to be in the best interests of the game and grounds-men should be instructed accordingly.

There were only twenty-five members present at the annual meeting when Dr Thwaite expressed his view that what was wanted to meet the competition there would be in the post-war world of sport was 'common-sense' cricket. The good doctor was elected President in succession to Sir Charles Hyde, with Colin Langley as chairman and Captain Cowan as honorary treasurer. The wartime executive received the Select Committee's recommendations with some reservations. The public, they thought, probably rightly, had no interest in first innings points. Wins only should count, with two points for a win and one for a draw, but they agreed that they would have to control the groundsmen to see that wickets were prepared to enable a bowler to utilise his pace and spin, but still be fair to both batsmen and bowler, an ideal still not achieved.

No such worries inhibited the players who took part in the 1944 Festival which proved easily the best yet. This time there was an additional two-day match between teams representing Australia and the West Indies, which brought such players as Miller and Constantine to Edgbaston, to say nothing of Workman, Sismey, Cristofani, C. B. Clarke, Ablack and Achong.

Despite atrocious weather the match proved a great attraction, 4000 people attending on the Saturday and 3000 on the Sunday, and it made £604 profit for the Royal Australian Air Force Welfare Fund and West Indian charities. There was one letter of protest—at Sunday play.

The Australian XI rattled up 304 for four declared in four hours, Sergeant C. P. Calvert missed at 25 and 58, going on to make 141 in as many minutes. Sergeant Keith Miller trod on his wicket after hitting 27 in twenty minutes, which was a pity. Constantine, of course, captained the West Indies and, although suffering from a pulled leg muscle, still managed to hit a characteristic 54. The West Indies had made 137 for three when rain ended play just after three o'clock on the Sunday afternoon, and 1000 people waited in the rain until 6 p.m. to attend a sportsmen's service conducted by a garrison chaplain from the balcony of the pavilion. It produced a collection of £40 which went to the Prisoners of War Fund.

That game took place in July and the Festival itself, which followed in August, was a great success. Throughout the week the weather was hot and sunny and no fewer than 42 000 people, including 6000 schoolboys, poured into the ground, 10 000 of them on the Saturday. Many of them, especially the boys, must have been seeing such cricket for the first time. When it was announced that I was to write this history I had a letter from a former newspaper colleague welcoming the news and saying he hoped I would include a chapter about wartime cricket, for it was during these matches, when he was still a youngster, that he saw his first glimpse of some of cricket's great men, including Frank Woolley.

The schoolboys were allowed to play all over the area during the intervals and, although it was not roped off, but was marked only with white circles, none of them trespassed on the wicket. Parties of wounded soldiers were given a specially decorated enclosure next to the pavilion, and before play began each day Scorer gave what he called 'crazy natters' over a loudspeaker system he had had installed. There were running commentaries on the play between overs and the fall of wickets and during intervals; there were plans of the fielding positions on the reverse of the score cards – one man said he had wondered for years where gully was and had never dared to ask – and Frank Woolley came out of retirement to play and delight everyone once more.

R. T. Simpson, then just making his name with Notts, was the player of the week. He was on embarkation leave, and in nine innings in various matches before it ended, five of them at Edgbaston, he scored 529 runs – 41, 69, 16, 79, 99, 86, 21, 47, and 71. No wonder P. F. Warner, who paid his first visit to the ground for twenty years and spoke to the crowd, wrote afterwards: 'I think Simpson is by far the most promising of the young batsmen and I guess he will be playing for England one day'. He guessed correctly.

Woolley turned out for the National Civil Defence XI which played a two-day match with the Festival side. In his own inimitable way he made 57 of the 290 total of the C.D. XI. When the Festival XI batted Woolley even bowled, but only one ball, for then he pulled a muscle.

By the end of the first day the Festival XI had made 181 for loss of only one wicket, C. S. Dempster, the backbone of the side having contributed 89 and Simpson 75 not out. Next day they took the total to 310, Simpson just missing a century in a partnership of 138 made in only 85 minutes. In the second innings the Civil Defence XI were without two of their batsmen, Lee and Guise, who, apparently thinking the match would end in a draw, left the ground. The C.D. XI were all out for 82, Hollies having a four for 14 spell in seven overs. The Festival XI had to make 63 to win and got 49 for four, so it was a good finish.

Dempster and Simpson also put on 146 for the first wicket for the Festival XI against the Royal Air Force side, who were beaten by 56 runs; and Walter Hammond, captaining an R.A.F. XI, made 70 not out against the Festival XI for whom Dennis Brookes got 100 not out and Simpson 47 and 71. Woolley wrote afterwards: 'I have played in a great deal of festival cricket during my career, but I have never enjoyed four days' cricket as much as I did during your week.' The financial results too – nearly £2000 for the Lord Mayor's War Relief Fund, £500 to the R.A.F. Benevolent Fund and £100 to other charities – were rewarding.

Scorer thought the loudspeakers had proved a great success and forecast, accurately as it turned out, that they 'will form part of the future equipment of all big grounds – it brings the game right to the spectator in a most intimate and instructive manner.'

Coventry also staged four big matches during 1944, which was the first year of the wartime Tests with the Australian teams. It was also the first year of the flying bombs, one of which, alas, struck the Guards' Chapel during a service there, G. D. Kemp-Welch being among the fatal casualties.

Quietly that October the second of Warwickshire's outstanding servants severed his official association with the Club. At the meeting of the wartime executive on 4 October, the chairman reported that he had received a letter from R. V. Ryder tendering his resignation as secretary. It was accepted with great regret and the Committee placed on record its appreciation of the great services rendered by him during nearly fifty years:

During that long time Mr Ryder has been untiring in his efforts on behalf of the Club and unceasing in his devotion to the best interests of the game. His record as a county secretary, both in length of time and ungrudging service, is unique, and as some slight recognition the committee has great pleasure in electing him an honorary life member of the Club.

It was not quite unique, perhaps, though until then only Mr A. J. Lancaster, who was with Kent from 1885 until 1935, had held the position of county secretary for a longer period, retiring after completing fifty years in office, a period later completed by Mr W. T. Taylor, of Derbyshire. Ryder would have exceeded that period but for the war, but it was remarkable enough. It is difficult for anyone who did not work with him during that long period to assess his value to the Club, but tremendous is the word that comes to my mind.

I met him only once when I was a young cricket reporter come to cover a Test at Edgbaston. I had written for, but not received, a Press ticket. I had heard something of Ryder's reputation as a bit of a Tartar and it was with some timidity that I knocked on the door of his office and stated my business. He was alone in a room which seemed to be full of papers from which, with an air of detachment, he extracted a ticket and gave it to me. He looked at me over his spectacles, which were almost off his nose and said something, though I cannot now remember what it was, and I thanked him and went away feeling that I had committed an intrusion into privacy and rather glad to escape.

He made an even more overwhelming impression on Alec Hastilow who first encountered him when, as a boy, he haunted the ground:

It cost only threepence for a boy to get into Edgbaston in those days [he said], but it wasn't always easy to raise the wind. I used to do it by acting as ball boy to the tennis players in Cannon Hill Park. Then I would get under the turnstile and through the railings. I would field on the outskirts of the nets and once Hargreave invited me to have a knock at the end of a practice. Then Ryder asked me to go into his office. I was terrified, thinking he had got to hear of me getting through the fences, but all he said was: 'You're very keen. Would you like to be a member?' I told him no, thank you, as I couldn't pay the subscription. 'Well', said Ryder, 'I will start a junior membership. Could you find five shillings?' I said 'Yes', so I went and held the horses' heads at the tennis club to earn the money and I became the first junior member – on a ladies' transferable ticket.

The reference to getting under the turnstiles and through the railings reminded Leslie Deakins of the dedication Ryder once penned to a book he always intended to write. Alas, he got no further, but it seems worth reproducing here:

To those regular spectators whose consistent support is beyond computation, and can never be repaid; whose pertinacity and ingenuity are beyond compare; whose courage laughs at locks, bolts and bars, and even spikes – *they who climb over the fence*.

Eric Hollies was another who approached him in awe, but to whom he showed his human side. Hollies recalls that Ryder always wore his hat in the office and his spectacles at the end of his nose. He lost both one day when Eric, pulling on the rope used to stop people walking behind the bowler's arm, found that he had tripped up no less a person than the Club secretary; he was soon transferred to other duties.

Canon Parsons, who had served during the Second World War as an Army chaplain, and after being invalided out of the Army in September

1944, was appointed an honorary chaplain with the rank of major, remembers him as 'a very aristocratic old gentleman' who told him when he first reported to the ground after being engaged in 1910: 'I am sorry. You will have to go home. The king has just died.' Another old Warwickshire player thought Ryder was a very clever man in the office, but did not understand what went on in the middle. This latter view is questionable, but there is no doubt that a number of players, of whom Wyatt was the most prominent, did think that Ryder interfered in matters on the field which were not his concern as secretary. This was, perhaps, a weakness, but he would have been a remarkable man indeed if, holding office as long as he did and wielding so much executive power, he had not felt that everything that appertained to Warwickshire cricket was his affair.

Certainly no one could have worked harder or longer for the Club than he did. Had he been paid according to the hours he put in he would have retired a rich man and he could probably have done that in any case had he accepted some of the offers made to him, including, for instance, the secretaryship of the Royal and Ancient, but nothing could lure him away from cricket. He must be regarded as the central figure of the three chief architects of the Warwickshire Club, the first, of course, being William Ansell, and the third Leslie Deakins, who succeeded him. Ryder must have derived enormous satisfaction from what he achieved yet one is left wondering if, at the end, he was not a disappointed man in that, for all his efforts to build up membership in particular and attract people to the ground in general, he never saw more than 11 000 spectators on the ground on any one day. Five years before he died he wrote these words:

Birmingham has shown nothing like the passionate interest in cricket which has marked the attitude to the game in Manchester, Sheffield, Leeds, or Nottingham.

Ryder was forced to believe that Birmingham had given its heart to football. If it had, it was not Ryder's fault. He had done his best to make it fall in love with cricket and he had set the example, remaining ever steadfast to the game in general and that of his adopted county in particular.

But let Leslie Deakins, who for fourteen years had grown up under Ryder's wing and probably knew him more intimately than anyone alive today, have the last word about him. For him Ryder was not only an eminent Victorian, but as a match manager and cricket administrator 'he was probably the best there has ever been in the game'. Somehow or other R.V.R. and L.T.D. bridged the generation gap of those days and worked admirably together. Ryder soon told his young assistant that he, Ryder, had never learned the first rule in such a job, which was to suffer fools gladly, for he was apt to be peremptory in manner and intolerant of some of the wilder ideas which Warwickshire members sometimes brought forward. He was autocratic – he once ordered no less an official than a police superintendent off the ground – and austere, but to L.T.D., who spoke of him with warm affection, he was 'a first-class man of the highest integrity, completely honest'.

Deakins was the obvious successor, but he had to be appointed *in absentia,* for he was still serving as a writer in the Navy when Ryder announced his retirement, and at once the Club set about trying to secure his early release. The prospects of some cricket in 1945 were also discussed and it is an indication of how conservative the Club still was in its attitude to the game that the annual report for 1944 could express satisfaction that the Select Committee did not believe any radical changes in its conduct were called for, and unanimously decided that Sunday cricket should not be introduced. On matters nearer home, the report was more realistic and a special sub-committee was appointed to prepare a comprehensive scheme of ground development. 'The playing pitch', the report stated, 'has few superiors in the country, but the same cannot be said of the pavilion, stands, etc.'

It was also decided to approach eleven of the pre-war players and to inquire whether 'Tiger' Smith was prepared to act as coach, a position he eventually accepted and held until Dollery relinquished the captaincy. Hollies asked for a five-year agreement, including a benefit, and was eventually given one for three years, a guarantee of a minimum salary of £500 – the highest figure yet paid by the Club to a player, and a benefit.

A few matches in 1945 were recognised as first class by the M.C.C. It was a summer in which the Empire teams played some of the most attractive cricket ever seen in this country and of wonderful hitting by Miller and Pepper, the Australians, and by Hammond and Martin Donnelly, who was a major in the New Zealand forces and was to stay on at Oxford and later assist Warwickshire. For the Dominions he hit two centuries, scored 348 runs and averaged 87·00, though it was Wyatt who emerged again at the head of affairs.

But it was Miller and Pepper whose innings will always be remembered by those blessed enough to see them, and not least by Eric Hollies whose six wickets in the matches ranked first class cost him 56 runs each. It was off him, in a wonderful match at Lord's between England and the Dominions, which the latter won by 45 runs with eight minutes to spare, that Miller hit one of the biggest sixes ever seen on the ground. The ball landed on the roof of the small broadcasting box above the England dressing-room. Hollies got him lbw for 26 in the first innings, but in the second Miller hit a glorious 185 and Eric had 115 runs hit off him for his three wickets. Hammond also hit two hundreds and Donnelly one in that match.

Hollies had the rough end of the stick also in the Scarborough Festival game between H. D. G. Leveson Gower's XI and the Australian services. Pepper hit six sixes and eighteen fours in an innings of 168, one of the sixes off Hollies clearing the four-storied houses into Trafalgar Square. Hollies took one wicket for 135 and I suppose that he can always console himself with the thought, if a bowler who has been severely hit can ever do so, that he contributed to the gaiety of nations – and there was precious little of that about at the time, thanks to the flying bombs.

Not least of the pleasures of this season was to see Dollery back in action again. He returned to England to play in several matches for the Central Mediterranean Forces XI, making 92 in one match out of a partnership of 196. Playing for them also was a young fast bowler from New Zealand, Tom Pritchard.

The county, captained by Cyril Goodway, and including five 'regulars', played single-day home and away games with Lancashire in August. At Edgbaston on a sporting wicket Lancashire were routed by Hollies and Grove for 78 and Warwickshire won by four wickets, C. S. Dempster making 58 out of 106. At Old Trafford Lancashire had their revenge by ten wickets, Eddie Paynter, after being missed twice in the deep, making 82.

But the best cricket in the Midlands came in what proved to be the last of the wartime festivals – the most successful of all. Festival week proper was preceded by three other games. First there was another two-day match between the Royal Australian Air Force XI and a West Indies XI in which the Australians this time had much the better of it. They scored 275, of which Miller made 30. Constantine, not bowling fast, but mixing them as only he could, took four for 46. The West Indies collapsed, however, and were all out for 55, so an exhibition match was played in which Constantine hit a ball from Cristofani so far out of the ground that it was never found.

Then on 8 July came a Sunday match between W. R. Hammond's XI and New Zealand which caught the public's fancy as only a Test Match had done so far. The weather was ideal and 14 000 people crowded into the ground. At one time traffic was held up by the queues and the main gates had to be opened, six men with bags taking £140 in twenty minutes – at 2s a time. They saw a wonderful match. Donnelly, driving superbly, made 100 not out, and the New Zealanders were able to declare at 236 for eight. Hammond's side, which included Herbert Sutcliffe, then on the verge of retirement, Edrich, Wyatt, J. G. Dewes, Hollies, Goddard and Cyril Goodway, had two hours thirty-five minutes to get the runs and did so with ten minutes of the extra half-hour remaining, thanks largely to Edrich, who, although a trifle lucky, hit a very enterprising 132 not out.

The following Sunday, Scorer took a Warwickshire XI, which included most of the regular county players, to Northampton, where they won by five wickets after getting Northants out for 68 – Grove five for 31 and Hollies four for 15.

'Cricket with a Laugh in it' was the slogan for the Festival itself. There were seven days of it and neither cool winds nor occasional rain were able to put a damper on them, though the Lord Mayor of Birmingham and several visiting mayors and chairmen of councils were unlucky enough to attend when play in the Royal Australian Air Force XI game with the Festival XI was limited to 100 minutes, and even then sometimes took place in sharp rain.

Constantine came again for two matches against Sussex, had five fours and two threes in an innings of 29 in the first game and took six for 60 in the second. Among the guests at another match was Sir Home Gordon, the administrator and writer on the game, who afterwards in *The Cricketer*, wrote that 'what the Chamberlains were to politics in Birmingham, he [Scorer] is to festival cricket'.

For the R.A.F. in a Saturday match against the Festival XI Edrich made another century, 165 in two and a quarter hours, and Hammond and Washbrook half-centuries, nearly 500 runs being scored in a day which ended with a variety show and dancing on the ground. Eight thousand people came to see this game and another 7000 turned up on the final Sunday for another game between the same two sides; Hammond this time making 63 not out and Wyatt 58.

Scorer ended his final broadcast on the festivals with these words: 'And so my wartime festivals come to an end – for me happy memories of wonderful sportsmen, great cricket and happy crowds bringing money for those who need it. I give you a toast – to Cricket.'

It had been a remarkable achievement. Over the four years, 140 000 people had come to watch cricket at Edgbaston and nearly £10 000 was raised for wartime good causes – £1701 from the last effort. Birmingham was the only city or town in the country which held an annual festival during those years and *Wisden* thought they had proved that Birmingham possessed a big public for the game.

There was one more match before the season ended. On Saturday and Sunday, 18 and 19 August, Scorer's XI met New Zealand at Edgbaston in aid of the Queensbury Club, which had been generous with its hospitality to visiting players. On the Saturday, when about 1000 spectators came, New Zealand, with Dempster and Donnelly, made 147 and Scorer's XI, 171 for two wickets. They then shuffled the packs of players for the Sunday game, which drew a crowd of 2000, but again Scorer's side won – 251 to New Zealand's 154, Hollies taking six for 55. This performance followed his eight for 92 in a match against an Australian Services XI at Blackpool on the Friday, in which he bowled

Keith Miller twice – revenge must have been sweet – and seven for 26 for West Bromwich Dartmouth in the Birmingham League on the Saturday. After the match the New Zealanders stayed on to attend a thanksgiving for victory service at Birmingham Cathedral.

It was a fitting finale to the festival, which a good many people were reluctant to see end. Both M. F. K. Fraser in the *Birmingham Evening Despatch*, and Claude Westell, in *The Birmingham Mail*, had complimentary articles asking if this need be the last of festival cricket in Birmingham. Fraser commented on 'how uninterested (seemingly) the County Club authorities have been about it' and suggested that Birmingham should strike its own note and have a week in the middle of the summer to avoid clashing with the seaside festivals at the end of the season. Westell ended his article with these words: 'Is Festival cricket in Birmingham to die with the end of the war? Then a host of stout Birmingham cricket-lovers should know the reason why.'

A week later Fraser wrote that Dr Thwaite had sent a letter saying that he and E. George Payne, chairman of the Ground and Buildings Sub-committee, known as 'Old Hammer and Nail', his remedy for all ground repair work, had been examining the idea of a festival as a permanent feature; that suitable matches had been envisaged and that as soon as it was possible to get the Club machinery working, various possibilities would be explored. Dr Thwaite added that if necessary he was prepared to take over the management and organisation. He paid tribute to Scorer's work and 'agreed that some county members have felt that there has been a lack of interest by the committee in the festival idea and that a few have gone so far as to resign on that account', but he added that if it had not been for the efforts of Mr Payne and other 'back-room boys' there would not have been a ground available for these wartime fixtures.

Wyatt also wrote to Scorer, saying he was certain the matches were appreciated by thousands 'and I can assure you that those who matter at Lord's thoroughly approved of your festival. Quite apart from providing money for charity and keeping up morale, it kept the game before the public and proved that it was by no means dead in Birmingham . . .'

The question of the festival came before the General Committee in September when the President said he had received a number of inquiries from the Press and individuals asking whether it was their intention to continue them. He felt that in the interests of the Club and Warwickshire cricket generally, this was a matter which should receive careful consideration.

The Committee unanimously agreed and it was decided that it should be further considered by the executive committee after the fixtures for next season had been determined. Perhaps they had forgotten that in the previous March the special executive had unanimously agreed that such an arrangement 'would be impracticable', though no arguments for or against were given. Eventually it was agreed that the August Bank Holiday matches should be regarded as a Festival Week, though it was hardly on Scorer lines. Perhaps the series could have happened only in wartime. His final verdict, given on the occasion of his 80th birthday, was: 'I must have been mad, but I'm glad I was.'

BOOK THREE

LESLIE THOMAS DEAKINS

1945—

Reconstruction
(1946–1948)

THRILLING and entertaining as the cricket was during the last year of the war, matters of much more moment for the future of the Warwickshire Club were being decided. The main business of the year was planning a programme to bring the ground to a state in which Test Matches, of which there had not been one since 1929, could again be staged there.

Dr Thwaite told the annual meeting that post-war planning could be divided into two parts – capital outlay on premises and an income adequate to meet reasonable expenditure. The aim was to increase the capacity of the ground to 20 000 at a cost of £200 000 spread over ten to twenty years.

The President also took the opportunity to convey good wishes to Ryder and his compliments to Leslie Deakins. 'When the war started', he said, 'I snapped him up as my secretary and until he joined the Navy he did a lot of county cricket work in his spare time.'

A report on the reconstruction of the ground was prepared by Mr Frank Wager, the Club's honorary architect, who, so to speak, acted as midwife to the plans nearing birth, the child being reared in later years by his successor, Mr John Suggitt, of Essex, Goodman and Suggitt, of Birmingham, who became the Club's professionally employed architects.

Another report by Colin Langley and J. A. Lones for the General Committee was presented to them, received and approved on 15 May. It provided for four blocks of accommodation: a double-deck stand, with seating accommodation for 6800 – 2400 under cover and 4400 in the open – on the popular side, plus buffet bars, luncheon-room, kitchen, dressing-rooms and lavatories; a second double-deck stand, with seating for 1200, plus a luncheon-room, small gymnasium, squash courts, a new house for the groundsman and a cricket shop; a members' pavilion with covered seating for 2400 and 800 in the open, including a ladies' section, luncheon-rooms, buffet bars, a committee room and accommodation for the secretary; terracing with open seating for 4000 on the east side and for another 1000 on the remainder of the ground; a third double-deck stand, seating 950 under cover and 2750 in the open, with a snack bar and lavatories; and a car park for 700 vehicles as a priority. All this would give total accommodation for 21 000, about one-third of them under cover. The cost of the whole scheme, including land acquired, would be £201 150.

An appeal for the first £50 000 required was launched to coincide with the home match with Lancashire. Dr Thwaite gave it a good start with a generous personal contribution of £2500, and by the end of the year £10 871 had been raised. Part of this money was spent in acquiring six acres of ground between the existing west boundary and the Pershore Road, the former Birmingham Rugby Football Club ground, for £3100. A plan of the proposed new lay-out for the ground, visualising the new Pavilion, was published in August.

Naturally the Calthorpe Estate was consulted about the changes. The relationship between the Club and the Estate had always been a pleasant one since the earliest days when the Edgbaston ground was first acquired. The Club has invariably consulted the estate before taking any action concerning the ground itself – a continuing acknowledgement, as it were, of the most generous terms under which the freehold was originally sold to the Club – and it was a happy coincidence that on both occasions when purchases were made from the estate the agents involved, apart from members of the Calthorpe family, were also lovers of the game – Mr Frank Newman and his son, George, the latter of whom played for Middlesex and at the time of writing was President of that club.

Ideally, it would have been better if the whole ground could have been cleared and a new start made from scratch, as some of the bombed cities were able to do to their advantage. Had that been possible the new Edgbaston could have been built very much more quickly and efficiently than it has been possible to do it piecemeal over the years, and many of the pitfalls involved in that sort of rebuilding would have been avoided. That, however, could not be done. First-class cricket had to be resumed as soon as possible and no delays could be tolerated other than those imposed by lack of finance and the building licence restrictions which remained in force for some time after the war and greatly hampered reconstruction and development.

Despite all the efforts made to get him home earlier, it was 30 October 1945, just a year after he had been appointed, before the new secretary could attend his first meeting and begin to put into effect the plans for reconstruction he had dreamed about during the dog watches at Scapa Flow, and which he had been sending back to the President so that they could begin to take shape in his absence. He brought with him a new assistant, Sydney S. Harkness, who had served with him at the destroyer depot at Scapa. Then, as now, Leslie Deakins was always ready to talk cricket when he could get anyone to listen to him and, in Harkness, he found a ready listener to his ideas for creating the Edgbaston he hoped to see after the war. Harkness had played club cricket, but not worked in the game before; now, like Deakins, he was to devote his life to it.

The first plan for the new Edgbaston had been drawn up on a piece of Royal Navy notepaper in 1943. It developed into a 40-page treatise on the development of the ground as he saw it which he sent back to Dr Thwaite. It provided the basis for the development plan announced in 1945. It has been modified many times since, but always three fundamental spectator requirements have been kept in mind: first, comfortable seating; second, a good view of the play from anywhere on the ground; and third, every reasonable amenity.

There were many other matters to be dealt with even between that first committee and the end of the year. It was decided that the old system under which the professionals had been paid on a match fee basis should be abolished and that in future they should be given agreed fixed sums each year; that subscriptions should be increased despite the fact that the numbers had dropped from a peak of 2700 to 700. Now the fee for an ordinary member was to be increased from £1 10s 0d to £2 2s 0d, country membership to £1 5s 0d, ladies' tickets to £1 1s 0d, car park to £1, transferable season tickets for the popular side to £1 1s 0d and boys under 15 to 10s 6d. These rates were agreed at a special meeting of members, the first since the start of the war, on 18 December. And in ten years, by 1955, the number of members went up to over 10 000.

Sunday cricket was discussed, but the Committee decided against it for the time being, and the question of the captaincy was deferred, though invitations to play were sent to a number of amateurs, including Peter Cranmer, Bob Wyatt, Cyril Goodway, J. R. Thompson, R. Sale (the Oxford University left-hander), R. H. Maudsley, and others.

There was also a fixture change to be introduced. Each county would play the same number of matches against each of the counties on the list and would be allowed to name four sides who would become its 'permanent opponents' to be met home and away each season. Warwickshire chose Worcestershire, Derbyshire, Leicestershire, and Lancashire and forfeited three home games with Middlesex, Surrey and Gloucestershire for one season in four, though this also meant the return of games with Essex, Somerset and Notts. Coventry was allocated two matches.

Another project started this year was a new form of annual report which Leslie Deakins has compiled ever since and which has gradually blossomed into one of cricket's most remarkable publications, with a world-wide circulation of 9000–10 000, to which I, in common with many others, have had much cause to be grateful. The first issue, appropriately enough, contained an appreciation of Dr Thwaite, a member since 1909, honorary treasurer in 1930, chairman in 1939 and President in 1943. There was also a not untimely reminder, in view of the proposed developments, that the premises on the ground at that time were largely of wood. Edgbaston was about to move into the concrete age.

Not only a ground, but a team, without which the finest cricket ground would have been but an empty shell, had to be reconstructed after the Second World War. The Committee began by reappointing as captain Peter Cranmer, who had been demobilised with the rank of major, and it was expected that he could count on such amateurs as Wyatt; C. S. Dempster (who had transferred his allegiance from Leicestershire and would play when business permitted); Cyril Goodway as wicketkeeper, Buckingham having retired; Dick Sale and J. R. Thompson, a schoolmaster at Marlborough, when the summer term ended.

Of the former regular professionals, the war had ended the careers of Buckingham, Santall, Mayer and Croom; and only Dollery, Hollies Ord and Ken Taylor were available at the start of the season, with the registration of Tom Pritchard being infuriatingly held up, and, looming up on the Coventry horizon, the sturdy figure of Fred Gardner. Grove was still in the forces. 'Tiger' Smith, of course, was coach and Alec Hastilow agreed to captain the second XI for the season.

As things turned out, the county called on many amateurs as well as club players – an average of six played in every game in 1946 – for Wyatt moved to Worcestershire and after three matches at the start of the season Dempster departed once more to New Zealand on business, while Sale was not available until after the University season ended. No fewer than thirty-three players had one or more innings for the county and twenty bowlers were called on. But vary the team selection as they might, it was virtually a four-man side – Cranmer, who never lost hope, Dollery, Hollies and Ord.

There was one other old retainer who did not report for duty at the start of the season – Chloe, the last of a long line of distinguished drawers of the heavy roller, though none, I think, achieved a retirement notice such as she was accorded by Claude Westell, cricket correspondent of *The Birmingham Mail*, on 14 May of that year:

When at long last county cricket again goes along the old sweet way at Edgbaston, a familiar and faithful servant of the Warwickshire Club will be missing from the ground. She has fallen a victim, not of the war, but of the ruthless and relentless machine-age which is no respecter of faithful old servants. The advent of a motor-driven roller will mean that no longer shall we see Chloe, the Edgbaston mare, standing patiently in the shafts, waiting for the end of the innings, plodding her customary way to the middle, at the day's close, providing a mount for the groundsman's daughter.

Through many a summer before the war, she had gone about her pleasant task, the successor to a long line of Chloes, who had been similarly and pleasantly employed. She had more than a mere nodding acquaintance with the most inept of county batsmen and the most expert of county bowlers, and she had the rare distinction of having been interviewed by that peer of county cricket writers, Neville Cardus. On that unforgettable occasion she discoursed delightfully in the pages of *The Manchester Guardian* on her long and honourable cricket career, asserting with positive feeling that oats were not what they used to be – and neither were last-wicket batsmen.

The engagement of the first Chloe, more than fifty years since, was a somewhat tragic affair. Mr R. V. Ryder has told me how, in his fifth year as Warwickshire's secretary, he set out with a committee man for a horse repository, 'there to buy a most absolute and excellent horse'. Neither of them knew the first thing about horses, but they did their best in the cause of county cricket. As the Psalmist has told us, a horse is a vain thing for safety, and this one had scarcely set foot upon the pleasaunce of Edgbaston than she fell down dead; a sad blow to a struggling club.

Her successor, happily, proved to be of sterner stuff. True, there have been lapses. For instance, there was an occasion in 1928 when there was no small cause for anxiety, but the circumstances were both exceptional and extenuating. Warwickshire were playing against Yorkshire on a June day that was really flaming. Only Sanders remained to bat, and as he walked out to join Santall the mare moved instinctively into the shafts of the roller, but the last man in did not run true to form. He stayed on until after lunch and into the middle of the torrid afternoon, to help in the scoring of 128 runs and the setting up of a Warwickshire last wicket record which still holds.

It is related, with what truth I know not, that, what with the intense heat, the long and unaccustomed period of waiting and the shock to Chloe's deep-rooted conservative principles, caused by so revolutionary a procedure on the part of the batsmen, she fainted for the first and last time in her life.

There was another occasion, not long before the outbreak of war, when Chloe, in a literal sense, blotted her copybook. It happened on one of those mornings, so irritating to the cricketer when the dry intervals between the showers were constantly raising hopes, which did not materialise, of play being started. In the periods between umpirical visitations to the middle, Leyland, the groundsman, had laboured long and arduously in his endeavours to dry the pitch, only to have his work ruined by rain.

At last came a longer spell of clear sky than any that had gone before. The umpires decided that if there was no more rain play should begin after lunch. The little group of impatient spectators cheered. Yet again Leyland and his staff got busy with absorbent roller, sawdust, blankets, and all the familiar resources of the groundsman who has to deal with wet weather situations.

The sun shone as the mare went out, drawing behind her the iron roller which marked the final stage in the preparations for cricket. But in mid-wicket Chloe behaved in most unladylike and inconsiderate manner, and Leyland perforce had to begin anew to the accompaniment of as choice a selection of peculiarly pungent Yorkshire invective as ground staff, Chloe included, had ever had to listen to, whereon a literary-minded cricket lover was constrained to quote John Gay's

> *Why vent ye on the generous steed your rage?*
> *Does not her service earn your daily bread?*

And now yet another old retainer has passed from the Edgbaston scene. It has been truly said that that which happened on the other side of war is ancient history, but we who knew those happy yesterdays will linger fondly on memories of Chloe, placidly champing the grass on the boundary's verge whilst awaiting the inevitable end of the innings. Will she, I wonder, feel a little sad when, as the summer moves towards its crown, she thinks of Edgbaston and what is there afoot?

I like to think that when at last she takes her long rest it will be on an Elysian cricket field among the game's Immortals, that she will be surrounded by equine friends who, too, have drawn cricket rollers and tasted happiness, that the sun will fall warmly upon her and that the pasturage will be good.

Wyatt's unhappy departure was really a continuation of the sad story of disagreements with the Committee. He says that he had always intended to continue playing for Warwickshire after the war and the Committee is on record that they wanted him to do so, but relations were never 'particularly harmonious', as he put it. There was an incident at a luncheon, but that alone would not have prevented him from continuing to play; it was 'the general atmosphere and attitude adopted towards me by certain members of the Committee' that decided him to move to Worcestershire, where he had gone to live at the beginning of the war.

There was disharmony even about the manner of his going. There was no mention of his intention to do so at the annual meeting. The first reference to it comes in the minutes of a meeting of the general committee on 18 April when it was decided to return the form for his registration for Worcestershire, recently handed to the secretary. This was done under Rule 10 (1) which related to players not required by the county for which they were qualified. The form, it was stated, was returned because 'it had been very apparent at all times that he was wanted by Warwickshire', to which Wyatt might well have retorted that sometimes they had a curious way of showing it.

According to the minutes, Wyatt met the executive committee after a preliminary discussion during which it became evident that the committee did not wish to retain him against his will. When he was admitted to the meeting Wyatt expressed a wish to play for Worcestershire 'as he felt a change would be mutually beneficial in view of past incidents and the strained atmosphere that was likely to ensue'. The chairman – Alec Hastilow presided in the absence of Colin Langley – stressed that Warwickshire wished to retain his services if possible, but when Wyatt reaffirmed his wish to go a statement was drawn up, mutually agreed and issued to the Press.

The text of it was:

Mr R. E. S. Wyatt, at his own request, met the Executive Committee at the Club today and intimated that he did not wish to accept the invitation already given to him to play for Warwickshire and desired registration under Rule 10 (1) to enable him to play for Worcestershire. The Committee, although they very much regretted the decision, did not wish to stand in the way of so able a cricketer remaining in the county game, and informed him they would not oppose his decision. The final decision, of course, would rest with the M.C.C.

According to Wyatt, it was said in Committee that he was not qualified for Worcestershire because when he went to live in that county he had not notified Warwickshire of his intention of qualifying; a minor point, he thought, if technically correct. I have not found any reference to this in the minutes, but, far from being a minor point, it was an essential preliminary to qualification by residence – indeed, under the then rules of county cricket the qualification could not begin to run until the date was decided by Wyatt's letter.

The M.C.C. therefore suggested that he should qualify for Worcestershire under the then new registration rule, but for this Warwickshire had to agree that they no longer required his services. Warwickshire, indeed, delayed signing the registration form in the hope that Wyatt would change his mind. Wyatt said that when he met the Executive he told them that they could prevent him from playing for Worcestershire if they wished to do so, but not for Surrey, for whom he was, of course, qualified by birth, and that if he did go to Surrey he would consider it necessary to give publicly his reasons for leaving Warwickshire, who could not have had any objection to him doing so.

As it was, however, the chairman, on behalf of the Committee, and of Warwickshire cricketers generally, wished Wyatt all good fortune with his new county and that was that. Wyatt never again played under the Warwickshire emblem, except for the Old County Cricketers' Association, though he often visited the ground to which, after his retirement from the game, he was a welcome visitor. The Committee, however, never reconciled itself to electing him an honorary life member, which was proposed several times, but was always turned down on the ground that such an honour should be conferred only on an unanimous vote.

Wyatt, despite his failings, to which his somewhat dour and uncompromising personality may have contributed, served the Club well according to his lights and by any reckoning would have to be one of the first choices for the best Warwickshire eleven of all time.

At least Wyatt had nothing but the happiest recollections of the men he led and played with.

I could not have played for a nicer side [he said]. There was Len Bates, master of all the shots. He should have played for England, but he lacked concentration. He *looked* an England player. 'Tiger' Smith was a great wicket-keeper and even in my day, when he was obviously past his prime, he was still a useful batsman. Jack Parsons was a fine forward player and Norman Kilner another very fine bat. Reg Santall played some very good innings and should have been fifty per cent better. Croom was a fine opening bat and I hardly ever saw him miss a catch. As for Tom Dollery, I would put him as the best player Warwickshire had in the latter part of my day, though he played too much on the on-side. He was a beautiful hitter of the ball. Howell was a fine fast bowler and Hollies very, very accurate.

Warwickshire having withdrawn their objections, the M.C.C. agreed to Wyatt's immediate registration for Worcestershire for whom he played later in the season in one of the matches against Warwickshire, though not at Edgbaston. It was at Dudley where he went in first wicket down, scored 4 and 27 and took one for 42 in the second innings. He continued to play for Worcestershire until the end of his career. In his last county match against Somerset he had the satisfaction of hitting the six Worcestershire needed to win; and in his last first-class match of all, in 1956, when he was 55, for D. R. Jardine's side against Oxford University, he had M. J. K. Smith, his successor years later as Warwickshire's captain, caught at mid-off.

In all, for the second county of his adoption, he scored 5647 runs, including six centuries, and took 73 wickets. In 1950 he was appointed an England selector; in 1951 elected captain of Worcestershire a few weeks before his 50th birthday; in 1954 became a vice-president of the Worcestershire Club and president of Warwickshire Old County Cricketers' Association, and continued to serve cricket in a variety of capacities.

Cricket came back to a cold douche from the weather, the season being one of the worst experienced, but still most counties did well, for the public, long starved of the first-class game, was anxious to watch it again. There were record attendances at many grounds where players really did show a desire to get on with the game, as they had been urged to do, and in their anxieties to get a result there were more freak declarations, in one of which Warwickshire figured. The county's membership rose spectacularly – from just over 600 to over 2000, though only thirty members let their enthusiasm carry them away to the extent of attending the annual meeting at which Colin Langley appealed for a membership of 8000 to 10 000. 'Seldom has public support been so keen and so strong,' the annual report commented.

All the counties played twenty-six matches. Warwickshire won seven of theirs, but lost fifteen, and only Derbyshire, Northants and Sussex finished below them in the table. Nevertheless, Captain Cowan, reviewing the season later, disagreed with *The Birmingham Post*'s description of it as disappointing. To win seven matches, he said, was more than he had dared to hope for and he thought Cranmer had captained the side well, despite seldom having the same team two matches running.

Hollies even thought that only a man of Cranmer's type and outlook could have seen the Club through such a season. He 'remained his bright and cheery self, and through his ability to laugh at the worst problems maintained a wonderful team spirit . . . He opened the bowling, he opened the batting, he scored more runs than anyone with the exception of Tom Dollery, and made light of a great many weaknesses.' And no one could ever accuse him of prolonging his own innings at the expense of the side. More than once he declared when in sight of a century.

The spirit in which Cranmer played the game was evident in the match against Hampshire at Edgbaston in which, after the loss of a day's play, there were three declarations. The first came after Warwickshire had scored 252 for eight, of which Cranmer had hit 83 in eighty-five minutes. Then Hampshire made 154 for eight before E. D. R. Eagar also declared. As an indication that he was willing to try anything, Cranmer opened the bowling himself with Hollies, who could bowl a useful seamer with the new ball, and took six for 52. Then Cranmer hit 81 not out, including five sixes off Bailey's left-arm slows, before declaring a second time, at 154 for two. Then they got Hampshire out for 179 and won by 73 runs. This time Hollies took five for 71.

One gamble that did not come off was in the Yorkshire match at Bradford which was reduced to one day. Yorkshire, sent in, declared at 104 for seven and then Smailes and Booth routed Warwickshire for 56, of which Fantham, who twice hit Bowes for six, was the only man to get double figures. The result counted as a win for Yorkshire.

Hollies had begun the season as he was to go on with seven wickets for 77, including three in five balls, against Sussex at Edgbaston. He was virtually a one-man attack, bowling altogether during the season 1433 overs, more than any other bowler in the country. Among them were 416 maidens, an astonishing proportion for a bowler so hard-worked, and he had no fewer than 175 wickets, the highest number ever taken in one season for the county, easily beating George Paine's previous record of 156 in 1934. His average was the extremely low one of 15·16. Altogether this must rank as one of the best of all post-war bowling performances anywhere.

There were few matches in which he did not bowl sixty overs or more and in one he bowled seventy-one. Regularly, he has told us, he was so tired that he went to sleep in the dressing-room and had to be woken up when it was his turn to bat. 'Nevertheless,' he said, 'I enjoyed the action and there were few times indeed when I wished someone else could take over.' As 'Tom' Dollery once said of him, 'Hollies would always say, "I shall get him out next over." ' You could say he loved bowling, and against Notts that season he had his just reward – taking all ten of their wickets himself without the aid of a fieldsman. He bowled seven of them and the other three were lbw. It was the finest performance of his career and for once an outstanding feat by a Warwickshire player was done at Edgbaston.

Warwickshire batted first and were all out for 170, Fantham making his first 50. When Notts went in Hollies found that he could turn the ball hardly at all, yet this was the analysis he achieved, such was his skill in length and flight:

O	M	R	W
20·4	4	49	10

He took the wickets of batsmen nine and ten with consecutive balls and says he was so excited at the prospect of getting all ten for the first time in his life that he forgot he was 'on' a hat trick as well. But he did not get it then, nor did he ever do so for the county.

Even so, Warwickshire lost the match. In the second innings they collapsed for 113, and Notts hit off the runs for the loss of three wickets. This time Hollies bowled twenty out of the forty-one overs sent down and took one for 29. The President had the ball with which he took all ten mounted and suitably inscribed and it was presented to him at the next annual meeting, but soon afterwards another gift reached him which I imagine he treasures just as much. It was a copy of *English Cricket* by Neville Cardus, and on the fly-leaf are pasted cuttings from *The Birmingham Post* of the scores in the match and a leading article which appeared the day after the performance. Written beside them are these words in R. V. Ryder's handwriting:

To an English cricketer who, playing for his county, Warwickshire at Edgbaston, on July 14 1946, took all 10 wickets against Notts 'without help from fielders', this souvenir is offered in appreciation and admiration by a friend. R.V.R. 25/7/46.

The strange ins and outs of cricket form were vividly illustrated in the return match at Trent Bridge. R. T. Simpson – on embarkation leave – finished his wartime cricket with that wonderful run of scores which culminated in the 1945 Edgbaston Festival. When Warwickshire came to Trent Bridge he was on demobilisation leave, but had played ten innings and made only 82 in all. Perhaps he had just got news of his release, for now he made 201 in four hours five minutes, hitting two sixes and twenty fours without giving a chance.

Warwickshire's bowlers had to put in more long and arduous toil against Essex at Southend where D. M. Wilcox and R. M. Taylor put on 263 for the eighth wicket.

Warwickshire just did not have two opening bowlers this season and Hollies was often pressed into service, sometimes to good effect, as in the second innings of the last match of the season against Surrey at The Oval. He and Ron Maudsley took the new ball and, bowling unchanged, skittled them out for 97 in ninety minutes. Maudsley took six for 54 and Hollies four for 34. In the match Hollies had eleven wickets for 124. As for Maudsley, Cranmer gave him his county cap as he walked off the field.

Both Dollery, who pulled Warwickshire's batting chestnuts out of the fire on numerous occasions – Cranmer was the only other player to make over 1000 runs – and Hollies played in the Test trial at Lord's which was spoiled by the weather, Dollery making 39. They also played against the Gentlemen at The Oval, but without success. Both were extremely unlucky not to be chosen to go to Australia that winter. Had they done so their careers might have gone very differently, though both were essentially what, for want of a better term, one might call 'home boys'.

The two matches at Coventry this season were the first since 1932 when they had been given up because of the cost of staging matches there compared with Edgbaston, though, as Ryder had admitted, the Club had never felt comfortable about depriving Coventry of first-class cricket and had been anxious to resume fixtures there.

There were some fine players in the All India side – the first to tour after the war under the captaincy of the Nawab of Pataudi – among them being V. M. Merchant, who became their first batsman to score 2000 runs on a tour, and a great all-rounder in Vinoo Mankad, who did the double. At Edgbaston in August they won the toss and sent Warwickshire in, only to see them make their highest score of the season – 375 for nine declared. Sale, down from Oxford, opened the innings – he was one of eight opening batsmen tried during the season – and made 157. Merchant let us see his quality with 86 not out, but probably Warwickshire followers were more interested in Tom Pritchard, who was making his first appearance for the county. Although there was considerable rain on the second day, he worked up a fine speed, sent back Hazare, Mankad and Mohammed without a run being scored off him and took four for 46. He bowled no fewer than five consecutive maiden overs to Merchant. It boded well for the future, for Warwickshire badly needed a good fast bowler – two, in fact.

One of the members of the Indian team was named Abdul Hafeez, a slow left-arm bowler. The next year he returned to England to study at Oxford University where he then announced that his full name was Abdul Hafeez Kardar. He got his Blue at Oxford where he was a contemporary of Ron Maudsley, who introduced him to Warwickshire cricket. Subsequently he played two seasons for Warwickshire, appearing also for the Gentlemen, before he became captain of the first Pakistan side to tour this country and, much later, President of the Board of Control for Cricket in Pakistan, as well as a Minister in the Government.

In mid-summer *The Birmingham Post* had published a review of the county's post-war prospects, in the course of which it said that had there not been a Great War and had not Foster met with a crippling accident, the story of Warwickshire cricket would have been very different. 'That leads to the real moral,' the paper went on, 'that what Warwickshire needs more than anything else is the stimulus of three or four really good seasons consecutively. Without that, no improvement in the amenities of the ground will bring prosperity. The pre-condition of these good seasons for a struggling county is a captain of something better than good quality. Since the earliest years Warwickshire has had only one. It is now hoping for another.'

The paper did not name the one, but presumably Foster was meant. Well, there was not long to wait for both the good seasons and the captain. It is interesting to contrast this point of view with that of someone who saw it all from the inside – Eric Hollies.

Considering the trials and difficulties of 1946 [he wrote in his book], Warwickshire made a remarkable post-war recovery, for five years later they won the County Championship. The swiftness of the recovery can be gauged from the fact that the county were seventh in 1949 and fourth in each of the two seasons before the final triumph in 1951 . . . . The summers of 1947 and 1948 were the building up years, with 1947 being Peter Cranmer's last year in the captaincy. I said earlier that he was the unluckiest Warwickshire captain under whom I played and that was true enough. He had the worst of the thirties, when we were weak in the last two pre-war years, and certainly the worst of the post-war period.

In appreciation of Dr Thwaite's great services to Warwickshire cricket it was decided to open a subscription fund to provide new entrance gates in Edgbaston Road and to name them after him. The President's latest gift was sound equipment over which Peter Cranmer gave lunchtime chats, as 'Rusty' Scorer had done during the wartime festival games.

On a lesser scale the Committee at last got around to buying a second typewriter and even a filing cabinet 'as existing facilities were proving very inadequate'. Also, in view of the heavy cost of cricket balls – 193s a dozen – it was decided to use secondhand balls for Club and Ground games and, at the request of the M.C.C., the bat shortage was brought to the attention of the players. One of Syd Harkness's jobs at this time was to look after the rationing of cricket equipment which was still difficult to get. Clubs had to apply to Warwickshire for the necessary permits printed by the Board of Trade.

It is strange to read of such minor items of equipment in almost the same context as the announcement of a £200 000 scheme, to which by now over £12 000 had been paid or promised. By October it was known that receipts for the season had reached £16 850, compared with expenditure of £12 976; Warwickshire's share of the Test profits of £4500 was £460; and there was also the little matter of damage done by the A.F.S. during their occupation of the ground, which was finally agreed at £807. The value now put on land and buildings at Edgbaston was £11 400, with furniture and implements at another £1297, and it was decided that the dining-room should be used for small functions in the winter months if there was any demand – a forerunner of the Pavilion Suite development.

At the annual meeting in March Dr Thwaite had promised extensive trials for young players; the Club applied to join the Minor Counties Competition in 1947, but had to withdraw owing to failure to obtain qualifying fixtures, so notice of entering the competition in 1948 was given. Another move to encourage the young players Warwickshire so badly needed was the reorganisation of the Public Schools Cricket organisation with the Jackson Cup for competition. This later became the Warwickshire Clubs' Schoolboy Association and was run in conjunction with the Warwickshire Youth Cricket Council. Later came the Warwickshire Young Amateurs side which, under the chairmanship for many years of Harry Harper, and in conjunction with the Colts' XI, selected by Derief Taylor, with the assistance of Norman Sharp, Derek Salberg and Leo Deamer, produced many future members of the county eleven.

Warwickshire were not represented in the M.C.C. team which went to Australia in the winter of 1946–7, though one would have thought that Dollery had just as good, if not better, claims to inclusion than, say, Fishlock, Hardstaff or Ikin, and Hollies than Wright; but at least the county got something out of it, for the M.C.C.'s profits from the tour came to £50 000, of which Warwickshire's share was £850.

From the point of view of income from subscriptions and gate receipts – 2 500 000 people watched Championship games in 1946 – the Club had never been better off, though in the annual report for 1947 the Reconstruction Appeal Fund stood at no more than £16 412, described as 'a totally inadequate sum for the programme your Committee has in mind'. Early in 1947 the Committee applied for its first licence to

277

spend £10 600, but it was declined, though later they were granted one of £2800, a mere morsel.

The report also paid tribute to 'the joie de vivre' that Cranmer had brought to Edgbaston, Colin Langley going so far as to say that the line between the amateur and the professional had been 'completely erased'. When he moved the usual resolution of thanks to 'Mr Cranmer and the other amateurs' he amended this to 'other players'.

Cranmer continued to contribute to the spectators' delight with some very bright and breezy innings, but they were not enough to bring the sort of success on the field the Club was looking for and needed, though it was a season of fast, lively wickets and exciting matches. Warwickshire often began well, but seemed to lack the penetrative power which made the difference between winning and losing, or winning and drawing.

In the middle of July they were sixth in the Championship, but then they did not win another match all season, which ended with five defeats. They lost twice as many matches as they won and fell from fourteenth to fifteenth position. Dr Thwaite later blamed the team's ups and downs on 'rash and hasty batting, intended to be attractive, but it must be allied to success if the county is to stand high in the estimation of members and the public'. Peter Cranmer, expressing his regrets, said he could only attribute the general failure to over-confidence.

Their failings were despite the fact that at last they had a pair of opening bowlers in Pritchard and Grove, the latter finally demobilised. Between them they took 173 wickets and relieved Hollies of more than a little of his burden. After his exhausting labours of the previous season, it was not surprising that he was not able to reproduce the form that had gained him getting on for 200 wickets, and his total for the county now fell to 96, though he passed another milestone – his 1000th wicket in first-class cricket.

Dollery, too, suffered some loss of batting form, scoring 716 runs fewer, with the result that his average dropped from over 40 to less than 26. This may well have been partly because he had other responsibilities this season, for in the very first match he took over the task of wicketkeeping – something he had not done for sixteen years – when Cyril Goodway was suffering from a poisoned leg. He did very well at it, too, catching thirty-nine batsmen and stumping twelve.

Ord had the highest aggregate among the batsmen, 1399 runs, and Ken Taylor, who had also been in the Army, and Hill, who had returned to the first-class scene, also got their 1000 runs, though Hill received a rebuke in the annual report for his running between the wickets – 'Hill ran himself out through slow starting far too frequently. It must be almost unique for a first-class batsman to be run out four times in six consecutive innings.'

Pritchard, probably not yet fully acclimatised to the continual stresses of an English season, to say nothing of the weather, missed several games through strains, but when he was fully fit and bowling flat out there were few faster bowlers in the country, despite the fact that more arm than body went into his action. He showed one penchant very welcome in a fast bowler – the ability to polish off tail-end batsmen, of which he gave two striking demonstrations. He clean bowled the last five Kent batsmen in nineteen balls at Gillingham, though that did not prevent Kent winning by nine wickets, and he swept the last five Cambridge University batsmen out of his way at Edgbaston for a mere eight runs. Perhaps it was the bottle of Mackeson he insisted on with his breakfast.

He and Grove, who did the hat trick against Somerset – seven for 48 – blossomed out as opening batsmen at Brentwood. This was one of Cranmer's gambles, aided and abetted by Tom Dollery, that did come off. There was a tie on the first innings and Warwickshire took third knock on a wicket they felt sure would take spin sooner or later. So after an overnight discussion it was decided to send in Pritchard and Grove in the hope that they might be more effective against the new ball than they would against the spinners, Ray and Peter Smith. The plan worked. Each made half a century and contributed an opening stand of 107, Warwickshire winning by 34 runs.

Gardner made a very promising start by sharing in partnerships of 81 and 111 with Hill against Gloucestershire. When Lancashire came to Edgbaston Warwickshire were without all their three principal bowlers, so George Paine was pressed into service again and showed he was still a force to be reckoned with by taking five wickets for 75.

Both Dollery and Hollies were selected to play against the South Africans, who were beaten in three successive Tests. Dollery made 9 and 17 in the first match and was then dropped, but Hollies played in three matches, with a best performance of five for 123. In his first home Test at Trent Bridge he took part with Martin, of Kent, in a last-wicket stand of 51. Hollies must be the only player who has ever used a bat with a nail in it in a Test match. It was one which all the Warwickshire team had used at times – it had scored 2000 runs in May! Hollies liked the feel of it because it was very light and when it split under the pounding it had received he put a nail in it to hold it together and took it with him to Nottingham where it served him very well indeed.

Warwickshire scored 330 against the tourists at Edgbaston, Cranmer hitting 101 in 90 minutes, but it was a quite inadequate score, South Africa running up a total of 520 for seven before declaring. Dudley Nourse made a not out double century, 205, and Viljoen 113, Hollies having 144 runs hit off him without taking a wicket; a rare occurrence indeed. Worse still, Warwickshire collapsed in their second innings

279

against Tucket and Dawson, and were all out 76, no fewer than 58 of which were made by Cranmer and Jack Hossell, the Aston Unity and Stratford-upon-Avon amateur.

One Monday in August the players appeared wearing black armbands out of respect for Arthur Croom, who had died on the Saturday, aged 50. Before play was resumed they stood in silence and Peter Cranmer paid a tribute to him. Though he never quite made the highest grade, Croom was a stylish opening bat who scored over 1000 runs in every season, except 1936, from 1927 until the outbreak of war – he had been severely wounded in the First World War – with a highest innings of 211 against Worcestershire at Edgbaston in 1934. He was one of the best fielders in any position the Club ever had.

There was one unique occurrence at Edgbaston just before the match with Northants in July. There had been rain in the night and when Eric Hollies arrived early on the ground he was astonished to see what appeared to be steam rising from the wicket. The cause was Fred Pope trying out as a wicket drier a flame gun used to kill weeds which had been bought from a local firm. The newspapers inevitably christened it a flame-thrower, which led to a polite but firm inquiry from the War Office as to where it might have been obtained, and Syd Harkness had the job of reassuring them that it was not the military type. It certainly had an effect on the wicket, the only sticky one that Hollies can ever remember at Edgbaston, for the match was over in a day and a half.

In August 'Tiger' Smith, reporting on the team's 'very disappointing' form, attributed it to the players' 'casual attitude' to the game, which, in his opinion, was largely due to poor practice conditions, including lack of nets on match mornings and to the absence of serious competition for places in the side. (There were then only seventeen players on the professional staff.) He undertook to get in touch with old players of his acquaintance to keep him posted on promising youngsters, and to watch as much local cricket as possible.

Various steps were taken to find new players – engagements were offered to Cannings, a fast medium bowler from Hampshire; R. T. Spooner, a batsman-wicketkeeper from Durham; Alan Townsend, an all-rounder also from Durham; Norman Horner, of Yorkshire, who, like Gardner, had been a Bevin boy – and it was also reported that J. V. Wilson, of Yorkshire, was seeking his release and was interested in an engagement. Yorkshire, however, refused permission for Horner's special registration and he later took a business appointment in Bradford, though his arrival was to be not long delayed.

The difficulty with Wilson, who decided to remain with Yorkshire whom he later captained very successfully, was that he insisted on a house and smallholding being provided before he would agree to move; this was a great problem at this time, so much so that the Committee considered adapting premises as flats (which came later), or setting up a communal residence if a suitable place could be found, and bought or rented at reasonable cost, but no fewer than fifteen estate agents were approached without result. Housing difficulties nearly cost them the services of Spooner, too, but happily these were resolved by a loan to him to buy a house.

Some differences of opinion on team selection had become evident among members of the Committee, though it was generally agreed that selection of the best eleven, irrespective of age, should be the main consideration for the first team; but for the second eleven some members strongly favoured a preference for youth, while others wanted a blend of both youth and experience. The Committee decided to convey their views to the selection committee, which at this time consisted of Captain Cowan, Alec Hastilow and Peter Cranmer.

Towards the end of the year Hastilow, who had been making strenuous efforts to secure the services of Donnelly, now at Oxford, was able to announce success and that he would be available in 1948. He had just had a very successful season, in which he scored five centuries, and he figured as one of the Five Cricketers of the Year in the 1948 *Wisden*. Kardar, who was also now at Oxford, received a cordial invitation to play in second eleven and Club and Ground games.

The Committee still set its official face against Sunday cricket at Edgbaston, though it was agreed that for 1948 professionals should be allowed to play in not more than six Sunday games for benefits, but evenly spread over the season. Benefits, it was stressed, were to be regarded as at the discretion of the Committee as they had always been, not as a right. Hollies was granted one against Kent in 1948 with a guarantee, which was not to be regarded as a precedent (of course) but which might also operate in Dollery's case.

One other interesting question which came before the Committee was a suggestion in a letter from Miss Margaret Pugh, of Edgbaston, that ladies should be allowed full membership 'as they used to be'. A minute on the matter said that it was regretted no one could recall the time when ladies were accepted as full members, and an examination of the Club's rules did not disclose an authority to elect them as such at any time in the Club's history. Miss Pugh's suggestion was politely declined, but the matter did not rest there, so a potted history of negotiations with the gentler sex may not come amiss. I am indebted, as for so many other things in this history, to Leslie Deakins.

The very first rules agreed, on 14 February 1885, made no mention of female, only male, membership, but two years later it was decided that every member might, if he wished, buy transferable tickets for use by ladies, for 5s each. Two further years later, on 22 March 1889, membership for ladies was approved.

When the Club's rules were revised in March 1902, the subscription for lady members was raised to 10s 6d at least and their transferable tickets to 5s, and these amounts remained unchanged for nearly twenty years when they were increased to 12s 6d and 7s 6d respectively.

When after being in existence for twenty-four years – from 1899 to 1923 – ladies membership tickets were abolished (in November, 1923) no one protested, perhaps because the number then holding them was negligible. Transferable tickets only remained and these, like everything else, gradually rose in price to £1 10s 0d.

There was something a little more in keeping with the times, however, when the Club applied for a music and singing licence to regularise the playing of gramophone records through the amplifiers and loud-speakers which Dr Thwaite had generously had installed. They were, it was stated conservatively, intended for use during intervals and wet weather, providing there was no nuisance to neighbouring residents.

At the end of the season Cranmer notified the Committee that because of increased business calls he would be unable to continue to captain the side. Perhaps no one with a temperament better suited to cope with the frustrations of the years immediately preceding and following the war could have been found than this ebulliently extrovert young man. He took over at a very difficult time from a much older and more experienced cricketer and captain, who continued in the side under him; a situation which could have been highly embarrassing, to say the least, and, at worst, a cause of serious trouble. It says much for both men that it was neither, partly because Cranmer was not the worrying kind, outwardly at least, and because Wyatt, to quote Cranmer, 'was first rate under my captaincy and a great help to me'.

Cranmer rightly felt he was unfortunate in that in the years before the war several of the players were rather too old and that after the war he was left with only Dollery, Hollies and Ord who had had pre-war experience. There were also times when, like Wyatt, he had to suffer some pressure from committees and his non-belief in selection committees doubtless stems from those days. Teams, he thought, should be run by the captain and the vice-captain.

Happily Cranmer's cheery services were not lost to the Club and in his 41st year with Warwickshire and nearing 60, he was leading the second eleven with the same gusto, seasoned now by long experience, that has always marked his play. He took part in practically every match, going to the gymnasium once a week to keep fit and attending the evening sessions in the Indoor School, as well as serving as chairman of the Cricket Committee.

Joint Captaincy
(1948)

❖ ❖ ❖

BEFORE the Committee finally chose Cranmer's successor they called in Eric Hollies as senior professional and sought his views – as, in fact, they sought those of several others – about a plan for Dollery to take over the captaincy for the first half of the season and then for him to hand over to Ron Maudsley, the Oxford Blue – who, of course, was not available until the end of the University Trinity term – in mid-June.

Hollies thought it a good idea, though there was one point which he said would concern him if he were in the Committee's position – what would happen if, half-way through the season, the team was on top of the Championship table – would it be wise to change captains then? It was a question to which he did not receive a decisive answer, though it had doubtless occurred to the Committee also, and, as it happened, such a situation almost did arise.

In January 1948, the decision, which was unanimous, was taken, Maudsley and Dollery being chosen as joint captains. Maudsley was appointed captain, but in view of the fact that his law appointment at Oxford would prevent him being available until 23 June, the side until then would be led by Dollery, who thus became the first Warwickshire professional to be appointed captain, though the county had, of course, been led occasionally by professionals in the past, most recently by Bates. There did not appear to be a precise parallel for a dual appointment, however, though Essex had once appointed four amateurs to be captains for different parts of the season. Dollery was also appointed joint senior professional along with Hollies.

Maudsley was born in Cheshire, but his home was at Quinton, Birmingham. He had gone to school first at West House and then Malvern, where he did well in some school matches, first as a bowler,

283

then as a batsman and then as a bowler again. Then came Birmingham University, for whom he played three years, being captain in 1939. He had played in some Warwickshire second eleven matches in 1938 and 1939 and in the latter years he had a chance of going to Oxford for two years, but instead joined the Territorials. He was a private for the first few years of the war, but, as he put it, 'promotion was pretty quick in the Western Desert', and he became a major just before the Battle of El Alamein and held that rank until the end of hostilities. He even managed to get a little cricket at the famous Gezira Club in Egypt.

Maudsley returned to Oxford in 1946 and one day when he was home in Birmingham he met Leslie Deakins in the street. He was asked to come to the ground, thus renewing the association with Edgbaston. Maudsley had two years in the Oxford side, at the same time as Dick Sale, Donnelly and Kardar, and was afterwards awarded a Fellowship at Brasenose. According to Maudsley, it had been planned to ask Dollery to become captain in 1950; however, when Cranmer gave it up he, Maudsley, was approached, but could not be free until June, hence the compromise, which it had been intended should be for two years. But events changed that.

Maudsley had a high regard for Dollery as a captain. 'Perhaps he was not the ideal man to be in charge as a tactician', he once said, 'but I have never known his equal in other respects. He had every batsman and bowler buttoned up. He knew who was nervous of Pritchard at the beginning of an innings – and Pritchard *could* be frightening – and who didn't know Hollies's googly, and he had a wonderful facility for getting matches finished off.' He was certainly known as a master in timing a declaration.

As for Dollery, he told us in his book* that he hesitated about accepting the offer, though he agreed that he 'could not have had a more favourable opportunity, for the county's need was to tide over the problem for the first twelve matches until the University vacation . . . If that short period did not prove to be a success I could return to my role as a player pure and simple and no harm would have been done. I was to be a stop-gap for the time being with the possibility, if all went well, of succeeding Ron Maudsley when he had to give up.'

Dollery's hesitation was because it was 'a revolutionary step' and he wondered whether he would make himself the object of controversy.

I was happy playing as a batsman for Warwickshire and I enjoyed fielding. It would have been different if I had been younger, with possibilities ahead of me; but as it was it seemed that I had reached the straight leading to the finish of my career and I was not keen on suffering any interruption or disturbance . . . Others who had been approached [there had been one camp in favour of appointing Ken Taylor, but Hastilow opposed this and got his way] had all

Professional Captain, Stanley Paul and Co. Ltd.

turned the post down, one of them on the odd grounds that amateur captaincy was not a sufficiently long career. Somebody had to head the side for the first twelve matches and there appeared to be no one else to do it. For my part, I was very conscious of the honour Warwickshire did me.

So far from being anywhere near the finish of his career, the appointment gave Dollery greater authority, not only as a captain but as an individual, and led him to the greatest heights he had achieved in the game, though he probably had a few qualms – albeit only in an early season trial game – when he found that the umpires were Alec Hastilow and Captain Cowan. Later, in his first county match as leader at Trent Bridge there they were again, this time in the pavilion balcony, where they had been joined by the President, Dr Thwaite, all come to lend him moral support. But in the first county match at Edgbaston in which he was captain, Warwickshire beat Yorkshire for the first time on that ground since 1893, and that was to be off to the best of all possible starts.

Dollery himself made 95 in that game, but he would be the first to admit that the two outstanding innings in the match, played on a decidedly tricky wicket, were Ken Taylor's 30 and 81 not out. There was some match-winning bowling by Hollies, Grove, Pritchard and Alan Townsend, from Minor Counties cricket with Durham, who, at a very early stage in his career, gave evidence of that enviable facility he had for taking a quick wicket or two when they were most badly needed – he had three for 18 in Yorkshire's second innings and Warwickshire won by 54 runs. Some very caustic remarks about his colleagues' shortcomings were heard coming from Frank Smailes in the Yorkshire dressing-room until someone discreetly pulled down a window.

Dollery was greatly blessed in his first season as captain in that he returned to something like his best form. In Championship matches alone he scored 1649 runs for an average of nearly 50, which took him past his 10 000 runs for the county. Ord also had his best-ever season, opening with two hundreds against Notts, which earned him the gift of a clock from the Club; overall he scored 1421 runs, averaging nearly 40. They were the only batsmen to get over 1000 runs, but Spooner made 759 in his first season and Donnelly 738, though he never reproduced for Warwickshire the form he had shown for New Zealand, or for Oxford; his highest score in fifteen matches being 96. Dollery attributed this to the fact that, in this season, Donnelly never quite adjusted himself to other less perfect wickets after The Parks and played too adventurously at the start of his innings.

The new captain was fortunate, too, in that Pritchard was at his best, taking 163 wickets for only 17·47 runs, a remarkably low average for a fast bowler. Hollies, too, set up a Warwickshire record by taking over

100 wickets for the seventh successive season – 128 of them also for under 20 runs each and passing his own 1000 for the county alone. Grove was rather less successful with only 58 wickets. Of the 385 taken by Warwickshire bowlers, Pritchard and Hollies were responsible for 291. If they had only had a slow left-hander, or a good off-spinner as well, Warwickshire would have had the best attack in the country.

Pritchard began in May like a whirlwind out of season, clean bowling six Essex batsmen at Edgbaston in a first innings analysis of seven for 71 and then adding four for 70. In June he ran riot against Leicestershire. In the first innings he took six wickets for 33, four of them for 2 runs, and in the second innings he did the hat trick to finish off the innings, a match record of eleven for 80. This was the first match since 1925 in which Warwickshire's opening bowlers had bowled unchanged. He followed this with six for 59 against Worcestershire, with Wyatt one of his victims for 25, and in the next match against Northants he had thirteen wickets for 153 – eight for 43 and five for 110.

Hollies took his benefit against Kent in July after a handsome tribute had been paid to him in the annual report by J. C. Clay, of Glamorgan, who knew something about slow bowling:

'Thank goodness for Hollies' must have been a frequent exclamation at Edgbaston. When the wicket has been too hard for Alf, too soft for Bert, or too dead for Perce, the ball has been handed to Eric and he has carried on. For herein lies his merit – an ability to bowl effectively, untiringly, cheerfully, no matter what the conditions. Lucky captain; one end, at any rate, will be well and truly looked after.

Hollies's colleagues did their best to ensure that the match lasted three days by scoring 478, to which Gardner contributed a first century in what was to become for him the more or less typical time of four hours forty minutes, and Dollery 93. The beneficiary made one run before being stumped, no doubt trying to force the pace. He did not have much bowling success, taking only two for 49 in Kent's first innings of 198 and one for 70 in their second venture which ran to 287 for two; Todd, missed when two, made 127 and Fagg, who had got 99 in the first innings, 106. In all, Fagg batted eight hours – shades of ten years before when he performed his unique feat of scoring two double centuries in the same match.

The benefit brought Hollies a rich and well-deserved reward of £4896 and it could have been still richer if he had availed himself of all the opportunities for collections. It was the county's first post-war benefit and easily the best so far. It was at one and the same time an indication of how the Warwickshire public had taken Hollies to their hearts as a player and of the changed value of money the war had brought about. But the crowning triumph of his season was still to come.

Warwickshire outplayed and defeated the prospective first-time Champions, Glamorgan, by 183 runs; Ord having one of his best matches with innings of 101 and 72 not out. At one time Warwickshire were third in the table and in June, seeing how well things were going, Maudsley wrote to the Committee saying that he would be happy to stand down if that was their wish. The reply was that they wanted the arrangement they had made to stand, so Maudsley duly took over.

Then there was the anticipated falling away in form and the general consensus of opinion was that this was largely due to the unsettling effect of the change of captaincy, but, of course, no one could be certain. Maudsley appropriately captained the team for the first time against his old university and made 59 against them, which must have pleased him. Kardar got 40 for them, but he did not take any wickets which, no doubt, he would dearly have loved to do. The first time Maudsley led the side in a Championship match was against Lancashire at the end of June when Dollery (to whom, on relinquishing the captaincy, the Club had made a gift of £100 in appreciation of his service) was away playing in a Test. Maudsley made another 40, but the match is more likely to be remembered for the fact that in making his maiden century Kenneth Cranston, the Lancashire amateur, hit a glorious straight six off Hollies which struck the clock on the Pavilion balcony, smashing the glass and leaving its impression on the face. The clock stopped at 2.25 p.m. – Cranston must have been well fortified by his lunch – and another ball had to be obtained. The clock required some attention, too. It was a feat which not even Jack Parsons achieved, though he came near it on several occasions.

Edgbaston, still without a Test, had to be content with a trial in June, but it was spoiled by rain. No Warwickshire player was invited, though both Dollery and Hollies played in one or more of the Tests, of which Australia won four out of five on Bradman's last tour and remained unbeaten throughout, a record. Dollery in the second Test made nought and 38 before being bowled by Lindwall, and in the third his only innings produced one run.

Bradman, in his book, *Farewell to Cricket*, wrote that he could still,

picture the unlucky Dollery. He had not that season faced a bowler anything like as fast as Lindwall and had to play him immediately he arrived at the crease. The first ball found Dollery much too late. Fortunately for him it was not straight, but Lindwall doesn't waste opportunities and one more ball was enough.

Without wishing to detract from Dollery's ability, for he is a good, sound batsman [Bradman added] I thought the Selectors were asking too much of a new man whose eyesight and reflexes were possibly on the decline [At 34? – L.D.] to handle Lindwall first up in a Test. Simpson was much younger and had already played our fast attack with considerable success. Theoretically, he looked to be a better selection.

Hollies was not called on until the last Test at The Oval, but before that he had a fascinating duel with the Australians at Edgbaston at the beginning of August. Bradman sent Warwickshire in on a wet pitch and got them out for 138. When Australia batted, Hollies got both the opening pair, Brown and Morris, hit wicket playing back to him – and that cannot often have been seen in a scorebook. Bradman came in and hit three fours off the first over bowled to him. Maudsley says that Brown tried to keep Bradman away from Kardar's left-arm slows, turning from leg, but it was Hollies who got the great man, bowling him for 31. The new ball was due, but the conditions were not right to take it. Maudsley later frankly admitted that he did not know what to do, for Hollies had been bowling all morning, but he gave the ball to him with the remark: 'Have one more over and if you don't have a bit of luck we'll take the new ball.'

With his fourth ball Hollies got Hassett and so he kept on and on – for over four hours, bowling more than forty overs. His control of length and spin was masterly to a degree. Maudsley regards Hollies's all ten against Notts as the greatest thing he ever saw in cricket and one of the great bowling performances of history, but, considering the quality of the opposition on this occasion, I do not see how his Nottingham feat could be better. I did not see the Notts match, but I saw Hollies against the Australians and I regard this as probably the best piece of bowling seen since the war.

There is some doubt whether Bradman had succeeded in picking out Hollies's googly in his first innings. In *Farewell to Cricket* he does not give any clue as to whether he did so. Of the match he merely says that it was 'played throughout on a wet pitch – not dangerous, but most responsive to spin and hardly anybody batted with confidence . . . Outstanding feature of the match was the bowling of Eric Hollies, who delivered 43·5 consecutive overs and took eight for 107. He bowled beautifully. The pitch gave him just that little bit of assistance he needed, but even so his control of length and direction were admirable. His performance must have earned him a place in the fifth Test.'

Warwickshire were all out very cheaply again in the second innings and Australia made the 41 they needed for the loss of one wicket, Bradman this time being 13 not out. It is generally believed that he came out again to have another look at Hollies, so in this brief second innings Eric did not bowl the googly, thinking to keep him guessing in case they met again.

I was so impressed with Hollies's bowling that day, and it stayed so vividly in my memory, that not long afterwards I wrote the following description of it, intending one day to use it in a book; never thinking that it would be in a history of Warwickshire, but what more appropriate place could there be? I headed it 'Great Bowling' and that, truly, is what it was:

There is an absurd notion that the really great performances of cricket are done only in Test Matches. True, these have a certain cachet not possessed by the others because of the quality of the opposition and the circumstances, but there have been many great exploits outside Tests and I count myself to have been fortunate enough to have seen one of them – Hollies against the Australians at Edgbaston, August 1948 – and no one is going to question the quality of that opposition.

The Australians had nearly two hours' batting before the close of play on the first day on a wicket which was drying out slowly but naturally. There was no sun, but it was taking spin a little more quickly than at the start of the day. Brown and Morris gave them a slow but steady start before Hollies came on and got them both. The manner of their going should have been a warning to others – they were both out hit wicket – *playing back*.

Bradman was not out 20 at the close, not a very confident 20, and Hassett 3, and when Hollies went on to bowl immediately play was resumed the next morning the writing was on the wall. It was obvious from his first few balls that the wicket was drier than it had been overnight and that it was taking spin more quickly. Every bowler, even the lowliest club cricketer, has had the feeling at least once in his life that he can do anything with the ball. Barnes had it at Melbourne in 1912 and so it seemed with Hollies.

Flighting the ball beautifully, varying his pace and spin and apparently able to pitch the ball where he wanted at will, Hollies soon had both Bradman and Hassett playing with the light of acute and uneasy speculation in their eyes. Bradman had added only 11 runs to his overnight score in a manner not at all becoming the world's greatest run-getter, when Hollies deceived him into playing for spin which wasn't there and bowled him with a top spinner.

The next one comprehensively beat and bowled young Neil Harvey who seemed hardly able to believe that the ball, pitched a foot outside his off stump – it would have been a leg-break to a right-handed batsman, of course – could have turned enough to hit the wicket. He obviously thought the ball had rebounded from the wicketkeeper's pads, but he was wrong and he had to go.

Hassett, realising what the Australians were in for, called upon every ounce of his skill and knowledge of English wickets and although beaten several times he contrived to show his bemused colleagues how they at least ought to try to play Hollies by getting to the pitch of the ball before the spin could take effect.

McCool tried aggression, which succeeded for a time until he cut a leg spinner from Kardar, the slow left-hander at the other end, into slip's hands. Lindwall, no slouch with the bat, knew nothing whatever about the first three balls he received from Hollies. His bat clove the air, but somehow the ball missed the stumps. The third ball he snicked just past the leg stump. He then recovered some semblance of composure and made several hefty punches, but he, too, went eventually, caught; Hassett died the death in high Yorkshire fashion, leg before, after a valiant 60 or so; and Saggers and Johnson were both hopelessly beaten and bowled.

In his last three overs Hollies took four wickets for 14 runs and at the end this was how his analysis read:

O	M	R	W
43·5	8	107	8

It was the just reward of over four hours' bowling, but if he had taken only one or two wickets I should still describe his bowling that day as great. He had made the cream of the Australian batsmen look very ordinary harassed mortals indeed and his success proved once more what I shall never tire of repeating – that accurately flighted leg spin is the most deadly kind of bowling to right-hand batsmen because there is no logical answer to it except to get out and hit it before the spin bites. And that, if the bowling really is well flighted, as it was that day, is extraordinarily difficult for even the most quick-footed batsman to do.

The mistake most of the Australians made – a surprising one for them – was in playing back, especially when the wicket began to dry and take spin more quickly. Then was the time to get out to the pitch of the ball, but Brown, Morris, Bradman (of all people), Hassett himself eventually, Harvey, Saggers, and Johnson were all out playing back. I don't think Miller would have played back, but he wasn't in the Australian team for this match.

This was great bowling by any standards and I consider myself privileged to have seen it.

The story of Bradman's dismissal by Hollies for a duck in his farewell Test Match at The Oval has been told many times, but even though it did not happen in a Warwickshire match it must have a place in the Club's history because of the circumstances. It very nearly did not happen the way it did at all. When the invitation to Hollies to play arrived he told Leslie Deakins he would rather play for Warwickshire. The rubber had already been decided and it would have meant that he would have missed two county games when he could ill be spared. It was the Warwickshire Committee who persuaded their 'home boy' to play; if they had not succeeded cricket history would almost certainly have been different.

Before leaving Birmingham for the match Hollies had a talk with Tom Dollery, who agreed with him that Bradman had not spotted the googly and Hollies made up his mind that if he had to bowl to Bradman, he would give him the googly second ball – just in case he was expecting it first ball. Bradman, as it happened, came in to bat in the middle of an over by Hollies. As he was walking to the wicket Norman Yardley, England's captain, remarked, 'We'll give him three cheers when he gets on the square.' Then he turned to Hollies and added: 'But that's all we'll give him – then bowl him out.'

And that was exactly what happened. The first ball Hollies bowled to him was a leg break which Bradman played defensively down the pitch. The second was a good-length googly to which Bradman had to play forward. Hollies says he moved three-parts of the way forward to it, but not far enough to smother the spin, which he seemed to anticipate would come from leg, but the ball broke in and hit the off and middle stumps, though, in fact, Hollies did not see it do so – the wicket was hidden by Bradman's legs.

Afterwards, Bradman who, to do him justice, may well have been a little unsettled by his reception, said it was 'a perfect ball' that had bowled him, but, says Hollies, he has never admitted it was a googly. That evening when he got home Hollies rang up 'Tom' Dollery and told him triumphantly: 'He never saw it, Tom.'

But did he? In *Farewell to Cricket* Bradman wrote that he 'dearly wanted to do well, but it was not to be. That reception had stirred my emotions very deeply and made me anxious – a dangerous state of mind for any batsman to be in. I played the first ball from Hollies, though not sure I really saw it. The second was a perfect length googly which deceived me. I just touched it with the inside edge of the bat and the off bail was dislodged. So in the midst of my great jubilation at my team's success, I had a rather sad heart about my own farewell as I wended my way pavilion-wards.'

Leslie Deakins adds the perfect footnote to this historic episode. He says that the morning after the match Hollies popped his head round his door and said triumphantly: 'Did you notice who was left not out?' He had made none not out and none – out – and that, it seemed, was of far more consequence than bowling the world's greatest batsman for a duck in his last Test, and depriving him of the honour of becoming the only batsman in cricket history to average 100, instead of 99·94, in Test cricket.

It is interesting to reflect that Maudsley regarded Hollies as one of the best No. elevens one could find and there were many last-wicket performances of which he had every right to be proud. One of them came in the return match with Leicestershire. Grove was 60 not out when the ninth wicket fell and Hollies stayed with him until he reached his century – the only one of his career – and Warwickshire won by an innings and 43 runs.

Warwickshire recovered their poise before the end of the season. One of their best wins was over Hampshire at Southampton. Hollies and Pritchard twice bundled them out for 114 and 192, and Warwickshire needed 147 to win in 95 minutes and got them for the loss of five wickets with five minutes to spare. Dollery gave a perfect demonstration of how to take control of an innings. In just over an hour he hit four sixes and four fours and at the close was not out 76, slightly more than half Warwickshire's score.

The Indian Board of Control had given Kardar permission to play for the county and he made his first appearance for them against the Royal

Navy, taking six wickets for 37 runs, a promising beginning for the kind of bowler Warwickshire badly needed.

All in all, it was a good season for Warwickshire, who won two more matches than they lost and rose dramatically from fifteenth to seventh in the Championship table. Nevertheless, in November the executive committee decided that it was not sound policy to divide the captaincy and as Ron Maudsley could not undertake it throughout the 1949 season, it was decided to recommend Dollery's appointment. This was a view with which Maudsley himself concurred, for he had written stressing his inability to give full time to the captaincy and asking for his name to be deleted from the list from which a choice would be made. 'The team', he wrote to the Committee, 'achieved great success in the early part of last season and towards the end; a rather less successful time was during the middle of the season immediately after the changeover. Such a change inevitably has an unsettling effect on a team as a composite force.'

It was a self-sacrificing gesture which one is sure the Committee appreciated. Happily they were to have Maudsley's occasional services for some seasons to come.

Dollery in Command
(1949–1950)

THE choice, inevitably, fell on Dollery. The decision to have a joint captaincy had had a mixed reception from the Press, though *The Birmingham Post* had welcomed Dollery's appointment in these words:

Our grandfathers might well have looked in pained surprise at even the notion of a professional leading a county side, but thank goodness we have advanced far since the days the amateurs and professionals left the pavilion by different gates. It is the game which counts and if a man is a good sportsman, a first-class cricketer, a born leader and appeals to the crowd, then he is the man to skipper the team . . . We have every confidence in the new skipper.

When Dollery was appointed captain in his own right the newspaper expressed further confidence in him: 'No man, we believe, could get more out of the Warwickshire XI, either in bulk or quality of work; under no man is the team more likely to be a real team.'

The annual report expressed the view that Dollery 'manifested considerable ability and aptitude for the position when he captained the side in the early part of the season', though it had some reservations about the team's performance as a whole: 'The bowling lacked variety with no one at all to exploit a rain-affected surface and the batting was still deficient in solidarity.'

But for the first time in the history of the Club membership had to be limited – to 6000 – the Committee deciding that the accommodation was quite inadequate for the additional demands made on it, and that more space must be allocated; in the meantime the right to introduce a friend must be restricted. The same limit was imposed for 1949. In 1947 membership subscriptions had amounted to £8521, nearly twice as much as in the previous season, and gate money to over £10 000, so that it was possible to carry out ground repairs and improvements cost-ing £5000. In 1948 that sum rose to £11 000 and 150 000 people paid to watch the play at Edgbaston. The reconstruction was beginning.

The Club suffered a severe loss during the year through the death of Colin Langley at the age of 59. His fast bowling had made a decided impression when he first played, though he had never repeated the success of his first season in 1912. He was lost to the active side of the game because of war injuries, but his services continued to be available in many capacities, including those of honorary secretary, honorary solicitor and later chairman of the Committee. He bequeathed his library of cricket books to the Club, a gesture for which I and many others have had cause to be grateful. It has since been added to by annual gifts from the Supporters' Association and is under the direction of Mr Peter Handford, the Club librarian.

Alec Hastilow was appointed to succeed Langley as chairman and honorary secretary and he also became chairman of Warwickshire Youth Cricket Council, appointments which crowned a lifetime's passion for the game. The flames had first been fanned when, as a small boy, born in Birmingham of humble parents, he found a broken bat in Cannon Hill Park one day. He went to the Central Secondary School (later the Central Grammar School), which he was later to captain for three years and made, literally, the lowest of entries to Edgbaston – underneath the turnstiles. He joined the Moseley Club and in 1912 he played his first game with the Club and Ground side and got a 'duck', but that did not deter him. When Warwickshire appointed the engaging G. J. V. Weigall to coach the players before the season started, Hastilow and Len Bates were among them. Weigall asked him: 'What are you going to do?' and Hastilow told him: 'I want to play for Warwickshire,' to which Weigall replied: 'I don't see why you shouldn't. Are you likely to be able to go to a university? That's the best way.'

Young Hastilow did go to a university, winning a scholarship to Birmingham where he took his B.Sc. degree in chemistry and he played for the University side, which he captained in 1914, and for Moseley until the war came. He then joined the 2nd Birmingham Battalion, in which were also serving several Warwickshire players, including Bates, 'Tiger' Smith and Jeeves. Later he was seconded to the chemical com-pany of the Royal Engineers, and then found himself at a government factory at Oldbury for manufacturing T.N.T., where, unhappily, he had an accident in which he was burned in the face by acid and was fortunate not to lose the sight of one eye.

He got some cricket during the war with the Battalion team and with King's Heath, Moseley having had to suspend activities, and afterwards he returned to the University where he took another degree, this time in commerce, and was again captain of cricket. In that season, 1919, playing for a variety of clubs, he did the 'double' for the first and only time – 1015 runs and 148 wickets – though half a score of times afterwards he took 100 or so wickets with his off-spinners. He played two innings for the Warwickshire first eleven in 1919, but pressure of business – he was appointed chief chemist at Docker Bros, the Birmingham paint firm – prevented him from playing first-class cricket, though he used to play for the second eleven in Bank Holiday matches.

When Captain Cowan gave up the captaincy of the Second XI, Hastilow was invited to take it on, which he did very happily from 1935 until 1947, apart, of course, from the Second World War years during which he was seconded to the Ministry of Supply, whose team he captained from 1945 to 1947. He had been elected to the Warwickshire Committee in 1933, helped to keep the Club going during the war and in 1946 accepted an invitation to be vice-chairman. Now he was chairman and was to remain so during some of the most momentous years of the Club's history, including the winning of the Championship and the restoration of Test Match status, two of his dearest ambitions.

The new salary structure adopted for the players this season had three categories and rates – men who had appeared in representative cricket, £500 to £600; men who had been awarded their county caps, £400 to £500; uncapped men under £400. There was also a proviso that the award of county caps would be strictly controlled, although still only on the captain's recommendation, and the executive committee agreed to recommend that, as a general rule, they would not undertake to find employment, or accommodation, for players as a preliminary to an engagement. They did, however, still help players with equipment allowances – £15 to those first joining the Club and a further £10 if they were retained for a second season. Often in the past, players had had to be granted loans to enable them to play at all; when Tom Pritchard arrived he had no cricket boots.

Earlier in the season there had been some concern about the condition of the ground – bare patches, unevenness – and Pope was instructed to deal with these satisfactorily in future, but by the end of the year Pope had resigned, and after one candidate had declined an offer of the appointment, K. Boak, formerly at Trent Bridge, was engaged.

Hollies had been invited to tour South Africa during the winter, but he had to decline owing to an injury to his right knee – a pattern of ill-luck in international cricket to which by now he had become almost accustomed. The mishap occurred in mid-July and it took him four months to get it right, but it always retained a tendency to go out of joint and he played with it strapped up.

Wisden described Warwickshire's rise up the table to seventh position in 1949 as 'a splendid advance'. It was, in fact, their best season since 1934. For much of it they looked likely winners and in August they were second, but a crushing defeat by Yorkshire at Scarborough put paid to their chances. One had the feeling that if Donnelly had been playing for Warwickshire, instead of for his own country touring here, the Championship would have come to Edgbaston a little earlier than it eventually did. As it was, the crowds showed their appreciation of the team's improved form by flocking to the ground in still greater numbers – 152 000, including members; 35 000 for the New Zealand match. There was now a waiting list of 600.

Of Dollery's own role as professional captain, *Wisden* had this to say: 'He never lacked courage and his tact and genial disposition made harmony complete. Though still young in a cricket sense, he was the "father" of the side. As a batsman he stood above the rest in his benefit year.' He made six centuries, including his first double, scored over 2000 runs for the first time and headed the county's batting averages for the fourth time. As he also became the first county captain to play in his own benefit match, which was a record of £6362, and had, of course, been elected to the Committee of the Club, his first season as captain was indeed a memorable one. The Club's annual report said of him:

He was the country's outstanding captain and at all times led the side with quiet dignity, marked technical skill and splendid personality ... The side was everywhere described as one of the happiest in England and certainly one of the most attractive to watch.

The batting generally was better than it had been for some time, Gardner, Ord and Townsend being the others to make over 1000 runs, though no regular opening partner was found for Gardner. Wolton, another Berkshire product who had been playing with the Aston Unity Club, made his first century and Spooner's wicketkeeping and batting both improved.

A cheerful dark countenance, which was to be around Edgbaston a long time, looked in for the first time and made a hundred. The owner of it was Derief Taylor, who had met 'Tom' Dollery while serving in Italy during the war. One day he sold his taxi business in Jamaica and turned up at Edgbaston to see if English cricket had anything to offer him. It had – a permanent post on the ground staff, though this only happened because Dollery intervened on his behalf. The Committee had decided to dispense with his services as a player, but in view of his improved form towards the end of the season and his latent abilities as a masseur, he was retained for 1950 and, in fact, was on the playing staff for three years. When, later, there was a vacancy for a full-time masseur he was appointed, but he found the true outlet for his talents as a coach, especially of young cricketers. Apart from that century in the 1949 season he took a fantastic catch while lying on his back among the crowd who had encroached over the boundary.

Once again Hollies bowled over after over – more than 1000 of them, for the fifth time – and more than one-third of them were maidens. He was so accurate that at the end of a four-hour spell in Dick Howorth's benefit match at Worcester his figures read: 46 overs, 23 maidens, 50 runs, 3 wickets. Altogether he took 128 wickets for just over 20 runs each. Pritchard was not quite so penetrative, though he did the hat trick, but his total of Championship wickets fell from 163 to 97. 'He never succumbed to the modern fetish of swing,' *Wisden* said of him. If he had only been able to get a little more back into his action and less arm he would, despite his comparatively slight build, have been a great fast bowler instead of a very good one. Whenever John Snow bowls he reminds me of Pritchard – their build and actions are very similar. Grove's tally of wickets rose to 84 and Kardar's to 48, and Taylor supplied some badly needed left arm guile and spin. And a 16-year-old named 'Roly' Thompson gave promise of developing into a good fast bowler.

On the morning of Dollery's benefit in the match with Middlesex W. E. Hall, George Egdell's successor as cricket correspondent of *The Birmingham Post*, wrote this very handsome tribute to him:

In nine seasons since he first played for the county in 1934 he has scored 11 354 runs for Warwickshire in 351 innings, 34 of them not out, for an average of 35·78 and made 22 centuries. Before the war he was one of the best cover points in the country and once ran out three successive batsmen from that position. Dollery [he went on], heralded the new professionalism and his cricket was so characteristically English that if ever we seek the incarnation of the 'Boys' Own' cricketer, his name might well be Tom Dollery.

Unhappily only ninety minutes' play was possible on the first day of the match, but eventually Warwickshire were able to declare at 279 for seven, of which Dollery contributed 32. Middlesex, too, declared – at 231 for nine – and it was during their innings towards the end of the second day that Edgbaston saw some of the finest cricket it has been my privilege to enjoy.

Compton and Edrich were at the very peak of their form – 1947 had been their golden year when runs flowed from their bats in what seemed a never-ending stream – and now they were opposed to two of the best spin bowlers in the land, Hollies and Kardar. The batsmen were just as anxious to push the score along as the bowlers were to restrain them. The wicket was giving a little help to the bowlers and the struggle for mastery was on – two great batsmen against two fine bowlers 'and the modern game', as a note in the annual report put it, 'has nothing better to offer than the exciting and tense struggle that ensued between four masters of their respective arts.'

There were a few not very perceptive spectators who barracked

Compton and Edrich because they were not scoring quickly enough for their liking. The truth was that they could not. There were no spectacular figures in this classic confrontation. Compton made 71 and Edrich 64, and I would wager that they never had to work harder for their runs. Hollies took five wickets for 104 and Kardar one for 72, figures which were no reflection at all of the skill of the latter's bowling. This was connoisseurs' cricket which will not be easily forgotten by anyone who saw it and each bowler in the end was justly rewarded – Hollies had Edrich caught and Kardar bowled Compton. Hollies also bowled five overs of off-breaks round the wicket in this innings just to give the Warwickshire attack a little variety – and show his own versatility in the process. The match was drawn, but it did not matter; we had seen greatness.

The return fixture at Lord's was also a fine match. In the previous game, Compton's benefit, he had made a glorious 182. Next day he was bowled by Hollies for 14, and in the second innings by Pritchard for the same score – such are the vagaries of a batsman's life even when in form. Warwickshire bowled and fielded finely and, despite 72 by Edrich, Middlesex were all out 135 – Grove four for 29, Hollies three for 35 and Pritchard three for 57. Warwickshire did little better with 155 and then Middlesex piled it on – Edrich 114, which enabled his captain to declare at 340 for six. Warwickshire had to get 321 to win and when the eighth wicket fell at 215 there were 75 minutes left. Wolton and Pritchard stayed while 65 were added and then Wolton and Hollies played out the last 25 minutes of extra time. Wolton was not out 72 and Hollies – not out 2.

There was another wonderful match when two professional captains, Dollery and Ames, were opposed to each other at Maidstone. Pritchard bowled Todd with the first ball of the match and then Fagg, 68, and Ames, 69, put on 137 and brought Kent to the respectability of 265. Kardar arrived late from an Oxford examination, but was in time to take two for 60. There was a similar sort of partnership in Warwickshire's innings between Dollery, who got 95, and Ken Taylor, 89, the stand of 152 taking them comfortably to 289.

On what was by now a wearing pitch, Ames hit a superb 160 in Kent's second innings and then Pritchard produced his hat trick. Even so, Kent were able to declare at 300 for nine and Warwickshire had to get 277 in three hours to win – 92 an hour. Dollery made it possible with a great innings of 118, and it was a close run thing to the very end for he was fifth out at 262 with only eleven minutes left. It looked odds on Warwickshire, but with only one run added, Wolton, Pritchard and Grove all went and there were eight men out. The last over arrived with 5 runs wanted and two wickets left. Off Dovey's first ball Ken Taylor was caught; off the second Bromley should have been stumped.

Then Bromley and Spooner each got a single and off the fifth a leg-bye was run. But with only one run wanted, Spooner could do no more than play the last ball back to the bowler and the match was drawn instead of being won or lost. Spooner will probably regret to his dying day that he did not hit that ball for four, or get out in the attempt. But it was a great game.

Dollery played another match-saving innings against Derbyshire at Edgbaston. After Hollies, with four for 24, and Townsend in a deadly little spell of 5 overs, 2 maidens, 4 runs and 3 wickets, had demolished Derbyshire for 86, Warwickshire, too, were in trouble, losing their first four wickets for 7 runs. But Dollery, as he so often did, pulled the game round. He had got to 83 when last man Hollies came in and again Eric stayed with him until his captain had made exactly 100 and the total had reached 172. Derbyshire recovered in the second innings with 292 and Warwickshire this time were left with 207 to get to win. They only just did it and for the second time in the match Hollies helped to save the day. Two runs were needed when the ninth wicket fell, but Hollies, although opposed to Gladwin, saw that the tenth one did not, while Ord, 75 not out, made the winning hit.

Against Hampshire at Bournemouth, Warwickshire, for a change, had plenty of runs on the board when Dollery came in – Maudsley having made his first century for the county – so there was nothing to restrain him. His hitting that day was the fiercest Hollies ever saw in a long career. He made 50 in eleven minutes, 20 of them in one over off Bailey, and the scoreboard operator, working by hand, could not keep up with him. Altogether he made 121 and in the last hour Ord, Dollery and Pritchard between them added 161. Warwickshire's total was 498 for five, their highest for ten years.

It was against Gloucestershire that Dollery made his double century exactly – and that took him only 205 minutes. It was made out of 400 for nine declared and contained four sixes and 22 fours. In the second innings his 73 out of 157 for nine declared was made in 65 minutes. Five times he hit Tom Goddard for six, one of them going over the pavilion. Both Hollies and Goddard got their 100th wicket for the season in this match, which, although Crapp made 102 and 50, Warwickshire won by 112 runs.

J. R. Thompson showed what an asset he could have been to Warwickshire had he been able to play all the summer by scoring 97 and 102 not out on his first appearances against the Combined Services, who included a young batsman, P. B. H. May, whose 98 and 41 gave promise of higher things to come. Thompson also had 77 and 103 against Somerset at Taunton.

Two Warwickshire records were set up in July. When Hollies got Barrick's wicket in the Northants match he brought his total to 1216, and thus beat Sydney Santall's record. It was another ball to add to his collection of souvenirs. Santall, then 75, and living in retirement in Sussex, sent him a telegram of congratulations – but did so prematurely. When it arrived Hollies still needed six wickets. The second record came to Esmond Lewis, a fine amateur wicketkeeper who, making his début against Oxford, had nine victims in all, eight batsmen being caught and one stumped.

During the winter of 1948–9 between 25 000 and 30 000 tons of rubble from bomb-sites in the city, had been dumped on the ground, the first instalment towards providing additional seating for 15 000 to 20 000 people without which the Club could not hope to be allotted a Test Match instead of the trial match they were given. This stirred Dr Thwaite at the annual meeting to say that perhaps in future years Edgbaston's 'Hill' on the north side of the ground would be as famous as Sydney's; *The Birmingham Post* commented that the Club was surely right in putting the interests of its supporters as a whole before even those of so important a section as the members 'and not only in the hope that improved accommodation will bring Test Matches as well as Trial games to Birmingham. It is, indeed, much to be regretted that the second city in Britain should still not be able to stage a match between England and Australia. That objective will be achieved only by attending first to the needs of the mass of cricket-lovers whom the magnet of a Test Match attracts from all over the country.'

Whether because of the newspaper's comments or not, Captain Cowan felt it necessary to say that he was afraid some members might think that the Club had done too much for the public in improving the ground and not enough for the members, whose turn would come next.

The weather for the Test trial turned out to be poor and the cricket tedious and none of the best performers in the game – Simpson, with 69, Robertson, with 126, and Jackson, who took six for 37 in the first innings – were eventually chosen, so one was left wondering what was the point of it all. Hollies played for the North and took two wickets in each innings for 25 and 62.

In fact, he played in all four Tests as well, taking ten wickets at a cost of 38·5 runs each, and only Trevor Bailey, with sixteen, had more. In the first at Leeds which, like all the others, was drawn, he did not take a wicket, and had 90 runs scored off him, so it is perhaps surprising that he survived to play in the others. In the second game at Lord's he bowled no fewer than fifty-eight overs and despite the fact that he was unlucky enough to run into Donnelly at his best, eighteen of them were maidens and he took five wickets, though he had to concede 133 runs to get them. Against Donnelly in the form he showed that day it was very good bowling. He made 206 and as he came off the ground the pavilion rose to him. Robertson-Glasgow ranked this among the great Test innings of all time. Like A. P. F. Chapman, Donnelly had now scored a century at Lord's, a century in the Oxford-Cambridge match and a century in a Gentlemen v. Players encounter and now a double in a Test Match. 'No left-hander', wrote R. C. Robertson-Glasgow, 'has excited less expectation in the slips. His place is undoubtedly among the few truly great players of the present, a view in which I know W. R. Hammond concurs.' What a pity Edgbaston did not see more of him in this mood.

In the third Test Hollies was again wicketless and in the last at The Oval he had one for 51. He fared better against the tourists at Edgbaston with four for 84, Donnelly making 106 this time; and he had five for 32 and three for 51 against the Gentlemen, though Pritchard took the honours with six for 96. Kardar, who was also honoured for the other side, scored 2 and 16, and took one for 37. Why Dollery was not selected for one of these representative encounters passes comprehension.

Worcestershire's Roly Jenkins just pipped Hollies for two honours. He was first in the race for 100 wickets – he finished with 183 to Hollies's 166, which were gained more cheaply – and as one of the Five Cricketers of the Year. But two of Warwickshire's old players W. G. Quaife and 'Tiger' Smith were honoured this season. For the first time a member of the Royal Family, the Duke of Edinburgh, who had been known to turn his arm over, was President of the M.C.C. and they decided to elect twenty-five veteran professionals to life honorary membership. Smith was the only Warwickshire player who qualified, though they included S. F. Barnes. Both Smith and Quaife were similarly honoured by Warwickshire later in the year.

And in September, as the season ended, R. V. Ryder died at his home in Birmingham at the age of 76 years, two-thirds of which had been devoted to Warwickshire cricket. Although he had been retired some time there was a deep sense of loss at Edgbaston on which he had imprinted his personality for so long, and there were many tributes, verbal and written, to his memory. Strangely enough, though, there is nothing on the ground which stands as a memorial to him – except the ground itself.

How reluctant clubs were to consider any breakaway from tradition in the game was shown when Glamorgan suggested the introduction of a trophy for annual competition. It was not approved because it was felt that the proposal was not in accord with the traditions of county cricket. Neither, perhaps, was the importation of 'foreign' players. With two New Zealanders, a Pakistani, and a West Indian, not to mention men from Durham and Cornwall in the side, it was perhaps not surprising that Warwickshire were being dubbed in some quarters 'a League of Nations team'. M. F. K. Fraser first referred to it in an article he wrote for the 1950 edition of *Wisden* and added that the Birmingham public, 'nurtured on the liberal transfer system of soccer, will not worry where their cricket favourites come from so long as they play attractively and win matches.'

The theme was taken up at the annual meeting in 1950 both by the President and the chairman. Dr Thwaite said that for too long Warwickshire had been content with mediocre play and he was by no means on the defensive about the Committee's policy of seeking the aid of Colonial and other outside players, insofar as the introduction of these men was stimulating interest throughout the county and breeding a spirit of emulation in Warwickshire youth in town and village.

This was putting it a bit strong, perhaps, but the fact remained that the county had never had so many excellent young players coming along, Alec Hastilow mentioning that in one second eleven match six of the team were under 21 and seven of them born in Warwickshire. Earlier he had drawn attention to 'the splendid record' of the second eleven who had been defeated only twice in four seasons.

Dr Thwaite described the Club's financial position as strong, but deplored the lack of support for the Test trial, which he regarded as a serious setback to the Club's prospects of securing a Test Match in the near future. He thought the Committee had been badly let down. 'We are frustrated by our own public', he was reported as saying in *The Birmingham Post*, 'and, be it remembered, a public which enjoys the best popular side amenities of any county ground in England, bar none.'

The public, however, showed that when there was what they considered a worthwhile attraction at Edgbaston they would come to see it. They did so in record numbers for the visit of the West Indies, for whom Frank Worrell proved to be in superlative form. By the time they came to Edgbaston they had beaten England twice and thousands flocked to see them, 19 174 people paying for admission on the second day, 10 August, and, with members, making a record attendance of 25 000 – all with a good view of the game and seated in comfort. The annual report made the point that only two, or possibly three, grounds could equal this, as most clubs expected several thousands to stand all day, or sit on boards.

There were queues from 7.30 in the morning, three and a half hours before the start of the match – and a woman led them. Altogether, 45 440 people, additional to the 163 751, who watched the county games, paid to see this match, in which Warwickshire did what England seemed to have some difficulty in achieving – they beat the tourists by three wickets. They were the only county to do so and, indeed, the first county to beat a touring side since Worcestershire defeated the South Africans in the opening match of 1947.

That they did so was largely due to Grove who, using a green wicket magnificently, achieved his best performance in first-class cricket:

O	M	R	W
26·4	9	38	8

Worrell thought it the best piece of fast-medium-paced bowling they had met on the tour. Since a week's rest at the end of July, Grove had taken twenty-four wickets in six days of cricket.

The West Indians were all out for 156 and Warwickshire's 284 gave them a comfortable lead. In their second innings it was the turn of Hollies. He found a worn patch no more than six inches in diameter just about on a length outside the middle and leg stumps and exploited it to the extent of taking six wickets for 57. Warwickshire had rather a fright before they got the runs, losing seven wickets in the process largely because of some fine catching by the West Indians, but they got home with three wickets to spare.

The second scoreboard given by Dr Thwaite, this one in memory of his wife, who had died two years before, and had been a gracious and generous supporter of the Club in her own right, was opened in time for this match. Dr Thwaite, who had offered a £10 prize to the first batsman to have a century recorded on it, had said that he hoped the West Indians would not work the board too hard. As it happened, he need not have worried.

The guests at the dinner Dr Thwaite gave during the match spanned more than sixty years of the Club's history. They included J. Ernest Hill, aged 82, who had made a century against the West Indies in 1900; J. F. Byrne, aged 79; Cecil Hands, aged 63; Frank Stephens, aged 61; the Rev. J. H. Parsons, aged 60; 'Tiger' Smith, aged 64; and the Rev. E. F. Waddy, aged 70.

Hollies had several other encounters with the tourists in the Tests. In the first game at Manchester, which was played on the roughest wicket he had ever seen, one ball from him pitched on middle and leg and went over the heads of the slips. Frank Chester called a wide because the batsman could not reach the ball – he said it was the only time he had ever done so of a ball pitched on the wicket. Hollies took three for 70 and five for 63, and England won by 202 runs. Dollery had also been selected, but failed, making only 8 and nought, and he was dropped for the next game, as was Hollies, surprisingly.

Hollies was back at Nottingham, however, where Worrell cut loose with some of the finest batting Hollies ever saw – and he had a good view of it from the other end. Worrell made 261 and Hollies, who was one of three bowlers who had to bowl over forty overs each, had 134 runs hit off him for two wickets. Even so, he was more fortunate than Roly Jenkins: he bowled only thirteen overs, but 75 runs were hit off them. Hollies was dropped again for the last Test, probably to his relief, for the West Indies had another total of over 500, Worrell this time making only 138. Wright, who was preferred to Hollies, got a taste of the medicine – 141 runs for his five wickets.

There was one other representative match this season in which both Hollies and Dollery played. This was Gentlemen v. Players at Lord's where Dollery had the honour of following in the footsteps of Dick Lilley and leading the Players. He showed himself worthy of it, too, for once doing himself full justice in a representative game, scoring 123 and 20, and so becoming the first Warwickshire professional to score a century in this famous series which can never be played again.

Hollies had a modest bowling match, one wicket in each innings, but once again he took part in a superb finish and prevented a win by the Gentlemen in the last over. When Hollies – last man, of course – joined Wright 11 runs were needed and there were five balls left. 'Amidst tense excitement', *Wisden* recorded, 'Hollies managed to keep the last deliveries out of his wickets and away from the clutching hands of ten fieldsmen crouched in a circle only a few yards from him.' During the match F. R. Brown was invited to captain the side to go to Australia in the winter, but even after his showing in this game Dollery did not get an invitation to go, though Hollies did, with disappointing results all round.

As for the County Championship, Warwickshire began as if they meant to walk away with it. They set the pace, won eight and lost only two of their first seventeen matches and were leading until the end of June, but then a rot set in and they did not win one of their last eleven county fixtures. Even so, for the second season in succession, they finished fourth. 'Enigmatic Warwickshire', *Wisden* dubbed them, and it is difficult to put one's finger on why they did not do better. Dollery made four centuries, but did not score so prolifically as in 1949; and he undoubtedly suffered from staleness towards the end of the season to such an extent that in the last five weeks he made very few runs, a loss of form which may very well have cost him the trip to Australia. His leadership of the team did not suffer, however, and the President described him as 'undoubtedly the best captain of a county side in the country'.

Some of the younger players disappointed, but not Gardner. He made a double century, as well as a century in each innings of a match, the sixth Warwickshire player to do so. In all, he scored nearly 2000 runs and headed the averages with nearly 50, Dollery being second. Spooner was tried as an opening bat and his aggregate rose from 559 to 1254; he also caught forty-five batsmen and stumped sixteen and got into the Test trial. It was Ord's benefit year, but he disappointed, failing to reach a four-figure aggregate. Donnelly could play in only four Championship matches, but in one of them, in which he led the side, he made a glorious century against Yorkshire.

As for the bowling, Hollies again sent down over 1000 overs and his 117 wickets cost him well under 20 runs each. He was third in the race for the 100. Pritchard just failed to get 100, Grove had 84 and Kardar 55, as well as scoring his first Championship century – and at Lord's, too. His decision to return to Pakistan was much regretted by his captain and colleagues on the field, for his left-arm spin had given a much-needed variety to the Warwickshire bowling.

Dollery's four hundreds were among the best he ever made. His first against Derbyshire was a true captain's innings for he took command of the game when three wickets were down for one run and hit three sixes and twelve fours in a fine knock of 163; against Kent he made 100 in exactly the same number of minutes and nearly enabled his side to get the 282 in 170 minutes they needed to win; and in Ord's benefit match against Middlesex he scored a magnificent 185 without the semblance of a mistake, completing his 1000 runs. The beneficiary got only 2 but a 20 000 crowd on the Saturday must have consoled him, as the result – nearly £5000 – must also have done. He was a batsman, who, if he never reached the heights, was always entertaining to watch. There was never anything depressing about an Ord innings, and that could not be said about everyone who played for Warwickshire. Dollery's fourth century was a fine 150 against Somerset.

Gardner's double century, 215 in the return match at Taunton, was a monumental affair of nearly seven hours' concentrated effort. It contained his first six in county cricket, but only fourteen fours. He followed it in the next match at Northampton with 126 and 28 not out, and he was at his most stubborn against Leicestershire at Coalville – 95 in the first innings and a century partnership with Spooner, and then 58 not out in the second. They had another century stand against Yorkshire at Edgbaston, but it was Donnelly's superb 120 which took the eye in this game – half of the runs made in only fifteen strokes.

Young 'Roly' Thompson, taking his chance in the absence of the injured Pritchard, showed what he was capable of in the match with Gloucestershire on a damp pitch at Edgbaston. In seven balls he bowled two such excellent bats as Emmett and Young and had B. O. Allen caught, at a cost of 4 runs, and in the innings took five for 16. He was soon to have another young rival in the seam-bowling department in Jack Bannister – one of the few really good cricketers who have sprung from the Wolverhampton area – who was engaged during August.

By the end of that month it was evident that both gate receipts and members' subscriptions would again be records, and numbers of the latter had again to be limited. Even so, there was a constant struggle to make income equal, let alone exceed, expenditure, and year by year the value of the ground that was slowly being built rose steadily, though the funds to do it were even slower to accumulate.

The Club lost no fewer than three former captains in 1950: T. S. Fishwick who made twelve centuries for the county and in 1905 set up a record of 40 catches in a season; A. C. S. Glover; and G. W. Stephens, who had resigned from the Committee only three years earlier and whose place had been taken by his twin brother Frank. Both brothers had been members of the 1911 Championship team and it was a pity that G.W. could not have lived a little longer to see Warwickshire's second triumph, though F.G. did. Vacancies on the Committee at this time were made good by the election of James McDowall, later the Club's honorary treasurer and legal adviser, and H. W. Homer, former captain of Staffordshire, both men whose advice in different spheres was invaluable.

Dollery was otherwise engaged coaching in New Zealand during the winter of 1950–1 and at least one person, *Wisden*'s correspondent, missed him from the Australian scene. 'People in Australia with England's cause very near to heart', he wrote, 'regretted the absence of the stability in batting which might have been provided by such men as Robertson and Edrich, of Middlesex, Ikin (Lancashire), Hardstaff (Notts), Dollery (Warwickshire), Emmett (Gloucestershire) and Brookes (Northants).'

Hollies was one of three leg-spinners in the side – the others being Wright and, of course, the captain, Freddie Brown – but it was not a happy tour for him. 'Hollies', said *Wisden*, 'did not enjoy bowling on Australian pitches on which pronounced spin was essential to make the ball turn. Usually, he pitched his English length and direction, which, in Australia, meant short of a length on the leg stump. The best batsmen found time to play him off the back foot and they exposed the many gaps in his leg-side field. Few people could have hidden disappointment better than Hollies and his "ground staff" companion, Berry, who seldom looked likely to fulfil his mission as a left-hand stock bowler to pin down the opposition.'

Hollies was not selected for any of the five Tests in Australia, or either of the two in New Zealand. Indeed, he played in only nine first-class matches on the tour. In these he bowled 1576 balls for 858 runs and twenty-one wickets, an average of 40·85, which was far below his England standard. His best performance was four for seven against a Combined XI in New Zealand after he had changed his style, keeping the ball up to the batsman and attacking the off stump.

Hollies himself has written that soon after his arrival in Australia he found that he could not make the ball turn as he did in England – 'a great amount of wrist and finger spin was needed to make the ball turn at all.' Nor was it just a matter of flighting and spinning the ball more. It was not until he began to push it through with a lower trajectory that he bowled more accurately and became more difficult to play. But by that time it was too late. Oddly enough, when he was allowed to take the new ball for a few overs 'to see the shine off' he made it move about like a boomerang.

His experience made Hollies doubt the wisdom of taking any leg-spinner, or off-spinner, to Australia 'unless he is a player out of the ordinary – he must have proved in English cricket that he genuinely has something different and can spin the ball viciously if necessary.' Two left-arm spinners bowling a good length would be his solution to the problem.

Spooner got his first tour this winter – in a Commonwealth side visiting India – which, unfortunately, he was not able to complete because of illness. He played in two of the five unofficial Tests, but had only one innings, in which he made 62 not out. This was also his highest score for the tour in which he played in eleven matches and made a total of 269 runs, doing well both as batsman and wicketkeeper.

Champions Again
(1951)

EXACTLY forty years after they had first won it, the Championship came again to Edgbaston and by a greater margin – thirty-two points over Yorkshire, the only other county to win more than ten games – than it had been gained since the scoring system was altered immediately after the war. Warwickshire took over the lead on 1 June and never let it go. Lancashire were the only team to beat them before the Championship was decided, though Essex did so afterwards.

It should not have been an occasion for surprise, for, as *The Birmingham Post* said in the special supplement they published to mark the event, 'it had been coming these last four seasons', though there's many a slip 'twixt the cup and the lip, especially in cricket which is, after all, known above all other sports for its glorious uncertainty. Perhaps the players had sensed that it was in their grasp but were keeping their fingers crossed, as it were, for did not Dollery, at the annual meeting before the season began, deplore the fact that the side was frequently labelled as potential champions even before the 1950 season started, thereby tending to make the task more difficult for them? But here came victory with her wine at last, and who shall say it was not fully deserved?

What had they done to warrant it? No player enjoyed that *annus mirabilis* that comes to the blessed among cricketers. Dollery himself described his colleagues as 'an extraordinary team of ordinary cricketers playing purposeful cricket'. No batsman made over 2000 runs, though five of them got well over 1000 in Championship games alone – Spooner (1767, average 43·009), Dollery (1491 – 41·41), Gardner (1338 – 31·85), Ord (1311 – 31·21) and Wolton (1011 – 30·60) – and six batsmen had averages of over 30 an innings.

True, two bowlers took over 100 wickets in Championship games –

Hollies 145 for 17·69 runs each, and Grove, for the first time in his first-class career, 103 for 18·78; while a third, Pritchard, took ninety-three for 21·65, though he did so in an extraordinarily uneven way not conducive to the winning of titles. In his first thirteen games he took no more than thirty-eight wickets and they cost him dearly – 31·55 runs each. Then in the next four games he took almost as many, thirty-six, but at a cost of only 10·88 runs each. Then an injury kept him out of all the August matches except two.

Happily, his young replacement, 'Roly' Thompson, only 18, seized his chance each time Pritchard's misfortune gained him a place in the team, and another youngster – a 21-year-old slow left-arm bowler, Ray Weeks, replacing Kardar – did so well in his first season that he took sixty-eight wickets for 23·88 runs in Championship games and ninety-four for 21·75 all told. It was not Weeks's figures which impressed so much as the way he bowled against even the best batsmen in the country, hardly ever allowing himself to be hit off his length. He provided invaluable relief for Hollies who, says *Wisden* (though he himself does not mention it), because of an injury to his right ankle, 'was often obliged to bowl more slowly, with a run of only two or three paces. The ball, tossed higher in the air, turned more than usual and the majority of the opposing batsmen, stuck fast behind the crease, prodded apprehensively and fatally.'

This admirable variety of penetrative bowling was largely responsible for the fact that Warwickshire won no fewer than six of their victories in two days – thus bearing out the classical Yorkshire dictum that it's bowling that wins matches. Their fielding, too, was often brilliant, Townsend, at slip, recalling the sleight of hand of a Hammond, and in the last match of the season setting up a club record of forty-one catches. In the outfield Wolton excelled and threw in beautifully, while Spooner showed himself the most improved wicketkeeper in the land, stumping twenty batsmen and taking fifty-three catches. He was never the most stylish nor the most acrobatic of keepers, but he was extremely efficient, especially on the leg-side – he was left-handed, of course – and tremendously keen. By the end of the season he had risen to fourth place in the Fielding Statistics Table, only Yarnold, L. H. Compton, and H. W. Stephenson being above him.

But perhaps the most important factor of all in Warwickshire's success was the fact that they needed no more than thirteen players, all professional with the exception of Esmond Lewis, the wicketkeeper, and he played in only one game. They were able to do this for two reasons: freedom from injuries; and the fact that it was their good fortune that there were no calls on them for Tests or other representative games, though, goodness knows, the form of more than one player was good enough in all conscience to warrant it. It is not without significance,

I think, that both these factors entered largely into the 1951 success. They meant that Warwickshire were always a team and this, probably more than anything else, accounted for their success. Dollery certainly thought so. What he could not say was that every team, if it is to fulfil its function, must have a leader and that in him they had the best there was. Happily there were others who did not hesitate to say it for him and one of them was the Club's annual report:

It was success in the best traditions of the game for a team playing perfectly together as a co-ordinated entity under the man who proved himself the greatest professional captain the game has known and one of the greatest natural cricket leaders of all time ... when necessary he inspired them with the brilliance of his own personal achievements – magnificent slip catches, great fighting centuries against the near rivals, Lancashire and Yorkshire, and superlative cricket judgment.

Only twice so far in Warwickshire's history have the Fates conspired to bring all these factors and qualities together at one and the same time and on each occasion they brought the Championship, too.

But let us go back to the beginning and savour the story in its proper sequence. The year began sadly enough with the news of the death of Sir Leonard Parsons, one of the many distinguished men of medicine, whose allegiance Warwickshire have been fortunate enough to attract, and the further dampener that though the membership subscriptions had risen by £1200 and the gate receipts by a similar amount, the large increase of work done on the ground had resulted in a loss on the 1950 season of £4267.

This brought a warning from the President that the efforts to build a new Edgbaston had exhausted the Club financially and that they might temporarily have to rest on their laurels until they got their second monetary wind. Then came the usual inquest on the previous season's play which brought a verdict from the President that the decline in late summer had been caused by uncertain middle-order batting and the lack of an off-spin bowler. He added a rider, as it were, that Peter Jackson, the former Worcestershire player, had been engaged to coach potential bowlers of this type on the staff, especially Wolton, Bromley and Don Taylor.

All this must have been rather depressing for the players, though doubtless they took pleasure in the presentations to Charlie Grove of the ball, mounted on three stumps, with which he had taken eight for 38 against the West Indies: of another ball to Pritchard for his eight for 20 against Worcestershire; and of an inscribed silver plate for Gardner's presentation bureau to mark his two centuries against Essex.

Before the main drama of the season began there was a curtain raiser of some note on 30 April between an Old England XI and a Warwickshire XI, which had been inspired by Councillor Edgar Hiley, of Solihull, then appeals organiser for the Birmingham and Warwickshire branches of the National Playing Fields Association which was celebrating its silver jubilee. His name was soon to figure largely in the history of the Club.

The scores in the match do not really matter – except one by D. J. Knight, the former England and Surrey opening batsman, who for Old England made 112, including eighteen fours, out of a total of 206, and moved W. E. Hall to describe it as 'a bright light' of an innings and a good deal more. Knight, who was within a fortnight of his 57th birthday, was missed at square leg when he was four, one of those missed chances for which the player responsible might well be singled out for praise in, say, the annual report because thereby cricket-lovers were providentially able to catch a glimpse of the sublime. Knight took 19 runs from two overs by Eric Hollies, which not many batsmen have done, and made his second 50 in forty minutes.

Preliminary publicity about the match had made much play with a reported announcement by Canon Jack Parsons that he proposed to hit Eric Hollies further than any batsman had done before – first bounce into Cannon Hill Park. Alas, for the plans of men – the doughty Canon, who was then aged 61, was bowled by Jack Bannister for 15, but Bob Wyatt's score was only three runs short of his age – half a century.

Warwickshire's first victory at the beginning of May was over Sussex by the convincing margin of eight wickets. Pritchard, Grove and Hollies got rid of them for 158 and Warwickshire then scored consistently – Dollery 71, Don Taylor 66 and Spooner 46 – to make 266. Sussex, with 10 runs fewer – Hollies and Pritchard again – could do no better than ask Warwickshire to make 149 in two and one-quarter hours, and Spooner showed the way with 94 not out, the match being won with a comfortable twenty-five minutes to spare.

There followed draws at Swansea and at home to Derbyshire, the first a low-scoring affair marked by an astonishing feat of endurance by Grove, then 39, who bowled for three hours broken only by the tea interval, sending down twenty-six overs and taking seven wickets for 53. This was followed by a sparkling piece of hitting by Pritchard, whose 43 in twenty-five minutes included three sixes – two of them out of the ground – and three fours.

The second draw, far from being the tame affair so many draws are, provided an exciting climax. Warwickshire made a comfortable start with 276, which Derbyshire bettered with 313, thanks – no doubt – to a joyless innings by Kelly, who somehow occupied three and a half hours over his first 50 and nearly five hours over 97. Everybody there wished they hadn't seen Kelly, to misquote the old song. The upshot of it was that Warwickshire had to score 174 in two hours to win and once more

Hollies found himself in the position where everything depended on him. Warwickshire had made only 157 when he came in so it was impossible for him to get the runs in the time, but he played out the last over from Morgan and saved the game. Of such things are Championships compiled.

On then to Huddersfield and the first of two grand wins over Yorkshire. This was a bowlers' battle on a rain-affected pitch and for once Yorkshire, who have always specialised in such things, did not win it. Thanks to Gardner, digging in for 30, and Ord, aggressive for 37, and a ninth-wicket stand of 46 by Pritchard and Weeks, Warwickshire struggled to 171. Yorkshire, bad-wicket revellers though they were supposed to be, could not cope with Hollies, four for 53, and Grove, three for 31, despite a 61 by Billy Sutcliffe; but they put the pressure on mightily when it was Warwickshire's turn to bat again. They fared even worse against Appleyard and Wardle and were all out for 92, of which Gardner made a defiant 27.

The sun shone warmly on the wicket for the fourth innings and the machinations of Hollies and Grove utterly did for Yorkshire, who were all out for their lowest score of the season, 49. Only J. V. Wilson got double figures – just – and Hollies this time had five for 12, four of them off one stroke. He bowled with marvellous accuracy and, in fact, he himself rates this as the best performance of his career:

O	M	R	W
20·5	12	12	5

Grove's figures were almost as good – 18 overs, 8 maidens, 25 runs and 4 wickets. Their devastating bowling wrung a *cri de cœur* from some poor soul in torment in the crowd which 'Tom' Dollery remembers to this day. 'Tom', it cried, as Warwickshire were changing places in the field, 'for God's sake take one of 'em off.'

Leaving Huddersfield mourning, Warwickshire came back to Edgbaston to meet their nearest neighbours. Once more Hollies was in at the death, this time as a bowler, and he literally won the match with five minutes of extra time to spare with an inspired spell in which he took six wickets for 24 runs – six for 62 in all. Spooner, 122, and Gardner, 73, had a first-wicket stand of 156, which largely helped Warwickshire to a first innings total of 389 for eight wickets. In the end Worcestershire wanted 275 to win, but with only seventy-five minutes left for play they were no more than 118 for one wicket. Then they decided to try to catch up with the clock, but the attempt failed dismally, four wickets being lost for the addition of only 7 runs, so they then tried to settle for a draw.

Problem – what was Dollery to do? Answer – he had the kind of inspiration which comes only to a master of timing and the art of declarations. He had plenty of runs to play with so he suggested to Hollies that he should bowl 'donkey drops', but to a close-set field. This meant that the Worcestershire batsmen could have hit the bowling easily enough, but that time would be taken up in retrieving the ball. Hollies was already saving it for Warwickshire by bowling from almost a standing position. But Worcestershire's batsmen stayed rooted behind the crease, pushed defensively and gave easy catches. Only four minutes remained to play when the last wicket fell to Hollies.

After the match Wyatt, who was leading Worcestershire against his old county, said to Hollies: 'Fancy getting us out like that when you weren't even taking a step to bowl.' To which Hollies rightly rejoined: 'The trouble was that *your* people didn't take a step when they were batting.'

Next came another exciting win, which many thought the best of the season, this time with seven minutes to spare, over Middlesex at Lord's. When Middlesex had made 335 for eight declared – Compton, 172 and Edrich, 71 – they seemed safe enough. This was the severest test young Weeks had had so far and he came through it well. He bowled nineteen overs, four of them maidens, for 57 runs and three wickets, and he never lost his control – even against Compton on the rampage.

With Warwickshire out for 185, of which Spooner made a fine 96, they were 150 behind and Middlesex looked certain to win, even though their second innings was kept down to a total of 192. Warwickshire were faced with the seemingly impossible task of scoring 343 in just over five hours, but again Spooner took matters in hand. He put together his highest score so far of 158, and with a 53 from Gardner and 40 not out from Dollery, Warwickshire just did it. It was a weary Spooner who changed at the end of the game for he had been on the field for all but an hour of it.

Weeks came creditably through another severe ordeal against Cambridge University where, although May was in form with 156 not out and 42, he bowled his left-arm slows with such notable accuracy and direction that in the match he took nine wickets for 120. Back to the more serious business of Championship cricket, Warwickshire had the worst of a draw with Essex at Edgbaston, where too cautious batting against the leg-breaks and googlies of Peter Smith nearly cost them the match after they had been left to get 248 in two hours.

Then came Grove's benefit against Notts, which provided a perfect example of how a piece of inspired fielding can change the course of a game. The match went more or less placidly on its way until the last innings, in which Notts needed to score 243 in three hours ten minutes, a by no means superhuman task. With 100 passed in less than an hour, it looked as if they would do it easily, but then Hitchcock (another New Zealand import – he worked his passage – recommended by Pritchard), ran out Stocks with a magnificent throw from the boundary. Hollies then went through the tail, taking five for 60. Grove derived nearly £5000 from the benefit.

Eight matches, five wins, three draws – so far very, very good, but the first defeat lay ahead at Old Trafford, where Warwickshire never recovered from two bad starts against Statham, who was always one of their bogey bowlers. He took only five wickets in the match – three for 13 in the first innings and two for none in his first five balls in the second – but the explosive impact was shattering. Warwickshire were all out 101 in the first innings; and though Ord and Wolton had a century stand in the second it was not enough, Lancashire winning by nine wickets.

A bold declaration by Simpson when Notts were 148 behind transformed the return game at Trent Bridge. Warwickshire had begun with 387, which included Townsend's maiden Championship century of 112. Simpson himself counter-attacked with 148 not out and then declared at 239 for five. Dollery took up the challenge and rattled up 172 for three, Don Taylor making 90 not out. Notts needed 321, but it was too many for them against the guile of young Weeks – seven for 70. In four hours and forty minutes of playing time on the last day 425 runs were scored.

Another astute declaration, this time by Dollery, turned the scale against Gloucestershire at Bristol where he got them in on a wearing pitch. Graveney made the kind of graceful century of which only he among batsmen of that time was capable, but another Gardner-Spooner opening stand, of 129, gave Warwickshire a very good start in reply. When Dollery saw wickets falling quickly after tea he declared although he was only 44 in the lead, and he got Gloucestershire in – and out – for 163, leaving Warwickshire with only 121 to make.

Grove, with five for 20 and six for 54, almost beat Leicestershire on his own at Edgbaston, Warwickshire winning by six wickets; and then there was another thriller at Coventry in the return game with Gloucestershire in which the lead frequently changed hands. At first, when Gloucestershire were got rid of for 163, it looked easy. This was when Pritchard started his remarkable return to form with five for 55. Then a not out 157 by Wolton, who, with Ord, put on 143 for the fifth wicket, took Warwickshire to a comfortable 313. However, when Gloucestershire batted again, Emmett, by a superlative display of forcing strokes, added a 93 to his first innings effort of 78, and Gloucestershire, too, were over the 300 mark. Warwickshire wanted only 179 to win, but they lost four wickets for 26 and when Wolton left at 80 their chances seemed pretty thin. But then Hitchcock transformed the innings with a splendid half-century in thirty-eight minutes, and Warwickshire were home by three wickets.

It was their fifth Championship success in a row, a record for the

Club, and it was followed by another over Somerset at Edgbaston, their bowling proving altogether too strong for the visitors. They were all out 113 in the first innings – Hollies six for 23 – but in the second innings, against Pritchard and Grove, their score approached the preposterous. They had five wickets down for as few runs and seven had gone for 13. Had it not been for one man, Redman, who made 25, they would not have reached even their meagre total of 50. Warwickshire won by the ample margin of an innings and 115 runs.

Gardner did not lighten the gloom of a cold and rainy game at Dudley by taking six hours to amass 144 out of Warwickshire's first innings total of 343. After that there were more interruptions than play, but somehow Cooper managed to survive no fewer than eight of them to carry his bat through the Worcestershire innings of 154. Nor could he be got out in the second innings either, so that in the match he made 102 without being dismissed. Warwickshire had to be content with first innings points.

Warwickshire won the next three games in a row, all in two days. The bowlers put on another firework display at Edgbaston where they got Glamorgan out before lunch for a mere 60. The innings began well enough with an opening partnership of 31; but the next nine wickets went down like ninepins for 29 against Pritchard and Grove who, in their last ten overs, sent back seven men for 6 runs, Pritchard having six for 38 and Grove four for 20. Pritchard bowled the last two Glamorgan batsmen with successive balls, and when they went in a second time after Warwickshire had made 285 (Spooner, 102), he had Emrys Davies caught off the first ball he sent down – a split hat trick, so to speak. He went on to an even better performance in the second innings than in the first – eight for 55 – Glamorgan being all out this time for 157.

Then down to Maidstone for a match which Arthur Fagg had chosen for his benefit. In reply to Warwickshire's 322 Kent could make only 93, Grove taking six for 41 and Weeks finishing off the innings with two for none in six balls. Following on, Kent reached 260, of which Fagg made 80. The winning runs were made almost as extra time expired – and they were two leg-byes made into six by an overthrow to the boundary.

Middlesex came to Edgbaston without Compton, Robertson and Edrich, all appearing for the Players, and they were tumbled out for 181 and 85 by Pritchard in the first innings and Hollies in the second, Warwickshire winning easily by ten wickets. Perhaps it was the absence of the Middlesex stars which, despite the fact that Warwickshire were hot-foot on the Championship trail, kept the crowds away. Their absence prompted *The Birmingham Post* to the comment that Warwickshire now had a big lead in the Championship and that wherever they played outside the county they commanded widespread interest, but

315

that when they played at Edgbaston the story was different. That week for the two-day match with Middlesex they had taken £1000.

They interviewed Leslie Deakins and quoted him as saying: 'We are a little disappointed. We have had a remarkable season and we feel that if we had been Yorkshire playing at home we should have had 25 000 people at a match. At Maidstone there were 11 000 spectators . . . It is rather galling to find Aston Villa able to command a following of 50 000 a week during their season, whereas we are finding it difficult to get a tenth of that number.'

He would have far greater cause for lament in years to come, but he soon had his immediate answer. Perhaps it was because of what he said, or the three wins in a row, but the next game at Edgbaston against Lancashire, on a perfect summer's day, really brought the crowds – almost 30 000 on the first day – still a record for the ground – when Tattersall tied Warwickshire up with six for 53 and they could make no more than 184. Lancashire, too, made a bad start, but Washbrook chose this occasion for a timely double century – 209 out of 333 for nine declared.

Warwickshire's opening pair failed in the second innings, but Dollery, like the superb leader he was, took command and for three and a half hours held off Statham, Wharton, Hilton and Tattersall and saw Warwickshire out of danger in a struggle which brought intense excitement. He was not out 108 at the close of play and if any innings can be said to have won Warwickshire the Championship it was this. The match was drawn but the paying attendance for the three days was 32 091. What would the Committee not give to see half that number at any county match today?

The next game against Somerset at Wells brought a decision in Warwickshire's favour in a curious way. After they had scored 397 for nine declared – Ord 123, Hitchcock 80 and Wolton 94 – Hollies and Weeks, each with eight wickets, routed Somerset for 173 and 102. Weeks, who bowled for four and a half of the five and three-quarter hours of play, conceded a total of only 128 runs off fifty-eight overs, a performance which almost out-Hollied Hollies, so to speak. Two minutes before the close of play on the second day Somerset, in their second innings, were 83 for five. Rogers, their captain, was batting and Dollery, though not very hopefully, suggested the extra half-hour. Rogers agreed to play a quarter of an hour, but said that if Warwickshire did not take two wickets in that time stumps would be drawn, but if two wickets fell he would play the second quarter of an hour.

Hollies has described how, on the stroke of the quarter-hour, there were three balls left of the over he was bowling. Somerset still had five wickets left, but with each of the next two balls Hollies took a wicket; stumps were not drawn and Warwickshire went on to get the remaining wickets down, winning by an innings and 22 runs. It was their fourteenth win of the season and the fifth gained in only two days.

Once more the crowds, perhaps now scenting blood, swarmed into the Edgbaston ground when Yorkshire came for the return match, even though they were without Hutton, Lowson, Watson and Brennan, all playing for England. They did so in such numbers on the second day that the only way to get them all in was to allow them to overflow on to the grass. This, however, meant putting Yorkshire at a disadvantage for they had had their first innings on the first day with the full boundary in use. When this point – which was one of some importance since both teams were battling for the Championship – was put to Norman Yardley he simply said: 'Good heavens, don't consider that. It's a treat to see so many people wanting to watch cricket. Pack 'em in.' And they did, to the tune of another 28 000 crowd.

Even without three of their batting stars, Yorkshire occupied the crease all the first day in scoring 249. However, although they were not without their regular bowlers – Trueman, Whitehead, Wardle, Leadbeater, Yardley and Halliday – Spooner and Ord put on 134 for Warwickshire's second wicket and Dollery followed on with his second successive century, 111, on the ground. They reached 362 and on a by now worn wicket Yorkshire found Hollies and, even more so, Weeks, too much for them. Hollies had five for 47; but Weeks, in five overs and five balls, three of them maidens, took three wickets for 3 runs.

Yorkshire were all out for 97 and as the Warwickshire players, victors by an innings and 16 runs, came off the field, 8000 spectators rose in their seats and cheered them home. It was Warwickshire's first double over Yorkshire for sixty-one years, and they were the first county to achieve the feat since Gloucestershire did so in 1947. An aggregate paying attendance of 43 000 saw this match and with members the total for the three days must have exceeded 55 000.

That win made Warwickshire's position at the head of the Championship table almost, but not quite, unassailable and it was as well that it did so for they drew their next three games. At Leicester, Spooner and Gardner, each scoring 101, had an opening partnership of 195 and with Dollery contributing a modest 77 they totalled 375. Once more in Pritchard's absence 'Roly' Thompson proved an able deputy with six for 63. Leicestershire followed on, but Vic Jackson saved them with 119 not out.

Despite rain at Derby both captains tried hard to reach a decision, each making a declaration, but without effect. The weather was also the decisive factor at Wellingborough where Warwickshire looked like winning – Northants having lost six wickets for 190 in their second innings when only 100 ahead – when they had to call it a day. The return match followed immediately at Coventry and this time Warwickshire made as sure of the Championship as it lay in their power so to do. They did so first by building up their highest score of the season, 456 for five, by batting of remarkable consistency – Gardner six hours as anchor man for 139 and sharing in stands of 90 with Spencer (57), 105 with Ord (74), 121 with Hitchcock (60) and 59 with Dollery (42), while Wolton added 46 not out and Townsend 19 not out for good measure.

Then the bowlers did their share by disposing of Northants for 117 – Hollies four for 49 – and 170 – Grove five for 22, which included his 100th wicket of the season. It was all over in two days again and it was just as well they won, for of their three remaining games one, with Essex, brought their second defeat of the season, and the last two against Hampshire at Edgbaston and Surrey at The Oval were drawn.

As it was, Warwickshire had to wait on tenterhooks for twenty-four hours before they knew whether the Championship was coming back to Edgbaston or not, and by a curious coincidence it was their greatest rivals in Yorkshire and their nearest neighbours in Worcestershire who were concerned in the finish with them. Yorkshire had to beat Worcestershire at Scarborough to stay in the hunt and the thought of what might happen there had been worrying W. E. Hall, the *Post*'s cricket correspondent, on and off all that second day at Coventry. As it ended 'it seemed', he wrote in the last paragraph of his account of Warwickshire's win, 'that there was but one place to go. So to Scarborough after a wrestle with the railway time-table, and if train meets train as British Railways hope it will, to see what may be the last day of Warwickshire's journey to the Championship.'

British Rail, for once, was as good as its time-tables and Hall arrived at Scarborough in time for an early breakfast. 'It was very overcast', he said later, 'and when I turned up at the ground there was a certain kind of ribaldry from the Yorkshire Press, as you may well imagine. Yorkshire wanted 250 to win, the wicket was slow and easy and there was, in fact, more rain during the morning. Yorkshire seemed certain to win or draw.'

But nothing is certain in cricket. Worcestershire had begun the match with a first innings of 271, of which Kenyon had made 145 and Howorth 45 not out, and had then dismissed Yorkshire for 114, Perks taking six of their wickets for 29. R. E. Bird, once of Warwickshire, who was leading the side, had not enforced the follow-on in order that Worcestershire would not have to bat in the fourth innings, though, in fact, it might have paid them to do so for Appleyard and Wardle got them out in their second innings for only 92.

So that was how the stage was set for the final day – 250 needed in 250 minutes. Yorkshire went for the runs, as they had to do, from the start, but rain caused a 25-minute break. They caught up with the clock again, however, and by 3.30 p.m. the match was going the expected way, with Yorkshire 232 for five and needing only 18 to win with half an hour in which to get them. For what happened in the next twenty minutes I cannot do better than quote Hall's vivid account which appeared in next day's issue of *The Birmingham Post*. Even though it was not a match in which Warwickshire took part, I make no apology for including it, for it had a vital bearing on the Championship and it was cricket history in the making both on and, to a lesser degree, off the field:

Leadbeater came in (at the fall of Wardle's wicket) and swept Jenkins for one and Howorth luckily for four; but in the same over, when he tried to sweep Howorth, he was given lbw. Yorkshire needed 12 and had twenty-five minutes – an abundance of time. At 240 with 10 wanted and twenty minutes left, Booth, defending sedulously, was well caught by Outschoorn in the slips when Howorth made one pop. Now the air was electric. Yorkshire's victory had seemed so certainly assured that it was unbelievable that they could be denied. Wilson took a single off the second ball of the over from Jenkins and every Yorkshireman said, 'Nay, lad; nay, lad'. They were right. Appleyard pushed the next ball back at Jenkins.

Trueman survived three balls while the field was close around him and then, with nine wanted, Wilson faced Howorth. Wilson was inscrutable; Howorth, who had been bowling beautifully, was remote and nonchalant; and off his second ball he had Wilson caught by Yarnold. It was that most deceitful of balls – the one going with the arm and it was bowled perfectly and a little faster, a little wider of the off stump so that Wilson was drawn forward uncertainly playing for a break which was not there. A splendid finish which was exciting beyond words in the last twenty minutes.

One factor outside an intensely exciting game made the day memorable for its irony. One of the umpires was E. Paynter, of Lancashire; the other – the first thing one noticed as the formalities of play began – was Emmott Robinson, who has seen so many triumphs of cricket in the Ridings. How his old Yorkshire heart must have been torn beneath the white coat of the non-partisan as Yorkshire had the game snatched from them.

And by a Lancashire lad at that, as Hall had earlier made clear, who took six Yorkshire wickets for 63 runs and was more than forgiven for the hat trick he had inflicted on Warwickshire only a few seasons before.

Hall gave me a footnote to his enthralling account of a fine finish, for, like the conscientious journalist he always was, he was worried, years afterwards, lest he had not done justice to Howorth's bowling.

As you will see [he wrote], the game ended at ten to four. By ten past I had finished my piece – which must have run to 1400 to 1500 words – had given it to a telephonist and was rushing down to a waiting taxi. Inevitably it is a chronological story of the game and when the course of a match changes as suddenly as this one did it is possible to record it accurately only by dint of doing a very great deal of rewriting. This there was no time for, and as a result I have not done justice to Howorth, or to Bird's captaincy. Worcestershire played a remarkable waiting game. Time and runs were going, but the wicket was gradually drying and getting a little quicker, a little more awkward. The question really was whether Worcestershire could hold on long enough for the ball to start turning destructively. Howorth therefore bowled defensively – beautifully. Bird's preoccupation, as I do say, was to keep the other end as tight as possible. I well remember appreciating this as it was going on and I still feel the thrill of seeing that first ball from Howorth pop, and wondering whether there was, after all, a chance of victory; but I haven't brought it all out in the copy.

I remember thinking about this in the train and reflecting that I might be able to alter the introduction, or phone through a Page 1 piece after I had arrived in London. But the train which left Scarborough at half past four, I think, was twice halted by what rumour said were engine breakdowns – this was in the sadly declining days of steam when pre-war engines were puffing themselves to pieces – and I arrived at my hotel at around 2 a.m.

Then to The Oval to see the Test rubber settled. Three consecutive days and the ends of three first-class matches which decided the County Championship and a Test series. Others may have seen as many first-class matches end consecutively, but could they have been matches of such consequences? I hope not; it's my only cricket record. I also travelled something like 500 miles and lost a lot of sleep.

P.S. It's an interesting fact that I remember very little of Laker in the Test. (He won the match by taking six South African wickets for 65.) My memory is dominated by what I regard as Howorth's superb bowling and tactics the day before.

It was an exciting day in Birmingham, too. Some of the Warwickshire officers and players had gone to the ground, gleaning news from the radio and the offices of the Birmingham newspapers, and hundreds of supporters gathered outside the ground. Within a few minutes of the last Yorkshire wicket falling, the Warwickshire flag was flying proudly from the pavilion, bottles of champagne were popping and toasts were being drunk, and the messages of congratulation were beginning to arrive, the first from Yorkshire. The reporters and the photographers were already there, seeking interviews and photographs.

Dr Thwaite told *The Birmingham Mail*: 'I am gratified and overwhelmed with feelings of satisfaction and delight at Warwickshire's achievement and I express to Tom Dollery and his team my heartiest congratulations and sincerest thanks on winning the County Championship. Tom Dollery has established a new epoch in cricket, the brilliant success of a professional captain.'

Dollery himself paid tribute to teamwork, but it was probably from Leslie Deakins that the most heartfelt message came: 'This is the day I have been waiting twenty-five years for,' a sentiment shared, I am sure, by Alec Hastilow.

One person who had had more than most to do with Warwickshire's triumph had the greatest difficulty in finding out what had happened. Eric Hollies had bought all the editions of the evening papers as they were published, but could not find out what had happened to Yorkshire when with only five wickets down they needed only 25 to win. He tried ringing up the newspapers and, of course, the county ground, but all the lines were engaged. So he went to the local office of a newspaper near his home, told the manager who he was and asked if they could give him the result of the match.

'But either he did not believe me', Hollies wrote, 'or else he was the most zealous worker in the Black Country.' Hollies was not to know that staffs of newspapers have the strictest instructions not to pass on news to members of the public, so the manager was only doing his job; though if he was satisfied of the identity of the person who was asking – and he should have known Hollies by sight – he might have stretched a point, especially as he admitted he had the news on a slip of paper in his hand ready to be stamped into the next edition.

Hollies offered to buy half a dozen copies in advance, but it was no use. The one result he wanted to know more than any other in twenty years of cricket was not for him. So unable to bear to wait until the next edition came out, he went back home just as a friend arrived to give him the glad tidings, phoned by Leslie Deakins with additional information about where the team were meeting for their celebration that evening. Eric did not wait until then – he and his friend had their celebration at the friend's wine and spirit shop!

In a leading article *The Birmingham Mail* described Warwickshire not merely as worthy champions but as 'exceedingly polished ones. Without turning the game into a carnival knockabout, Dollery and his men have generally succeeded in playing forceful and attractive cricket . . . Indeed this may well be Warwickshire's special contribution to the post-war game, for if English cricket is to flourish there is need for more clubs that will show the same spirit of sensible enterprise.'

The Birmingham Post, in its leading article in the special supplement, after saying that the side had been 'superbly led', took the view that winning the Championship was 'a triumph for team spirit':

This extraordinary team of ordinary cricketers, one commentator [it was in fact 'Tom' Dollery] called them; and, though their supporters, will accept the word 'ordinary' only with certain reservations, it is no mean compliment. Warwickshire have not relied on one or two 'stars'. They have been solid all through.

They have proved themselves the possessors of the most formidable attack among county sides – formidable because sufficiently varied to maintain hostility . . . All have had their individual triumphs; but their greatest success is that between them they have been a balanced force such as no other county could deploy. They could not have succeeded, however, without the support of admirable fielding, and it is in this, the excellence of their out-cricket, that Warwickshire have most clearly proved themselves a team.

The Times cricket correspondent, after proffering his congratulations, answered the cynics who had criticised Warwickshire for their importations of Commonwealth players and others from outside their own boundaries, though not from other first-class counties, and said that this was 'part of a long-term policy . . . Warwickshire have set out to provide the success which would gain support for the Club and at the same time quicken the playing interest of youth in the county so that some day soon, so they could hope, many young players from within their own borders will be fighting for places in the side. And beyond this plans have been laid for further improvement and expanding the accommodation of the Edgbaston ground, so that some time it may be again the scene of a Test Match. Nothing succeeds like success and Warwickshire, after a long interval, have tested it once more. All honour to them.'

The last comment, perhaps, should be from *Wisden*. In the 1952 edition Dollery was one of the Five Cricketers of the Year – the seventh Warwickshire player to be so honoured – and the Editor also had some flattering things to say of him. Warwickshire's triumph, he wrote,

emphasised the importance of skilled leadership, for in Tom Dollery they possessed a man able to get the best out of his team both on and off the field. Dollery, a professional, led an all-professional eleven, and while twentieth-century conditions rob the game of the real amateur Dollery showed that a paid player can become a captain in the real sense of the word. By his astute work, Dollery has raised the status of the professional just as Hobbs did in the days when every county had one dressing-room for the paid and another for the unpaid.

There were no stars in the Warwickshire team – none of their men was chosen for England – they were a well-balanced side splendidly equipped in bowling. Perhaps the match-winner was Eric Hollies, a grand leg spinner in this country, but the whole attack was capable of exploiting any type of pitch and they did not pursue the fetish of in-swing and off-break. Much credit for Warwickshire's achievement must also be given to the Committee and Secretary, L. T. Deakins, for shrewd team-building. Warwickshire certainly played dynamic cricket. Twice they beat Yorkshire and six other games were won in two days.

Wisden also returned to the importation of players charge and commented: 'It would be a sorry day for cricket if players were bartered in the transfer market, but no one need fear such a happening for already the problem has been tackled and Warwickshire were one of the counties represented on the small committee which has tightened the Special Registration rules. Now only two registrations are permitted each year by any county and from 1953 no county will be allowed more than ten specially registered players on their list, including eight professionals.'

The climax of the celebrations came at a Championship dinner given by Lord Iliffe and the directors of The Birmingham Post and Mail, Ltd, at the Grand Hotel, Birmingham, on the night of 23 October in the presence of as distinguished a cricketing company as had ever been seen in the city – 'this tribute from all England', as Lord Iliffe described it. Some of the Warwickshire players were unable to be present because of playing and coaching commitments – Spooner was touring with the M.C.C. team in India; Ord and Hitchcock were coaching in South Africa; 'Roly' Thompson was in the Forces – and the fact that a General Election was going on prevented some M.P.s, including Mr Anthony Eden, as he was then, from attending.

W. G. Quaife had lived to see the second Championship triumph and paid his tribute, but died only ten days before the dinner. His son Bernard was there, however, as well as J. F. Byrne, who had celebrated his 80th birthday during the summer; J. Ernest Hill, 'a legendary figure in Warwickshire cricket', as Lord Iliffe described him; and Charles Barwell, who became a member when the ground was opened in 1886.

Lord Iliffe welcomed the guests, who included the Lord Lieutenant of the county, Lord Willoughby de Broke; the Lord Mayor, Alderman R. C. Yates; F. R. Brown, the England captain; and Neville Cardus; and he read a telegram from Sir Pelham Warner, who wrote of Dollery: 'He created a band of brothers and everyone will acclaim him.'

Dr Thwaite paid a glowing tribute to 'that splendid fellow Tom Dollery', and presented gold watches to all the members of the team present. In his reply, Dollery said the Championship had been won by 'honest endeavour, great enthusiasm, and some very fine bowling'. He had very much in mind Eric Hollies,

that very fine bowler who undoubtedly bowled us to victory and who can adopt his technique to any type of wicket. I am proud not only of the fact that we won the Championship, but of the way we won it. We did not resort to any tactics other than those which were in the true spirit of the game. For instance, I never allowed any of my bowlers to bowl the new ball called 'the beamer' which has developed over the last season. You will see many better cricket teams, but I doubt if you will see a keener one. And I know there has never been a more loyal one, not only to the Club but to its captain.

In turn, Dollery presented to Dr Thwaite a silver cigarette box which bore this inscription:

Presented to Dr Harold Thwaite, President of Warwickshire County Cricket Club, by the players and administrative staff in grateful acknowledgement and appreciation of his inspiring leadership, example and personal interest throughout the years and particularly in this the Club's Championship Year, 1951.

Among other speakers were F. R. Brown, who disclosed that if Dollery had not been visiting New Zealand to coach in the coming winter he would possibly have been going with him as vice-captain of the team to tour Australia; and Neville Cardus, who, characteristically, spoke of the spirit of the game which he wanted to be of the period when it was not regarded principally as a competitive game, but as a spectacle. 'We regarded it then', he said, 'as a game which produced great artists.'

The Club's annual report carried an illuminating comparison of figures in the two Championship years:

	1911	1951
Subscriptions	£1866	£15 543
Gate money	£2858	£20 318
Match expenses	£2239	£9487
Ground staff and groundsmen's wages	£1132	£11 479
General expenses	£855	£8805

All of which went to show that in forty years running a first-class county cricket club had become a very expensive business indeed. And it was to become more costly still.

There were two more receptions the following month, the first at Coventry, where the Lord Mayor, Councillor Harry Weston, presented each of the players and George Austin with silver cigarette boxes, the cost of which had been defrayed by local firms; and the second given by the Mayor of Warwick, who that year was the Earl, in the Georgian ballroom of the Court House, where a distinguished gathering of county notabilities assembled to pay tribute to fourteen of the players, officers and officials of the Club.

A testimonial fund to which members and the general public were invited to contribute, eventually realised nearly £1000, which the Club made up to £1350. This was divided between the players taking part in the matches, in proportion to the number in which each had played, and the secretary.

Even twenty years afterwards when I asked 'Tom' Dollery what came first into his mind when he thought about that Championship year, his answer was the bowling of Eric Hollies. 'You knew he was never going to let you down,' he said, 'though all the team seemed to pull out a bit extra whenever we got into trouble. But Hollies – well, against Yorkshire at Headingley on a bad wicket he opened the bowling. "I can spin a new ball as well, you know," he said.'

There were some lessons for the Committee in the success that came the Club's way at the gate. Influenced no doubt by the fact that many of the people who came to the Yorkshire and Lancashire matches had to watch the play from positions on the turf, all the bank seating being occupied, the Committee reviewed the accommodation likely to be needed if the ground was again to be chosen to stage Test cricket.

They took the view that they had an obligation to the Birmingham public to bring the highest class of cricket back to the ground and, on Alec Hastilow's suggestion, decided to appeal to industrial and commercial organisations for funds which would permit further ground developments in recognition of the Championship achievement. They would certainly be needed if work was to go ahead, for although gate receipts and subscriptions continued to run at record levels, expenditure was high because of the money being spent on the ground and, despite receipts from the Test pool, the overdraft at the bank was in the vicinity of £10 000.

Hastilow, then a vice-president of Birmingham Chamber of Commerce, became the driving force behind the appeal, which realised just over £10 000. Another of his many activities at this time was his appointment as one of the original members of the M.C.C. Youth Cricket Council under the chairmanship of H. S. Altham.

Before it was known which county would win the Championship a prominent member of the Club had suggested that there should be a Championship pennant, which would bear the name of the winning county, and the year, on a triangular flag to be flown on the grounds where the Champions were playing. The Committee liked the idea and decided that the secretary should canvass it among the other counties. Their reaction, too, was favourable, so the suggestion was passed on to the Advisory County Cricket Committee. The result – Warwickshire's offer to provide a pennant was accepted, as later was their idea for one to be awarded to the winners of the Gillette Cup.

There are a few i's to be dotted and a few t's to be crossed before the 1951 season can be closed. As *Wisden* had reminded everybody, Warwickshire were not called upon to provide any players for the Tests, but they met the South Africans at Edgbaston and gave them something of a fright, even though lacking the services of Spooner, Pritchard and Hollies. Athol Rowan bowled so well – eight for 106, his best performance of the tour – that Warwickshire, who had been put in, were dismissed for 230; only Don Taylor, 73, and Dollery, 52 (who hit Rowan for two successive sixes), playing him at all comfortably.

However, against Grove and Weeks South Africa fared much worse. They had eight wickets down for a mere 39, due largely to an early breakthrough by K. R. Dollery, but Mann and Chubb made a stand which took the total to 77. Had they been made to follow on, the South Africans might well have been beaten, but there was the public (not to mention the gate) to think of, so Warwickshire batted again and Taylor took another 69 off their bowling in an innings which realised 201. Then Cheetham came along with a not out 116, so it was a draw.

The Lord Mayor gave a dinner to the tourists at which Dudley Nourse paid the Warwickshire team and their captain a nice compliment. 'Tom Dollery,' he said, 'has with him ten other triers and I think you will agree that eleven triers in a side are better than eleven champions.' That was on 9 August when Warwickshire were leading the table, but the result was not yet known. There was a further compliment to come, a letter from S. J. Pegler, the South Africans' manager, who wrote: 'I can safely say that I have never heard such universal praise from members of this 1951 side as on your organisation,' a nice feather to put in Leslie Deakins's cap.

Wisely the Committee negotiated a new contract with Dollery. Under this he became the first Warwickshire player to be paid a four-figure salary, including captain's expenses allowance. He was also to be appointed chief coach and team manager when he ceased playing. At the other end of the scale, the Club engaged a promising 16-year-old all-rounder from Coventry named Tom Cartwright at £5 a week for the twenty-two weeks of the summer, plus an equipment allowance. More-over, George Austin's salary was raised from £180 to the princely sum of £200; though a decision to give a joint testimonial in 1954 to him and to 'Tiger' Smith, who had had the satisfaction of playing in one Championship team and coaching another, was deferred so that it would not clash with one to Eric Hollies. Instead the honorary officials decided to make a gift to Smith for the time being.

December brought a depressing report from Lord's that the aggre-gate attendances at all first-class cricket matches was down by a quarter of a million compared with the three previous years and that the gates for the South Africa Tests had been 30 per cent lower than those for the West Indies the previous year.

The report was depressing in general but bright in particular for Warwickshire, for they had enjoyed the highest daily aggregate attendance – 5389 – of any county. They were one of the six whose figures were up. The Club had contributed £1911 from three days' play to the South African Cricket Association, whereas Glamorgan (£1935), and Yorkshire (£1668), the only counties with comparable figures, had needed five days' cricket to produce their returns. The Warwickshire Club's share of the tour profit was £210, and there was a loss on the Australian–New Zealand tour of the previous winter. Was the decline setting in?

By way of a footnote to a memorable season, there were four pieces of unfinished personal business when the Warwickshire team arrived at The Oval for the last match. Four players had opportunities to dis-tinguish themselves – Hitchcock needed 28 runs for his 1000, but did not get them; Townsend wanted one catch to equal T. S. Fishwick's record of forty, in a season – and took four; Pritchard needed six, and Weeks ten, wickets to get their 100s, but neither succeeded.

In the early part of the winter Hollies had an invitation to fly out to India to replace A. E. Rhodes, who had gone out with the M.C.C. team and had been taken ill, but he declined for he was still nursing his knee injury. Spooner was a member of the party, which visited Ceylon, India and Pakistan, and this time he did not suffer any interruptions. He played in all five Tests, scoring 319 runs with a highest score of 92 and an average of 35·14. In all first-class matches he made 886 runs, including a 168, and averaged 36·91, showing himself much happier when going in first. It was a good note on which to finish the year.

The Flowers Fade
(1952)

❖ ❖ ❖

Thousands of plants arranged to form the Bear and Ragged Staff emblem went into beds in Cannon Hill Park, opposite the ground and in Malvern Park, Solihull, to commemorate the winning of the Championship, but the sweet smell of success faded even more quickly than the flowers. Warwickshire, unlike Yorkshire, Surrey and, in their greater days, Notts and Lancashire, have never acquired the Championship-winning habit and in 1952 history repeated itself. Just as in 1912 after the success of Foster's team they slumped to ninth in the table, so now in 1952 Warwickshire slipped even lower, to eleventh position, though it is true that if one match in which they made a bid to get twelve points had been won instead of lost they could have been sixth.

It is difficult even now to put one's finger with any certainty on the cause; if, indeed, there was only one. In 1912 Foster came back a very tired young man from an arduous tour of Australia in which, following a Championship season here, he had shared the brunt of the bowling; and for two other Warwickshire players, Smith and Kinneir, it had not been exactly a rest cure. Moreover, the 1912 season was very wet, producing conditions totally unsuited to the Warwickshire attack of those days, and both Foster and Smith were away again playing in the Tests of the Triangular Tournament.

No such excuses could be advanced in 1952. True, Hollies had been on an Australian tour – the winter of 1950 – but he can hardly have been exhausted with the amount of bowling he had to do, though he had borne much of the burden in 1951; Spooner had been to India and Pakistan, where he had his first taste of Test cricket, and several other players, including Dollery, had had coaching engagements during the winter – but in themselves these were not sufficient to account for a marked decline in form. Nor were any players called on for the home Tests against India, or for other representative matches.

Always, of course, there is a psychological reaction, an easing-up, after the strain inseparable from anything so prolonged as a county cricket or a football season – which is why it is much harder to win the League Championship than the F.A. Cup. It is also true that every side wants to beat the Champions, a point stressed in the annual report, which, after admitting that the team might wilt under the pressure in the face of a succession of 'keen and determined opponents', added another factor – 'a certain nervous tension on the part of various members of the side which manifested itself in a temporary but marked deterioration in ability . . . Your Committee deeply regrets that in some quarters the failure was attributed to dissension in the Club (a rumour without a vestige of foundation) while a season-long Press controversy concerning the captain's future did nothing to help matters.'

The President, at the annual meeting of 1953, 'bitterly resented' what he called 'the unfair criticism, veiled innuendoes and general attitude adopted by some Club members and a section of the public in attempting to attribute the team's failure to dissension among themselves', and emphatically denied that any such dissension existed.

But making the Press the scapegoat for what happened was surely a little too facile a way out. Dollery himself, at the same meeting, said that the early-season batting was 'beyond belief' – by the middle of June only one batsman averaged 30 – and he admitted that he had considered resigning the captaincy at one period when he felt his batting was on the decline, but his experiences in the latter part of the season suggested to him that this was a little premature. There was no dissension in the dressing-room, he said, 'but there might have been a little depression – the batsman out of form is a very unhappy person'.

If any of this leaked out – and it is almost inevitable that it would be talked about both in and out of the dressing-room – it is not surprising that there was speculation, and it would not be confined to the newspapers. *Wisden*, while allowing that the decline was 'most surprising', put it down to being 'unable to capture the team-work which gave them the Championship in 1951', while the county introduction, like the Club's own annual report, likened the loss of form to that of other Championship winners since the war, spoke of reactions to stress and emphasised that only Gardner, of the batsmen, and Hollies, of the bowlers, was really consistent.

As for the captain's own loss of form, in his first twenty-two innings he scored only 562 runs and the others – Spooner 489 in twenty-one innings, Ord 655 in twenty-one and even Gardner, 956 – were certainly far below their form of the previous season. The bowlers were not much better, Hollies having taken only fifty wickets by 28 June when only one match out of twelve played had been won. But then came a remarkable transformation. In his last twenty-nine innings Dollery made 1511 of his total of 2073 runs for the season and brought his average up to 42·41, and both Hollies and Grove went on to take over 100 wickets, the former 118 for 20·27 and the latter 113 for even fewer runs, 17·49. It was, indeed, Grove's best summer. Unhappily, it was Pritchard's worst; he lost both his pace and his accuracy, and took only thirty-seven wickets, which cost him over 30 runs each. At the same time young Weeks not only failed to fulfil his high promise, but fell away so badly – to thirty-seven wickets for 31·22 – that although he was offered a further year's engagement he was sent for an interview with the chairman, who drew attention to his lack of enthusiasm and physical fitness. 'Roly' Thompson, however, had the distinction of heading the first-class averages even though it was with only eighteen wickets for 12·72 runs each – that absurd qualification of ten wickets!

So, after the end of June, three out of the next four matches were won and altogether in the second half of the season Warwickshire had seven wins, one of them over Surrey, who ultimately became the first county club to fly the Championship pennant Warwickshire had so thoughtfully provided. The depression lifted a little.

In January the appeal to industry went out to between 3000 and 4000 firms, 300 of them in Birmingham; and it was none too soon for because of expenditure of over £13 000 on repairs, maintenance and development of the ground, the accounts were indicating a loss of £5369 on the previous year and this despite the Championship success and record gate receipts and subscriptions. Such are the fruits of victory.

The annual meeting in 1952, as was only to be expected, was a very happy affair. Between 350 and 400 members were present, a record attendance which proved that they would come in good times as well as bad, and Dr Thwaite and the players, who occupied seats immediately in front of the Presidential chair, were greeted with great acclaim. Dr Thwaite was able to speak of the present happy position of Warwickshire and the possession of two essential assets – 'a great team and a fine ground'. On developments, he said that over 100 000 people had watched the games with Lancashire and Yorkshire, an indication that still more accommodation was needed for 'the ever-growing public interest in good cricket'.

Speaking of Dollery's part in the team's success, Dr Thwaite was in a prophetic mood: 'It may be that in the next decade most counties will be prepared to profit by our experience and have their sides led by their most able professional player . . . He should go down in history as the leader of a time that must surely come.'

In this respect, at least, Dr Thwaite was right, though the manner of its coming about, with the abolition of amateur status, was very different from the way in which he visualised it. It makes sadly ironic reading now, but perhaps Dr Thwaite, basking in the full sun of a Championship-winning team, could be forgiven for not paying more heed to the chill wind that was beginning to blow over the cricket grounds of England.

When Peter Cranmer proposed the vote of thanks to the players, Dollery again deplored the publicity which had been given to his share in the triumph, paid tribute to Cranmer's own work in helping to create the side and said that, in his opinion, Hollies and Spooner were the two outstanding players. He had complete faith in the future of the game to attract a public provided the wickets were kept favourable to bowlers. The Edgbaston pitch must not be allowed to revert to its old paceless self.

Then Dr Thwaite presented the testimonial cheques, amounting to over £100, to each player, an inscribed wristwatch to 'Tiger' Smith, and – this was a personal gift from him – a ball mounted on three silver stumps to Pritchard for his fourteen wickets against Glamorgan, including the hat trick. It was Dr Thwaite's turn to be a receiver for once when 'Tiger', on behalf of the players, presented him with a replica of the county badge, the Bear and Ragged Staff, inscribed with the players' signatures as a mark of 'appreciation and affection', a gift which the President said had 'set the seal on a magnificent Warwickshire season for me'.

During April two pleasant post-Championship functions took place. On 4 April 'Tom' Dollery and members of the team and officials attended Birmingham Council House to present to the Lord Mayor a photograph of the Championship team and officials, together with an autographed bat for inclusion in the city's Art Gallery and Museum.

The other was on Wednesday, 23 April, which had been set aside as a day on which members and their ladies could celebrate the winning of the Championship. It took the form of a match between teams captained by J. M. A. Marshall, deputising for 'Tom' Dollery, who was indisposed, and Eric Hollies; a demonstration of youth coaching; a show of cricket films; and a general inspection of the Club's amenities. One imagines a pleasant time was had by all the 1500 people who were there.

There was a further honour for Dr Thwaite when, on 15 May, the gates named after him were opened by Mr W. Findlay, President of the M.C.C., who spoke of 'this fine ground, now one of the greatest in the country' and said that Dr Thwaite had played a major part in making Edgbaston what it was today.

The car of the Lord Mayor, Alderman R. C. Yates, a vice-president of the Club, was first driven through the gates which had the Warwickshire badge in stone on the supporting pillars, and then stone plaques on either side of it were unveiled by the captains of the sides playing at Edgbaston that day – 'Tom' Dollery, and Wilf Wooller of Glamorgan. The carvings were the work of Maurice Norman, the Cheltenham sculptor.

The good doctor, who had been accorded honorary life membership of the Club he had served so well, made his usual modest reply. As he had said when he first learned the gates were to be named after him: 'Anything I may have done for Warwickshire cricket has been done happily, freely and with a deep sense of gratitude that I have been able to help.'

Probably the most remarkable match of the season was a tie with Sussex at Hove. It was a low-scoring game in which the bowlers had the upper hand throughout. Warwickshire reached 138 in their first innings only because Dollery, as he had done so often, saved them from collapse. He batted two hours (although he was missed when he was 23), and without his 55 Warwickshire's score would have been a sorry effort indeed.

When Sussex batted it was John Langridge's turn for the innings-saving act, though it took him a little longer, three and a half hours, to make 65. Sussex got to 123, Grove taking four for 42. Warwickshire's second innings began even more disastrously than the first – half the side was out for 13. This time Townsend and Grove retrieved the situation slightly with a stand of 60 for the seventh wicket; even so, with a total of 116, Sussex had to get only 132 to win.

Before he had scored Cox played a ball into his wicket without moving a bail and he survived to make 27. With Oakes scoring the same number, Sussex had got to within 51 runs of victory with seven wickets still to fall, but then Grove and Hollies caused a collapse and with the last pair together they needed 12 to win. They got 11 of them and then Hollies had West lbw – his sixth victim for 49 runs. The matches that man won or saved at the last ditch!

Hollies figured in two other end-of-the-innings affairs. Against Yorkshire at Bradford he was in a last-wicket stand of 46 and at Maidstone helped in another which produced exactly the same number of runs. He also had a race with his friendly rival, Doug Wright, as to who would be the first to take 1000 wickets in first-class cricket and Hollies just won it – by clean bowling his rival with a googly. It was the only wicket he took in the innings.

It was also at Maidstone that Townsend demonstrated what a useful all-rounder he was, for it was thanks to him that Warwickshire won by seven wickets. He made 61 and 50, both not out; the stroke which gave him his half-century being also the winning hit; took four for 47 and one for 41; and held five catches. At Lord's he returned the remarkable analysis of four wickets for 3 runs in three overs, two of the four being

Edrich and Compton with his first and fourth balls after lunch. The last six wickets fell in five overs for 5 runs – Townsend five for 27 – and Warwickshire won by 72 runs.

There was another remarkable affair of a different kind at The Oval where Dollery played another fine bad-wicket innings. The wicket showed signs of breaking up, especially at the Vauxhall end, even on the first day when twenty-one wickets fell. At the close Surrey, who had gained a first innings lead of 49, were 37 for one. That evening at a dinner at the House of Commons given to the team by two Birmingham Members, Sir Edward Boyle and Sir Peter Bennett (later, as Lord Bennett of Edgbaston, to be President of the Club) the wicket's uncertainties were the subject of some good-humoured banter; but it was a different story when the teams assembled on the ground next morning and found that broken parts of the wicket had been patched up and were a different colour from the rest of the pitch. By whom, or how, this was done is still a mystery, officially at any rate, even though the position was discussed by both Surrey and Warwickshire officials. It was Surrey, though, who won the match. They made 138 in their second innings and then dismissed Warwickshire, who, although losing their first four wickets for 17, reached 115, thanks to a fighting 50 by Dollery.

Twice Warwickshire players batted through an innings. After scoring 114 and 92 for once out against Glamorgan at Edgbaston, Gardner went to Liverpool for the next match but one and for the third time in his career carried his bat, this time for 184 out of 286, a splendid innings. Then Spooner did it for 98 out of 210 against Worcestershire. Horner, who had finally joined Warwickshire and who had no sooner arrived than he got himself knocked out while in the Indoor School, made 140 against Oxford University and, with Ord, 143, put on 238 for the second wicket.

Grove had the best figures of his career in the return match with Sussex and only just missed taking all ten wickets. He did, in fact, get the first eight and the last; Hollies, probably rather reluctantly, nipping in for number nine. Grove's analysis was:

O	M	R	W
19·1	3	39	9

Another Warwickshire bowler to take nine wickets in an innings was 'Roly' Thompson, who celebrated a leave from the R.A.F. by playing against Notts at Edgbaston and returning this analysis:

O	M	R	W
22·1	4	65	9

His pace off the pitch beat most of the Notts batsmen and he had two more wickets for 31 in the second innings. Dollery conserved his energies wisely, using him in four spells, with eight overs the most at any one time.

Pritchard had his benefit against Essex, but took only one wicket in the match. Grove got rid of the opening pair in both innings. Bromley, former captain of Warwick School, now 21, got his first century – 121 out of 346 for six declared, Warwickshire winning by ten wickets. Proceeds for Pritchard came to nearly £4000.

Dollery was at his scintillating best against Leicestershire at Edgbaston. Half the side was out for 140, but then he and Hitchcock took command and added 204 in what *Wisden* described as '135 minutes of exhilarating stroke play'. Dollery went on to his second double century, his 212 being made out of 437, with one six and 24 fours. In the very last match of the season against Notts, Cartwright, a Coventry school product aged 17, making his first appearance in first-class cricket, scored 82 and 22 not out, a foretaste of things to come, though he did not bowl on this occasion.

The match with India was drawn, only six and one-quarter hours of cricket being possible because of rain. In that time India made 172 for seven declared and Warwickshire, whose innings was largely a formality, 96 for two. Gardner was run out for 27 and Spooner was not out 8, and one spectator did not think much of it. He wrote calling for an apology to members and the public for the way they had batted.

It was a tour which had little profit in it for anyone. The counties which did not stage a Test were informed that their share would not be likely to exceed £100. Pakistan had now been given Test status and were to tour England in 1954. Kardar, remembering old friends, had urged the claims of Edgbaston for a Test, but without success and Warwickshire had to be anything but content with a Trial allocated for 1953. Six counties applied for the four Tests and Yorkshire agreed to stand down, but they went to Lord's, Manchester, Nottingham and The Oval.

Ronny Aird, assistant secretary to the M.C.C., said that the Board of Control was 'extremely sympathetic' to Warwickshire's claim, but added, oddly, that they felt those counties which had invested a great deal of money in building stands, particularly Trent Bridge, which were used mainly, if not entirely, for Test Matches, should not be deprived of the big financial return that Test Matches brought. What on earth did he think Warwickshire were doing? Dr Stanley Barnes had just announced the gift of a whole new stand. Aird added that if there had been five Tests he thought Birmingham might have been awarded one of them, which was no consolation at all. They would be given a Test trial and he added: 'We must see how the Birmingham public will support it. We know you have a big population, but are they cricket-minded?'

Leslie Deakins recalled that when Edgbaston lost its Test status in 1929 the Club was selling £800-worth of tickets in advance compared with Nottingham's £7000-worth, but returns from Tests today were in the region of £20 000, of which most clubs could guarantee £10 000 in advance sales.

Work in progress at Edgbaston always occupied more space than any other subject in the committee minutes. They showed that since 1946 £71 000 had been spent on repairs, alterations and improvements; though the Development Fund stood at no more than £38 406 and Edgbaston was still a long way from becoming the ground Leslie Deakins visualised in an interview he gave to *The Birmingham Mail*.

He said that if he had £250 000 and he could get the necessary licence to build he would make Edgbaston 'a terrific place'. He did not mind being called a showman, for he would always be interested in putting on another show to serve the game and the Warwickshire Club because he felt Edgbaston was the ideal setting for the finest ground in the country. He wanted visitors to Birmingham to come to see Edgbaston even in the winter.

With a quarter of a million pounds he would first like to build a modern pavilion backing on to the Edgbaston Road, with every conceivable amenity for members. It would be of two storeys, with the stand roofed, and a Long Room similar to that at Lord's, and up-to-date dressing-rooms and offices. Dining facilities would be first-class, so that it would be a top-grade club for members in the winter as well as in the summer. Clubs which supported Warwickshire should feel that the Edgbaston pavilion was their natural venue for annual meetings and dinners and their social functions – the home of all cricket in the county area where every club would have its family reunion. He wanted Edgbaston to be the envy of Lord's. Though nobody knew it at the time, a possible means of providing the money to turn this dream into a reality was just around the corner.

Towards the end of the season there were conflicting reports about Dollery's future – he had said when he signed his new agreement that he did not wish to commit himself beyond a year – and the President undertook to see him, with the result that he was reappointed captain. He had had a book, *Professional Captain*, in which he had collaborated with W. E. Hall, published during the summer and a fascinatingly thoughtful study of the game it proved to be. It disclosed, among other things, that he was once asked to consider becoming an amateur, to which he replied: 'I cannot imagine that I should do the job any differently, or play differently, if I were known as an amateur.'

In fact, as he told me, he felt that his becoming a professional captain improved the status of professionals generally, though he did not notice any difference in the treatment he received from his own team mates, or from his fellow professionals generally. When he was appointed he declined to change dressing-rooms and he feels that even today, when the official distinction between them has been abolished, there is still what he calls a hangover of prejudice against players who were professionals before the changeover and a tendency to favour gifted amateurs.

It became all too clear at the end of the season, when the gate receipts were totted up, that the Birmingham and Midland public soon lost interest when the team was not playing so well. There was little or none of that loyalty for the county cricket club that the football fan shows for his club, win, lose or draw. True, membership subscriptions reached a new high level at £18 435 compared with £15 389, but gate receipts were down by £7880 to £12 351. There was a drop of as many as 30 000 in the number of scorecards sold, though they still made a profit of £890, and Warwickshire were still fifth in the table of county attendance figures for the season, with 144 000 against Yorkshire's 216 000.

The chairman had certainly been justified in his comment that the Committee's carefully planned policy on membership – now 9508 – had carried the Club safely through a year when gate receipts fell badly. The appeal to industry and the public had realised £10 000, £8650 of it from concerns and the rest from individuals. Even after increases, the charges for admission to Championship matches were still only 2s, and, after 4.30 p.m. 1s for adults and 6d for children, so the public was still getting its cricket very much on the cheap.

During 1951 a country-areas coaching scheme had been introduced and in 1952 sessions had been held at the grounds of the Coventry and North Warwickshire Club, Shipston-on-Stour, Knowle and Dorridge, Tamworth, Shirley, Stratford-upon-Avon, Bedworth, Rugby, Sutton Coldfield, Leamington and Warwick, so no one could say that the Club was not on the look-out for promising youngsters; though Dollery in his book had said Leslie Deakins had told him that, of 427 youngsters to whom trials were given in 1951, 400 were wasting their time. The M.C.C. Youth Cricket Association was also formed, but Warwickshire continued their own arrangements and, *pour encourager les autres*, presented a shield to the Birmingham Public Parks Cricket Association for annual competition.

During 1952 there was formed an organisation which, over the years, brought the delights of cricket to many thousands of people unable to go and watch it because they were in hospital. The Birmingham Hospitals Broadcasting Network, with its own commentary box, changed all that.

It began this season with a ball-by-ball account of all home county games to three hospitals, but expanded to cover over twenty, with a potential audience of over 12 000 patients, and its own studio in the Press Box Stand at Edgbaston, from which emanate a whole range of special programmes as well as cricket.

This season came to an end on a curious sartorial note. Grove found that his blazer was too small for him and applied for another one. What is more, he produced the evidence, but his first request was deferred pending an inspection by the secretary of existing blazers and his recommendations. Then 'it was felt that a blazer might reasonably be expected to serve a player ten seasons at least'. The secretary was therefore asked to use his discretion, bearing in mind the need for stringent economy, but also the desirability of the players' appearance being in keeping with the Champion County. Presumably Grove got his new blazer, though the minute does not record the fact. He was not to wear it for much longer, at least in the service of Warwickshire.

Y

Pool of Plenty
(1953)

THE means to finance the reconstruction of Edgbaston for which Leslie Deakins had been sighing and seeking came quite out of the blue in 1953. And it is safe to say that although football pools have long been an established feature of the English scene, with a turnover of millions of pounds (much of which, of course, finds its way to the promoters), not one of the people responsible for the idea of applying one to serve the needs of The Warwickshire County Cricket Club had the slightest idea that the baby they brought into the world then would develop into the giant it has become – the means of raising, up to the end of 1972, well over £2 000 000 for cricket as a whole, including £1 000 000 spent on building projects at Edgbaston, and nearly £400 000 of investments and generous help to many other clubs. No wonder it has been the envy of every other similar organisation in the country. In addition it has provided the Government with over £4 000 000 in Betting Duty, a sum more than sufficient to have solved all cricket's financial problems.

Warwickshire cannot claim credit for the original idea, nor, indeed, can Worcestershire, who were the first county cricket club in England to run a sweepstake or pool, though Sussex had something they called a players' welfare fund, which was not at all the same thing. Mr W. E. Poulton, chairman of the present Worcestershire scheme, freely admits that they got the notion from, of all places, a Roman Catholic Church, that of St Ambrose, in Kidderminster, one of a number of churches of this denomination which had seized on the pool idea to raise the money they needed to build new schools.

Most of the clergy concerned originally with the St Ambrose pool are dead now, but it is believed to have been started around 1950 during the priesthood of Father M. Rudman. Members paid a shilling a week and

I have details of a coupon for 17 April 1954, which shows that at that time the number of members was 26 821, and that there was a gross pool of £1341. The expenses came to £57, leaving £1284. Of this the organisers took 25 per cent, £321, which went to a central diocesan fund, and the remaining £963 was paid out to the winning members in four prizes. Up to that date the Society had paid out £11 000 in prize money and in due course, though I do not know how long it took, they got their new school for £50 000.

Worcestershire, recognising a good money-raising idea when they saw one, embarked on a similar scheme – Mr Poulton helped draft the rules – and although prizes to begin with were only about £100 they got up to 75 000 members.

Hereford United Football Club also had a very profitable pool and through the good offices of a native of that city, Mr Frank Owens, then Editor of *The Birmingham Mail*, officials of the Warwickshire Club obtained a valuable insight into its working and administration.

Even so, the Warwickshire Committee's approach was very cautious at first, almost as if they suspected that the carrot being held out to them might be poisoned.

The matter was first brought to the notice of the Advisory Committee by Leslie Deakins, who sought instructions with a view to forming a supporters' club in Warwickshire. After considering the matter, the committee decided that no action should be taken for the time being, but that the position should be reviewed in twelve months. 'The opinion was expressed', a minute of the meeting recorded, 'that it was an undignified method of obtaining funds, that the legal aspect was very uncertain and that the officials of such a club would undoubtedly in time wish to influence County Club policy.'

This seemed a little like prejudging the issue, to say the least, but the general committee also decided against doing anything at that time. However, later, someone must have had second thoughts, for it was agreed that the proposal should receive serious consideration at the meeting on 11 August. That committee, 'bearing in mind the financial results achieved by various counties operating a Supporters' Club', decided to appoint a sub-committee, consisting of Messrs C. C. Goodway, James McDowall and Ran Smith, to investigate the possibilities and report back.

They duly did so on 12 September to the effect that the revenue from an organisation of this kind (with its attendant sweepstake) was such that it could not be disregarded 'however distasteful it might be to true lovers of cricket'. The sub-committee, therefore, was asked to investigate still further, with the idea of putting a firm recommendation before the next meeting on 24 October.

Before then, of course, the sub-committee, plus the secretary and assistant secretary, met again, but were not prepared to make a firm recommendation, preferring to leave the decision to the general committee. However, 'in view of the vast potential financial assistance to be derived from an organisation of this sort, with its attendant football sweepstake [This was obviously the nettle they were reluctant to grasp – L.D.] it was felt that such a scheme might be favourably reviewed by the general committee, and the funds to be derived therefrom be utilised for the benefit of the further development of Edgbaston as a cricket centre and of the game throughout the county.' It is worth noting that even at this very early stage Warwickshire were not selfishly thinking of themselves alone.

If this proposal proved acceptable to the Committee, the sub-committee was prepared to put nine recommendations before it. These were:

1 That the organisation should be known as The Warwickshire County Cricket Club Supporters' Association.

2 That it be controlled and governed by an organising committee of five, three of whom should be members of the General Committee of the Cricket Club.

3 That this organising committee should have power to appoint one or more paid officials to administer the affairs of the Supporters' Club and that their duties be confined to supervision and general control and not to actual administration.

4 That the scheme be launched by a series of advertisements in the local Press and elsewhere (after an initial approach to suitable members) rather than by an inaugural meeting and that such advertisements should contain invitations to individuals to apply for appointment as agents at an agreed commission of 10 per cent. [This was later increased to 15 per cent.]

5 That the credentials and standing of all agents be carefully checked before appointment.

6 That when sufficient agents have been appointed, an agents' meeting be convened and the scheme officially launched. It was felt that a minimum of 5000 members would be necessary to justify launching the organisation, i.e. say 50 agents each securing 100 members.

7 That each member on joining be asked to pay 1s entrance fee and 1s per week to enter the sweepstake, and in consideration each member be admitted to one day's play in a county Championship match per season free of normal admission rate upon production of his Supporters' Club membership card.

8 That members be encouraged to pay their weekly shillings in a lump sum, say 5s or 10s at a time, to facilitate the work of the agents.

9 It would be clearly understood that certain preliminary financial negotiations would have to be met in order to put the organisation in being and the County Club would need to advance a sufficient sum to cover these outgoings until the Supporters' Club was self-supporting. If subsequent Government, or other official, legislation prohibited continuance of such schemes it must be appreciated that a loss of this initial sum might be incurred, if the legislation was passed within the first six weeks, or two months, of the scheme's operation.

For a sub-committee not prepared to make a firm recommendation, they certainly went into a great deal of detail and it is given here in full as an indication that the Warwickshire Club did not rush blindly into the venture without proper investigations and safeguards.

The general committee, meeting on 24 October, had a full discussion on the scheme from which it emerged that some members, notably Messrs P. G. Whitehouse, T. E. Hurst, E. J. Dodd (then the Chief Constable of Birmingham and understandably likely to be wary of anything which might conceivably fall foul of the law in any way) and Col. P. N. Dingley, 'found the creation of such an organisation distasteful to a point where no financial considerations, however large, would make it worthwhile'.

On the other hand, Messrs McDowall and J. M. A. Marshall 'felt that advantage should be taken of the psychological reactions in the minds of people today and that in consequence the best interests of cricket would be served and the position of the clubs strengthened if this source of substantial regular income was accepted'.

Ultimately Guy Heaton proposed, and J. A. Lones seconded, the following resolution:

That whilst this Committee would be very thankful to receive donations legally obtained from any source, it does not see its way clear to sponsor a Supporters' Club at the present time.

This was carried by seventeen votes to three, but the secretary was instructed to raise the matter again at the next meeting with particular reference to a possible referendum of the whole membership of the Club. Before that could take place, however, there came a letter signed by five prominent members of the Club – the second 'Five Men of Warwickshire' as it were – seeking the Committee's blessing for an Association which they proposed, with Ray Hitchcock as the paid organising official. The five were M. F. K. Fraser, the Club's publicity officer, Councillor Edgar Hiley, of Solihull, who had also been helpful in this sphere, Aubrey Lewis, Councillor E. H. Richardson, and Derek Salberg, of the Alexandra Theatre.

It seems that Hitchcock had discussed the idea of helping the Club with 'Tom' Dollery and a few other players. They encouraged him to forward his scheme to the Warwickshire authorities, so he mentioned it to Leslie Deakins, who assisted him in getting some influential backing for it and then in bringing it forward again. This was done in the letter of the five signatories. Hitchcock's playing career was progressing well, but he obviously saw possibilities of a new career in this comparatively fresh field of activity.

On receipt of the letter the general committee appointed yet another sub-committee, consisting this time of Alec Hastilow, the chairman,

James McDowall and Colonel Dingley, to interview the five signatories and find out exactly what they proposed and what form their organisation would take.

However, in December the members of the sub-committee and the secretary met four of the signatories of the letter over lunch, Councillor Hiley sending apologies for not being able to be present. From their talk the following points emerged:

1 That the County Club was in need and could make the fullest use of funds of the nature of those to be derived from a Supporters' Association.

2 That if the County Club approved the scheme, it was reasonable to assume that it would loan a sufficient sum of money to inaugurate it.

3 That the organisation should have a separate and clear identity quite apart from the football sweepstake which would be the chief source of revenue.

4 That in view of recent Press references to the Gloucester City F.C. Supporters' Fund and the possibility of legislative action by the Chancellor of the Exchequer, it might be unwise to form a Supporters' Association until September 1953, when the question of legality and subjection to tax might well be clarified.

5 That R. E. Hitchcock, who had shown marked interest in the matter, be given an opportunity to identify himself with it as a paid organiser. [One would have thought that he might well have been invited to the lunch.]

6 That there was a certain urgency in so far as some other form of sport, such as speedway racing, might 'steal the market' in this city if there was much further delay.

M. F. K. Fraser undertook to draft a proposal to contain rules and operating instructions for the organisation, secure the full approval of his fellow signatories and submit the draft to the committee of the County Club through the secretary, all this in time for the next meeting of the general committee in January 1953.

Eventually an eight-point memorandum set out the principal objects of the proposed Association. It stressed that the new body should be separate from, but closely allied to, the County Club; that it would provide financial and other direct and indirect support for the Club through competitions, or other approved means; that there should be an advance from the Club of £300, which has an amusing ring about it now in view of the vast sums the Association was later to make over to the County Club; and that the financial support would be provided mainly by means of a weekly competition among such of its members as wished to take part. This would be based on the result of football matches and the most expert legal advice would be obtained in order that the competition would conform fully with the law. In return, the Association sought such perquisites as occasional free admission to the ground, assistance in obtaining Test Match tickets and, possibly, reserved accommodation for members.

Both the sub-committee's report and the memorandum were before the general committee when it met on 21 January 1953, and on the proposition of James McDowall, seconded by Cyril Goodway, the following three points were agreed:

1 To recognise the proposed body as the official Warwickshire Supporters' Association under the sponsorship of the five signatories to the original request.

2 To accept the proposed constitution, with the exception of the last clause, where it was felt that such concessions as proposed should be the subject of separate application by the Association when it was in being.

3 To request the sponsors not to launch the Association until a date after 30 April next and in the meantime not to publicise it in any form.

So after some trials and tribulations the Association was formed. It seems a far cry now to the days when the modern counterparts of the original Five Men of Warwickshire held their first meetings in the scorebox and then in a hut, no larger than ten feet square, in the Thwaite scoreboard, though it soon had to be doubled in size. In the first three weeks of the first competition in the autumn and winter of 1953–4 the share of money to be devoted to the further development of the ground was £240. By the end of the 1953–4 season the number of entries to the competition was 39 000, the prize money £30 000 and the turnover £46 000.

With the Association's help, a new Bituturf wicket, which the captain had wanted for early season practice, had been laid down and was expected to be ready by the following spring, and the annual report was already forecasting that 'the advantages to the Club of an organisation of this nature should be tremendous', a comment which seemed more than justified in the light of the £8170 which had already become available for developments. This was in addition to the prize money paid out, the cost of erecting temporary offices on the ground for the officials' use, offering £5000 towards a new Indoor Cricket School, and entertaining the touring Pakistani and Canadian touring teams to dinner.

There were teething troubles, of course, especially legal ones, including one competition which the Chief Constable had warned did not satisfy the law, and speaking at the dinner to the Pakistanis, M. F. K. Fraser, who had been elected chairman, was moved to say: 'We envisaged a number of years stretching into infinity in which we could go on doing no harm and raising vast sums for the benefit of the Warwickshire County Cricket Club, and found we were operating under a number of archaic and inequitable laws which operate in such a way that one man may steal a horse while another cannot look over the stable door.'

Season by season, however, the Pool attracted more and more entries until it had outstripped all others in the country. The huts had long been outgrown as offices and the pavilion (East Wing) was built to house the growing Association which had its offices downstairs and on part of the first floor. Within two years that accommodation also was too small and so, when the splendid William Ansell stand, built partly to house the Association, partly to provide a ballroom and partly to complete the accommodation for members, was finished, the Association moved in there. 'If only all one's enterprises had borne such splendid fruit,' sighed Edgar Hiley when it was completed. By that time he had succeeded to the chair.

How did this surge of growth come about? It was partly due to the fortunate fact that they were operating from the centre of the highly populated area of the West Midlands, the bulk of the support coming from Birmingham and its environs; though it also extends out to the north as far as Wolverhampton, Lichfield, and Burton-upon-Trent, eastwards to Coventry and Nuneaton, and south and west to Solihull, Stratford-upon-Avon, Bromsgrove, and Stourbridge, and even beyond the West Midlands to Oxfordshire and Leicestershire.

Population obviously has been an important factor, but Edgbaston is the centre also of county cricket for the same area, but it did not regularly attract anything like such numbers of spectators – though, of course, the Club was not offering any prizes. But when I asked Mr Poulton, of the Worcestershire Club, why he thought Warwickshire had left all the others behind, he summed it up in three words: 'Damned good organisation', a forceful tribute to all those who have built up the Association. Among these are Ray Hitchcock, the first organiser and particularly his first assistant, Miss Winifred Crook, daughter of a Birmingham solicitor and a former Birmingham League cricketer, who took over from him, and David Blakemore, formerly assistant secretary-accountant of the County Club, who married Miss Crook and became secretary of the Association some three years later, with his wife, formerly a teacher, continuing as organiser.

In all but the early days she has carried out that task with such skill and devotion that more than one visitor, seeking to discover why the Warwickshire scheme has been so successful, has been tempted to try to lure her away. Edgar Hiley told how one famous football club manager quickly assessed her capabilities and made her a lavish offer to join his club organisation and run their pool. Winnie Blakemore looked at him in amazement. Then she said: 'Mr ——, I play for Warwickshire.' As Edgar Hiley commented: 'Such people are beyond price.'

Fright for the Australians (1953)

In the spring of 1953 came news of the death of a man who had been
referred to as 'that great sporting figure' – J. F. (Fred) Byrne,
whose name will always be remembered in Warwickshire cricket history, if only because he shared what for many years was the record
opening stand for the county – 333 with 'Sep' Kinneir at Edgbaston in
1905, Byrne making 222 of them; figures which make both totals easy
to remember. But perhaps a memory he treasured even more was having twice bowled 'W.G.' in a match at the Crystal Palace. Byrne was
a link with the days when Warwickshire, whom he captained for four
years, 1903–6, were still a second-class county. His bluff and breezy
personality was reflected in his batting, which was hard-hitting, and in
his bowling, which was fast, as well as in his rugby, as befitted a
former captain of England.

There were two matches in 1953, one at Edgbaston and the other at
The Oval, which would have been memorable in any season. The
Australians were here under that astute captain Lindsay Hassett, and at
last after four drawn Tests England recovered the 'Ashes', but none of
them provided as thrilling a struggle as the August game with
Warwickshire, who came nearer to beating the tourists than any other
county.

Warwickshire began reasonably enough on a soft, damp pitch, which
drew some, but not all, of the sting out of Lindwall. Gardner dug in
from the start – no, that is not the right word in this case for he and
Horner scored 43 off the first seven overs, 100 in eighty minutes and
finally 143 before Horner was out for 61. This was easily the best opening partnership of the season against the Australians; but then Gardner
remembered who and where he was and altogether spent three hours

345

and fifty minutes in making the first century, 110, ever scored by a Warwickshire batsman against the Australians.

Dollery was emboldened enough to declare the Warwickshire innings closed when eight wickets had fallen for 270. Hassett and McDonald promptly replied with another century stand, 104, their first of the tour; but then Hollies got to work, and the remaining wickets fell for 77 more runs. Hollies had five of them for 45 and Wolton's off-spinners accounted for three for only 20 runs. The Australians were all out 181, Warwickshire having a lead of 89 – and that was something no one else had achieved against them.

Dollery had seen what he had seen and he wasted no time about getting the Australians in again. He declared for the second time – and nobody had done that against them since Wyatt had dared to do so in the third Test in 1934 – when the Warwickshire total was only 76 for three. This time Gardner got 33 – 143 for once out in a match which he will always remember with pleasure. The Australians were left with 170 minutes in which to score 166 on a pitch which was taking spin appreciably at one end. 'Lindsay', Dollery told him, 'it's all yours.' And Hassett replied, briefly but pungently, 'You bastard.' He knew what to expect.

Had Warwickshire been playing against another county, Dollery would probably not have declared so soon. Hollies, indeed, thought he was giving the Australians the match, but then he always was a modest man. But Hassett knew that Dollery had – as he suspected – set them a task which was beyond them, for he, too, had seen how poorly his colleagues, with less experience of English wickets, had fared against spin bowling in the first innings. So, like the good captain he was, he took it upon himself to look after Hollies and, if possible, play out time.

Over after over he played him and, whenever he could, he took a single towards the end of an over so that his frailer brethren, with each of whom he had a word when they came in, might be kept away from the terror that bowled by day. Perhaps not unnaturally, the crowd – and there were 22 000 of them – who were avid for Australian blood, resented the slow scoring and twice play was held up by the noise of the protests they made and the slow clapping. It was the worst barracking Hollies had heard anywhere. When Hassett suggested to one of the umpires that he should have a word with the noisiest section of the crowd, the latter told him: 'You go and ask them to be quiet – you're the cause of the trouble.'

Hassett took off his cap with a mock flourish to the crowd, but he was not to be swayed from the course he had set himself, though it must be said that some of his colleagues were guilty of showing exaggerated respect for the bowling, good though it was, on a pitch never so bad as they made it seem. Hollies took two wickets and Wolton two, but not even the former could run through such a side, and in the end the Australians, although they lost half their wickets for 53 runs, scraped through to safety – at least from defeat. Safety from the incensed crowd was another matter. Hollies says that when the barracking was really hostile he said half-jokingly to Hassett: 'It won't be long now before they come on the pitch.'

'Do you really think so?' asked Hassett.

'I'm certain of it,' said Eric.

'Well, the first one that comes for me I'll wrap this bat about his head,' retorted Hassett.

'Ah yes', said Hollies with an impish smile, 'but what about the second one?'

It did not quite come to that, but the police thought it advisable to provide an escort for the Australian batsmen just in case. One lone spectator, probably a Yorkshireman, patted Hassett on the back as he went through the gate into the pavilion. He had batted 165 minutes for his 21 not out and only once did Hollies get through his defence, missing his stumps by a hair's-breadth. Dollery, who knew a fine innings when he saw one, shook Hassett by the hand. Miller batted twenty-seven minutes for his 10 runs, probably an all-time slow record for him.

The bowling analyses of Hollies for the two innings, especially the *Maidens* column, shows the grimness of the struggle:

	O	M	R	W
First innings	33·3	15	45	5
Second innings	22	16	14	2

Eight of the fifteen overs Wolton bowled in the second innings were also maidens. No fewer than 41 855 people paid to see this splendid match, the receipts being £8323. This was nearly half the total of those who attended the county games during the season – 88 113 – an indication of how vital the visits of the touring teams were to all the counties. In the Championship year the comparative figure was 204 000. Fortunately there was a greater membership than ever, bringing a revenue of £20 321.

The author of the Club's annual report could not find it in his heart to criticise the Australians. After pointing out that of the fifty-eight overs bowled in their second innings thirty-one were maidens, he commented: 'It was fortunate indeed that the Australians had a great fighting captain in A. L. Hassett, who stood firm on the final afternoon and was undefeated at the close after opening the innings and meeting the main force of the attack on a turning and difficult wicket. It was a great game of cricket.' It was, indeed.

There was another astonishing game which was all over in one day – 16 May – something that had not happened since 1857. It was at The

Oval, where on the first day play was delayed until noon because of a damp pitch. Then the fun began, at least for Alec Bedser, who found it difficult to keep his footing on the wet turf, so he slowed his pace and attacked the leg stump with catastrophic effects for Warwickshire. He took eight wickets, seven of them caught and the other lbw, for 18 runs, and Laker had the other two for 9 runs. Warwickshire were all out 45, of which Spooner got 16.

Despite accurate bowling by Keith Dollery, a Queenslander recommended by Hollies, and Hollies himself, Surrey managed to get 146, which gave them a very useful lead. They did not need it, for Warwickshire again collapsed and were all out 52 in seventy-five minutes – five minutes fewer than they had lasted in the first innings. There were five consecutive 'ducks' in the middle of the innings and seven batsmen were caught, two lbw and one run out, so that not one Warwickshire batsman was bowled in either innings. This time Bedser had four for 17, but Laker did the hat trick in his five for 29. Hollies was on 'a pair' when he went out to bat in the second innings and as he passed Bedser he asked him to give him one to get off the mark, promising not to hit it far. Bedser obliged by bowling one down the leg side for him – and Eric put it straight into the hands of short leg.

Throughout the season Warwickshire were handicapped by indifferent weather and inability to force decisions in matches they should have won. Their record of wins, in fact, six, was the lowest since 1947, though they took first innings points in as many as eleven of their drawn games, several of which were really moral victories. These, however, did not enable them to rise higher than eighth in the table. Five batsmen made over 1000 runs in Championship matches, including Dollery, scoring most with 1871; Horner, 1334; Townsend, greatly improved, made 1127, and for the second season in succession, broke the catching record, making 200 in six seasons. Ord, whom it had not been intended to play in the first eleven, but to use for coaching, came into the side because of early batting failures and averaged 42.

Hollies missed some matches because of back trouble and for the first time since the war did not take 100 wickets. His total fell to eighty-three, the same number as Grove, which made the dropping of the latter at the end of the season appear all the more surprising to the many members who objected both to the act itself, its timing and to the way in which it was done. Keith Dollery took seventy-three wickets in his first full season and Bannister was coming along well, but Pritchard failed to recover his form and poor Weeks, far from profiting from his interview with the chairman, went from bad to worse, taking only fourteen wickets for 41·5 runs each.

Quite unintentionally, Hollies might have had something to do with Grove's misfortune. The selection committee decided to rest Grove for a match towards the end of June, giving him the choice of missing either the game with Gloucestershire at Bristol, or the one immediately following with Leicestershire at Hinckley. He asked Hollies's advice as to which one he should play in, and Hollies suggested that as batsmen had been scoring pretty consistently at Bristol, whereas Hinckley was an unknown quantity, Warwickshire not having played there since the war, the latter might be the better bet for him.

So Grove missed the Bristol match where, as luck would have it, Bannister, taking his place, had eight for 55 in the match. So an unchanged side went on to Hinckley, where Bannister did the hat trick, and Grove did not get back into the side until Hollies was injured two weeks later. The number of appearances Grove made this season figured prominently in the controversy that was to follow over his fitness.

'Tom' Dollery was involved in two double-century partnerships: one of 275 with Gardner against Somerset at Coventry, in which he made 173 and Gardner 137; and 250 for the seventh wicket against Kent at Maidstone with Ord – Dollery 169 and Ord 109 – which still stands as a record for the county. The previous one by W. G. Quaife and Glover had lasted since 1899. Dollery, with Gardner again, also put on 180 for the fifth wicket against Derbyshire. His score had gone up to 100 on the board when he was run out, and it was then corrected to 99. Gardner's contribution was 143.

Horner appropriately chose the Yorkshire match in which to make his first Championship century, 115, in an opening stand of 182 with Gardner, and he made another 75 against them when they came to Edgbaston. How exiled Yorkshiremen like to take it out on the old county! Even more appropriately, the last match of the season was decided by the last ball of the match. It was at Clacton against Essex, who began by dismissing Warwickshire for 120. They declared when they had a lead of seven and this time, thanks to 122 by Horner, Warwickshire made 203 for six before they, too, declared. Essex had to get 197 in two hours and twenty minutes and 8 were still needed when the last man came in, Saville ending the match heroically with two fours off the last two balls from Keith Dollery.

This was 'Tom' Dollery's twenty-first season with the Club and during the course of it he scored his 20 000th run in first-class cricket. He also became the second Warwickshire batsman to aggregate over 2000 runs in all matches for a second time. They were notable milestones in a distinguished career. At the annual meeting he had promised that whatever else happened, Warwickshire would play bright and attractive cricket and he had kept his word.

In view of the appointment of chief coach to come, it was noted that he was one of six Club nominees to gain the M.C.C.'s newly instituted Advanced Coaching Certificate – and he did it by obtaining the highest

marks of anyone taking the examination. The other successful candidates
– and Warwickshire now had more holders of the certificate than any
other county – were 'Tiger' Smith, J. M. A. Marshall, Ord, Spooner,
and Derief Taylor, who began this year the job he has since done so
well, the coaching of boys and youths. To encourage them the Club
offered a scholarship for boys attending secondary modern schools
in the city. These granted privileges and facilities to junior membership
and a chance to develop their cricket under Taylor's guidance free of
charge. Considerably fewer members were now coming to practise than
used to be the case. At one time this was one of the principal reasons
why a man joined a county club, but although all male members were
sent a circular about their availability to play in Club and Ground matches
only 37 forms out of 6300 were returned completed.

Revised salary scales were agreed this season. Under them players
who had appeared in representative matches were to be paid a minimum
of £525, capped players in the range of £475–£575, uncapped
players up to £475, with a further £25 for pace bowlers and all-
rounders in the last two categories. In view of the team's achievement
against the Australians, it was also agreed to raise the award for a win
on the first innings from £2 to £5 a man.

One great financial boon to clubs was the abolition at last of the
Entertainment Tax which, at £8356 in the seven post-war years,
would almost have balanced the Club's losses of £9439. Two trends
continued to dominate finance – the decline in revenue from gate
receipts and the increase in revenue from 10 000 members' subscriptions, now £20 321, second only to that of Lancashire. So, with a record
overall revenue, despite the further fall in attendances, and £10 000
from the industrial appeal, the Club was able to reduce its liabilities
from £17 000 to £5000 and leave a small profit of £659.

The paradox of the fall in the numbers of people paying at the gate
and the rise in membership had now become one of the outstanding
phenomena of post-war cricket. Perhaps because nobody looks a gift
horse in the mouth, no one troubled to investigate the contradiction of
why some people would pay membership fees a good deal in excess of
the 2s admission other spectators paid, to see exactly the same sort
of cricket. On the face of it, the reasons seemed to be that those who
become members are the diehard corps of faithful supporters, come what
may; the growing facilities and amenities being offered by county clubs
generally; and the certainty, if one was a member, of being able to see
a Test Match, or Test trial, though only the latter were coming
Warwickshire's way at this time, the last one having attracted 13 223
spectators even though no Warwickshire players took part in it.

In later years, of course, memberships, too, began to decline even
though grounds and amenities did continue to improve, but still no one

has explained exactly why, perhaps because the experts, the survey takers, have tended to concentrate on the man on the popular side rather than the man in the pavilion. Or perhaps it is just simply that (apart from the obvious division between those who can and those who cannot afford to be members, and without wishing to be class-conscious about it) members and other spectators are basically different kinds of people, with different backgrounds and outlooks, for whom love of cricket is the chief, if not the only, common denominator.

In June one of Warwickshire's most colourful and best loved characters died – Crowther Charlesworth. The previous season it had become known that he was living in Huddersfield in reduced circumstances and the Club tried to find someone nearby willing to administer a small fund for him. F. E. Greenwood, the former Yorkshire captain, kindly undertook this at Warwickshire's request and he was sent a grant of £52 a year to be paid to Charlesworth at the rate of £1 a week and to be used, 'having due regard to Charlesworth's weakness', to buy clothing and other necessities. Early in the year came a report that Charlesworth was fit and well for his years, 76, although he was not much disposed to look after his appearance; Greenwood continued to look after his clothing needs and allowed him 10s a week pocket money.

A member of the Committee suggested that as the Club was not giving a benefit in 1953 a collection might be made, the proceeds to be divided among former members of the staff; but it was felt that this was rather a dangerous precedent – that word again – and there were difficulties about who would benefit. Not long afterwards Greenwood reported a marked deterioration in Charlesworth's condition and the end came on 15 June in a Salvation Army hostel.

In his time for Warwickshire he had scored nearly 15 000 runs, including fifteen centuries, and taken nearly 300 wickets. As a Lancastrian – he was born at Swinton – his 206 out of 283 against a Yorkshire attack which included Hirst, Rhodes, Booth and Drake, must have given him as much pleasure as if he had made them for his native county. His benefit in 1920 was the first one for Warwickshire to realise over £1000, an indication of his popularity both among his colleagues and the public. Canon Parsons and 'Tiger' Smith, to whom he had been very helpful when they were youngsters, as he was to all of them, were especially fond of him. Parsons borrowed a bat from him for his first second-eleven game at Worcester and damaged it beyond repair. Hesitatingly, he tried to tell Charlesworth what had happened, but Charlesworth interrupted him to ask: 'How many did ta get, lad?' 'Two hundred,' said young Jack, whereupon Charlesworth slowly got up from the locker on which he had been sitting, took out one of his own bats and gave it to the youngster saying, 'See if tha can do it agen, wi' this 'un.'

351

Let the Salvation Army major who came to tell Frank Greenwood that Charlesworth was dead provide his epitaph. 'You know, Mr Greenwood,' he said, 'he was quite a remarkable man – a fool to himself maybe, but he never did anyone else any harm and very often offered a helping hand. The world would be an infinitely better place if more men were like him and had his philosophy.'

The Grove Affair
(1953)

WHAT might be called 'The Grove Affair' began with a letter dated 14
September 1953, informing Grove, who would have been 41 that
December, that he would not be retained because the Club wished to
give younger players an opportunity. It is interesting to speculate now
whether, if such a decision to a man who had served the Club so well,
had been conveyed to him earlier, at the end of July, as was customary,
and in person rather than in a formal letter, there would ever have been
any affair at all. As it was, it came to be linked quite irrelevantly, except
insofar as the action of the general committee was concerned, with the
departure of Lobb to Somerset and of Boak, the head groundsman, for
totally different reasons.

The first the public knew that Grove was not to be re-engaged was an
announcement in *The Birmingham Post* on 17 September, and at the
same time Dollery publicly acknowledged 'what a great bowler he has
been to me during my captaincy'. Next day Grove was reported as saying that he had no complaints and would certainly continue to play in
league or club cricket. 'It is one of those things which come to all professionals in time', he said, 'but I didn't expect it yet. I am sure of one
thing, though – I can still bowl forty overs in a day.' Worcestershire
seemed to agree with him for on 22 September he signed a two-year
contract with them.

After this, letters began to appear in the newspapers criticising
Warwickshire's decision to dispense with Grove's services, and the
matter really came to a head when one appeared in *The Birmingham
Post* on 23 September over the signature of Ted Hampton, the Club's
honorary statistician for many years, bluntly accusing the Committee of
'sacking' Grove. 'His figures for the last three years can only condemn

z   353

their action,' he wrote. 'It is surely now clear to all members that the decision was arrived at quite a while ago. Members have it in their own hands and it is up to them to act in the proper way at the proper time.'

This drew a reply on 25 September from Alec Hastilow, the chairman, in which he said that although it was neither the Club's practice, nor in the players' interests, to give detailed reasons for not offering re-engagement, he felt it necessary to depart from precedent. After expressing the Club's appreciation of Grove's services, he said they had been faced with the responsibility of deciding which of seven pace bowlers should be offered re-engagement – Grove, Pritchard, Dollery (K.), Bannister and Lobb, who were on the staff the previous year, together with Thompson (R. G.) and Carter now returning from the Forces.

The Committee, he went on, decided that a maximum of five of these players could be re-engaged, for reasons of expenditure but more because of the necessity of giving young players of decided promise regular matches in the first and second elevens. It was with great regret, therefore, that the decision was made concerning Grove, but it was felt to be in his own interest as well as that of the Club. There were indications last season that the physical effort of playing cricket six days a week was beginning to tell on Grove – he had to miss a number of matches owing to a strained Achilles tendon (in his left heel) and it was expected he would take an engagement in league cricket, where, playing only one half-day a week, he would be able to prolong his active cricket career for many years. Critics were reminded that because Grove's career was seriously interfered with by the war he was granted a benefit after only five years in the first eleven.

This was the first intimation that there were any real doubts about Grove's fitness, and Hampton, in a further letter on 29 September, contended that Grove had been fit and that Warwickshire won only one of the six matches they played without him. There was another letter from Hastilow on 30 September saying that the Achilles tendon strain had occurred in August during the Derbyshire match and the player submitted a doctor's certificate showing him unfit to play. He added that Grove did not feel he had been unfairly treated in any way.

Hampton replied to this by denying that a grievance had been artificially manufactured and that he had been in touch with Grove almost daily to the day on which he had notice from the Club. Hampton, as he had written in his original letter, had not envisaged any action being taken in the matter except perhaps at the annual general meeting, but others had different ideas and the next move came on 19 October when twenty members signed a requisition for a special meeting. It perhaps ought to be made clear here that Grove himself had no part in the events which led to this step being taken. Two days later it was confirmed that a resolution expressing 'no confidence' in the Committee would be moved at it. The requisition and the resolution were in these terms:

We, the undersigned members of the Warwickshire County Cricket Club, request that a special meeting of the members be convened in pursuance of Rule 29 for the purpose of discussing the following motion: 'That this special general meeting of the Warwickshire County Cricket Club deplore the recent action of the Committee in respect of the retention of the professional staff and records its lack of confidence in the Committee as at present constituted.'

Ted Hampton in the meantime had resigned as honorary statistician, though he said he was prepared to resume in that capacity after the special meeting had been held. When the requisition and the resolution were reported to the Committee they deplored the action of the rebel group, taking the view that they 'appeared to have acted very rashly and in a manner involving the Club in considerable expense over a comparatively trivial issue'. It was agreed, however, that the meeting must be convened and that no private approach to the group should even be contemplated. The secretary, however, was instructed to include on a subsequent agenda the whole question of the Committee's approach to players' engagements, with particular reference to much earlier notice being given to those ending county careers and likely to be seeking league engagements, which was partly the cause of the trouble.

It was also decided to include the question of more rapid release of information to the Press after decisions at meetings so as to avoid 'scoops when leakages occur', and to reconsider Rule 29 to prevent a recurrence of the present position whereby twenty 'malcontents' could involve the Club in expenditure of this magnitude (in fact, it came to about £100) instead of using more normal channels to ventilate their complaints. Lastly the Committee agreed to resign *en bloc* if the vote of 'No confidence' was passed. It was also decided that the meeting should be confined to members and that professional players should not be admitted, as had been customary at annual meetings, unless they were members in their own right.

The attendance at the meeting, held at the Grand Hotel, Birmingham, on 19 November, was the largest ever known in the history of the Club. It was estimated that 1600 members were present – notices had been sent out to 7300 – and two overflow meetings had to be held in antechambers linked to the main room by loudspeaker. To begin with, Dr Thwaite, as President of the Club, presided, but intimated that since he was a member of the Committee, he would vacate the chair. He proposed that Alderman Yates, the former Lord Mayor, should preside and this was agreed, the new chairman beginning the meeting by making an appeal that personalities should be avoided.

It was Councillor Denis Howell, not then an M.P., who moved the resolution. He said they did not criticise the Committee on the grounds that it did not feel it necessary to retain 'this great bowler', but the method by which it dispensed with the services of 'one of the greatest bowlers to come out of Warwickshire'.

Grove, he went on, felt he had been treated badly, but he did not desire to become involved in any public discussion. The letter notifying him that he would not be retained, just after he had returned the two best seasons' averages of his career, gave the impression of a 'mercenary approach' – it was suggested that he had been adequately compensated for his services. One would have thought, Councillor Howell said, that a representative of the Club would have talked to him and explained the position. It had not been intended to announce his non-retention until October, whereas in September almost every club had already engaged, or re-engaged, a professional. The Committee must have known early in the season that it was to be able to retain only five fast bowlers. On physical fitness, Grove was in no doubt he could still give a good season's cricket; and, more important than the way Grove was treated, the cricket public of Warwickshire were entitled to know when he would have been playing his last match so that they could have been there in large numbers to show their appreciation of his magnificent services.

Councillor Howell said that Lobb* should have been released earlier and that Boak† had had a letter suggesting he should apply for a position open in Coventry and that if he did not do so he would be exposing his family and himself to a risk. There were cries of 'Shame' at this. 'All these three cases', Councillor Howell went on, 'are bad enough individually; taken together they present to us an extremely doubtful attitude of mind in which to deal with players and other professional staff in this mercenary manner.'

To Alec Hastilow, as chairman of the Committee, fell the main task of replying. He said the Committee's opinion had been unanimous.

*A minute of the Committee meeting on 9 September said that Somerset sought information on players not likely to be engaged on 18 July, but were told on 22 August that Lobb would not be released.

†In September, Boak had been notified of the Club's intention to advertise the post of head groundsman, was told that he was an unsatisfactory employee, that his tenure of employment was precarious and that his continued employment was dependent on the quality and skill of the applicants who might respond. Boak complained about the inadequacy of his staff for the work expected. His attention was later drawn by Syd Harkness, as ground committee secretary, to a vacancy at Coventry and it was suggested that he should apply for it, but he declined to do so. The secretary was then instructed to send him a letter setting out clearly the circumstances and indicating the position he now placed himself in by his action if the Committee decided in the future to dispense with his services. The clause in the letter to which exception was taken at the special meeting was: 'By declining this opportunity you may well be exposing your family and yourself to serious risk.' Boak, it should be remembered, was in a special position in that he lived on the ground so that his home and his job were inseparably linked. Some years later he was killed in a motoring accident.

Normal gates were down by £1000 compared with last year and the Committee had to think seriously of the expense for next year. Referring to 'an embarrassment of seam-bowling riches', he said they had seven to consider and it was decided there was no point in having more than five quick bowlers. They had an obligation to take back Thompson and Carter, two young players from the Forces, and Keith Dollery and Bannister both had exceptional records. That left Lobb, Pritchard and Grove. Lobb was a promising bowler who might make the county grade and do well for Somerset, but at this stage he was not as useful as the others. It was therefore decided that he was one who would have to be released. That left Grove and Pritchard.

He denied that they had considered the matter before September, or that there had been any suggestion in the Committee's mind that Grove was not going to be retained, but Grove broke down at Derby with a strained Achilles tendon and they had a medical report that he was unlikely to go through another complete season. It was thought to be in the Club's and in his own interest that he should not play another season of six-days-a-week cricket, but should secure a league position.

Councillor Howell intervened to say that Grove did not know of this report.

Hastilow, continuing, said that in a letter Grove was told that Mr Deakins had been asked to see him on behalf of the Committee. The same morning that he received the letter he saw Mr Deakins and they discussed a new engagement. Five league clubs were seeking professionals and Grove was interested in these. Grove, he contended, had been handsomely treated at all times, securing a benefit after only four full seasons of cricket and when he had taken only 383 wickets in first-class cricket. Including the proceeds of his tax-free benefit, Grove's earnings since the war had amounted to £12 500, an average of £1800 a year for five months' cricket. 'Surely it cannot be suggested that Grove has been unfairly treated,' he added.

After being rested for eight matches in the early part of the season, he went on, Grove broke down at Derby and could not play against the Australians. His physical condition had to be taken into account when considering a renewal of his engagement, particularly as medical opinion suggested he might not be fit to undertake a full season's cricket in future. As for Lobb, he could not agree that the delay had prejudiced his chances unduly; and, with regard to Boak, on his engagement he was second choice, he had not fulfilled expectations, and numerous requests for salary increases had been turned down, so he must have been well aware of his precarious position with the Club. This fact was emphasised again and again when it was suggested he apply for a post in Coventry. Correspondence needed to be in direct terms, but in no way did it constitute a threat.

Then the chairman played his trump card. If the Committee resigned *en bloc*, as indeed they must do if the vote went against them, he visualised a period of chaos, disastrous to the future of the Club, which would be without leadership, since the requisition was purely destructive, with no constructive suggestion whatever to bridge the gap created by their possible success.

After this dire threat the result was pretty well a foregone conclusion, though Mr Edgar Hiley did move an amendment deploring the action of those who had requisitioned the meeting as not being in the best interests of the Club, considering the elected Committee the best judge of those interests, but expressing the hope that in future the Committee would consider making an earlier announcement concerning re-engagement of players. He had one word of criticism – he wished that at times the Committee was not quite so aloof from the membership and it was a little high-handed.

Mr Tom O'Loughlin said that where they had failed was in human relationships with the players. After further discussion, Edgar Hiley withdrew his amendment and the motion was then put to the meeting. About 100 hands were raised in support and the chairman declared it defeated by a substantial majority.

There are a good many things that could be said about the affair that were not said at the meeting. One is that when the Committee, rightly as it thought, made the matter one of confidence, some members were embarrassed by the announcement in advance that if the vote went against them the Committee would resign *en bloc*, which they felt precluded a completely free and frank discussion. There was also a feeling that it was irrelevant for the chairman to refer to the Club having seven seam bowlers when, after all, it was the Committee who had engaged them.

Some people also thought that to invite a man to an interview in the same letter which told him that his services were no longer required was not an ideal way to approach the problem, and that it was also inappropriate and inaccurate to include the proceeds of a benefit in a player's earnings since they fell into entirely different categories, the benefit proceeds being an entirely unsolicited – so far as the Club is concerned – public acknowledgement of his services and no part of his contract.

On the other hand, Councillor Howell surely got his priorities wrong when he said that more important than the way Grove was treated was the fact that the public were entitled to know when he would be playing his last match. Remarkably, no one recalled a precisely similar omission on the part of the then Committee in the case of W. G. Quaife. To the Committee's comment that the special meeting was 'an unfortunate event in the Club's history without virtue or value' other than the obvious 'sensationalist interest', it could be rejoined that it was certainly not without value inasmuch as it caused the Committee to revert to their established and well-tried procedures, especially those affecting players' future engagements.

In a leading article next day *The Birmingham Post* also described the meeting as 'valuable and necessary', with strong feelings 'subjected, as they should be, to frank, public discussion'. The paper felt that the increase in mutual understanding between Committee and members fostered by the discussion 'should result in an access of even greater strength . . . Of the present vitality of the Club the attendance at last night's meeting is plain evidence', a dubious argument, surely.

The *Evening Despatch* was more positive: 'There may now be some whispering criticism of the 20 members who signed the requisition for the meeting. It may be said that they were badly advised, or that the Club will suffer for this public discussion of its "family quarrel". Such a view would be quite wrong. Rather should "the twenty" be thanked for the service they have rendered the Club.'

The *Sports Argus* asked the question: 'And what above all else is the key to success in professional sport?' The answer they gave was that 'No club or organisation can do anything without money and when finance begins to creep in sentiment starts on the way out.'

Dick Knight, in the *Despatch*, reported that one of the twenty had said, ' "The committee can sack whosoever they like, but not howsoever they like," and that about sums it up.' Perhaps 'whensoever' would have been more accurate.

Now came the internal 'inquest'. There were hints of legal action following certain statements made at the meeting, but fortunately these came to nothing. Very sensibly, the Committee reviewed matters on which it had been criticised. It agreed that, in regard to players' engagements, a meeting of the full Committee should be held early in August (later changed to July) but that the September meeting, at which for the three previous years the engagements had been decided, should also continue; that information should be offered to the Press immediately after the meetings; and that the secretary should be appointed the Club's public relations officer (which, in effect, he had long been) if such an office should be considered necessary.

Regarding Boak, the secretary emphasised that the controversial letter sent on 22 July 1953, was written by him, the assistant secretary having nothing to do with it. He considered it a right and proper letter based on his five years' knowledge of Boak and contended it was sound advice, if accepted as a private letter and in the spirit in which it was written – an endeavour to make Boak appreciative of the precarious nature of his appointment and the fact that his home responsibilities were literally allied to, and part of, his job. Leslie Deakins emphasised that he had been prepared to make these facts known at the special meeting, but had been denied the opportunity.

The Committee decided not to take any action on Councillor Hiley's suggestion that it was too aloof in its relationship with members and that the ground 'was plastered with too many restrictive notices', or a member's suggestion that a questionnaire should be circulated annually to all members on which they could register complaints, criticisms or grievances. That would have been too much to expect of any committee.

There was a reference to the affair at the annual meeting in 1954 when the President – who had gone to live in Surrey, though he did not let that interfere with his interest in the Club – expressed the hope that if a group of members ever again felt the urge and necessity to convene a special general meeting they would first of all afford the Committee the opportunity to meet and consult with them on the issues involved.

Alec Hastilow added that he believed this was now a closed chapter in the Club's history and he looked forward to a resumption of the hitherto very happy relationship between members, players, committee and officials in furthering the high aims and ideals of the Club.

But the inquest was not over. The question of increasing the number of members whose support was necessary to convene a special general meeting was discussed and deferred several times on the ground that it would be premature at that time, but eventually a new rule was proposed to be substituted for Rule 29 under which the last meeting had been called:

The Committee shall, on the requisition of fifty (or 1 per cent) of its members, or of their own authority, call a Special General Meeting, of which not less than seven days' notice specifying the object, time and place of such a meeting shall be given. This notice may be given by Press advertisement in not less than three local newspapers. At such Special General Meeting the chairman shall be nominated by the Committee; voting on the resolution shall be by ballot, or otherwise at the discretion of the chairman, and no business may be discussed at the meeting other than that contained in the resolution of any amendment arising therefrom.

Adoption of this rule, however, was also deferred until information had been obtained from other counties on whether a fixed number, or a percentage, of the members governed the calling of their special general meetings. This, of course, took some time and it was not until early in 1955 that it was eventually reported that only one county had a percentage system. It was then decided to amend Rule 29 only in so far as the method of advising members of such a meeting was concerned, and to substitute four Press announcements instead of individual postal distribution. This was finally agreed at the annual meeting that year.

And Grove, the principal but unwilling figure in all this? Well, in 1954 he went to play for the county of his birth – he had discovered that, in fact, he had been born in Yardley, in 1912 just before it officially became part of Greater Birmingham – and had one more season in first-class cricket with Worcestershire. This was *Wisden*'s verdict on it: 'Grove, secured from Warwickshire in the hope that his pace would give Perks additional support, achieved little after a reasonable start.' His figures in all matches for them were:

O	M	R	W	AVE
548·2	144	1275	43	29·65

After that he was mostly concerned with the second eleven and did, in fact, captain them in some games, as well as coach players such as Flavell. He was offered the job of coaching, but declined it for personal reasons, but he afterwards enjoyed several seasons in league cricket with the Old Hill club and he was one of the founder members of the Warwickshire Old County Cricketers' Association in 1958, acting as fixtures secretary for a time. Eventually he moved to Penzance, where he and his wife took a guest house overlooking Mount's Bay, to which he gave the appropriate name of 'Dunbowlin'. From there he wrote me saying that his association with Warwickshire was always a happy one and that if it were possible to start all over again he would, without hesitation, join the Edgbaston club.

I must admit [he went on], that I was deeply hurt at the way I left, but this has long been forgotten and I would rather it remain so. I often look through my Press cuttings and action pictures and memories come flooding back of some really great days ... The present-day player seems to have lost sight of the fact that cricket is still a game to be enjoyed by both player and spectator and that the ball is meant to be hit [– generous words, indeed, from a bowler].

I am convinced that if our team of 1951 could take the field again today we could draw much larger crowds than they will see at Edgbaston this coming season because of the *way* we played. I'm afraid the game here is not very good. I had a go last summer in the league, but after a two-year lay-off and having to get used to playing in 'specs' I didn't enjoy it very much. The bowling and fielding on the whole were poor and catches went astray to an alarming degree, so I doubt if I shall bother this time. I got so —— stiff I couldn't move for days and the practice area was hopeless; one needed danger money. I think at my age it's time to call it a day.

So for one man at least 'The Grove Affair' ended happily for the time being beside the seaside. Whatever else was at issue, no one ever questioned Grove's unswerving – no, that is the wrong word for as good a new-ball bowler as he was – wholehearted efforts on behalf of the Club for which he turned in this record:

O	M	R	W	AVE
6533·4	1606	15 484	697	22·21

He also scored 2968 runs, some of them at very timely moments, with one century, 104 not out. He was always a hard-working bowler – 'I used to keep him at it', said Tom Dollery once, 'because he was a thick-set man who needed to bowl to keep moving' – and, like Statham, he was often unlucky. Perhaps among those cuttings at which Grove glances occasionally is one in which W. E. Hall wrote of him:

If a special Hereafter awaits professional cricketers it will have wickets pitched on a gentle slope with a fresh, gusty wind blowing down it, and Grove, as soon as he arrives, will know that his place is at the bottom of the slope, bowling up.

Well, he doesn't have to bowl up or down now if he does not want to do so and he can reflect that his captain once said of him that 'he had the great quality of getting the good players out'. There can be no higher praise of a bowler than that.

Perhaps the final verdict on the affair might be that the Committee's decision to dispense with Grove's services was justified from the playing strength point of view, whatever criticism there might have been of the way the matter was handled, and the perfect ending came when Grove returned to the Edgbaston fold in the role of scorer.

Dollery Departs
(1953–1955)

DURING the winter of 1953–4 Dick Spooner exchanged the fairly even tenor of his life at Edgbaston for the bottle-throwing tour in the West Indies, where he allowed only six byes in an innings of 681; and in the spring of 1954 a team from Pakistan, led by A. H. Kardar, whose experience with Warwickshire stood him in good stead, came and won a Test at The Oval, a feat without parallel for a side on its first visit here. 'He made few mistakes and led the side in a quiet orthodox manner,' *Wisden* said of him.

Despite Kardar's efforts, Edgbaston had still not been allotted a Test, nor was any Warwickshire player chosen for any of the four games played, but good news was only just around the corner. So, too, unfortunately, was the information that the Club was soon to lose the services of two of the greatest players ever associated with it – Dollery and Hollies.

It was in October at the end of one of the wettest seasons since 1903 that Dollery, who had earlier declined nomination as an England selector because it would mean missing eight county games, wrote intimating that he did not wish to renew his engagement, giving two grounds – increasing business responsibilities (in January he had become tenant of a licensed house) and a decline in his playing ability owing to age – he was 40. True, his aggregate for the season in Championship matches had fallen to 1236, but he passed Wyatt's aggregate of 21 597 runs and he had an average of over 35. Moreover, he had several times sacrificed his wicket going for runs, trying to make up time lost by rain, and one would have thought that he could have gone on comfortably for another two or three seasons, though it was understandable that a player of his ability and standards would not want to suffer a slow decline.

The news was a severe blow to Warwickshire and the chairman was asked to see Dollery, point out the difficulties that would be created by his decision and try to persuade him to play for at least one more season. The outcome of this was another letter from Dollery seeking a ten-year engagement – one more as a player and nine as head coach.

The executive committee thoroughly discussed the matter and Dollery was offered an agreement for five years, which he accepted, though it transpired later that had he stood out for it he could have had one for seven years.

Hollies also discussed his future with the Advisory Committee. He, it seems, had been offered a league appointment as well as a close season job, but he wished to remain with Warwickshire and after some discussion he decided to do so. It was agreed that an all-out effort would be made to find him a job, and that when the time came for his retirement, the public would be given six weeks' notice so that they would have ample opportunity to see his final games at Edgbaston. Even if Hollies was not aware of what had happened to W. G. Quaife, 'the Grove Affair' was still fresh in everyone's mind.

Despite the weather, Warwickshire rose three places in the County Championship. This was during Surrey's great run of seven successive wins. Warwickshire beat them at The Oval and shared the leadership with Middlesex until June when Yorkshire took over from them. By the second week in July they had won nine matches, but largely because of the rain they won only one more and three others ended without a decision, even on the first innings. Altogether they lost 100 hours of cricket in home matches alone and, not unnaturally, the gates suffered.

Aggregates of runs were on the low side, but Wolton, who had now consolidated his position at No. three, scored 1685 and headed the averages with 41·09. Gardner, Horner and Spooner barely got their 1000 and Townsend no more than 846. Only Hollies took more than 100 wickets – 117 for 19·19 – though Bannister climbed to 80, Keith Dollery 65, and Ian King, yet another slow left arm bowler, 58. Pritchard played in only three games. An off-spinner was badly needed.

There were several good finishes, two of them against Worcestershire. At Edgbaston Worcestershire needed 31 in eighteen minutes and Jenkins won the match by hitting friend Hollies for six off the first ball of the last over. At Dudley it was Flavell's turn. He took seven for 91 and then won the game by hitting 54 in thirty-two minutes by means of twenty-two scoring strokes. Wolton made his highest score, 165, and Hollies had thirteen wickets for 131.

Essex were beaten with four minutes to spare at Edgbaston – Dollery 109 and 43 – and against Sussex, King and Hollies put on 65 for Warwickshire's last wicket in the first innings. This match must go into the records, for in it Hollies made the highest score of his career in first-class cricket, 47. Moreover, it contained a six off Jim Parks and four fours. His previous best had been 24 made as long before as 1937. Keith Dollery, too, had the best figures of his career in this game: 22·3 overs, 5 maidens, 42 runs and 8 wickets.

Against Yorkshire at Leeds Gardner played what the annual report described as 'one of the great innings of Warwickshire cricket', in the opinion of opponents and colleagues, though no one would have guessed it from the account in *Wisden*. He made 70 of Warwickshire's 281 for six and they were able to force the follow-on, but had not enough time to drive home their advantage.

Kardar did not bowl against his former colleagues in the Pakistan match, which did not escape the rain. He did not need to do so for his two spinners, Zulfiqar Ahmed, off-spin, and Shuja-ud-Din, leg-spin, got the county side out for 170, and they were again collapsing in the second innings when the end came. Pakistan, one of whose countrymen, Khalid – soon to be changed to 'Billy' – Ibadulla, had joined Warwickshire to qualify, also failed against Hollies and were all out for 165.

The penultimate match of the season at Edgbaston was the occasion for a courtly and probably unique little ceremony. During the course of it Wilfred Wooller, the Glamorgan captain, completed the 'double', whereupon, Alec Hastilow, in his capacity as chairman, took out cele-bration glasses of champagne which were quaffed at the wicket. But there was no nonsense about the result – Warwickshire won by 56 runs. Hollies, three for 66 and six for 40, saw to that.

The spectre of slow and negative play walked again to such an extent that in the autumn Warwickshire sent a memorandum on the subject to the M.C.C., with special reference to its effect on the early stages of the game. But they might as well have banged their heads against a brick wall. At the annual meeting, Dollery, replying to the vote of thanks to the players, had said that he would like to see a rule to prevent a side which had been batting all day from continuing their innings on the next, but whenever he tried to persuade county captains at their meetings to 'gee up' the first innings he got little response. Most people, he said, seemed to think there was nothing wrong. But, as he said in a speech the following year, it was no use building new pavilions and terracing unless clubs tried to attract spectators. Warwickshire did not want a magnificent ground for two matches in five years.

Warwickshire, in fact, were trying hard both to build pavilions and attract spectators. Dr Stanley Barnes had given £5000 – the largest single donation ever made to the Club – for reconstructing the pavilion (centre) conditional on the work beginning before the end of 1954. It was long overdue. The pavilion had been built nearly seventy years earlier when membership was below 1000; now there were 11 000 members.

It was proposed that it should include new dining-rooms for both members, seating 280, and players, a snack bar, accommodation for ladies and additional seating for 1400 members. There was some criticism of the proposal to build a dining-room costing £10 000 to £12 000, but it was stressed that the desire to stage a Test Match was not an overriding factor in the Club's future development; the membership was entitled to consideration in amenities and comforts.

Nevertheless, the Test position did loom largely on the horizon. When the announcement came in November that Tests against the Australians in 1956 had been allocated once more among the 'big five', there were letters of protest in the Birmingham newspapers and one writer in *The Birmingham Mail* suggested that when five Tests were to be played Yorkshire and Lancashire should each have one, the final game should be at Lord's and the remaining two should alternate between Edgbaston, Trent Bridge, Gloucestershire, and Glamorgan, presumably at Bristol and Cardiff.

The annual report regretted that one of the Tests in the Pakistan series could not have been offered to Edgbaston 'in view of Mr Kardar's dual association, for all Warwickshire would have appreciated the opportunity to welcome him here again – this time as captain of his country's XI – for only a few seasons ago his skill and enjoyment of the game were marked features of Warwickshire cricket.'

There was one cheering feature, however. Although attendances at county matches during the summer dropped by some 239 000, Warwickshire were one of only two counties – Yorkshire were the other – who had higher gates, and this despite the weather which had cost them £5500 in takings. This included a loss of £1000 on the Pakistan game, though this was more than counterbalanced by the amount received from the Test Pool, £1444. But for the lifting of the Entertainment Duty, the report pointed out, 'such a season as 1954 might well have spelt financial ruin for most counties'.

The testimonial to Hollies, including gifts of 100 guineas each from the Club and the Supporters' Association, realised £2000 and after deducting expenses this left £1796.

The Club was glad to welcome back to the fold Ted Hampton, who not only resumed his invaluable services in the statistical field, providing all the figures for the Annual Report booklets and answering the various queries which cricket-lovers are ever raising on the subject, but also helped organise matches for players' benefits and testimonials. In particular, he now helped with the Smith–Austin testimonial, though in later years he was forced to relinquish this work for a time owing to health difficulties, including eye trouble. They culminated in a severe operation in 1971 from which he happily recovered.

A belated attempt was made, on the initiative of Leslie Deakins, to get Austin's salary raised from £200 to £240 for the season. Some of the Committee members felt he might be offered annual employment at an increased salary, but the secretary said he did not feel he could justify an all-the-year-round arrangement at a figure of between £300 and £400, and he was left to discuss the position with Austin with a view to helping him if at all possible.

In view of the later importations of overseas players, it is worth noting Alec Hastilow's point made at the annual meeting that whereas in 1946 only one native-born player was on the county's books, in 1955 ten out of the twenty professionals were born either in Warwickshire or Staffordshire.

The South Africans were here in 1955, but, though there was no Test for Edgbaston, there came just in time for the annual meeting the announcement that the Club in general, and Alec Hastilow and Leslie Deakins in particular, had worked and waited for twenty-eight years – the return of Test Match status with a match against the West Indies for 1957. Earlier in the spring the Club had proposed a rota for all touring sides which normally played five Tests here – one at Lord's, and the others to be allocated between The Oval, Old Trafford, Headingley, Trent Bridge and Edgbaston. Under Warwickshire's scheme, each of these latter five grounds would get four Tests over a period of five years and seven over ten years. The proposal had been put forward at a meeting of the Board of Control the previous year but had been deferred. This time, as 'Citizen', writing in *The Birmingham Mail* put it, it proved to be the key which unlocked the door.

Even though this meant that Warwickshire would have to wait until 1961 for the Australian plum, everyone was delighted, but especially Leslie Deakins, to whose work in trying to bring Test cricket back to Edgbaston, Alec Hastilow paid a particular tribute. 'Naturally, I am delighted,' the secretary told the Press. 'It has been an ambition of my Committee and myself and we hope thoroughly to justify not only the Board of Control's decision, but also their faith in Edgbaston. All Warwickshire is elated at the prospect and it is a great fillip to the game in the Midlands.'

But there was some sad news, too. Just before the annual meeting was held there came a letter from Dr Thwaite announcing that, owing to ill-health, he had decided not to seek re-election as President. The decision was most regretfully received, many tributes were paid to him and he was elected an honorary life member. The names of both Dr Stanley Barnes and Lord Bennett of Edgbaston were proposed, and Dr Barnes, who was on the ground at the time and who, earlier in the month, had also been elected an honorary life member, accepted the nomination.

He was duly elected at the annual meeting, though he was to hold office for only a few brief months. That August, he died, aged 80, and the Club had lost one of its greatest benefactors. A brother of Dr E. W. Barnes, the former controversial Bishop of Birmingham, he had captained the Camp Hill School XI in his early days and had been a member of the Warwickshire Club for many years. In his chosen profession he won a European reputation as a neurologist and in 1931 had given up practice to become Dean of the Faculty of Medicine at Birmingham University, where he was largely instrumental in the development of the Queen Elizabeth Hospital. That and cricket were his great interests.

Now, on the only occasion on which he was to be in the chair as President, he asked for support for the pavilion reconstruction scheme. About half the £30 000 needed to complete the first phase had been raised, but £100 000 in all was needed. Dr Barnes also mentioned that membership subscriptions had risen *following* an Australian visit, an unprecedented occurrence. The news that Dollery would take over as coach when his playing days were over was received with loud applause. The change was not to be long delayed.

No time was wasted in making further preparations for the coming Test. The general committee, meeting early the next month, decided to summon the ground and building sub-committee forthwith and a memorandum was prepared on all the work considered necessary, the secretary taking the view that priority should be given to an all-out effort to increasing the accommodation which could be booked in advance on the popular side. Later a special Test Match sub-committee was appointed to deal with the thousand and one things that have to be done before a Test Match can be staged – reservation of seats; catering and toilet facilities; car parking; dressing-room accommodation; umpires' accommodation; hotel and dining arrangements in the city; Press and TV facilities and not least the wicket.

This was a special sub-committee, but the work was going on all the time. The agenda for just one meeting of the ground and buildings sub-committee contained these items: pavilion (west wing) reconstruction; popular side development between implement store and Hill Bank peak; Indoor Cricket School; dressing-room alterations; former members' dining-room; resiting of head groundsman's house; playing area report; the Thwaite Scoreboard; TV commentators' box; groundsman's equipment to be overhauled.

This last was now the responsibility of T. Williams, of St Dunstan's School, London, who had taken over the appointment after Boak's departure, but he had to resign in June 1955, because of the ill-health of his wife. By the end of the season, after an acceptance and withdrawal of two, Bernard Flack, formerly at Cambridge and head groundsman to the Darlington Cricket Club, was appointed largely on the recommendation of D. J. Insole, of England, Essex and Cambridge. He took up his duties in October that year and since then everything on the ground, so to speak, has been, if not always lovely, at least comparatively peaceful and progressive and under expert control.

Flack found there was a considerable amount of repair work to be done at the bowlers' ends and 500 square yards of turf had to be bought for the square. Flack was not overburdened with instructions from the Committee since they had every confidence in him. They left it largely to him to get on with the job of getting the ground into the best possible condition so that bat and ball could have equal chances. And that, and to increase the pace of the wicket, is what he has been trying to do ever since.

True to his word, Dollery, in mid-August announced his retirement, though his form suggested that he could have gone on considerably longer. He had even declined the captaincy of the side to tour Pakistan during the winter. He was very nearly the first batsman to reach 1000 runs this season, being beaten by a matter of hours by D. J. Insole; in July he made the fiftieth century of his first-class career – 151 against Notts at Edgbaston – and perhaps he thought that was an appropriate pinnacle from which to say farewell. In all, he scored over 1500 runs and was second in the county averages to Hitchcock; finally he appeared for the Players at Lord's and made the highest score in the second innings, 82.

Dollery was one of no fewer than six Warwickshire batsmen to make 1000 runs or more, though the scoring was not very heavy considering it was a good summer. Hollies took his usual century of wickets (111), one of which was the 2000th of his career; and he also set up a new batting record for himself, making two double-figure scores in one match for the first time in a career that had lasted twenty-five years. At long last, in the 1955 *Wisden*, he was one of the Five Cricketers of the Year. He was 43 – a truly astonishing neglect of this 'fair-haired Peter Pan of Warwickshire cricket', as they called him, 'first and always a team man.'

The article went on to record some of the records (up to 1954) of 'Warwickshire's master craftsman of spin': most wickets for Warwickshire (previous best Santall's 1215); 100 or more wickets in a season twelve times, Howell next with six; most wickets in a season of any Warwickshire bowler, 180 in 1946; more than 1000 overs a season nine times, compared with the four times of George Paine; all ten wickets without the help of a fieldsman, an unprecedented feat in first-class cricket; two of the finest ever performances against the Australians – eight for 107 in 1948 and seven for 59 in 1953.

'Teams visiting England', the writer commented, 'have not been alone in wondering why Hollies has been chosen for only thirteen Tests. Above all, his unswerving length and direction are most rare for anyone bowling out of the back of his hand.'

Bannister took ninety-one wickets this season and Thompson, just out of the Forces, eighty-four, but Warwickshire, winning only one more match than they lost, slipped to joint ninth in the Championship table with Lancashire. The great need was still an off-spinner.

Bannister showed his class by taking nine Yorkshire wickets for 35, including a hat trick of Wilson, Yardley and Lester, at Sheffield in May. Yorkshire were all out 73, but they still won by five wickets. Thompson showed how very useful he was to be with ten wickets for 85 in the match against Leicestershire, off whose bowling Dollery took his sixth century in seven seasons.

The Thompsons – Warwickshire's with a *p* and Sussex's without – had what might be called a seam bowlers' ball at Hastings in July, 'Roly' taking six for 61 and five for 47, and Ian six for 36 and four for 59. Dollery's 82 was the highest score on either side and Sussex won by 56 runs.

Hitchcock several times played the kind of innings which once caused W. E. Hall to write that when he was in the mood 'the knowing spectator at square leg makes sure that the breakables are under the seat'. He hit 123 not out in as many minutes against Surrey at Edgbaston including seven sixes, five of them off Laker – whom Wolton also hit for three sixes – and twelve fours. Laker got seven wickets, but 95 runs were hit off him in the first innings and 90, for three, in the second. So for the second year Warwickshire beat the Champions, this time by 131 runs.

Against Derbyshire Hitchcock got an even quicker century – in 78 minutes, one six and sixteen fours – and he played another dashing innings of 128 against Essex at Edgbaston, scoring all but 58 of a partnership of 191 for the fifth wicket with Townsend. Dollery had a great match against Essex at Westcliff – 156 and 65. Then he made a declaration which, with Hollies taking eight for 42 in the second innings, enabled Warwickshire to win by 142 runs. Two matches later, against Notts at Edgbaston, Dollery almost exactly reversed his innings – 65 and 151.

On the other side of the coin were the games with Gloucestershire at Edgbaston in June and Northants at Northampton. These were prime examples of how-to-play-cricket-and-drive-the-spectators-away. The first innings points at Edgbaston were not decided until the third day and then there were declarations and rushes of runs to the heads of both sides. There were compensations. Gloucestershire had to make 206 to win in two hours and, to their credit, they got them, Emmett scoring 113 in 92 minutes, but it was all very belated.

The same thing as far as first innings points were concerned happened at Northampton. There were three declarations in the game and Hitchcock made 82 and 59, not out on each occasion; but the result was a draw. This was the sort of cricket Dollery had vainly condemned – two days of dull cricket and a harum-scarum finish on the last day. It was the kind which also provoked Lord Cobham, President of the M.C.C., when welcoming the South Africans in Worcester's Guildhall, to ask: 'Can we get rid of those awful bores who prod doubtfully at half-volleys and let every long hop pass by? They are the ones who are emptying our cricket grounds. We must get rid of them.' But no county did. It was easier said than done.

There was a curious episode in the Yorkshire match at Edgbaston in July. When he had made 54 Wilson was adjudged run out, but as he started to return to the pavilion spectators protested that the ball had struck a boundary flag and therefore was dead when the fieldsman, Horner, picked it up and threw it in. One umpire, Spencer, after consulting the fielder and his colleague, Pothecary, signalled a boundary and recalled Wilson to continue his innings, which he did to some tune, he and Padgett putting on 288 for the third wicket. A young tearaway fast bowler named Trueman twice broke the back of Warwickshire's innings with five for 31 and four for 68, though Wolton made 107 in the second innings.

Only Spooner of the Warwickshire players got a chance in the Tests against South Africa, who beat Warwickshire by ten wickets. The county made only 188 – Gardner taking three and a half hours over 58 – and 201, whereas the South Africans scored 382 for nine declared. Spooner stumped two batsmen, caught two and did not allow any byes, form which no doubt led to his selection for the final Test at The Oval when Evans was injured and unable to play. Unhappily Spooner got 'a pair', bowled by Tayfield in each innings, but he caught two batsmen in the first and did not allow one bye in the whole match. The attendance at Edgbaston was the largest at any county game the tourists had played and the cheque Warwickshire handed over was the largest they received except for a Test. It augured well for Edgbaston's own coming Test.

Dollery did not retire without more efforts being made to change his mind, but he said that he had found that the physical effort of cricket six days a week, allied to looking after his business interests, were making unreasonable demands on him. Not even the inducement of a testimonial had any effect, so his decision was accepted with regret and glowing things were said about his 'magnificent services' over the past twenty-one years as player and captain.

The Committee recorded that 'few counties have been blessed with a player of the personality and ability of H. E. Dollery, and he has undoubtedly left his mark for all time, not only at Edgbaston, but in the game generally where he has given a new status and dignity to the professional player both as a cricketer and a leader.'

A special tribute to him in the annual report recalled him 'once again lifting with easy grace and yet boyish blushing apology a delivery from Bill Bowes off his back foot for a six at Edgbaston; and, incidentally, to visualise the solemnity with which Bowes put a man out deep twelve months later when he came to Edgbaston and Tom came in to bat, indicating to the fielder the precise spot where the previous hit had soared over the pavilion rails a brief year before.'

It was unanimously decided to elect Dollery an honorary life member of the Club, so that he joined the small but distinguished gathering of Captain Cowan, F. R. Foster, S. Santall, E. J. Smith, C. A. F. Hastilow, Dr Thwaite, Dr Stanley Barnes and, later in the season, Canon J. H. Parsons; Dollery was also appointed a member of the selection committee with Hastilow and H. W. Homer.

His retirement gift from the Committee and members was a silver tea set inscribed 'in recognition of his outstanding services to Warwickshire cricket as player and captain'. It was presented at the next annual meeting, and from the proceeds of a Shilling Fund, organised by Ted Hampton, he was presented with a cocktail cabinet.

Judged from the highest possible standards, I do not think it can be said – nor would Dollery himself have said it – that he ranked among the greatest captains of all time. Nevertheless, he must be rated very highly as a leader and for his gift of inspiring any side he led with complete faith in his judgment. This sprang from his profound knowledge of the game, tactically and strategically, and of the players – his own men no less than his opponents – their strengths and weaknesses, which enabled him to read and pace a match often with uncanny perception. He and Hollies especially were a truly formidable combination. But above and beyond the basic skills necessary in any good leader, he had many of those flashes of brilliant inspiration without which no captain can be successful – and he was successful even though Warwickshire won only one Championship under his leadership.

Peter Cranmer at the annual meeting after Dollery retired said he rated him one of the four best batsmen in England on all wickets, but if he lacked the divine spark of absolute greatness as a bat, as his record in international cricket shows, he was an enormously accomplished player, highly efficient technically and tremendously strong on the leg side, and revelling in playing match-winning, as well as match-saving, innings which were a feature of Wyatt's captaincy, though to be fair to the latter he was often forced into them by circumstances.

Like many others who scored their thousands of runs in county cricket, however, he lacked the temperament which singled out, say, a no more technically accomplished player such as Sutcliffe; though – who knows? – had Dollery been given the chance earlier he might have succeeded in the highest class of cricket. But he thinks he was past his best when he was selected and he preferred the friendlier atmosphere of county cricket, whereas with Sutcliffe the greater the dog-fight the better he enjoyed it.

To be fair to him, Dollery always tended to belittle his batting. 'I've never been a really great cricketer, you know', he once told John Tarrant, of the *Green Mail*. 'I would describe myself as a very average player judged by the best standards.' Well, he may not have been in the Hobbs–Hammond–Bradman class, but he was very, very much 'above average'. He rarely failed Warwickshire when they were in trouble, and, a completely unselfish player, he sacrificed his own innings many times in the interests of the team. His fielding, whether at cover point, or in the slips, was always of the kind that inspires. He was what Isaac Walton in another context would have called 'the compleat county cricketer'.

The value of such a man and player to a club cannot be measured in runs, wickets, or catches, but since this is a history it must be recorded that he played 679 innings for Warwickshire, scored 23 457 runs, including 49 centuries and a highest score of 212, and averaged 38·07. In all matches his total of runs was 24 406; there was one more hundred to make the nice round figure of fifty, and his average was 37·54. There were also 276 catches and thirteen stumpings as well. These, of course, are his figures in first-class cricket; he went on playing for several seasons more in charge of the second eleven and in Club and Ground games.

Difficulties often arise when a new head of a department is appointed and when Dollery took over as chief coach was no exception. Naturally he had his own ideas of what should be done and how. He felt, for instance, that too much emphasis was being put on defence and that coaches should aim at teaching, first, the grip of the bat, second the stance and then some measure of defence and how to hit bad bowling. There were some teething troubles, which came before the Indoor School sub-committee where they were eventually sorted out. The effect was that 'Tiger' Smith, then 69, was retained in a liaison and scouting capacity, but without any responsibilities for coaching, and Ord, who had been running the nursery eleven, was appointed deputy coach on the ground during the summer.

Ord had made nearly 12 000 runs for the county, none of them in less than gracious style, and one would have thought he would have been a good model for youngsters to emulate. However, the nursery staff, it was reported, had been rather a disappointment. The boys were enthusiastic cricketers, but over-anxious to do well. The failure, it seemed, was one of temperament rather than ability and there were grave disadvantages in making professionals at too early an age. Of 500 boys six were selected to form the nucleus of the nursery staff.

Another problem the secretary reported was getting young pace bowlers to give up lucrative employment during the winter to take up muscle-developing, labouring type of work to build up their strength. He suggested organising special P.T. classes, and that winter Bill Slater, the former Wolverhampton Wanderers international and physical culture expert, recommended bar and weight-lifting equipment for a course designed to develop muscles to withstand the strain of a season's strenuous cricket. This, it was thought, would be more valuable than routine bowling at the nets.

Some inducement to the players to work and play harder was given in an all-round salary increase of £25 a year to all staff in view of the increased cost of living. This, in the case of players, included the price of hotel rooms for away matches which the secretary said had risen from 23s in 1954 to 28s in 1955, partly due to the rising cost of living, but also 'in part to the exalted level at which certain professional players had suggested, through their captain, that they should be maintained during the course of away games.'

It was agreed that the secretary's office should continue to book accommodation, but that players should be responsible for securing bed and breakfast terms only, at the most reasonable rates they could obtain. There would be an evening meal allowance of 8s 6d a player for each night spent away from home – and no one would paint the town red on that.

Meanwhile the Smith-Austin Testimonial had brought in £2091. Expenses were £294 and the secretary was authorised to hand to each of these old servants of the Club cheques for £898. The annual report contained this pleasant tribute to them:

When the internal combustion engine was in its infancy and a motor-car on the roads of England was a rare sight, young Jim Smith and young George Austin came to Edgbaston. They joined a club that was but 22 years old when they themselves were only 17 and 14 years old respectively. Down the years that followed, despite the interventions of two wars and the calls of more lucrative occupations they remained faithful to the game and their Club.

Sooner or later the colour question was bound to raise its ugly head and when it cropped up in Committee it was agreed that at present the approach should be realistic and engagements should be offered to men with the required ability irrespective of their colour. It was felt, however, that it would not be appropriate for the county club to field regularly more than, say, one or two coloured players, and the following season the view was expressed that the side should never contain more than four Commonwealth players at a time, though that term, of course, covered both white and coloured players.

It would be true to say that the Club has always scrupulously maintained an attitude of objectivity to this prickly question, even to the point of allowing coloured players on the staff to decide for themselves whether they wished to be considered for selection when the apartheid issue was raised during the proposed visit of the South Africans in 1970.

For another servant of the Club this season, too, was farewell. Tom Pritchard, whose loss of form had been almost catastrophic, had to be advised that the Club could not offer him re-engagement as a first-team player; eventually he took up a business appointment, though he did play another season with Kent, for whom, however, he took only eleven wickets for 39·54 runs each. On his day he was a devastating fast bowler and although he relied mainly upon the strength of his good right arm he was for a time probably the fastest bowler in the land. Altogether he took 695 wickets and scored 2827 runs for the Club, serving it well during the difficult days of reconstruction of the team after the Second World War.

Ian King, too, retired from the professional game. He and Ray Weeks had both seemed highly promising slow left-hand bowlers and it is not easy to say even now why they did not develop as everyone hoped they would. Even allowing for any defects there may have been in their make-up, temperaments and skills, one feels bound to wonder whether some reports that they were urged to bowl more quickly than their true style demanded, or at least flatten their trajectories so that they would provide a contrast with Hollies, can be entirely discounted.

As one player went, another took his place. A promising young fast bowler from Walsall, Staffs, David Brown, who had been specially registered during the season, was engaged. The Committee also learned that Ray Illingworth, the Yorkshire all-rounder, had agreed to give Warwickshire first option on his services if he decided to leave his native county, but he changed his mind when shortly afterwards he received his county cap. Years later, of course, he moved to Leicestershire, but by that time his undertaking to Warwickshire could reasonably be regarded as having expired.

But the best news about a player came almost at the end of the year when Alec Hastilow was able to tell the Committee that his efforts to persuade M. J. K. Smith, the Oxford University captain, to leave Leicestershire, the county of his birth, and throw in his lot with Warwickshire, had succeeded. Smith, who wished to make cricket and its administration a full-time career, as well as to tour and see the world, accepted a five-year appointment on the office staff at Edgbaston beginning on 1 July 1956, when he came down from the University.

Leicestershire, to whom what they described as 'an absolutely correct' approach had been made were, of course, extremely sorry to lose him and naturally did everything they possibly could to persuade him to stay, but they could not offer him a sufficiently attractive job. 'We were prepared to offer him administrative employment', said a spokesman for the Leicestershire Club, 'but the attraction did not measure up to that of Warwickshire. We cannot, and do not, grumble at his decision.'

The official announcement of Smith's appointment made no reference to his future as a player, but to Warwickshire members and supporters, of course, it meant only one thing. Here was the next captain of the Club and it was undoubtedly a feather in Warwickshire's cap to have secured his services, for he was rightly regarded as the most gifted young amateur batsman in the country.

'M.J.K.'
(1956)

❖ ❖ ❖

WARWICKSHIRE has never had a batsman – and it is doubtful if any other county has had one either – who has scored runs so prolifically as M. J. K. Smith. In his first sixteen seasons he exceeded the aggregate of every previous Warwickshire batsman except Quaife, taking his total to 24 562, compared with Quaife's 33 872, which took him more than twice as many seasons – thirty-five. Dollery in sixteen seasons made 23 457 and the only other batsman to have topped 20 000 runs is Wyatt – 21 597 in seventeen seasons.

Michael John Knight Smith was born at Broughton Astley, Leicestershire, and was educated at Stamford School, where he won a place in the first eleven when he was 13. Even from school he appeared in three county games, but without making any scores that caused raised eyebrows – they were, in fact 4, 0, 5, 4, 1 and 25. He did his National Service in the Army with the R.A.S.C., and played for the Corps, but not in any kind of representative cricket for two years until after he went to Oxford in October 1955, where the principal of his College, St Edmund's Hall, once likened him to 'a model of the Admirable Crichton', for which 'M.J.K.' probably never forgave him.

The following spring in a University trial game he scored the first of those centuries that were to stud his Oxford career like gems. In his very first match for the University, against Gloucestershire in The Parks, he made 104 not out. In the first of the three Varsity matches in which he was to play he opened the innings with J. M. Allan. Between them they were dropped three times in the first two overs and one wonders what might have happened if those catches had been held, but they went on to make 145 for the first wicket and eventually Smith took his individual score to 201 not out.

That season Smith, whose captain was Colin Cowdrey and by whom he was much influenced, scored 1065 runs for the University alone – an average of 48·40. This was almost certainly a record for a Freshman – he was the only one in the Dark Blues' side – and he also played in ten matches for Leicestershire, scoring 475 runs for an average of 27·94.

His second season with Oxford began badly and his aggregate fell to just below 1000 – 943, average 36·26 – but in the Varsity match he made another century, 104 this time. For Leicestershire he played in fourteen matches, scoring another 688 runs and finishing fourth, with 26·46, in the averages for the county for whom he often opened the innings. The year after he had agreed to join Warwickshire he was Oxford's captain and crowned his career there as a cricketer by making yet another century, 117, against Cambridge; the only player to achieve the triple-century feat in Oxford and Cambridge matches. His aggregate for the three games against Cambridge was 477, which comfortably beat the previous record set up by the Nawab of Pataudi, 457.

People have often marvelled that a player wearing spectacles could have performed such scoring feats as have marked Smith's career. He first had them when he was 17 and expressed a quiet but firm conviction that they had never been a disadvantage to him. Not unnaturally, he feared what might happen if his glasses were damaged, so he wore plastic lenses – indeed at one time he doubted whether he would have risked playing at all with glass lenses – and he had his eyes tested once a year. He admitted his weakness against fast bowling, especially at the start of an innings, but contended it had nothing to do with his eyesight.

It is difficult to believe that anyone with even slightly defective sight, glasses or no glasses, could have made a tithe of the runs he has made, or taken the hundreds of catches he has taken, especially at short leg where they are apt to come at you with the speed of light and where he had no superior in the country. As for his not inconsiderable exploits at rugby which, of course, he played without spectacles, it is said that he was as blind as a bat, but that he had a built-in radar system of his own so that he rarely fumbled a pass.

Unfortunately, both for him and for Warwickshire, the M.C.C. did not approve his special registration and he had to spend a year qualifying to play for them, so when he did come to Edgbaston, after he came down from Oxford, he played in just a few non-Championship games and otherwise immersed himself in youth cricket. Meanwhile, several names for the captaincy were canvassed and the chairman suggested that Hollies should be asked to bridge the gap. It was a compliment to a respected player, of course, though it was an onerous responsibility to place on a man who was in his 45th year, especially following the departure of a key figure such as Dollery.

From a playing point of view, the result, not unexpectedly, was disappointing to say the least, Warwickshire finishing in their lowest position in the Championship table, fourteenth, since 1947. Not that this could be laid at the door of Hollies. Not only had the side lost its batting mainstay – and only three of the remaining players made over, though not many over, 1000 runs – but the bowling was unbalanced. In one of the wettest seasons on record, there were few pitches to suit Hollies, upon whom responsibility sat heavily, and he took no more than eighty-two wickets. That would be enough for most young bowlers, let alone one of his years, which is an indication of how his form had been taken for granted. He had indifferent support, Bannister taking only seventy-five wickets, Thompson fifty-nine and Weeks twenty-one. It was no surprise when Hollies announced that he would retire at the end of the 1957 season – he himself had foreshadowed it.

There was even a mid-season inquest on the team's poor performances in particular and slow play in general. Hollies naturally emphasised what the loss of Dollery had meant to a side never over-strong in batting without him. That was the main cause, but he also expressed the view that some of the young players would never develop to the right standard. The coaches were making big efforts to help players who were out of form, but intensive net practice was made difficult by the absence of good practice wickets. The side was undoubtedly dispirited, though they were trying hard, perhaps too hard.

Everyone felt that the introduction of new players – Smith, Brown, Youll, Ibadulla and Shirley Griffiths, a West Indian – in 1956 would lift the county's stock, and it was agreed that in the meantime there was not much more that Hollies could do except make the best use of the material he had available. He was not helped by the fact that Gardner played for most of the season with a fractured finger – less loyal and stout-hearted players would have given up – and finally he had to do just that when he went one worse and fractured his elbow at Nottingham.

There were some brighter moments. The season had begun with a defeat by eight wickets at the hands of Sussex at Edgbaston despite centuries by Gardner – who got two of them in his first five innings – and Horner; and Keith Dollery did the hat trick against Kent, one of the trio being Tom Pritchard, who opened Kent's bowling with Ridgeway and took one for 39 and one for 38 against his old colleagues.

Another hat trick came to Thompson in the return match with Sussex at Horsham where Spooner snapped up his 500th victim. Horner hit a century before lunch against Leicestershire, thus joining the select company of Diver and Fishwick (both of whom had also done it against Leicestershire) and Reg Santall, whose 173 against Northants is the highest score ever made by an individual batsman before lunch in a first-class match. Fishwick also did it against Gloucestershire.

Dollery was especially missed on bad wickets, as at Lord's, where

Warwickshire lost six men for 27 and were skittled out for 55, and even more so against Hampshire when Shackleton shook everyone, probably himself included, by taking Warwickshire's first five wickets for 1 run in forty-five balls. Half the side was out for 7 runs, but Spooner came to the rescue with a hard-won 76, worth many a century, and the total staggered to 112. There was no one, however, who could save them at Bradford, where they were got out for 86, or at Trent Bridge, 94; and they got the slow handclap at Portsmouth where, on a perfect pitch, Wolton took four hours over 50.

Smith, whom Warwickshire met in the match with Oxford, for whom he made 37, showed bright promise of what was to come. First he made 76 against Scotland – Youll, another left arm spin bowler, one of the five youngsters qualifying at this time, took four wickets in fifteen balls for 6 runs – and then when the Australians came to Edgbaston Smith, with innings of 55 and 14, twice tried to stem Warwickshire collapses against Benaud, who had five for 44 and six for 31. Warwickshire were all out for 194 and 103, and then the Australians savaged their bowling to the extent of taking 424 for four off it, Burke making 194 and Harvey 145. Not even Hollies could keep them in check this time – he had to concede 128 runs without taking a wicket, though he got some compensation by hitting a six into the pavilion.

Wisden's verdict on Smith, who also played for the Gentlemen at Lord's in the 150th anniversary match with the Players and made 16 before being lbw to Lock, was that he should be 'a valuable acquisition, indeed one around whom the county can build for the future. It would certainly be appropriate if the re-emergence of Warwickshire as contenders for Championship honours coincided with the return of Test cricket to Edgbaston in 1957.'

There had been a first-day crowd to see the Australians of 20 000–21 000, nearly as many as on the first day at The Oval, and 50 000 altogether, but the annual report remarked on the fact that gates at county games, even on the best days, were modest indeed. The paying attendance at the Northants match on Saturday 12 June, was only 722 people and the gate £79. True, it was a shocking day weatherwise, but even on a lovely day only 755 people came. By 23 August the Club had lost £7000 in gate money owing to the weather. At one time they used to insure against it, but now the rates were considered too high.

The weather, however, was not the only thing blamed in the report. The poor gates were attributed mostly to:

the slow tempo of the game, which was often characterised by tedious, stroke-less batting, engendered, as batsmen aver, by negative bowling down the leg side to a packed on-side field. It is strange, therefore [the report pertinently pointed out], that two of the most attractive stroke-players and aggressive run-getters in the game today occupy two of the first three places [in the averages] T. W. Graveney (Gloucestershire) and L. Livingston (Northants), with aggregates of 2397 and 2006, reflected a very positive approach to negative bowling and perhaps the proof that an assertive batsman can score against any form of attack.

Just about the time I was reading this I came across a report that in the game between Middlesex and the Australians at Lord's in 1899, the Australians batted so slowly – Darling, who said he had a painfully bruised heel, took three hours to make his first 38 runs – that at one time the crowd whistled the Dead March from *Saul*. At least Edgbaston was spared that.

But were lack of enterprise and negative bowling the only causes of slow play? Ted Hampton wondered whether or not Edgbaston's wicket was not too docile and he produced some figures he had worked out which tended to show that the Club's bowlers achieved their best results away from home. Of eighteen scores of over 300 made against Warwickshire in the previous season, six were at Edgbaston; of the twenty-one scores of under 200 only three were made at Edgbaston; and the figures of the county's most effective first-team bowlers showed these comparisons:

HOLLIES: At Edgbaston, 44 wkts at 22·31 each – elsewhere 71 at 14·84.
THOMPSON: At Edgbaston 27, at 27·55 each – elsewhere 65 at 18·81.
BANNISTER: At Edgbaston 23, at 41·82 each – elsewhere 68 at 17·32.
HITCHCOCK: At Edgbaston 5, at 58 each – elsewhere 30 at 16·56.

Hampton said his report was not intended as a criticism, but he contended that from a bowler's point of view the Edgbaston wicket was 'very unfriendly' and that for the last ten years it had been getting worse.

Alec Hastilow admitted that 'it is not a really good cricket wicket'. It was too friendly to batsmen since it lacked pace and seldom deteriorated to any marked degree to give the spinners a chance later. The position had not been helped by constant changes in groundsmen, but they were making experiments.

During the winter of 1955–6 a special committee under the chairmanship of H. S. Altham had been studying the future welfare of first-class cricket. The counties had directed the committee not to consider the possibility of playing on Sundays – Alec Hastilow, reporting on an Advisory County Cricket Committee meeting at Lord's, said there was negligible support for it – but on other subjects the committee now recommended not changing the lbw law; limiting the on-side fieldsmen to five, with no more than two behind the wicket; limiting the number of overs in the first innings to eighty-five in 1957; tightening up the rules about time-wasting; no county to have more than two overseas first-class cricketers in any one season; and, at long last, a knock-out competition though of two-innings matches.

381

Two important events took place on the ground during 1956. In March the Lord Mayor of Birmingham, Alderman A. Lummis Gibson, opened the new Pavilion Suite, which he described as 'the finest room of any cricket club in the country', though he admitted that he had not been in the Long Room at Lord's, from whence came a telegram of good wishes. The suite embodied a reception-room; a dining-room to seat 196; a ballroom to accommodate 220 dancers; bars, one of them 27 yards long; kitchens and cloak-rooms; all of which were available for hire during the winter months when dinner-dances for 140 people could be accommodated.

Before the winter was out the Club might easily have lost this latest addition to its amenities. On the night of 5 October Tom Symm, a 75-year-old night watchman who was in his glass-fronted hut at the side of the main gates, saw a light in the new bar and ran 440 yards across the ground to the home of Syd Harkness, the assistant secretary, who, despite fumes, tackled the fire with a stirrup pump with the assistance of Bernard Flack, whom he had roused on his way to the fire. Thanks to their efforts, the suite was saved at a cost of about £100 in damage to the bar. It was a fortunate escape. In its first operational winter there were only a few nights when it was not booked and it earned revenue of £2690. It has since been developed enormously, and has added to the Club's income, as well as providing a much-favoured amenity.

The other event took place on 16 July when M. F. K. Fraser, chairman of the Supporters' Association since its inception, handed over to Lord Bennett, who had succeeded Dr Barnes as President, the new Indoor Cricket School, erected at a cost of £13 000 provided by the Association. This, the Association's first major contribution to the redevelopment of the ground, provided three practice nets; and after Lord Bennett had cut a tape in the Club colours, Eric Hollies bowled an over to 'Tom' Dollery to demonstrate the varying pace of the pitches. Fraser paid tribute to the work of Ray Hitchcock as first organiser of the Association, which by now had 500 agents and 40 000 members of the pool.

Hitchcock, however, had to give up the work this year to devote his full time to his sports outfitting business, and he was succeeded by Miss Crook, who thus got the chance to show herself one of the most capable organisers Edgbaston has ever had. In November Fraser was elected to a vacancy on the general committee.

There was one financial blow, for the ground was reassessed for rates at £2280 compared with a previous figure of only £990. The Club's first appeal against this was dismissed by the Birmingham Valuation Committee, and it was now to go to the Land Tribunal, the Committee deciding to fight the decision to the last ditch. From the bank, too, there came a request that there should be strict economy measures to keep the overdraft below £20 000, the agreed figure; the anticipation being that by the end of the year it would have risen to £27 000. On the other hand, there came a cheerful letter from a lifelong member, Mr E. Frank Cook, of Northfield, Birmingham, saying that he had intended to leave the Club a legacy in his will as his brother had done before him, but he had come to the conclusion that it would be better to pay it now – which he did with a cheque for £500.

Test Triumph
(1957)

IT is a moot point whether Warwickshire supporters were more concerned in 1957 with the return of Test cricket to Edgbaston after twenty-eight years, or with how the county side would conduct itself under its new captain and how he would play.

The place of honour here, I feel, must be given to the Test Match from 30 May to 4 June for, although it was a draw, it proved to be, as *Wisden* said, 'one of the most remarkable matches of all time', which saw a wonderful recovery by England when they seemed on the verge of defeat, 288 behind, and in the end it was the West Indies who had to fight for survival. The game also produced a variety of records, not least from Warwickshire's point of view the highest attendance, 30 000, the ground had ever been called upon to accommodate.

There were 13 000 bookable seats and even by 25 January some £6000 worth had been taken. Some letters contained requests for as much as £100 worth of tickets. By 5 March, when the bookings had reached £10 000, the success of the match was assured; by April they had swollen to £16 000 and orders were still pouring in, so there was even a change of design made in the new Hill stand so that 1000 more people could be seated instead of having to stand. One man of 'outsize proportions', as he described himself, asked for a gangway seat so that he could spread himself and he was duly accommodated. Altogether the advance bookings totalled £22 000, a far cry from the £300 to which they had amounted at the last Test in 1929.

Fortunately the weather was fine throughout, though the last day was cold. On the first day crowds queued from an early hour, and the gates were opened at 9 a.m. It was the first Test of the series and P. B. H. May won the toss for the thirteenth time in sixteen Tests. The wicket, prepared by Bernard Flack and his team, was perfect, but to everyone's surprise, except, perhaps, the West Indians, England were all out for 186. The tight-sleeved Ramadhin foxed everyone as to whether he was bowling leg-spinners, top-spinners or googlies; or, indeed, all three at the same time, judging by the way some of the England batsmen played, or, rather, did not play him. According to *Wisden*, he spun the ball very little and most of his wickets were taken with straight balls, proof positive of Wilfred Rhodes's old dictum that if the batsmen *think* they are spinning they are. Only Peter Richardson did not wholly disappoint, but he could manage no more than 47. Ramadhin bowled thirty-one overs in the innings, seventeen of them maidens, and he took seven for 49.

After a shaky start and various casualties, the West Indies ran up a total of 474, largely the work of Walcott, who made 90 despite a pulled muscle which was so painful he fainted when it happened, and Collie Smith, who, in his first appearance against England, hit a magnificent 161. He had done the same thing against Australia at Kingston, Jamaica, in 1954–5, a feat exceeded only by Compton, who made hundreds on his first appearance against Australia, the West Indies and South Africa. I can still see in my mind's eye a hook Smith made off Trueman, and hear the crack of it like a pistol shot. It was a very fast rising ball which would probably have scalped him if he had missed it, but he hit it a magnificent blow high into the crowd at square leg. Smith's untimely death in a motoring accident was a great loss to cricket.

Pairaudeau, the West Indies opening batsman, had a remarkable experience in this innings. He was out for one, yet he spent eight and a half hours at the wicket acting as runner, first for Walcott for three and a quarter hours and then five hours for Worrell, who also went lame and could not bowl again in the match. So, too, did Gilchrist, who bowled well in the first innings.

When England's second innings began, Ramadhin dismissed Richardson for 34 and Insole for none and it looked as if the second innings was going to be a repetition of the first, but Close and May stayed together until the end of the day when the score had been taken to 102. Next morning Close left when the score was 120. Cowdrey joined May and not another wicket fell that day. Both batsmen used their feet to Ramadhin, which was what all the England batsmen should have done in the first place, and they 'read' him so well this time that his analysis for the rest of the day was: 48 overs, 20 maidens, 74 runs and no wicket.

At the end of the day England were 378 for three, May 193 and Cowdrey 78. Next day the stand continued until it had lasted eight hours and twenty minutes and then Cowdrey was caught for 154 by one of the substitute fieldsmen. In the next half-hour May and Evans put on 59 more runs before May declared the innings closed at 583 for four. May had batted five minutes short of ten hours for his 285 not out, a truly astonishing innings, and he had seen the total taken from 65 for two to 583.

In the second innings Ramadhin bowled 588 balls, more than in any innings in first-class cricket. Curiously enough, the previous record was 552 sent down by his colleague, Valentine, at Trent Bridge in 1950. In the whole match Ramadhin bowled 774 balls, the most ever delivered by any bowler in a Test, the previous highest being Verity's 766 against South Africa at Durban in 1939. The only record Ramadhin did not break was C. S. Nayudu's 917 balls for Holkar against Bombay in 1944–5. Ramadhin's final figures for the second innings were:

O	M	R	W
98	35	179	2

It was an astounding feat of endurance and accuracy, for even over such a long spell he conceded fewer than 2 runs an over. May gave the West Indies two hours and twenty minutes in which to score 296 and they soon ran into trouble against Lock and Laker and were lucky to escape at 72 for seven. Ramadhin's were not the only records established during the match. The others were:

May's 285 was the highest score made in Test cricket in this country since the war, the previous best being Compton's 278 v. Pakistan at Nottingham in 1954; it was his own highest score and the best ever made by an England captain, the previous record being Hammond's 240 v. Australia at Lord's in 1948; and it was the highest individual score made on the Edgbaston ground, beating Kinneir's 268 against Hampshire in 1911.

Cowdrey's 154 was his highest in Test cricket and his first century in a Test in England.

The partnership of 411 between May and Cowdrey was the highest for the fourth wicket in any Test Match and the highest stand ever made for any wicket for England. It was only 40 short of the highest Test stand ever, 451, by Bradman and Ponsford, for Australia against England at The Oval in 1934. Roy and Mankad had an opening stand of 413 for India against New Zealand at Madras in 1955–6.

So much for scoring records. The ground record, too, had gone, the total paying attendance being 64 977, plus 26 500 attendances by members, and the gross receipts were £31 571, of which the Club retained £2075. This was a wonderful result and it must have been enormously heartening to all those who had striven for the return of Test cricket to Edgbaston. It had been agreed in 1956 that the six grounds now staging Test Matches regularly should have equal shares from the Test Pool, irrespective of whether they staged a match or not, and in all under this arrangement Warwickshire received £9125, compared with £5222 to other clubs.

The Club received many letters of congratulations, including one from Colonel R. S. Rait Kerr, former secretary of the M.C.C., who referred to 'your wonderful organisation on a great occasion', and *The Birmingham Post* described it as 'a truly memorable game in its own right'; and added that 'the Warwickshire Club and the secretary and his staff in particular have acquitted themselves triumphantly'. There was also praise for the groundsman and his staff.

No sooner was the game over than work began on the replacement of the 55-year-old double-decker stand by terracing, representing a gain of 2000 seats. This was the beginning of a four-year plan of reconstruction and new construction, of covering seating and of providing more catering facilities in readiness for the next Test with Australia. The Supporters' Association continued to devote its funds to the reconstruction of the whole of the West Bank of the ground which, when completed at a cost of £60 000, would represent, it was claimed, the greatest single gift ever made to a county club in this country.

The Association also favoured giving higher priority to the rebuilding of the Pavilion (east wing) and more consideration to aesthetics, when designing future buildings, in order to preserve the natural beauty of Edgbaston. It was agreed that in future there must be much greater control over early planning schemes and estimating. It was felt that no effort should be spared to destroy the impression that the Association had unlimited funds at its disposal, and that a more definite form of procedure must be laid down giving the Association the opportunity to express its views on the order of priority, nature and design of any project, although the final word must rest with the general committee of the Club.

One piece of reconstruction neither the Club nor the Supporters' Association had to worry about was the commodious new Press Box provided by the Hon. E. Langton Iliffe (now Lord Iliffe) – who had been elected a vice-president – and his co-directors of the *Coventry Evening Telegraph.*

Strangely enough the second visit of the West Indies to Edgbaston did not prove anything like the attraction it had been expected to be after the success of the Test. Although the West Indian community in Birmingham about this time numbered 27 000, it seemed that the public as a whole was not satisfied to come and watch even such a side as they had brought unless the opposition, too, was of Test class; and this Warwickshire, with the best will in the world, could not provide.

The county tried all they could to repeat their success of 1950, but rain prevented play on the last day. Horner gave them a good start with 98, but then Ramadhin broke through and the last seven wickets fell for only 19 runs, the county being all out 184. Ramadhin took seven for 43. The tourists' reply was 212, of which Kanhai, showing flashes of that brilliance that caused Warwickshire later to engage him, made 74 out of 112 in 85 minutes. Gilchrist hit his fellow-countryman on the ground staff, Shirley Griffiths, for 2, 4, 4, 4 and 6, but Hollies had five for 55 and the West Indies lead was kept to 28. In the second innings Warwickshire had made 204 for six when the weather ended it, M. J. K. Smith making 50 out of 82 put on with Stewart for the third wicket. Stewart was born in Wales, but came to Warwickshire as a product of a Coventry school through Mr E. Branson, a schoolmaster there who took the greatest interest in sport. He was to make his mark – literally – on the cricket grounds of England in no uncertain manner.

On the Championship front, the year had begun with a letter from Hollies sugesting that it would be in the best interests of the Club if Smith took over the captaincy in the coming season. He felt that he could render the Club and the proposed new captain better service as senior professional 'in what will probably be my last season in the county game' than by retaining the captaincy himself. Hollies amplified these views in a meeting with the Committee, and then both he and Smith left the room. The Committee expressed warm appreciation of Hollies's suggestion, which was adopted, Smith then being appointed the new captain before he had played a single match for them in the County Championship. 'It is a question of age,' Hollies told a reporter. 'One cannot go on indefinitely.'

Before the season began the secretary had to point out that Smith was not a capped player and that, according to the Club rules, he would have to recommend himself for this honour! As usual, Leslie Deakins also found the way out. He suggested that to appoint a player captain should, if necessary, carry the award of a county cap, since the greater honour should include the lesser. This view found favour and the award of a cap was approved. Smith was then called back into the room and formally told of the Committee's decision.

High as the hopes entertained for Smith's success with Warwickshire, no one was foolish enough to imagine that he could wave a magic wand over the team and transform it into a Championship-winning side again overnight. In fact, during his eleven years as captain, the longest period anyone has so far held the position, Warwickshire never did win it, though they came close to doing so several times, notably in 1964, when they were runners-up; in 1962, when they were third and in 1963 and 1969 when they finished fourth. Their average position in the table during Smith's régime was, roughly, eighth, compared with sixth in Dollery's eight years; ninth in Wyatt's eight seasons; and eleventh in Calthorpe's ten seasons. During Foster's brief reign the average was best of all – fourth.

In 1957 there was an improvement – they could hardly have done worse – for they went up by three places to eleventh and if their form in the second half of the season had been a patch on that in the first half they would have finished near the top. Early on they won six matches in succession and were running second to Surrey, who, although there had been a change of leadership (May having taken over from Surridge), won it for the sixth successive time. But of their remaining eleven games Warwickshire could win only one.

From a personal point of view, Smith could hardly have made a worse beginning. His first three innings were 0, 0 and 0. Two of these blobs were while playing for the M.C.C. against Yorkshire at Lord's. Trueman bowled him in the first innings and he was caught at the wicket in the second. His first innings for Warwickshire in the County Championship was against Worcestershire at Dudley and Flavell had him lbw before he had scored, but in the second innings he broke the spell with a brilliant 77 made in ninety minutes, which perhaps also helped to inspire Townsend to make 154, his first century in a Championship match since 1953.

After this Smith began to score as prolifically as only he of all Warwickshire batsmen has done, making 2074 runs in all matches for the county and 2125 altogether, including three hundreds. It was the first of a wonderful run of six successive seasons in which he scored over 2000 runs, reaching a peak in 1959 when he had an aggregate of over 3000, the first time any player had achieved such a total for any side for years. Of course, he easily headed the county batting averages and was twenty-first in the national list.

Generally, the county's batting was inconsistent, although three other players made over 1000 runs: Gardner; Horner, his highest aggregate for the county; and Townsend, a welcome return to form for him. Spooner made only 755 and was unlucky to miss his benefit because of injury. Ibadulla showed what a useful all-rounder he was by scoring 508 runs and taking 53 wickets for 17·20, figures sufficient to put him at the head of the bowling.

This, of course, was Hollies's last season and he finished it as he would have wished, with another 100 or so wickets for the fourteenth time in his career – 123, to be exact, for 19·35; and after bowling more overs, one-third of them maidens, than anyone else in the country. Cartwright, back from the Forces, had not yet shown signs of the greatness to come. He played in thirteen matches and scored 328 runs, but took only one wicket for 35 runs, though no one can take wickets if they are not asked to bowl.

At this time Cartwright looked upon himself primarily as a batsman and at the end of the season he told the Committee he wanted to be an opening batsman, but had not been given any opportunity in this capacity in the first eleven. For the second eleven, which, under Dollery's leadership, finished second to Yorkshire, he was fourth in the batting averages and topped the bowling with twenty-five wickets for only 8·84 runs each. He was given an increase in salary, but this hardly proved the right answer. Dollery, incidentally, played sixteen innings for the second eleven and scored 344 runs, with 50 his highest score.

Altogether, Warwickshire had a very up-and-down season. Twice they had the misfortune to run into Statham when he was in top form. At Coventry he rattled them out twice for 71 and 90, taking thirteen wickets for 89 and giving Lancashire the easiest of wins – in the second innings he took the first seven wickets in ten overs for 22 runs. Then at Old Trafford in August he did it again – three for 46 and six for 22.

Two other bowlers Warwickshire had allowed to go took the opportunity to remind them of it. Vic Cannings, returning to the Hampshire side after missing nine matches, enjoyed a spell of five wickets in 28 balls for 15 runs; and when they met Somerset Lobb took the first three Warwickshire wickets for 13 runs.

Graveney and Hollies had two wonderful duels in which the Gloucestershire man ran out winner with two centuries, and Gardner answered them in his own fashion with 163 and 73 not out. Against Oxford he not only made 157 for once out, but won the match with a six off the last ball. The Varsity match, incidentally, had in it two players later to be associated with Warwickshire, O. S. Wheatley and R. W. Barber, both of Cambridge. The former played five matches when he joined the county later in the season and took fourteen wickets.

Stewart made his first century in a Championship match against Leicestershire. The previous season there had been a reference to his 'somewhat nervous disposition which was holding back his cricket development'. Presumably to encourage him he was given a salary increase of £25 over and above the original offer made to him, and perhaps it was this that did the trick. He was soon to repay the investment in the most spectacular manner possible.

Spooner was unhappily unable to play in his benefit match against Middlesex, Esmond Lewis deputising for him, and he was unlucky, also, in that only eighty minutes' play was possible on the first day. Still, the benefit realised £3784, so there were compensations. This summer, incidentally, the M.C.C. made amends for their neglect of Lewis by inviting him to play for the Gentlemen and he rewarded them for their confidence by catching one batsman in the first innings and three in the second.

Bannister, who had shown himself a thoughtful young bowler, believed that the context in which a performance was achieved was often more important than the achievement itself, and he once instanced the match against Derbyshire at Derby in 1955 when he bowled 36·4 overs for 99 runs and five wickets in an innings of 172 runs. Now against Kent at Dartford he performed what he thought was the best of his career. Kent needed 209 to win and because some other bowlers were indisposed Bannister had to keep one end going. In the first innings he had bowled twenty overs and taken two for 57; now he bowled thirty-six consecutive overs from one new ball to the next – it was seventy-five overs then. He was almost punch drunk, he says, when 'M.J.K.' said to him: 'Take the new ball next over – unless you want another one with the old one to get loose.' One hopes he smiled when he said it; in any case Bannister had no breath left to reply. He took seven wickets for 95, and Warwickshire won their fifth consecutive Championship victory by 19 runs.

Hollies showed that even at 45 his accuracy was unimpaired. He had a spell of seventy-eight balls – thirteen overs – without a run being hit off him by the Leicestershire batsmen, and then towards the end of August he played his last county match at Edgbaston. It was against Surrey, who won by ten wickets, and as he went out to play his last innings the players formed a guard of honour for him. He had made none not out in the first innings and he got 7 in the second, compelling Surrey to bat again and some of his colleagues to change back into flannels – they had all thought it was over, but they should have known him better than that. His two final analyses at Edgbaston were:

	O	M	R	W
First innings	33	9	82	2
Second innings	2	1	2	0

Very fittingly, the last of those two overs was a maiden. His last match of all was also against Surrey, at The Oval, where he bowled in one innings, returning these figures:

O	M	R	W
15	2	35	2

Warwickshire were dismissed for 95 and 86, and Hollies's last contributions were 1 and none not out, which was as he would have wanted it to be. Crowd and players applauded him off the field.

So ended the career, in first-class cricket at all events for he never attempted a come-back, of the most successful bowler who has ever played for the county. But he was more than that. There are some – and I am among them – who would say that he was the most accurate and least expensive right-arm leg-spin bowler the game has known. It is a big claim, but his career figures in all first-class cricket are a very powerful argument in support of the contention:

O	M	R	W	AVE
21 449·4	6775	48 640	2323	20·93

I have not been through the records of all the bowlers who ever were, but I have seen most of the leg-spin bowlers of the last fifty years or so, the period in which they have nearly all flourished, and I have never known one of his kind who bowled as many maiden overs as Hollies did – nearly one-third in a career lasting twenty-six seasons. It is difficult for any bowler consistently to bowl so accurately that batsmen find it difficult to score from him, as they generally did off Hollies, but for a bowler of right-hand leg-breaks and googlies, who, as a tribe, are notoriously prone to waywardness of both length and direction, it is phenomenal. Because of his nagging accuracy, Dollery used to call him 'the toothache bowler', and said that he dropped the ball so often on the same spot on the concrete wicket at his father's home that it had to be recemented.

The only other bowler of his type I would compare with Hollies for putting the ball where he wanted it was Grimmett, but Hollies maintained his high standards over a much longer period of time than the Australian. E. M. Wellings, in an article on googly bowlers which appeared in the *Wisden* of 1958 after Hollies's retirement, expressed the view that 'there has never been an English googly bowler with such control of length and direction'. Not that Hollies bowled the googly all that frequently. He bowled fewer of them against the good batsmen, who could pick it out – or thought they could – and knew, in theory at least, how to play it, and more against the lower-order batsmen less able to cope with it. For the rest he bowled leg-breaks and top-spinners, two of the latter an over on average.

Like most bowlers, Hollies did not particularly relish bowling against left-handed batsmen, but there were others to whom he was a positive bogey. One of them was George Cox, of Sussex, who was wont to fail against him even in the middle of a run of good scores, and Jack Parker, of Surrey, whose wife, it was said, rather unfeelingly used to ring him up and ask: 'How did he get you out today?' – he, of course, being Hollies.

Astonishingly, although he took all ten wickets in an innings, he never did the hat trick, and although he headed the Warwickshire bowling averages almost as a matter of right, he was never at the top of the first-class averages for the country. His Test career is also quite unrepresentative of his record. He was unlucky in the matter of injuries, but, like Dollery, was always more comfortable at home in county cricket. Like some wines, he did not travel very well, but among the home vintages he ranked among the best, for his skill was founded upon the basic principles of length, length and length again, plus subtle flight and spin. Throughout his career the wickets he took outnumbered the runs he made, but he was probably the most popular No. eleven in the country – and not the least skilful.

Just as 'Mike' Smith always believed he could bowl a bit, so Hollies believed he could bat, but Fate (and captains) usually decreed that seldom, if ever, did he appear other than at No. eleven. However, there was one occasion at Derby when Cliff Gladwin, bowling beautifully, was reducing the Warwickshire batting to shreds, and Norman Horner, who had been in and out, suggested to Eric that it might be his day to show what he could do with the bat.

'What's he bowling?' asked Eric, whereupon Horner flattened out the inside of a cigarette packet and with a stub of pencil wrote on it a brief description of each ball as it was bowled by Gladwin. Needless to say, he gave his imagination full play and soon had down almost every kind of ball that could have been bowled by any type of bowler. Then to his astonishment the list was snatched from his hand by Hollies, who had seen that the ninth wicket had fallen.

Out he marched to the middle, walked up to Gladwin and handed him the list. ' 'Ere you are, Cliff', he said, 'bowl 'em in that order and I'll deal with 'em.'

Hollies was elected an honorary life member of the Club and for several years after his retirement he and Grove helped with coaching the young at Edgbaston – the M.C.C. should have had him at Lord's every season with a roving brief to find and cultivate young leg-spin bowlers – and he continued to play very successfully in Birmingham League cricket. When I last saw him at his home he looked years younger than his then age of 59 and he had just taken his fiftieth wicket of the season. He would go on playing, he said, as long as he got pleasure out of the game and could do himself justice. Few cricketers have given more pleasure to the Edgbaston crowds, but unhappily, because of a misunderstanding, he ceased to go to the ground.

The annual report contained this tribute to Hollies who, at the next annual meeting, was presented by the Earl of Warwick with a cocktail cabinet:

We at Edgbaston will always remember him in the mind's eye as we saw him in his great days with the ritual never varied – removal of the cap, sweater, the marking of the run, the reflected pleasure in the feel of the ball, the easy run, the smooth action and that unexpectedly vicious follow-through.

Dollery found himself in a curious position this season. There was an early inquiry from the M.C.C. asking if the Committee felt disposed to nominate him for the Board of Control Selection Committee. Dollery, however, had been informed by the Warwickshire Committee that he was no longer a county selector and he found this somewhat baffling. He told them so in a letter in which he said that as county coach he saw more of the players and their form than anyone and considered his judgment second to none, yet he heard nothing from the coaching sub-committee. He went so far as to offer his resignation if the Committee thought he was not the right person to carry out the job.

After the Committee had discussed the letter, it was decided to nominate Dollery for the Board of Control Selection Committee and grant him leave of absence, but to ask the chairman and vice-chairman to meet him and discuss his grievances. The matter was satisfactorily resolved after further adjustments had been made in the coaching arrangements and running the Indoor School, which left him in full control of the professional playing staff throughout the year.

There was another special general meeting in 1957 – on the subject of ladies' membership. This had been raised at the annual meeting by Mr John Godrich, who said the right had existed in the past and had been discontinued owing to lack of support. Now, however, in view of the high percentage of ladies attending matches, he thought the position should be re-examined. The President said that this would be done, though when there were women members between 1902 and 1924 there were no more than nineteen applications.

Only about 100 members attended the meeting, held in the Pavilion Suite, when Mr Godrich proposed that ladies should be admitted to membership. Today, he said, they represented 25 per cent of the total subscribers. Mr Michael Hastilow, who seconded, said he felt that as many as 500 of the 2800 holders of ladies' transferable tickets would take up full membership if given the opportunity. Of the thirteen out of fifteen county clubs which had replied to their questionnaire, only Lancashire and Middlesex still restricted ladies to mere ticket-holding; five of the fifteen withheld admission to the pavilion; three withheld voting rights; and seven specifically barred ladies from serving on the Committee; none had any ladies on that body.

James McDowall revealed that some years earlier the Committee had been placed in a most embarrassing position in trying to deal with a lady ticket-holder against whom complaints had been made. She insisted – and, with legal aid, successfully – on her right to be issued with a ticket and special legislation had to be introduced to prevent a similar situation arising again.

Mr W. Leslie Jones urged full membership for ladies, and this was seconded, but defeated, only thirteen members present voting in support; and when the chairman called for a vote on the original resolution as it stood, embodying the phrase 'without certain rights', this was approved by eighty votes to twenty. It was finally agreed by sixty-eight to nineteen that ladies should be accepted as members, but without the right to accept nomination for an official appointment, or for a seat on the Committee; and – and this by an overwhelming show of hands – that they be not allowed to use the centre pavilion, the club-room, or the bar.

Later when a sub-committee met to make alterations to the rules following this decision, James McDowall said he thought it most unfortunate that such a major issue of Club policy had been decided by a bare one per cent of the total membership; the decision, he thought, might well have been reversed if there had been a more representative attendance. By the time came for the annual meeting of 1958, 688 ladies had transferred to membership and about twenty of them attended the meeting, though none of them ventured to speak, let alone take up the cudgels (or knitting needles) against Mr McDowall. And, as before, after the first flush of enthusiasm, numbers dwindled again year by year until the total of ladies holding membership in their own right had fallen to about fifty. A pity, for they lend glamour to the ground.

The Club suffered grievous losses by deaths this year – in October of Lord Bennett, its President, the second in succession to die in office, after fifty years' membership and thirty years as a vice-president; Sir Fitzroy Hamilton Anstruther Gough-Calthorpe, Bt, the senior vice-president, who had sold the freehold of the second section of the ground to the Club in 1945; and in November at his home in Surrey, Dr Thwaite, at the age of 74.

Dr Thwaite's association with the Club dated from his days as a medical student and he had served as Committee member, honorary treasurer and President, holding the last position from 1942 to 1955, so that he had been at the helm in the testing post-war period. His death, as Leslie Deakins wrote in a tribute to him in *The Birmingham Post*, marked 'the passing of a man who, more than any other, was responsible for the resuscitation of Warwickshire cricket from the doldrums of the 1930s to the Championship of 1951 and the restoration of the Edgbaston ground as a Test Match centre in 1957.'

A still older servant, Sydney Santall, died at his home in Bournemouth at the ripe old age of 83. Until Eric Hollies came along, he had taken more wickets for Warwickshire than anyone else – 1206 for 23·98 runs each. He also scored 6490 runs, average 15·45 and took 150 catches. He and W. G. Quaife were the Club's first real all-rounders, although it is sometimes forgotten that in only one of twenty-one seasons did Santall take 100 wickets. Nevertheless, his steadiness and reliability over a long period stood the county in very good stead, to say nothing of his coaching.

During the winter 'Mike' Smith went on the first of his many tours abroad, though he missed the chance of a rugby cap to do so. This was to East Africa with a team of amateurs captained by F. R. Brown. They played nine matches, won three and did not waste any time, scoring regularly at the rate of 60 runs an hour and sometimes 100. Smith made 403 of them and was second in the averages with 36·63. *Wisden* said he 'looked the complete player throughout, on-driving with exceptional style and effect'.

Ill-Advised Experiment
(1958)

THE start to Smith's next home season in 1958 could hardly have been in greater contrast to what had happened in his first. This time he made two centuries in his first three innings – 131 against the Combined Services at Edgbaston and 160 for the M.C.C. in an opening partnership of 299 with another Smith, D. V. They made a shaky start and each gave two chances, but it may well have been this innings that influenced the Board of Control Selection Committee to make a request which had an unfortunate effect on the Warwickshire side's performances.

This was that Smith should gain experience of opening the innings in county cricket before his appearances in Test Matches against New Zealand, who were here this year. His selection, incidentally, made him only the second man in this century (and now the only living one) to play for England at both cricket and rugby football, the first having been R. H. Spooner.

The idea sounded admirable in theory; in practice it worked out badly. It did not produce results in the Tests, and it upset the Warwickshire batting order, breaking up the by now fairly well-established partnership between Gardner and Horner – the latter of whom volunteered to go in lower down the order – and depriving the side of badly needed strength at No. four; usually this season Horner went in No. five.

Smith opened in three of the five Tests, the first of which was at Edgbaston in June, but in four innings he made only 57 runs, 47 of them in one innings, and was then dropped; a not very auspicious beginning to his Test career. Freed of these worries, Smith's batting greatly improved and for the second season he had an aggregate of over 2000 runs. He was one of only three batsmen in the country to reach this total and he was fourth in the first-class averages with 2126 runs for an average of 44·29, a tribute to the resilience of his temperament.

How far the juggling with Warwickshire's batting order affected their decline it is, of course, impossible to say. The fact remains that only two other of their batsmen made over 1000 runs and only one of the six regular batsmen had an average of over 20. *Wisden*, which made no bones about laying the principal blame at the door of the M.C.C.'s request, also mentioned Gardner's loss of form at the start of the season, his benefit year; the failure of young batsmen of whom much had been hoped; the lack of an effective new-ball attack; and the enormous gap left by the retirement of Hollies, which Leadbeater, of Yorkshire, hopelessly failed to fill with only twenty-five wickets. No bowler got anywhere near 100 wickets, one of Warwickshire's own ground boys, R. G. Carter, judiciously mixing seam and spin, being the best with seventy-one, though a new slow left-arm bowler, G. H. Hill, discovered by 'Tiger' Smith at King's Heath, provided a ray of hope with 54 wickets for 20·92 runs.

Behind the bald statement in the Warwickshire report in *Wisden* that Bannister had back trouble and took only thirty-five wickets during the season, lay the story of a man's long struggle to overcome a physical handicap by modifying his style of bowling, a very difficult thing to do at the best of times, but most of all when one's livelihood depends on it.

Towards the end of the 1957 season, while playing at Clacton, Bannister had a long bowl and felt muscle pains in his back which caused him to miss the last few games of the season. In the winter he went to South Africa for three months to coach and had a complete rest apart from minor club games, but these started the trouble off again – pain in the lower rib on the left side of his back. He had intensive treatment – deep heat, injections, massage. Then he came home, but within a week of starting net practice at Edgbaston in April the trouble began again. So the Club sent him to Professor W. Gissane at the Birmingham Accident Hospital, who gave him an X-ray, which showed an original displacement of a vertebra of about one-eighth of an inch which had been aggravated to one-quarter of an inch by his bowling action.

Professor Gissane's verdict was that, surgically, nothing could be done about it and for most men that would probably have meant the end of his cricket career; but, as I have said, Bannister was a thoughtful young man, and still more important in his case, he had determination. He began to wonder if changing his action to reduce the pivoting of the body would help. He was told that it might. The Club gave him all the time he wanted and he set to work to change his bowling action, first cutting down his run from thirteen to nine paces and trying various modifications. Eventually he tried himself out in the nets. Everything seemed to work all right, so he played against Oxford University in

June and, despite his long lay-off, took seven wickets for 43, including that of A. C. Smith, a young amateur, Birmingham-born and future captain of the Club. He also played in some Championship matches. Bannister found that he had to bowl much more slowly, being now more of an arm- than a body-bowler, with the outswinger and what he called a slow floater as two of his chief weapons. Even so, he had one other very good performance – five for 30, including four for 8 in four overs, and four for 28 against Hampshire. Thanks to his determination and perseverance, he looked to be well on the way to recovering his best form.

Warwickshire won only three games during the season and finished next to the foot of the table, sixteenth, their lowest position for thirty-one years. It was strange to have Test Matches in consecutive years at Edgbaston, which had been allocated the first Test against New Zealand in June. England won by 205 runs on the Monday afternoon with a day to spare, but it was no thanks to 'Mike' Smith. He opened the innings with Peter Richardson and was leg before in the second over before he had scored. England lost her first three wickets for 29 runs and would have been in a sorry mess had it not been for May and Cowdrey again. May scored 84 and Cowdrey 81 in a stand which took the total to 150, but then the last six wickets fell in just over an hour for 71 and England achieved the barely respectable total of 221.

Fortunately, Trueman was at the top of his form and New Zealand, who were without their best batsman, Bert Sutcliffe, who had broken a bone in his left wrist while fielding, collapsed and were all out for 94. In one spell Trueman took four wickets for 7 runs, and he had five for 31. In England's second innings Smith was out for seven, but Richardson went on to make exactly 100 and, with Cowdrey 70 this time, England were able to declare at 215 for six, leaving New Zealand to make 343 in two and a half days. They did better than in the first innings, but Loader, Bailey and Lock saw to it that they did not get more than 137.

It was one of the wettest summers anyone could remember. There had been a phenomenal week of rain before the match began. The day before was Birmingham's wettest day for fifty-seven years, 1·8 inches falling in 24 hours, and how Bernard Flack and his assistants mopped that up only they could have told. Nevertheless, there were 10 000 people present on the opening day and, on the Saturday, despite showers, 25 000. Altogether nearly 60 000 people paid £18 941 to see the match, compared with £31 571 for the West Indies game, and, with members, there was a total attendance of 91 000; this was exactly the same as the figure for the game at Trent Bridge, where the receipts were slightly higher because of the greater prices of admission. More people paid to see this match than all the county games at Birmingham and Coventry. 'Edgbaston', *The Birmingham Mail* proclaimed, 'has fully justified its claims to Test status, its facilities are unsurpassed and the wicket is one of the best and fairest in the country.'

In the second Test Smith was in better form, and made 47 in the one innings he played, though they took him 230 minutes, but in the third he got only 3 and was then dropped. England won the rubber by four games to nil, the fifth being drawn. By the time the New Zealanders came to Edgbaston again in August, Warwickshire were bottom of the table, but managed to give one of their better displays. Gardner and Horner began the game with a century partnership and Smith, free from Test responsibilities, made 67, the county being able to declare at 316 for seven wickets. It was only the third total of over 300 made against the tourists, who got 265, young Hill bowling well to take four for 51. Warwickshire declared their second innings at 117 for three and New Zealand had made 116 for six in reply, the game being in a very interesting position when the end came.

Smith had better fortune as an opener for the county, but from Warwickshire's point of view he was of more value going in lower down the order and for once he gave the lie to those who said he was suspect against really fast bowling by making 76 out of 231 against Northants, for whom Tyson bowled with greater pace and accuracy than he had shown all season, taking six for 76.

But unquestionably the best match of the summer was against Yorkshire at Edgbaston. It was drawn, but only after a really nail-biting finish. Like nearly all the most exciting games, it was one of low scoring. What it boiled down to in the end was that after Warwickshire had made 142 and 229 and Yorkshire 208, the latter had to score 164 to win with nearly three hours and a half remaining. When the final over of extra time came they still needed 9 runs with three wickets in hand. The first five balls provided two singles, a four and two wickets, those of Ryan and Binks. That left one ball to go and 3 runs still wanted. With Bannister about to bowl the last ball of the match, this was the position – if he took a wicket that meant a win for Warwickshire and a hat trick for him; if Yorkshire made two runs it was a tie, a three or a four and they had won. What happened was that Pickles hit the ball hard into the covers, but the batsmen ran only a single, so stumps were drawn with Yorkshire one run behind and one wicket left.

There were two maiden centuries – 116 by Leadbeater, though Warwickshire, while grateful enough, would doubtless have preferred some wickets, and 128 by Cartwright in an opening stand of 218 with Gardner against Kent. Cartwright, who had been scoring prolifically with the second team – he had won the Wilfred Rhodes trophy for heading the Minor Counties batting averages – had now been awarded his county cap, but he was still not happy about his future at Edgbaston.

Indeed, he went so far as to ask for his release with the intention of seeking his fortune where there might be opportunities for him as an opening batsman. But Cartwright had a qualification to play only for Warwickshire and, in view of the cost they had borne in developing him as a player, the Club was not willing to let him go and he was told that he would not be released to play for another county. However, after his salary had been increased and he had been assured of regular consideration for a permanent place in the first eleven, he accepted the offer.

Carter also got his cap after two particularly fine performances against Somerset – six for 54 and eight for 82 – and he had a great day against Worcestershire at Edgbaston. Their last nine wickets went down for 69 runs and Carter had five of them for 7 runs in what *Wisden* described as 'a shattering spell' of 8·4 overs, six of them maidens. Wolton's 102 in this match was his first century in two seasons.

Gardner's benefit against Lancashire was so affected by the weather that the gate receipts were only £250 and it was only through gargantuan efforts by his fellow players, notably his former captain, 'Tom' Dollery, that eventually £3750 was raised. The beneficiary scored 26 in each innings, but Bob Barber made 115 and Pullar 157 not out.

One thing to be cheerful about was the form of O. S. Wheatley, who while at Cambridge, set up a new University record for the number of wickets taken in a season – eighty for 17·63 each – the previous best having been A. G. Steel's seventy-five as long ago as 1878. In the Varsity match he had two for 39 and two for 47 and he took a few wickets for Warwickshire as well, crowning his season by being chosen for the Gentlemen. His total of wickets for Cambridge included seven of Warwickshire's after he had put them in. Another cause for congratulations was that Alan Smith had been awarded his Blue at Oxford and been appointed captain for the 1959 season. Indeed, Smith, an old boy of King Edward's School, Birmingham, led the University side for two seasons, something that had been done only twice before this century – by E. L. Wright in 1907–8 and by Alan Melville in 1931–2, though it has happened several times since.

What with the weather and Warwickshire's indifferent cricket, the Club had its worst financial season since the war and for the first time since then the membership showed a slight decrease, a trend which, unhappily, has continued. Despite the Test, gate receipts were down by £4000, one consequence being that the four-year plan of development had to be shelved for the time being. The 1959 annual report was blisteringly critical, not only of the Warwickshire team's display – the defence of a number of batsmen, it said, 'seemed inadequate to permit them to survive at the wicket until scoring opportunities came along', and the bowling was also inadequate, and the fielding, with the notable exception of Horner, 'deplorably bad' – but also of the state of the game generally. The report went on:

. . . the tempo of the game slowed down to a degree where, in the early stages of many games it was difficult to define actual movement; the Laws of the game were more than ever disregarded, and throwing and dragging by bowlers became all too commonplace . . . and, most depressing of all, no apparent action was taken to rectify the position; as a culminating effect there was a very grave diminution of public interest and county match aggregates fell from just over a million in the season before to practically half that figure . . .

There can be little doubt left that . . . the changes instituted twelve months ago* almost entirely failed in their purpose and that further legislative action must now be taken, among other things, to ensure that the laws of the game are upheld, and, if necessary, an incentive given to ensure that the bat is applied to the ball with the basic idea of scoring runs.

If cricket is to continue as a spectacle to interest a public and provide them with entertainment, the great majority of players will have to show far more zest and attacking ability. Your Committee is at one with the authority that declares there is nothing wrong with the game, but only with the players' approach to it; unless this is remedied soon, most players will have lost the ability, through lack of practice, to play strokes and the game will face an age of strokeless batsmen opposed by throwers and draggers . . . a complete prostitution of the art of cricket.

This was easily the strongest broadside ever delivered in an official report about Warwickshire cricket and one is tempted to wonder what the Committee's reaction would have been had it appeared in a newspaper. Leslie Deakins did, in fact, amplify it in a Press interview. He said he felt that the situation about throwers – M.C.C. had not notified Warwickshire that they were considered to have any – was so serious that now it must be tackled from the top and each county invited to list those bowlers with suspect actions and to give an undertaking not to include them in representative cricket until such time as they corrected their actions.

The annual report added that the Committee was considering proposing action through the County Advisory Committee in the best interests of the game unless steps were taken very soon. At the season's end the Committee took some of their own. A sub-committee, which had been inquiring into the team's lack of success, deplored the fielding, with Horner an outstanding exception – though, surely, this department of the game was the captain's responsibility in conjunction with the chief coach – and recommended that pre-season training should be introduced. Both Hollies and Grove were engaged to coach during the

---

*The number of leg-side fielders to be limited to five, with no more than two behind the wicket; eighty-five overs in the first innings; bonus points for faster scoring in the first innings; boundaries standardized at seventy-five yards; and elimination of time-wasting were among the changes.

winter. It was also felt that there were too many young players on the staff so that there were too few opportunities for them, especially the young amateurs.

One of these youngsters, who had accepted an engagement on the nursery staff at the age of 15, was named Dennis Amiss, a product of Oldknow Road School, Birmingham, of whom 'Tiger' Smith said: 'This lad could reach great heights.' But there were others who had shown promise like Weeks, King, Thompson, Ratcliffe and Youll, who appeared almost to go back in development – if that is not a contradiction in terms – though the Committee agreed that the head coach's approach to the game was beyond praise. Nevertheless, it was decided to co-opt Messrs Edmund King, T. W. Durnell and M. J. K. Smith to the coaching and indoor school sub-committee and, with Dollery, to ask them to reconsider the Club's methods of finding and developing players, as well as other factors which might have a bearing on the lack of success.

All this had followed the August meeting on players' engagements when there was a general discussion on the Club's policy towards its playing staff after the chairman had said he agreed there were too many players, but that he would not recommend the release of any of them. The one thing everyone seemed agreed about was that the fielding was 'unbelievably bad' for a county side, but no clear feeling emerged at this time whether the policy should be to concentrate on finding and developing young players, which the Club had been trying to do for some time with disappointing results, or to try to secure the services of more mature cricketers.

This was not the only 'inquest' held during the summer. With what seemed to be another financial crisis looming ahead, a long, hard look was taken at Club policy in this field, too. It revealed a sharp cleavage of opinion between the Committee and the secretary, which, in a less flexible and less tolerant organisation, might well have resulted in a resignation or two. On the one hand, it was felt that the Club already had a magnificent ground and that some time a halt must be called to the spending of large capital sums which could bring only a limited return, especially in view of the overdraft (now nearing £30 000), and that the rating appeal might be lost, to say nothing of the spectre of such a calamity as the closing down of the Supporters' Association – the taxation and legal positions were delicate to a degree about this time.

Leslie Deakins, on the other hand, thought the Club's position stronger than it had ever been. A reduction of the overdraft by £5000 a year had been promised to the bank. Would not the Supporters' Association subsidise the Club to such an amount each year to sustain this? It was eventually decided to call a halt to further capital development until the financial situation was stabilised; to ask the Supporters'

Association to make a grant of £25 000 to the Club to put its finances on a sound basis and to eliminate the overdraft; and that the question of seeking an annual endowment, or grant, from the Association to cover maintenance and a possible rating increase should be deferred pending the result of the rating appeal.

The secretary, however, recorded his complete disagreement with these decisions, which he felt were neither warranted by the facts nor were in the best interests of the Club, either then or in the future. His view found some support at the end of the year from Edmund King who, commenting on the fact that the accounts showed a deficit of £2870 – the Club's share of the Test Match profits had, for the first time for many years, been credited to the income and expenditure account – said he felt that to meet an expenditure of £48 000, all but £2870, in a year as poor as 1958 and without calling on the Supporters' Association funds, was a clear indication of the Club's ability to pay its way under normal conditions.

Meanwhile, the Association, too, had been considering its position. They recommended that cash should not be transferred to the Club, but that payments should be made for capital developments. They, therefore, advised the transfer of £21 324, the balance outstanding on the Club's reconstruction and development programme. Creation of an endowment fund to cover maintenance costs with money provided by the Association might be fraught with many difficulties and, it was thought, should be approached with considerable care.

M. F. K. Fraser, the chairman, also felt that for the Association to finance a project rather than make a cash grant to the Club would prevent any suggestion that the Association might claim to influence Club policy, or even have a voice in its running. He reiterated that his committee's constant desire was to be of service to the Club without in the slightest degree interfering with the management or policy.

For deaths of cricketers and those associated with the game 1958 must have been one of the worst of all years. Warwickshire lost F. R. Foster, Captain Cowan and the Rev. E. F. Waddy; and over a wider field there were C. G. Macartney, C. P. Mead, George Gunn, D. R. Jardine, J. R. Mason, C. L. Townsend, Vernon Ransford and R. K. Nunes.

Foster's later years had been clouded by ill-health and unhappy incidents which are best forgotten. What will always be remembered as long as Warwickshire cricket is talked about will be those four electrifying years in which he led the county side, especially 1911 when they first tasted the sweets of Championship success. No one could take that away from him.

Because of ill-health, Captain Cowan had only recently resigned the honorary treasurership which he had held since 1942, and he had been elected to honorary life membership and a vice-president as some

recognition of his services to the game over fifty years, including leading the second eleven when it produced such players as Dollery, Hollies
and Ord.

The Rev. E. F. Waddy, who died at Evesham, was a link with great
Australians such as Victor Trumper, M. A. Noble and S. E. Gregory.
In 1904–5 he had headed the inter-State batting averages and his 308
for Melbourne against Sydney in 1904 was the highest score ever made
in Australian inter-university cricket. After he came to England in 1915
to become a master at Rugby, it was unfortunate that he could not play
more first-class cricket than he did, for he headed the county's averages
in 1921 and made 109 against Middlesex at Lord's, which must have
pleased him mightily.

Happily there were old Warwickshire cricketers still hale and hearty
and they now formed themselves into the Warwickshire Old County
Cricketers' Association, believed to be the first body of its kind in the
country. The idea was born between Hollies, Grove and Pritchard at a
social gathering and an inaugural meeting was held in November 1958.
It was calculated that, since the first County Championship match in
1894, 350 men had played first-class cricket for the county up to 1958,
and that about 190 of these would be eligible to join, though the whereabouts of many of them were not known.

However, there were about thirty present at the first meeting which
elected – who else? – J. Ernest Hill, then 91, as the first president;
Cyril Goodway as chairman; Grove as honorary fixtures secretary, and
J. M. A. Marshall as honorary treasurer. The first committee included
four former England players – S. F. Barnes, then 86; 'Tiger' Smith;
'Tom' Dollery, and Hollies. The membership soon rose to over 100 and
letters came from as far afield as India, South Africa, Australia, New
Zealand, Canada and America. The members chose a tie in the same
colours as the Club's, but in equal proportions of dark blue, gold and
silver, with a single silver crest of the Bear and Ragged Staff.

The Association's aims are to bring together, in and out of season,
in good fellowship and the true traditions of cricket, those who have
played first-class cricket for Warwickshire; to organise cricket matches,
outings and functions; and to do everything possible to foster interest
in, and love of, the game. All splendidly laudable ambitions, and all
achieved.

The first annual dinner was held in December the following year
when they were the guests of the Supporters' Association, whose new
chairman, Alderman Edgar Hiley (who had succeeded M. F. K. Fraser
on the latter's death in the summer of 1959), referred to the occasion
in a happy phrase – 'thanks for pleasures given' – and Canon Parsons
replied. Since then the presidency has changed each year, but Cyril
Goodway continued as chairman and honorary secretary, with his wife

helping him, and it became a cause dear to both their hearts. The Supporters' Association has also been their very good friend. There are now about 140 members.

That dinner had been held in the Pavilion Suite, the accounts of which, to 31 October 1958, showed a profit of £6014. To cover expenditure the Suite needed to be booked on approximately one-third of the times and it showed a reasonable profit if it was half booked. The work entailed in running the Suite and the increasing number of other social activities on the ground led to the appointment of Mr R. L. Walker as club superintendent, and he later became social manager as well.

Champagne from Cavaliers (1959)

THERE was probably some very hard thinking in many quarters during the winter of 1958–9, for it had become evident that the team's poor showing in the previous season and the consequent serious decline in public interest – as shown in the gate receipts – had led at least some people in authority to ask themselves for the first time whether too much emphasis was not being placed on building a super Test ground and too little on building a more successful team, without which no club can exist, no matter how magnificent and palatial a ground they have to play on.

Probably the first drop in membership figures had had more effect than anything else, for this was the first indication that even those most loyal of all supporters were perhaps less concerned with the amenities provided for them than with what was going on in the middle, and that if that was not worth watching then the surroundings were of comparatively little importance.

If any of them did think these things they did not trouble to express their views, except in the most telling way of all by not renewing their membership. Not one member at a crowded annual meeting said a word, and if anyone had done so the Committee could always have retorted that the Test Matches were the one certain way the Club had of making the sort of money needed to keep going, and that unless the ground was maintained in a condition to stage Tests, bang would go one of the main sources of income.

Alec Hastilow did, however, reassure those who might have feared that cement and concrete were being put before the flesh and blood of players by saying that the Committee felt that, having reached Test Match status, it was not necessary to spend all the Club's funds on ground development. 'We think it our duty', he said, 'to build up a Championship side and to spend money on cricket, to develop it throughout the county and to see that no promising player suffers from lack of adequate coaching – in fact, to make cricket at least as important an objective as the further development of the ground.'

Retrenchment, indeed, was the theme at the annual meeting, at which Lieut.-General Sir Oliver Leese was elected President in succession to the Earl of Warwick, who had had to relinquish the office because of ill-health. Sir Oliver, of course, was best known to the general public as the former Commander of the famous Eighth Army, but his interest in the game was almost lifelong, certainly dating back to the time when he played in the Eton eleven. Though his life had been devoted to soldiering, he had never lost his interest in the game and his world-wide travels in search of rare and exotic plants for his gardens at Worfield in Shropshire, enabled him to keep in touch with cricket on a wider international scale than any other previous holder of the office.

Alec Hastilow, who presided, said that each year hitherto a substantial amount had been set aside for development, but in the year under review this had not been possible, and it had been decided for the time being to curtail development expenditure and try to improve the liquidity of the balance sheet by building up a reasonable reserve – to which the new honorary treasurer, Edmund King, added the comment that while the Supporters' Association was the Club's fairy godmother the various jobs it financed did need maintaining.

Playing methods came in for more comment. Hastilow deplored the marked increase in throwing and dragging and said that if players could not adjust their actions to conform with the laws then they should be ostracised, for already youth was beginning to follow their unfortunate lead.

Peter Cranmer, who had also been elected an honorary life member, thought more risks could be taken and he agreed with a colleague that there was nothing wrong with the game, only with the players' approach to it. Strategy and tactics had improved enormously in recent years, though running between the wickets and taking quick singles had become somewhat lost arts.

'Tom' Dollery, too, had something to say to the point in May when he spoke at the Midlands Club Cricket Conference and wondered whether the three-day game was getting out of date. Perhaps crowds could be attracted back if they could be sure of seeing both sides bat on the first day. 'If the county captains', he said, 'would only attack the game in the summer in the same spirit as they did at dinners they attended during the winter, when they declared time and again that they would play brighter cricket, then we should have some wonderful cricket this summer.'

Even the old cricketers felt stirred to intervene in the slow play problem, their Association sending a good luck message to 'Mike' Smith: 'Best wishes to you and the whole staff for an enjoyable and successful season. May you all ensure that the ragged staff refers only to the Club's motif and that the Club's motive is purposeful and attractive cricket irrespective of results.'

Perhaps the players, too, spent the winter cogitating on their sins and omissions and they may even had read the annual report and the speeches. Whatever the cause, play in 1959 underwent a transformation the like of which is usually seen nowadays only on the stage of a theatre during the pantomime season. At the end, the annual report, so critical previously, now rhapsodised about 'every sign of a revival in the game . . . the best summer for 200 years . . . modern players caught some of the spirit of the Hambledon men . . . it was champagne cricket'. And even the M.C.C. was moved to write a letter to the President warmly congratulating him on the manner in which the Warwickshire XI under the captaincy of 'Mr Michael Smith' was playing cricket this season.

The cricket correspondent of *The Birmingham Mail*, Bill Wanklyn, hailed Warwickshire as the leaders of the drive to bring cricket back to life. In this, he wrote, they 'succeeded gloriously' and he gave three reasons for it: 1. The brilliant batting of M. J. K. Smith; 2. The first season of covered wickets; 3. A fine dry summer. The players, he said, had earned the title of 'The Cricketing Cavaliers'.

The season of 1959 saw no fewer than 337 centuries made in first-class cricket and 23 batsmen, the highest number ever, scored over 2000 runs. Far outstripping them all was the aforesaid Mr Michael Smith, who played sixty-seven innings, more than any other batsman, was eleven times not out, scored 3245 runs, more than half of them in boundaries – and he was the first man to make 3000 runs for ten years – had a highest innings of 200 not out and averaged 57·94, which put him easily at the top. He reached his 3000 runs by 21 August, passing on the way Wyatt's previous record season's total for a Warwickshire player of 2630 twenty years before. By only one day he missed beating the fastest 3000 aggregate held by Tom Hayward and Walter Hammond, and at 26 he was the youngest batsman ever to reach such a total, a record previously held by the great 'Ranji', who did it when he was 27.

Smith made eight centuries, six of them for Warwickshire and two of them before lunch, and he hit twenty-two sixes; but the man to whose head the champagne really went was Stewart, whose confidence had been in doubt, but who now ran riot in a manner which put him into the record books for all time. And Smith and Stewart were not the only ones who had things going for them, as they say today. By July no fewer than four of the county's batsmen, from No. one to No. seven, had made centuries; Horner had his best season ever; Cartwright reached 1000 runs for the first time; and Wolton celebrated his benefit year by hitting nineteen sixes.

Not much was seen of Gardner this season, however. He had wintered in South Africa and then suffered hand injuries. It was also felt that he 'would not fit so neatly into the quick-scoring pattern of the season', as *Wisden* tactfully put it, and Stewart was such a success as an opening bat, that Gardner played only nine innings, scoring 409 runs.

The bowlers, too, recovered something of their lost fire. No one took 100 wickets but Thompson, who had been on the verge of not being re-engaged, staged a comeback with ninety-three for 17·90, which took him to the head of the averages. Wheatley had ninety-one for 24·82 and Cartwright seventy-five, so that for the first time he fulfilled something of his potential as an all-rounder. Bridge, former captain of the Birmingham Schools XI, with much-needed off spin, took sixty-three wickets, and Bannister, though not yet back in full cry, forty, including all ten against the Combined Services.

Warwickshire rose meteorically to fourth place in the Championship table and would probably have been still higher but for losing their last two matches. At one point they shared first place with Gloucestershire, but it was Yorkshire who finally ended Surrey's fantastic run, clinching the title with an out-of-this-world innings against Sussex in which they scored 218 runs in 98 minutes.

Wisden, rather grudgingly, said that if Warwickshire had won the Championship they would have been flattered, but at least they congratulated the team on playing enterprising cricket. The Editor wrote:

For many years Warwickshire had been noted for their cautious methods. [This was certainly not true of Dollery's régime.] Their batsmen made defence the first principle and rarely departed from playing down the line of the ball no matter how perfect the pitch, or how easy the bowling. Last year under the captaincy of M. J. K. Smith, they discarded their safety-first ideas and decorated their cricket with a gay abandon. Their performances were worthy of the well-equipped new home they have built for themselves on their old site at Edgbaston. No longer did they play in front of empty terraces; even on the third day the crowds went to watch them with the certain knowledge that there would be enterprising cricket to enjoy.

From their first eight home games £2800 was received in gate money, more than the total income from this source for the whole of 1958; and by 28 August the receipts had passed £10 000, more than double the 1958 figure, though only just half the 1951 Championship year amount of £20 205. Cricket with a punch obviously paid.

The fun began very early in the season with Stewart hitting a century in 85 minutes against the Combined Services and going on to make 151, including five of the thirty-three sixes he was to hit during the summer, and nineteen fours, all in 145 minutes. In the second innings, however, he was bowled for a 'duck'. The Services caught it from all sides. Bannister, his back all the better for a winter's rest, bowled to such good effect that he took all their wickets for 41 runs, a feat which not only gained him the ball suitably mounted, but a 100-guinea cheque and a cup for the best bowling performance of the season. His full figures were:

O	M	R	W
23·3	11	41	10

Bannister was the third Warwickshire bowler to take all ten wickets, Howell and Hollies having preceded him; but even this feat did not get him into the team for the next match against Gloucestershire, Thompson and Wheatley, who had been bowling consistently well, being preferred.

Wolton's benefit match against Surrey proved a most exciting game in which there were two declarations. Ken Barrington hit two fine centuries, 186 and 118 not out; 'Mike' Smith, 130, Horner, 98 not out, and Cartwright two half-centuries, the beneficiary, no doubt, being reasonably content with a modest 49 and 2. Only nineteen wickets fell in the match in which 1159 runs were scored, Warwickshire making the 234 they needed in 155 minutes. Townsend made the winning hit, a six off Laker into the members' pavilion. It was a challenge flung down and boldly taken up.

Even so, this is probably one of the matches E. M. Wellings had in mind when he suggested that more than 10 per cent of all the points gained in the County Championship this season had been won as a result of generous declarations, and he suggested that these contrived games were not good for English cricket. He calculated that Warwickshire had benefited from them by thirty-six points and Gloucestershire by thirty. Not good or otherwise, there was no doubt that the crowds preferred a result to a draw any day.

Smith followed in the footsteps of many Warwickshire players in playing many of his best innings away from home. At Stroud, for instance, when Warwickshire wanted 318, he got most of them off his own bat, scoring 182 not out in four hours, with five sixes and twenty-eight fours, Warwickshire bringing off a remarkable win by four wickets. He did come home, however, for his next big innings – 184 not out against Leicestershire, though it was not quite as brilliant as the one he played at Stroud. He followed with 72 and 200 against Worcestershire, also at Edgbaston, though the visitors took the only points there were in the match for the first innings lead. Smith's double century was scored out of 300 and an indication of how he monopolised the scoring is shown by the fact that the next highest scores were 60 and 10. He did not hit a six this time, but he had thirty-two fours, his last four scoring strokes all being boundaries.

The other Smith, Alan, playing his first match of the season against Scotland, and leading the side, declared when 83 behind, but the Scots accepted the challenge, set Warwickshire to get 210 to win and got them out with 53 runs to spare. Stewart had had rather a lean time after his first explosion, but found his fireworks again at Neath with 155 and a partnership with Horner, 126, for the third wicket of 175. He followed this with 156 against Essex at Coventry, hitting twenty fours and then at Blackpool he provided his own illuminations with a pyrotechnical display that is never likely to be equalled.

Not only did he hit a century in each innings, 155 and 125 – and hit is the word – but he set up a new record for first-class matches with seventeen sixes. In the first innings, driving with incredible ferocity, he got ten of them, one short of the record for a single innings. At one point eleven consecutive scoring strokes produced these figures: 4 4 4 6 4 1 6 1 4 1 4 – a total of 39 runs. Five of the ten sixes came off Hilton, who took nought for 60, but they were well spaced out. The second innings had this sequence – 4 6 6 4 2 1 1 6 1 2 6 6 – 45 in twelve strokes. In two overs from Dyson he hit 16 and 18, 34 runs. There were also such minor matters as twelve fours in each innings.

After all this the match was drawn, Lancashire even taking four points for first innings lead – 389 for six declared, to 322. Lancashire declared again in the second innings at 222 for four and Warwickshire was only 32 short of victory when the game ended with their total at 247 for six. When Lancashire came to Edgbaston Stewart helped himself to another hundred runs in innings of 70 and 32, but this was Thompson's match – four for 10 in fifteen overs at the start and seven for 52. And Smith took his forty-third catch of the season, thus setting up another Warwickshire fielding record.

Smith even shook off his Test Match cares, playing in two of the five matches against India, although he was not called on until the fourth at Manchester, by which time the rubber had been decided. This time he batted at No. four and scored 100 exactly without giving a chance. When he had made 50 in the last Test at The Oval he completed his 3000 runs and he just missed another hundred – 98 – in the only innings England had. When they came to Edgbaston he made 52 and 43, hitting four consecutive balls from Surendranath to the boundary, though the latter had his revenge later at Scarborough when he twice got Smith, playing for T. N. Pearce's XI, leg before for 6 and 2. Smith also had a fine Gentlemen v. Players match, making 79 and 166, the highest score in the series since the war. One hundred of the runs in his second innings came from boundaries. Finally he made 77 and 25 for The Rest against the Champion County. His *annus mirabilis*, indeed.

As the second eleven led by Dollery won the Minor Counties Championship and were fifth in the newly constituted Second Elevens Championship – the players received silver salver mementoes – it was the best season from the playing point of view for years. By way of celebration, the Club also presented a Championship pennant to the Minor Counties competition, and Douglas Turner, the former honorary treasurer, gave a dinner at which there were over 200 guests.

Nevertheless, if anyone had tended to get too proud of the county's achievements some statistics produced by Ted Hampton should have had a sobering effect. They showed that, in the sixty-five years' history of the Club so far, only eighteen batsmen had scored more than 10 000 runs and only fourteen bowlers had taken over 500 wickets, from which the inference could be drawn, not unfairly, one would suggest, that Warwickshire had produced few players of really outstanding ability, but many of mediocre attainments. Doubtless, however, similar figures could be produced for most other counties.

All the same, the improved playing record produced much better gate receipts, and an increase in total revenue from £48 088 to £52 829; but there was still an overall loss on the season of £3258, largely due to the stiff increase to £7548 in rates and an assessment raised from £990 to £3200. The Club was thus being penalised for trying to improve its amenities. The rating appeal had resulted more or less in stalemate; the Club failed to get the figure of £3200 reduced and the Valuation Officer failed to get an amount of £4250 reinstated. Meanwhile, there was a rate demand from the city for £7548 up to April 1959, which, however, was met by a generous loan from the Supporters' Association.

So on 2 November 1959, a special general meeting of members was called to consider an increase in subscriptions for the first time since 1945 – from £2 2s to £3 3s for ordinary members; from £1 10s to £2 2s for country and family members; those for old age pensioners remaining at £2 2s. These amounts still compared favourably with those paid by members of the Surrey club (£5 5s), Lancashire (£4 4s), Notts and Yorkshire (£3 3s), with Lord's in a class of its own at £6 6s. The increases, it was estimated, would bring in an income for Warwickshire of £9000.

As usual where increases in anything are concerned, there were two schools of thought about the proposals. There were those who took the view that the subscription had remained too low for far too long and that the present increases could have been avoided had earlier opportunities been taken at more favourable moments. The first could have been in 1951 after the team had won the County Championship when, it was argued, an increase from the then figure of two guineas could have been increased to three, and would willingly have been accepted because money was plentiful and people like to be associated with a club at the top. This school of thought also contended that a second increase from, say, three guineas to four, could probably have been made palatable in 1957 when Test cricket returned to Edgbaston after an interval of twenty-eight years and members had the right of free admission to the ground and the pavilion for Test cricket. By not taking the plunge then, so the argument went, the Club lost in revenue from subscriptions over a period of ten years something in the order of £100 000.

The other school of thought, which had prevailed, was that it was preferable to have a large number of members at a low rate of subscription than a smaller one at a higher rate, and that low subscriptions would encourage popular-side supporters to become members. Supporters of this view could point to the fact that membership income rose steadily from £11 041 in 1948 to £23 079 in 1956, though it had declined a little in the last three years. Moreover, during the period concerned, some substantial items of income never figured in the Income and Expenditure Account, but were credited directly to the Development Fund. Had they been included, there would have been a substantial surplus from 1948 on.

Whichever school of thought was correct, it was obvious that the time had come when an increase could no longer be avoided.

For the first time General Sir Oliver Leese presided at a Club meeting and Edmund King, who had succeeded Douglas Turner as honorary treasurer, apologised for having to touch members' pockets in his first year, but said that, apart from a 5s increase in country membership and transferable tickets in 1952, it was remarkable in a period of inflation that subscriptions had remained at the same level since 1945. In the postwar period expenditure had risen from £14 000 in 1946 to £52 000 in 1959 and despite success in playing and in the weather, income had not kept pace. The liquid reserve of £2500, which was all the Club held, was valueless in the event of a real emergency.

For once, members raised a variety of questions on junior and country memberships, one favouring a return to more rural surroundings instead of continuous development to fit the ground for Tests; returns from the Pavilion Suite; catering criticisms; season tickets for the popular side; and the plight of the pensioners. One of the latter, however, actually spoke up for the Committee, pointing out that the subscription in 1900 was £1 so that the increase had been modest over the years.

After Edmund King had said that the Pavilion Suite brought in £7000 a year and that the membership in 1946 was 600 and now totalled 11 300, the increases were approved by 117 votes to 41. The member who moaned about continuous development had his answer in a heartfelt comment in the annual report – and there are no prizes for

413

naming the author. He expressed the view that the Committee was 'fortunate to enjoy the services of an administrative staff which can survive the rigours of winter in such premises. They do so in the belief that this structure will one day be demolished to make way for a pavilion worthy of the ground and, indeed, of the county of Warwick.'

Some of the ladies who had taken up membership had now intimated that, as there was no Test Match this year, they wished to revert to transferable tickets. There was nothing in the Club rules to prevent this, or from stopping them from taking up membership again in 1960 when the South Africans would be here, or in 1961 for the Australians, but it was pointed out that changes of this kind would cause chaos in office records, as well as making a mockery of the rules, so the secretary sent out letters stressing that persons sacrificing membership might not always be able, very readily, to secure re-election.

Following some teething troubles as to who was responsible for what, there was an exchange of views between the Club and the Supporters' Association which resulted in a new code being drawn up governing their relationship. This laid it down that the Association continued as a separate entity from the Club, but formed and run for its benefit; that the Club would not interfere in any way in running the Supporters' Association, but would work in close collaboration with it in disposing of the latter's funds; the Association appreciated it had an obligation to underwrite losses, if they occurred, on buildings given to the county Club; and undertook to provide capital, as circumstances permitted, for investment in a fund to endow the properties of the Club. The income from this would be at the absolute disposal of the Club, which agreed that the Association should help cricket in the county generally, assist youth cricket and schools, assist former players who might suffer misfortune, and make gifts for prizes and other incentives.

By this time the Association had a membership of 200 000 and was so badly in need of permanent administration offices that the list of building priorities was amended to give first place to these, preferably in the Pavilion (east wing).

Early in the season Dollery had intimated that he did not wish to be nominated again as an England selector, as he felt the duties took up too much time which he would prefer to devote to his work for the Club, which he did with very good results; but at the end of the season he indicated that he did not seek a further engagement as coach because of the demands made on his wife by his absences from the hotel he tenanted. Eventually, however, he was persuaded to carry on for another year, from April 1960.

In April, Warwickshire had tried out a white ball – first thought of years before – to overcome objections from batsmen who complained of the dark, gloomy background of the terraces opposite the pavilion.

The matter had been raised the previous season in a book by Peter Richardson, the Worcestershire player, who criticised the sightscreen arrangements. It was stated, however, that to provide alternative screens would mean a loss of up to £3000 in bookings in a five-day Test because they would block out seats for 800 spectators. It was then decided that a screen should be provided for all matches and the ground and buildings sub-committee, of which Cyril Goodway was now chairman, was asked to examine the various types available and recommend one. There were second thoughts about this, however, and a resolution was proposed reversing the original decision. The voting was nine–nine, and the chairman gave his casting vote against the resolution and in favour of sightscreens largely because he felt it incumbent upon him to support the Club captain, so no more was heard of the white ball, though the screens were not forgotten.

Various deaths during the year – of M. F. K. Fraser, chairman of the Supporters' Association and an ardent worker for the Club, especially in the publicity field; and of Percy G. Whitehouse, a former player and chairman of the ground committee from 1957 to 1959 and a Committee member for seventeen years, who is commemorated by the score indicator board on the pavilion – created vacancies on the Committee, which were filled by the election of Edgar Hiley and A. K. Jackson, a former amateur fast bowler who had played for the county.

A decision which was to affect the status of every cricketer came before an M.C.C. conference. That body issued a memorandum on the subject of amateurs and professionals and Warwickshire decided that its delegate should support the removal of all distinction in the classification of players and that all should be known as cricketers. The proposal, however, was defeated by fifteen votes to two. The general consensus of opinion at the conference favoured retention of amateur status, with a little more license allowed on reasonable expenses, but with the introduction of a top limit. The matter was then referred back to a special sub-committee, but it was not long before it was raised again.

Warwickshire nearly, but not quite, secured the services of Colin Milburn, who, with another Durham cricketer, R. Cole, came for a trial. An offer was made to Milburn, but he replied saying that he wished to complete a student teacher's course and to link this profession to his cricket in future. He later went to Northants, who, it was said rather surprisingly, could offer him better opportunities to combine the two. One would have thought Birmingham could have offered better facilities in both fields.

After all the financial worries of the season, the question of whether male spectators should be allowed to remove their shirts on hot days seemed rather academic, especially when it was pointed out that it was seldom warm enough for the question to arise. Perhaps this was the first intrusion of the permissive society into the purlieus of Edgbaston.

During the winter 'Mike' Smith went to the West Indies with an M.C.C. team captained by Peter May, who, however, was taken ill and had to return home, Cowdrey taking over the captaincy. It was, literally, a riot of a tour, with bumpers being bowled and bottles thrown in about equal proportions. To *Wisden*, Smith was 'the enigma of the tour. Quite often he was dismissed early and the West Indies bowlers came to realise he was susceptible to the well pitched-up ball, either yorker or half-volley, as soon as he went in. If able to settle down, he was extremely difficult to dislodge as he varied his game with long defensive spells and sudden bursts of free scoring. Trinidad was his favourite ground, for he hit a century there in the second Test and missed another by only 4 in the fifth.'

He played in all five Tests, scoring 308 runs, with a highest innings of 108, for an average of 34·22. In all matches he made 649 runs, average 38·17. His Test scores were 39, 108 and 12, 0 and 10, 0 and 23, 20 and 96. Both ducks were 'b Hall', hence, no doubt, *Wisden*'s comment.

The Sad Season
(1960)

If 1959 had been the champagne season, 1960 was, in *Wisden's* phrase, largely 'the sad season'. Not only did rain spoil many matches, but there was also much dull play, including during the Test Match with South Africa at Edgbaston, factors which led to an alarming decline in attendances. It was also a season of bitter controversies – alleged throwing by Griffin, the South African fast bowler, in a disappointing tour; the dropping of Syd Buller as a Test umpire, one of the most deplorable happenings in post-war cricket in this country; Graveney's dispute with Gloucestershire, which led to him coming to the Midlands; and Laker's book, which for a time cost him his M.C.C. and Surrey privileges, though, happily, they were restored.

Wisden disclosed that while, in 1947, attendances, exclusive of members, at county games throughout the country were 2 300 910, the figure in 1960 fell to less than half that number, 1 046 104. It was a decrease of 323 569 compared with even the previous year. Gates were down on every day of the week, with Saturday showing the biggest decline, from which it was argued that it was dull play rather than other factors which kept people away, though this was surely to ignore the fact that there are far more rival attractions – and distractions – on Saturdays than on other days. Monday showed the next worse fall in attendances.

The editorial in *Wisden* said bluntly what many people had been saying for years – that there was nothing wrong with cricket that the county captains could not put right. At least one of them, 'Tom' Dollery, had told them that a long time ago.

It is useless them going to Lord's in the winter [the Editor noted], and agreeing that it is essential for every county to adopt a dynamic attitude to the game from the first ball to the last, whether batting, bowling or fielding, and then deliberately ignoring the agreement on the field. And I am afraid this accusation can be levelled against some county captains ... Some county committees, too, should be more realistic and not pick players on the form shown by the weekly averages, but by their actual deeds on the field.

Wisden instanced what an outstanding player can do for a side by citing the case of Dexter and Sussex, whose membership went up by 1200 and the gates by £2000 in his first season as captain. 'I did not see anyone standing close to the bat when Dexter was in full cry,' the Editor commented. 'The plodders and the prodders have allowed the fielders to creep nearer; they soon disperse to safer regions when a genuine batsman appears. There are too many county professionals who reckon they have done a satisfactory job if they scrape 1200 runs in a season for an average of about 30. They pay no heed to the way they make their runs and it is time they were clearly told that unless they are prepared to think of making the occasional hundred in two and one-half to three hours their services will no longer be required. The decline in professional batsmanship since the war is one of the main reasons for the alarming fall in public support.'

Every county club had this kind of so-called batsman and it really was surprising that not one of them had sacked a player in mid-season and announced why they were doing it. Occasionally they dropped players from their sides, or did not re-engage them at the end of the season, but none of them dared to grasp a nettle which might have had more effect than all the special committees and inquiries into the state of the game and all the law-changing. The players had done more than anyone to cash in on the game and they could hardly have complained if the rules of commerce had been made to apply – do your job efficiently or go elsewhere. But we still liked to think of cricket as a gentleman's game, embodying all that is best in the British tradition, instead of recognising that it was becoming increasingly big business, with all the disillusionment that brought.

Wisden's words were echoed in Warwickshire's annual report which was prefaced by a photograph of an empty litter bin against a background of empty seats with the following caption: 'Empty seats – empty litter baskets – empty coffers at the season's end – a sad reflection on a disappointing season, emphasis on the financial risk in cricket.' The Committee, the report said, was very sorry to see teams and individual players putting 'the prize above the game'. Many of the seats remained empty, incidentally, but the litter bins did not and Mr Walker, the ground superintendent, and his staff, had the job of removing three and a half tons of litter after the Test Match alone at a cost of £105, the sort of item of expenditure of which the public never thinks.

The Warwickshire eleven, the report contended, made regular and conscientious efforts to play entertaining and purposeful cricket, but they were often thwarted for one reason or another. 'On the individual side it has long been apparent that the highest rewards of the game go to players who develop the Test Match temperament and approach, and this has a disastrous effect on the county game for they regularly use it as a practice ground to prove their suitability for the grim struggle that has been Test Match cricket in recent years. It is becoming increasingly clear that variations should be made in the laws and playing conditions governing the two classes of cricket, so that county cricket may not be used in this way, but remain a separate game in its own right.'

The outcome of all this, as might have been expected, was yet another committee set up by the M.C.C. to examine the state of the game – the fourth such inquiry in the last twenty-five years, the others being the Findlay Commission in 1937, Sir Stanley Jackson's inquiry in 1944 and H. S. Altham's in 1957. Alec Hastilow was appointed a member of it, as well as of the pilot committee, which sifted the ideas.

One of the main sources of the complaints about slow play was the first Test with South Africa at Edgbaston in June, which led to the old cry going up again: 'Does Birmingham want Test cricket?' By this time the word 'apartheid' had become part of the English language and the Club had had warning as early as mid-January that Birmingham Young Socialists would picket the Test if there was any colour discrimination in the selection of South Africa's team to come on the tour.

A Socialist member of the Club, Councillor A. E. Benton, said he would come and do likewise, though at the annual meeting Alec Hastilow had hoped there would not be any boycott, or untoward incident. It was evident to straight-thinking people, he thought, that sport was not a medium through which to express political views, or racial prejudice.

What in fact happened was that a silent protest was staged by about forty anti-apartheid supporters before the match began. Police with dogs were on duty, but they were not required. Leslie Deakins was satisfied that the political boycott, if it could be called that, was not sufficiently strong to affect the attendance at the match. Nor did he consider the weather, unkind though it was, as a serious cause of the comparative lack of interest in the game. He thought, too, that except perhaps for the first day, the cricket was full of interest, though there were some who would not have agreed with him. What, then, was the trouble? Was it too soon after Whitsuntide, or did the dreary play of the first two days scare people off? 'It all makes one wonder whether Birmingham really wants Test cricket,' Leslie Deakins reflected sadly.

The answer to that, surely, was that Birmingham certainly did not want Test cricket in which only 175 runs were scored on the first day, 231 on the second, 161 on the third, 234 on the fourth and 89 on the fifth, even allowing for interruptions caused by the weather. Canon

Parsons, when asked for his views, could not trust himself to speak and, allowing for the strength of his feelings on slow play, perhaps this was the most graphic comment of all.

It is also true that the South African team of those days, unlike that of more recent years (if we could have been allowed to watch it), contained no more than four players of world rank in McGlew, Goddard, Adcock and Tayfield and, on the whole, Midland people had firmly shown in the past that only the best would bring them to the ground.

It was England, however, who were responsible for the first day's dullness – 175 for three in five and a half hours' play. Of those Dexter made 52, including eight fours, the one bright flower of compensation. On the second day the remaining seven wickets fell for 117, Tayfield bowling unchanged from 11.30 a.m. until England were all out at 3.10 p.m. for 292. 'Mike' Smith, going in at No. five, made 54 this time, Subba Row also getting a half-century.

Thanks largely to Trueman and Statham, South Africa were then dismissed for 186, only Waite, their captain, offering much resistance. For many spectators the outstanding recollection of this day's play, if not of the match, was the catch which Statham took to get rid of McLean. The batsman hooked a full toss high towards long leg and Statham raced forty yards from the leg trap and took the ball as it came from behind him over his head.

England's second innings was a feeble affair of 203, to which Smith contributed 28; but playing against Trueman and Statham, a total of 309 was beyond the tourists, and they were 100 runs short. In five days both sides made only 890 runs at 2·2 runs an over, which hardly suggested that the cricket was full of interest and incident, though admittedly the games in which most runs are scored are not always the most gripping.

The attendance on the first day was only 6775; on the second it rose to 8385; and on the third to 12 373; but after that it slumped to 5984; and on the last day, though this was to be expected, to 2074 – a total of 43 137. Receipts were £16 664, less even than those for New Zealand (£18 936 in 1958), and very much less than the £31 568 for the West Indies in 1957.

There was a second anti-apartheid demonstration outside St Ambrose's Church near the ground on the Sunday when the Rev. Nicholas Stacey, one-time Olympic athlete and then chaplain to the Bishop of Birmingham, declined to preach, though one would have thought that by doing so he missed an opportunity of putting over the Christian message and making his protest.

Griffin bowled throughout the Edgbaston Test, during which he celebrated his 21st birthday, without complaint, but also without much venom; and at the end of the match Mr G. W. A. Chubb, President of the South African Cricket Federation, after discussing the matter with members of the team, telephoned his Association and asked for an additional bowler to be sent, but the request was turned down. In the second Test at Lord's, Griffin did the hat trick, 'Mike' Smith, who had then made 99, being one of his victims. In his one innings in the third Test Smith got a 'duck'; he did not play in the fourth, and made nought and 11 in the fifth.

He had another run-less first innings against the tourists when they came again to Edgbaston in August and drew comfortably, but he made 29 in the second innings. On the whole, he had a very good season, scoring more runs, 2551, than any other batsman in the country for the second season in succession and being third in the first-class averages. *Wisden* for 1960 had honoured him as one of the Five Cricketers of the Year in a portrait by J. M. Solan, by then the cricket correspondent of *The Birmingham Post*, who wrote that he 'often turned what looked like defeat for Warwickshire into victory'. Solan thought it 'fair to say that no other county captain gave quite the same personal inspiration to his side', though on the field he was the least demonstrative of leaders. Quiet consultations were usually the only obvious sign that he was in charge.

Neither Smith's batting this season, nor that of the four other members of the Warwickshire side who got their 1000 runs, was reflected in the team's performances as a whole, though *Wisden* said 'there were few more attractive sides to watch in the country'. In no fewer than nine of their drawn matches they led on the first innings, and in two of these they lost; but their reputation for sprightly batting may have cost them dear, for, as *Wisden* suggested, one reason for their decline to fifteenth place in the table might have been that opposing sides were disinclined to set them accessible totals to get in the second innings – and several times they fell just short of victory when trying to get runs against time.

The bowling was disappointing, even though for the first time since 1951 two bowlers each took over 100 wickets in Championship matches alone – Bannister exactly 100 for 21·48 runs and Wheatley 109 for 24·86. Wheatley was the first amateur bowler to take more than 100 wickets in a season for the county alone since the days of Frank Foster, and his departure at the end of the season on taking up a business appointment in South Wales, where he later played very successfully for Glamorgan, was much regretted.

Unfortunately Bannister and Wheatley had little support. Thompson, Cartwright and Bridge, who between them in 1959 took over 230 wickets, now had fewer than ninety. Thompson and Cartwright were both unlucky with injuries, but Bridge was in poor form and could not keep his place in the side. It was the lack of support for the seam bowlers that prompted James McDowall to ask in Committee if there was any special reason for the falling-off, after a period of success, of so many of the Club's slow bowlers – Weeks, King, Youll, Hill and now Bridge – but no explanation was forthcoming except that there was a shortage of good quality slow left-arm bowlers in the country and that even England often had to take the field without one. It was not a very satisfactory answer and so far as I am aware none has ever been given. Hill gave up the first-class game this season and went into business.

It was these and other failures which gave rise to the legend that 'Mike' Smith did not trust, or could not handle, slow bowlers, but he hardly had them to handle, except for Eric Hollies in his last season. The criticism was similar to that made of him that he was too much an on-side player. The trouble was, as he once told John Arlott, that he was really an off-side player who had been born into an on-side age.

A notable new record went into the Warwickshire statistics this season – a first-wicket stand of 377 by Horner and Ibadulla at The Oval. It was not only a county record, beating the 333 made by Kinneir and J. F. Byrne in 1905, but the highest unbroken partnership in first-class cricket and a record for The Oval ground, previously set up by Washbrook and Place for Lancashire seventeen years before.

Each batsman also had the best innings of his career – Horner 203 with twenty-eight fours, and Ibadulla, a much improved batsman who, since Gardner's decline, often opened the innings, making 170, with twenty-one fours. They batted for five hours twenty minutes against a Surrey attack consisting of the two Bedsers – Alec had 87 runs scored off him without taking a wicket – Sydenham, Allom, and Lock, who also had nought for plenty – 82.

Warwickshire declared at 377, but even then Surrey got first innings lead before the rain came. John Edrich made his highest score up to then, 154. Horner and Ibadulla followed this with stands of 174 against Somerset at Edgbaston and 70s against Notts and Gloucestershire. Amiss made his County Championship début in the Notts match, being run out for none in the first innings, but making 36 in the second. Altogether he scored 135 runs in nine innings.

Townsend got both runs and wickets in his benefit against Northants – three for 17 to break the back of their batting and then 26 – and in the same match 'Mike' Smith took his first wicket in first-class cricket. He always cherished a secret passion to be a bowler and nearly always at the end of the season appeared under *Also bowled* in the averages.

A Birmingham-born left-hand batsman, B. E. Fletcher, released from National Service, played several good innings, including a maiden century of 102 not out against Oxford. With Spooner having largely dropped out of cricket in favour of business, Fletcher kept wicket at times until Alan Smith, down from Oxford, took his place. He had regularly kept wicket there, though he preferred to bowl, which he did very usefully at times. *Wisden* commented that he did not have much luck with his batting – 424 runs with a highest score of 80 – 'but his wicketkeeping was beyond reproach and from him sprang the keen spirit, attention to fielding and general efficiency of the side' when 'Mike' Smith was absent on Test duties.

Both of them played for the Gentlemen against the Players, A.C. keeping wicket, under Cowdrey's captaincy. He had only one innings in which he made 5, while M.J.K. got 17 and 28 not out.

There had been thirty-two matches in the County Championship, each county meeting the others twice, and for the first time for twenty-five years a match, with Derbyshire, was played at Nuneaton, the County Club later joining the Griff and Coton Sports and Social Club, on whose ground it was played, in making a gift of a silver bowl to the Borough of Nuneaton to commemorate the return of first-class cricket to the town.

At Edgbaston provision was made for a sightscreen on the North side of the ground, about which there had been complaints. It was 48 feet long and 15 feet high, with 80 yards of track, costing £2000, and obscured nearly 800 seats at a Test Match. Another notable change on the ground was the departure of the old clock on the pavilion, which, after more than fifty years' service, was replaced by an electric one. The original, appropriately, was given to the Warwick Cricket Club, on whose ground had played Warwickshire Gentlemen, forerunners in an amateur sense of the County Club.

As a result of the discussions with the Supporters' Association, which was now paying £4000 a week – 30 per cent of the weekly stake money of £13 500 – in betting duty to the Commissioners of Customs and Excise, it had been decided that there should be three trustees from each organisation for the Endowment Fund. It was also agreed that there would have to be complete unanimity before action could be taken; that the total amount disbursed to clubs within the county could be increased from £2000 to £5000 in any one year; and that the approval of the Club's Committee must be obtained before gifts for prizes and other incentives were made to the playing staff.

David Blakemore, who had married Miss Crook, now left his post with the Club to become secretary of the Association, a departure to which the Club reluctantly consented; and a former player, George Paine, joined the Association's committee in succession to Councillor Richardson, one of the founder members, who had resigned because of ill-health. A report on constructional development now listed no fewer than twelve projects completed, or introduced, with the aid of the Association, and half a dozen others in the 'proceeding' category.

To compensate players for possible loss of pension rights through playing cricket instead of going into business, the Club now introduced an insurance scheme, and other benefits were increased – the appearance awards from £2 to £4 per player per match and the win awards from £7 10s for one-to-five wins, £10 for six-to-ten, and £12 10s for eleven wins and upwards.

Mr James Parsons, F.C.A., the Club's honorary auditor, retiring after sixty years' association with the Club, was elected a vice-president, and the Club found a valuable adviser in Hubert Bewlay, a friend of Edmund King and an expert on rating. He was appointed honorary rating consultant, a post in which he was of great help not only to Warwickshire but to many other county clubs and the game at large.

The Old Cricketers' Association, whose president this year was S. F. Barnes, played a match in July which produced a notable innings. It was against Solihull School, which was celebrating its quater-centenary, and five old county players, whose combined ages came to 265 years – Canon Parsons, now 70, D. L. Clugston, Peter Cranmer, George Paine and J. J. Hossell – turned out for the Association. And the top scorer in age was top scorer in the match, Canon Parsons making 65 runs in 43 minutes. He hit four straight sixes and a number of drives which left schoolboy hands tingling – when they could move quickly enough to reach them. What a pity they could not have seen Barnes bowl as well. At the Association's annual dinner that year Lieut.-General Sir Oliver Leese was able to greet five former county captains – Wyatt, Cranmer, Dollery, Maudsley and Hollies.

Stewart had his first tour abroad during the winter, visiting New Zealand in a side led by D. R. W. Silk, and averaging nearly 40 in the first-class games, while in the spring of 1961 Alan Smith went to the West Indies with E. W. Swanton's XI and had a successful tour both as batsman and wicketkeeper.

Australia Again
(1961)

AFTER a lapse of over fifty years Australia again played a Test Match at Edgbaston, their visit setting up a new financial record for the ground. Two months before the game took place in June, every ticket for the third day, Saturday, had been sold and the receipts that day totalled £13 096. Police even had to ask people to go away, and this despite the fact that the weather was cold, windy and showery – there was rain on three of the five days – which seemed to suggest that it is not primarily poor weather which keeps people away from Test Matches. The game was drawn, so England maintained their record of never having been beaten at Edgbaston, a good argument, one would have thought, for allocating more Tests to the ground.

Australia, led by Richie Benaud, won the series and retained the 'Ashes'. There had been much speculation about who would succeed May as England's captain, but M. J. K. Smith's name was not mentioned among the possible candidates. He played in only one match, at Edgbaston, and could scarcely have fared worse. In the first innings he went in sixth and without scoring he was bowled by Mackay, who took three wickets in four balls and was largely responsible for England being dismissed for so poor a total as 195, of which Subba Row made 59.

Then Australia's batsmen, especially Harvey, who hit a superb 114, took apart an England attack consisting of no less bowlers than Statham, Trueman and Illingworth, each of whom had more than 100 runs scored off him. Australia were able to declare at 516 for nine wickets. Fortunately, when England batted again, Dexter was at his punishing best, hitting a splendid 180, while Subba Row did even better than in the first innings with 112. Smith did not get the chance to retrieve himself, being 1 not out when the game came to an end with England's score 401 for four.

The total attendance, including members, was 83 000, compared with the 91 000 who had come to see the West Indies. True, that match had been played in five days of sunshine, but there was a clear indication that what the Birmingham public wanted was flashing bats, which they certainly got from Harvey and Dexter. The gross receipts, £38 482, were a record for Edgbaston and the profit was second only to that from the Lord's game. Among the spectators were those four grand old men of English cricket – Barnes 89, Rhodes 84, and 'Tiger' Smith and Woolley 75 – and this may well have been the last time they were all seen together at a Test Match.

Two temporary stands had been erected to provide 1000 additional seats for the game and the Australians were loud in their praises of the ground on which in the preceding five years nearly £200 000 had been spent. *Wisden*, too, was complimentary: 'The Warwickshire officials and their Supporters' Association deserved the highest praise for the excellent conditions provided for the players, spectators and commentators.' It was not surprising, therefore, that Leslie Deakins regarded it as a setback, even if a minor one, when Headingley was raised to the same status as a Test ground as Lord's and The Oval, the effect being that Edgbaston in future would get six Tests instead of seven over ten years.

Since returning to Test status in 1957 Warwickshire had paid over to the Test Pool more than Yorkshire – £36 631, compared with £29 443, an average of £12 201 to £9811 in Warwickshire's favour. The Club's annual report found the decision difficult to understand, particularly as it was supposedly made on financial grounds, though it seemed much more likely to be to avoid upsetting the powerful Yorkshire club, whose proposal for seven Tests of three days each Warwickshire decided to support. They thought the idea would bring better returns and deprive counties of their best players for only twenty-one days instead of twenty-five.

By a nice stroke of irony, M. J. K. Smith, who had signed a new three-year agreement, under which he was to be known as assistant secretary, was graciously permitted to play an innings of 53 against the Australians when they returned to Edgbaston in August. He and Benaud did their best to get a result, but there were only three hours' play on the last day. Cartwright nearly emulated Gardner's performance in taking a century off their bowling – he made 93 – and Bannister had 66 in a Warwickshire total of 251; but again it was Harvey who took the eye, this time with 115 not out, he and Simpson, 132 not out, sharing in a partnership of 202 in two and a half hours. Horner made a nice 77 in Warwickshire's second innings, but there was no getting beyond a draw. 'Mike' Smith played against the tourists twice more, scoring 21 and 90 for the Gentlemen at Lord's and 2 and 30 for T. N. Pearce's XI in the Scarborough Festival, all of which went to swell his aggregate for the season to 2587. His average of 41·72 put him tenth in the national list.

He began the season with 145 against Essex (who arrived the day before to have net practice before the start, something even Leslie Deakins could not recall happening in thirty years); then he made 12 and 90 not out against Sussex, 83 and 57 against Gloucestershire, 93 and 82 against Somerset, 41 and 9 against Sussex again, and 27 and 40 against Leicestershire – a total of 678 runs which gave him an average of 60·70.

The Somerset game was an amazing affair. Bill Alley, their Australian, scored 221 not out in the second innings and yet Somerset finished the losing side by 47 runs. In under four hours Alley hit six sixes and thirty-one fours, the 221 being made out of 341 after Somerset had been asked to get 389 to win.

With five batsmen getting over 1000 runs – Alan Smith improving to 864 and Stewart getting back to some extent to his six-hitting ways – Warwickshire made lots of runs, even though Ibadulla fell away badly to an aggregate of only 675. Cartwright, with 1670 runs, seventy-seven wickets and eighteen catches, established himself as one of the best all-rounders in the country, but perhaps the most startling development was the form of Bridge.

From taking thirty-four wickets at a cost of 40·47 runs each in 1960, he now became the first spin bowler in the country to take 100 wickets and finished with 121 for 22·75. His success was saddened, however, by the death of his father, who came to see him play only a few days before. Thompson and Bannister, too, were back to something like their old form, the latter bowling more overs – 1197·3 – than any seam bowler had ever done for Warwickshire, and that by a man who, some had thought, would never bowl again. David Brown, from Walsall, still in the nursery, also showed promise.

As a result, Warwickshire improved their position in the table from fifteenth to twelfth and would have done better but for a poor run in August of two defeats and four draws. Against Kent at Maidstone, on a drying pitch in the second innings, Bridge was almost unplayable and had an analysis of 5·1 overs, 4 maidens, 2 runs and 5 wickets, and he gained his county cap at Swansea where he followed a performance of five for 48 in the first innings with seven for 49 in the second. In this match M.J.K. took five catches in one innings, and he then took four in succession at short leg off Bridge at Northampton to take his season's total to 53 and break his own record.

Perhaps the best win of the season, though, was at Old Trafford where Warwickshire won for the first time since 1936, Lancashire being beaten by 84 runs by good batting and sound bowling. Play did not begin until late on the first afternoon and then it was in bad light, but this did not trouble the two Smiths. Alan, who opened the innings, made 78, and M.J.K. 112 not out, the pair putting on 164 for the third wicket. Warwickshire were able to declare at 244 for five, and then Bannister, Thompson and Bridge put Lancashire out for 208. Warwickshire quickly added another 136 for seven before declaring and then rattled Lancashire out for 88, Bannister taking six for 31 and Bridge four for 33. But in the return match at Edgbaston Warwickshire could only draw despite hundreds by Hitchcock, 145 (and 53 in the second innings), and Cartwright 119 not out in a partnership of 170 for the fifth wicket.

Stewart got back into the six-hitting vein against Somerset at Street with innings of 104 and 55 not out. He carted Langford for six sixes, three in one over, and altogether hit eleven sixes and fourteen fours, the last six winning the match. At Southampton, against Hampshire, eventual champions for the first time in their history, he made 143 in three and a half hours, a long time for him, with four sixes and nineteen fours, and then against Derbyshire at Edgbaston it was four sixes and fifteen fours in an innings of 135.

The strength of the youngsters coming along was shown in the match with Cambridge at Edgbaston where, with only one regular first-team man in the side, Warwickshire won by 51 runs; M. S. Cook, on his début, Fletcher and Kennedy all making half-centuries.

Both Smiths ended the season by playing for the Gentlemen against the Players at Scarborough, M.J.K. scoring 92 and 43, and A.C. 37 not out and 16 and taking three catches in each innings. Let it also be recorded for posterity that in 1961 M.J.K. headed the Warwickshire bowling averages with these figures:

O	M	R	W	AVE
3	1	3	1	3·00

And it would take a good man to have a lower bowling average than that in first-class cricket. Not even Barnes, specialist in low averages, achieved it in league cricket. But I still do not know what sort of stuff he bowled, never having been present on one of those momentous occasions, though I have heard it described as 'right arm indifferent'.

There was a further decline of over 76 000 in the number of people who attended county games, a fact which the author of the Club's annual report found amazing in a season with the Australians here. It was 'disappointing because of the failure, despite administrative activity in the close season and the many promises made by county captains and others to sponsor a more attractive and purposeful game, to draw back any appreciable measure of the public support lost in recent years.'

On the other hand, the total membership of the Club had doubled since 1955, partly, one imagines, because membership ensured getting a comfortable seat for Tests and other representative games. It was also a clear indication, one would have thought, that most people would stir from in front of their television screens only for the top attractions in sport, for television almost invariably gave a perfect view of the game from directly behind the bowler's arm without any of the discomfort sometimes entailed in visiting even the grounds with the best amenities and surroundings.

The Warwickshire report, on the subject of slow play, thought it 'unreasonable to rectify the position under the existing laws when to do so frequently acts against the career interests of several of the players in their teams by making demands on individuals to adopt a style of play for county games which largely preclude their selection for Test Matches or overseas tours.'

At least the M.C.C. committee inquiring into the structure of the game agreed with Warwickshire to the extent of recommending limiting the number of games (though only to twenty-eight) and that a knock-out competition should be introduced (but not until 1963 – it was considered that more time was needed to bring in these innovations). Warwickshire welcomed these proposals as a step in the right direction, but regretted that nothing had been done to brighten up the first day's play, such as limiting the first innings of both teams so as to ensure that the Saturday visitor, able to come only on that day, would see the major part of the innings of both sides.

As for Sunday cricket, Warwickshire favoured bringing the Lord's Day Observance Act up to date and decided that, before committing itself, it would hold a referendum. One held by the Birmingham Press, to which 450 people replied, showed that they were about evenly divided; members of the Club being mostly against; those who frequented the popular side of the ground being mostly in favour.

At the end of the season three members of the 1951 Championship side – Gardner, Townsend and Wolton – decided to retire from county cricket. They had been three stalwarts indeed. Batsmen with more strokes and a greater sense of urgency than Gardner have played for Warwickshire, but none with more courage and perseverance. It may surprise even some close followers of the county to realise that he ranked sixth among the county's batsmen in the number of centuries made – 29. Only Dollery 49 and M. J. K. Smith 45, of modern players, are ahead of him, the others being Quaife 71, Wyatt 51, and Parsons 35. In all first-class cricket he scored 17 826 runs at an average of 33·82.

Townsend always looked, but too infrequently played, as if he ought

to be one of England's greatest all-rounders. He had that rare gift –
Basil D'Oliveira had it, too – of inestimable value to captains of sides
deficient in bowling, of being able, amazingly often, to break up stubborn
partnerships and take a few quick wickets. His slip fielding reminded
one of Hammond's and there could be no higher praise than that; but
both he and Wolton, who played some fine innings and whose fielding
also could not be faulted, lacked that drive and consistency which could
have taken them to the top. Townsend scored nearly 12 000 runs, with
an average touching 25 and took 323 wickets at 28·60, and he made
410 catches, the last a feat of surpassing consistency. Wolton made
nearly 13 000 runs at an average of 31·00, but bowled only occasionally
and took no more than thirty-seven wickets.

Dollery, too, decided that as he was 'no longer mobile enough in the
field' it was time for him to give up playing and concentrate wholly on
coaching, and it could easily have happened that this season Cartwright,
too, might have gone. He must have done more worrying than most
players about his future, for early in the year he had again written at
some length to the Committee seeking the top-rate salary and some
assistance in securing what he called a progressive and lucrative
appointment to run parallel with his cricket.

The Committee, while appreciating his value as an all-rounder whose
services should not be lost to the Club, nevertheless felt that to grant
his request would be a dangerous precedent (what shivers that word
sent down the spines of successive Warwickshire committees) and it
was ultimately agreed, on a fourteen to six vote, that if he did well in the
first half of the season his salary would be raised to £700, retrospective
to the start of the season, and to invite him to discuss employment with
Derek Salberg, now a member of the Committee, who thought he might
be able to help.

The Committee also decided unanimously that if he declined this
offer Cartwright should be advised that, in accordance with the rules
of county cricket, permission could not be granted for him to approach
other counties, a ban which puts professional cricketers in a category
unique among employees. Prompted by some observations from the
chairman, who obviously thought the offer unfair to other and equally
deserving players, the Committee had second thoughts, agreed to
rescind the earlier minute and reaffirmed the original offer. This was
after an amendment suggesting a salary increase to £675 (again
subject to good performances in the early months of the season) had
been defeated. Before the season opened, Cartwright accepted re-
engagement on the terms originally offered, but it is doubtful if anyone
really thought this would be the end of the affair and it was not.

Both T. W. Graveney, if he were released by Gloucestershire, and
T. L. Goddard, the South African all-rounder, were considered as

possible additions to the playing strength, the latter as a potential captain should there be any uncertainty about M. J. K. Smith's future. However, both present and former players on the Committee were opposed to such engagements at the expense of young players and it was agreed that Club policy should be to encourage youth as a first principle, but at the same time not to neglect any opportunity to approach any outstanding player whose services became available. The main aim of the Committee, it was felt, must always be to build up a winning team. In these circumstances it was decided not to approach Graveney, who in any event, decided to join Worcestershire. An offer was made to Goddard, who, however, settled the matter by deciding to take up a business appointment in the South of England and to play in the North Staffs League.

But the names of two youngsters were added to the staff – those of John Jameson, captain of Taunton School, who was brought to the attention of Alec Hastilow by his son, B. W. Hastilow, a master at the school, and played for Smethwick when he was not needed by the county; and R. Miller, from Durham, yet another slow left-arm bowler.

A major piece of reconstruction decided on was the rebuilding of the Centre Pavilion, for which the Club and the Supporters' Association, whose weekly entries now totalled 290 000, decided to set up a Trust Fund. The cost was estimated at £250 000, but it was not before time. The Pavilion was now over seventy years old, having been built in 1885–6 as suitable to a private club for some 400 gentlemen – but now there were 11 000 members.

It was also decided that more seating was necessary to accommodate the crowds, who, whatever they thought about the county games, obviously wished to see Tests. The value of the freehold land and premises now known as Edgbaston was £271 195. Was it, as Alec Hastilow at the annual meeting said someone had told him when the South Africans were here, a white elephant – 'Deakins's Folly', as it had been described – which would probably never, or only rarely, be needed? The previous year, he said, they had been told there was too much seating; this year with the Saturday of the Test sold out, it was said that the seating was inadequate. To provide one new seat cost £20 and the return from it was limited because some of the seats were used only on rare occasions.

But it transpired that Australian legislators visiting the ground for the Test had criticised it because, in their view, the covered seating was inadequate. So the ground and building sub-committee was asked to look into the possibility of remedying this by increasing accommodation by 10 000 and enlarging the cover. Eventually the general committee decided to invite tenders for additional cover on the Rea Bank side at an estimated cost of £10 000, an amount which, although it was more than double the total paying gate for the whole of the season, was thought justified for Tests alone.

There were objections to providing more seats on the popular side which would seldom be used, but when it was suggested that, if necessary, people should be allowed on the turf, Leslie Deakins asked that his objection to such a move should be recorded. He regarded it as a very retrograde step after the Club had established a post-war reputation for seating comfort and excellent views of the play. To adopt this method of accommodating spectators would be putting the clock back.

Although the Club had benefited to the extent of £12 761 from the Tests, there had been an increase in expenditure of nearly £10 000, due to spending on repairs and maintenance, and there was a profit on the year of only £522. It was obvious that the Club could not hope to continue to meet annual outgoings of £64 000 from the income sources available to it, in particular a revenue from county matches of only £8 000, so the establishment of an Endowment Fund was regarded as of paramount importance.

The Edgbaston wicket had come in for some criticism at the annual meeting. Everyone, as the chairman said, was trying to get faster pitches, but no one seemed to know how to achieve it. M. J. K. Smith said one needed to work like a horse to get wickets on 'that unresponsive turf', so it was decided to hire a heavier roller, a three-tonner immediately christened 'Big Bertha' by the newspapers, in the hope of finding the happy medium between the flier and the featherbed.

The man who, by his devotion to the family business, had allowed Frank Foster to give more time to cricket, much to Warwickshire's benefit, died during the year. He was W. H. Foster, Frank's brother, who was a vice-president. At the end he was still thinking about the Club for he left it £200 in his will.

After twenty-five years on the selection committee, during which time he had exercised considerable influence on the teams that had represented the county over the years, Alec Hastilow decided that it was time for a change, so he resigned. Bert Homer was elected in his place and, with 'Mike' Smith, Esmond Lewis and 'Tom' Dollery, constituted the Committee.

The various bars on the ground had now been given the names of fielding positions – Slip In, Third Man, Gully, Cover Point, Long On and Long Leg. *The Birmingham Post*'s commentator, drily recording the change, said that cricket 'widows' would be glad to learn that Long Stop was not contemplated.

M. J. K. Smith was off on his travels again during the winter, this time to Ceylon, India and Pakistan, with the M.C.C. team led by Ted Dexter; but his name was not mentioned in *Wisden*'s account of the tour, not surprisingly in view of his moderate performances. He played in four of the five Tests against India, but scored all told only 126 runs and got 'a pair' in the second match. In three Tests against Pakistan he did slightly better and made 199, with a highest score of 99. In all first-class games he scored 789 runs, with an average of 34·30.

Room Near the Top
(1962–1964)

In the next three seasons – 1962–4 – Warwickshire came nearer to winning the Championship than at any time since 1951. Oddly enough, only one of them coincided with a summer in which 'Mike' Smith scored over 2000 runs. In 1962, the last of the six consecutive seasons in which he exceeded this total, Warwickshire finished third in the table; in 1963, when he scored over 1000 fewer, they were joint-fourth and would have been higher but for rain-spoiled matches at the end; and in 1964 they were second in both the County Championship and the Minor Counties Competition; also for the first time in their history they beat the Australians. It was an astonishing sequence of events which produced an unusually high proportion of records for the county.

There was a Test against Pakistan at Edgbaston in 1962, but for the most part, with all due respect to the visitors, it merely provided batting practice for England, and for once the county game was much the most absorbing, especially for batsmen. No fewer than three Warwickshire players made over 2000 runs during the season – Smith 1988 for the county, 2090 in all; Ibadulla, 1863 and 2098; and Stewart, 2100 and 2318 – an astonishing record considering that in the whole history of the Club only seven batsmen previously had accomplished the feat.

Moreover, four others – Cartwright, Hitchcock, Horner and A. C. Smith – also made over 1000, and Cartwright became the first Warwickshire professional to do the 'double' with 1082 runs, average 31·82, and 101 wickets, average 20·31. It had not been achieved for the county since Foster accomplished it in 1911 and 1914. In addition, two other bowlers, Bannister and Wright – the latter had joined Warwickshire when he was 14 straight from school at Arley, near Nuneaton, had developed into a very useful bowler rather faster than Cartwright, and this was his first full season – took over 100 wickets – Bannister 106 and

434

Wright 111, the first time the county had had three bowlers with such figures in the same season. They were, however, deficient in spin. Bridge underwent an operation which restricted his appearances to six matches and the brunt of the support from this direction fell on Hitchcock, who took thirty-five wickets, and Miller, who had forty-one. Brown, too, suffered from injury, but managed to take fifty-three wickets. And last but not least Alan Smith equalled Esmond Lewis's record by taking six catches in one innings. It was a pity the rest of the fielding was not up to the same standard.

In the circumstances, it is surprising that, despite injuries and the weather, Warwickshire did not finish even higher up the table than third. The lead, indeed, changed hands several times during the summer and Warwickshire did not drop out of the running for the title until late in August, whereupon Worcestershire and Yorkshire engaged in a life-and-death struggle which the Northerners, ten points behind, won in the last few hours of the season – a revenge for that crucial defeat at Scarborough way back in 1951. Both Warwickshire and Worcestershire, however, had some compensation, the former winning the Minor Counties title for the second time, with the help of Amiss, Jameson, Kennedy and 'Roly' Thompson, and Worcestershire the Second Elevens' Championship.

On the whole the batting honours went to Stewart for he scored over 2000 runs for the county alone. In full cry, he was, as M. J. K. Smith said at the annual meeting, 'one of the highlights of the modern game', and it was unfortunate for Warwickshire supporters that so many of his best performances were away from Edgbaston. At Folkestone, for instance, he made 133 not out in a third-wicket stand of 212 with 'Mike' Smith, 124, despite which Kent won by 12 runs nine minutes from the end; and at Leicester he went one better still, scoring 182 not out and 79 not out – 261 without being dismissed. This time his partner was Ibadulla – and, incidentally, Horner and Ibadulla were the only two Warwickshire batsmen dismissed in either innings in this match. In a second-wicket stand of 223 Stewart hit 23 off one over from Savage – 4 4 4 6 4 1 – who was not taken off although in the next over there came another 11 runs.

In the next match, at Edgbaston for a change, he got another century and reached his 1000 runs fifteen days earlier than any Warwickshire batsman had ever done. He followed this with 59 and 61, also at Edgbaston, and then at Hove, after M.J.K. and Cartwright had had a first-innings partnership of 199, Stewart and Ibadulla, in an unbroken stand lasting only 135 minutes, made 211, which enabled Warwickshire to win the match after being sent in to bat. Both of them also hit centuries off the Sussex bowling at Edgbaston, and in the second innings on the last day Warwickshire actually scored 122 in 48 minutes.

Cartwright came to his full flowering as a batsman with 210 out of 387 against Middlesex at Nuneaton, where he and A. C. Smith, just missing his first century for the county, shared in a stand of 244 in just under three hours. Warwickshire finished only three short of victory with one wicket standing.

Horner's benefit against Worcestershire was a dull affair, for both sides were among the first teams in the table and neither would take a risk. It took Worcestershire nearly six hours to score 175 and Warwickshire also struggled for 115. Horner himself was out of touch, making 9 and 0. He was also unlucky in the weather, but financially he was in favour, for the benefit as a whole produced £6465, yet another new record for the county, just beating Dollery's £6362. Enterprising batting and fielding had earned its reward.

There were two promising débuts – Jameson made 73 against Derbyshire at Edgbaston; and a 22-year-old West Indian medical student at the Medical School of the Queen Elizabeth Hospital, Birmingham, rejoicing in the name of Rudi Valentine Webster and bowling extremely quickly, twice 'operated' drastically on the Cambridge batting – six for 70 and four for 71. The Club had had favourable reports on him from two of their players who had encountered him when playing for an M.C.C. side against Scotland, for whom he took seven for 56 and four for 44, and he also took two of the Australians' wickets for 67, so he was a very useful acquisition to the bowling strength.

England, as usual at Edgbaston, won the Test, Pakistan being beaten by an innings and 24 runs with a day to spare. The touring side had met with very indifferent success – they won only four of the thirty-nine games they played on the tour – and no one got excited about their visit. The advance bookings were the lowest since Tests had been resumed at Edgbaston, amounting to only just over £5000, even though there were estimated to be 18 000 Pakistanis and Indians living in Birmingham at this time, though it is doubtful how many of the latter would have attended in any case. True, the weather was not very kind, the sun shining only on the last day, and the best attendance was 16 000 on the Saturday, the grand total being 35 000 and the receipts £11 000.

At least England's batsmen had some practice, Cowdrey 159, Parfitt 101, Graveney 97 and Dexter 72, helping to compile 544 for five declared. Four of the Pakistani bowlers tried had centuries of runs scored off them, including Intikhab Alam, who was to captain the 1971 side with such success. The match was notable for one unusual event – a wayward fieldmouse suddenly appeared at the feet of Dexter, of all people, and stopped play. There must be a moral in that somewhere; one could have understood it with So-and-So or Such-and-Such at the wicket.

England won four and drew one of the Tests, in none of which any

Warwickshire players were called upon to take part. Pakistan lost to Sussex, Glamorgan, Somerset and Essex, among the counties, but not Warwickshire, the game at Edgbaston being drawn in miserable conditions.

At the end of the season, though Warwickshire would have liked him to continue, 'Roly' Thompson decided to go into business. At 16 he had taken five Gloucestershire wickets at a run for every year of his age and he continued to be one of the liveliest of fast-medium bowlers in first-class cricket until plagued by injuries in his later seasons. In all, he took 470 wickets for 23·02 runs each, a good record.

Although the weather on the whole was unkind, Warwickshire's bright batting earned its reward in slightly better gates, totalling nearly 70 000. Twice in county matches, against Worcestershire and Northants, the receipts exceeded £1000, an indication that the neighbourly competitive element did make a difference. Warwickshire were fourth in the attendance table – Yorkshire leading with 131 121, Middlesex second and Surrey third – and their batsmen scored at a higher rate than those of any other county except Kent – 2·89 per over to 2·76.

Nevertheless, the overall attendance position in the country as a whole was worse, a breakdown of the figures showing this progressive decline:

1947	2 200 910
1957	1 197 979
1962	933 871

The figure had fallen below a million for the first time in 1958, but it had been going down steadily before that. In 1959 and 1960 it was back to a million again, but then fell below that mark in 1961 and 1962. Daily attendances at county matches compared with 1961 showed decreases on all days except Friday. The figures were 232 000 down even for Tests, a clear indication that Pakistan did not as yet possess the drawing power of the other countries.

Warwickshire suffered a drop of £4378 in its share of Test profits, and this year, for the first time for several years, were able to accept more members, seating being now available in the Pavilion (east wing). In 1939 the income from members' subscriptions had been £4019; now it had grown to £26 315, nearly, but not quite, half the sum Warwickshire needed annually to cover normal expenditure. Largely because of the drop in Test profits, the accounts showed a loss at the end of the season of £5327.

The Supporters' Association found itself confronted with one of those legal pitfalls with which those who run pools of any kind could find themselves threatened. In December 1961, the Association had celebrated reaching a membership, or at least weekly entries, of half a million, more than double that of all other similar organisations, and of having given £250 000 to the Club, an astonishing record.

But in March 1962, summonses were taken out against them under the 1934 Betting and Lotteries Act, and also against the Birmingham firm which printed the weekly lists of teams and statement of accounts and against two agents. The summonses were under Section 22 of the Act, which dealt with the sale, printing and distribution of lottery tickets, and two former policemen were named as informants on the summonses. There was a total of fourteen alleged infringements.

The summonses were down for hearing on 23 March, but only two days after they had been taken out representatives of the Association were informed that they would not be proceeded with and on 23 March all ten summonses were withdrawn. The Stipendiary Magistrate expressed disappointment because, he said, he had been assured that this was going to be a most interesting case on a very interesting point of law.

There were important administrative changes during 1962. Alec Hastilow relinquished the positions of both chairman, a position he had held for fifteen years, and honorary secretary, to make way for a younger man in the person of Edmund King. Bert Homer also resigned as vice-chairman, his place being taken by Cyril Goodway, so there was a double change at the top.

The chairmanship now became a Club, as distinct from a Committee, appointment, and the office of honorary secretary, which had long been an anachronism – a view held sixty years earlier by William Ansell – was abolished. The posts of secretary and treasurer were amalgamated in that of the general secretary, which Leslie Deakins continued to be, with James McDowall honorary treasurer and Hubert Bewlay, who had successfully intervened to get an Inland Revenue assessment of £6288 reduced to £3500, much to the Committee's pleasure, continuing as rating consultant.

Alec Hastilow's services were happily not lost to the Club, the Committee electing him an honorary life member and a vice-president, and his advice continued to be available. Hastilow had held the reins of office during one of the most important periods in the Club's history. Once, referring to the fact that during that time Warwickshire won the Championship for the second time and Edgbaston was restored to Test Match status, he said: 'I am very proud to say that I played well enough to get both of them.'

At the complimentary dinner given to him by the Club and the Supporters' Association later in the year there were representatives of every major sport in the Midlands. Ronald Aird, secretary of the M.C.C. was there from Lord's, where Hastilow had done some of his best work for the game and the Club. Lieutenant-General Sir Oliver Leese, the

President, who was in the chair, said there could be no man who had given so much time to study the many diverse problems of the Club. John Arlott had called him 'The Squire of Edgbaston' and said he had been a perfect host. Mr Aird, recalling his work at Lord's, said that sometimes 'he has been a jump ahead of the rest of us'.

Hastilow, who was presented with a cocktail cabinet, said he thought no one should have too long a monopoly of the position of chairman and he commended to them his successor, Edmund King. That morning in an interview with J. M. Solan in *The Birmingham Post*, Hastilow had permitted himself a glimpse of the Edgbaston he hoped to see in the future – a comprehensive sports and social club, used in the winter for athletics, hockey, or boxing, with a membership of 20 000, paying 10-guinea subscriptions.

Because of the demands of his profession, Edmund King, in his younger days, had been able to play far less cricket than he would have wished, though he made a number of useful appearances in the county side in the late twenties and the early thirties. He was one of many accountants who, in recent years, have risen to high office in fields other than that of their chosen profession, and the success that marked his chairmanship of the Warwickshire Club led to many demands on his services in the wider field of cricket administration as a whole.

Some indication of how important a financial part television had come to play in first-class cricket was given when a new fees agreement was negotiated with the B.B.C. – £75 000 for a series of Tests with Australia, £50 000 for the West Indies, and £25 000 for Pakistan covering 1962–4 tours – but even their eventual share of these amounts did not lure Warwickshire into trying to secure the services of Jim Laker. It was known that Surrey would have released him, but that he would have been available for only a limited number of games, and in view of the success of Bridge – which, alas, proved only transient – it was agreed that no action should be taken.

A. C. Smith, who had had a very good season for the county, stumping three men – the preponderance of seam and swing bowling did not allow many chances of stumping – and catching seventy-five, within two of the Club record held by Jack Smart, had another tour during the winter, this time to Australia and New Zealand, with the M.C.C. team led by Ted Dexter. J. T. Murray was the other wicketkeeper in the side, but *Wisden* said that Smith showed the sounder, if less classical, style and became first choice. He played in all but the third Test against Australia and in two out of three in New Zealand, and though he scored only 47 runs against Australia and 71 without being dismissed against New Zealand, he nevertheless contrived to share with Cowdrey in a record stand of 163 for the ninth wicket in a Test Match. Because of a damaged finger, Cowdrey did not go in until No. eight in the second

Test. By close of play on the second day he and Smith had put on 145 and they were allowed to go on next day until they had increased the stand to 163, Cowdrey being 128 not out and Smith 69 not out, including eleven fours. During the series Smith stumped one batsman and took thirty-seven catches to Murray's one stumped and eleven caught.

Nineteen sixty-three was a most exciting season, even though it was a poor summer. They were all players now, the amateur status having gone for ever during the winter; the West Indies were here, with a Test at Edgbaston; there was a thrilling struggle in the County Championship; it was the first year of the Gillette Cup; and an exciting new player, in R. W. Barber from Lancashire, joined the Club and celebrated his arrival by doing the hat trick – the first slow bowler to do so for Warwickshire at Edgbaston. Warwickshire had approached him when he was a schoolboy at Ruthin because they had heard that he and his brother were very promising players, but he indicated then that his county allegiance would be to Lancashire. When he became unhappy there, however, the opportunity occurred again and this time he decided to come.

The season opened with a lament in the centenary issue of *Wisden* for the abolition of the amateur, advocated long before by Bob Wyatt, and at last decided on at a meeting at Lord's only five years after it had been rejected:

By doing away with the amateur, cricket is in danger of losing the spirit of freedom and gaiety which the best amateur players brought to the game.

It was in danger of losing much more than that, and this decision, while rectifying many anomalies, probably hastened, contradictorily enough, the funereal progress of the game towards the vacuum in which, despite the Gillette Cup, the John Player League, and the Benson and Hedges Competition, it is still all too frequently becalmed. It was a far cry, indeed, from the day in 1879 when the M.C.C. appointed a sub-committee to inquire 'into the Definition and Qualification of Amateur Cricketers' and concluded, among other things:

We are of the opinion that no Gentleman ought to make a profit by his service in the cricket field and that for the future any cricketer taking more than his expenses in any match should not be qualified to play for the Gentlemen against the Players at Lord's, but that if any gentleman should feel difficulty in joining in the match without such assistance he should not be debarred from playing as a Gentleman by having his actual expenses defrayed.

There were no lamentations, however, at Edgbaston where they had been campaigning for the change for some time, as well as for alterations now made to the rule to permit overseas players at universities other than Oxford and Cambridge to play cricket while in residence, which meant that Webster could play immediately. There were efforts to restrict this relaxation to Oxford and Cambridge cricketers, but Alec Hastilow fought for equal rights for all university players and eventually won the day.

The annual report paid graceful tribute to the 'tremendous service' of all the amateurs of the past, but it welcomed 'this sound and logical step' under which there would be three classes of players – the present regular staff; those who could make themselves available for a limited number of matches; and those who did not want to be paid, for personal reasons. 'No player', the report observed, 'will lose or gain in stature, but the game itself and its administration will benefit enormously, albeit in many respects indirectly.' Has it done so, one wonders? Alec Hastilow at least has no doubts that 'all underhand payments to so-called amateurs and resultant hypocrisy have been eliminated'.

The President went out of his way at the annual meeting to dispel any fears there might be that the Committee with the longest purse strings might attract all the best players. Legislation apart, he would say at once that, assuming Warwickshire to be one of the wealthier counties (with the aid of its Supporters' Association), anyone feeling that their policy would run along these lines could not be more wrong. He felt confident that it was the wish of all who loved the game to prevent men from seeking transfers mainly to improve their own financial position.

The change in status involved corresponding changes in the terms of players' engagements and it was recommended, from Lord's, that match fees payable to contract players for Championship matches and against touring sides should be £35 for those who had appeared in representative cricket, £25 for players who had been awarded their county caps, and £15 for other players, mainly young cricketers. In addition, players would also be paid win, but not appearance, money, and be reimbursed for out-of-pocket expenses. For the knock-out competition the match fee would be £15 irrespective of grading.

John Solan, cricket correspondent of *The Birmingham Post*, obviously had Edgbaston particularly in mind when, in the same issue of *Wisden*, he took a look at the cricket ground of the future in an article aptly entitled 'Through the Crystal Ball'. After remarking that 'a county cricket ground used solely for cricket will soon be an insupportable luxury', he went on:

The county cricket ground of the future, therefore, can be expected to be a comprehensive sports centre, the extent of whose activities will be limited only by the space and facilities available. Members will make it their club, not merely their cricket club, and by paying a fatter subscription, will be able to enjoy amenities in and out of doors.

It can be envisaged as a family centre, too, although one imagines that

Bingo would not be wholly acceptable, say, at Lord's. Such attractions as boxing promotions should not be beyond the scope of the bigger grounds, and such games as squash, for the energetic, and snooker, for the idler elements, will be laid on. Out of doors in the winter, hockey comes automatically to mind, but greyhound racing would possibly come under the same headings as Bingo and Ten-pin bowling. To many people such a development may seem a desecration of some of the country's loveliest spots, but needs must when the devil drives.

A devil, he might have added, very much of cricket's own making.

Considering the injuries which afflicted several players at the start of the 1963 season, it was remarkable that Warwickshire played as well as they did. In an operation during the winter Stewart had the misfortune to lose the big toe of his left foot, with the result that he had to wear a special boot, a considerable handicap to a man who was fond of getting out to the pitch of the ball. He missed some of the early matches, though when he did return at Lord's he hit a brilliant 93, including three sixes and twelve fours, which gave rise to hopes that he would be as good as ever – but he could never quite recapture that first fine careless rapture.

Then M. J. K. Smith broke his wrist while fielding against Yorkshire in only the second match of the season and though he made a very rapid recovery he was absent for a month, missing half a dozen matches. In the circumstances, it would have been surprising indeed if he had reached 2000 runs; even so, his 1566, at 47·45 an innings, was good enough to enable him to head the first-class averages again, though he was not selected for any of the Tests, partly, no doubt, because he was out of action when most of the teams were being selected.

Among the bowlers, Bannister had knee trouble and Brown a stomach operation, so that two men who had taken 165 wickets between them in 1962, now bowled no more than 200 overs altogether. Wright was out of form and Bridge could not even get a place in the side. So Barber's arrival under special registration was a godsend both for his batting – he was one of four players to score over 1000 runs – and his bowling, which brought him sixty-five wickets, including a hat trick against Glamorgan.

Notwithstanding all these handicaps, Warwickshire splendidly kept up the challenge to Yorkshire and had they won their last three games it was possible for them to have drawn level, but against Northants they were held up for two and a half hours at a vital time on the last day; at Bournemouth against Hampshire the teams were not even announced and the players never opened their bags; and in the last match of the season at The Oval rain prevented play on the first and third days.

Yorkshire, on the other hand, were able to complete their last two games and that was that. Warwickshire finished joint fourth with Sussex, but there might still have been a different tale to tell if in that early match in which Smith broke his wrist Warwickshire had not allowed Trueman to rout them twice. In the match he took ten wickets for only 36 runs, Warwickshire making no more than 35 and 55, their lowest aggregate in first-class cricket and their heaviest defeat since 1922. Oh for a Quaife, a Wyatt, or a Dollery! These are the times when such men are worth their weight in gold. On this occasion only four men reached double figures in either innings.

Barber began badly enough – in his first match he was run out for 2 and then made nought and took none for 41 and none for 57 – but he soon ran into form and though his personal contribution was not great he must have been very pleased when Warwickshire again won at Old Trafford, this time by six wickets. There was no need for him to bowl, the seamers disposing of Lancashire, who were going through an unhappy period in their history, for 140 and 121. The previous match had been against Scotland and for the first time in the Club's history the team had flown to fulfil a fixture, first from Birmingham to Edinburgh and then to Manchester.

Over 1100 runs were scored in Hitchcock's benefit against Worcestershire, but only 37 of them by the beneficiary. Warwickshire made 339 for seven before declaring, Horner being responsible for 113 of them, and Cartwright, whose batting fell off a little – though in all matches he took over 100 wickets – made 81. Worcestershire topped that total with 351 for seven, D. W. Richardson 104; and then Warwickshire declared for the second time after rattling up 266 for seven in only sixty-three overs, an average of four runs an over – good practice for the knock-out cricket to come. Worcestershire, invited to score 255 in 163 minutes, had a bold try, and, while Graveney was hitting sixes and fours had a chance, but with their last pair together they still needed 22 – a splendid match.

The latter half of the season was marked by the return of the young hurricane from the West Indies. Freed from his university studies, Rudi Webster came into the side at the beginning of July and in sixteen matches took no fewer than seventy-seven wickets for only 17·44 runs each, figures more than good enough for him to head the county averages. He had a five-for-5 spell – seven for 40 in all – against Glamorgan, eight wickets against Gloucestershire and six for 36 against Worcestershire – really tearaway stuff.

Webster and R. B. Edmonds, a physical education student from the Club's nursery, added tremendous fire to the attack. Edmonds headed the Minor Counties bowling averages and Amiss the batting, winning the Wilfred Rhodes trophy. Miller did not have to bowl so much, though he took forty-five wickets. His batting improved and he also took forty-four catches. M. D. Mence, a Bradfield College boy, regarded as the outstanding schoolboy cricketer of 1962, also showed promise.

Edgbaston had been allotted the third Test, which unfortunately clashed with the Royal Show at Stoneleigh, Warwickshire. Before they came to Edgbaston the West Indies had won one and drawn one Test and, as usual before a Test here, they were welcomed by a deluge of rain, so that neither side was able to have any pre-match practice. Fortunately the wicket had been covered, but even so the ground staff had to work like beavers, even Mrs Flack's washing machine being pressed into service to supplement the ground mangle and wring out blankets used to soak up the water.

Then another downpour prevented play beginning until after tea on the first day, and play on the second was cut to an hour and fifty minutes. On Saturday the gates were closed with an estimated 25 000 or more people on the ground, 21 266 having paid £13 054, just short of the record. They saw two hours and forty minutes' play, but nothing after tea. On Monday there was a full day's play at least and 17 500 people came along. On the last day there were 11 000. Altogether 86 500 people saw the match and the total receipts were £36 349.

Despite the interruptions they got value for money. Dexter won the toss and elected to bat, though in the light of what happened he probably wished he had sent the West Indies in. Sobers at least found the wicket to his liking and if it had not been for some stout defiance by Close, who scored a very valuable 55, England would not have made anything like the 216 they got. Sobers's five for 60 was his best bowling performance in a Test up to that time.

The West Indies had to struggle even harder against Trueman – who had taken eleven wickets against them in the previous Test – and Dexter, who took nine of their first innings wickets between them. But it was in the second innings, after England had declared at 278 for nine, that Trueman showed that at the age of 32 he was still a great bowler. Bowling swingers from a short run because of foothold difficulties, he had the last six wickets in twenty-four balls at a cost of one four by Lance Gibbs, and in the end he took seven for 44 – twelve for 119 in the match – the best Test performance of his career. The West Indies were all out for 91, only Kanhai offering serious resistance, and losing by 217 runs. Thus once more Edgbaston's success record was sustained. John Solan, in *The Birmingham Post*, commented that 'the impression grows that they [the West Indians] are fair-weather cricketers', but at least they made strokes to the end and of how many sides could that be said?

There was a sequel to this match because of an overflow of spectators on the Saturday, which caused a breakdown in the arrangements for the popular side. Because of the weather there was a delay in opening the gates and play was resumed at too short notice to allow the large crowd waiting outside to get into the ground before play began again. The result was that, despite all the efforts of the staff, the ground was virtually overrun at one point and more spectators were admitted than could be comfortably accommodated, even with an overflow on to the grass, where people standing interfered with the view of those with reserved seats in the Rea Bank stand.

Over thirty letters of complaint were received after the match and a full report on the incident was submitted. This showed, in the chairman's words, that 'some things went wrong, but many things went well'. As a result, Warwickshire decided to make future Tests all-ticket affairs if other Clubs staging them would do the same, and there was another argument about whether spectators should be allowed on the turf, which had not been allowed for forty years. There were differing opinions about this, but the view that to allow people on the grass would mean more work for the ground staff and that the turf should be for 'players only', which was Leslie Deakins' opinion, prevailed for the time being.

The West Indies doubtless derived some consolation for their Test defeat by beating the county side in August by seven wickets, fiery bowling by Hall and Griffith proving too much for Warwickshire, who were all out for 210 and 187. Only 113 in the first innings by Barber – his first century for his new county (though he should never have got it for he was dropped three times) – and a stand by 'Mike' Smith, 68, and Barber, 40, in the second, prevented two worse collapses; Griffith, in his last seven overs, taking five wickets for 6 runs, and the last six wickets going down for 29 runs. Cartwright, who had been twelfth man in the Edgbaston Test, puzzled the West Indians with his swing and took four for 36, their first five wickets falling for seven. They were all out 270, but in their second innings Kanhai gave Warwickshire further reason to like the look of him by making a not out half-century.

Whatever reservations the purists may have had about the kind of cricket the sponsored Gillette Cup competition produced, there was no doubt that it aroused enormous interest, 25 000 people watching the final at Lord's – a splendid sight to see with the great ground full to the brim – in which Sussex beat Worcestershire by only 14 runs. From all the rounds in the competition £13 771 was taken in gate money, the final balance left for the counties being £17 614. Warwickshire's annual report saw the competition as possibly proving 'a financial salvation for many clubs, for in this initial year the winners benefited by almost £2000, whilst a side eliminated in the initial round made £773'.

That was Warwickshire's fate. They were drawn against Northants at Northampton where they were put in – and out – for 140 runs in fifty-six overs and two balls out of the sixty overs allowed to each side. They were without 'Mike' Smith and Stewart, and only Amiss and Jameson, two of the younger members of the team, made even respectable scores – 34 and 29 respectively. Mostly the Warwickshire batsmen tried to score too quickly, but at least they learned the lesson of one-day cricket – 'Don't run out of batsmen before you run out of overs'.

Northants needed to score at no more than just over two runs an over and they took it very leisurely, Reynolds spending an hour and three-quarters over 34 and Prideaux two hours for 52, which was not exactly what the promoters of the competition had in mind.

Notwithstanding all the excitement and the novelty, attendances all over the country dropped still further – from 933 871 in 1962 to 719 661. Warwickshire were still fourth in the list, with 48 785 for Championship matches, compared with 68 000 the season before, there being five blank days in the last week of the season. But they headed the fastest-scoring table – 45·94 runs per 100 balls – and they were third in the rate of overs bowled per hour with 20·88. Thanks to the Test Pool share, which amounted to £6137, there was a surplus on the year of £1748.

It was a busy year for the ground and buildings sub-committee, quite apart from the work that had to be done for the Test. During the previous winter Bernard Flack had been appointed to serve on a national committee appointed by the M.C.C. to consider the question of faster pitches, though no one ever took the trouble to explain just exactly how these would benefit both batsmen and bowlers and produce brighter cricket. The sub-committee produced the following recipe for the ideal type of pitch on which to play a three-day game:

1 Must have considerable pace which must be maintained throughout the match.

2 Should have a fair degree of bounce which should be reasonably consistent.

3 Should during the early part of the match give the faster bowlers a fair chance to move the ball off the seam.

4 A wrist spinner should be able to turn the ball a certain amount on the first day and increasingly as the game progresses.

5 It should wear sufficiently to give the finger spinners some assistance by tea-time on the second day and greater assistance on the last day.

6 The pace and bounce should at all times encourage the batsmen to play shots.

What the sub-committee did not do – and no one else has yet succeeded in doing either – was to produce a recipe to guarantee production of such a wicket, allowing for difficulties of weather and variations in soil and turf on different grounds. They were, in fact, trying to do the impossible. Warwickshire's feeling was that too much had been done for seam bowlers and too little for spin bowlers. It was decided that, as even Big Bertha's weight had not proved a panacea at Edgbaston, two areas of the square each two pitches wide, should be lifted at the end of 1963 and the sub-soil changed to see if this would bring about any improvement.

446

The Test Match had brought some twenty-five letters on the subject of protecting and drying pitches and criticising antiquated methods, though, goodness knows, Bernard Flack and his boys would have tried anything, short of setting fire to the pitch, which might have done the trick. However, the letters did lead the Committee to suggest to other counties that a body should be set up to investigate the position and to experiment, Warwickshire offering a grant towards the cost. The counties agreed, and Cyril Goodway was appointed chairman, a tribute to the wide experience and knowledge he had acquired as chairman of Warwickshire's ground and buildings sub-committee.

The new Press Box stand had been completed in time for the Test, providing seats for another 1000 spectators and including two private boxes which industrial concerns could book and reserve for their guests. Tenders were also invited for the first phase of the Pavilion (west wing) extension. The Club had rejected the idea of an overall plan for development because of factors it could not control and had long been working on the principle of providing dual-purpose buildings which would pay for themselves throughout a full year, not just in the four months of the cricket season – in short, making the ground a club, not solely a cricket club.

The game lost heavily by deaths during the year, the obituary columns recording the passing not only of such national figures as Sir Pelham Warner and Sir Jack Hobbs, but also of three Warwickshire members of very long standing. First in length of years was 'the grand old man of Warwickshire cricket', J. Ernest Hill, who had first played for the county in 1888 and scored the first century made on the county's entry into first-class cricket. He was in his 97th year and, in the chairman's words, 'his life ran parallel with the Club's full history'. He was the last survivor of the famous match with Yorkshire in 1896, and he was always happy to end his reminiscences of that famous occasion with the remark, 'They didn't win the match, you know.'

Another link with the earliest days was broken by the death of Miss Mabel Ansell, last surviving member of William Ansell's family, who died at Edgbaston at the age of 87. She was very knowledgeable about Warwickshire cricket and she remembered her mother once telling her on the balcony of the old pavilion that however good the play it was 'not seemly for a young lady to applaud in public, even with gloves on'.

The third was George Austin, aged 73, faithful chronicler of Warwickshire's doings on the field for fifty-two years and associated with the Club for even longer than that, having been engaged as office boy when he was 14. It was said that he never missed a ball until illness overtook him during the Essex match a week before his death, an astounding record, and I, for one, have had cause to be grateful for his neat caligraphy. His appearance was always so youthful that he was always known to his intimates as 'Chicko'. Of kindly manner, he loved the game to distraction; only such a man would have gone on all those years for the salary Warwickshire were able to pay him. Although not strictly entitled to membership, he was the only man ever honoured by the Old Players' Association with a standing invitation to attend their functions. He died in the spring of the year and all the players stood in silence for him on the ground he loved. I only wish I had had an opportunity of talking to him before he died. He was succeeded by another old cricketer, Jack Wilkinson, aged 70, the second-eleven scorer, who once played for Worcestershire, and had played for Dudley, in the Birmingham League, for thirty-seven years.

Mr Michael G. Parsons, who had succeeded his uncle, James C. Parsons as auditor of the Club, when the latter died the previous year, now left the firm with which the family had been associated for many years following a merger and set up practice on his own account. The 70-year-old link between the Club and the family, however, was maintained.

Following illness, 'Tiger' at last relinquished full-time coaching duties at the Indoor School, though he remained as supervisor, Cartwright taking over his coaching work. 'Tiger' was 77, but to have retired completely would have been unthinkable to him and Edgbaston would not have seemed the same without him. His coaching colleague, Derief Taylor, was meanwhile honoured by an invitation, which the Club allowed him to accept, to return to his native Jamaica and coach for two months for the Jamaican Board of Cricket Control.

No fewer than three Warwickshire players were also on tour that winter – Ibadulla as a member of the Commonwealth XI which toured Pakistan and for whom he made scores of 50, 40, 19, 103 not out, 40 and 76 in representative matches; and M. J. K. Smith and Cartwright, both of whom went to East Africa – Smith as captain – and had successful tours.

Warwickshire were not only runners-up both in the County Championship and the Gillette Cup in 1964, but for the first time in their history they beat the Australians at Edgbaston. This match was a thriller, the margin being a mere 9 runs with only two balls left to play, after both captains had sportingly declared. It was the fifth time the county had beaten a touring side – South Africa in 1910, India in 1911, and the West Indies in 1928 and 1950.

The tourists had been beaten in the previous match with Glamorgan, but probably few people would have bet on them losing two matches in succession. The foundation for a notable victory was laid by Barber, who hit a brilliant century before lunch on the first day and completed 138, including twenty-two fours, out of 209 in two and one-quarter hours. It was only the second century made by a Warwickshire player against them and 384 was their highest total. On the second day, when three and one-quarter hours were lost through rain, the Australians had five wickets down for 169 and might have been in real trouble but for a not out hundred by Burge. Young Mence did most of the damage – four for 48.

Booth, who was captaining the side in the absence of Simpson, declared at 253 for eight – there was obviously no point in batting out – and then Warwickshire added 63 to their first innings lead of 131, leaving the Australians to make 195 in two and a half hours at a rate of 76 an hour. Some Australian teams would not have attempted it, but, all credit to the 1964 side, they batted adventurously to the last man. They began poorly, but Potter and Burke added 95 in an hour and with 60 minutes remaining they still needed 47, which should have been within their powers. Then Potter was brilliantly caught by Miller at mid-wicket, and when Edmonds began the last over of the match 14 runs were still needed. Martin hit the first ball for four, then skied the next and was caught at mid-on. Sellers played one ball and was bowled by the fourth and with Grout unable to bat Warwickshire were home and dry. Edmonds, aged 23 – and on vacation from King Edward's School, Birmingham, where he was teaching physical education – took five for 68, with two wickets in one over, and Bannister three for 25, the Australians being all out 185.

It was not Edgbaston's turn for a Test this year, but Cartwright was chosen to play in two of them. He came in for the fourth match at Manchester where Australia piled on the agony of a total of 656 for eight declared, and had the mortification of having Simpson missed at the wicket on the leg side when he was 23, after which the latter went on to make his mammoth score of 311. It took him twelve and a half hours and is the longest Test innings ever played in England. *Wisden* recorded that Cartwright's 'control of length at medium pace and some movement off the pitch occasionally worried the batsmen', but it did not worry them enough. All the same, he was England's most successful bowler with five wickets, though they cost him 45·60 runs each.

M. J. K. Smith, who had been among the twelve chosen for the match but was left out, probably regretted missing an opportunity to take some runs off the Australians when England piled up another huge score – 611. It took twenty-eight and a half hours to get a result on the first innings and if that was not reducing Test cricket to a farce it is difficult to imagine anything more boring. In the last Test Cartwright did not score, but he took the wickets of Simpson, O'Neill and Grout for 110 runs.

M. J. K. Smith led an M.C.C. team on a short spring tour of India and earned high praise. Smith and D. G. Clark, the manager, said *Wisden*, formed an exceptionally good team and their conduct of this tour should serve as a model for all such ventures ... they made themselves and the team popular visitors wherever they went. Inside the party they quickly developed a degree of team spirit which is not common among England teams abroad and that spirit proved its sterling worth when illness laid low several of the players. It was proof against the crisis of Bombay, where the second Test was played against a hospital background.

Barrington broke a finger, Mortimore, Edrich and Sharp were affected by stomach trouble and Wilson was nursing an injured back but played. By tea-time Surrey's Stewart was also down with stomach trouble and a substitute fielder had to be borrowed from India who nevertheless were fought to a level draw. 'Only a team possessing that team spirit that stems from good leadership and sound management could have risen so superior to the depressing difficulties', said *Wisden*.

Later in a letter to the Warwickshire Club came Clark's own tribute to Smith:

It is difficult to imagine a better person to captain a side in India. Under conditions where leadership is a first essential, he could not be faulted. When conditions were difficult he was completely unflappable. On the field he set a fine example, being a great fielder, and always tried to score runs fast when the occasion demanded it. Although at times he must have been very tired, he never showed it. He was the greatest help to an inexperienced manager and any success that the tour achieved must largely be due to his efforts.

High praise indeed.

Troubles did not spoil Smith's form either. Although he did not make a century – his highest score in a Test was 75 not out – he averaged 51 in the Tests, scoring 306 runs. These encomiums proved to be the start of a run of M.C.C. team captaincies which also took him to Australia and South Africa.

At home Worcestershire won the County Championship by the largest margin of points since 1957 – 191 to 150 – but for most of the season it was a tremendous fight – with Warwickshire. Worcestershire took the lead in mid-May, then lost it and Warwickshire, apart from one series of games, hung on to it until early in August. Then Worcestershire forged ahead again and finished so strongly that they had made sure of the title when they still had three games to play, whereas Warwickshire won only one of their last five games. Worcestershire had no fewer than four bowlers in the first twelve in the first-class averages, illustrating once more the truth of the old saying that bowling wins matches – and Championships.

Tired or not, Smith again headed the Warwickshire averages, though with fewer runs, 1586, average 39·65, and only one century. Barber improved greatly and usually opened with Ibadulla, who, while he was out coaching in New Zealand the previous autumn, had scored 166 for Pakistan against Australia. Horner also reached 1000 runs, but Stewart was inconsistent and Jameson too impatient at the start of an innings, though he and Amiss, who was also disappointing, shared in the highest stand of the summer, 255 against Oxford.

Cartwright was a model of accuracy and took 128 wickets for only 13·78 runs each, a fantastically low average. Brown would probably have taken 100 wickets for the first time except for injury – he was almost as unlucky as Field – and had seventy-six for 19·72, but Barber's tally fell to forty-one and Bridge, for whom even psychiatric treatment had not brought a return to form, played in only two matches.

'Mike' Smith began by scoring 109 for once out against his old county, who were beaten by five wickets at Leicester and at Edgbaston by nine wickets. Hampshire were shot out for 89 and 99 at Edgbaston, first by Brown and Miller, and then by Bannister and Cartwright; at Old Trafford they got rid of Lancashire for 168 and 157; and Notts were routed for 34 and 57 at Edgbaston, where Cartwright had first-innings figures of 5 overs, 4 maidens, 3 runs and 4 wickets, and nine for 40 in the match.

But there were even more remarkable happenings at Worthing. First, Thomson, of Sussex, took all ten Warwickshire wickets for 49 and followed this up with five for 26 in the second innings. Even so Warwickshire won by no fewer than 182 runs, for Sussex were first dismissed for 120 – Brown four for 50 – and then for the quite incredible score of 23, their lowest total for forty-four years. The innings lasted only fifty-five minutes, and five batsmen failed to score. It is safe to say that no three Warwickshire bowlers have ever produced analyses like these in the same innings:

	O	M	R	W
BROWN	6·0	4	7	2
BANNISTER	6·0	2	16	6
CARTWRIGHT	0·2	0	0	2

The mystery here is why Smith troubled to change the bowling.

After this at Edgbaston in the first innings against Kent Cartwright had figures of O: 13, M: 9, R: 7, W: 2 and then in the second innings took the last five wickets in seven overs for 8 runs – seven for 56 in all. It was devastating bowling.

No quarter was asked for or given in the two blood battles with Worcestershire. The first one at Worcester was a hard-fought draw and, it must be admitted, a dull affair, Worcestershire batting on so long that Warwickshire, facing a total to win of 243, were given only seventy-three minutes' batting, a farcical declaration by Kenyon. Worcestershire had gained first innings lead by one run after Warwickshire's last pair had made 9 of the 11 runs they needed when they came together. So great was the interest in the struggle between the two sides that there were 13 000 people present on the first day, and the aggregate attendance was 24 500, the best ever for a county match at Worcester and the highest gate since the Australians were there in 1948 – which just shows what a bit of needle can do.

Bannister was lucky to have chosen the return match with Worcestershire for his benefit, even though, because of a knee injury, he was prevented from playing in it. The match receipts alone brought him nearly £3000 and other efforts took the figure to £8846, yet another record for the Club. This time the Champions-to-be won by the handsome margin of 219 runs. Twice Warwickshire's batting broke down against Coldwell, Standen, Gifford and Horton on a pitch which increasingly gave help to the bowlers – and it was their turn to be put out cheaply for only 72 and 86, the former score one of their lowest ever totals against Worcestershire. Dick Richardson took four brilliant catches. Cartwright had ten wickets in the match for 84 runs, but they were not enough to offset two such batting failures.

After Notts had caught another cold at Trent Bridge, being dismissed for 49 before lunch, Webster returned fresh from qualifying as a doctor and celebrated by giving Warwickshire a tonic, wrecking Yorkshire's innings at Edgbaston with this remarkable analysis:

O	M	R	W
12·4	7	6	7

Yorkshire, wondering what had hit them, were all out for 54, of which one man, Padgett, made 28, and then Webster, just to show them that it was no fluke, took five more of their second innings wickets for 52. When Warwickshire went to Harrogate both Barber and Ibadulla took centuries off Yorkshire's bowling, but could not force a win.

A dashing young batsman named Colin Milburn, who might so easily have played for Warwickshire instead of Northants, scored 117 and 31 against Warwickshire at Northampton, and although there was a near-record stand for the last wicket by Hitchcock and Edmonds of 115, only 13 short of the record by Santall and Sanders, Northants won by 64 runs.

Warwickshire's Championship hopes were finally dashed at Southampton where Hampshire beat them by 17 runs, though they went down with colours flying for they very nearly succeeded in scoring 314 to win at 90 an hour. With fourteen minutes and two wickets left they needed only 26, but that old schemer, Shackleton, with White, each took a wicket. Shackleton had taken six for 55 in the first innings in which Ibadulla had made 100 out of a total of 175.

According to *Wisden*, the knock-out competition, as had been hoped, had 'proved a money-spinner in filling some grounds', though the Editor was not enamoured of most of the cricket it produced. 'In this one-day tournament', he wrote, 'most captains aim to bowl defensively to keep down the run rate for with the number of overs limited in each innings there is no need to make special effort to dismiss the opposition.' Surely this could have been foreseen.

M. J. K. Smith had told Warwickshire's annual meeting: 'We went the wrong way about it last year. This year we intend to devote at least one full day's practice to this type of game.' Well, whatever it was they practised, it was undoubtedly M.J.K.'s defensive field placings which triggered off *Wisden's* condemnation. They caused a rumpus and the blame was laid fairly and squarely by *Wisden* at Warwickshire's feet:

The sides successful in knock-out cricket generally use a battery of seam bowlers and defensive field placings. This playing pattern has received criticism from many quarters and the defensive tactics used by Warwickshire and the counter-measures adopted by Lancashire in the semi-final caused the crowd to barrack. There was talk of legislation to make captains adopt a more attacking outlook in the field. [This would have been the supreme irony – L.D.] A negative attitude can only do harm to one-day cricket, as it has to the first-class game.

The Minor Counties were brought into the competition this time, which brought an increase in the sponsors' grant to £8000. Warwickshire had a bye in the first round and in the second easily beat Hampshire at Edgbaston by 172 runs, Jameson making 100 not out and M. J. K. Smith 88 – 127 in an hour for the fifth wicket. In the third round at Northampton, they got their revenge for the defeat of the previous season, disposing of the home team by 147 runs, Barber saying 'Thank you' for being put in to bat by hitting a fine 114, which won him the man-of-the-match award. He and Horner took 134 off twenty-eight overs for the first wicket and Stewart and Jameson added 58 in eight overs.

This took them to the semi-final at Old Trafford where the real fun began. It must have pleased Barber greatly to give his new county a splendid start with 79 out of 119, and Warwickshire's batsmen generally so attacked the bowling that they rattled up 294 for seven wickets in their sixty overs. With such a total under his belt, it might be wondered why Smith should trouble to set defensive fields, but Lancashire made a bold reply and it was Smith's efforts to clamp down on them which caused the trouble.

Clayton, the Lancashire wicketkeeper, chose to protest against the defensive field placings, first by appealing against the light and then often refusing to go for runs. He scored only 17 while seventeen overs were bowled and he was not out 19 at the end when Lancashire's score was 209 for seven. Both sides were heavily barracked in the closing stages and one can hardly blame the spectators, for this was the very negation of the kind of cricket the knock-out competition had been devised to present. Clayton was later dropped by the Lancashire committee, to whose officials he afterwards apologised, as he did to Warwickshire's.

Smith's defensive field settings in the final against Sussex at Lord's, though far more justified than they were against Lancashire, earned him a mild reproof from Herbert Sutcliffe, the adjudicator, and this time they did not pay a dividend. Warwickshire, facing Thomson on a green wicket in a humid atmosphere which enabled him to swing the ball about like a punctured balloon – I have never seen such acute swing – were dismissed for 127, despite a valiant not out 35 by Alan Smith. Thomson took four wickets for 17 in his first eight overs and four for 23 in all, and rightly got the man-of-the-match award. Sussex had no difficulty in hitting off the runs for the loss of only two wickets.

Not all the criticism of Smith's tactics came from outside the Club. The annual report was strangely silent on this aspect of the matter, but Peter Cranmer, for one, had sufficient doubts about the wisdom of methods which obviously tended to defeat the whole purpose of the competition to speed up the game and provide brighter cricket, to raise the matter in Committee. Their verdict was uncompromisingly in support of the captain's actions:

After batting attractively to score nearly 300 runs, it had been suggested in certain quarters that it was wrong to set a defensive field so early in the Lancashire innings [after ten overs]. The Club captain, members of his team, and the cricket world at large saw nothing wrong with this strategy which had been employed a number of times in cup matches already and, in any event, it was felt that a defensively set field should encourage short singles, which could be as effective as the occasional boundary. Consensus of opinion was that no official action whatsoever was called for, but it was confirmed that the Committee was unanimously behind the Club captain in his action and indeed in his general control and running of the team throughout the season.

Well, *Wisden* had certainly seen something wrong. On the other hand, the criticism was also made that fieldsmen were often brought too close in to prevent the single and thus conceded fours, the theory being that it is easier to run in to a ball than to have to turn and chase it.

If anyone needed evidence to support a contention that Midland people as a whole cared little about the *quality* of the cricket they saw, unless there was something at stake and it was exciting, this was forthcoming in a match played at Edgbaston towards the end of the season. The Committee was invited to stage a game between an England XI captained by Dexter and including several Warwickshire players, and Sir Frank Worrell's West Indies XI, which meant that in a season in which there was no Test at Edgbaston the public still had a chance to see some of the world's greatest players.

Yet, as the annual report regretted, the 'gate' was 'wholly disappointing' and in three days no more than £773 was taken in receipts and Warwickshire's half share of the profits was no more than £606. Not that this mattered overmuch because the match was partly sponsored by Rothman's, but the Committee had agreed to put on the match 'in the hope that in bringing international cricket to Edgbaston at that time [8, 9 and 10 September] it would, in part, satisfy a demand that has been expressed on so many occasions for a season stretching into September – or at least a good match coinciding in timing with the Festival cricket played at seaside resorts.'

Well, the public by and large missed what the report went on to describe as 'the perfect cricket match, with a decision well within the prescribed three days and offering literally everything this wonderful game can provide when properly played. Perhaps the very fact that there was nothing at stake beyond providing entertainment for a public and enjoyment for the players, gave freedom of mind and body to the participants and they certainly revelled in it.'

The West Indies were disposed of for 137 in the first innings, thanks to some finely controlled bowling by Worcestershire's Coldwell, who took six for 36. England did not do much better with 183, of which Dexter made 84, but the second innings of Worrell's XI positively scintillated with superb batting, especially by Kanhai, who hit a brilliant 170, with six sixes and twenty fours. 'On the second day', the Warwickshire report stated, 'when Rohan Kanhai was at the crease, those present saw batting of a talent and quality they are seldom, if ever, likely to see equalled.' No wonder Warwickshire later engaged him. The West Indies declared at 408 for six and then Dexter gave another taste of his quality with 110 out of 210; but the West Indies won easily by 193 runs after a great game which those who had the luck and the foresight to go and see were very grateful to Warwickshire for presenting.

On the whole, though, since it was an Australian year, attendances throughout the country were better than they had been in 1963 – 832 993 compared with 719 661 – and Warwickshire were second only to Yorkshire with an aggregate of 81 175, though it is ironic that whereas 204 000 paid to see them when they won the Championship in 1951 fewer than half that number came to see them try to win it – and very nearly succeed – in 1964.

Despite the absence of a Test Match, there was an increase in income from cricket of £2561 to £30 125, largely due to £13 235 from the Test Pool and £2325 as the result of getting to the final of the Gillette Cup. The general income, however, fell from £19 276 to £16 497 mainly because of reduced earnings from the Pavilion Suite, but the accounts showed an overall surplus of £5617.

All this was small beer compared with the money the Supporters' Association were making. Their overall surplus on the year's working was £167 891 and their membership three times that of the combined total of all other supporters' associations linked with game. There was some criticism of their action in giving help to other counties, especially an interest-free loan to Essex to enable them to buy the Chelmsford ground, but Edgar Hiley defended it by saying that Warwickshire's gesture had been acclaimed throughout the country, one national newspaper describing it 'as the happiest sports story of the year'.

Following the West Indies Test complaints, Warwickshire had the bright idea of sponsoring a novel competition, with prizes of £500 and £100, to try to find an answer to the problem of protecting pitches from the weather, the area to which suggestions should apply being sixty by forty yards. They got a little more than perhaps they bargained for – 563 entries from a dozen different countries in all parts of the world, including two from as far away as Australia and one from Malta.

Mr John Porter, architect, and Mr Bill Langdon, engineer, had the job of sorting out the entries, which included a suggestion for a cover for the whole ground, which, unfortunately, was not mobile; a balloon hovering over the square so that the game could go on even in a downpour; hovercraft to cover the wicket; tunnels under the pitch to let the water drain into them like sewers; a vacuum system for sucking the rain down as it fell; and finally an offer of help from a reputed African witch doctor, who claimed (in quite reasonable English) to be able to stop rain with the same ease as the rain-makers of film and fiction make it come.

The entries were reduced to a short-list of thirty-three, but none of them was considered sufficiently practical to win the first prize outright, so they shared awards ranging from £75 to £10, amounting to about £500 in all. The bright ideas were not the monopoly of the competitors, however. Cyril Goodway had one to provide perhaps 1600 more seats at Tests by means of sheets of white-painted plywood installed behind the wicket at both ends, so that only the faces of the spectators would be visible to the players. John Nash, the Yorkshire secretary, whose retirement in 1971 left Leslie Deakins the longest-serving county secretary in the country, called the system 'The Jury Box', but it worked and had the effect of adding £2000 to £3000 in gate receipts from seats previously unusable.

There were more comments during the season about that wicket, and the annual report agreed that 'one or two wickets towards the season's end proved to a degree dangerous'. The Derbyshire captain, Derek Morgan, wrote to the M.C.C. in August, about sifted soil and grass cuttings on the wicket. This brought a strong letter from the Advisory County Cricket Committee who were told that the wicket had been prepared in conformity with the Committee's own directive. The pitch in the following match against Surrey also brought complaints, this time from Barrington, the acting captain, that the ball knocked pieces out of the pitch. Again Warwickshire replied that the pitch had been prepared in accordance with instructions. They contended it was a good cricket wicket and that its variations were due to the effect of the weather during the game.

However, in October a strip of the square was dug up and it was found that there was only a very thin layer of turf cover, with stunted root growth, over compacted soil on top of damp clay. One would have thought that this would have become evident in the ordinary course of repairing bowlers' footholds. Anyway, it was replaced with approximately eight inches of rubble, topped with fine ash, and then loam.

A singular honour came to Dollery during the summer. He was elected a member of the general committee, the first paid officer of the Club to hold such a position in his own right as distinct from through his work. He was still officially captain of the second eleven, although he had not played for some time, and still watched every match.

When the time came in the autumn to choose the M.C.C. team to tour South Africa, the country was in the middle of a General Election in which the reigning England captain, Ted Dexter, was a candidate, so the Selection Committee had to look elsewhere for a captain. After the praise lavished on him for his leadership in India, it was fairly obvious that their choice would fall on M. J. K. Smith; and as Alan Smith was also selected to lead a team to South America, Warwickshire supplied captains for two overseas tours in one winter, which is probably unique.

M.J.K. had with him county colleagues in Barber, Cartwright and Brown, and Dexter joined the party after being beaten at the polls. Donald Carr, assistant secretary of the M.C.C. was manager and he and Smith hit it off as well as Clark and Smith had done. The series, which England won, was a success from the playing and every other point of view. 'At once', wrote *Wisden's* correspondent, 'Smith welded his men together and instilled confidence. As captain of Warwickshire for eight seasons, Smith had already proved those qualities of leadership first displayed at Oxford ... Supporting him was D. B. Carr ... between them they formed a happy partnership which greatly benefited English cricket and may have begun an upsurge of England's Test fortunes.'

Basil Easterbrook, one of the Press correspondents on the tour, thought that the M.C.C. might have sent out more powerful teams, 'but never one superior in terms of corporate effort on the playing pitch and harmony in the pavilion. Manager and captain set the tone by behaving naturally and unchangingly to all with whom they had to deal . . . They were as near ideal executives as anything can be in this imperfect world.'

Easterbrook also thought Smith 'a wily and phlegmatic captain', though he mildly criticised him for his reluctance to use his leg spinners more. Smith scored nearly 900 runs on the tour, averaging 58, but Barber had the better record in the Tests, with an average of no less than 71·50. Cartwright, unfortunately, revived an old soccer injury and bowled in only one Test in which he took two wickets for plenty – 196 – and he had no more than twenty-five on the whole tour, though he had better fortune as a batsman, averaging nearly 50 in all matches.

In his last match before he left England, Brown, playing for the President of the M.C.C.'s XI against the Australians, had bowled Simpson for a 'pair', the Australian captain's first such distinction. However, Brown could not adapt his bowling to South African conditions, being much too prone to bowl down the leg side, so that he did not get a chance in the Tests, though he took twenty-three wickets on the tour and averaged 20 with the bat.

The team Alan Smith led to South America, the first to go there for six years, was composed mostly of public-school-reared cricketers and won fourteen of its fifteen matches. The captain averaged 34 and acted as deputy wicketkeeper after M. G. Griffith had broken a toe.

Decline and Fall
(1965)

JUST at a time when their supporters had reasonable hopes that they would again win the Championship, Warwickshire, in 1965, suffered a marked decline and it was again their near neighbours, Worcestershire, who pulled it off for the second year running, winning ten of their last eleven games and clinching the title with but ten minutes of extra time to spare. Three of their bowlers – Coldwell, Carter and Gifford – did the hat trick, a feat without parallel for three bowlers of any one county in the same season.

Warwickshire, in the person of their President, Lieut-General Sir Oliver Leese, had an interest in their success, for in his capacity as President of the M.C.C. this season, it was his privilege and pleasure to attend their celebration dinner and congratulate them.

The Presidency of the M.C.C. was the highest honour in the game that had yet come to a Warwickshire man, and it was the latest in a long list of M.C.C. appointments dating back to H. W. Bainbridge, who was a member of the M.C.C. Committee from 1906 to 1909 and again from 1913 to 1916. He had been followed by the Hon. F. S. G. Calthorpe (1926–9), R. E. S. Wyatt (1951–3), C. A. F. Hastilow (1965–7) and later Sir Oliver was also to be a member from 1968 to 1970. Members serve for three years only at a time and are not allowed immediately to seek re-election, though they may do so for another three-year period if proposed and seconded.

There were no celebrations in the President's own county. So far from giving Worcestershire even a run for their money, Warwickshire fell to eleventh position. They won only five matches and the number of draws doubled compared with the season before, to eighteen. This was partly due to the weather, which several times prevented them from going for victory when in a favourable position on the last day. But there were other reasons. For the first time since the Triangular Tournament of 1912, there were two touring sides in England this summer, New Zealand and South Africa, each having three Tests. M. J. K. Smith and Barber played in all of them, thus missing twelve county matches, and no side could release players of such calibre for so long and not miss them. Cartwright and Brown were also called on and four other players missed matches through injury or illness. Hitchcock had retired from the game to devote more time to his business, Horner had gone into turf maintenance and Ibadulla was not at his best.

Only one century was scored for Warwickshire all season in the County Championship. That came from Stewart and it was his first in three years. With M. J. K. Smith also losing form and not scoring a hundred for the first time since he joined the county – was he having too much cricket? – Stewart headed the averages, but with no higher figure than 39·16, and the three batsmen who made over 1000 runs only just did so.

In all matches Cartwright managed to get his 100 wickets, but both Bannister – although he became the county's fourth bowler, and only the second of their pace men, to take 1000 wickets in his career – and Brown fell away. Bridge's loss of form had been so devastatingly complete that he played in only one Championship match and at the end of the season he retired from the game, leaving the mystery of his decline unsolved. Miller was handicapped by injury, so the spin bowling was almost non-existent.

Thus Alan Smith, during his namesake's absence, was left to lead a sadly depleted side which obviously lacked stability, especially as none of the younger players tried seized what should have been golden opportunities for them to make their mark. No fewer than half a dozen combinations of opening batsmen were tried and, in the early part of the season, Amiss virtually held together what batting there was. Both the acting captain, who had an impossible task, and Jameson were called upon to bowl and both did it so successfully that each did the hat trick, Smith's against Essex being the only known case of the feat being performed by a player who had taken off his wicketkeeping pads to bowl.

This was at Clacton, where Webster was injured and could not go on in the second innings. With the new ball, which he swung to some tune, Smith dismissed Barker, G. Smith and Fletcher with consecutive balls and when he had added Trevor Bailey to his collection he had taken four wickets in thirty-four balls without a run being hit off him. Subsequently he conceded 36, but ten of his twenty-one overs were maidens. Essex just saved the game with the last pair at the wicket.

Jameson's hat trick was against Gloucestershire and it finished off the innings. He bowled only four overs and two balls and had only 3 runs scored off him. Warwickshire had an extraordinary second innings against Derbyshire at Edgbaston. It reached 185 for nine, and only two players got double figures and five did not score at all. Rhodes sent back the first two batsmen for 4 runs and had a spell of four overs in which he took five wickets for 7 runs, but then Ibadulla, 85, and Jameson 79, put on 163 in 95 minutes. Then came Rhodes's deadly spell, and he finished with seven for 38. 'Mike' Smith had the misfortune to have nought against his name in both innings.

There was a thrilling finish at Taunton where Somerset won by one wicket, Hall, the last man in, hitting the two needed to win off the last ball but one of the match. Virgin, adding 82 to the two hundreds, 124 and 125, he had made off the Warwickshire bowling at Edgbaston, joined the band of batsmen who loved to face the county's bowling. All the same, Warwickshire won by three wickets, Stewart this time hitting a four off the fourth ball of the last over to do it.

Cartwright, released from the Test twelve against South Africa at The Oval, took six for 46 and six for 54 against Middlesex at Edgbaston; he then went on to Derby where he had seven for 48; and he finished the season by taking five for 47 against Middlesex, again at Lord's. This put him fourth in the first-class averages with 108 wickets for 13·93 runs each.

There was one Test Match at Edgbaston in this wet and windy summer – against New Zealand – and it was quite spoiled by the weather – 'seldom in England has a Test been conducted in such cold, cheerless weather', noted *Wisden* – even though England won by nine wickets. Smith, as captain, Barber and Cartwright all played, Barber taking the honours with innings of 31 and 51 and two for seven and four for 132. In the first innings he had a first wicket partnership of 54 with Boycott.

England made 435, mostly due to 137 by Barrington, but it was an innings of such boring inertia that he was dropped as a disciplinary measure. On the Thursday it took him three and one-quarter hours to get to 61, with only three fours, and altogether he was at the wicket for seven and one-quarter hours – just over one-third of a run per over. He was on 85 for over an hour while twenty overs were bowled. Not even the cold – the temperature was 47° F (8.5° C) and hot coffee was twice served – or the fact that J. R. Reid, the New Zealand captain, described the wicket as 'the slowest in the world' (for which Cyril Goodway blamed the Arctic conditions before and during its preparation) could justify play such as this. The England innings lasted nine hours and it would have been enough to drive everyone screaming from the ground even if the weather had been perfect. It was ironic to a degree that when M. J. K. Smith went out to bat in the midst of all this gloom and despondency he was lbw for nought, his fourth cypher in his last six innings and his tenth in Test cricket.

New Zealand, perhaps overcome with weariness, if not boredom as well, obviously could not cope with Titmus, Cartwright and Barber and they were disheartened by losing Bert Sutcliffe, their outstanding batsman, in a most unfortunate manner. Trueman, trying to force some pace out of the wicket, had bounced one or two and Sutcliffe ducked into one that did not rise and was hit on the right ear. The game was held up for eight minutes and though he tried to continue his innings he became dizzy and had to go off. New Zealand were in such a plight, however, that he came back for a few minutes before lunch, but during the interval it was decided that he was not fit to continue and the innings closed for 116.

Smith, no doubt thinking of the Edgbaston gate, did not enforce the follow-on, but declared after England had added 96 more runs to their first innings lead of 319. New Zealand made a brave attempt to get the runs. Sutcliffe had recovered sufficiently to be able to bat in the second innings and he made a very useful 53, sharing with Pollard in a record stand of 104 for their seventh wicket. Trueman had the grace and sense to keep the ball up to him on or outside the off stump and he played some fine strokes, though he was never again quite the same batsman. Pollard made 91 not out and New Zealand reached 413 before the last wicket fell.

Only 21 000 people attended the match, New Zealand's share of the receipts being no more than £1000 and on the final day, when England had won by a quarter to one, only 107 people paid to watch the finish.

Barrington was back for the third Test and made 163, somewhat more rapidly this time, but two years later Boycott also suffered the indignity of being dropped against India for his negative approach and that after scoring 246 not out; but, he, too, came back after missing one Test. The 'sentences', if one can call them that, were not extensive enough. Smith was very much out of form in both series of Tests in 1965, making only 46 runs, 44 of them in one innings against New Zealand and only 112 in six innings against South Africa. Barber, on the other hand, had 142 against New Zealand and 172 against South Africa.

In the second Test Snow was preferred to Cartwright, thus making his first appearance for England, and taking four wickets in the match for 80. Brown got his first cap against South Africa, when he took three for 44 and three for 30. He was injured and missed the second Test against them, in which Cartwright, after taking six for 94 in the first innings, broke his right thumb stopping a hard return and did not bowl again. South Africa won the match by 94 runs; it was only the first defeat in fifteen matches in which Smith had led England. In all the Tests Barber scored 314 runs, with a highest score of 56 for an average of 28·54; and Smith, 158, highest 44, average 22·57. Cartwright headed the bowling with eight wickets for 120, while Brown had eight for 200.

The New Zealanders provided Warwickshire with their best match of the season at Edgbaston at the end of June. The county won by nine wickets, though at one time, when they had lost four for 64, they seemed well on the way to defeat. New Zealand batted first and declared at 297 for nine. Warwickshire's reply began badly, but then Jameson and Cartwright came together and in the next three hours and forty minutes they added 255, only 13 short of the county record for the fifth wicket made by the Quaife brothers in 1900. Jameson's share was 137 and Cartwright made 112.

Warwickshire were able to declare at 319 for four wickets, and then they got New Zealand out for 219 despite a fine innings by Reid, who hit 22 off one over from Bridge, though the latter caught and bowled him in the end. Warwickshire had to make 198 at 77 an hour and thanks to a stand of 132 in 75 minutes by Ibadulla and 'Mike' Smith they did it with twelve minutes to spare. A fine match and a fine win, and Smith's 61 not out must have been some consolation for his earlier lack of form.

The game with South Africa in August was ruined by rain and left drawn. There was no play at all on the Saturday and another downpour on Tuesday ended the match just as South Africa were going in to try to make 180 to win in two hours and five minutes. In between times Warwickshire had scored 217 for seven declared, South Africa 208 for four declared and Warwickshire 170 for nine declared. No one could say the captains did not try to get a result.

Warwickshire again got to the semi-final of the Gillette Cup and then let Yorkshire put them out in a match which, the strongly critical annual report said, 'was literally thrown away by utterly inept batting and ill-judged running between the wickets'. In the first round Warwickshire easily beat Cambridgeshire by ten wickets, and they then disposed of Lancashire by six wickets at Edgbaston. Lancashire lost four wickets for 37 and never recovered. Edmonds took four for 33 and then Ibadulla and Amiss both made half-centuries. There was another comfortable win, this time by 74 runs, over Hampshire at Edgbaston in the third round. Ibadulla, despite several interruptions by rain, made 75 and then, with pacy off-breaks, took six for 32 and again was named man-of-the-match.

Because of the weather three days passed before Yorkshire and Warwickshire were able to bowl a ball in the semi-final at Edgbaston. Then on a drying pitch Yorkshire lost six wickets for 85, and that ought to have cost them the match; but Illingworth, 45, Binks and Trueman halted the collapse and took the total to 177. The Warwickshire batsmen then succumbed to an epidemic of what can only be called run-out madness. Beginning with Ibadulla, no fewer than five men lost their wickets in this way, and despite a valiant 39 by Alan Smith, who always seemed to be trying to pull chestnuts out of the fire in this sort of cricket, Warwickshire deservedly finished 20 runs behind. Yorkshire then went on to beat Surrey in the final. As M. J. K. Smith said when he apologised for this result at the following annual meeting, it was a moment when he felt, as someone had said before him, 'you did not necessarily have to be mad to survive such circumstances, but it helped.'

The Edgbaston wicket had come under fire earlier in the year from Brian Statham, who, in an article in *Wisden*, attributed most of his success in the previous season – 137 wickets for 12·52 runs each – to present-day pitches. He contended that the practice of leaving grass on them to help fast bowlers,

has proved a complete failure. Instead of every county possessing at least two genuine fast bowlers, as was the case twenty-five years ago, there is now a race of medium pacers, who bowl short of a reasonable length and rely on the seam to deviate the direction of the ball. Lush green outfields help to keep the shine on the ball and unless something is done the slow bowler will disappear from English cricket . . .

Surely it is time the groundsmen returned to the old method of using marl, cow manure and the heaviest possible roller. The way back to better first-class cricket is to remember that the state of the pitch governs the play. Fine weather is essential and when the sun shines batsmen should be able to know the ball will behave reasonably as it comes off a fast, true surface. Bowlers will learn that accurate length and direction, allied to speed and spin, are the main ingredients of success.

Edgbaston was listed as among the pitches in England considered worst: 'Edgbaston which had once the reputation of being the finest wicket in England, for batsmen at least.'

M. J. K. Smith took up the theme at the annual meeting. In his opinion a good deal of the trouble in the game throughout the world stemmed from pitches without pace. The problem was a vital one, but tremendously difficult of solution. He thought Edgbaston had a wonderful groundsman in Bernard Flack, but he could do little to alleviate the problem without leaving a lot of grass on. Originally, groundsmen had been told that wickets must last five days, for financial reasons, and this factor now guided Test Match wicket preparation. A little give-and-take on both sides would go a long way towards redressing the position.

Following Reid's complaint about the slowness of the wicket in the New Zealand Test, the matter was considered at the June meeting of the Committee when the secretary quoted a contrary opinion from C. D. Ingleby-Mackenzie, the Hampshire captain, that the pitch prepared for the Gillette Cup match was 'a thoroughly good wicket, one of the best

464

I've seen here and quite quick', a comment confirmed by one of his fast bowlers, David White.

The Committee reiterated their complete faith in Flack and decided to try the experimental wicket they had had re-laid, not in a match, because the turf had not knitted properly, but in a practice game. The verdict was that it was much firmer than the surrounding area of the square and that the ball came through more quickly and at a more consistent height. This led to a decision to re-lay one-third of the main square, which was excavated to a depth of two feet. Two-inch gravel was then laid to a depth of eight inches for drainage – the opportunity was taken to install a new drainage system along all four sides of the square – followed by ten inches of specially selected King's Norton loam, and finally turf from Staverton, near Northampton, was laid in a binding soil. Each September, over a three-year period, it was decided, one-third of the square would be similarly re-laid.

Few people except the groundsman have any idea of the wear and tear to which county ground pitches are subjected. There are twelve central wickets at Edgbaston on which Tests and first-eleven matches are played, and four others on either side making twenty, but even this is none too many in view of the number of games played on the ground – Tests, County Championship matches, Gillette Cup ties, John Player League games, Club and Ground, school games and various finals and friendlies traditionally played at Edgbaston.

The Advisory County Cricket Committee, reporting in November on wickets, noted with dismay the poor quality of pitches on county grounds and added: 'The pitches produced for Test Matches were good apart from Edgbaston, which was slow and turned early on.'

The Club's annual report, however, took leave to doubt whether hard, fast, true pitches were necessarily the sovereign remedy for cricket's ills, since the game usually came much more alive for the spectator when the bowlers had the upper hand; and in the Gillette Cup, when everyone was concerned with getting on with the game, the pitch was taken for granted and very little was heard about it as a decisive factor in the game.

The report sought different reasons for the further decrease in the number of people who came to watch cricket which, in Warwickshire's case, had been almost halved – from 81 175 to 42 421 – more marked than the overall drop from 832 993 to 659 568, though Warwickshire were still sixth in the attendances table. The remedy, in the report's view, was first to reduce the length of the first innings and to get the players making a positive approach from the first ball, and second, less cricket, with all matches starting on Saturdays. This, in turn, would remove the need for retaining a playing staff throughout the season. Players would be given a generous match fee for each game of, say, a sixteen-match programme and this would enable clubs to save 'enormously' on the vast salary bill they had at the moment to meet.

Some hints of what might happen in the future came in the last month of the year when David Clark, chairman of the Structure Sub-Committee set up by the Advisory County Cricket Committee, issued an interim report. After mentioning the fall in gates and disclosing that in 1965, for the first time, club memberships had shown signs of declining, the report said that despite this some counties were now more prosperous than ever before in their history, but that some might have to consider reducing their staffs. So far, however, the counties had agreed on only three points:

1 Hard, fast true wickets were in the best interests of the game, but while fifteen counties were trying to produce such wickets, only three were satisfied with the results obtained.

2 The need for a good over rate. Counties could help by including slow bowlers in the side, and by trying to reduce the run-ups of fast and fast-medium bowlers. All captains should aim at twenty overs an hour.

3 Alterations in the structure of the game necessary to change the attitude of players and make them realise that only by a positive approach and en- thusiastic and quick movement in the field, allied to aggressive batting and bowling, were they likely to interest the public again.

Points put forward by individual counties included more positive cricket on the first day, suggested by Sussex and Warwickshire; only one new ball an innings, put forward by Glamorgan; and complete covering of wickets, also put forward by Warwickshire and referred to the Clark sub-committee.

Sunday cricket, it had been decided, was to be allowed in twelve three-day matches in 1966, but no money was to be taken at the gates, though it could be received for seating, scorecards and car parks, which, incidentally, had brought in £50 000 in revenue to Warwickshire in the twenty years since the war. The Club had sought the views on Sunday play of Brigadier Sir Richard Calthorpe, then head of the Calthorpe Estate, who replied saying that it was a matter entirely for the Club and if they decided on it for the future the Estate would not object. 'I cannot think in this day and age,' he wrote, 'that a healthy game of cricket on a Sunday afternoon can do anyone any direct harm; indeed, it might keep some out of mischief.' Consequently, the Warwickshire Committee decided to seek the opinion of its members at the next annual meeting.

The most important development on the ground for many years was completed during the summer – the £400 000 stand designed as a memorial to the Club's founder, William Ansell, and named after him. It was officially opened in June, 100 guests making a tour of the dual-purpose building, which contained a ballroom, bars and refreshment rooms linked with the redesigned banqueting room in the adjoining west wing of the Pavilion (centre) as well as the new headquarters of the Supporters' Association, which had financed it. The President described it 'as just about the most modern and exciting stand on any cricket ground in this country – possibly in the world'.

No one was disposed to argue with him, though there had been some structural troubles, for which no one was anxious to accept responsibility, and in its natural anxiety to get the stand finished, the Club mortgaged for some time ahead the amount it could expect for reconstruction from the Association. This led to a revival of the finance subcommittee, which had not functioned since 1939, to keep an eye on such things. One of them was a deficiency of £13 781, largely due to a fall in income of £10 784 resulting from smaller receipts from the Tests and county matches. Another item which needed watching was the overdraft, now swollen to £41 000.

A move which could have had – and may still have – important implications for Club development came with discussions between the County Club and the Tally Ho! Lawn Tennis Club, with a view to a possible merger and the development of land on lease to the tennis club as a multi-indoor sports centre. The cost was estimated at around £750 000 and Leslie Deakins, enthusiastic for the scheme, regarded it as the most ambitious yet discussed for a Test cricket ground.

Edgar Hiley, on the other hand, while strongly convinced of the desirability of developing the ground on multi-sports lines, but fearing that, apart from squash rackets, few of the probable activities could be self-supporting, was very concerned lest the Club encumbered itself with an extremely costly venture which would mean an even greater drain on its funds. He also feared that if the Club went into it alone, without public money in order to preserve its independence, the Club would have to spend its invested funds and so lose the income, both in dividends and in capital appreciation, derived from them. The Club's architects were given authority to continue investigations into the possibilities, especially as Birmingham City Council, the Midlands Arts Centre in Cannon Hill Park, and the Government itself, through its Regional Sports Council, were also interested in possible developments there.

The talks went on for some time, but when it was found that the Arts Centre thought it could develop the area within three years, the County Club withdrew, since it was not in a position to undertake such a large-scale development in such a short space of time. As it happened, the Arts Centre, because of financial stringencies, was not then able to develop the area either.

While the discussions were going on about restructuring the game, what of the players' salaries? Some taxable income tables produced at this time showed that the maximum for a capped Warwickshire player was now £1000, the average basic salary being £700. Lancashire came next at £859. Warwickshire's equipment allowance for players just joining the Club was £30, twice as much as any other club, and other allowances for travel and meals compared favourably.

In some counties, supporters' clubs assisted the players in various ways, as they did in Warwickshire, with the Club's approval. Several players on the Warwickshire staff had insured themselves against injury with the result that under the salary scheme then in force they were better off not playing than playing, a state of affairs not unknown in the wider world of unemployment. They also had a car mileage allowance for travelling to and from away matches.

At the start of the season Deryck Murray, the West Indies wicket-keeper, had inquired through Rudi Webster if there was any chance of playing cricket with Warwickshire after the end of the Cambridge University term, but no offer could be made to him at that time in fairness to other wicketkeepers on the staff. No engagement was recommended either in the case of Intikhab Alam, later to play for Surrey and captain the Pakistan touring side.

A voice which had rebuked even the great ones of cricket with the stern injunction 'Sit down, please', was heard no more with the retirement at the end of August of Harry Mold, pavilion attendant, at the age of 74. He was a nephew of Albert Mold, the old Lancashire fast bowler, and he once told no less a person than Sir Learie Constantine, as he then was, not to move about.

For the first time that autumn a Warwickshire player was invited to captain an M.C.C. team in Australia and New Zealand. It was, of course, M. J. K. Smith, and though his side did not return in triumph with the 'Ashes', they did more for cricket, in the words of *Wisden*,

than the majority of international touring teams in recent years ... M.C.C. were anxious that each game be approached in a positive way; that a challenge be accepted if the faintest chance of winning existed; that the team should never contemplate tactical time-wasting. To make sure their wishes would be carried out the M.C.C. appointed their secretary, Mr S. C. Griffith, manager and granted him authority to over-ride the captain in matters of tactics, but it seems that only rarely did Mr Griffith find it necessary to criticise adversely. Right from the beginning of the tour, the M.C.C. played positive cricket, and when they had their occasional bad days these were usually due to excessive caution.

Perhaps only a player as unassuming and as easy to get on with as 'Mike' Smith would have tolerated such an arrangement. One can easily think of captains who would have refused flatly to take a team out under such a restriction, for it suggested that the M.C.C. had little faith in the judgment of the man they had invited to lead the team. By inference, their own judgment was thus sadly at fault, but Smith did not seem to mind and *Wisden* later had occasion to refer to 'M. J. K. Smith and his gay cavaliers'; two of whom were Barber and Brown.

Smith's success was one of leadership rather than of personal performances which, in fact, were poor in the matches that mattered – no more than 316 runs in the Tests against both Australia and New Zealand; though in other games he was more successful, scoring in all first-class matches 1079 runs at an average of 46·91. He did not escape criticism, especially from E. M. Wellings, who described the tour for *Wisden*. Wellings agreed that Smith and his men were 'widely acclaimed as an enterprising side', that Barber played attacking cricket from start to finish and that his 185 off only 225 balls in the Sydney Test was the superlative achievement of the whole tour.

But in the field Wellings thought Smith a cautious captain – 'his policy was based on defensive measures which played on the patience of his opponents . . . Smith's great virtue lay in his ability as a tour leader to take the players along with him. He had no tricks of leadership – in the modern idiom, no gimmicks. Yet he had a flair for leading and binding the team together.'

It was with good reason that Smith was regarded by his colleagues as pre-eminently a players' captain. David Brown once said of him: 'Without driving, he draws more reserves out of a player than any other captain I've known.'

Towards the end, however, wrote Wellings, his leadership was flagging and in the last three matches was a spent force. Wellings questioned the wisdom of Smith having his wife and two young children join him – the care of a family in a strange country was, he thought, a crippling additional burden. Wellings also roundly condemned Smith on one score – which in his view was vital to the health of the game – 'he did little or nothing to stir dawdling bowlers and fielders to maintain a satisfactory over rate. In only one first-class match did this reach the bare minimum of satisfaction – 120 balls an hour.' He also, in Wellings's opinion, did not use his spin bowlers enough, especially Barber, who was regarded as 'a luxury for occasional use at a probably high cost', but Wellings thought Smith himself played fine cricket during the first half of the tour and his catching at short leg was outstanding, though he did little in the big matches; whereas Barber scored over 1000 runs in Australian matches alone, 328 in the Tests. He averaged just over 50, but did not play in New Zealand.

Brown, who was one of the alleged dawdlers and was still rather injury-prone, took eleven wickets in the Australia Tests at a cost of 37·18 runs each, and only Jones took more. In all first-class matches in Australia Brown had twenty-nine wickets at 31 each and six more in New Zealand for 21 each.

Winds of Change
(1966)

THE season of 1966 was one of administrative turmoil in which the game itself – despite a visit of the West Indies led by the dynamic Sobers, by then generally regarded as the world's greatest all-rounder, and the fact that Warwickshire won the Gillette Cup – tended to be submerged. This was largely because of what came to be known as the Clark report on the structure of the game – a phrase much to be bandied about in the next few years – and the argument which will doubtless always be with us.

The report made both short- and long-term recommendations, the former, as already foreshadowed in the interim report, suggesting that greater efforts should be made to get hard, fast, true pitches; to step up the general tempo of the game by a better over rate; a more positive approach by all the counties; more standardised covering of pitches; a ban on players polishing the ball; and a limit of sixty-five overs on the first innings of certain matches. Long-term, and, most important, the report envisaged yet another survey of county members and associations and, subject to its results, a County Championship with a minimum of sixteen three-day matches, a separate Championship of sixteen one-day games and retention of the Gillette Cup competition.

The sub-committee went further than any previous inquiry had ever done in saying that the players should be made to realise that unless they adopted a more positive attitude their livelihood was 'in real jeopardy', but this, presumably, meant the game as a whole, not that of the individual offender. Hutton, Barrington and Boycott had all been disciplined in their day, but quickly restored so that the stigma had no salutary effect on other players as it should have had.

Generally speaking, the sub-committee had found that a large majority of club members and the public condemned the modern game as dull and unattractive, largely owing to the attitude of the players, who blamed the pitches and the system of averages; that there was an overwhelming demand for Sunday cricket; that a large body of the public favoured one-day cricket; and that most players favoured sixteen three-day games and sixteen one-day games in separate championships, the last a point on which Warwickshire had reservations, though they were prepared to accept it for the sake of the rest. The danger seemed to be that in trying to find something to compensate for the loss of some three-day games the authorities would tend to crowd in too many substitute competitions and that the counties would end with more, instead of less, cricket.

The Editor of *Wisden* saw cricket 'flourishing everywhere except in England' where 'the standard . . . has never been so low; not even after the First World War when England lost eight consecutive Tests to Australia was the outlook so depressing.' Of the Clark report he had this to say:

For the time being the three-day County Championship remains unaltered, but although I would like to see it cut down, as was proposed, it cannot last much longer in its present form without public support which has dwindled from next to nothing. Considering there is more leisure than ever with the five-day working week and universal annual holidays, there must be other reasons besides the motor-car and television that have caused attendances at county cricket to fall so alarmingly. Even members, though still paying their subscriptions, do not appear with any regularity.

Surely it is because the pattern is always the same. One can scarcely tell one county from another; just a succession of seam bowlers against numerous batsmen static on their feet, ready to use their pads as a main line of defence against the ball directed at the stumps, with a few deflections behind the wicket for the odd single . . . The way county cricket has been allowed to drift towards disaster is surely a reflection on the Advisory County Cricket Committee . . . For the past twenty years we have had one change after another . . . Small wonder that the ordinary follower of the game has become so utterly confused . . . And what about the players? Surely this constant tampering with the rules has been of little benefit to them. Is it too late to put the clock back thirty years and begin all over again?

Charles Bray, the former Essex player, cricket correspondent and a member of the Clark Committee, also had an article in *Wisden* on the plan which he said had been killed before it was born. 'Its main recommendation [the reduction of the County Championship programme] was defeated by sixteen votes to four, a majority so emphatic that the counties may have signed their own death warrant.'

He went on to point out that in 1950 close on 2 000 000 people paid to see Championship cricket. In 1966 the figure had dropped to 513 578.

In 1964 members totalled 141 707; in 1965, 139 964; and in 1966, 135 045. 'It was then obvious to all,' he commented, 'except those with their heads firmly buried in the sand, that first-class cricket was only solvent because of the efforts of supporters' clubs with football pools and Test-Match profits.'

Like every other county, no doubt, Warwickshire had prolonged discussions in Committee on the plan and the future of the game. Many differing opinions were expressed, but all agreed that too much cricket was being played. It was suggested, for instance, that time allocated to Tests in future should be based on hours – thirty for each match – rather than days. On the over rate, a former chairman felt that not enough had been done by the Committee, or the Club captain, to reduce the inordinately long curving run taken by David Brown; another member said attempts had been made to cut 'Roly' Thompson's run-up, but without success; and a third wondered whether it was really necessary anyway, as for years the Club's bowlers had maintained an over rate of approximately twenty an hour.

Members generally thought that the attitude of Warwickshire players to the game 'had been extraordinarily good' over a number of years. There was a general majority against one-day cricket, in or out of the Championship, other than the Gillette Cup, and it was felt that it was extremely bad for the game to mix the Championship as between three- and one-day cricket.

As for Sunday cricket, a vote taken at the annual meeting showed 146 in favour, possibly with reservations (such as that play should not start until after 2 p.m.), and 67 against, a verdict which was reflected in the referendum taken of the members which had this result:

In favour	2420
In favour with reservations	460
Against	668

Six thousand members refrained from voting, but even after this apparently decisive vote the Club was reluctant to take the bull by the horns as far as Edgbaston was concerned, for a variety of reasons, partly concerned with the legal position and the estimated costs, which had been something of a shock. Ground staff and gate stewards all required double pay for working on Sundays and the caterers also had to pay double wages, though they were not allowed to charge more for meals. Income could not be collected in the normal manner and it was considered doubtful whether people in an industrial city, many of whom took the opportunity to move out to the country or to the seaside for weekends in the summer, would come to watch cricket instead. It was calculated that a crowd of at least 10 000 would be needed to make Sunday afternoon cricket financially worthwhile, and several members of the Committee felt that although Sunday cricket was sure to come Warwickshire should be the last to adopt it. Pioneers, O pioneers!

So action was deferred until the autumn to see what would happen in games played by other counties. The Club raised no objection, however, to players taking part in Sunday games away from home, and the first of these were played this season. In fact, the first Sunday match at Edgbaston was played on 6 June when Warwickshire's Old Cricketers played their opposite numbers from Nottingham. It did not provide much of a clue to future attendances. The weather in the morning was not helpful, the match was limited in its appeal. But some stewards offered their services free and after payment of £161 in expenses there was a profit of £117 to be devoted to the two benefiting charities. In the event, the Supporters' Association bore the expenses, so £278 was raised. In view of what had happened in Committee it was interesting to find the annual report commenting that 'possibly the most pleasing feature was to see Bob Wyatt at the wicket again, carrying his 65 years very lightly and batting with much of his old skill'.

A National Opinion Poll taken in August showed that no fewer than 43 per cent of those questioned did not attend first-class games because of 'dull play', and 68 per cent said they would watch it more often if it were played on Sundays; 31 per cent saying that they would not. Seventy-seven per cent said they would watch more one-day cricket and 22 per cent would not.

In October Warwickshire issued their own questionnaire to members on what they would like to see from the game. With 320 of the 550 forms sent out completed, 65 per cent were in favour of Sunday play and 31 per cent against. TV, they said, had little influence, no fewer than 81 per cent saying that it did not keep them away, which must have surprised a good many people. Only 16 per cent said that it did keep them away. What, then, was it? Why did attendances at Warwickshire's county games slump even further during the season from 42 421 to only 22 627?

Somehow the general unease felt about the future of the game seemed to find its way into the cricket itself. Most of the short-term recommendations of the Clark report came into force for the 1966 season, but the 65-over limit on the first innings was dropped for 1967, after too brief a trial, one would have thought, but the sub-committee itself felt that the changes had very little effect on the tempo of the game.

Perhaps the fact that not only did England have three captains in one season, but called on no fewer than twenty-four players all told, was a symptom of the general malaise. After M. J. K. Smith's successful tour in Australia, there was no need to look further for the captain, at least to begin with. Smith was captain for the first Test against the West Indies, but was then dropped with such unseemly haste that the selection

473

committee's action was criticised in a much wider area than that of his own county. Richie Benaud, for instance, described it as 'the most drastic chop' in post-war cricket.

Cowdrey took Smith's place and he, in turn, made way for Brian Close, who was successfully leading Yorkshire. 'In the case of Smith and Cowdrey', commented *Wisden*, 'the selectors probably felt that their diffident batting did not set the example required to inspire their men, compared with the authority and brilliance that their rival, Sobers, exercised immediately he reached the crease. One of the biggest disappointments was the failure of the fast bowlers, I. J. Jones and D. J. Brown, to reproduce the form they showed earlier in the year against Australia.'

The decision to drop Smith was all the more surprising in view of the fact that he began the season by making a century against the tourists – 140 – for the M.C.C. at Lord's. Next day it was announced that he would captain England, but in the first Test at Manchester he failed, scoring only 5 and 6, out to Gibbs each time, the West Indies winning by an innings and 40 runs, after Sobers had made 161. He was missed four times, however, once by Brown, who had 84 runs hit off him without taking a wicket.

Neither M. J. K. Smith nor Brown played again in the series, but Barber, somewhat belatedly, in view of his striking success abroad, was brought in for the fourth Test at Leeds when he made 6 and 55, and took one wicket for 55. At The Oval, where England won by an innings after the West Indies had already won the rubber, Barber got 36 and took three for 93 and two for 78. Amiss, who had made 69 and 47 against the tourists for the M.C.C. President's XI, as well as 19 and 160 not out – the innings of the season – for Warwickshire, got his first England cap in this game in which he scored 17.

Despite Amiss's century, the West Indies beat Warwickshire at Edgbaston by ten wickets with as many minutes to spare. The county, sent in to bat, were all out for 173, and then the tourists hit up 441, Butcher making 128. Warwickshire recovered well – Amiss and Smith putting on 109 in 84 minutes – though not quite well enough.

The first innings in 102 matches out of the 238 in the County Championship – twelve for each county – were limited to sixty-five overs, but on the whole, in *Wisden*'s view, the experiment did not succeed, although some games produced excellent cricket. Perhaps it was a combination of the new rule and the wet summer, but only two batsmen in the country reached 2000 runs, and only eight averaged 40 and over, compared with twenty-three and thirty-two respectively in the dry summer of 1959.

The Warwickshire annual report said the experiment was very popular with spectators, but players did not like it. They argued that the over limit gave little opportunity to middle-order batsmen and that fielding sides tended to bowl defensively rather than trying to get their opponents out. The report firmly laid the blame for the failure of the experiment at the door of the players 'who gave it not a chance', a comment which seemed a little severe. Jameson certainly seemed to be one of the batsmen most affected, either not getting in to bat at all, or doing so only when the pressure to score runs quickly gave him little chance to settle down.

Some new ball bowlers certainly felt it a handicap not to be able to polish the ball, and they tended to bowl a shorter length. Whether this was the reason or not, Cartwright, who missed some early matches because of injury, took only twenty wickets in the first two months, but recovered his form and topped the hundred again before the season ended.

Changes and weather notwithstanding – there was snow nine days before the season began – Warwickshire managed to improve on their 1965 performances and went up to sixth place in the Championship. When they had won four of their first seven matches it looked as if they would be challenging again for the leadership, but Barber was able to play in only ten matches, and though M. J. K. Smith, Jameson, Amiss and Abberley, a product of the county nursery and of the Moseley Club, all got over 1000 runs, the batting tended to be uneven and the bowling not penetrative enough, often failing to get sides out. Brown was handicapped by wet, slow pitches, Webster suffered from injuries and Miller, after an indifferent season in which he took only twenty-five wickets in Championship matches, decided to retire from first-class cricket at the early age of 25 – yet another slow left-hander who failed to develop and was now lost to the game. Mence, too, whose play had been disappointing, was released to go to Gloucestershire, with whom he hoped to get more first-team chances, but he stayed only briefly before returning to his native Berkshire.

The county's best win of the season was undoubtedly against York-shire on a drying wicket at Hull on which the bowlers had much the best of it. After a dour struggle, Yorkshire got a first innings lead of just four runs, but then Bannister, five for 38, and Cartwright four for 44, put them out for 101. Even so, they would probably have won but for an innings of great stubbornness by young Abberley, who defied all the Yorkshire bowlers for two and a half hours and carried his bat for 54, a fine innings which saw Warwickshire home by three wickets. Abberley may play many innings and score many more runs, but few will be more creditable to him, or more valuable to his side. He had a remarkable start to the season, his first seven innings producing scores of 56, 26, 31 not out, 117 not out, 81, 29 and 43.

Webster gave us something to remember him by with his best

performance, in figures at least, he ever did for Warwickshire, eight for 19 against Cambridge University. He followed this with three for 36 and five for 46 against Middlesex and then, against Glamorgan, went in at No. ten, scored 47 and then, with six for 30, bundled Glamorgan out for 52.

Warwickshire played two matches on pitches of somewhat dubious quality, one at Edgbaston and the other at Coventry. The game at Edgbaston against Notts was played on a portion of the square dug up two years earlier. Brown and Cartwright certainly got more bounce out of it and Notts were got rid of for 103, the last eight wickets going down for 21 in little over an hour. This was a 65-overs-in-the-first-innings game and Warwickshire did slightly better with 115, but they could not force a win.

There were many ups and downs in the match at Coventry which was against Derbyshire. The visitors lost four wickets for 24 and were then allowed to make 281, whereas Warwickshire were routed for their lowest score of the season, 38, of which M. J. K. Smith made 15. The man who did the damage was Jackson – eight for 18 – and he also polished off most of Warwickshire's second innings, Derbyshire winning by eight wickets. The pitch drew unfavourable comment even from the captain of the winning side and Bernard Flack was asked to co-operate with the Coventry authorities in trying to improve the wicket for next season and to eradicate moss on the square.

Pitches generally continued to be criticised by the Advisory County Cricket Committee and Board of Control. Indeed, they concluded that those in 1966 were the worst ever. Batsmen used to control the groundsmen – e.g. Edgbaston in Bates's time – then it was the turn of the bowlers, but now the Board thought groundsmen should be instructed to prepare good batting wickets and use ten-ton rollers. They, too, preferred criticism only from umpires and took the view that captains had too little knowledge of pitches and were inclined to be prejudiced.

When it came to the last county match of the season against Northants at Edgbaston, Cartwright still needed thirteen wickets for his hundred and the odds must have been heavily against him getting them. But in the first innings, with six for 46, he was largely responsible for Northants being dismissed for 89 and in the second he went one wicket better still and took seven for 57, which gave him his hundred exactly. He owed four of them in this match to the co-operation of Alan Smith, who caught two batsmen in the first innings and stumped one and caught one in the second.

Whatever their failings in the three-day games, Warwickshire carried all before them in the Gillette Cup, which they won for the first time after beating Glamorgan, Gloucestershire, Somerset and, finally Worcestershire in the final at Lord's. They excelled both in batting and bowling and all the games were won by comfortable margins. The success gave their captain particular satisfaction because, until the cup competition had been devised, there had been no chance to win anything in cricket except the County Championship.

Against Glamorgan on their own ground at Swansea they hit 266 for eight off their 60 overs; Amiss, 113, and M.J.K. putting on 126 in 85 minutes. Then Brown took five Glamorgan wickets for 18 and earned himself the title of the man-of-the-match. Only two Glamorgan batsmen reached double figures.

Everything else in the fourth round against Gloucestershire at Edgbaston was dwarfed by a magnificent innings of 113 in 125 minutes by Barber, which Cyril Washbrook, the adjudicator, said was the best he had seen in the competition. He had no need to look any further for his man-of-the-match. Warwickshire's first 50 were scored off fourteen overs, their second off nine overs and their third off only six, a perfect acceleration of the scoring rate.

When Somerset were 97 for one at lunch in the semi-final, it looked grim for Warwickshire, but then Bannister took three wickets in four balls and Somerset were all out 189. Barber again began the reply well with 45, but it was Amiss, with 80 not out, and M. J. K. Smith again, in a stand of 109 off twenty-nine overs, that finally turned the scales. Amiss got the award this time.

Worcestershire, who had only just failed to win the County Championship, began the final badly. Kenyon hit his wicket and then Cartwright removed Horton, Ormrod and Graveney, the last named superbly caught by the diving Ibadulla, for a mere 16 runs. Though Gifford helped to add 50 in the last eleven overs, the total reached no more than 155. Barber then hit 66 out of 95 in thirty-nine overs, which got him his second man-of-the-match award of the season and his fourth in all since the competition had started, from Peter May. Amiss contributed a useful 44, but it was left to Alan Smith, when Warwickshire still needed 17 from seven overs, to see them home with an invaluable 21 not out.

Nothing, of course, could have given Sir Oliver Leese greater pleasure during his year of office as President of the M.C.C. than to present the trophy to the captain of Warwickshire. The Lord Mayor, Alderman Harold Tyler, gave the team a civic reception on their return to Birmingham.

As winners of the Cup, Warwickshire again met the West Indies at Edgbaston at the end of the season in a one-day challenge match of fifty overs and this time they were beaten by 19 runs. The West Indies paid the cup winners the compliment of playing their Test side and a wonderfully free-scoring game resulted. They made 257 for four wickets in their fifty overs, Nurse hitting 102 not out in four minutes under two hours and being named man-of-the-match. Warwickshire's reply was 238, which contained another brilliant innings by Barber, whose 63 included 23 off the only two overs Charlie Griffith was able to bowl before he had to retire, and 76 by Amiss. Warwickshire passed 200 in the fortieth over, but then the batting broke down. This, incidentally, was Webster's last appearance for the county, for he emigrated to New Zealand to set up practice there. This was a distinct loss.

Barber had more than proved himself now in both kinds of cricket, a point made in *Wisden*'s portrait of him as one of the Five Cricketers of the Year. Since his departure from Lancashire he had really enjoyed his cricket and so had those who had been fortunate enough to see it; and not least his fielding in the leg trap with M.J.K., with whom he formed as good a close-catching combination as any in the world. The pity of it was that he could play so little first-class cricket.

Faced with a deficiency of over £13 000 in 1965, it was only to be expected that the Committee's thoughts would very soon be directed to trying to make up at least some of this, and very early in the year it was decided to increase subscriptions and have a membership drive. Edmund King surprised some of his fellow-members of Committee, perhaps, when he told them that on recent visits to Lord's he had heard of embarrassment caused to other clubs by Warwickshire's low subscription rates, which strongly supported the view held in some quarters that the Club, backed by a powerful Supporters' Association, was more or less indifferent to membership revenue. To announce increases, he said, would show that the Club wished to stand on its own feet, cover its financial responsibilities from income and leave the Association to help with ground development and stimulate funds, the income from which would help to cover the increasing maintenance costs on a growing ground and its premises.

The increases proposed were from £3 3s 0d to £5 for ordinary members, from £2 2s 0d to £4 for country members within a radius of fifteen miles, from £2 2s 0d to £4 for family members, with concessions for old-age pensioners, and from £1 5s 0d to £2 10s 0d for juniors. When they came before the annual meeting Edmund King took the opportunity to give the 200 or so members who troubled to attend a little history. He reminded them that before the Second World War the full membership subscription had been £1 10s 0d, which was increased to £2 2s 0d on the resumption of cricket after the war. In 1960, when the ground had again become a Test venue, it had been raised to £3 3s 0d and it had been possible for the Club to carry on with this until large-scale developments came along; these meant additional maintenance responsibilities and costs, and the whole concept changed. Gate returns now were lower than ever – 22 000 only paying for admission in 1966 to a ground which would hold 30 000 for a single match.

Golf club subscriptions, he pointed out, had increased by as much as three to five times since the war.

It would be three years at least before the Club could clear its deficit, he said. The only alternative was to cut costs, which would mean a big curtailment of playing staff and of amenities and the possible loss of Test Match status. The Club was at the crossroads and all it could do was to appeal to the loyalty of its members. Even after these increases they would still be the lowest of any Test ground in the country, with the exception of Headingley, which the Yorkshire club did not own. The proposed increases would amount to only 8d a week for a full member and 6d a week for a pensioner, who, incidentally, had more opportunity than anyone to watch cricket regularly.

Edmund King said there had been rises in income from membership (£500), cricket (£2000), Test Matches (£3400) and generally (£1000), but county finances were altogether too much dependent on Test Match profits which fluctuated considerably. The deficiency on 1966 of over £19 000 followed a loss in the previous year of over £13 000. There were only two possibly non-recurring items – the membership drive, £1900, and players' salary adjustments, £1400.

Several members spoke against the proposed increase for juniors, who were being asked to pay 100 per cent more, and an amendment that junior subscriptions should be £2 and that the age limit should be left at 19, was carried by an overwhelming majority.

By the end of the year it was also decided to increase admission prices to 4s, an increase of 1s. Warwickshire were one of the last three counties to keep the price down to 3s. Admission for an Australia Test would go up from 7s 6d to 10s 0d and for the county match against them from 5s to 6s, all sums which surely no one could have called extortionate. In short, as the annual report put it, members 'had had it too good for too long'.

There was a good deal of frank but friendly discussion during the year between the Club and the Supporters' Association. At the annual meeting, for instance, the Club chairman followed up his earlier remarks in Committee by saying that in his opinion the Club should come much nearer paying its way without the very special form of investment income. He much regretted that he could not dispel the erroneous impression that 'Warwickshire was a wealthy club', which was based entirely on the fact that substantial capital development had been possible, thanks to the Supporters' Association, but that body could not influence the day-to-day running of the Club. The Association should not, nor should it be expected to, underwrite the revenue side of the affairs of a Club that was member-owned.

The chairman finally urged support for the membership drive which, led by A. K. Jackson, and a small sub-committee of which he was chairman, and with the energetic drive and efficiency of Anthony Haycock, the membership secretary (who distributed 20 000 brochures), eventually added about 1000 to the total.

Edgar Hiley also took the opportunity to state the Association's point of view. The Club and the Association, he stressed once more, were two entirely separate bodies, separately governed and separately run. The Association's present standing challenged comparison with that of any similar body in any sport in the world and, as a result of its endeavours, the Club and its members enjoyed a measure of comfort superior to that available on any other cricket ground in the country.

The Association's activities, however, were strictly confined to capital assistance, mainly in the development of the ground, but the national Press was insistent in referring to the Club as a wealthy body. The tag, 'Wealthy Warwickshire', had stuck, though there was not a grain of truth in it. The Association had declared from its inception that it could not in any circumstances subsidise the Club's income, which would involve serious problems of taxation and other matters with which they had no wish to become involved. The time would come, he hoped, when the Association would be able to create an Endowment Fund, interest from which would cover the maintenance costs of structures given as gifts to the Club.

He had not exaggerated when he referred to serious taxation problems, for shortly afterwards it became known that, in counsel's opinion, trusts created for endowment and pavilion reconstruction funds were void. The trustees, therefore, returned the assets of the trusts to the Association who, in order that the funds should be used to the best advantage of the Club, had agreed to make them an unconditional gift for capital purposes.

The Club naturally expressed its gratitude and it was then decided that these and all other funds received from the Association for capital purposes should be managed by a special sub-committee, to be called the Capital Investments Sub-committee, with full powers; the committee consisting of the Club chairman, honorary treasurer, and Cyril Goodway, with Edgar Hiley; W. Leslie Jones and J. A. C. D. B. Wildsmith representing the Association. (The last named's five initials stand for Joseph Aubrey Clarence Donald Bolton, but as they referred to a man of some physical stature they all naturally boiled down to 'Tiny'.)

Warwickshire were not the only county Club the Association was helping. Edgar Hiley was able to report that Essex, who had been lent £15 000 to buy their ground at Chelmsford, would repay it on the date due, 30 June, which he thought a splendid gesture, so much so that

Above: Protest. The man who made his physical presence felt by sitting on the pitch during the tour of Mr Wilfred Isaac's XI from South Africa, which preceded the cancellation of the tour in 1970.

Below: No apartheid here. West Indian Gary Sobers presents the Cricketers' Cricketer award to Mike Procter, a South African member of Rest of the World team which beat England at Edgbaston in 1970 after South Africa's tour had been cancelled. Behind is another South African, Tony Greig, and on the left Dennis Amiss, of Warwickshire.

Top left: Edgar N. Hiley, M.B.E., formerly prominent in Midland industrial and local government affairs, one of the founders of the Warwickshire County Cricket Supporters' Association, and its chairman since 1959. He also became chairman of the West Midlands Sports Council in 1969.

Top right: James McDowall, vice-chairman and hon. treasurer.

Above: Peter West, the TV and radio commentator, opening the modernised premises of the Warwick Social Club. He was presented with a table lighter by the chairman of the Association, Edgar N. Hiley, with whom is J. A. C. D. B. ('Tiny') Wildsmith, chairman of the social committee.

Top: H.R.H. The Duke of Edinburgh being received by the Club President, Lieut-General Sir Oliver Leese, at the entrance to the Pavilion Suite where in June, 1970, he attended a conference on his awards scheme. The Duke thought it 'a splendid setting' for the meeting.

Bottom: The President, Lieut-General Sir Oliver Leese, and the new chairman, Edmund H. King, admiring the presentation gift to C. A. F. Hastilow (left), on his retirement from the chair.

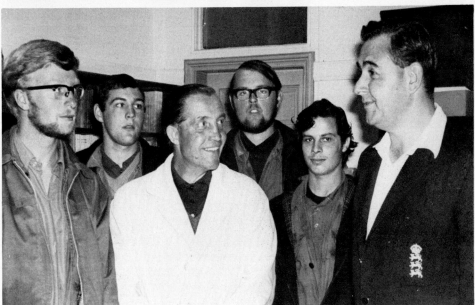

Top left: 'Mike' Smith was captain of the first Warwickshire side to win the Gillette Cup in 1966. He is seen here with the trophy after the final at Lord's.

Top right: Another Gillette Cup for Warwickshire, this time in 1968, when Alan Smith not only led the side to victory, but also won the 'Man of the Match' award.

Bottom: Congratulations from the England captain, Colin Cowdrey, for Bernard Flack, the head groundsman, on the valiant efforts he and his staff of six – they were afterwards dubbed 'The Magnificent Seven' – made to get the ground fit for the Test with Australia in 1968 after torrential rain.

L. T. Deakins, general secretary of The Warwickshire County Cricket Club and only the third holder of the office. He represents the Club on many other bodies, notably at Lord's, and is one of the most widely known figures in the game.

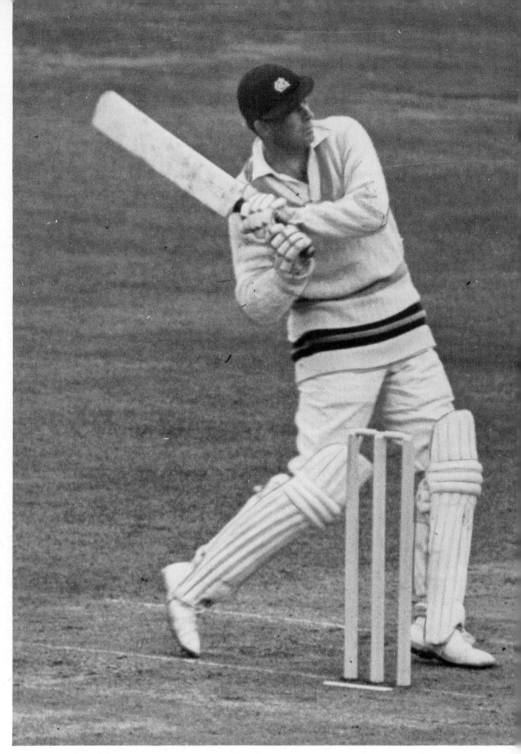

R. W. Barber who came to Warwickshire from Lancashire and proved both
a dashing bat and a very useful leg spin bowler.

Top: Alan Smith can be equally energetic and acrobatic as a wicket-keeper, as he showed here in running out C. T. Radley, of Middlesex, from a throw by W. J. Stewart against Middlesex at Lord's in 1968.

Bottom: Alan Smith's bowling action has been variously likened to windmills and white tornadoes, but, as these photographs show, no one could say that it lacked determination.

Top: An aerial view of the Edgbaston ground in 1966.

Bottom: Pitch inspection by two visitors from nearby Cannon Hill Park, often seen at Edgbaston especially on days like this.

Top: Edmund H. King acknowledging tributes paid to him on his retirement from the chair. On his left are the President of the Club, Lieut-General Sir Oliver Leese; Lord Nugent, former President of the M.C.C.; and Mrs King. Every county was represented at the dinner given in his honour.

Bottom: Three chairmen of The Warwickshire County Cricket Club – Edmund H. King (1962–72), C. C. Goodway (1972–   ), who succeeded him, and C. A. F. Hastilow (1948–62) who preceded him.

T. W. Cartwright, Warwickshire's most successful all-rounder with over 10000 runs and 1000 wickets to his credit while playing for them before he moved to Somerset.

Top: Historic Catch. This catch at mid-on by W. J. Stewart off J. B. Bolus (Notts) in 1968 gave Tom Cartwright (extreme left) his 1000th wicket in first-class cricket.

Bottom: Salute from a Century-Maker. Colin Cowdrey's 100th Test Match, against Australia at Edgbaston in 1968, had a story book flavour about it – he made 104 and not even the ranks of the Australian fielders could forbear to cheer.

Above: A fine action picture of Lance Gibbs, the West Indian off-spinner, who in 1971 took 131 wickets.

Opposite top left: The fast bowler's follow-through as demonstrated by David Brown. The umpire is J. S. Buller.
Opposite top right: A. S. M. Oakman, senior coach, formerly of Sussex and England, who uses the cine camera as an aid in his work of showing young players how it is done.
Opposite bottom: A sight to gladden any bowler's heart – the middle stump going down. The bowler is N. M. McVicker and the batsman, Standen, of Worcestershire.

Top: 'Farewell' to M. J. K. Smith. Australians joined with Warwickshire players to pay tribute to retiring captain, M. J. K. Smith, during the tea interval on the second day's play of the match with the tourists in June, 1968 when the President of the Club, Lieut-General Sir Oliver Leese, made presentations. 'Mike' Smith later made a successful return to the game.

Bottom: A unique gathering of cricket captains in the Pavilion Suite at Edgbaston on the occasion of M. J. K. Smith's 'retirement' – H. E. Dollery, A. C. Smith, his successor, Rachael Heyhoe, captain of the All England Women's XI, M. J. K. Smith and Eric Hollies.

Only W. G. Quaife has scored more runs for Warwickshire than M. J. K.
Smith, but not even he was stronger on the leg side. This boundary came
off M. Taylor, Notts, now with Hampshire. The batsman at the other end
is Kanhai.

Top: By Air to the Cricket. For the first time in the Club's history Warwickshire supporters flew from Elmdon, Birmingham's airport, to Manston in Kent to see their team in the Gillette Cup semi-final at Canterbury in 1971.

Below: Three of the most important members of the staff at Edgbaston – David Blakemore and his wife, Winifred, secretary and organiser respectively of the Warwickshire County Cricket Supporters' Association, and L. T. Deakins, general secretary of the Club.

he wanted to acknowledge it by making Essex an outright gift of one-third of the amount, £5000, to their appeal fund.

This caused a few raised eyebrows and some opposition; one member of the Club Committee suggesting that £2500 be given instead. When Edgar Hiley protested at the opposition after the joint committee (later known as the Warwickshire County Cricket Liaison Committee) had endorsed it, the chairman agreed that it was unfortunate that the Club Committee had not readily accepted the recommendation. But at least Essex were pleased and the three senior officials of that club – Sir Hubert Ashton, president, Tom Pearce, chairman, and Trevor Bailey, then captain and secretary – all sent letters of appreciation.

Since then the Association has given or lent substantial sums to outside organisations, including other county and local clubs, a striking indication of how it has spread its largesse for the benefit of the game as a whole, and it entered into agreements with five first-class counties – Worcestershire, Derbyshire, Leicestershire, Essex, and Hampshire – and seven minor counties – Lincolnshire, Staffordshire, Oxfordshire, Shropshire, Cheshire, Wiltshire and Dorset – to operate the pool in their areas.

This was not the last heard of financial matters that year. At its very end A. K. Jackson expressed grave concern about the Club's position. Despite all appeals for control of expenditure, he said, losses of £33 000 had been incurred over the past two years, though he realised that investment income would increase appreciably in 1967. He thought there were two lines of possible action – first, to let the *status quo* prevail until such time as the structure of the national game was altered to reduce expenditure, or until the subscriptions went up; second, to make a determined effort to examine every item of expenditure to see whether the Club could afford it or not.

He found support from Edgar Hiley, who expressed disappointment that the Pavilion Suite did not pay to better advantage – more lunch-time business should be sought. Vast sums had been spent on some buildings that were unoccupied for the greater part of the year, a development policy that was 'absolutely crazy'. He advocated leaving the Pavilion (centre) rebuilding until the Endowment Fund was created.

In view of the financial situation it was not surprising that, after considering a very ambitious proposal to erect the new pavilion, with all its ancillary features, on the north side of the ground where members would get the sun – but face the prevailing south-westerly wind – the Committee decided to stick to the present site.

The chairman and the secretary had worked out that the possible saving to Warwickshire, if the number of three-day matches were reduced to sixteen, would be from the current expenditure of £85 000 down to £50 000, so no wonder the Committee was in favour of fewer games; just as Edgar Hiley was at pains to make it clear that in his opinion the Committee was inclined to lavish expenditure because of the Association behind it and would do well to forget the existence of the Association as a rich uncle.

He warned that for the first time since it had begun there had been a slight decline in the pool income due in part, in his view, to redundancy in the motor industry and to increased competition from the new pool of Coventry City Football Club. Curiously enough, it was on the proposition of Edgar Hiley that the chairman of Coventry City, D. H. Robins, was elected to the Warwickshire Committee this season as country area representative for Leamington Spa. He was a former player of both the Coventry and North Warwickshire and Leamington cricket clubs, made one appearance for the county and would have played more but for business calls. Later he took over the responsibility of organising the Eastbourne Festival and some tours abroad.

Hopes of the structure of the game being revised were, however, dashed by the chairman, who reported sorrowfully on meetings of the Advisory County Cricket Committee and the Board of Control at Lord's, the whole tone of which, Edmund King said, were 'almost beyond belief' in this day and age. Any proposal which suggested progress, or meeting the needs of the time, was rejected virtually out of hand and the structure sub-committee was both embarrassed and depressed at the failure of its proposals to gain support.

The Committee were given something else to think about when in mid-summer M. J. K. Smith intimated that, as he wished to consider a career outside the game in the near future, he might end his engagement with the Club in the next season. Another engagement they had to consider was that of Lance Gibbs, the 31-year-old off-spinner and top Test-wicket-taker of the West Indies, who was signed after some to-ing and fro-ing and telephoning to France, where Edmund King, who had approached him during the West Indies match, was on holiday. Gibbs had begun as a leg spinner, but found that way of life too expensive in runs, so changed his style highly successfully. His fielding, especially to his own bowling, was often brilliant.

Another player anxious to join Warwickshire was Glenn Turner, the New Zealander, who had been recommended by Ibadulla when he was coaching out there. Dollery, too, had liked the look of him, but wanted to see more of him in matches, so he was advised to approach the New Zealand Board of Control, ask for his release and then get in touch with Warwickshire again.

In case it should be thought Warwickshire were looking too much to outside players, seven of the team at this time were Midland boys who started in the school side – Brown, Cartwright and Alan Smith were members of the Young Amateurs; and Abberley, Amiss, Stewart and

Edmonds had also played for the Amateurs while still at school. Another youngster in the offing was 16-year-old Hemmings, born at Leamington, who had taken ninety-six wickets and scored 500 runs for the second eleven in his first season.

Alec Hastilow, who had served the Club in various capacities for thirty-three years, shed further duties by resigning from the General Committee and all sub-committees. He had earlier given up the chairmanship of the cricket sub-committee, to which Peter Cranmer was elected in his place. Cranmer had long held the view that team selection should be left to the captain, who could consult with other Committee members, or players, as he saw fit. This was a view with which Dollery agreed, but they were in a minority, though not for long.

Leslie Deakins had an opportunity of going into more detail about his ideas for the future of cricket and putting them before a wider audience when he spoke during the winter to the annual dinner of the Forty Club, and *Wisden* of 1967 reported him at length. He made nine principal points:

1 The structure of the modern game defeats the possibility of it being self-supporting because far too much cricket is played at times when spectators cannot reasonably be expected to attend.

2 Cricket did not preserve the amateur status of the early days and so large salary bills for the players are the main item of expenditure with little chance today of income covering them.

3 Therefore it seems evident that if cricket wants the spectators it must do one of two things – play matches when people can come without loss of time from work, and play cricket of an eventful and purposeful nature that will appeal in the modern age.

4 To this end it is suggested that County Championship cricket should be confined to sixteen matches, eight home and eight away, all starting on Saturdays and continuing over Sunday and Monday; that professional staffs as such should be done away with and players be invited from clubs within the county to play at a fee of, say, £50 per man per match. This would mean that a man could follow his regular employment four days of the week (Tuesdays to Fridays) and if he could get sixteen Mondays off he could earn himself £800 a year from his cricket and yet not lose in a business sense, as so many do today.

5 In Warwickshire the playing staff has been costing £25 000 to £27 000 a year and under this new method it would cost £9000 to £10 000, and the difference between these two figures is approximately the loss sustained in recent years – something in the region of £14 000 to £19 000 a year.

6 It will be suggested that this would not offer enough cricket for the members of many counties, but do members prefer quantity to quality? The average member would much prefer stimulating weekend cricket to six days of masterly inactivity which we seem to get at the moment.

7 To ensure this we should, of course, limit the first innings, which is essential to good cricket, as otherwise the first innings of all county games are

turned into 'Test-Match practice' by the big boys to ensure a good average and continuity in the England XI.

8 With regard to the suggestion that we could not, under these methods, produce Test Match players, let us turn to Australia, South Africa, the West Indies and point out that there cricketers have developed on the half-day game with occasional inter-state matches.

9 We have lost 80 per cent of our watching public in the last twenty years, i.e. we have dropped from two and a quarter million in the boom period after the war to just over half a million now.

'We must face the fact', Leslie Deakins concluded, 'that we are providing a spectacle the public does not want. At the same time we must acknowledge that we know what the public *does* want – they have told us so through the medium of the Gillette Cup games – and if we want to survive and to preserve the happiest of games we should play it the way it was intended to be played and the way the public understand and love it.'

No fewer than three young Warwickshire players – Brown, Amiss and Abberley – were included in the Under-25 team's tour of Pakistan before the next English season opened, Brown being vice-captain to J. M. Brearley. Amiss, scoring two centuries, 131 against Pakistan and 102 against the President's XI, was second in the averages for first-class matches with 575 runs for 63·88, and confirmed the view of that gentle but astute judge, A. A. Thomson, that he was 'the brightest batting prospect for many a day'. Abberley, after playing good innings of 93 and 31, unluckily had a finger cracked by a 'beamer' and had to return home. Brown took eighteen wickets for 22·50 each, so both he and Amiss had a good tour.

The Time Wasters
(1967)

❖ ❖ ❖

THERE was much to occupy the cricket world during 1967 – the wettest May since 1773; another double tour, this time by India and Pakistan; the retirement of M. J. K. Smith and the election of a new Club captain; a deplorable exhibition of time-wasting at Edgbaston which indirectly cost another captain his job as England's leader; and the first Sunday Championship cricket at Edgbaston.

As expected, the Clark report was largely shelved, at least so far as its more important provisions were concerned, and this despite the fact that without the Test and Gillette Cup receipts the total loss by counties in 1966 would have been £150 000. It disappointed Warwickshire's President beyond measure, as he told the annual meeting, for he was confident it offered the salvation the game needed. If income could not be increased, then expenditure must be reduced and that could mean a lowering of standards; but if less cricket were played it would mean players would not get stale and it could be a stimulant to the game as well.

Sir Oliver felt that the Warwickshire Club met better than any other the day-to-day requirements of its members and the public, but although his opposite numbers and chairmen of other clubs were no doubt saying much the same sort of thing, nothing much seemed to happen as a result. *Wisden* reported no improvement on the general low standard of batting and bowling in the County Championship, and the new points system, amended over twenty times in the last fifty years, as the Warwickshire annual report reminded us, 'brought in with all too little thought', and designed to provide a genuine interest in the struggle for the first innings lead, had mostly the opposite effect. So many sides declined to take the slightest risk and, instead of aiming to make 400 to 450 on the

485

first day when winning the toss, too many merely crawled up to 350 by lunch on the second. Yet still no one was sacked, or even dropped.

Wisden seemed to think that the signing of Sobers by Notts might be a panacea for some of the ills of the game. The Editor, somewhat optimistically one feels, welcomed it as 'a bold move which could be the salvation of the three-day County Championship and I am only surprised that the plunge was not taken sooner'. He dismissed as groundless, fears that cricket was heading for a transfer system like football.

Certainly there could easily have been an auction, but Warwickshire declined to enter into it, though they did make inquiries about the possibilities of Sobers joining them. But when a sum in the region of £7000 was mentioned Warwickshire took the view that this was exorbitant and that the whole matter had become undignified and alien to the true image of the game.

With two touring sides here, six Tests were played during the season and Edgbaston staged the third one against India in July which England won by 132 runs with two days to spare. As usual, there was rain about and after England had made a comfortable 298 India were dismissed before lunch on the second day for 92, their lowest Test total since 1952. David Brown, who had had three wickets for 61 against them in the second Test at Lord's, took three more for 17, but strained a back muscle in the process and broke down in the second innings after bowling only two overs. Snow also had three for 17 and Hobbs three for 25.

Close, England's captain, did not enforce the follow-on because, he wrote afterwards, there was a West Indies tour in the winter and he wanted to give the England batsmen a chance to show what they could do before the team was chosen. When England batted again, India, although handicapped by the absence of their three opening bowlers – their wicketkeeper, Kunderan, having to bowl for the first time on the tour – got four of our wickets down for 66; but Close and Amiss, with a useful 45, retrieved the position and the total reached 203, which proved ample even though India's second innings showing was a much better 277.

Afterwards there was an inquest on the wicket. Close in his book, *Close to Cricket* (Stanley Paul), says that when India's captain, the Nawab of Pataudi, returned home he was reported to have said: 'The pitch at Edgbaston for the final Test was unfit even for a county pitch,' and Close himself then added these criticisms:

The Nawab and myself took one look at the wicket, glanced at one another and shrugged our shoulders. There was nothing we could do about it, but as the 'Noob' has said, it was scarcely good enough for a county match. Everything had been done, but I must mention the state of the pitch so that what followed can be fairly judged.

Some of the square had been re-laid and was not quite ready for use so that we were forced to play on a strip on the old part of the square which had already been used in a county match earlier in the summer. We could see from a glance that the pitch was not firm enough to last five days of a Test Match. The wicket was patchy, grass here and there with bare spots in between. Some spots were ready to break up and some did, in fact, crumble before the first morning was over ... Pataudi wasted little time in bringing on his spinners, Chandrasekar, Bedi and Prasana, and England's troubles started.

Nevertheless, they made 298 and as for India's collapse, was it due to the wicket – John Woodcock, in *The Times*, referred to 'an awkward pitch' – or to poor batting against Brown, Snow, Hobbs and Illingworth? The Warwickshire Committee's version of the affair was rather different. It had been decided that the Test should not be played on one of the new wickets because, although Flack was pleased with it, he felt it might not be up to Test standard. He based this view on what had happened in the match against Derbyshire, played on one of the new pitches, when twenty-two wickets fell for 141 runs in four hours and forty minutes. The Derbyshire captain had sent a report to the M.C.C. who wrote to the Club. The correspondence led to a visit from Bert Lock, former groundsman at The Oval and now the M.C.C.'s Inspector of Pitches. The Middlesex captain had also complained.

Cyril Goodway, chairman of the ground sub-committee, had later explained that it was possible the head groundsman had made 'a slight error of judgment' in using part of the re-laid area too early for these matches and that no further Championship matches would be played on the re-laid area in 1967. The explanation was accepted, but let the annual report take up the tale:

It was disappointing to your Committee, however, as it must have been to others further afield, to find criticism levelled against the Test Match pitch at Edgbaston, and that this was without reasonable foundation was readily demonstrated by the fact that India, who admittedly were dismissed in the first innings for only 92 runs, mainly due to indifferent and casual batting (five wickets falling to pace and five to spin) rallied splendidly in the fourth innings when set to score 410 to win the match and at one time were 180 for three wickets, with A. L. Wadekar and the captain, the Nawab of Pataudi, both not out and batting extremely well – in short, they were nearly half-way home, with two experienced batsmen well set – and to suggest that the pitch was responsible for their subsequent failure is unreasonable, for both the captain and later batsmen were out to rash strokes not warranted at that stage in the match, with time still on their side.

It is all too frequent that batsmen in the modern game blame either the pitch or negative bowling for their own failings, and there could be little seriously wrong with the Edgbaston pitch for this match, which in the end saw some 860 runs scored, offered an excellent contest and gave infinite pleasure to spectators. It would be as well for some batsmen, both at Test and County level, to realise that cricket is intended to be 'a fair competition between bat and ball' and that at no time is it the intention to prepare pitches that favour either unduly. It might even be argued that the pitches prepared in the early days of the century and continuing into the 1930s are the root cause of the game's loss of attraction for its public, for those plu-perfect pitches, giving so much advantage to the bat, gradually destroyed the Englishman's belief in a fair contest.

There were repercussions, too, of both the matches played at Coventry against Notts and Gloucestershire, and Lock had a look at these wickets as well and made some recommendations which it was hoped would bring about some improvements. Nevertheless, it was decided that in 1968 only one match should be played at Coventry and one at Nuneaton, a decision which brought a strong reaction from Coventry where it was considered an indignity that the seventh largest city in the country should have only one county game. They were told that it was partly on the grounds of economy and that the Club considered that three out of fifteen games played away from Birmingham, where all but 1000 of the 10 300 members lived, was out of proportion. The original decision was adhered to by fifteen votes to three.

The whole question of the condition of pitches and the right of captains to express an opinion about them received a thorough airing in the annual report. The Committee did not feel that the opinions of the captains should ever be invited on the subject since they were participants in the game. Players, though, might have been forgiven for thinking that that was a very necessary qualification for expressing an opinion. In the Committee's view 'the only worthwhile comment or criticism of pitches must come from qualified groundsmen or first-class umpires', this despite the fact that neither would have experience of playing on the wicket and so be able to judge it from the only point of view that mattered. Watching the game, whether from the middle or the boundary could not, it would seem to most players, give the same impression of how the wicket was playing as batting and bowling on it would do.

The report welcomed the appointment of Bert Lock, the ultimate result of whose inquiry at Edgbaston was

a warm commendation of the policy adopted by your Committee, which has been so expertly carried out by the Club's Head Groundsman, Bernard Flack. It was readily appreciated that the Club and its Head Groundsman had taken a very bold step in excavating so extensively on an established ground in order to try and put into effect the proposals of the Advisory County Cricket Committee and agreed that they should be both encouraged and commended in their endeavours.

Your Committee sincerely hopes that the area in question may play very much better, particularly from a pace point of view, in 1968, and results when the area is in use will be observed with the greatest possible interest, but at no time will your Committee have serious regard to the opinion of captains who must, of necessity, be partisan in their comments and who, in any event, have little or no background knowledge to sustain their statements, since they have no practical experience of pitch preparation, and are guided entirely by what happens during the game (and, being human, there must be a considerable measure of bias at times) with no regard to experiments that may be proceeding over a period (as at Edgbaston), or the weather conditions during the preparatory period, or immediately prior to the game.

In no other game is the opinion of the participants sought to this extent on the playing conditions, and to a marked degree acted upon. The game's administration at County level would do well to accept Law 46 in its entirety, and leave all the questions of fair and unfair play (which must of necessity include the pitch) to the only competent unbiased authorities, the umpires.

Surely the Committee were pushing at an open door here, for the Advisory County Cricket Committee, only a few months before, had said they preferred criticism only from umpires and took the view that captains had too little knowledge of pitches and were inclined to be prejudiced but voted for them to continue to complete forms. The captains, had they been given the chance, might well have replied that they knew as much about the preparation of pitches as the umpires did; that unfair play had little or nothing to do with the state of the pitch, since it is neutral; that if a pitch proves dangerous it is the batsmen, not the groundsmen or umpires, who take the risk of being hit; and that one does not have to have a groundsman's training to know a bad pitch when one plays on it, any more than one needs to be a brewer to be able to tell bad beer when one drinks it. And it surely was too much to expect, say, a visiting captain, on a ground for one match a season, to concern himself with long-term experiments, no matter how worthy or in the interests of the game, especially if his side had just been tumbled out on a beast of a pitch.

Warwickshire had the unusual experience this season of providing a player to appear against England in the Tests. He, of course, was Ibadulla, who first met his countrymen when they came to Edgbaston late in July. Warwickshire beat them by an innings and 101 runs, M. J. K. Smith making a fine 173 not out in a total of 439 for six declared. Pakistan were always struggling against Cartwright and Gibbs, who had played his first match for the county against the Indians, taking one for 38 in a travesty of a game of which the first and third days were washed out.

Against Pakistan Cartwright took five for 56 and Gibbs four for 19, and Ibadulla also helped to defeat his countrymen by dismissing Hanif Mohammed, their star batsman, for nought in the second innings, a feat which probably helped him to earn a place in the Pakistan side for the first Test which followed. He opened the innings with Burki and scored 8 and 32. In the second Test he could manage only 2 and 5 and was then dropped for the third, in which Amiss was recalled to the England side and made 26 and 3 not out.

The weather was so wet at the start of the County Championship season that in only one of Warwickshire's first nine games was it possible to get a result, five being abandoned without a ball being bowled and three drawn. It soon became obvious that no one was going to break any run-making records and only two Warwickshire batsmen, M.J.K. and Amiss got over 1000 runs, Amiss heading the averages with 54·88. Because of Test calls, which took away Ibadulla, Amiss and Brown (who also missed some matches through injury) and Barber's infrequent appearances, Smith never had a really settled team to call on and it was, therefore, not surprising that Warwickshire, winning only five Championship matches and drawing fifteen, with no decision in four, dropped from sixth to tenth place.

Their position would probably have been worse had not Cartwright enjoyed his best season as a bowler so far, taking in Championship matches alone 132 wickets at an average of only 15·84. In all matches he took 147 wickets, more than any other bowler in the country, and was fourth in the national averages. He also put himself into the statistical records by taking fifteen wickets in one match, eight for 50 and seven for 39 against Glamorgan at Swansea, where Warwickshire won by seven wickets. Cartwright thus equalled the feat of Hargreave in 1903. In five balls in the first innings he took three wickets without conceding a run and in the next match against Hampshire at Edgbaston he finished off Hampshire's second innings for 44 with these extraordinary figures:

O	M	R	W
9·4	7	6	5

There were three outstanding matches. The first was against Derbyshire at Edgbaston, which produced the complaints about the wicket. It certainly turned out to be a seam bowler's paradise. Four innings produced only 313 runs – Warwickshire 106 and 80 and Derbyshire 70 and 57 – and if I had been the Warwickshire captain, not to mention Derbyshire's, I should have been looking for something other than fine bowling or poor batting to account for such a quartet of analyses as these:

WARWICKSHIRE

FIRST INNINGS	SECOND INNINGS
Jackson 4 for 47	7 for 22
Rhodes 5 for 27	2 for 20

THE TIME WASTERS (1967)

DERBYSHIRE

FIRST INNINGS	SECOND INNINGS
Bannister 7 for 52	3 for 31
Cartwright 3 for 11	5 for 7

Both counties made their lowest scores of the season and Warwickshire must be regarded as lucky to have won by 59 runs. But it was infinitely better than both sides scoring, say, 400 runs each, and a tame draw.

The second game, against Essex at Edgbaston, had a tremendous climax and ended in a tie, only the second in the Club's history. Essex batted first and, with Barker making 124, reached 253, a total which Warwickshire managed to exceed by 6 runs, almost entirely due to a ninth-wicket stand of 51 between Brown and J. M. Allan, the former Scottish and Oxford University player, who was also to be involved in the tense finish. Essex declared their second innings at 208 for seven, leaving Warwickshire needing 202. When the last over was called they still wanted 13. Boyce was recalled to bowl and Allan then hit him for 4, 4, 2 and 1, and when Cartwright failed to hit the last ball Allan scampered to the other end and got home for a bye which levelled the scores.

Sussex called Allan the best No. nine in the business for, after he had made 153 against them for Oxford, he got 56 and 76 not out for Warwickshire at Hove, where he had also taken five for 11 in their first innings; the best performance of his career. He was played primarily as a bowler, but took only seventeen wickets in the entire Championship season, each of them costing him 54·52 runs each, although he bowled over 500 overs, over 100 of them being maidens. Once when opening for Kent he had made a century in each innings, a feat now performed for Warwickshire by Bryan Richardson, who got 126 and 105 against Cambridge. Richardson, who was only the eighth batsman in the county's history to bring off this notable feat, was the youngest of the three Richardson brothers, the others, Peter and Dick, long being associated with Worcestershire cricket. Bryan was born in Warwickshire, went to Malvern College and later came under the eye of Derief Taylor; but unhappily he never approached such form again.

The sensation of the season was saved for Edgbaston in the Yorkshire match in August. As usual, the northern side were well in the running for the Championship and in their eagerness to take away two points they indulged in what must be the most remarkable time-wasting tactics ever seen on a cricket field, which sullied the image of the game as a whole, injured Yorkshire's good name and, in conjunction with other factors, cost Close, their captain, the chance of taking the M.C.C.

491

side to the West Indies, which, in the opinion of many judges, was a thousand pities for he led England to five victories in Tests that summer.

I must confess that at first I was inclined to dismiss the accounts I heard and read as exaggerated and to think that if these incidents had happened in a Yorkshire-Lancashire match no one would have thought very much of them. But when I came to investigate more closely it became increasingly evident that what had happened was gamesmanship carried to a deplorable degree. It is one thing to try to draw, by legitimate tactics, a match one cannot hope to win, at which Yorkshire have always rather prided themselves; it is quite another to do it by deliberate time-wasting.

The match was not particularly eventful until the last day. Yorkshire won the toss and against some keen bowling by Brown, Cartwright and Allan reached the moderate total of 238, due largely to two men, Hampshire, 102, and Boycott, 57. Consistent batting by Amiss and Ibadulla, each of whom got half-centuries, and Jameson, 42, enabled Warwickshire to gain a lead of 4 runs; but when they routed Yorkshire for 145, Cartwright taking four for 26, the would-be champions were in real trouble.

Warwickshire, according to their scorer's note, had 102 minutes in which to get the 142 they needed to win. Naturally they went for the runs and Amiss, with 46, and Jameson, 36, gave them a good start – 100 in 82 minutes – but then time was wasted by Yorkshire in prolonged drying of the ball and setting the field. Yorkshire's over rate was never very high – only twenty-four were bowled in the entire innings – and in the last twenty-two minutes, during which the Yorkshire players once left the field to the batsmen and the umpires because of a shower, only two overs were bowled.

One of them from Trueman contained two no-balls, three bouncers and one wicket and, according to the cricket correspondent of *The Birmingham Mail*, took six minutes. The other was by Hutton, who also took a wicket, and the match ended with Warwickshire still 9 short of their target with five wickets in hand.

There had been a most unfortunate incident as Close came off the field at the lunch interval and passed through the members' enclosure on his way to the Yorkshire dressing-room. He has described how a loud remark was made, obviously meant for his ears, which he contended was not only personal, but slanderous and contained swear words 'which *might* have been excused on the Hill at Sydney, but not from a members' enclosure in England'. Close added that after asking the man he thought had made the remark, 'Was it you who said that?', and being told that it was not, he immediately apologised, as he also did to Leslie Deakins, who told him that no complaint had been made about the incident and that he should forget it. It should not, of course, have been raked up, in the way that it was in a Sunday newspaper ten days afterwards, for it had little, if any, bearing on the incidents on the field.

If the Edgbaston crowd had been exasperated with Hassett's Australians, they were livid with Yorkshire and one young man, it was reported, was so incensed that he rashly threatened with his umbrella Trueman, who, he said, swore at him. Trueman, in fact, said the young man did hit him on the arm with the umbrella. Generally, the crowd made so much noise in their indignation that Close said he had to walk nearer to players to make his orders heard. He strongly denied in his book that he ever instructed his bowlers deliberately to take their time when bowling and said that with a wet ball, which had to be wiped, a greasy pitch and run-saving field setting, a normal over rate was impossible. He argued that surely the fielding side must employ all the tactics they could to prevent their opponents from scoring the necessary runs – within the laws of cricket, a point that he stressed.

Close contended that Yorkshire fielded most of the time in a drizzle before they were rained off and he himself was last on the field again for personal reasons, not because he was deliberately wasting time. In the ten minutes that remained, he added, two Warwickshire wickets fell and Trueman bowled an eight-ball over because he was twice called for over-stepping. Only one other over was possible and Warwickshire failed by 9 to get the 16 runs they wanted to win. 'They deserved to succeed', wrote Close magnanimously, 'I don't deny them that' – which was generous of him.

Close listed the following time-table of alleged events which led to his being censured:

1 We bowled only twenty-four overs in ninety-eight minutes' playing time. [A difference of opinion here.]
2 We bowled only two overs in the last eleven minutes.
3 We changed positions slowly in the field between overs.
4 Bowlers walked back at less than their usual speed.
5 Bowlers waited at the end of their follow-through for the ball to be returned to them.
6 There were endless consultations between myself and both bowlers and fielders.

Perhaps Close did not realise that in listing the complaints he was drawing up a pretty formidable indictment. Of course, he refuted them all in detail, making the point that it was ten, not eleven, minutes for the last two overs, that two overs became 14 balls, that two wickets fell and 13 runs were scored, all of which took valuable seconds. Close wrote that he was not aware that they changed fielding positions more slowly than usual and that it was not until 'a few minutes' from time that anything was said to him by Charlie Elliott, one of the umpires.

So Yorkshire got their two points, though in the last resort they made no difference to the Championship. But were they worth it? The Warwickshire Club made no official complaint, but at the request of the M.C.C. Cyril Goodway, who saw that day's play, attended the inquiry at Lord's though he did not have a vote. Close put in a written statement to the Committee of Inquiry, before which he later appeared, in which he reiterated points he had already made, including the statement that Trueman's over took six minutes to complete and that what Elliott said to him when he ran across to speak to Hutton, who was bowling the last over, was 'Get on with it'.

The members of the Committee, which sat the day before the Test at The Oval against Pakistan in which Close was captaining England, were A. E. R. Gilligan, President-elect of the M.C.C., C. G. A. Paris (Hampshire), D. G. Clark (M.C.C. delegate), E. J. Gothard (Derbyshire) and A. B. Sellers (Yorkshire); D. J. Insole (chairman of the selectors) also attended, but without voting power. All were former county captains.

There was a two-hour hearing and the decision was unanimous – that Yorkshire had used delaying tactics, that these constituted unfair play and were against the best interests of the game, and that they held Close entirely responsible for these tactics. They severely censured him, and their decision was conveyed to the Yorkshire Club. Close has said he was thunderstruck by the decision.

The Yorkshire Committee gave an undertaking that the team would not again be involved in any time-wasting incidents – and that implied, of course, that they thought there had been some already. Close, however, has dismissed as absurd the suggestion that all would have been well and that the captaincy of the M.C.C. side to visit the West Indies would still have been his if he had apologised.

'But', he wrote, 'I could not desert my stand, my beliefs and my principles and apologise publicly for following a course of action that privately I thought was right in order to curry favour. I could not respect a captain who publicly admitted his guilt, but inwardly and sincerely believed in his own innocence.'

I was not there, so I have had to rely on the accounts of others as to what happened and I am prepared to let a Yorkshireman have the last word. He is J. M. Kilburn, the respected and experienced cricket correspondent of *The Yorkshire Post*, who, in his recent history of the county,* had this to say:

Yorkshire made no effort to disguise their delaying tactics. They walked slowly to bowling marks, to positions in the field and between overs. They were provocatively tardy in retrieving the ball from the boundary and returning it to

A History of Yorkshire Cricket, Stanley Paul and Co. Ltd.

play. Spectators grew increasingly discontented and abusive and the whole atmosphere of the game degenerated to disillusion with the basic principles of sport.

Were I a Yorkshire cricketer I hope I should be ashamed to have been a member of the team of which that was written and I have been given to understand that at least some of them were. Nor did *Wisden* spare Close and his colleagues, saying that their deliberate wasting of time, 'brought upon them and their captain a heap of adverse criticism and the image of cricket was besmirched'. The Warwickshire annual report let them off lightly, merely recording that Warwickshire, after having outplayed the ultimate Champions, were 'denied the fruits of victory', and recording the results of the inquiry.

Edgbaston had been an unhappy ground for Close. In his book he described it as 'the graveyard of my hopes', since what had happened in the match with Warwickshire 'sealed my fate and cost me the coveted captaincy of my country's cricket team', though, as he admitted, it had really nothing to do with his refusal to apologise; that was his own doing.

The Yorkshire Club, through its chairman and secretary, sent a letter of apology to Warwickshire's senior officers and its members. It would have been only poetic justice if Warwickshire could have gone to Middlesbrough for the return match, the last of the season, and walloped them good and hard, but they batted so feebly against Don Wilson, who, in the match, took thirteen wickets for 52 runs, that they were all out for 148 and 70, and Yorkshire won by 229 runs. But at least peace was restored between the two clubs. The chairman, Edmund King, Edgar Hiley and Tom Dollery all accompanied the team to Middlesbrough and if they did not smoke the pipe of peace they doubtless had a drink together, as did a number of the players with the result that, in the words of a Press statement issued afterwards, 'the whole matter was now happily and completely resolved'.

Warwickshire had only a short run in the Gillette Cup this season – one match only in fact – Somerset, who got to the final, beating them at Edgbaston by 25 runs. The game was spread over three days, no play being possible on the second. Largely because they missed four catches, Warwickshire allowed Somerset to score 206 for eight wickets. Virgin made 49 – he also had 150 against them in the county match – and Alley 45, as well as three wickets for 24, which earned him the man-of-the-match award. Warwickshire were all out 181.

The Club did not lose a match in the Minor Counties Competition, in which they were runners-up, and it was unfortunate that, for financial reasons, it was then decided to withdraw from the competition, particularly as it meant a saving of no more than £1300. The second eleven, which played eight Minor Counties games, was next to the bottom in their own competition and this programme for 1968 was cut by half, to eight games only. It was felt that the staff was too large, but that it should not be too drastically cut.

M. J. K. Smith officially announced his retirement towards the end of September and went to join Derrick Robins, the Coventry City chairman, in business. The latter clarified his position in the matter by informing the Committee that he had told Smith seven years before that as and when he wished to retire from first-class cricket he would be happy to discuss his business future with him. When Smith approached him earlier in the season with this end in view he (Robins) had at once advised the chairman of the Club of the fact in writing. Edmund King, confirming this, said it had been known that Smith wished to retire at the end of the 1967 season and after considering various offers had accepted that of Mr Robins, whose statement the Committee happily accepted.

Smith's 'very great services' both to Warwickshire and across the world were recorded in the minutes of the General Committee which said it had been honoured by his county allegiance. He had enriched the game throughout the decade he had played in it. Smith later self-sacrificingly declined the idea of any form of testimonial or benefit, for various reasons, one of which was that Cartwright was having one in 1968. He was, however, made an honorary life member.

That 'decade' should have been eleven years, counting only those in which he had captained the county, and he had also been playing abroad during the previous three winters. He had reached the stage, however, when he did not enjoy playing the game any more. 'Every cricketer', he said, 'feels he has got to do something else and I had changed my mind about going in for a career in cricket administration. As for the cares of captaincy, there is a lot in them but they didn't worry me even when I was skippering England, though I found the duties outside cricket trying.'

Everyone thought this was the end of Smith's career in first-class cricket and the Club's new scorer, Philip Pike, compiled a statistical summary which showed that in all first-class matches he had scored 31 580 runs, with a highest innings of 204 and an average of 41·99, including 55 centuries. He had also taken 488 catches, a record total for the Club; his 52 in one season being another record. His grand total of runs had been surpassed by only one other Warwickshire player, W. G. Quaife, who spent nearly three times as many seasons over them. 'Story book stuff all the way through', as Frank Bough said of his career.

Pike, who had been scoring for the second eleven, had succeeded Jack Wilkinson, who had collapsed and died during the lunch interval of the match with Scotland. He had been seriously ill during the winter, but his death at the age of 75 was a shock. The match continued with flags at half mast. 'We feel sure it would have been Jack's wish for the game to go on,' Leslie Deakins said.

The Committee carefully considered all the possible successors for the captaincy and then unanimously decided to invite Alan Smith to take over the leadership. An old boy of King Edward's School, Birmingham, and, like his predecessor, a former Oxford captain, he had impressed by his qualities of leadership whenever he had deputised for M.J.K. He had not scored as many runs as had been hoped, but he had proved a skilful wicketkeeper and he was a very useful bowler to be able to call on when an emergency occurred, as he proved on several occasions. He also took over the posts of public relations officer to the Club and the Association.

During September and October, the Club, for the first time, sent a touring side abroad. It went to East Africa at the invitation of Mr C. O. Oates, chairman of the East African Cricket Conference, and not only the players went. There were thirteen of them, but the party was sixty-five strong and it included the chairman and his wife, members of the committees of both the Club and the Supporters' Association, and the umpire, Charles Elliott and, as the saying goes, a very pleasant time was had by all. M. J. K. Smith wrote a long account of it for the annual brochure. All the matches were played on coir matting wickets, and Alan Smith, who was used as a bowler because Jack Bannister was unable to go, proved most successful because of his ability to cut the ball. M.J.K. said little about the batting, though, except to mention notable innings by Amiss, Cartwright and Abberley.

Because some of the games were boycotted by certain sections of the community – shades of troubles to come – there was a loss on the tour to the East African Cricket Conference of £1134, and as the chairman felt that in the circumstances the Warwickshire Club should make a gesture, the Supporters' Association made good the loss.

The Association was in the news on several occasions, notably for a further unconditional gift of £50 000 to the Club, which was placed towards the Endowment Fund. Edgar Hiley again expressed the hope that the Club would gradually begin to live within its income and not regard the Association either as a milch cow or as a prop, a point with which Edmund King agreed, though he felt the Club had been unfortunate in that it had developed a splendid ground, which of necessity had a high upkeep cost, at a period when the game was failing in its attraction for the public.

The *Daily Mail* had reported in May that the Association was on the point of embracing all the similar pools of other clubs, which brought from Edgar Hiley, who had now retired from business and was able to travel about more on the Association's affairs, a rejoinder that the proposal was in no sense a takeover bid for other counties' organisations. The Warwickshire Association, he said, were making £186 000 a year and no other county made £10 000.

The Association had had approaches from both Worcestershire, who had begun it all as far as the counties were concerned, and Northants, for co-operation, and a pilot scheme was being considered. Under this, 2d of every 1s which became available, less a ½d for expenses, would be evenly divided between Warwickshire and each sponsoring county – ¾d to each. This was the beginning of Operation 'Rescue Cricket', which may still lead to a pool on a fully national scale, under which the Warwickshire Assocation has links with those of five first-class counties – Worcestershire, Derbyshire, Essex, Hampshire and Leicestershire – and six minor counties on the basis of the original arrangement, except that in Staffordshire's case they received a contribution of £1000 a year. It cost £40 000 to promote the scheme, but in the first year alone, for example, Worcestershire received £12 000, the sharing arrangements being adjusted accordingly to the mutual benefit of all the clubs. In 1967 the Association opened its own social club in the Pavilion (east wing) and soon had a membership of over 1000 which has steadily grown, for both Association and County Club members belong to it. Known as The Warwick Social Club, it is open all the year round and provides facilities for meals, dancing, concerts, cabarets, snooker, table tennis, darts, badminton and cards, and runs its own sides at several of these games, as well as at cricket and football.

As the negotiations with the Tally Ho! club had come to nought, the Committee now concentrated attention on the overall plan the architects had prepared. Reconstruction of the Pavilion (centre) at an estimated cost of £750 000 naturally figured largely in their discussions, though it would take second place to the establishment of an Endowment Fund. There were also ideas for an hotel, or flats, on land belonging to the Club, or a multi-storey car park, but these were not regarded as acceptable; though a multi-purpose arena on the Old Edwardians' ground was thought worth consideration as this could produce revenue throughout the year. This dual purpose use of buildings was stressed by the chairman to Derrick Robins when the latter asked if thought had been given to developing Edgbaston as a general sports centre.

It was decided that future grants from the Supporters' Association should not be used for any capital development until the Endowment Fund had been built up to a figure which would provide sufficient income to meet the losses on running the Club – £13 000 in 1965, £20 000 in 1966 and an anticipated loss of at least £17 000 in 1967. These losses, it was agreed, must be rigorously tackled, wastages cut and savings made wherever possible. The Club was now in 'big business', but had a paltry income from cricket which was the whole object of its existence.

Nevertheless, it was felt that even during this period of severe restraint, and pending future clarification about the structure of the game, some money from the Supporters' Association should be allocated to improving the ground. Suggestions included making the Pavilion (centre) safe and improving it so that it would last for another ten years if necessary; generally tidying up; extending the cover and back walling of the Rea Bank stand; painting seats, and improving popular bars and catering arrangements.

When the views of the secretary were sought, Leslie Deakins was absolutely opposed to money being placed in an Endowment Fund since the Club held the freehold of the ground worth possibly £500 000 and in his opinion this was sufficient security for anyone. He thought that the only way to make a success of the Club was to continue building and developing the ground either for cricket, or for other purposes. Funds invested in the Endowment Fund would, he thought, be vulnerable to attack from outside sources unless they were spent on development. These views, however, were not accepted by the Committee. Their general feeling was that the Pavilion (centre) should be for cricket only and not a multi-purpose building.

Leslie Deakins also found himself called upon to defend his ideas of what Edgbaston should be when Leslie Jones, secretary of the Midlands Club Cricket Conference, speaking to the Northern Cricket Society in Leeds, said that over the years Warwickshire had built up a concrete mausoleum where players did not like playing because the ball echoed from the terraces. Asked for a comment by the Press, Leslie Deakins had this to say:

Mr Jones's reference to 'concrete mausoleums' prompts me to remark that such places still lie across the world and have been in place since before Roman times. The concrete arenas of today are the amphitheatres of yesterday in a modernised form. They offer the *only* means by which vast crowds can watch great events. That they will be empty on many occasions is inevitable; that they will justify themselves often is equally certain.

After long discussions it was at last agreed that the Club should sponsor four home Sunday games in 1968; two at Edgbaston, one at Coventry and one at Nuneaton. Because of legal complications over Sunday observance, all Club members, it was decided, would be admitted free to the ground and the pavilion; others would be made temporary or associate members for the day on payment of a subscription of 3s, giving access to the popular side of the ground only, with no half-price.

The engagement of Gibbs seemed to set off a spate of inquiries by, and about, cricketers, home and away. An approach was made to Barry Knight, the all-rounder, who wished to leave Essex, but that fell through. Inquiries were also made about Dexter, but he was available for only part of the season. Overseas players discussed were Graeme

Pollock and Eddie Barlow, of South Africa, both of whom stayed there; Clive Lloyd, who later joined Lancashire; Kanhai, who did join Warwickshire the following season on similar terms to Gibbs; Barry Richards, who came to Hampshire; Graham Mackenzie and Walters, the Australians; and Jawahit Patel, East Africa. Williams, a Cape coloured slow left-arm bowler, had been signed on a two-year contract, but his form was disappointing and at the end of his first season, when it looked as if there might be bigger fish in the sea than had come out of it, Warwickshire offered to end his contract and he was paid a sum in lieu of salary.

As for Warwickshire's own players, Barber was invited to play as much cricket as possible, but had said he would be able to make himself available only for approximately six weeks, preferably from the middle to the later part of the season. It was decided to offer him match fees, provided he was available for a minimum of twenty Championship games and all Gillette Cup games.

Stewart, who, unhappily, had to miss playing in his benefit against Worcestershire because of bronchitis – the match was drawn with honours to Worcestershire, both Headley and Graveney making centuries – was fortunate in his friends, for the benefit realised £8346, only £500 less than Bannister's record. Stewart also asked for a three-year contract. It was understood that an approach had been made to him by another county, and his request was turned down. One very promising young fast bowler who was offered an engagement was Norman McVicker, of Lancashire, who had not retained him, and Lincolnshire for whom he was leading bowler in the Minor Counties competition, but he proved hard to get.

The coming of Gibbs was also a beneficial thing from the point of view of at least some of the players, for it led to a levelling up of some top salaries. It was decided that the maximum rate for capped players would be increased, and at the end of the year Alan Smith submitted a memorandum on salary scales to the cricket sub-committee.

In it he pointed out that present rates were not high enough to attract the best home players; that it was becoming increasingly difficult to find half-year jobs outside cricket (for the first time for many years, it had been announced, some players were without winter employment and members were asked to assist); that the continuation of benefits was in some doubt; and that the arrival of overseas stars commanding much higher salaries than the home-bred player could create problems in the dressing-rooms.

Smith suggested an increase in bonuses for wins (these were later raised in Championship matches to a range of from £5 to £25 from one win to ten and over, and from £5 to £50 in the final of the Gillette Cup), and said that if the stars' services could be seen to be putting money into the players' pockets, objections to their salaries lessened. He also suggested that bonuses should be linked with crowds – that players should be paid for 1000 spectators above the norm and/or tied to the Club's Championship position, a novel approach which unfortunately has never been tried – though who would have decided what the normal gate was? He also urged an increase in the appearance money, which had been at £4 a match for the past eight years.

The players themselves took action to protect their own interests, forming The Cricketers' Association, which may well have received a spur because of the number of overseas players coming into the game. Some such body had been proposed many times in the past, but nothing had come of it. Its aims were set out as providing an organisation to which players could turn for advice and help on all matters concerning cricket; to seek ways and means of elevating the standard of living of cricketers without placing great burdens on county resources by negotiating with B.B.C., I.T.V. and the Press for fees and contracts, with business houses for bulk advertising – certain firms might supply gear and clothing free; forming an out-of-season employment exchange capable of placing those players in need of winter employment in suitable positions; finding business houses prepared to train the younger cricketer during the winter for a career when cricketing days were over; offering help in organising benefits and testimonials and generally becoming the county cricketer's agent; and for liaison between players and committees in times of dispute should the need arise.

The cricket sub-committee felt that it was not perhaps appropriate or opportune for them to comment on the formation of the Association, but subsequently the Club provided facilities for holding meetings at Edgbaston, and Jack Bannister became the Association's first honorary secretary and later its chairman, eventually becoming secretary again.

Promotion came to a lowlier servant of the Club, Derief Taylor, who, as an acknowledgment of his services over twenty years, was appointed coach in full charge of the Indoor School, with the assistance of 'Tiger' Smith, Cartwright and Alan Townsend, the last-named on Saturday mornings. Derief Taylor had shown himself to possess a skill, probably second to none in the country, of bringing the best out of boy cricketers. I liked especially the story Leslie Deakins has told about him many times. One Saturday one of his Under-13s ran all the way round the ground to tell him *he* had made 27. Derief asked him how many runs the team had made and, when the boy could not tell him, sent him all the way back to find out.

The sequel came on the Monday morning when two smartly dressed parents arrived on the ground and asked to see Mr Taylor. They were politely told that Derief was not there that morning, but that he would be in the afternoon. They said they would come back and when they did so and met Derief the father thanked him and said: 'You taught my son more in five minutes than we have taught him in twelve years.'

To which Derief replied: 'Not me, sir – the game of cricket.'

According to Dennis Amiss, who should know for Taylor began coaching him when he was only eight, Derief practises what Amiss believes is the only philosophy for a good coach – 'he brings out what you have got. He does not try to put in what you have not. He makes each of his pupils feel that he is an individual.'

In the very last days of the year there at last came to an end one of the most remarkable lives the game has known. The death occurred on Boxing Day of S. F. Barnes, whose long life – he was in his 95th year – had spanned almost the whole of the Club's history, for he had played for them as long ago as 1896. Though he left them, as he left so many other clubs, they were happy to have him back in later years at Test Matches and, in 1960, as president of the Warwickshire Old County Cricketers' Association. Of him, far more than of most people of whom it had been said, it was true that no one would look upon his like again. After his funeral at Cannock his son, Leslie, who wrote almost as good a hand as his father, presented the ashes to the Warwickshire Club and they were eventually enshrined in the pavilion garden.

West Indian Magic (1968)

SMITH's batting was not missed so much as Dollery's had been because there was an immediate – and very successful – successor to him in the magical person of Rohan Kanhai, the West Indian, who, unlike Gibbs, was able to play immediately under the new rule which allowed overseas players to appear without qualification delays. By the end of June he had reached his 1000 runs, the first batsman in the country to do so, and his final aggregate was 1819 runs, which gave him an average of 46·64 and third place in the national list.

Edgbaston, of course, had had previous entrancing glimpses of his batting genius during his appearances with West Indian touring sides, but in recent seasons it had been largely lost to first-class cricket, for he had been playing in the league game in Scotland and Lancashire. Warwickshire had long before been interested in him, but it was partly because Eddie Barlow, the South African all-rounder, remained impervious to all blandishments to persuade him to come and play regularly in England that the Committee thought again and decided to go for a great batsman and snapped up Kanhai.

Alan Smith had gone out to Jamaica in February 1968, to look at another player altogether, but he reported back unfavourably (though later the player signed for another English county) and then, on the instructions of the Committee, saw other players, including Kanhai, who was in outstanding form and had been strongly recommended by Lance Gibbs and David Brown who were out there playing in the Test series with and against Kanhai. An offer was made to Kanhai and in March he signed a three-year contract. It proved to be one of the best strokes of business Warwickshire had ever done. Kanhai was of Indian stock, for although he was born in British Guiana (now Guyana), his grandparents

503

had emigrated from India. For someone only five feet seven inches tall and stockily built, though still lithe, he hit the ball with astonishing power, the secret, of course, being timing, and he has always acknowledged his great debt to Worrell, who was a past-master of it.

As a schoolboy, Kanhai played without pads or gloves, a reason, he considered, why West Indian batsmen became less addicted to pad play than those of other countries – it hurt too much. He made his first century when he was only 16 and he was in the British Guiana team when he was 19, scoring 51 and 27 against the touring Australians. He got his chance to play against them by drawing lots from a hat. He lost, but next day the man who had won wrenched an ankle and Kanhai took his place.

His first visit to England in 1957 had been disappointing, for he made only 206 runs in Tests and averaged only 22·88. Even so, after that he rarely missed a West Indies Test. Against Pakistan at Calcutta in 1958–9 he made 256 and at Lahore 217, scoring 1518 runs on the tour. In 1960–1 – the famous tie tour – he averaged 50 in Tests against Australia, making centuries in two of them and 252 against Victoria; and during the 1963 tour to England he was the leading scorer on either side. Two of his outstanding innings produced no more than 32 and 38, but they were made against Trueman 'on the kill' in the Edgbaston Test.

I shall always feel a personal debt of gratitude to Warwickshire for engaging him, not so much because of the runs he has scored for them, though they have been entertaining enough in all conscience, but because I was able to see again in him what batsmen were like in the days when they still believed it was their main function in life to hit the ball hard – plus, of course, the personal panache he brought to the game. Sometimes he would let seemingly quite hittable balls pass him for no apparent reason, but then the tiger that always lurked beneath that seemingly benign exterior would stir and pounce and you would see a cut of blinding brilliance, or a drive that would make you instinctively draw your hand away from even the thought that you might be called upon to stop it. He was sometimes a man of moods – aren't we all? – but he let the younger generation of Warwickshire players and spectators see what real batsmanship could be, and I knew that I had not dreamed there really were such batsmen once. For that I shall be eternally grateful.

A system of bonus points for runs scored and wickets taken in the first eighty-five overs of the first innings of a match was introduced at the start of the 1968 season. It was the twenty-third alteration in the system of scoring in fewer than forty years, as the President reminded members at the annual meeting, and he was not alone in saying that he would watch its operation with some trepidation. The view was expressed in the annual report that it worked remarkably well in practice and it certainly led to some players pulling their socks up, but, as the report also said, it would need more than a new points scoring system, or a revision of the lbw law, to bring back spectators.

'It was remarkable', the report went on, 'to note ... how quickly counties realised that more bonus points were going to be won by bowlers than batsmen and in consequence there were several rapid reversals in policy on pitch cover.' Warwickshire was one county which decided not to cover during matches, but to let Nature take its course, thereby at least pacifying those doddering diehards (of whom the author is one) who believe that the effect of rain and sun on English turf is one of the most important factors in giving cricket its unique flavour. The policy, however, was not implemented for long. A year later it was decided that pitch-covering should be uniform throughout the country, thus conforming to the pattern for Test Matches.

Cyril Goodway, chairman of the appropriate sub-committee, was totally opposed to uncovering, believing that hard, true wickets were essential and that regard should be given to the watcher of the game rather than the player; a far cry in attitude from the days when man played cricket merely for his own enjoyment, though no one could quarrel in principle with his view that 'we owe it to them [the spectators] to provide as much cricket as possible in this variable climate'.

Kanhai soon made his mark for his new county, scoring 119 in his very first innings in the first match of the season against Cambridge. It was the first of the six centuries he was to make during the summer and in the next game he paid his compliments to the sister university by making 111. He followed these 'starters' with 59 not out against Sussex at Edgbaston. But all this was rather like Yehudi Menuhin tuning up by playing a few short pieces before tackling the major concerto. In Kanhai's case, this was played at Trent Bridge in the first three days of June in what might be called the match of transformations.

In their first innings Warwickshire made no more than 93 and Notts established a lead of 189. History looked like being repeated in Warwickshire's second innings when the wickets of Barber, Stewart and Amiss went for 6 runs. This left Kanhai and Ibadulla together, and that was how they stayed for the next six and three-quarter hours. During that time they broke not only the record for Warwickshire's fourth wicket, but for every other Warwickshire wicket as well – and those of Notts – by making 402. Of these Kanhai scored no fewer than 253 and hit one six and thirty-six fours. Ibadulla's more modest contribution of 147 not out included sixteen fours. That new Notts star, Gary Sobers – and how it must have pleased Kanhai to get such a score against the bowling of the captain of his country – took just one wicket – for 87 runs.

The previous fourth wicket record for Warwickshire, 319, stood to the credit of Wyatt and Dollery twenty-one years before and the record for all Warwickshire wickets was the undefeated 377 of Ibadulla and Horner at The Oval in 1960. Kanhai followed this mammoth effort with a mere 111 at Edgbaston against Yorkshire. At Middlesbrough, Yorkshire had won by an innings, but this time they were humbled by Cartwright, who took seven of their wickets in the first innings for 37 and three for 48 in the second. Kanhai was also involved, this time with Stewart, in a double-century partnership of 248, for the third wicket against Leicestershire. On this occasion he just missed the 200 – 193 – and Stewart got 117.

Another all-time Warwickshire record was established this season – for a benefit. Cartwright had selected the match against Worcestershire at the beginning of August and though he was absent – as he was for nearly half the season with knee and shoulder injuries – his share of the gate receipts and the proceeds of many other efforts on his behalf took the total to £9592, which was not only a Warwickshire record, but the twelfth highest in the history of benefits for all cricketers.

One of those efforts, a Sunday match with the International Cavaliers, the first of cricket's sponsored teams, the benefactors being Rothman's, brought in no less than £3246, compared with £885 from the benefit match itself. It was the first time this attractive side-of-all-the-stars had visited the ground, and they attracted the largest crowd, Tests excepted, seen at Edgbaston for seventeen years – over 14 000 spectators. The problem of not being able to charge them for admission in the ordinary way was overcome by making everyone an associate member for 4s, which gave them the right of entry to the ground. They saw Warwickshire win a fine match. The Cavaliers made 232, Clive Lloyd contributing 59, R. T. Simpson 47 and Saeed Ahmed 40; and Warwickshire hit off the runs for the loss of only five wickets, Amiss making 102 not out, Barber 43 and Cartwright 33 not out.

The success of this game prompted Leslie Deakins to point once more to the appeal of one-day cricket. 'Yesterday proved one thing,' he told the newspapers on Monday morning – 'the public want to see one-day cricket. They don't want three-day, mid-week cricket. I would like to see county cricket take a new form in future – a three-day match at the week-end – Saturday, Sunday and Monday – with a single-day competition on Wednesdays and supplemented by the Gillette Cup. This would give sixteen weekend matches with terms per match which would slash our wages bill.'

This is surely the most attractive and the most-likely-to-succeed programme that has yet been put forward as a solution to the game's present ills and the mystery is why it has still not been given an extended trial at the very least. Another is why the Morris Report has never been published. It was the work of Denis Morris, former Head of Programmes in the B.B.C.'s Midland Region and later Head of the Light Programme, who, at the behest of the M.C.C., made a comprehensive survey of the first-class game at all levels. There is reason to believe that some of its recommendations have since been adopted, but it is part of cricket history and could surely be made available for publication now.

Because of his frequent absences during the season, one of which was ultimately to have international consequences no one could have foreseen, Cartwright took only sixty-eight wickets in Championship matches, the first time for seven years that he had failed to get 100. He still managed to achieve the distinction of being the first Warwickshire player to score 10 000 runs and take 1000 wickets in first-class cricket, though he was still 50 short of the latter for Warwickshire alone.

He was not the only bowler without whose services Warwickshire had to manage during the season, the county's worst in this respect for many years. At one time all their front-line bowlers were out of action. Bannister broke down; Brown was away for four of the Tests against Australia; and Gibbs, in his first full season, found few wickets to suit him, was slow to adapt himself to English conditions, and suffered the frustration of numerous dropped catches, so that he took no more than sixty-seven wickets for 25·04 runs each. In the circumstances, the side did well to drop only one place in the Championship table.

Alan Smith proved a keen and enthusiastic captain, even if he did not particularly distinguish himself by his batting in Championship games, and he certainly showed a flair for one-day cricket, Warwickshire winning the Gillette Cup for the second time in three years. They had a bye in the first round and then beat Yorkshire by four wickets with thirteen balls to spare at Edgbaston, where the match had to be spread over three days and the ground staff worked all night to get the ground fit.

Hampshire were beaten by 27 runs after Kanhai, missed when 6, hit 92 and won the man-of-the-match award; and in the semi-final he made another 53, Warwickshire beating Middlesex by three wickets after an exciting finish in which 10 runs were needed from ten balls, and they scored 12.

Warwickshire got a fillip for the final against Sussex by beating them by three wickets in the Championship match at Hove the day before. And then, even without Cartwright and Bannister, both injured, they increased the margin at Lord's, where Alan Smith really came into his own as a leader before a crowd of 23 000 – more people than attended all the County Championship matches at Edgbaston.

Sussex batted first and off their sixty overs made 214 for the loss of seven wickets. Parks was their mainstay with 57, and Ibadulla took the bowling honours with three for 25. Amiss was pressed into service as a bowler, but was hit for 63 runs. His turn came when Warwickshire batted. Stewart began with a very useful 59, and then Amiss and Smith, running brilliantly between the wickets, put on 60 runs in an unfinished partnership which won the match. Amiss was 44 not out and Smith 39 not out; this innings and his inspiring leadership generally earning him the man-of-the-match award. No side batting second had previously made so many runs.

Amiss, Barber and Brown were all called on for various Tests against Australia, the third of which was played at Edgbaston. Brown was one of three fast bowlers the M.C.C. had taken to the West Indies under the leadership of Cowdrey in place of the deposed Close. The others were Snow and Jones. Snow proved the fastest and most dangerous, taking twenty-seven wickets in the Tests to fourteen each by the other two. Snow's cost him only 18·66 runs each, Brown's 32·71 and Jones's 46·84. In all the first-class matches Brown took sixteen wickets for 37·25 each, distinctly expensive, though England did win the rubber by the only match in which there was a decision.

Amiss would probably have gone on the tour as well, but after the one Test he played in 1967 he tended to cut out his shots and to dig in, a method which was becoming all too common in batsmen playing for a place in international cricket, though one would have thought that it would have given them a better chance of being selected if they had showed their strokes and got runs instead of grafting for them. It was an affliction from which Amiss suffered for some time until Alan Smith helped to talk him out of it; and he then began again to look like the batsman 'Tiger' Smith had prophesied he could be, and who should have established his place in the England side by now. Unhappily he had the misfortune to get 'a pair' in the very first Test of the series, a horrible thing to happen to anyone, but most of all in a Test at Lord's against Australia, and he was dropped for the rest of the series.

So, too, was Barber, though he made 20 and 46. Brown did not come in until the second Test at Old Trafford, in the first innings of which he had his best performance so far – five for 42. On a green pitch and in a heavy atmosphere, he and Knight, three for 16, were responsible for getting Australia out for 78. Brown did not take a wicket in the second innings and Australia went one up in a series in which they suffered from a poor summer.

Advance bookings for the Edgbaston game were disappointing – perhaps people had been put off by slow play at Old Trafford – and again the warning went out that apathy might cause Edgbaston to lose Tests. The day before the match was washed out – no less than 2·44 inches of rain fell – and so was the first day, despite Herculean efforts by Bernard Flack and his ground crew, all under 21, who by working all night again, earned themselves the titles of 'The Magnificent Seven' and 'The Water Babies'.

This was Cowdrey's 100th Test Match and I had ended an appreciative article about him for *The Birmingham Post* with the thought that if he made a century in this one it would be like something out of schoolboy fiction. And that, of course, is precisely what he did. Although he went lame after making 50, Boycott acting as runner for him, Cowdrey got to 104 not out in England's total of 409. This was his twenty-first Test century and it took him past the landmark of Hammond's record total of 7249 runs in Tests, though the latter had achieved them in fifteen fewer matches. The ball with which Cowdrey scored his 100th run was later mounted by the Warwickshire Club and presented to him by Derrick Robins, on behalf of the Warwickshire Committee, at the Kent centenary banquet the following year. It was a pleasant gesture which brought an appreciative letter from Cowdrey, a great admirer of the Edgbaston ground about which he has gone on record as saying: 'Anyone who set about trying to select three of the best-appointed cricket grounds in the world could never leave Edgbaston out of their three.'

Australia were got out for 222, Brown taking one wicket for 44 runs, and England, batting again, declared at 142 for three. Australia had made 68 for one on the last day when rain stopped play for good with the tourists still needing 261 to win. Despite the poor weather there was a 25 000 crowd on the Saturday of whom 16 953 paid £12 739. The total attendance came to 56 069, with receipts £35 393, which were £10 000 up on those at Old Trafford. Incidentally, with their smallest playing staff for twenty years, Warwickshire had some difficulty in providing a substitute fielder for England.

Brown took two wickets in the fourth Test and four in the fifth, which England won to square the rubber, but his twelve wickets at an average of 33·41 was not really England form. For a change, there were three days of sunshine when the tourists came to Edgbaston again in June. Warwickshire, for whom M. J. K. Smith turned out again, gave as good as they got, even though the tourists scored 394 for seven declared, of which Chappell made 202 not out, his last 100 runs coming off 100 balls.

Warwickshire's first innings yielded 257, Kanhai 60, M. J. K. Smith 45 and Jameson 56, and then, in the Australians' second innings, Brown had an inspiring spell of four front-line wickets for 9 runs in twenty-two balls. Half the side were out for 34, but they managed to declare at 161 for seven, Brown's final figures being six for 55. Warwickshire were left with 299 to get at 85 an hour and they made a brave try. Jameson hit 98 and 'Mike' Smith also got going again. The extra half-hour was claimed with Warwickshire still wanting 65 runs with four wickets outstanding, and in the end Smith and Legard, the reserve wicket-keeper, were left holding out and for once 'a draw provided a thrilling and just result', as *Wisden* put it.

In the presence of the Australians, who were only too delighted to be asked to take part, the President made a presentation to 'Mike' Smith in front of the pavilion during the tea interval. Earlier in the year he had been the chief guest at a reception attended by over 300 people at which other farewell presentations were made.

There was one other match which deserves to be mentioned, a remarkable affair with Essex at Leyton in August. Rain prevented play on the opening day and then three innings of under 100 and one of exactly that figure were completed in the remaining two days – forty wickets for 343 runs. Warwickshire's score was 98 in each innings. The last nine wickets in the first innings went down for 54 runs, mostly to East, a left-arm spin bowler, who had seven for 52, which he followed with eight for 63 in the second. The Essex totals were 47 – Brown five for 21 and Gibbs four for 10 – and 100, Gibbs this time taking five for 33, and Warwickshire were winners by 49 runs.

There was more trouble with the Coventry pitch which played dangerously in Warwickshire's second innings against Gloucestershire in June. They were all out for 78. In Gloucestershire's second innings Gibbs took seven for 49, but they won by 112 runs. A report by the umpires, Aspinall and Pepper, to Lord's condemned the wicket as 'unfit for first-class cricket' and Lock was again called in. Both the Lancashire match and a single-wicket competition, which was to have been held in July, were transferred to Edgbaston, and the Coventry ground was ruled out for first-class cricket for at least a season, possibly two; a decision endorsed by the County Pitches Committee. The report of the selection sub-committee on the new part of the Edgbaston square declared that there was more pace in it than in previous years, but that the ball turned sooner than was desirable.

Although the weather kept gates at the Gillette Cup matches down – for the first time profits fell, by £7000, although the sponsors increased their support from £10 000 to £15 000 – the Editor of *Wisden* thought that the competition 'has done much . . . towards shaking up slothful performers and now we have the new Players' County League each Sunday to implement that good work, reducing the number of three-day Championship matches from twenty-eight to twenty-four'.

'Players' referred to the tobacco company, not to the players on the field. They were the sponsors of this Sunday afternoon competition to the extent of £65 000, of which £29 000 would be available, either as direct payments to the players, or as prizes for distribution, and £36 000 for the counties. Warwickshire had doubts about this latest innovation, which they considered to be 'matches within matches' at the weekends, and in view of the travelling likely to be involved; and at one time they had been prepared to propose that the idea should be abandoned.

At the end of the season Cartwright underwent treatment to his shoulder for thickening of the tendons, which prevented him getting his arm high up, in the hope of being pronounced fit to go to South Africa with the M.C.C. touring team. Four days later in the match between Warwickshire and the Gillette Invitation XI he bowled ten overs without any apparent ill effects, but he later told the M.C.C. he dare not risk it – 'the hardest decision of my life', was how he described it.

Basil D'Oliveira was chosen in his place, but the South African Government declined to accept him and eventually the M.C.C. cancelled the tour, as, surely, they were absolutely right to do. Many people felt they should have told the South African Board of Control that the refusal to accept a player officially chosen was something that could not be tolerated. Had that been done then it is possible that there would have been none of the deplorable events of 1970.

Commenting in *Wisden*, Michael Melford, of *The Daily Telegraph*, wrote that,

when so many voices in England were discussing the political side of the affair, it was hard for anyone at a distance who did not know them to believe that D. J. Insole, A. V. Bedser, P. B. H. May and D. Kenyon, augmented by G. O. Allen, A. E. R. Gilligan and the captain, M. C. Cowdrey, were impervious to political influence and were picking the side purely on cricket qualifications.

It was harder still after the final readjustment of the team on 16 September. Cartwright had been unfit when picked originally, but the assurance given by specialists of his imminent recovery had been provisionally accepted and he had bowled ten overs for Warwickshire on 14 September without apparent discomfort. However, a subsequent medical report ruled him out and D'Oliveira was chosen to replace him.

In view of Mr Insole's previous statement that D'Oliveira had been considered only as a batsman, his substitution now for a bowler must have been final proof to the South African government that political influences were at work. Mr Insole's explanation that the balance of the side had to be entirely reviewed made little impact. No replacement of Cartwright's type, or experience, did, in fact, exist in England in the unavailability for different reasons of B. R. Knight, Illingworth and others.

This, however, was surely beside the point. It is difficult to conceive of circumstances in which the M.C.C. would have taken exception to any player chosen by the accredited ruling body of any country, and certainly not on the ground of the colour of his skin, and this should apply equally all round, otherwise cricket will have ceased to be a game in which all the players are equal in every respect other than their abilities in the field.

The whole structure of the hierarchy of the game underwent a major change this season which meant the end of the M.C.C. as the supreme ruling authority accepted by all the cricket-playing countries. They were superseded by the M.C.C. Cricket Council (later The Cricket Council), consisting of the President and honorary treasurer of the M.C.C., who appointed nine other members, plus seven from the Test and County Cricket Board and ten from the National Cricket Association, on which a large number of bodies and every class of cricket were represented. No one body could out-vote the other two.

Warwickshire supplied representatives to nine of the twelve standing committees of the new Board. They included Edmund King, the chairman, who was a member of the Cricket Council and was now also appointed to the extremely important office of chairman of the Finance and General Purposes Sub-Committee of the Board; and the vice-chairman, secretary and captain of the Warwickshire Club. Edmund King remarked that he regarded these appointments as a reflection of the Club's standing on the legislative side of cricket.

In the absence of any funds in the Test and County Cricket Board's account, at that time, Warwickshire offered the loan of £20 000 to cover the initial expenses of the South African tour, an offer which was warmly accepted, though the money was not, of course, needed. The Supporters' Association meanwhile underwrote the M.C.C. tour to Ceylon and Pakistan to the extent of £15 000, which was later repaid and reinvested. Brown was in the team, led by Cowdrey, and played in all three 'Tests', taking eight wickets for 19·87 runs each and heading the averages. He also had a batting average of 40. Even here the third match was abandoned because of rioting over something or other after England had scored 502 for seven.

Incidentally, the Advisory County Cricket Committee, which was merged with the Board of Control for Test Matches to form the Test and County Cricket Board, brought some good out of the unfortunate match with Yorkshire. In order that there should be no more deliberate time-wasting in the extra half-hour, Warwickshire had proposed that ten overs should be substituted, but the committee made it twenty overs in the final hour.

Warwickshire, too, formed its own County Cricket Association at the request of the M.C.C. and the National Cricket Association. Over ninety people representing all the bodies controlling cricket, or any aspect of the game, in the Midlands, were present at the inaugural meeting at the county ground, but everything did not go as smoothly as had been hoped.

The Midlands Club Cricket Conference, formed twenty-one years earlier and with a membership of 240 clubs in Warwickshire alone, but in itself a regional body with 700 member clubs, took the view that it should be asked to be the county association for Warwickshire and that the new body was not needed. The others, however, were not prepared to accept this and the meeting was adjourned until December, both Edmund King and Cyril Goodway deploring the Conference's attitude.

When the December meeting was held the Conference withdrew their proposal that they should take over the duties and responsibilities a county association would have, and a steering committee was then set up under the chairmanship of Alec Hastilow to draw up a constitution and establish the Association without the Conference.

A good deal more was heard on the subject of Warwickshire players' salaries, which had now risen to an annual sum of £53 000. Alan Smith, initiating a discussion on the subject at a meeting of the cricket sub-committee, felt that by bringing its salary structure more into line with modern ideas instead of waiting for a lead from somewhere else, the Club could lead the way for all other cricket in the country.

A man devoting his life to the game now was taking a much bigger risk than in days gone by, he considered, for it was extremely difficult to get a worthwhile appointment in business after the age of 36. The Club, he felt, would have to pay considerably more if they wished players to bear the responsibility of providing the type of cricket the individual wished to see. The chairman approved of these views. But was not this to acquiesce in having to pay the players more in order to induce them to play the sort of game they should have been playing anyway – dangling a carrot, as it were?

It was true, of course, that county clubs were now dealing more with the product of the grammar schools than the kind of boy who used to come into cricket the hard way via the elementary school, or the ground staff, but it might have been thought that players would have been chary of pushing their claims too hard in view of the possibility of the county programmes being cut, staffs reduced, or players being paid on a match fee basis.

Warwickshire players' salaries, including allowances and fringe benefits, were now much higher, if still below those paid to professionals in some other sports, or in the entertainment world, let alone industry and the professions, but they were understandably concerned about their salaries and prospects, though it has to be remembered that there was very little money in the game itself. They had also been pressing for better pay for Sunday games, and the Club had calculated that the arrangements they had made would mean a seasonal outlay of an additional £3300, the whole of the sponsorship fee to which each county was entitled. And this, of course, did not take into account payments they might have to make to office and ground staffs for the extra hours they had to put in. The Club had also agreed to release Gibbs and Kanhai for the Tests during the West Indies tour of 1969,

KK   513

though they were opposed to doing so for the whole of the tour; a fact which had been made clear at the time they were signed. Their salaries would have to be paid in their absence while playing in Tests.

Players also expressed some concern about the increased amount of travel involved in Sunday play, a spokesman of their Association saying that at one period they faced twenty-eight consecutive days of cricket without a break, which hardly sounded like the reduction in the amount of cricket for which Warwickshire had been pleading for years.

Meanwhile, with all these extra outgoings, it had become obvious that the overall income of the Club could not increase correspondingly without sponsorship in some form or another. It was variously estimated before the 1968 season had started that the increase in subscriptions had cost the Club between 15 and 20 per cent of its membership – 1250 compared with usual annual wastage of 500 to 600 – but that if all the remaining members remained on the list the total subscriptions would still be well in advance of any sum previously received from this source. In fact, at the annual meeting the chairman announced that the total income was only £66 000, resulting in a loss on the year of £17 000 and making the deficit for the last three years, £50 000, 'terribly depressing figures'.

They were, however, bettered as 1968 progressed. Income went up to £92 269, but expenditure was also up and the loss on 1968 was £9161. The total paying attendance was only 23 000, an average of just over 500 a day.

A table of match results between 1864 and 1968 published in *Wisden* provided some interesting comparisons between the records of the counties. This, for instance, was Warwickshire's, though, of course, they did not come into the reckoning until 1894:

PLAYED	WON	LOST	DRAWN	TIED
1569	425	466	677	1

The only counties with more wins than losses were Kent (761 to 634), Lancashire (844 to 417), Middlesex (682 to 466), Notts (612 to 490), Surrey (899 to 478) and Yorkshire (1183 to 328). Five counties lost more than one-quarter of their games – Glamorgan, Northants, Somerset, Warwickshire and Leicestershire, the last-named winning less than one-fifth of them. Notts had most draws, 804, but Essex, Glamorgan and Warwickshire each drew over two-fifths of their games.

Leicestershire were the fastest scorers in 1968 with 49·78 per 100 balls, and Notts second. Glamorgan bowled most overs an hour. Despite a wet summer, 1968, with 43·21, saw the highest average run rate of the last six seasons. Warwickshire bowled 18·83 overs an hour in 1967 compared with 18·56 in 1968. The county's runs per 100 balls figure was 45·72 in 1967 and 45·65 in 1968.

Regrettably, one of the longest-standing links in the Club's history, with the Royal Warwickshire Regiment, had to be broken during the season. The regimental secretary of the Royal Warwickshire Fusiliers as they had become known, wrote saying that, as from April 1968, they were to merge with the three other Fusilier regiments to form The Royal Regiment of Fusiliers, with headquarters in London; this meant the removal of the county's name from their title and therefore he felt the long link between the Club and the Regiment was broken and that the vice-presidency the Regiment had held should cease. The decision was received with the greatest regret for the two organisations had been associated throughout virtually the whole of the Club's existence.

The Cartwright Case (1969)

THERE were two happenings in 1969 which overshadowed everything else so far as Warwickshire cricket was concerned – the beginning of the John Player League competition on Sunday afternoons and the departure, despite all that Club officials could do to prevent it, of Tom Cartwright, which perhaps caused more argument over bars and dining-tables than anything that had happened since Grove had bowled his last over for the county. Between these two events, the fact that Warwickshire finished fourth in the County Championship and that both the West Indies and the New Zealand teams were here, got rather less attention than they deserved.

The traditionalists of cricket had found much to criticise in the Gillette Cup competition. It was not the kind of cricket they had been brought up on, they said, conveniently ignoring the fact that most of them had played only in Saturday afternoon cricket, or works knock-out competitions. It was not the three-day game, let alone the five-day Test; it was cricket for boys, not men, they said contemptuously. But the vast majority of the public, who had suffered long, if not always silently, from the push-and-prod school welcomed it with open arms and flocked to see it in their thousands. Soon all but the most encrusted of the diehards came to accept and enjoy it, too; but then when they watched the Sunday afternoon games and saw the sort of happy-go-lucky cricket it sometimes produced, old prejudices reasserted themselves and out poured the criticisms.

Some of them, it must be admitted, were justified. It was patently true, for instance, that the sixty overs of the Gillette Cup did give a batsman some sort of chance, if only a fleeting one, to have a quick look at the bowling before he started to try to score from it as rapidly as he could, but in the forty-over limit cricket of the John Player League it had to be bang-bang-bang from the start. Now your Sobers, your Lloyds, your Kanhais – odd that the names of three West Indians should come first to mind – can do this and still look the great class players they are (I have never seen a more perfectly played straight six than the one Sobers put *through* the sightscreen at Edgbaston in the summer of 1971) but lesser mortals have to resort to more unorthodox methods, and it cannot be gainsaid that the Sunday afternoon competition was responsible for bringing out the brute force and ignorance which lie latent in all but the most artistic of batsmen. 'All scramble and slogging' was Graveney's description of one-day cricket, though he conceded that it improved fielding and running between the wickets. The result was that the 'cow' shot, hitherto regarded as the copyright of the village green, or the works evening knock-out, came into all too common use on the county grounds of England. It was 'slap-bang-wallop cricket', as Edgar Hiley once described it.

Have we been any the worse for it? Well, it has offended the eye of the purist, but that is not so important as the fact that, more than ever, the indiscriminate among the crowd applauded even the rank bad shots if runs were scored from them and that these can be habit-forming among batsmen. Potentially good batsmen being spoiled in a frantic scramble for runs at all costs is not what cricket was all about even in its Hambledon days. The story of the young Compton, who was rebuked by his coach for having his feet in the wrong place when he made a drive which would have cut cover in half had he been so foolish as to try to stop it, and was bold enough to retort, 'Never mind my feet, look at the bloody ball', is well known. The trouble is that there has been only one Compton and genius has always made its own rules. Most batsmen are incapable of turning the sow's ear of their poor efforts into the silk purse of class batsmanship, though there might well have been more Comptons had there been fewer coaches.

Still, the Sunday afternoon matches produced some splendidly exciting finishes and, if nothing else, both the Gillette Cup and the John Player League proved what the criticis of the modern county game have always said, that players were not really suffering from paralysis, could get a move on if they had to do so and, moreover, play strokes they would never have risked in three-day games. Whether or not they will be any better cricketers from the point of view of technical skill, or whether, as many of them contend, these games are no training ground for the sterner stuff of County Championship games and Test Matches – ignoring the fact that some countries have done well enough in producing players of class on little more than this sort of game – is another matter. But then may not Test cricket itself have to brighten up its ideas if the crowds are not to forsake it, which they have shown signs of doing as they have largely forsaken county cricket? They have already shown that they refuse any longer to be bored to death by what should be the most joyous of games, which they have *paid* to see, and though there will always be a public for the star player, the man who can empty the bars, as W. G. Grace, or Jessop, used to empty the clubs, they are not going to put up with strokeless nonentities for much longer, even in Test cricket.

As it happened, in this first season of the John Player League, Warwickshire's supporters were not given stimulating cause to be excited except perhaps through watching the games they saw televised. Warwickshire, who, with their record of success in the Gillette Cup might have been expected to excel in the Sunday afternoon game, by no means did so. It must, after all, be somewhat unsettling, to a batsman particularly, to be constantly called upon to change the tempo of his game, a dilemma which produced a cartoon showing a batsman taking guard and saying to the umpire, 'Middle and leg, please, and would you mind telling me whether I'm playing in county, cup or league cricket?'

In their first sixteen matches in the competition Warwickshire struck their usual average – they won six, lost six and four were washed out by the weather, so they finished ninth in the table. Cartwright three times took four wickets in an innings and headed the national averages in the competition. In one match he had four for none in nine balls – four for 7 altogether. No Warwickshire batsman got in the first ten, but Kanhai brilliantly hit 102 in 35·2 overs against Notts, one of only five centuries made during the competition.

The school of thought that had argued that Sunday afternoon cricket, if played in the right spirit, would draw the crowds, was wholly vindicated by what happened at Nuneaton on 24 August where Lancashire had to win to become the first champions of the League. No fewer than 3290 people paid £882 to see the match – £200 more than the best gate at Edgbaston for a Sunday afternoon game. Indeed, only the day before, with Lancashire also the opponents, only £60 was taken at the gate at Edgbaston and that on a Saturday, the first day of a three-day match. The game at Nuneaton was won by Lancashire by 51 runs after a fourth-wicket partnership by Clive Lloyd, 59, and Sullivan, 60. There were a few complaints about the seating and the viewing and the Club apologised, but it must have been a long time since a crowd of anything like these proportions had come to watch cricket on the ground.

Altogether 280 608 people saw these Sunday afternoon games, compared with 326 927 who patronised County Championship matches; the figures for Warwickshire being 12 960 for the John Player League, almost as many in six half-days as came to see county matches on 36 full days – 13 780. There could have been few more convincing demonstrations of where the public's taste lay, even if its standards of appreciation of the finer points of cricket sometimes left something to be desired.

Warwickshire's annual report mentioned 'a growing school of thought that it requires more genuine cricket skill to prove successful in limited overs, single-day cricket, than in the three-day game', but perhaps this was rather making a virtue out of necessity. A different skill, certainly, but one unfortunate effect of it was to induce more negative bowling and field-placing in order to keep the runs down, so that with one hand the powers-that-be, or the promoters, were encouraging batsmen to go for runs, and with the other taking the chance away. The report was certainly on firm ground when it contended that 'in the very near future some form of compromise is necessary' and added: 'It is certain it cannot be, on current evidence, both a players' game and a spectators' game.' More's the pity. That would be the ideal solution and it should not be beyond the wit of administrators and players to find it.

Wisden thought the League 'an instant success . . . it is liked because both sides are seen batting, bowling and fielding on the same afternoon and at the end there is a definite result . . . The majority of these games produced wonderful fielding in the ways runs were saved, as well as superb batting. This was a feverish tempo'. But then the traditionalist emerged: 'Nevertheless, this one-day "instant" cricket must never be regarded as a substitute for genuine first-class cricket . . . the sense of urgency must stimulate the players.'

Not the least interesting feature of these Sunday afternoon games from Warwickshire's point of view was the re-emergence of M. J. K. Smith and the knowledge that he would again be available for first-class cricket in 1970. He was badly needed, for one thing to take the place of Alan Smith, who had been appointed a Test selector, which entailed absences, but there were many followers of the game who had always thought that he had left it prematurely and that he would find the pull of it too strong for him.

Warwickshire's run in the Gillette Cup was short-lived for they were beaten in the second round by Essex at Edgbaston. Edmeades took three wickets in nine balls, blows from which the Warwickshire innings never recovered, though thanks to a half-century by Stewart the total reached 146. Essex, however, hit these off in only 45·1 overs for the loss of three wickets; Fletcher, 54 not out, and Irvine, sharing in an unbroken stand of 88 to win the match.

It was Glamorgan's County Championship again after an interval of twenty-one years so no one could grudge them it. Warwickshire came with a late run, winning four of their last six games, which took them up to fourth place. They won only three other matches, being particularly unlucky in the weather, which was a big factor in the fourteen drawn games, so that their final position rather flattered them, though they were beaten only three times. Of the leading nine counties, only Gloucestershire earned fewer bonus points than did Warwickshire, the chief troubles, according to *Wisden*, being fragility in the middle-order batting and a lack of variety in attack.

It did not help that during the early part of June no fewer than eight players were either out of the side altogether for various periods, or severely handicapped by injuries and illnesses. The roll call of invalids read like this:

BROWN	bruised hand and leg strain
STEWART	pulled hamstring
KANHAI	food poisoning
JAMESON	tonsillitis
IBADULLA	groin injury
ALAN SMITH and BARBER	hay fever
AMISS	treatment for back

No wonder it was decided that the Club needed its own doctor, who was appointed in the person of Dr Glenn Lambert. On leaving the area he was succeeded by a member of a Birmingham practice, Dr W. A. Kerr, a former Scottish hockey international. For some years the Club had had its own physiotherapist in Bernard Thomas, whose standing and status in the game led to his appointment as physiotherapist for M.C.C. tours and as assistant to touring managers.

The side was handicapped in the first instance by Kanhai having to undergo a cartilage operation on his knee, through which he had to miss the whole of May. He scored only just over 1000 runs in Championship matches, though his average of 41·76 took him to the top of the county list. Amiss, although still playing too defensively for his admirers and seeming more concerned with staying in than with getting runs, was still the only other batsman to aggregate four figures – 1178 runs, average 30·20 – but it was not really good enough and no county can get far with its two leading batsmen scoring so moderately. Jameson still had not fulfilled his promise and his total was no more than 851, while Barber, playing only thirteen Championship matches, never found his touch and scored only 540.

Brown, showing considerable skill as a batsman, almost reached that total and was third in the averages. This, it may well be thought, does not say much for the recognised batsmen, but it speaks highly of Brown's versatility. On one occasion against Worcestershire at Dudley, when both Barber and Kanhai were injured, he opened the innings and made 47, and he did a dashing night-watchman act against Gloucestershire with eleven fours in an innings of 60.

In bowling, however, his total of wickets in all matches – he was away for three Tests against the West Indies – was only fifty-one, and McVicker, in his first full season with Warwickshire, who had spent eight years trying to persuade him to join them, overtook him and finished third in the averages to Cartwright, whose fitness had been in doubt all winter. Even the latter did not take 100 wickets in Championship matches, though he had 108 in all games at only just over 16 runs each. In total of wickets, Blenkiron, a sturdily built fast-medium bowler from County Durham, was second to him with seventy-nine in all matches; but Gibbs, after an exhausting Australian tour with his countrymen in the winter and absences in the West Indies series here in the early part of the season, bowled only 216 overs and took a meagre nineteen wickets. So far he was proving an expensive investment.

Alan Smith had to miss ten Championship matches because of injury and absences on selectors' duties, Cartwright and Amiss both acting as deputies at times. Two new wicketkeepers appeared on the scene – B. S. V. Timms, of Hampshire, who, for business reasons, wished to play only a limited amount of cricket, and J. I. McDowall, the Cambridge wicketkeeper, and son of James McDowall, the Club's honorary treasurer, who also played some useful innings when he came down from the university.

The match of the season was undoubtedly that against Yorkshire at Bradford, where, as so often was the case, the pitch was the answer to a bowler's prayer, especially Cartwright's. Warwickshire made no more than 167 in their first innings, but Cartwright then took five of Yorkshire's wickets for 21 and they could do no better than 115, even though Boycott carried his bat for 53, a notable innings. It looked a grim outlook for Warwickshire when they were all out in their second innings for only 72. Yorkshire had to get only 121 to win and they would surely have got them but for Cartwright, who at one point had taken six wickets for 5 runs and in all had seven for 34, a match 'bag' of twelve for 55. No wonder the Yorkshireman christened him 'Wheelwright' because of the smoothness of the action with which he so accurately wheeled them down.

Against Somerset he did the hat trick – five for 30 and two for 32 – in a match in which Warwickshire needed two wickets from the last two balls. Brown got one, but the last man survived and it was a draw. There was another exciting finish at Old Trafford, where Cartwright had his first experience of captaincy, and Warwickshire should have won. They had to score only 99 off an attack minus Lever, and when the last over was called they had to get no more than 5 and there were as many wickets outstanding, but Higgs bowled Cartwright and Hemmings; and Stewart, who, because of a leg injury, came in with a runner, failed to score off the last two balls – an ironic sequel to his famous six-hitting innings against the Lancastrians.

Ibadulla took a well-earned benefit against Worcestershire, who won by five wickets. He made 40 of Warwickshire's first innings total of 195, Brain taking four wickets in one over; but Worcestershire declared at 200 for five and then dismissed Warwickshire for 136. Ibadulla got no more than 6 in the second innings, but he was well recompensed with a benefit total of £7797. The return match at Dudley was a bowlers' match, in two ways. In Warwickshire's first innings Blenkiron made 62 and Brown 52; and then in Worcestershire's first innings Brown took three for 43; and in Warwickshire's second, opening with McDowall, he got the 47 already mentioned. Then it was McVicker's turn with five for 23.

A two-day match was played in July with an all-white touring South African side, Mr Wilfred Isaac's XI, which had come on a goodwill mission preparatory to the full tour in 1970, and it provided a slight foretaste of what was to come, though no one knew it then. Police kept a watch and there was a demonstration outside the ground, but one protester got in and sat down in the middle of the pitch. He was removed and afterwards fined £10 for insulting behaviour.

This episode led to a warning being issued to all counties to consult with their local police about security arrangements during the forth-coming tour. When Warwickshire inquired what the cost of these was likely to be, they were given fees – a police inspector £1 11s 9d an hour, sergeant £1 7s 6d an hour, constable £1 4s 9d an hour – and decided that, short of a dire emergency, such a service would be beyond the Club's financial resources, though it was realised that the situation might well have to be reviewed in the light of later events. Before the year was out the Club had lost at least one member, Mr Harold Marks, a well-known Birmingham trade unionist, who resigned after seventeen years as a member in protest against the proposal to stage a Test with South Africa at Edgbaston.

There were three Tests each against the West Indies and New Zealand, but none was played at Edgbaston. Brown was chosen for all three against the West Indies and the first against New Zealand, and was second in the averages with fourteen wickets for 22·21 runs each. His best match was the first against the West Indies in which he took four for 39 and three for 59; but he did not take a wicket against New Zealand, and Ward, of Derbyshire, was preferred for the other two Tests.

The West Indies made their appearance at Edgbaston in the anything but merry, merry month of May. The game was given up on the second day without even a start being made and a limited-overs match was arranged for the Tuesday, but even this had to be abandoned at lunch with the West Indies 113 for five wickets. The receipts were so poor that the Supporters' Association, whose membership had risen to three-quarters of a million, took pity on the tourists and gave them £1000 to offset the loss of gate money. It was more than they received from their first five county games put together.

The New Zealanders' visit in September was better favoured, the tourists winning by 50 runs; their first victory over a county side in the very last of their twelve matches against them. They looked like being beaten in two days, but Yuile and Dowling pulled them round and got the 197 runs they needed to win at a run a minute.

It was in this match that Cartwright took his 100th wicket of the season, a remarkable transformation from earlier in the year. For four months during the winter he had wondered if he would ever bowl again. Then on January 3rd he had a try-out in the nets of the Indoor School, where Warwickshire had given him a non-bowling coaching appointment. It was satisfactory and he began the season, but on May 9th he was injured again, though it was nothing to do with his shoulder. This time it was muscular trouble at the base of the spine caused in taking a spectacular catch against Middlesex at Edgbaston.

A month after the season had ended, on October 15th, it was reported in the newspapers that Cartwright had decided to give up playing first-class cricket. He was 34 and wanted, he said, to devote more time to his family, so he might decide to take a job in league cricket, though he added: 'I am liable to break down in any one of four places – knee, Achilles tendon and back troubles.'

The news was a considerable blow to Warwickshire, although perhaps in view of what had gone before they might well have been expecting some such development. By November 5th, however, Cartwright was reported as saying that he would much prefer to stay in the county game and that he would be perfectly happy to play with Warwickshire if they could offer him the future he was looking for. It had nothing to do with money – he simply felt he could not continue in what amounted to a dead-end job. What he would like best, he said, would be a post connected with the game, perhaps still playing for a county side, which might eventually lead to a coaching appointment at a public school. His main concern was to avoid upsetting his children's education.

This was the first of a number of necessarily guarded and sometimes contradictory statements that appeared in the Press during weeks-long negotiations that followed. Clearly Cartwright was completely unsettled. He said afterwards that he had never expected the Club to find him a coaching appointment and he had tried to obtain one at Rugby School, but the only opening was from April to July and he turned it down, though reluctantly.

Meanwhile, the Club gave him *carte blanche* to look around and even to approach other counties, although it was made abundantly clear to him that permission to do this did not mean that he could automatically play for another county without special registration. The Club also did all in its power to find an appointment locally which would suit Cartwright, but without success, and eventually he wrote declining the Club's offer of an engagement for 1970.

Edmund King visited Cartwright at his home to see if his decision was irrevocable and, among many suggestions, asked him if he had considered applying for the job of coach to the Club on Tom Dollery's retirement. After this interview, Edmund King informed the Press that the Club had never been approached by Cartwright previously to find him a coaching appointment at a school, or like establishment, and in any event such appointments were few and far between. With reference to Cartwright's comment that he felt his future with Warwickshire was a dead-end job, Edmund King said: 'This is very sad since we have offered him the best terms ever made to a Warwickshire cricketer.'

With regard to the coaching appointment, Cartwright told a newspaper correspondent that he would not be so presumptuous as to apply for such a job and stressed once again that it was the educational future of his children which was of primary importance. To which it might have been rejoined, however, that there was no reason whatever why he should have been so modest as not to have applied for the coaching post, for which he obviously had qualifications; and that surely his children's educational future could have been as well, if not better, assured in Birmingham as anywhere else and would not have been interrupted had he stayed.

Cartwright, of course, was not short of offers. Before the end of November he had the chance of an appointment at Millfield School in Somerset – the headmaster at that time was R. J. O. Meyer, a former Somerset player, who had Colin Atkinson, a former captain of that county, as his deputy (he later succeeded him) – and of playing for the county. Northants, Leicestershire, Sussex and Gloucestershire also made formal approaches to Warwickshire and there also came an offer from the East Lancashire Club at Blackburn.

It did not take him long to turn down the league club, but he began negotiations with the other interested parties. In December the Committee decided to have further talks with him, feeling it unfortunate that he had referred to his benefit as 'an acknowledgment of his services during the period he had been with the Club'. The Committee's view was that those services were, in fact, acknowledged by his annual salary and a benefit reflected popular appreciation by members and the public alike at a time when a player was contemplating leaving the game and starting a new career.

During these further talks Cartwright revealed that he had turned down the Millfield offer as he had had a more attractive one from Brighton College in Sussex. Later a short agreed statement was issued to the Press. This said that Cartwright 'put all his cards on the table' and added: 'It seems that some counties may have more to offer in the way of coaching opportunities outside the first-class game than we can find at the moment. Tom Cartwright has not yet made a final decision and we are exploring every avenue hoping that something will turn up which will appeal to him.'

Cartwright delayed his departure while the Club tried to find him the kind of engagement he wanted at a Midland public school. They made approaches to the authorities at King Edward's School, Birmingham; Solihull School; and Bromsgrove School, but no openings were available at the time and by the end of February Cartwright had made up his mind. He decided to take the post of senior cricket coach at Millfield because it was open at the time, whereas that at Brighton was not immediately vacant.

He had, of course, to apply for special registration to play for Somerset, but as Warwickshire still wished to retain his services the matter went before the Registration Committee at Lord's, who ruled that the move was in the interests of both the player and cricket as a whole.

Cartwright has since continued to enjoy a successful career with Somerset for whom, at the time of writing, he had not missed a game, having apparently overcome all the ills his flesh was heir to. When asked, when he had had time to reflect, whether he wished to add anything further to all that had been said at the time, he sent this reply:

The facts of my leaving Warwickshire are simply that I was looking for a coaching job for the future, a position that could not be found in that county. Had it been possible, I would still have been a Warwickshire player today. You will probably be aware that I delayed my move elsewhere for almost four months at Warwickshire's request to enable them to find a coaching position, which they were unable to do.

On the face of it, this was one of those cases in which the interests of the player and the club were irreconcilable and it is difficult to see what more Warwickshire could have done to retain Cartwright's services. It was certainly not their fault that there was no coaching appointment in the Midlands of the kind he was seeking, nor, indeed, would one have thought it incumbent upon them to try to find one, except that, if they had been successful, it would have been in the Club's interests also.

Incidentally, is there any other profession where an employer would be likely to find a dissatisfied employee another means of adding to his income and safeguarding his future? On the other hand, cricket is the only profession in which a player out of contract may find there are objections made to him following his employment.

Cartwright began with Warwickshire as a batsman who could bowl

– though even as a schoolboy at Coventry he did the 'double' – but because of the needs of the side he was developed, with Dollery's help, as an all-rounder. Whether he ultimately became the best the Club has ever had must remain a matter of opinion. He did not have Foster's flair and brilliance in either department of the game – who had?; the 'cricketer's double' twice in four seasons takes some beating – but he was the more consistent over a long period, though this is not to say that Foster might not have had a better record had his career lasted longer.

'Cartwright', *Wisden* commented, 'is certain of a place in the county records as he is the only player in Warwickshire history to have scored 10 000 runs and captured 1000 wickets.* He made his début as a batsman in 1952 and did not take a wicket until his fourth season. In 1962 he became the first Warwickshire player to perform the double since 1920. A magnificent bowler in England, his meticulous accuracy of length and line commanded respect even when the conditions offered little help.'

It was not to be expected that a player of Cartwright's calibre would be allowed to leave the Club without some questions being asked. There were letters in the newspapers and questions at the annual meeting in April 1970, at which the President referred to Cartwright as 'one of the great bowlers of the day', and the chairman commented that the school appointment seemed most important to him and county cricket secondary. He also disclosed that it was not until he went to see Cartwright that he learned for the first time that he was seeking an appointment outside the game which would secure his future and that of his family.

Looking back, the Club could hardly have been expected to have made Cartwright a higher offer than they did without having to restructure their salary scales. He always maintained that money was not the chief issue at stake as far as he was concerned and he said later that, in fact, he went to Somerset for several hundreds of pounds less than Warwickshire offered him, though it was no doubt some recompense to him when in 1972–3 he signed a three-year contract as coach to the Somerset County Club and was also appointed vice-captain.

*In all cricket up to the time he left Warwickshire, Cartwright scored 11 180 runs and took 1108 wickets.

Coaching and Cash
(1969)

❖ ❖ ❖

CARTWRIGHT was not the only player to depart. Before the 1969 season began Bannister intimated that he did not think he could complete another full season, but, as senior professional, he was appointed vice-captain to act when Alan Smith was away. The arrangement did not work, partly because the side was so well off in seam bowlers, and later Cartwright and Amiss took over these duties.

At the end of the season Bannister retired – with the best record of any seam bowler Warwickshire have ever engaged, 1199 wickets in all first-class cricket for an average of no more than 21·89, distinctly on the low side for a bowler of his pace. His total of 1182 for the county is the third highest, only Hollies and Santall having bettered it. He took five wickets in an innings on no fewer than fifty-three occasions and ten or more wickets in a match six times. He had 100 or more wickets in a season four times, his best year being 1961, with 137.

Stewart's affairs occupied a good deal of time. It had looked as if he was likely to go following 'Mike' Smith's departure and just after enjoying the second highest benefit in the history of the Club, but he was told that any request that might be made for his special registration to play elsewhere could not be granted.

In mid-July he was offered a final year's contract and given twelve month's notice that he would not be re-engaged, but some concern was expressed at this when his ability to play a full season was in doubt. Stewart's skill as a batsman and the Club's need for him at present were stressed, but his defenders found little support and the terms of the offer stood. By December he was undergoing a series of operations in a nursing home, but recovered in time to take up an appointment as part-time coach at Rugby School, and Warwickshire later agreed to release him to play for Northants where his stay, however, was brief.

There were two very promising young players to welcome in place of those who had left. One of them was a young leg-spin bowler with the extraordinarily appropriate name of Warwick Tidy, whom some judges thought the best prospect the Club had come across for years. He was only 16 and a product of the John Willmott Grammar School, Sutton Coldfield, and of the coaching of Tom Dollery and Derief Taylor. Eric Hollies had also had a look at him and improved his run. He had got his apt Christian name, not because of any association, or connection, with Warwick or Warwickshire, but after Warwick Armstrong. 'My father was a keen cricketer in his younger days,' he said, 'and I think he simply liked the name Warwick. I want to take wickets and take them for Warwickshire.' And what more laudable ambition could a young bowler have than that? The other youngster was a right-hand batsman from Nuneaton, John Whitehouse, who was at Bristol University and studying to be an accountant, and he was soon getting lots of runs with the second eleven.

'Tom' Dollery's resignation as chief coach could hardly have come as a surprise, for the previous season he had had second thoughts about continuing in view of the cutting down on staff and the decision to leave the Minor Counties competition, but Leslie Deakins had told him that the job was still there to be done. Now came letters of resignation from both Dollery and Hitchcock, the latter giving up the captaincy of the second eleven as from the end of the 1969 season. The chairman wrote thanking them for their services to the game and the Club for nearly forty years and twenty years respectively.

Very careful consideration was given to the appointment of a successor to Dollery and it formed part of a Club policy debate based largely on memoranda from the secretary and the captain. It was ultimately the considered opinion of the Committee that the new senior coach should not be identified with any other calling; that he should be willing to work seven days a week during the season; establish the closest liaison with other of the Club coaches, especially Derief Taylor; organise set trials once a month in the season and during the winter; and receive a salary equivalent to that of the highest paid player on the staff, the policy already adopted by some counties in making such appointments.

The advertisement which eventually appeared inviting applications for the position embodied all these points. In all, nearly twenty applications were received, mostly from older men, and the Committee felt that consideration should be given to a man aged 35 to 45 and that, if necessary, the appointment should be made from outside rather than inside the county. It was the suggestion of Derrick Robins that the position should be made an all-the-year-round, as distinct from a seasonal, one, and also that it should be brought to the attention of

Alan Oakman, the former Sussex player, then coaching in South Africa. It was he who eventually got the post.

There was another important administrative change during the season. Because of what was described as 'a failure of communication' between the selectors (the captain, acting captain and the travelling vice-captain), always difficult to maintain during the season with one or the other away, it was decided that in future the selection of teams would be left to the captain, except in the case of the second eleven, which would be vested in the senior coach. It caused a certain amount of controversy, but it was a policy which had long been advocated by former captains.

The sub-committee which had looked into this matter had also recommended that Alan Smith should be reappointed captain for 1970, and that since he might be appointed a Test selector – he was – Cartwright should be appointed vice-captain. As both would lead the team in the field they would constitute the selection 'committee' though they might consult others.

During discussions on playing strength and policy, the chairman of the Club expressed the view that the reduction in staff and the withdrawal from the Minor Counties competition might well have taught the Committee the bitter lesson that far more attention should be paid to second-eleven cricket and the development of young players. Concentration, he felt, must now be on building a team, not premises, and he had raised the question of a second-eleven knock-out competition at Lord's.

Peter Cranmer's view was that as the withdrawal from the Minor Counties Championship had saved only £1400, the decision was a bad one from a cricket point of view. Reduction in expenditure should be in other departments of the Club, he felt, rather than in the game itself.

Between forty and fifty boys appeared in the Colts side and it was generally felt that the Club probably had the best nursery staff and the best organised Colts in the country. According to Alan Smith, the Club 'could be reasonably satisfied' that no player under 19 escaped attention, though he doubted whether this necessarily applied to older players.

But what sort of material were these youngsters and was the best use being made of them? Harry Harper, associated with youth cricket in Warwickshire for a quarter of a century, was not so hopeful. He thought the play of the Colts was of poor standard. They used to be drawn from public schools and grammar schools, but now they were mostly from the comprehensives and they had many other interests and rival attractions such as tennis and golf, not to say part-time jobs to earn money, all of which were calculated to divert their attention from cricket.

More than half the Club's players at this time were 32 or over and, with one or two exceptions, there was a lack of really promising youngsters. Sooner or later there was going to be a gap. The question was: should it be filled by combing the country for players, or was there sufficient talent in Warwickshire?

There was a financial gap, too, which for the time being was even more important. Warwickshire had begun the season with a budget which showed how costs were rising:

	1968	1969
Salaries (16 staff, three coaches), pensions	£17 500	£19 667

The total figure of expenditure for 1968 was £30 302 and the estimate for 1969 £31 561, among the items which made up this amount being salaries, match fees, win awards, Gillette Cup payments, Players' League payments, national insurance, capped players' pension schemes, and evening bowlers, though precious few members now used the nets.

Some of the players were still dissatisfied with the terms for Sunday games, which they did not think sufficient to compensate them adequately for the disruption of their family life, and they wanted the Committee to be more specific about the terms for distributing gate receipts over a certain figure. Early in the year they held a staff meeting and before they got down to business they heard some straight-from-the-shoulder facts from the chairman of the Club in a letter in which he wrote that he was 'more than depressed about some of our cricketers and their present outlook'.

The letter went on to remind them of some of the facts of their life with the Warwickshire Club.

No club [he wrote], has done more for its cricketers than Warwickshire – huge, tax-free benefits; we have offered to pay over to them [the players] practically all the money we have received from the sponsorship of the League – the bit in reserve, if any, is the wise precaution any sensible employer would take. We have said we will look at the net income at the end of the season and if it is a success we will put aside a further sum for distribution to the players. My view is that our offer is as far as we can go; those cricketers who do not like it can opt out and be paid a match fee when selected without any security at all (injury, etc.). What match fees we pay is for the Committee to decide and none of our cricketers should have any say whatever in this decision except for the individuals we are negotiating with.

After this plain speaking, Alan Smith also reminded them of some of the benefits they enjoyed over and above their basic contracts – the capped players' gratuity scheme; the B.U.P.A. membership scheme; and the very high benefits of recent years. Under the B.U.P.A. scheme, as Peter Cranmer pointed out, all players were covered for up to £700 to £800 for nursing-home treatment and surgery if necessary, and families of all married players also received these benefits.

The total made available by the sponsors of the Players' League was £35 000 to be divided among seventeen counties, which worked out at

£2060 each, plus TV fees of £20 000, or £1170 each, making a total of £3230 for each county. In addition, there were gifts to the players hitting sixes and taking four wickets, plus amounts to the winning teams and the prize money at the end of the competition. All this made a grand total of £65 000, subsequently increased to £85 000.

It was calculated that after payments to players at the rates proposed, making total outgoings of £3072, the Club would be left with only a little in hand to meet an emergency, since if selections for any reasons involved more than the eighteen players provided for, further fees would have to be paid. In fact, it worked out at the end of the season that the players who had taken part in the matches benefited to the extent of an additional £500 divided between them.

Had they earned it? Alan Smith, at the annual meeting in March, had said he hoped all the players would try to play positive cricket and make an all-out effort to entertain the public – 'the restless public who seemed to have lost the art of relaxing', as the chairman said of them – though far too often one side seemed to be waiting for the other to open up the game without thinking of doing so themselves. This was precisely what 'Tom' Dollery had criticised them for doing twenty years before.

Somewhat belatedly the next month came word from the Players' Association – which had achieved 100 per cent membership and held its annual meeting at Edgbaston – that every player in the first-class game had given a firm promise that the new Sunday League would be 'cricket with the brake off'. One was tempted to ask them who had applied the brake in the first place and why, oh why, had they had to wait until the game was nearly dead before they decided to take it off? In one respect at any rate the Warwickshire players did not live up to their promises – they were at the foot of the rate-of-overs-bowled table, although fourth in the batting rate.

The Committee had to take an important decision on priorities during the year – whether to go in for a big new development proposed for the North side, or to reconstruct the Pavilion (centre) which had been talked of for years. Following World War I, Warwickshire, after having been 'left at the post' as Cyril Goodway put it, in the late 1920s, had taken the lead among English county clubs in ground development, but now the other counties were catching up.

Multi-sports developments of all kinds had been discussed at intervals now for some years, but the subject cropped up again following the appointment of Edgar Hiley as chairman of the West Midlands Regional Sports Council. James McDowall jibbed at the idea of Edgbaston becoming a 'fairground' and Ran Smith warned of conflicts which might arise between different sports organisations using a multi-purpose sports arena – it was a splendid idea in theory, but completely upset by human reactions when put into practice.

On the other hand, Cyril Goodway thought that continual hoarding of money was completely unimaginative and pointed out that if £40 000 a year was set aside for development a £200 000 scheme could be undertaken every five years. Eventually the ground and house sub-committee was empowered to go into the question of developing the North side with the architects and later the brief was extended to the ground as a whole.

By late May the general purposes and finance sub-committee had before it a £270 000 scheme for developing the North side, where high buildings would not cast shadows on the ground, involving a stand between the Press Box stand and the Rea Bank, with six squash courts, badminton courts and golf range, a health clinic, with treatment and consulting rooms, gymnasium, sauna baths, cold plunge, showers and dressing-rooms; nine private boxes with a seating capacity of 180 and communal dining-room and bar, to be let on five-year leases to business firms; 1560 seats on the upper terraces and 610 on the lower; and storage for wicket covers at ground level.

The scheme also involved demolition of the Stanley Barnes stand and the resiting of the Thwaite scoreboard on a new structure in the north-west corner of the ground, as well as new premises with every amenity for the Supporters' Association on The Hill. This would release to the Club the whole of the Pavilion (east wing), which many members had always felt should be for their use.

The chairman described all this as 'a beautiful conception', but Edgar Hiley thought it 'a grandiose scheme' and was opposed to any more accommodation being provided until what they already had could be filled. The alternative was the pavilion reconstruction scheme, which Cyril Goodway could not see being undertaken for at least another ten years, though he had put forward improvements and modifications. This face-lift was later adopted, the full scheme for a new pavilion, at an estimated cost of £500 000, being shelved for the time being as it was felt that it was impossible to justify such expense when the future structure of the game was so uncertain.

Edgar Hiley thought that if the North side development was to be long delayed, the Association committee might have to consider alternative proposals – the social secretary of the Association had already submitted a scheme to his own committee for the North side – but the Association had had its most difficult year to date and had been able to give the Club only £50 000 compared with the £90 000 of the previous year and larger sums earlier. No wonder the idea of 'wealthy Warwickshire' was so difficult to dispel.

Not surprisingly after all this, there were long discussions when it was disclosed that the Association proposed to lend Essex £20 000 for their pavilion rebuilding scheme at Chelmsford, the chairman commenting that it was pleasant for the Association to help other counties, provided there were safety measures to guarantee repayment. As for the Warwickshire Club, he conceded that the position was a peculiar one, for while it could be said to be 'sitting on £400 000' it could be equally correctly stated that it had lost some £60 000 on running its activities over the past four years and needed every care in financial matters.

This figure of £400 000 cropped up again in later discussion about future developments. It was the amount now in the Endowment Fund and the chairman thought it should remain intact. This led Cyril Goodway to seek clarification as to whether any new limit had been set on the Fund – £2 millions? He felt that if the annual loss was made the first charge on the Supporters' Association's annual cash gifts to the Club, the remainder might well be devoted to reconstruction of the ground, which was now slipping behind other Test grounds as a result of their progressive developments.

Edgar Hiley's view was that for the Association to make up whatever annual losses the Club incurred would amount to a blank cheque and an incentive to extravagance. There was general agreement with this view and the chairman made it clear that no limit had been set, but he would like the Club to enjoy what he called 'this background strength' until such time as the game stabilised itself. For the Association to cover the Club's annual losses would be for it to take a direct interest in the Club's affairs through supporting revenue and that could create an awkward tax position.

Another view put forward by Derek Salberg was that further development should concern itself more with amenities than seating – for instance, a swimming pool, a play area for children and sitting out facilities for other members of the family who did not want to watch cricket throughout a long day.

Ultimately it was decided that the Endowment Fund should be maintained at its then level at least, but that efforts should be made to make a proportion of future gifts from the Association available for the original purpose of ground development.

Financial relationships between the Association and the Club were the subject in September of a long memorandum to the general committee from Edgar Hiley, triggered off, no doubt, by the various comments made during the season especially on the subject of help to other counties. He began with a reminder that the Association's primary objective was to provide funds for the capital requirements of the Club, but that the Association could not be complacent about the strong financial position of Warwickshire alongside the perilous state of the finances of several other counties. 'The game', he commented, 'is a brotherhood and it is greater than any one county, and, in any case, we need opponents' – a point only too obvious when made, but apt to be overlooked.

Referring to Warwickshire's position, the memorandum recalled that in four years, 1965–8, the Club lost roughly £60 000 on its income and expenditure account. It received from the Association £10 000 per annum for the Minor Projects Fund and a further £50 000 was received from interest, or dividends, on investments, the funds for which were provided by the Association. Therefore, the true loss over the period was £150 000. These facts were stated to bring home to the Club its real position and to invite the Committee to consider what the position might be if there were a swing to Puritanism which caused the principal fund-raising activities to be terminated.

Since the Association was formed sixteen years ago, the memorandum reminded the Committee, about £850 000 had been spent on the ground and nearly £400 000 handed to the Club for investment. Originally these investments were in the form of two trusts of equal size. One for the pavilion was not to be limited until the required sum was obtained; the other was to be limited to £120 000, which was considered sufficient for an Endowment Fund, and this was to be inviolate unless there was a serious emergency in the Club's affairs. The two trusts, however, were not acceptable to the tax authorities which meant that income derived from them was taxable. To overcome this difficulty, it was agreed that the Association should make unconditional gifts to the Club from time to time.

'In doing so', the memorandum continued, 'it would appear to have surrendered its previous right to have some say in the expenditure of the moneys it has raised and this has given rise to some discontent in its ranks, in that interest has been lowered in consequence . . . It is, therefore, suggested that to a degree the former procedure be reinstated whereby the Club states its requirements to the Association and the Association shall have an absolute right, as it did for so many years, to consent or disagree to expenditure of its funds on capital projects and to express views as to the priorities of such expenditure.'

The memorandum emphasised that at no time did this earlier procedure involve any attempt on the part of the Association to dictate Club policy and the arrangement worked in complete amity. It was envisaged that a resumption of this procedure would mean co-operation in the same spirit as before. The Association therefore proposed that the Liaison and Investments Special Committees be set up again and that these matters should be the subject of friendly exchanges between the bodies, as before.

The Association also proposed that the surplus, as determined by the Association in the light of its known commitments, plus sensible retentions, should be handed to the Club as unconditional gifts with the tacit object of investment. An investment or endowment fund was regarded as vital to close the gap between income and expenditure, but it would appear necessary to place a limit to the size of the fund, which stood at approximately £400 000 against the £120 000 originally stated to be its limit.

Was it appropriate, the memorandum asked, to assume they had £280 000 in a development fund? Concern was felt lest the existence and continued flow of such large sums from the investments, the Supporters' future earnings and the Minor Projects Grants might well be inducements to extravagance, and whether the Club should not be far more mindful of the need to try to live within its income . . . 'one cannot escape the feeling that we are going to the other extreme'.

'By all means', the memorandum pleaded, 'let us go in for sensible developments, but let us not go on increasing accommodation for those who are not attending the ground and are unlikely to do so. We can have squash courts without a costly multi-purpose building to accommodate them.'

The memorandum went on to suggest that a ceiling should be placed on the Endowment Fund, that further development should be the subject of discussions between Club and Association; that the Endowment Fund should be inviolate save in the case of a situation in which the Club's future existence was imperilled; that no projects should be entertained until the money was available; and that unconditional gifts should be limited to the Association's surplus funds.

Commenting on the Association's suggestion that the ceiling figure of the Endowment Fund should be £250 000, Edmund King said that since the total of the Fund was then £400 000, this would leave £150 000 for transfer into a building fund.

It was agreed after some discussion to accept the proposals generally, but that the ceiling of the Fund should be made higher because it was felt that the income from it must be sufficient to cover the Club's annual losses and it was hoped, ultimately, to wipe out the accumulated deficit which stood at £40 000. Ultimately the figure was agreed at £350 000. The other proposals of the Association were adopted after some slight amendments.

On the question of reviving the joint committee, it was decided that the Club representatives should not include members who were already common to both committees and who, in consequence, might have divided interests. It was also agreed that the £35 000 needed to finance the Pavilion (centre) reconstruction should come from the Supporters' Association's surplus for the current year.

Edgar Hiley later suggested that the phrase 'a minimum figure of £350 000' should be inserted in the resolution of agreement instead of 'a ceiling figure of £350 000' and that the special liaison committee should consist of the chairmen of the Supporters' Association and the ground and house sub-committee of the Club; two club members not identified at committee level with the Association; and two Association members similarly not identified with the Club.

During the year the Association spent £160 000 on various projects not connected with the Warwickshire Club, including £42 000 in an attempt to spread the Association's activities in other counties and £40 000 and more in grants and gifts to organisations of various kinds and testimonials. They also made grants to three former players – Buckingham, Hill and Smart – none of whom had had benefits.

After all this clearing of the financial air, it was possible for the annual report to say of the relationship between the Association and the Club that 'never for one moment has it given rise to the slightest anxiety, and even thoughts of "tails wagging dogs" never arise since the joint interest is, and always has been, in a "healthy dog" '.

The annual accounts showed total income of £97 965, but expenditure of £106 705, a deficiency of £8740. The freehold value of the ground was now given in the balance sheet as £631 760 – big property business, indeed. Thanks to 'sensible action' by Michael Parsons, the Club's auditor, and R. W. A. James, the Club's investments adviser, the accumulated deficit had been reduced from over £46 000 to £28 000, with good prospects of a similar action in the new year. Investment income was up by £3000 to £19 333 and the Pavilion Suite takings increased. Test Match profits were estimated at £10 716 to £13 000, but Warwickshire's own two games with the tourists produced only £182. Returns from the Players' League games came to £5641, so that after deducting expenses of £3255, a profit of £2386 was left. One round of the Gillette Cup brought in £1858.

There was yet another administrative change in which the counties were divided into zonal committees whose aim was to work out the best possible structure for the game in future, each zone to draw up recommendations to go before the Test and County Cricket Board. Warwickshire, linked with Worcestershire, Northants and Leicestershire, appointed Cyril Goodway and James McDowall as its representatives, with 'Tony' Haycock, the membership and cricket secretary, as secretary to the Midlands Zone Committee.

One of the chief things to engage their attention was the fall in membership, now general throughout the country, amounting in 1969 to 6000 to a total of 121 140. In Warwickshire's case this meant an income lower by some £3000, which was a strong argument for developing the amenities of the ground on as widely appealing lines as possible.

The Warwickshire Cricket Association was at last duly formed from seventeen founder member organisations, with Mr Leslie F. Fellows, a member of the Club Committee, the first chairman. The Midlands Cricket Club conference was still unwilling to come in, but every other known cricket organisation of any consequence in the county had joined. The Association's objects were defined as producing further liaison between all the bodies controlling cricket, or having a direct interest in it, or service to offer in running cricket within the country. Leslie Deakins described it as 'the most important cricket event in the county since Warwickshire County Cricket Club was formed in 1882'.

During the winter, a team of women cricketers, captained by Rachael Heyhoe, of Wolverhampton, went on a tour to the West Indies and they were given permission to take with them as guide, and, no doubt, philosopher and friend, Derief Taylor, who was allowed three weeks' leave of absence on condition that his fare and expenses were paid.

The Coventry ground came back into favour for 1970, being given the match with Derbyshire in August, after encouraging reports about how the wicket played in a second-eleven game. Meanwhile the experiments at Edgbaston were coming along, with a scheme for fifteen wickets to be laid on the area of the old car park on the Colts' ground where they are being studied from the point of view of both batsmen and bowlers.

Finally a nature note: foxes were found in the roof of the old pavilion and the vixen and her two cubs were retrieved by an R.S.P.C.A. inspector, who removed them, released them in the countryside and earned a donation of £10 10s from the Club. The dog fox was seen making his getaway across the ground. Somehow one felt that wild ducks would have been more appropriate to a cricket ground, but, on second thoughts, perhaps not.

The Tour that Never Was
(1970)

ONE night in January 1970, the news desk of *The Birmingham Post* took a telephone call from a man who said he represented the Birmingham Ad Hoc Group for Solidarity with the Freedom Fighters of South Africa and that he had put weedkiller on the wicket at Edgbaston. In due time several bare patches appeared. Samples of the soil were sent for analysis and it was confirmed that a liquid had been put on the turf. Despite attempts to repair the damage, it deprived the Club of the use of five out of the twelve pitches for the whole season.

To change the simile, it was the cloud no bigger than a man's hand which presaged the second of the two great storms which have shaken cricket to its foundations. The first, of course, was the 'bodyline' tour of Australia in 1932–3; now there was to be the storm over the South African tour of 1970 that never was. But as the Warwickshire report pointed out, there was a difference. The cause of the first upheaval sprang from the manner in which the game was being played by England; the second had nothing to do with the game itself, but originated in the method of selection of one of the teams and was racial and political.

Warwickshire's President described the damage to the pitch as 'a monstrous impertinence'; it was one of several with which lovers of cricket had to contend during the year, described in the annual report as 'undoubtedly the most unfortunate in the game's long history'. Normally neither politics nor apartheid would have any place in the history of a cricket club and the historian would content himself with recording the effects, if any, on the Club of events in such spheres, but some statement of the basic facts is necessary to a full understanding of what happened and the issues at stake.

538

They had already made their impact on sport in this country through the South African Government's refusal to accept D'Oliveira as a member of the M.C.C. team which should have visited South Africa in the winter of 1968–9; in one or two minor incidents during the cricket season here in 1969; and in the interruptions and general harassment suffered from those who opposed apartheid during the Springboks' rugby tour of 1969–70.

What were the facts? Both the Cricket Council and the 'Stop-the-Seventy-Tour' Committee published leaflets setting out their case. The Council affirmed its total opposition to any policy of the South African Government which led to apartheid in sport, but stated that despite the 'widespread, natural resentment' at their refusal to accept D'Oliveira, over 80 per cent of M.C.C. members were in favour of maintaining cricketing ties with South Africa, and that all the first-class clubs and Minor Counties unanimously recommended that the invitation to the South African Cricket Association to send a team to Britain in 1970 should stand. They firmly believed that 'the severance of sporting contact would achieve nothing in terms of progress towards multi-racial sport, but that, on the contrary, it would have precisely the opposite effect'.

On the other hand, the 'Stop-the-Seventy-Tour' Committee took the view that it was no use assuring everybody that 'Of course, we don't agree with apartheid' and then going ahead and playing against apartheid teams. The Committee contended that if racialism in sport was rejected then it ought to be shown that it was, and the only obvious and effective way of doing so was by refusing to play against racially selected teams.

Nineteen-seventy was not very old when it became clear that life for cricketers and especially for those who administered the game was going to be far from easy. As early as 16 January, Leslie Deakins had received eight letters from members of the Club or the public either asking for the tour to be stopped, or for the Club to see that it went on, which indicated a conflict of opinion right from the start. The general committee made their position clear immediately – as a body they were right behind the Test and County Cricket Board decision that the tour should go on and that resignations of members would not influence their decision.

By 13 February the tour was still officially on, but it had become obvious that it would be impossible to ensure, except at enormous cost quite beyond the resources of the counties, that the full-length programme could be carried out, and it was curtailed from the original twenty-eight matches to twelve. The game with Warwickshire on 27 June was one of the three county fixtures which survived the cuts, the others being against Surrey and Lancashire.

The third Test was due to be played at Edgbaston on 16 July and the chairman estimated that the Club might still receive £5000 from the tour, though all income was to be allocated from a central fund on which the first charge would be for ground protection and for possible insurance against vandalism or disruption of games. The amount allocated for protection was £30 000 and for insurance £35 000.

In the meantime precautions had been going ahead at Edgbaston and elsewhere. Cyril Goodway reported to the general committee on the security arrangements that had been made. They were kept secret at the time, of course, though it was known that the Test Board was providing artificial alternative surfaces for use if wickets were damaged. The arrangements included, as the public subsequently discovered, a special night security system involving guards with patrol dogs, automatic alarms and floodlighting. Barbed wire was introduced at the request of the police as a precaution against vandalism, so that the ground had the look of a beleaguered garrison, and players and staff must have wondered sometimes what they were engaged in – a war, politics, or cricket, or all three at one and the same time. The laying of an artificial base on which matting could be placed, as well as a Tartan pitch in case of further liquid-pouring escapades, must have seemed peaceful experiments by comparison. The players also tried out new plastic-studded boots to be used if they had to play on matting. The bill for all this was reckoned at about £3000, which it was hoped would be repaid from the central fund.

Leslie Deakins reported that he had received several letters from local branches of the Labour Party and trade unions asking the Club to cancel its part in the tour and to refuse hospitality to the South African team. The Committee took the view that the writers of the letters were merely looking for ammunition for their cause and it was decided that replies should be brief and to the point. Edgar Hiley also disclosed that the Birmingham Borough Labour Party had asked its members to boycott the football pool, but, in fact, this had no effect.

On 31 March there was a demonstration in Birmingham, in which seven M.P.s took part, protesting against the tour, and a deputation came from the Council House to Edgbaston where they were received by the chairman and his deputy. The following day, the anniversary of the Sharpeville massacre, another deputation, ten in number, also met officials of the Club to whom they presented a petition against the tour.

The chairman reported to the annual meeting on these visits and said he had explained to the members of the deputations that no one in this country was in favour of apartheid, but that the Club felt it was much more likely to get this policy altered by inviting South Africa's cricketers over here into a multi-racial society than by ostracising them.

No one in the game, he told them, had any desire to enter into political issues, but all felt that in a democratic country the tour should be permitted to continue, with peaceful demonstrations accepted, but not organised interruption and vandalism.

Anyone who had anticipated that the meeting would be a stormy affair, with widespread argument about the tour and whether it should go on, would have been disappointed. About 300 members attended and only two of them asked questions. Sir Oliver Leese began the meeting by urging members to remember that 'we are a cricket club and a very privileged one because we are a Test Match cricket club. We have been given a Test this year against the best cricket side in the world today. Let us all work together as a team to make a success of this match. All I hope is that they will be allowed to play cricket.'

Edmund King reminded them that all the seventeen first-class counties, all the minor counties and the M.C.C. had voted unanimously for the tour to take place, as had the Cricket Council, the governing body for cricket at all levels. 'I don't suppose any cricketer likes apartheid any more than do those who administer the game', he said, 'but we think the end will come much more rapidly by inviting cricketers here and giving them a pleasant time and inviting them to our homes.'

One member, Mr Tony Engel, said the tour decision had led to several members resigning. It had been assumed that the majority of the members were in support of the tour, but that might not be so. What account had been taken of the views of those members? He suggested a referendum, or at least a survey, and that a tour should be offered to a Coloured Board of Control.

The chairman replied that the Committee was one of those of seventeen counties to vote for the tour to take place. Members who had resigned did not number more than 20 out of something like 8000. The question of whether to ask a coloured side to come over was being considered and it might well come about. The idea was welcomed by the meeting, but, in any case, it did not come off.

One former junior ticket holder, Mr Peter Jennings, rose to express thanks to the Committee for arranging for the South African side to visit Edgbaston twice during the season. He loved his cricket, he said, and did so want to see this great side.

Some anti-apartheid slogans were daubed on one of the main gates of the ground and there was an attempt to make capital out of a decision taken by the Committee that the Club's overseas cricketers – Ibadulla, Gibbs and Kanhai – would not be considered for selection in the county fixtures with the touring team. Mr John Darragh, secretary of the Birmingham Anti-Apartheid Committee, contending that this was a colour bar in reverse, complained to the Race Relations Board, who, however, ruled that the complaint was not valid under the Race Relations

Act, 1968, because it lacked the authority of at least one of the three players concerned.

Edmund King's comment on this was that the three players were 'relieved' at not being considered for selection. All three had received 'pressure' letters from campaign organisations urging them not to play again the South Africans and the Committee felt that this was putting an unfair burden on the players and their families. The players were probably thankful that the decision had been made for them.

The Committee had something of a shock, however, when some speakers at the Lord Mayor-making meeting of Birmingham City Council thought the Club should bear the extra costs of police protection for the two matches with the tourists. This was estimated at £250 000, of which £100 000 would be extra expenditure.

This was one burden which did not fall on them, however, for in May The Cricket Council, submitting to strong Government pressure, amounting almost to an order, most reluctantly cancelled the tour, much to the distress of many cricketers, administrators and followers of the game, including Edmund King, who said he was certain that it would only strengthen apartheid in South Africa.

In view, however, of the unpleasantness, to put it no worse than that, which might have occurred – it is so much easier to interrupt a cricket match than a game of rugby football and the atmosphere that could have been engendered is so alien to that in which cricket is normally enjoyed – that it was probably the wisest decision, but some people felt that it was made for the wrong reasons. What few seemed to realise was that for the first time a British Government had given way to threats of disruption directed at the peaceful activities of a section of the community who were not themselves breaking any laws, or, in this particular instance, not being guilty of racial prejudice – the reverse in fact – at which the protests were directed, but merely wished to watch a game of cricket.

This was something quite alien to the traditional English way of life, for it meant, among other things, that people in the older age groups were intimidated to the point of being deterred from booking to see the matches, and it filled at least one man, a barrister, Francis Bennion, with such perturbation that 'any individual should presume to interfere with the freedom of others in a way not sanctioned by law' that he took private action in the courts against Peter Hain, student leader of the Young Liberals and chairman of the 'Stop-the-Seventy-Tour' Committee.

The case lasted nearly a month and in the end Hain was found guilty on one of the four charges against him alleging that he conspired to disrupt rugby, cricket and tennis matches by visiting South Africans. The jury, out for seven and a half hours, were unable to agree on the other charges. Ironically enough, the charge on which Hain was found guilty by a ten-to-two majority related, not to cricket, but to the 1969 Davis Cup match at Bristol. He was fined £200 and ordered to pay £50 towards his legal aid costs. Subsequently he appealed against conviction, but his appeal was dismissed. Bennion later applied to the court for the costs of his private prosecution (estimated at £30 000) to be paid out of public funds and his application was granted.

When the tour was called off the anti-apartheid faction no doubt thought that they had won a great victory, but the Institute of Race Relations did not think so. In their annual report they took the view that the controversy worsened race relations here by highlighting the problem. The report said that it made people who had paid no attention to race problems aware of them (though that in itself was surely not a bad thing) and they were forced to take sides, usually with little knowledge of the facts and after little informed discussions.

Trying to ensure that the tour did take place involved county clubs in heavy expense they could ill afford, and cancellation of the tour made still more work for already harassed administrative staffs. Hundreds of letters – only some of the thousands the controversy provoked – had to be written to the holders of £1306-worth of tickets for the Test at Edgbaston; it was to have been an all-ticket match – but at least Warwickshire had the consolation of being allotted one of the England v. The Rest of the World games which were hurriedly substituted for the South Africa Tests, though this, in its turn, meant more work. This competition also found a sponsor, the Guinness Company, who put up £20 000 and a handsome silver trophy, a gesture which drew from John Solan in *The Birmingham Post* the anything but dry comment: 'Fancy English cricket being revived by injections of Liffey water.' But no stranger, surely, than receiving regular injections from the pool of the Supporters' Association.

The England XI for this series was selected by the Board's selection sub-committee, of which Alan Smith was a member, and they chose Ray Illingworth to lead the side. The Rest of the World XI was selected by F. R. Brown, who acted as manager, Leslie Ames, Kent's manager, and Gary Sobers, who captained a formidable team of international cricketers who won a series closer than it sounds by four Tests to one.

The wealth of talent on view should have made these games an even bigger draw than the Tests against South Africa would have been. In fact, five of the latter country's best players – the Pollock brothers, Eddie Barlow, M. J. Procter and B. A. Richards – played in most of the games, together with five great players from the West Indies – Sobers, Clive Lloyd, Kanhai, Gibbs and Murray, – plus Intikhab Alam. One of the pleasanter ironies of the situation was to see the marked friendliness on the field between the South Africans and their coloured colleagues, which showed more vividly perhaps than anything else could have done the absurdity of racial discrimination in sport, or in anything else. It is a pity that some members of the South African Government and the anti-apartheid agitators could not have seen it for themselves.

Yet for some reason, perhaps because no national pride was involved, the public did not take to these games as they normally did to orthodox international encounters, except for the final game at The Oval, though the cricket they provided was entertaining enough for anyone. Those who were fortunate enough to see the last hour or so of the second day at Edgbaston, when Sobers and Lloyd laid waste the England bowling and put on 139 runs between tea and the close of play, including 95 off the last hour with the new ball, went home rejoicing indeed. They made the England attack look like moderate club stuff, David Brown, in particular, taking a hammering and scarcely knowing where to put the ball.

The Rest of the World deservedly won this match by five wickets. Procter and Sobers got rid of England for 294, despite another rescue operation of 110 by D'Oliveira and a half-century by Greig, and then piled up a total of 593 for nine before declaring. England did better the second time, D'Oliveira again, Cowdrey and Knott, all batting well so that they rallied with 409, and The Rest lost five wickets in making the 141 they needed to win. During the match, some alert statistician informed the world, Sobers took his 100th catch and passed his 7000 runs in Test cricket.

Brown had a poor match – none for 65 in the first innings and none for 23 in the second. He had also played in the second Test with not much better results – two for 64 and one for 41. Warwickshire had released Gibbs and Kanhai for the Tests. The former played in four of them and had an even worse time than Brown, taking only three wickets which cost him 102·33 runs each; incredible figures for a world-class bowler, but he just did not bowl a tight enough line for English conditions. Kanhai played in all five Tests, hitting one century and scoring 284 runs for an average of 31·55.

So the financial results of the series was disappointing, though Warwickshire took twice as much gate money as the Trent Bridge match attracted. The Test and County Cricket Board, of course, had to seek compensation from the Government, since there is little doubt that had the South African tour taken place the clubs would have had a rich reward. The Board knew fairly soon the extent of the net profit from the series – £64 000, of which Warwickshire's share was £4491, whereas there would probably have been twice as much from visits of the South Africans – but the Board had some time to wait before it knew what Whitehall would do by way of compensation. It came too late in any case to save the Club from showing a deficiency on the year of £28 253, the heaviest loss in its history. This, of course, was primarily due to heavy expenditure on the Tests, offset by a lower return than expected, though it was hoped that this would be reduced when the Government made known its contribution.

Leslie Deakins prepared a very interesting memorandum which disclosed some fascinating information about the opposition to the tour. This showed that it had been primarily political, mostly from the Socialist and trade union movements, with some support from the Church of England, in which the former England cricketer, the Rev. David Sheppard, later Bishop of Woolwich, played a leading part. Written objections came from thirty-two individuals, most of them calling for cancellation of the tour, but some merely indicating that they would not support the matches. All but six of the writers were in the Birmingham area. Thirty-three members of the Club, one a vice-president, resigned, but six subsequently rejoined when the tour was cancelled.

Twenty-seven organised bodies, or collections of individuals, submitted letters, or signed petitions, which were forwarded to the offices of the Cricket Council. Of these twenty-seven, four were local branches of trade unions; thirteen were local branches of the Labour Party; three came from church groups; three from university groups and four from organisations brought into being to 'stop the tour', or for some similar purpose. The total number of signatures on the petitions was approximately 3000.

Taking the opposite view in favour of the tour, were seventeen individuals who took the trouble to write; and three organisations, two of whom offered help in providing stewards, or other assistance, to ensure that the tour went on. Subsequently two members resigned because the tour *was* cancelled, though this seemed rather pointless since it was not Warwickshire's fault.

This was the reaction from a county with a population of just over 2 000 000, or, to extend the area from which the Club draws support, the whole of the industrial Midlands, with a total population of 5 000 000 to 6 000 000. Not one organisation concerned with people overseas, the memorandum added, made any kind of protest (perhaps because others were doing it for them) although, of course, some of the signatures on the petitions might have been theirs. The evidence thus clearly showed that the protests and demonstrations were entirely politically based, the Labour Party as a whole being against the tour, the Conservative Party mainly in favour of it and the Church of England offering a minority view.

From your committee's point of view [the memorandum concluded], the tour represented the best attraction cricket has had to offer for many years, and it is sad indeed that it was ruined by extraneous influences that have at no time any part in cricket, aided by an inept Government which would not take positive action to ensure law and order, thus depriving the sport-loving section of the community of the normal freedom to pursue their lawful occasions which we have hitherto regarded as the first essential of true democracy. It should be emphasised that this is one county's experience and report on events and it is appreciated that the pattern may vary considerably elsewhere in the country.

For the first time for years during the season as a whole more people came to watch cricket, even County Championship matches, the attendance figure going up from 607 535, to 631 919. The biggest attraction among the counties was Lancashire – enjoying a revival under the leadership of Jackie Bond and winning both the Gillette Cup and Players' League – and Kent, who, in their centenary year, boldly challenged for the Championship and appropriately won it.

No doubt, also, the more attractive play helped. The new lbw law – under which the batsman was out provided the ball pitched, or would have pitched, in a straight line between wicket and wicket, or pitched outside the batsman's off stump and, in the opinion of the umpire, he made no genuine attempt to play the ball with his bat – seemed to give the batsmen more freedom. Certainly there were fewer lbw decisions and I sometimes found myself wondering how the poor bowler ever got one given in his favour, or how the umpire decided what the batsman's intentions really were. As it was, only four bowlers in the country took 100 wickets or more and there was not a seamer among them – two off-spinners, one slow left-hander and one right-handed leg-break bowler.

Lancashire's total attendances were up by 13 507 on those for 1969, which showed what enterprising cricket could do, and on the Sunday on which they clinched the John Player League title by beating their old enemies, Yorkshire, at Old Trafford, there were 33 000 spectators on the ground, their biggest crowd for years. Even so, they reported a loss for 1970 of £13 692. Kent's attendances were up by 15 331 and Warwickshire's from 13 780 in 1969 to 14 771. Not one county, however, made a profit, largely because of the cancellation of the tour.

As a team Warwickshire were inconsistent. They lost ground in the Championship table, falling from fourth position to eighth, were again knocked out in the first round of the Gillette Cup, but moved up four places in the John Player League table to fifth. *Wisden*'s verdict was that the middle batting was suspect. This makes rather strange reading in view of Kanhai's fine form, though he was absent from a number of matches, and the fact that M. J. K. Smith seemed to take up the game as if he had never left it, making nearly 1500 runs in Championship games alone and, in all matches, getting on for 2000 again, despite the cares of captaincy when he had to deputise for Alan Smith.

He thought the game was in a healthier state than when he had left it. For one thing, more spin bowlers were being used, an interesting comment in view of his reputed aversion to putting much trust in them. 'I think we are getting more of them into the game all the time,' he said. 'One-day cricket has done a lot for the game and for dour players like Bob Barber used to be. I think we should reorganise the game in this country – regionalise it in some competitions to bring in the Minor Counties players who normally never get a chance of playing against men in first-class cricket. We should let everyone in the country who is good enough play.'

Three other batsmen, Amiss, Jameson and Abberley, also scored over 1000 runs, so one would have said that the bowling was the weakest aspect of the side, especially as three matches, in which big early advantages had been gained, were drawn because opponents could not be got out twice. This is borne out by the fact that in the table of bowling points the team dropped from second place to sixteenth, but at least they led the over rate table.

Blenkiron, who bowled more overs than anyone for Warwickshire in the Championship, was more a stock bowler than the spearhead of an attack, but was still top wicket-taker with sixty-eight; Brown, absent from four matches because of a broken bone in his foot, had sixty-six; Gibbs improved on 1969, but could still take no more than forty-eight wickets; McVicker was even more disappointing with only twenty-eight wickets for nearly 50 runs each.

The one bright feature was the promise of the two youngsters, Warwick Tidy and off-spinner, Peter Lewington, who had come from Berkshire, Tom Dollery's native county. Three times Tidy had five wickets in an innings and altogether took forty-six for 32·02 runs each, not a bad rate for a young leg-spinner in his first season. He even succeeded in keeping that fine attacking bat, Clive Lloyd, quiet for a time and he was duly rewarded by winning the Sir Frank Worrell trophy for 'the outstanding young cricketer of the year'. Lewington had fewer chances than Tidy to show what he could do, but looked very promising, so much so that although he took only fifteen wickets at 21·86 each, it was good enough to put him at the head of the county bowling averages.

Although he was away in five Tests, Kanhai was Warwickshire's batsman of the year. He reached his 1000 runs by 13 June, the first player in the country to do so, and only three batsmen made 2000 runs and beat his aggregate of 1894 runs and average of 57·39. He played two really memorable innings. The first was against Derbyshire at Coventry, where he made 187 out of 232 put on while he was at the wicket, including 124 out of the last 126, an amazing indication of how he took charge of the innings. Out of a fifth-wicket stand of 53 with Gibbs, Kanhai made 50 – and the other three were extras. He hit Ward, the England fast bowler, for four fours in one over and altogether he had seven sixes and twenty-six fours, a staggering performance.

The second innings, which his colleagues said was even better than that at Coventry, was against Kent at Gravesend, graveyard of many a batsman, and they rated it more highly because it was played against Underwood on a wicket which was helping him, though the first ball he sent down to Kanhai went for a tremendous six. Warwickshire batted first and were all out for 204 and where they would have been without Kanhai's innings of 107 is anybody's guess. Half the side were out for 131, but Kanhai found a useful partner in Amiss and both astutely mixed aggression and defence. Amiss's 36 was worth a good many innings in which he has scored far more runs. As it was, Underwood's seven wickets cost him 103 runs, which would probably have been more like 33 had it not been for Kanhai. Leslie Ames said afterwards that he had never seen a better innings and coming from a man with as long an experience as his that was high praise indeed.

In the second innings Underwood took seven more wickets, this time for 110, when it was Amiss's turn to take the honours with a fine 91, which he rated his best innings so far, Kanhai's contribution being 35. Thanks to them, Warwickshire won a fine match by 93 runs, for they got Kent out for 227 and 130, McVicker doing his best work of the season in the second innings with five for 16.

Amiss, it will be obvious, had found his strokes again – his Championship aggregate of 1351 runs was his highest so far – and he got into the England team again for the last Test in which he scored 24 and 35. Had he done just a little better he might well have gone to Australia, a tour which would probably have done him a world of good by giving him more confidence to play his shots, but his closest rival, Hampshire, was preferred. As it was, Bernard Thomas, the physiotherapist, was the only Warwickshire representative on the tour; he also acted as assistant to the manager, David Clark.

Kanhai followed his Gravesend innings with 165 at Derby where Alan Smith took six catches in the first innings and one in the second. Smith had a poor season with the bat; he missed eight matches through his Test selection duties and scored only 261 runs in Championship games. Providing England with a captain, or a selector, can be very expensive for a county.

Jameson was given his head as an opening batsman and he showed his appreciation and his liking for the role by making nearly 2000 runs in all matches. He began the season with a fine flourish – 194 off the Cambridge bowling; four sixes and twenty-three fours, his third 50 coming in thirty minutes – and by taking three of their wickets for 4 runs with his sometimes more than useful off-breaks. He then took 61 off Notts and 73 and 60 not out off Essex. Kanhai had another brilliant innings of 105 against Notts, sharing a partnership of 182 with M. J. K. Smith, who made 83, and then had 153 not out against his old university.

Gibbs, despite his lean season as a whole, had a career-best performance against Glamorgan at Edgbaston – five for 9 in his first nine overs and ending with three in eight balls – eight for 37 – in the second innings. After five for 22 against Leicestershire, everyone hoped that he was in for a good season at last, but he fell away badly.

It was very appropriate that it should be against his former colleagues that Cartwright should be awarded his Somerset cap. This was at Taunton where he scored 60, but did not take a wicket, though no one found it easy to score off him – at one point he bowled sixty-nine balls without conceding a run. Altogether this season he made 766 runs and took eighty-six wickets, which Warwickshire could very well have done with. He was badly missed, not only for the wickets he himself took, but, as his former captain, Alan Smith, pointed out, for those he helped the bowler at the other end to take. When they escaped from Cartwright's nagging accuracy, they were much more liable to try to celebrate their relief by taking risks they should not have taken.

Virgin, who was becoming inordinately fond of Warwickshire's bowling, scored 151 this time, and Tidy collected nine useful wickets for 152. In the return match at Edgbaston, a ground for which he has confessed his 'great affection', Virgin got another century, 111, and Lewington made a very encouraging Championship début with three for 47 and four for 82. Another débutant in the first eleven was Whitehouse, who also gave good promise with 77 and 53 against Scotland.

There were several most exciting finishes – a win by two runs over Northants at Northampton, Blenkiron getting two wickets with the first two balls of the final over after three declarations; a win for Warwickshire in the return game with eleven balls to spare; a draw with the scores levelled with a bye off the last ball against Surrey at The Oval; and a catch off the last ball of the game to give a 31 runs victory over Lancashire after M. J. K. Smith had made a declaration by which he set them to get 179 to win in twenty-five minutes plus twenty overs. Lancashire nobly responded, but Gibbs took their last three wickets for 1 run in two overs and Smith, very appropriately, made the last and winning catch.

In the return game with Lancashire Pilling took a century off the Warwickshire bowling in each innings, though there was a flavour of the farcical about the second one. No fewer than ten Warwickshire bowlers were tried in this innings – shades of Calthorpe – in an attempt to force Lancashire into a declaration, but it was not made until Warwickshire were placed in the preposterous position of having to make 280 in 100 minutes, a state of affairs which rankled so much with one spectator that months later he was provoked into writing an article for *The Cricketer* which ended with these words: 'One of us, watching the silent ritual, was asking himself if this was the dance of cricket's death wish.' Jameson at least would have pleasant memories of the match for he made 158 not out.

Turner, the New Zealand batsman Warwickshire had not been able to engage because their quota of overseas players was complete, took his tenth century of the season off them at Worcester – and I have no doubt the Warwickshire bowlers wished it had been for them, while Graveney said his graceful farewell to English cricket, Kanhai saluting him with his seventh century of the season, 132 not out.

There was another sad farewell of a more final nature at Edgbaston in August after the match with Notts. Within ten minutes of leaving the field during a stoppage for rain, Syd Buller, former Worcestershire wicketkeeper and the best and most courageous umpire English cricket had seen since the days of Frank Chester, collapsed and died in the Pavilion. Sadly, too, the Club learned of the death in his 82nd year of another of its early stalwarts – F. G. Stephens, twin brother of G.W. and, like him, a member of the 1911 Championship side. Both had also played for Rossall School and Moseley, had served in the Forces and on the war emergency committee. Frank will be remembered not only for the immaculateness of his appearance both on and off the field, but for the elegance of his batting and his splendid fielding. It was a reproach to the modern game that in his later years he derived more pleasure from watching tennis than he did the game he had adorned. He must have felt as C. G. Macartney did when, not long before his death in 1958, he was asked why he had ceased to be a regular spectator at cricket matches, and replied: 'I can't bear watching luscious half-volleys being nudged gently back to bowlers.'

It was Notts who knocked Warwickshire out in the first round of the Gillette Cup. Both clubs protested at the game being played so early in the season – 25 April. That day was washed out and the fact that the rain also dampened the ardour of the Birmingham-Stop-the-Tour Committee was small compensation. The Monday was rained off as well and the match was eventually played on 28 April when there were only 600 spectators and a £200 gate. Warwickshire scored 215 for nine, Jameson, Kanhai and M.J.K. being the only batsmen not tied down by accurate bowling, but with the Warwickshire bowlers handicapped by a wet ball Notts hit off the runs in fifty-three overs; Sobers with a not-out 70 was the obvious candidate for man-of-the-match.

Country-wide, the receipts in the John Player League games went up from £66 000 to £72 500, or 286 205 spectators compared with 280 608, but payments to players were such that clubs derived little profit. Warwickshire won exactly half their sixteen games, the out-standing performances being 97 and 87 by Jameson; 91 not out from M.J.K. and 80 not out from Amiss, both the latter against Yorkshire; and 83 out of 136 by Kanhai against Glamorgan. And partly by way of a reminder, no doubt, Cartwright got top score of 44 against them when Somerset beat them by four wickets.

At the ripe young age of 56, Peter Cranmer again took over the captaincy of the second eleven. In a note he wrote for the annual report – those responsible for different sections of the Club's activities were now making their own contributions to it – he recalled that fifteen years before, on being asked to take over the second team, he asked the Committee: 'Do you want me to win matches, or bring on individuals? – you can't do both.' The reply he got was: 'Do the best you can.' To which he now added the comment: 'Times haven't changed.' Well, the team won only three matches out of the sixteen they played, but everyone got a good bowl, no matter what the state of the wicket, and there is no doubt that this most enthusiastic and ebullient of all Warwickshire's captains had more than a little to do with bringing along such youngsters as Tidy, Lewington, John Whitehouse and Rouse, a fastish left-hander, who had come from the groundsman's staff, a much more common gateway to big cricket at one time than it is now.

Whitehouse was a modest young batsman from Nuneaton, a product of his father's back garden coaching and the Indoor School under Derief Taylor, who had never expected to play county cricket. Then while playing for Bristol University, where he studied economics and accountancy, he also attracted the attention of Glamorgan, but, of course, he had a birth qualification for Warwickshire.

The Warwickshire Young Amateurs, Harry Harper's pride and joy, made up almost entirely of Colts, had a good season, winning a new trophy presented by Mrs Hilda Overy, wife of the chairman of the National Association of Young Cricketers, which was open to competition among twenty-seven counties.

It is difficult to avoid the conclusion, however, that Warwickshire could have done with more of the spirit of the young Northern professional who asked Arthur Booth, the former Yorkshire player who had been appointed Warwickshire's scout in that part of the world, whether, assuming Warwickshire accepted him, he would be allowed to continue playing as professional for a club in the north. When asked why, he said he had noticed that at Old Trafford the ground staff played only friendly cricket, whereas he would prefer to play competitive cricket which would help keep his game 'sharp'.

Booth put in a long report – after seeing no fewer than sixty matches in eighteen different leagues in nine counties; five inter-league games, one Test, nine Minor Counties games, one international match (Scotland v. Ireland), and four cup finals; so he had got about a bit. Some players he watched four times. He said there had always seemed to him to be a certain amount of complacency in the Warwickshire eleven – he was not alone in thinking this – as though the players felt there were no outstanding members of the ground staff who might win a regular place in the side. 'Anything which seems leisurely, to me a Northerner, does not win matches,' he reported. 'It is amazing what the fear of losing one's place can do – it makes a player take his finger out.' Not perhaps an elegant way of putting it, but there was no doubting his meaning.

Booth had given up his seat on the Lancashire committee to take up this work for Warwickshire. The Committee was asked if some former Warwickshire player could not have been given the position, but it was pointed out that no Warwickshire player could possibly hope to have Booth's knowledge of the game in Lancashire and Yorkshire, where there was a combined population of 15 millions, almost one-third of the population of the country, most of whom they could hardly hope to use.

His report eventually went to Alan Oakman, who in April had taken up his position as senior coach, the first man from outside the county to hold the position. Aged 39, he had played for Sussex from 1947 to 1968, as opening bat and off-spinner, scoring 21 000 runs, taking over 500 wickets, and making 550 catches. He had twice appeared for England against Australia, and in 1956–7 toured South Africa where for the previous five winters he had been coaching. Film-making was one of his accomplishments and his record of cricket at Edgbaston was one of the features of 'Cricket Occasion' at the county ground, organised by the Warwickshire Cricket Association, at which Alec Hastilow, Leslie Deakins and M. J. K. Smith were the speakers. Oakman generally made such an impression in his first season that his contract was renewed for five years.

More overseas players were considered – Eddie Barlow again, but still he would not be tempted; Lee Irvine, the South African wicket-keeper-batsman, who had returned there; Mushtaq Mohammed, the Pakistan all-rounder, who made an approach to the county, though to have engaged him would have meant displacing Tidy; Greg Chappell, the Australian, though he would not have been available when the Australians were due in 1972; S. Dik Abed, a promising fast bowler in the Lancashire League, who, at Alan Oakman's invitation, played in two second-eleven matches and took seventeen wickets and also batted well, though it was not then possible to make him an offer; Ted Dexter, about whom another inquiry was made – no doubt because Barber, through business calls, was able to play less and less cricket – but Sussex refused permission to approach him even about Sunday cricket.

All this followed an assessment of the Club's playing strength, which suggested that immediate needs were one or two 'strike' bowlers – cricket was borrowing football's jargon now – and an all-rounder who could combine attacking middle-order batsmanship with seam bowling and lively fielding. But nothing came of any of the inquiries. The only young new player to whom Warwickshire did decide to give an extended trial was a young West Indian fast-medium right-hander, William A.

Bourne, aged 17, whom they had noted while he was touring with young cricketers from the West Indies.

As other clubs were now beginning to offer capped players contracts up to three years, Warwickshire, on the advice of the chairman, decided to offer their staff two-year contracts with one year's notice at the Committee's discretion. By now several of the senior players were receiving salaries for a season's cricket round about, or approaching, the £2000 mark, and with Test Match fees going up from £120 to £150, the first increase since 1966, the top men in cricket generally were for the first time making money comparable with that earned by the lower executive grades in industry and the professions, though, of course, the latter work all-the-year-round for it.

Apart from the loss of revenue caused by cancelling the tour, Warwickshire's great worry was continuing loss of membership, which had amounted to 2600 over the last four years; a fall of 35 per cent. Between them the seventeen counties had lost 6000, so Warwickshire's loss had been considerably above the average. What it amounted to was that people were being asked to buy something which lasted for only four months in the year and sales resistance was increasing, so once more the emphasis was on all-the-year-round use of the ground.

Subscriptions were down £3320 and income generally by over £8000, but the Club's investment list at 10 November 1970, showed 55 securities with a valuation figure of £300 070. Thanks to the wise advice of their expert, Roy James, the Club had benefited to the extent of a £66 000 surplus on realisation of certain of those investments over the past three years. The freehold value of the Club's properties was now £652 162 and though the Supporters' Association had given the Club a short-term loan of £30 000, the call was for the strictest economy in every direction, for, with all sources of income down, 1971 was being looked on as 'a real danger year'. Cyril Goodway, however, had good cause to congratulate the chairman on persuading the Australians to accept the guarantee principle for future tours, which he regarded as 'a tremendous step forward which would free the home country to derive the best returns from its own endeavours'.

The Supporters' Association, too, was having certain difficulties though its record to date was a truly astonishing and highly creditable one – since its inception it had made available to cricket no less than £1 500 000 – £900 000 of it for building projects at Edgbaston – and had paid £3 000 000 in betting duty to the Government. Its accounts in 1970 showed a surplus on the past year's working of £135 065.

A far more serious problem for the Association, especially in its possible implications for the future, was a decision in the House of Lords, in which a football pool in South Wales similar to Warwickshire's had been judged illegal, which could have had the effect of putting all such pools beyond the law. This would have been 'a major disaster to cricket', in Edgar Hiley's phrase. The Warwickshire Association was quick to see the danger and took the lead, not only in alerting other sporting organisations to the threat, but by quickly preparing a brochure for circulation to members of the House of Lords and M.P.s, one of whom, Denis Howell, the former Minister of Sport, tabled a motion in the House calling for an amendment to the law which would safeguard the position of such bodies as the Warwickshire Association, whose case was undoubtedly helped by the generosity it had shown to other counties, leagues, clubs, schools and youth cricket.

This led to the passing of the Pool Competitions Act of 1971 which protected the position of pools operated for sporting or charitable purposes for five years, during which a Home Office Committee would review all aspects of betting legislation and, no doubt, recommend some changes in the present complicated legal situation. In the opinion of David Blakemore, 'it is difficult to imagine any Government killing off organisations which do good work by raising much-needed funds and thus avoid the necessity for some sports or charities to seek government aid.'

One of the Association's benefactions this year was an unusual one, indeed. For the first time the laborious job, over which county secretaries, notably Geoffrey Howard and his predecessors at The Oval, had toiled for years, of arranging the first-class fixtures was done by computer. Now the Association footed the bill for its services, and it also undertook sponsorship of a new 'Under 25' Knock-Out Competition, proposed by Cyril Goodway to encourage young players; teams being limited, except for the captains, to uncapped players under 25, with Alan Oakman acting as both secretary and treasurer.

As any large-scale development on the North side had been deferred, the Supporters' Social Club also abandoned its idea of moving there and took a seven-year lease of their premises in the Pavilion (east wing) where they continue to operate happily under the affable chairmanship of that five-initial man, 'Tiny' Wildsmith.

Although it had nothing directly to do with Warwickshire cricket, one of the highlights of the season was the visit on 11 June of the Duke of Edinburgh to attend a conference in the Pavilion Suite attended by some 400 delegates of bodies identified with his awards scheme. His equerry subsequently congratulated Sir Oliver Leese, who received the Duke on his arrival, on the setting for the conference and the arrangements made.

The old problem of spectators on the playing area cropped up yet again when Edgar Hiley expressed the very downright view that, as then administered, Edgbaston was 'the most oppressive ground in the country in a variety of ways' and seemed to be 'run for the administration'. Nearly all other grounds, he claimed, allowed spectators on the playing area without ill-effects.

Needless to say, he was strongly opposed by Cyril Goodway, who naturally looked at the question from the point of view of the additional work it might give the ground staff, and by the staff themselves as well as a section of the membership. Nevertheless, although no request was received either from members or spectators for this departure from tradition, the 'let them play' school got their way – during intervals in the play except at Test Matches, the privilege to be withdrawn depending on weather conditions and the possible effect of plebeian feet on the turf.

Perhaps the Committee would have been wiser to have concentrated their attention on the Nuneaton ground, which had had to be ruled out for matches in 1970 following adverse reports submitted by both umpires and captains after the Leicestershire match on 17 June. Owing to labour problems, the ground conditions had deteriorated considerably in the past twelve months. In the county pitches table Edgbaston was now listed eleventh for County Championship matches, but joint first with Derbyshire in the John Player League, which suggested that the judges, whoever they were, at least regarded them as sporting wickets.

The old 'uns elected as their new president Len Morris, a director of Birmingham City Football Club, who had played occasionally for the county in the 1920s as a left-hand bat and a lively fast bowler. He succeeded Alec Hastilow.

Almost There (1971)

For most of the 1971 season Warwickshire were at the head of the County Championship and for a long time looked like winning it. Indeed, it was not until Surrey played their last two matches in mid-September, unusually late in the season, that it was known they had taken the title and then only because they had won more games, for the clubs were level on points, 255 each from 24 matches. Surrey still needed fourteen points from their last two matches and six from the last game of all and only just got them.

However, since Surrey lost only three games and Warwickshire nine, it could be said that Surrey deserved the title, and their supporters were not slow to say that, had Warwickshire won, it would have been with one of worst 'losts' records for any champion county. In reply, though, Warwickshire could point to the fact that Surrey drew ten matches and Warwickshire only six and that, because of the bonus system, the Midlanders' points total was the highest achieved by any county during the three years of the 24-match programme. As Alan Smith said: 'We are interested in the points we win, not the points we deny to others' and it was true that Warwickshire lost some points by taking risks in trying to force wins including the early match against Surrey at The Oval. This, of course, made for good cricket even if the verdict sometimes went against them.

Warwickshire also reached the semi-final of the Gillette Cup, from which, however, they made an ignominious exit after having the worst of the weather and the wicket, and they still could not hit on the winning recipe for the John Player League in which they sometimes had to rest bowlers who had been carrying on despite injuries. They finished at the foot of the table, though, if it was any consolation to them, they had a crucial hand in who did win it.

Before a ball was bowled there was much clearing up to be done of the mess left by the cancellation of the South African tour, and there was even more anxiety than usual about finance. Shortly before the annual meeting, the chairman, perhaps with the notion of softening the blow he knew was to come, a loss of over £28 000, listed those of other counties in 1970. These were the melancholy records in alphabetical order:

Derbyshire	£12 000	Middlesex	£6500
Essex	£11 000	Northants	£9000
Glamorgan	£9000	Notts	£9000
Gloucestershire	£15 000	Somerset	£13 000
Hampshire	£18 000	Surrey	£9000
Kent	£7000	Sussex	£9000
Lancashire	£5000	Warwickshire	£28 253
Leicestershire	£2000	Worcestershire	£9000
		Yorkshire	£8000

Surrey, in particular, despite their success, were in dire trouble, being in immediate need, their president, Maurice Allom said, of £50 000 if they were to avert extinction in the next two years.

At long last the Government announced that it would give £75 054 in compensation for loss of the tour, an amount which fell far short of the £200 000 the Cricket Council had originally asked for and caused bitter disappointment among the counties, Leslie Deakins pointing out that, after all, the tour had been cancelled at the instigation of the Government.

The chairman told the annual meeting that preparations for the tour cost the Club £4500 and they would receive £3500 to £4000 from the Government. (This later became £8156.) Even so, the loss on the year of £28 253 was still 'a dreadfully heavy figure'. They had received another £5000 from the match against The Rest of the World, how-ever, so the loss could have been down to £15 000. All the counties were in trouble, but a Test ground such as Edgbaston was harder hit than non-Test grounds and they were 'so terribly dependent' on Test receipts that the position would be quite hopeless were it not for the membership and the income from other activities.

Perhaps the scent of the spring flowers sent every year by Richard Lethbridge, the Club's far-flung member in the Scilly Isles – there were so many daffodils decorating the Pavilion Suite that a rugby follower remarked that it was more like Glamorgan's annual meeting than Warwickshire's – so sweetened the atmosphere that any possible critics were overcome. At any rate, although about 300 members were present, nobody said a word about the record loss, or asked a question. One can imagine what might have happened had it been the annual meeting of a commercial company. In this case, the members' silence seemed to argue that (*a*) they appreciated it was not the Committee's fault; (*b*) that in any event they had implicit faith in them; (*c*) complacency because of the warm, comfortable feeling the backing of the Supporters' Association gave them; or (*d*) that they did not care. One hoped that '*a*' and '*b*' were uppermost in the members' minds, but, though they might not admit it, there was almost certainly more than a touch of '*c*' in their attitude.

Four causes for the decline in membership were listed in a circular letter sent out by A. K. Jackson, whose death during the year while on holiday abroad deprived the Club of one of its staunchest workers. The letter showed that, in the three years 1968–70 inclusive, membership had dropped by over 1500 and by over £7000 in contributions, a very serious loss. He put the causes as, first, death; second, removal from the area; third, inability to attend matches; and, fourth, financial stringency. Some people would have put the last first and added another – unenterprising play generally, a failing of which Warwickshire were not often guilty.

A survey of the membership of other counties, incidentally, showed that Sussex and Kent had surprisingly large membership revenues considering that neither had a ground which enjoyed Test status, or any very large centres of population. The probable reasons, it was felt, were that both counties have a high proportion of retired people and that there are neither large football, nor other top-ranking sports clubs, in the area offering competing attractions. I have learned since that they have Committee members who are very active canvassers.

Warwickshire, it was decided, would consider a form of industrial membership on an incentive basis – first-class dining and lounge facilities with a view of the playing area. free parking and other facilities at a subscription of, say, £100 for four tickets, Cyril Goodway thought this might bring in £5000 to £10 000 in subscriptions. It was also considered that there were possibilities in sponsorship of matches by industry under which firms would have a private box, or boxes, where they could entertain, with, possibly, an interchange between the firm's guests and members of the Committee and players, and temporary advertising facilities.

In fact, in the last week of the year the Club was able to announce its first scheme of industrial sponsorship for the County Championship game against Middlesex at Edgbaston in 1972. The arrangement was made with a firm based in nearby Oldbury, Schoeller-Bleckmann Steels (Great Britain) Ltd, and it included for the first time in such games a man-of-the-match award.

Of even greater moment for safeguarding the future of the Club and its membership was the most far-reaching step of its kind ever tried by Warwickshire in this field – the introduction for the first time in

English cricket of shareholder memberships, limited to 2500, at £10 each, comprising a full membership card, a guest card, a junior membership ticket and a car park pass, with a reduced rate to country members and pensioners of £8. When this new form of package membership was put to a special meeting of members in October only 20 of the 300 present voted against the idea which, it was felt, would give members a vested interest in the Club. The meeting also approved an increase from £5 to £7 in the ordinary membership rate and abandoned the entrance fee of £1 payable by new members, though a proposal to extend the country membership limit from fifteen to twenty miles was withdrawn.

Running ahead of the story a little, these measures were so successful that the 1972 annual report was able to announce that membership income rose from £27 000 to £36 000, although the limit of 2500 shareholders was not quite reached and there was a decline in numbers 'through the very style of the new membership'.

Members heard from Edmund King that the cost of running the Club was now in the neighbourhood of £105 000 a year, that the income was £85 000 and that they were losing at least £20 000 a year. The average amount from members in the last ten years was £30 000; from the Test Match Pool £11 000; from the Gillette Cup and sponsorship £3000; from gates £6000, and from lettings for social functions £15 000. But the main worry he put in the form of a question: 'How on earth do we get the Birmingham public to come through the turnstiles and watch cricket?'

Even a successful team was evidently not the sole answer, for Warwickshire's long run at the head of the table did not bring large crowds flocking to the ground, except for the Test Match with Pakistan, the Gillette Cup and some John Player League games. The recipe the Structure Sub-committee had prepared for 1972 with a trial period of three years, based on the reports supplied by the four zonal committees, which had gone into the subject very thoroughly, consisted of twenty three-day County Championship matches, with at least six Saturday home starts.

This was four fewer than in 1971, but still four more than Warwickshire wanted; the Gillette Cup and the John Player League were to continue as before, except that the Cup matches would be later in the season; and there would be a new early-in-the-season League Cup, based on four zones of five teams each, the balance being made up by Minor Counties and University sides, with a final at Lord's in July. In addition, there would be three one-day 'Tests' against the Australians in 1972 and six Tests instead of five in future single-tour years.

The sub-committee felt that twenty County Championship matches was the minimum requirement and that if this number was to be reduced the possibility of playing four-day matches should be carefully examined, though it might have been feared that such games would further slow down play and have made the decline in interest in the County Championship even more pronounced. The sub-committee was also of the opinion that 'a movement towards more one-day cricket would widen public interest without adversely affecting standards of play', the latter a questionable assumption perhaps.

One point that emerged from the sub-committee's report was that the introduction of the Gillette Cup and Players' League competitions had provided £100 000 additional income, but it was felt that too high a proportion of one-day, as compared with three-day, matches could lead to a lowering of standards in terms of Test cricket – a contradiction, it would seem, of the earlier statement – have, possibly, an adverse effect on existing one-day competitions and possibly lead to a loss in county membership.

On the whole, the proposals pleased Leslie Deakins, except for the retention of twenty County Championship games, which he thought an illogical compromise, as indeed, did the sub-committee itself, though it was also, of course, concerned with providing an adequate programme for the Australians. Leslie Deakins wanted every county to play all the others once, something the public could understand, but Jack Bannister, chairman of the Cricketers' Association, preferred the County Championship to be retained as the nucleus of the season and thought the plans struck a happy medium. Not so Derrick Robins, who saw the whole thing as merely 'an aspirin' when what was needed, in his view, was the surgeon's knife for that very sick patient, cricket. The success of the Sunday League, he argued, had shown the way and he wanted another similar type of Championship to be run on Saturdays.

In fact, however, the gates for Sunday cricket had not proved as large as had been hoped and the profits had been largely swallowed up in players' pay and costs, even though these were only one-sixth of those of three-day county games. And would Saturday afternoons, when there were more counter-attractions, be as popular and as financially successful as games on Sunday afternoons?

In the fresh of the year, when the sweet smells and sounds of cricket were providing an overture to the season ahead, the ashes of one of the Club's best loved sons, Len Bates, were scattered on the Edgbaston turf on which he had trodden, boy and man, for many years. He had died at his home in Sussex after long years of incapacity patiently borne and it was his wish that his ashes should be scattered on the playing area he had graced so often.

By one of those strange quirks of coincidence it was just at this time that the bedroom in which he had been born was being reconstructed in the first phase of the Pavilion (centre) scheme which was completed in June at a cost of £20 080. The second phase was estimated to cost £16 973, certainly much cheaper than building a new one at what would almost certainly have worked out at something in the neighbourhood of three-quarters of a million pounds. Other developments on the ground, the freehold of which was now valued at £656 060, were still being discussed, notably the possibility of residential property development inside the ground, and on this the views of the Calthorpe Estates were sought. There were also discussions with the Pattison-Hughes Catering Company, Ltd, the Club's caterers for over fifty years, who asked about the possibility of establishing their central office and stores on the ground. Subsequently, however, they found other accommodation.

A suggestion from the captain that the Indoor School should be turned into offices enjoying an Edgbaston Road frontage and that a new building embracing the School and squash courts should be erected on the North side, brought from Edgar Hiley another reminder that extra sports facilities on the ground should be considered in relation to other similar developments in the area. (In fact, the Midlands Arts Centre and another private club installed squash facilities, which rather took the wind out of Warwickshire's oft-talked-of scheme.)

Edgar Hiley added that he was in favour of a multi-sports centre, the development costs of which could be covered to a great extent by Government grant, but he was concerned about the cost of maintaining such a venture, which experience obtained from the Sports Council showed could not be viable. The Council, he said, had recommended that such enterprises would always need public funds to keep them going. The Government made grants for capital expenditure, but not for subsequent maintenance, and to obtain such money from local authorities could mean their having a big say in administration and the Club could thus lose its independence to some extent.

The Indoor School, run by Derief Taylor, was now full to capacity from 2 p.m. to 10.30 p.m. each and every day from 1 January to the end of April, and requests from as many as fifteen clubs and a number of individuals had to be turned down, a happily extraordinary state of affairs in view of the number of people drifting away from watching the game, though it could also have been the case that Alan Oakman's appointment had stimulated interest.

The Club had always considered the West Indies to be the most fruitful recruiting ground for both top-ranking overseas cricketers and likely youngsters, partly because the financial rewards for them, with their lower home standards of living, were more of an incentive than for Australians, New Zealanders, or South Africans, though this also applied to some extent to India and Pakistan. However, judging by a photograph published during the summer in the *Daily Express*, Warwickshire would soon not have to look further than its own doorstep.

The picture showed the finalists in the junior schools championships in Birmingham, played in Cannon Hill Park, just across the road from Edgbaston, in which only one white boy took part. All the others were coloured, mostly West Indians, some Pakistanis and one Turkish-Cypriot. The coach to one of the teams was quoted as saying: 'These boys have a natural aptitude for sports,' and he visualised the day when England, to say nothing of Warwickshire, might be represented by coloured players born in Britain, though their ambition, according to the coach, was to play for England at soccer – or for Birmingham City. On the other hand, Mr Stanley Pittman, general manager of the city's Parks Department, said the number of games of cricket played in the parks each season had dropped in the last ten years by more than a third to fewer than 2000, and he had to cancel a coaching course because of the lack of demand. Perhaps they were all going to Edgbaston in the hope of being 'discovered' by Alan Oakman, but a more likely explanation was that the quality of some parks and school pitches left something to be desired and were hardly calculated to give young players confidence. There was evidence of this when they came for coaching for some of them were found to flinch even from slow bowling.

This was another two-country tour season and it was unfortunate in view of the political situation in Pakistan and India that they should have been the countries involved, for it meant more demonstrations outside the ground, this time by East Pakistanis, chanting over and over again a word that was to be heard for many months – 'Bangla Desh'. But at least they did it in a very orderly fashion, something to be thankful for in these violent days, though one could not help feeling that they would all have been happier inside the ground watching the cricket.

There were the usual appeals by the chairman and secretary, well in advance, that unless better support was forthcoming for the Test with Pakistan the ground's status might be imperilled. Perhaps the fact that the county first met Pakistan helped to keep people away from the Test, but even if the visitors seemed unlikely to set the Rea on fire with the brilliance of their play, one would have thought that the first England team to have won in Australia since Jardine's day would have merited a better welcome. But, as Leslie Deakins reminded us in a speech he made at the Wolverhampton Cricket Club dinner, we now seemed to take no pleasure even in our victories.

As it was, no more than 23 000 people attended the match which, most unfortunately, coincided with some of the least June-like weather for years. It hit county clubs all over the country. For instance, Worcestershire, after two days of their match with Middlesex, had realised takings of as little as £35, and on the last day admitted people free to avoid having to pay turnstile attendants. The receipts at Edgbaston were only £6977.

562

Had more people come, especially Pakistani supporters, they would have had much to enthuse about, for their countrymen ran up the highest score ever made in a Test at Edgbaston – 608 for seven declared, which beat the previous record of 583 for four made by England against the West Indies in 1957. They would also have seen the personal triumph of one of their young batsmen, Zahir Abbas, making his first appearance in a Test against England, who took his score of 159 not out made on the opening day, to 274, the highest individual innings by a Pakistan player against England; a record previously held by Hanif Mohammed's 187 at Lord's in 1967. Only three batsmen – Bradman (twice), Simpson and Cowper – have made higher scores against England.

With Mushtaq Mohammed, who got 100 exactly, Zahir put on 291, the highest stand for any wicket for either side in seventeen years of Tests between the countries. He also reached his 1000 runs for the season earlier than it had been done for twelve years and at a faster rate than Bradman, which is going it more than somewhat. Zahir's was a monumental innings, though it must be reported that it was made off one of the weakest attacks which had represented England for some time. Ward, Shuttleworth and Lever all suffered strains during the match, so it was perhaps not surprising that all lacked length and direction and did little with the ball, either in the air or off the seam. Underwood, trying to push the ball through quickly, consistently pitched short and Illingworth grossly underbowled himself, especially in the first innings when he sent down only four overs in his first spell. If he was not fit to bowl more, he should either not have been playing at all, or some announcement should have been made.

Pakistan unfortunately batted on and on until England had nothing but a draw to play for, which ruined the match as an attraction. Not that England ever looked like making a real fight of it, except when D'Oliveira and Knott were together in the first innings, and when Luckhurst was batting in the second. Edrich was out twice from edged shots off a bat dangled naïvely outside the off stump – it was incredible that a player of his experience could still allow himself to do it; Cowdrey was out in a manner a batsman of his experience should have been ashamed of, 'shouldering arms' to a fast in-swinger; Amiss got another similar ball and in the second innings savagely mis-hit a fast long hop into the hands of mid-on. He just could not get going in a Test.

Luckhurst was, well, Luckhurst; anonymously dull and strokeless in the second innings, though at least he stayed there against bowlers who, although unused to English conditions, especially Masood, got infinitely more out of the wicket than England's did. There had been some talk before the game began that the wicket, most of the preparations for which had fortunately been completed before Bernard Flack had to go into hospital after a heart attack, would not last; but as J. M. Solan, in

The Birmingham Post commented, all the counties should have been grateful to him that it did last and that, moreover, it proved a wicket on which batsmen who could bat got runs and bowlers who could bowl took wickets.

It was a moral victory for Pakistan, who would probably have won if it had not been for the rain and bad light on the last day when the ground was almost empty. There were some complaints about the slow over rate – 96 on the Thursday and 98 on the Friday – a fact lamented by Robin Marlar who asked: 'What's to be done?' He got an answer from Jack Fingleton in Australia telling him that what's to be done should have been done years ago – limit the bowlers' run-ups. 'There is nothing more wearisome to spectators and batsmen alike', he wrote in *The Sunday Times*, 'than waiting for a medium-fast bowler to go through his 30-yard run.'

One has often disagreed about cricket with Jack Fingleton, but he was certainly right about the wearisomeness. Returning to watch cricket regularly after at last escaping from office routine, one found this aspect of the game, which had got steadily worse, much the most irritating feature of it, and seeing John Price on his 'outer circle' run brought to mind several captains who would have told him firmly that either he must cut it out or go and play cricket somewhere else.

There had been a suggestion before the Test and County Cricket Board that counties failing to average nineteen overs an hour throughout a season should pay a fine of X pounds, the amount to be decided by the Board, and that those averaging more than nineteen should receive a similar award, the sub-committee suggesting that £200 should be a suitable sum in both instances.

Why either penalties or inducements should have to be regarded as necessary almost passes comprehension. Warwickshire thought it 'a dreadful incentive' and even took the view that it was a bad example for all other cricket that the over rates in the Gillette Cup (sixteen in 1970) and the John Player League (nineteen) should be given publicity at all. But surely to have published the figures showed that clubs could cut out the dilly-dallying when time was pressing, which meant that they could do it at all times if they really got down to it. At one time one would have defended a bowler's right to any style he cared to adopt provided it was within the law, but by now matters had got so out of hand that players had only themselves to blame if the legislators took action. Some bowlers walked so slowly back to their marks that they almost appeared to have dozed off on the way. As it happened, Warwickshire, in 1971, bowled their overs more quickly than any other county – 19·3 an hour.

There were some really engrossing games in all three competitions and M. J. K. Smith, in addition to leading the side well in the absences of his namesake, had another splendid season, scoring 1951 runs, and bringing his total in all first-class matches to 35 475, only 546 short of the figure in all games put up by Warwickshire's other most prolific scorer of runs, W. G. Quaife, though Smith was still well behind him in runs scored in Warwickshire matches only. It was a remarkable performance considering the difference in the lengths of the careers of the two batsmen.

Looking at the game from the point of view of the Club's playing future, however, the most encouraging features were the successes of the young players, notably John Whitehouse, as an opening batsman, with 1295 runs in his first full season; and Alvin Kallicharran, a 21-year-old Guyanan left-hander, looking rather like a pocket Kanhai, whom Alan Smith flew out to the West Indies to sign in face of keen competition by other counties after he had been warmly recommended by Derrick Robins, who was on holiday in Barbados, and by Kanhai, his captain out there.

Tidy was troubled by a back injury in the early part of the season, though he had some good performances later, while Lewington did not get as many chances as before since Gibbs at last found his real form.

To look at Whitehouse with his most open stance, an exaggeration of 'Mike' Smith's, one might at first have thought it impossible for him to avoid playing with a cross bat, but his feet moved into the correct positions before the ball reached him and he hit very hard on both sides of the wicket. He showed that while he might never win awards for stylishness, he would earn high praise and much gratitude from spectators for punishing innings of the kind he played in his first game in first-class cricket against Oxford in The Parks. He reached three figures in ninety minutes, the second 50 coming in half an hour, and altogether made 173, including thirty-five boundaries. It was the highest score made this century by any player on his début in first-class cricket for his county.

Before and after taking a degree, Whitehouse played for the Nuneaton Club and made ample runs for Warwickshire's second eleven. He became articled to a firm which generously allowed him time off to play cricket in the summer, and for the county's sake one hoped they would continue to do so. The principal of the firm was reported to have said that 'he knows that when he's 40 and can't play cricket he will need other qualifications'. The Club was happy to think that if he could play for Warwickshire until that age both would do very well indeed.

He very well earned his selection, after only eight county games, for the England Under–25 side to meet an England XI at the Scarborough Festival, but he was not able to play, Warwickshire requesting his release for their last vital match of the season against Yorkshire. There was some compensation for him when he was chosen as 'The Young Cricketer of 1971' by the Cricket Writers' Club.

The bulk of Kallicharran's cricket to begin with was, of necessity, played with the second eleven, but his name often got into the smaller headlines because of the aggressive brilliance of several innings he played, astonishing in one who had never set foot on English turf until the 1971 season.

Two other causes for some jubilation were the continued success as an enterprising opening batsman of John Jameson, who was first to reach 1000 runs for the season, altogether scored 1765, and eventually won a place in the England side against India, which ought to have been his for keeps; and the best season Gibbs had had since joining Warwickshire, in which he took 100 wickets for the first time for them and was the first bowler in the country to reach that figure.

Gibbs's loss of form since starting to play county cricket had puzzled many people. Obviously he found the change in conditions and in the pace of wickets disconcerting, and he no longer had the enormous advantage of coming on first change in the wake of such a devastating pair of fast bowlers as Hall and Griffith, which can make a great difference to a bowler's morale. Looking at it from the batsman's point of view, even a bowler as subtly clever as Gibbs would seem a relief by comparison and even the most enterprising batsman would be unlikely to seek to hit him out of the firing line for fear of bringing back Hall, or Griffith, or both.

So there was a psychological difference, even a handicap, for Gibbs to overcome; he had to learn to bowl a tighter line and, on our slower wickets, to push the ball through more quickly so that batsmen did not have time to come out to him and kill the spin; he also had to learn how to circumvent the pad play experts, from whom he suffered a good deal in his first seasons with Warwickshire and until the lbw law was changed. Dropped catches were also one of the crosses he had to bear.

But suddenly, in 1971, everything seemed to fit into place, and nothing succeeds like success for bowlers who thrive on it. Gibbs's original five-year contract was due to end when the 1971 season was over, but, not surprisingly in the circumstances, Warwickshire tried to persuade him to stay on for another season. Gibbs was to return to Guyana to take up a coaching post with the National Sports Council there, to which he was appointed by the Prime Minister, and where also he was having a new house built. Happily for Warwickshire, he was granted a further two years' leave of absence, which also gave Lewington a further chance to blossom out.

It was as well for Warwickshire that Gibbs 'came good' again in 1971, for they were without Brown for all but ten matches because of shoulder trouble and the attack sometimes lacked the bite it needed to gain victories after the batsmen had given them a reasonable chance.

McVicker's 74 wickets was the highest total after Gibbs's 131. Three times at the start of the season Alan Smith set targets for Warwickshire's opponents and three times he saw them achieved. One of them was against Surrey at The Oval where John Edrich got centuries in each innings and Surrey made 257 in 105 minutes and 20 overs to win in the last over.

Perhaps encouraged by his success for Oxford Past and Present against Cambridge Past and Present under John Player League rules at Fenners, when he bowled Dexter, May and Prideaux with sharply curving in-swingers, Alan Smith more than once put himself on to bowl to help out Warwickshire's depleted attack, and, in two matches towards the end of the season, picked himself as a bowler, leaving Timms to keep wicket.

Jameson, who was born in Bombay and was therefore qualified to play for Mother India, no doubt played himself into the England side by his massive 231 against them at Edgbaston early in July. He made his runs out of 377 declared, but despite this Warwickshire lost the match by as wide a margin as an innings and 3 runs. The Indians, too, took heavy toll of Warwickshire's bowlers – 562 runs – and then dismissed them for 182. Bedi bowled left-arm spin so beautifully, catching and bowling both Kanhai and M. J. K. Smith in the classical manner, that he conjured up wistful memories of Wilfred Rhodes.

One had it on Alan Smith's authority that the England selectors, when they picked Jameson, had the good sense to ask him to play his normal attacking game and he duly did so; the result being several innings of an aggression not seen in an England opener since the days of Charlie Barnett – of whom Jameson was strongly reminiscent in style – Gimblett or Colin Milburn. The fact that he was bedevilled by being run out three times, once in the unluckiest manner possible from a deflection when backing up, did not diminish the splendour of his batting by one jot. He even dared to hit two sixes before lunch and earned from J. M. Solan the title of 'the harmonious blacksmith'.

Warwickshire were involved in more wicket trouble, but happily this time not on one of their own grounds. It was on a pitch of rugged rural eccentricity at Glastonbury, where they suffered an innings defeat by Somerset, twenty wickets falling in one day, the side being out twice for scores of 95 and 69. They were lucky to escape without someone being injured, for Kanhai alone was hit on the chest, arms and frequently the hands.

True, on the Saturday, Somerset had scored 258 and Warwickshire 52 for no wicket. Even so, the umpires reported it and Bert Lock came to inspect it. By Monday, after a Sunday League match against Hampshire, there were broken patches on the pitch and even a bowler of Cartwright's pace was making the ball lift head high off a good length. Brian Close, fielding at suicide corner two feet from the bat, grabbed no fewer than five catches during the day in which Cartwright, bowling unchanged for 42 overs, took eight wickets for 37, while a young West Indian, Moseley, had eight for 68. Later in the season Cartwright completed his 100 wickets.

After it was all over Alan Smith reported: 'This does not conform to the sort of pitch which should be prepared for first-class cricket.' Edgbaston's own wickets, incidentally, have been regarded in late years as easy-paced batting wickets, but some of them now have more pace than they used to have, so that they have a little more tendency to help bowlers, though still not so much as the Committee would wish.

The end of the Championship season at Edgbaston was enlivened by two splendid finishes, which those few spectators lucky enough to have seen them will long remember. The first was against Lancashire, when Warwickshire lost to a leg-bye, frantically scrambled off the very last ball of the match. Warwickshire began with 252 for eight declared, which Lancashire failed by 4 runs to reach in 85 overs. M. J. K. Smith then rattled up his sixth century of the season, giving his side a second chance to declare at 182 for six, which left Lancashire with 187 to get to win.

Warwickshire had their young leg spinner, Tidy, in the side and in the first innings I had mentally criticised 'Mike' Smith for not giving him a bowl until Lancashire had scored 207 for six wickets, though his answer would probably have been that there was no need to do so as Gibbs was getting wickets – he finished the innings with six for 70, one of them being his 100th wicket of the season. Tidy's contribution was two for 31, one of them being caught and bowled from a hard return which split his left hand and must have caused him considerable pain.

In Lancashire's second innings Smith bravely – some would have said rashly – brought Tidy on at a crucial stage in the innings when Lancashire needed only 30 or so runs to win and Warwickshire had no margin for error. A Committee member on the balcony was overheard to say, 'Well, I might have risked it with Eric Hollies, but not with young Tidy.' But Tidy justified his captain's faith in him by getting a wicket with his third ball, and then he tried to take another hard return wide of his left hand which made him wring it in agony. But he kept pluckily on, and saw what might have been a crucial catch dropped off him in the long field, but another one thankfully accepted by his captain. And if he was not then near to tears of joy one is very much mistaken. One's heart warmed to the boy.

It was not his fault that Lancashire won – Gibbs had the nerve-racking job of bowling the last over, which, despite all that the West Indian's skill could do, yielded just the 10 runs Lancashire needed to win –

but Tidy had played a worthy part in what might have been a famous Warwickshire victory. It had been a challenge flung down and boldly taken up and a young cricketer had been subjected to the literally painful fires of experience and had come through them splendidly. What more could anyone ask of a game?

The second match was against Yorkshire and it provided a positively and magnificently Newboltian end to the last Championship match of the season at Edgbaston. Here were almost all the famous poem's ingredients – a blinding light for most of Yorkshire's second innings and the last man in with only a few minutes to go. Only the bumping pitch was absent and the margin of runs – 22 – a little greater.

Alan Smith throughout the game handled his forces with both decision and flair, bravely bringing Tidy and Jameson into the attack at crucial moments, but it was the art of Gibbs, with white shirt sleeve flapping in the encircling gloom like the trappings of some dark ghost, who broke Yorkshire's heart when he bowled Hutton with a beautiful ball and spun yet another to produce a third catch for Ibadulla and see Warwickshire home with three minutes to spare, everyone being on tenterhooks, hardly daring to breathe.

It was a great game of cricket and if anyone had any doubts as to who was the most technically accomplished English batsman, they must have been resolved once and for all by the two superb innings by Boycott, who played every stroke in the book like the master he had become. In the first innings he carried his bat for 138 through an innings of 232 and in the second he paced the innings beautifully and seemed certain to get another century.

Then he mis-hit a full toss from Tidy, whom he had punished cruelly at times, and Ibadulla raced for and held the catch. Never was revenge more sweetly earned, for the boy had bravely kept the ball up to him even when he was being hit. It was a wicket he would long remember and he had no need to be ashamed of the fact that it was a full toss. Cecil Parkin used to say that every ball which got a wicket was a good ball and that may well be said of any ball which gets out a Boycott when he is well and truly set and in sight of a hundred.

Boycott might not be the greatest captain Yorkshire have ever had, but his batting in 1971 added lustre to the game and we were lucky to see it. At the end of a summer in which he made thirteen centuries he became the first Englishman ever to have a batting average of over 100 in an English season. He also pipped M. J. K. Smith in the race for 2000 runs, and thus deprived Warwickshire of what would have been a novel form of hat trick – the first batsman to reach 1000 runs, the first bowler to take 100 wickets and the first batsman to score 2000 runs.

The pity of it was that these two wonderful matches were watched by mere smatterings of spectators. Warwickshire, in fact, though they made mistakes and dropped some catches – and the Sobers of this world simply must not be dropped as they dropped him – played entertaining cricket all season, yet no more than 15 116 people all told were inclined, or took the trouble, to come and see Championship games. It was yet another clear indication that even success almost to the point of winning the Championship and getting there by playing very watchable cricket was not sufficient to bring the crowds back in mid-week, and that change of habits, including the five-day week, as well as dull play (which might have led to the change in the first instance, of course) was largely responsible for the decline of the three-day game.

That success was not the sole criterion was also borne out by the fact that their home games in the John Player League, in which Warwickshire had their worst season, attracted just over 1000 spectators fewer, 13 743, than the Championship games, though the Gillette Cup, in which they reached the semi-final did bring its own shared reward.

After a bye in the first round of the Cup, Warwickshire entertained one of the Minor County sides, Lincolnshire, for whom the once-great Ramadhin was playing. But it was another bowler, a former Lincolnshire player, too, in McVicker, who, somewhat unkindly against his old county, took the bowling honours with five for 26, including the hat trick, and won the match award. Kanhai took the batting honours with a brilliant 126, he and 'Mike' Smith – with an adventurously made 88 not out, in which in one eventful over from Plaskitt, he was dropped twice and hit three fours – putting on 157, a record stand for the third wicket in Gillette Cup cricket. Obviously Ramadhin had no terrors for the batsmen on this occasion.

A win by 95 runs over Hampshire at Edgbaston in the third round took Warwickshire into the semi-final for the fifth time in nine years. Jameson celebrated his 30th birthday with what J. M. Solan described as 'a gift of an innings' of 96, which made him man-of-the-match – by now Warwickshire players had won fifteen such awards – and despite a fighting 69 by Barry Richards, Hampshire could not get the better of Gibbs and Ibadulla.

The semi-final against Kent was at Canterbury and for the first time the Club chartered a plane to take supporters to a Warwickshire match – at a cost of £10 a head. They formed part of a record crowd for the ground of 15 000 and it was a pity they did not receive a better reward for their trouble and expense. The start of the match was delayed for two hours and fifty minutes by overnight rain, some of which got under the covers and made the wicket soft and easy. Then Kent, whom Warwickshire had beaten comfortably in the Championship at Edgbaston only a few days before, batted for all the rest of the day.

They were aided at the start by some misdirected bowling from Blenkiron, who, although he took four wickets in his 12 overs, conceded an average of more than 4 runs an over – 51. This was one of the few matches in which Brown played and it was felt that it would probably be better if he bowled all his overs in succession. After a pain-killing injection he did so and did not seem in any discomfort. But it was no pitch for fast bowlers. He did not take a wicket and 40 runs were scored off him.

Had it not been for Gibbs who, coming on later, had a drier ball on which he could get a better grip and took three wickets for 9 runs in his last fifteen balls, Kent would probably have scored more than the total of 238 which they reached in just two balls short of their sixty-over ration. The imperturbable Luckhurst was the chief architect of the innings with 84 and received the man-of-the-match award.

Warwickshire had one over before bad light stopped play on the Wednesday evening and the match was continued on the Thursday, a day best forgotten from Warwickshire's point of view. With the single exception of Jameson, whose 48 included six desperately-hit boundaries, not one of Warwickshire's batsmen showed determination, technical skill, or the cricket *nous*, to overcome the problems of a pitch which, under the influence of some sun, was playing a few tricks, the ball kicking occasionally and coming through at an uneven pace and height – though not so unplayably as Warwickshire's largely inept batting would have led one to believe. Even Kanhai seemed hopelessly at sea to such an extent that he was in while thirteen overs were bowled yet scored only 1 run. Kent did not even call on Underwood, the bowler best suited to the conditions, until seven wickets were down, Warwickshire being dismissed for a mere 109 runs in only 44 overs.

One could not help wondering how far Warwickshire's disappointing display could be attributed to the custom of covering wickets to safeguard gates, so that batsmen got hardly any chance to learn how to contend with what used to be natural hazards in a country with a climate such as ours. It was another indication that one of the great arts of cricket, which all the masters had to learn in their day, had been almost lost, so that spectators rarely, if ever, had the chance to see one of the sights of cricket – a duel between great bad-wicket batsmen like Hobbs or Sutcliffe, and masters of slow left-hand spin such as Verity of Yorkshire, or Parker of Gloucestershire.

The other semi-final between Lancashire and Gloucestershire at Old Trafford proved to be one of the most astonishing cricket matches played since the war – indeed, there can never have been anything like it. To begin with there were no fewer than 35 000 people on the ground and the game went on until nearly 9 p.m. when the lights were on in the adjoining railway station. The match will stand out in the memories of those who saw it, even on television, for that incredible match-winning innings of only 26 not out by Hughes, who hit Mortimore for 6, 4, 2, 2,

4, 6 in one over. 'If I can see them I can hit them,' he told his skipper, Jackie Bond, and he did, though Mortimore should never have been kept on in such a situation. The one bowler the wise captain does not have bowling when someone is hitting at everything like this, as Hughes had to do if Lancashire were to win, is a slow off-spinner, no matter how good he may be normally.

After that, Lancashire certainly deserved to win the final at Lord's, resplendent in sunshine and with a capacity crowd; though again the match ended in the gloaming, turning this time on a superb, but positively sinful, diving catch by Bond just when Asif Iqbal had the bit between his teeth and looked like winning the match for Kent. It was all splendid cricket.

Although Warwickshire did so poorly in the John Player League, they were in a position in both their last two matches against Essex and Worcestershire to influence who won the title. But they had their moments before that. Some of them came when Kanhai hit the fastest century of the season in fifty-eight minutes against Northants. The crowd of 1500 had to wait two hours for the game to start because of rain and Kanhai began modestly enough, for him, with 50 in forty-nine minutes. Then he really cut loose, the second 50 coming in an incredible nine minutes in which he hit Sarfraz for 28 in one over – 6, 4, 6, 0, 6, 6. Altogether he had eight sixes in his 112 and there were thirteen altogether in the match; no wonder the crowd loved it all. 'I know it was a Sunday,' J. M. Solan wrote, 'but what a Sunday.'

Unfortunately I did not see those hits, but if any were better than the six Sobers put through the sightscreen off Hemmings in the Sunday League match with Notts I should have been surprised. So perfect was the timing that the stroke seemed almost effortless. Blenkiron's two enormous blows off Taylor, one of which cleared the Rea stand and the other hit the ironwork, seemed like the labours of Hercules by comparison.

Controversies over the interpretation of the rules in the John Player League, following curtailment of overs and batting time, drew attention to the need to clarify them, or to provide umpires and/or scorers and adjudicators with portable computers. There was a quite fantastic game between Warwickshire and Somerset at Edgbaston when there was even some doubt about how many runs Warwickshire needed to win after a stoppage caused by rain, and Alec Hastilow, the adjudicator, had to go out on the field in an effort to sort things out.

Three Warwickshire players were run out in the last over of the game (though the umpires later ruled that one of them had been stumped), feats of self-destruction in the frantic scramble for runs which can be compared only with the achievement of Blenkiron in being run out while attempting a fourth run in the Gillette Cup semi-final. This was an astonishing match in several other respects. Jameson was out in the nineties for the fifth time and the usually safe Barber, at long leg, dropped Close no fewer than three times, which was carrying generosity to ridiculous lengths. It was the last game for Warwickshire of a player who, on his day, was one of the most effective of modern batsmen. Leslie Deakins was fond of citing him as a batsman who disproved the theorists who regarded it as essential for a man to play three-day cricket if he was to be a success as a Test player. For Barber the one-day game proved a happy release from the dry run-accumulating atmosphere of the county game. In the seven seasons he played for Warwickshire he scored nearly 6000 runs, averaging almost 30, and took 197 wickets, but, as with all the cricketers most entertaining to watch, it was the manner rather than the mathematics of his playing that will be remembered.

Worcestershire were also involved in mid-field conferences both at Derby and at Cardiff, where the Glamorgan captain had to seek clarification of a point from the scorers, and by the end of the season the situation at the top of the table had become so complicated that before they met Warwickshire at Dudley, Worcestershire sought guidance from Lord's as to their exact position. There some mathematical genius worked out that if they got four points to tie with Essex, Worcestershire had to score at 5·67 runs an over to go ahead. They got Warwickshire out for 126 and thus had to make 127 within 17·5 overs to beat the Essex scoring rate by three-thousandths of a run, and they did it with two balls to spare. To such mathematical niceties – or absurdities, according to how one regarded the game – had cricket descended.

Two men who turned the scale for Worcestershire were D'Oliveira, with a spell of three wickets in seven balls, and Ron Headley with an innings of 58. No wonder he said later that cricket had been given the 'kiss of life' by the one-day game. The 9000 people who paid £1500 to see this computer-calculated game would doubtless agree with him, but there were others who were tempted to cry halt and ask: 'Is this cricket?'

This was Worcestershire's last match and it put them four points ahead of Lancashire, winners in the two previous seasons, who could still overtake them if they beat Glamorgan, for they had a superior scoring rate. This, however, they failed to do, so it was Worcestershire's title and they completely clinched it by winning the forty-overs match to which Lancashire challenged them at Old Trafford. Their success was a nice parting gift for their secretary, Joe Lister, to take with him to his new job with Yorkshire in succession to the retiring John Nash.

Worcestershire gained £1800 during the season from forty-overs cricket, which was such a success nationally – attendances rose by five per cent to over 300 000, bringing £75 000 through the turnstiles – that John Player renewed their sponsorship for a further three years.

But there ought surely to be some simplification of the scoring system. For a side to win a title by ·0037 of a run is a state of affairs to which a once noble game should never be reduced, for gate money or anything else. As Michael Blair commented in *The Birmingham Post*:

How absurd. Who would have thought that cricket would go computer-crazy? An electronic calculator had to be brought in to decide how Worcestershire had to beat Warwickshire to get above Essex . . . What if the machine had not been there? Who would have worked out the sum? Could it be that cricket will soon have to appoint its captains from among the senior wranglers at Oxford? Of course, it is all so silly, so unfair and so unnecessary.

Mention of Oxford is a reminder that one of the direct results of the creation of the National Cricket Association was a request to the Warwickshire Club, in conjunction with the British Universities Sports Federation and the Warwickshire Cricket Association, to stage a cricket tournament at Edgbaston bringing the eight major universities in the United Kingdom in a knock-out competition spread over four days.

Courtaulds were approached and readily undertook to sponsor the event as well as providing a very beautiful and original trophy created by a member of their design staff. The tournament took place in July and the trophy was won by the Universities Athletic Union team, which defeated Cambridge University in the final. Thus was begun what it was hoped might prove a fascinating annual competition serving to bring together players from the old traditional universities and 'the Red Bricks', to the lasting benefit and enjoyment of both and of cricket generally.

The competition afforded one novelty in the person of a member of the Oxford University side who had such long hair that he wore a Red Indian-style headband, perhaps the only device that would have kept it out of his eyes. It was interesting to speculate what his captain would have said had he proffered as an excuse for missing a catch that his hair got in his eyes.

It was no doubt a relief to statistically-plagued John Player League adjudicators to learn that the new League Cup competition which, it was announced, yet another tobacco company, Benson and Hedges, was to sponsor in 1972 to the extent of £80 000, the largest amount yet (later to be increased to £90 000 and £100 000 by 1976), would be played under far less complicated rules. It was to be on a zonal basis, with five teams in each of four zones, which introduced an element of regional competition. Each county would play four zonal matches – Warwickshire against Worcestershire, Leicestershire, Northants and Cambridge University for instance – with the two leading teams in each zone qualifying for the quarter-finals. From that point onwards it would be a knock-out competition with the final at Lord's in July.

Winners of the competition were to receive £2500; the runners-up £1250; the losing semi-finalists £625 each and the losing quarter-finalists £400 each. Winners of all the forty preliminary matches in the four zones would get £150 each. There were also special awards of £250 to 'the team of the week' and 'man of the week' awards of £25 in zonal matches, £75 in the semi-finals and £100 in the final. The prizes totalled £15 000 a year, the rest of the sponsorship money being divided among the twenty teams taking part, about £3000 each.

This latest example of sponsorship brought the total amount of money being put into cricket from these outside sources, mostly from tobacco companies, to £1 000 000 over the next three years, a far cry indeed from the days, almost another lifetime ago, it seemed, when wealthy benefactors offered gifts to players who made the fastest century of the season, or hit the most sixes. It was a far cry even to when Rothman's began it all by sponsoring the International Cavaliers, and the M.C.C. took a leaf out of their book by accepting Gillette's offer of a cup competition, though that idea, of course, went back many years.

It was this state of affairs that provoked one of the most respected commentators on the game, J. M. Kilburn, of *The Yorkshire Post*, to write in an article headed 'Care for Cricket,' which appeared in the winter annual of *The Cricketer*, that 'cricket has turned to the money-lenders', the truth of which even D. G. Clark admitted in a following issue, though he added that the commercial sponsors and the TV authorities would not care for the comparison. He then went on to point out, however, that if public interest in, and support for, the game declined beyond a certain point, all sponsorship would cease, or be materially reduced.

The one activity in the game no one had so far rushed to sponsor was the County Championship, although there had been nibbles, such as taking over financial responsibility for individual county matches, a growing practice. But would any form of sponsorship, without changing the Championship out of all recognition, make it appealing or effective enough to regain the affections of the cricket public? Sad though it might be, the fact had to be faced that, except on special occasions, the only spectators who were still faithful to it were the last hard-core remnant of the retired and pensioned followers of the game, the only ones who could still be found sparsely, if regularly, populating the corners of pavilions up and down the country and exchanging reminiscences of the good old days when cricket really was cricket.

So far sponsors had been scrupulous about not interfering directly with the structure of the game, or with how it should be played if not run; though indirectly the fact that they offered financial support for a particular cup, league or any other form of competition there may still be to come, might well have had an influence on what kind of cricket was played and when. After all, they were unlikely to go on putting up money if they did not think they were getting value for it. As it was, one wondered sometimes what their shareholders thought about it.

Certainly cricket as a whole would have been in a sorry plight but for their support, which could well be the only way in which even a remnant of the three-day game has a glimmering of a hope of being preserved, even though the players themselves cling to it; but for that matter it could be that even Test Matches will have to undergo some changes if they are to continue attracting public support.

In the autumn of 1971 Warwickshire took a step towards solving the problem of finding a wicketkeeper for when Alan Smith was away on other duties, and at the same time strengthened their batting, by engaging Deryck Murray, the West Indies Test wicketkeeper, who, since he had first approached the Club some years earlier, had played some county cricket for Notts and was taking a course in industrial economics at Nottingham University. He had first toured England in 1963, having thirty-four victims in the five Tests; had captained Cambridge University in 1966; and played in the England v. the Rest of the World series the previous summer.

Shortly afterwards they added another fast bowler in Bob Willis, of Surrey and England, to their strength. Their interest in him obviously stemmed partly from anxiety about the future of David Brown, who, during the autumn, underwent an operation on a torn cartilage and for the removal of a cyst from his left shoulder which had been the cause of his absences during the season.

Brown was awarded a benefit in 1973, rewards which Warwickshire have usually given after ten to fifteen years' service. The next three players in line were Brown (ten seasons), Jameson (eleven seasons, 1974) and Amiss (eleven seasons, 1975). Up to the end of the 1972 season Brown had taken 620 wickets for 23·11 runs each; Jameson had scored 11 832 runs for an average of 30·81; and Amiss 12 287, average 36·03. It had been agreed that the Club would not allocate a John Player League match for a benefit.

The interest shown in Willis by Warwickshire and other clubs prompted a statement by Jack Bannister, then secretary of the Cricketers' Association, to the effect that some counties in seeking Surrey's permission to approach Willis, as Warwickshire did, for instance, were still observing rules which had been changed in 1929; and that it was no longer necessary for a county interested in a player to seek his county's permission to approach him, but merely to inform them that they were doing so. Warwickshire, however, said they preferred to observe the code of conduct. One notable achievement of the Association, with its

Above: Man of the Series. 1972 was a season for Dennis Amiss to remember for he won the 'Man of the Series' award for his performances in the three one-day matches played against Australia. He is here seen being congratulated by Ray Steele, manager of the Australian team. On the left is Mr Kenneth Usherwood, chairman of the Prudential Assurance Co. Ltd which sponsored the series.

Below: Championship Commemorated. During the celebrations on winning the County Championship and other successes in 1972, George Paine, the former Warwickshire player (centre) presented to the Club a model he had designed and made of the Bear and Ragged Staff emblem mounted on a ball and plinth on which the success was recorded, much to the admiration of Alan Smith, the captain (left) and C. C. Goodway (chairman), right.

Above: The Under-25 Champions. Middlesex won the Under-25 County Cricket Competition, sponsored by Warwickshire Supporters' Association in 1972, and after the final at Edgbaston they received the Association's trophy from Edgar N. Hiley, its chairman (on the left) and presentation ties from C. C. Goodway, chairman of the Club, on the right.

Deryck Murray holds aloft the Courtauld Trophy won by the University Athletics Union side which he captained in the competition at Edgbaston in 1971 organised in conjunction with the National Cricket Association and the British Universities Sports Federation. Fourth from the left is another Warwickshire player, John Gray.

Above left: Rohan Kanhai, captain of the West Indies touring team of 1973 and one of four Warwickshire players who played for their country, with the Wisden Trophy awarded to the winners of the series.

Above right: The body leans beautifully into and over the stroke as Kanhai plays an off-drive. The wicket-keeper is E. W. Jones, of Glamorgan.

Below: This must be one of the most remarkable cricket photographs ever taken. It shows two Cambridge University batsmen, P. Edmonds and P. Johnson, reaching desperately for the same crease, where Deryck Murray, the Warwickshire wicket-keeper, playing for U.A.U. obviously ran both of them out, but it was Johnson, on the right, who 'walked'. The incident occurred in the final of the Courtauld Trophy.

Top: Past and present mingle in this Pavilion balcony trio – Alan Oakman, senior coach, Canon J. H. Parsons, and E. J. ('Tiger') Smith.

Bottom: Warwickshire's three Championship winning teams are represented respectively in this group enjoying a talk together – E. J. ('Tiger') Smith (1911), Dennis Amiss (1972) and Tom Pritchard (1951).

Opposite: Dennis Amiss, Warwickshire and later England opening batsman and the first Warwickshire-born player to score a century in a Test Match at home or abroad.

Top left: S. S. Harkness, Assistant Secretary (Administration) and Treasurer.

Top right: J. M. A. Marshall, former Warwickshire player and one of the Club's country representatives, covering Warwick and Warwick School.

Bottom left: Derief Taylor, coach, guide, philosopher and friend to Edgbaston's younger generation of players.

Bottom right: A. ('Tony') Haycock, membership and cricket secretary.

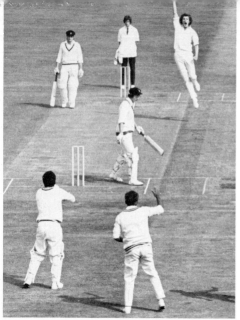

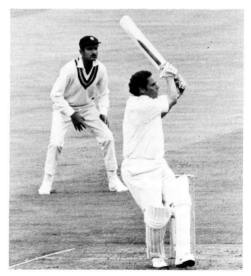

Top left: R. G. D. (Bob) Willis wound up the 1972 season with his best performance for the county up to then – eight for 44 against Derbyshire including the hat-trick. This victim was caught at the wicket.

Top right: 'Billy' Ibadulla in a rare moment of repose. He was always in the game as batsman, bowler or fielder.

Bottom left: A six from the moment it left the bat – Rohan Kanhai in the aggressive mood with which he so often delighted Warwickshire supporters – and many other spectators.

Bottom right: John Jameson making a big hit to leg during the highest score of his career, 231, against the Indians at Edgbaston in 1971.

Top: Championship Winners 1972. Back row: B. W. Thomas
(physiotherapist), W. Blenkiron, N. M. McVicker, J. Whitehouse, D. L.
Murray, J. A. Jameson, R. G. D. Willis, D. L. Amiss, S. J. Rouse,
A. Kallicharran, W. Tidy, P. Pike (scorer). Front row: R. Kanhai, L. T.
Deakins (general secretary), M. J. K. Smith, Lieut-General Sir Oliver Leese
(President), A. C. Smith (captain), C. C. Goodway (chairman), D. J.
Brown, A. S. M. Oakman (senior coach), L. R. Gibbs.

Bottom: Pavilion Reconstruction. The Pavilion at Edgbaston as it appeared
in 1970, a compound of the old – the original structure was built in 1886 –
and the new. It has been reconstructed in three phases at a total estimated
cost of £100,000.

Above: An all-clean-bowled hat-trick. Bob Willis brought off a remarkable hat-trick against Yorkshire in the John Player League match at Edgbaston in June 1973 – Richard Hutton (middle stump), Bairstow (leg stump) and Carrick (middle stump again).

Right: Princess Anne at Edgbaston. H.R.H. Princess Anne visited Edgbaston on July 28th, 1973, for the Ladies' World Cup Final between England and Australia. Here the Lord Mayor of Birmingham, Councillor Mrs Margery Brown, is presenting to her Mr C. C. Goodway, chairman of the Club, behind whom is Mr Aidan Crawley, President of the M.C.C.

Above: A Warwickshire reunion in the dressing room at The Oval after the West Indies had beaten England in the first Test in 1973. England's Dennis Amiss joins his four West Indian colleagues – Lance Gibbs, Alvin Kallicharran, Rohan Kanhai, the tourists' captain, and Deryck Murray – in a champagne toast.

Opposite top: Warwickshire's chairman, Cyril Goodway, welcomes Rachael Heyhoe, the captain, and the England Women's Cricket Team to Edgbaston for the final of the World Cup with Australia at Edgbaston in 1973.

Opposite bottom: International Sextet. Six Test cricketers were captured in one picture from the match between Warwickshire and Yorkshire at Edgbaston in 1973. It shows the dismissal of Boycott, who played a ball on to his chest from which it rebounded and was snatched up just before it touched the turf by M. J. K. Smith's left hand. The other players are Amiss, Jameson, Kanhai and Murray.

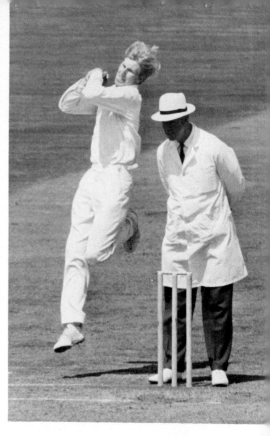

Above: Railings, steps, seats and canopies make geometric patterns in this photograph of the Ansell Stand, named after the prime founder of the Warwickshire Club.

Opposite top left: Charlie Grove, one of the hardest triers as a bowler Warwickshire ever had. On Philip Pike's retirement in 1973, he took over as scorer.

Opposite top right: Youth in Action. A Warwickshire bowler of promise, Peter Lewington, off-spinner.

Opposite bottom left: A study of John Whitehouse, one of the most promising batting discoveries of the 1970's. An accountant by profession, he gave up cricket for a year in 1974 to concentrate on his final examinations.

Opposite bottom right: Alvin Kallicharran, Warwickshire's latest acquisition from the West Indies, who soon proved himself to be one of the most exciting left-hand batsmen in the game.

Opposite: On the social side – the splendidly appointed ballroom and dining room of the Pavilion Suite.

Right: The forecourt garden with its flower beds, shrubs, coloured umbrellas and bar has a most inviting aspect. It was a project introduced by Edmund King during his chairmanship.

Below: The Committee Room in the pavilion at Edgbaston. It was formerly a bedroom of the groundsman's flat and in it was born Len Bates, one of the finest batsmen who ever played for the county. When he died in 1971 his ashes were scattered on the ground.

The Committee Room balcony.

100 per cent membership of 300 players, was to get the counties to agree in principle to a group pension scheme for its members, maturing at age 40.

There was one major change in the rules which home-grown players certainly welcomed. In recent years there had undoubtedly been a tendency by some clubs to regard every overseas player as an incipient genius, with the result that in the last five years the number of them registered in this country grew from 37 to 65. Considering that there are no more than about 200 men playing first-class cricket in England at any one time, this was a fairly high proportion.

Moreover, enough of them had been given middle-order batting places to cause anxiety in some quarters – notably to the selectors in the person of Alec Bedser, their chairman – about England's deficiencies in this aspect of the game. So the rule was changed, making the residential qualifying period ten years instead of five for all but the two overseas players already allowed each county. Ten years, though, seemed rather a long period considering how comparatively brief is the playing life of a professional cricketer.

During the autumn and winter of 1971 Australia's Cricket Board of Control not only followed England's example of cancelling a South African tour, but took a leaf out of our book in substituting for it a series with a Rest of the World XI, which included Kanhai. He played some fine innings, but was literally hamstrung by an injury which kept him out of some games. He also had the unusual experience of encountering a colleague, Billy Ibadulla, in the unaccustomed role of captain of Tasmania, where he was coaching.

Again the irony of the series was the fact that the Rest of the World side at one point included no fewer than four South Africans – the Pollock brothers, Hylton Ackerman and Tony Greig – but those who had all along thought that continuing to meet the South Africans at cricket was the best way of getting their Government to mollify its apartheid policy found little support for their point of view in an interview given by Peter Pollock on his arrival in Melbourne.

Certainly he gave out the good news that 'the Government has relaxed its attitude towards mixed racial sport and the future is a lot brighter than a lot of people think', but could anyone doubt that it was partly the effect of cancelling tours and the general blacklisting of South Africa's sportsmen from international competition which had helped to bring about this more tolerant attitude?

The opening of the 1971–2 football season brought the first major change in the Supporters' Association pool since its inception. The cost of the weekly entry was increased from the old 1s (5p) to 10p, but this gave automatic participation in nine pools compared with five previously, so that although the stake was increased so were the chances of winning a prize. The result was a slight decline in membership, but financially the position was much better.

One individual to whom some regular spectators at Edgbaston might well have been willing to see apartheid applied was the gentleman, reputedly from Worcestershire, who blew blasts on a hunting horn whenever he thought applause was called for. By comparison, transistor radios seemed comparatively innocuous. Disappointment was expressed in Committee that no action had been taken to silence him, but no official complaint had apparently been received and when an attendant tried to silence a transistor the people in its vicinity asked for it to be kept on as they were enjoying it.

Doubtless the blower of the hunting horn and the transistor fans would all have been thoroughly at home at a pop festival, a request for which was made by a commercial group in 1972. Mercifully the Committee turned this down. To some that would indeed have been the end.

Momentous Year
(1972)

IT had been planned that close of play in this history should be the end of the 1971 season, but 1972 proved to be such a momentous year that the story would have been lamentably incomplete without another chapter, so publication was delayed until it could be added and statistics brought up to date. In this respect at least the present author has been much more fortunate than his predecessors, neither of whose accounts was lucky enough to coincide with a rising tide in the Club's affairs which led on to such good fortune.

What, then, occurred to make 1972 what the President was happy to describe as 'a great season'? First, Alan Smith, with the assistance of M.J.K., crowned his fifth season as captain by leading an undefeated side to the third County Championship in the Club's history, and one can leave it to posterity to decide whether winning the title or doing it undefeated – with all due respect to Oxford University their win by two wickets in the very first game of the season is irrelevant in this connection – was the more meritorious performance.

Secondly, the side reached the final of the Gillette Cup for the fourth time and were beaten only after a superb innings by Clive Lloyd, of Lancashire and the West Indies; thirdly, despite poor weather in the early rounds, Warwickshire got to the semi-final of the new Benson and Hedges competition; fourthly, the Under-25 XI also figured in the semi-final of their competition, which Warwickshire had inspired and which the Supporters' Association had sponsored, as well as providing a unique trophy. It should also be recorded that the county's second eleven finished third in their Championship table and that the Club and Ground eleven went through the season without being defeated once in fifteen matches. Only in the John Player League, in which success persistently eluded the Club, were performances not at top level, though even here there was an improvement to eleventh position in the final table.

The annual report for 1972 thought the lack of success in the John Player League was 'doubly unfortunate' because it is so popular, especially to followers of the game in the cities, and added this comment: 'It is essential, therefore, that the team should make every effort to establish a better approach and pattern to its play in this Sunday competition, for if they did, it is reasonable to assume that they would command strong public support,' words later reinforced by speakers at the annual meeting in April 1973, when there were rueful reflections that in good weather as many people could be attracted to Edgbaston on a single Sunday afternoon as saw the County Championship games in an entire season.

Naturally the annual report also extended 'warm congratulations' to Alan Smith, who had led the side 'with his customary zeal and marked ability . . . Captaining a county side these days', the report added, 'is an intense and demanding occupation, which few men can hope satisfactorily to contend with, and at the same time to achieve results . . . and in particular in 1972 he showed rare courage in some of the decisions he had to take.'

Two of the most remarkable reversals of form, one up, one down, which any county can have experienced, also made the season noteworthy. Amiss, who could not command a place in the first eleven at the start of the year, blossomed out as an opening batsman and was eventually named as England's Man-of-the-Series in the first one-day international matches with Australia; but unhappily Jameson, who, the previous season, had seemed certain to figure as one of England's opening pair for many years to come, was the victim of one of those inexplicable losses of form which occasionally afflict the best of batsmen.

On a happier note, 'Mike' Smith, after six years in the wilderness, was recalled to the England side for three Tests, and Lance Gibbs was not only voted Cricketers' Cricketer for 1971 by the Cricketers' Association, but figured as one of *Wisden*'s Five Cricketers of the Year.

Administratively, there was a change at the helm, Edmund King deciding that ten years was long enough for one man to remain as chairman and relinquishing the office in favour of his deputy, Cyril Goodway. Happily, he remained a member of the Committee, from which, however, 'Tom' Dollery resigned, thus giving up his last office with the Club after an association lasting forty years, although, of course, he remained an honorary life member.

Warwickshire won the Championship by such a large margin – 36 points – and put the issue beyond any reasonable doubt well before the end of the season, that their success did not, alas, stimulate the kind of interest which showed itself in increased attendances at matches. For most of the time Gloucestershire were their only serious rivals, but as Warwickshire's winning impetus increased, Gloucestershire's declined, and in the end Kent overtook them and finished second. Such normally serious challengers as Yorkshire, Middlesex, Surrey and Lancashire were ultimately well down the table, and whereas Warwickshire would perhaps have been rather flattered had they won the title in 1971 there was no question about their mastery in 1972. 'Day in and day out', wrote E. W. Swanton in *The Daily Telegraph*, 'there has scarcely been a better side to watch,' a comment which must have pleased the captain, who was surely not alone in thinking that Warwickshire played the most positive cricket of any side in the country – and that despite losing the toss in sixteen out of twenty matches and electing to field in two of the other four games.

It was generally agreed that it was primarily a team effort, no matter which of the two Smiths was leading or Kanhai or Brown, both of whom also acted as captain on occasion. 'A.C.', because of his England selector and other commitments and a leg injury which plagued him during the latter half of the season, was absent not only from six Championship games, but did not play in a single round of the Gillette Cup competition and was able to turn out in only four out of sixteen Player League games. Nevertheless, despite the differences in temperament between the captain and his deputy, their approach to the game was identical – to win in the most attractive manner possible – so, despite the inevitable changes in leadership, the team always remained a team, not a collection of individuals.

Individually, Kanhai, with seven centuries in first-class matches, and Amiss, with five, both had wonderful seasons and Kallicharran fulfilled his early promise. 'Mike' Smith had a poor season for him, making only 1107 runs in all first-class matches – 743 in the County Championship – and scoring only one century, but he did more than enough to take him to the pinnacle of having scored more runs in all first-class matches than any other Warwickshire player, W. G. Quaife included; his grand total at the end of the season being 36 722. His record of 541 catches in all first-class matches was another reason why his name will always remain high in the annals of Warwickshire cricket.

None of the bowlers came anywhere near taking 100 wickets, a feat which will become increasingly difficult as the programme of three-or-more-day games is reduced. McVicker was the most successful with sixty-three, but no fewer than six bowlers took twenty or more wickets, which emphasised once more what a co-operative effort the team's success was.

Heading the bowling averages was Alan Smith, who was largely freed for the work he has always loved best on the cricket field – bowling, with that windmill action of his – by the arrival of Murray, who, because he had not played for his previous county, Notts, for three years and was not registered with them, was given immediate registration for Warwickshire. This made it possible to field what A. C. Smith described as a five-one-five combination – five batsmen, a batsman-wicketkeeper, and five bowlers – four seamers and a spinner.

David Brown's shoulder, to everyone's relief but mostly to his own, stood up to a fairly full programme of matches, though he suffered from an ankle injury late in the season. It was only to be expected that after such a long lay-off he would have lost some pace, but that was supplied by Willis when he was finally released to play for his new county on 1 July. He then took twenty-five wickets in the Championship, another fifteen in the John Player League and he also bowled well in the Gillette Cup, especially the final when he was very economical even against Lloyd at his most aggressive. The fact that his wickets in first-class cricket cost him 28·67 runs each was due, not to wildness or inaccuracy, but to the fact that he was nearly always bowling to an attacking field which inevitably meant more runs if the ball penetrated the inner ring.

There was something of a battle royal between the Club and the Registration sub-committee of the Test and County Cricket Board and the Cricket Council over his registration. First, the sub-committee decided that Willis could be specially registered, but only with effect from 1 July, which meant a two-month qualifying period. The position was made all the more unsatisfactory because the sub-committee declined to give any reasons for its decision, or to state why it had differentiated between the cases of Tom Cartwright (who, although Warwickshire still wished to retain his services, as Surrey said they did Willis's, had been allowed to play for Somerset without any delay) and R. M. H. Cottam, of Hampshire, who was given leave to play for his new county, Northants, two weeks earlier than Willis.

The Club appealed to the Cricket Council, but after a five-hour hearing at which Warwickshire were represented by A. C. Smith and Leslie Deakins (who were twice asked to retire, as was M. J. C. Allom, chairman of the sub-committee) and at which they refuted any suggestion that they had not wished to retain Cartwright, the decision, as announced by F. R. Brown, President of the M.C.C., who presided as chairman of the Council, went against them.

Naturally the Club was 'bitterly disappointed with the outcome of the appeal', as Sir Oliver Leese put it at the annual meeting, and it brought a call from the Committee for a drastic revision of the rules governing such cases – normally twelve months' registration was required unless it was considered in the best interests of cricket and of the players to waive them – and for them to be brought into line with the modern requirements of the game.

The Club's view was that although no one wanted to see a transfer system, with its astronomical fees, such as afflicted football to be applied to cricket, players should not be prevented from playing for the county of their choice, provided the rights of the club they wished to leave were adequately safeguarded.

Accordingly the Club submitted a memorandum to the Registration Sub-Committee of the Test and County Cricket Board advocating that 'in the best interests of English cricket' the county qualification system, based on birth and residence, should be abolished, but that the registration of players for their respective counties should be retained.

Warwickshire's views were summarised under six headings – that birth qualification should apply only insofar as the England XI is concerned and that only a man born in the United Kingdom, or, if abroad, of English parentage, may play for England; that in order to ensure the standard of the England XI in future all counties competing in the County Championship must play in all matches at least nine players holding such a qualification for England; that any player born in England, irrespective of current residence, or the nationality of his parents, should be free at any time to register for any county cricket club of his choice, and that any county club should be free at any time to approach any cricketer with an offer of an engagement, provided he was not already engaged by another county; that any player approached in this way should be offered engagement for a set period which should be notified to the Test and County Cricket Board as and when the player is registered, and that at the end of each season the Board should circulate a list of those players whose contracts had expired and not been renewed so that other counties should approach them; that any contracted player not wishing to remain with his registered county, may present a case to the Board when his contract expired seeking registration with another county, though generally his request would be granted only on the score of restricted opportunity, or remuneration inappropriate to his standing in the game; and, finally, that all cases disputed should be submitted to the Registration Sub-Committee, sitting with a representative of the Cricketers' Association, who should be the sole and final arbiters.

Perhaps not surprisingly, the Registration Sub-Committee thought all this was too far-reaching for them to consider unless they were specifically briefed to do so, and they therefore suggested that if the Warwickshire Club felt sufficiently strongly it should submit a firm resolution to the full Board. This the Club decided to do, but had some difficulty in finding a seconder, so instead decided to submit a memorandum to all the counties calling for a special sub-committee to be set up to consider the whole matter. In this move they had Worcestershire's support.

The dispute also led to the Cricketers' Assocation holding a referendum of their members, and many of them took the view that the players concerned should miss part of the season. Later, however, the Association urged the appointment of a three-man commission to look into disputes between clubs and players before they came before the sub-committee.

It could have been argued that the loss of two months' first-class cricket in the case of so young a player as Willis – he was 22 at the time – was no great handicap, but it might well have cost him the chance of playing in the Tests against Australia. He had begun the year in what some people might have regarded, in the light of later events, as a rather unfeeling way by saying in a newspaper interview that he liked to frighten batsmen a bit: 'If you hit a bloke with the ball you're sorry afterwards, but I think you're entitled to fly a few around his ears.' This, of course, is the creed of all fast bowlers, particularly when pitches favour the bat.

Certainly he did that on not a few occasions, notably in only his second game for Warwickshire against Yorkshire at Headingley, when he forced some life out of the pitch and sent down what J. M. Solan, in *The Birmingham Post*, described as 'a nasty lifting ball' which hit Boycott, who had been having trouble with batting gloves of his own design, on the right hand with such force that the flesh of the top of the middle finger was separated from the bone and he had to have ten stitches put in it. The injury put him out of two Tests and several matches for his county.

John Whitehouse began his year on rather a different note, taking first place (equal) in the Order of Merit, Part 1 of the Final Examination of the Institute of Chartered Accountants of England and Wales and sharing equally the Robert Fletcher prize. In answer to those who wondered how he had managed to study so intensely as to achieve those honours as well as play cricket all the previous summer, the Nuneaton chartered accountant to whom he was articled told a reporter: 'He worked enormously hard in the winter of 1970–1.' It is a recipe that also pays on the cricket field, but despite the fact that his success in his profession should have taken a load off his shoulders, it was not reflected in his play during 1972, in which he scored well under 1000 runs. His form was doubtless affected because he was not able to play his preferred role as an opening batsman. Such are the vagaries of the game.

Before the playing season got under way, there were several financial matters to be disposed of, some favourable, some not so welcome. First came the announcement that the Prudential Assurance Company would sponsor to the extent of £30 000 the first three one-day matches to be played between England and Australia – £26 000 to the Test and

County Cricket Board, the first-class counties, the Minor Counties and the Universities; and the other £4000 to the winners of each match (£3000), £200 to each Man of the Match, and £200 to the player on each side contributing most to the series.

The not-so-welcome financial news came in the Club's annual report which disclosed that, despite an increase in income from £88 000 to £103 000, another record loss, this time of £30 000, £1000 more than in the previous year, had to be reported, plus a warning that there were no grounds for thinking the position would improve. Indeed, the report commented that 'one can visualise the day when figures such as were never dreamed of will be a regular feature of the accounts'.

Once more, however, realisation of astute investments brought in just over £20 000, reducing the overall deficit to just under £9000. The decline of interest in three-day cricket was shown in the fact that, even excluding players' salaries, it cost £13 000 to run and brought in only £3000, whereas income and expenditure for one-day cricket were just about evenly balanced.

Edmund King told the annual meeting that the costs of running any club were continually rising and while their policy was to field the best side in the country, in the best setting, and to remain a Test ground – the order in which he placed his priorities was reassuring – he could not honestly say they would be able to cover their costs very much, if at all.

He went on to answer a question which many people had asked – why Lancashire could produce a handsome profit. 'The answer', he said, 'is gates. Lancashire have a following which is far greater than anything in Birmingham. This is sad because it used not to be so.' Nevertheless, Mr King ended on a cheerful note. 'With the Australians here,' he said, 'I am optimistic about our finances, but it is genuine support through the gates that we want rather than sponsorship money, and the Committee believes that only a successful side will bring it.'

More pleasant reading as an appetiser to the home season was of the successes of Kallicharran in his native country against the New Zealanders. First, playing for Guyana under the captaincy of his Warwickshire team-mate, Lance Gibbs, he made 154, including fifteen fours, out of a total of 493 for four declared and followed this in the second innings with 51. Then when New Zealand batted, another Midlander-by-adoption, Glenn Turner, of Worcestershire, excelled this with 259.

Kallicharran was called on for the fourth Test and joined the select band of players who have made a century in their first international game – in this instance exactly 100 not out. He did not bat in the second innings, but in the last Test he made 101, hitting a six and thirteen fours, and in the second innings 18. His innings in the first Test was described by correspondents on the spot as easily the best of the match, despite the fact that he had to come in when the crowd was in a bottle-throwing mood after Clive Lloyd had been run out. Gibbs played in the first two Tests, but took only three wickets, though he had the free-scoring Turner missed off him at 47 when he went on to make 223 not out. After that Gibbs was dropped, though he was to find compensations when he returned home.

It was midway through April that Edmund King announced that he was retiring from the chairmanship after ten years' distinguished service in that office. The move was not unexpected, at least to members of the Committee to whom he had intimated the previous season that he wished to retire after another year. Happily he remained a member of the Committee as well as being appointed the ninth honorary life member of the Club, and he also retained his chairmanship of the finance and general purposes sub-committee of the Test and County Cricket Board, one of the numerous national bodies on which he had served with distinction, while later he was elected a member of the M.C.C. Committee. He himself proposed as his successor, Cyril Goodway, deputy chairman for the past ten years and another widely experienced cricket administrator, and that James McDowall should be the new vice-chairman, while at the same time continuing as honorary treasurer. These proposals were unanimously endorsed.

The Committee, of course, put on record its own appreciation of his 'wonderful record of service' to the Club and his part in finding solutions to many of the game's problems at both national and Club level. At the end of June members were able to pay their tribute at a dinner given in the Pavilion Suite by the Club and the Supporters' Association at which the President, Lieutenant-General Sir Oliver Leese, presided, and the M.C.C. was strongly represented by Lieutenant-Col. Lord Nugent, a past President of the M.C.C. and of the Surrey County Cricket Club; Mr S. C. Griffith, secretary; and Mr D. B. Carr and Mr J. A. Bailey, assistant secretaries. All the counties were represented.

Lord Nugent spoke of the high regard felt in all circles of cricket administration for Mr King, 'the most modest and charming of men' and acknowledging presentations of silver from the Committee and vice-presidents and furniture from the Supporters' Association, Mr King referred to his 'ten wonderful years' as chairman and said that 'despite those losses, which are so terrific and so regular, I rather like presenting them'. After the laughter had subsided, he recalled that Sir Oliver, when told of the biggest loss so far, remarked: 'You will probably get a better ovation than usual,' and he was absolutely right.

Mr King thanked the Committee, the administrative staff, especially Leslie Deakins ('He is never ruffled and is the embodiment of courtesy and everything he does is for cricket and Warwickshire cricket in particular'); the team ('No nicer crowd of chaps'); the groundsman,

Bernard Flack; Edgar Hiley and the Supporters' Association ('for all the lovely lolly'); the Press in general and *The Birmingham Post* and *The Birmingham Mail* in particular, and he especially commended to them his successor, Cyril Goodway.

The new chairman was born a Staffordshire man, at Smethwick, for whose club he played as a notable wicketkeeper-batsman for thirty-seven years and of which he is a past president and life member. He also played for the county of his birth before throwing in his lot with Warwickshire. One of the most experienced administrators in the game, his list of appointments at national and Warwickshire levels is extensive, but probably none has been dearer to him than the Warwickshire Old County Cricketers' Association which he helped to found and of which he is chairman and honorary secretary, with his wife, Wyn, as honorary organiser and assistant secretary.

A tacit acknowledgement of the place Jameson had earned in the hierarchy of cricket by his performances in the previous season was shown by his selection, first, for the Duke of Norfolk's XI in the opening fifty-overs match of the Australian tour at Arundel, but more so, of course, for the M.C.C. against them at Lord's, but he scored only moderately on both occasions and these innings seemed to set the pattern for him, not only in the early part of the county competition, but also for the rest of the season. In all first-class matches he played twenty-eight innings, but could make no more than 543 runs, with a highest score of only 78 and finishing with an average of just over 20. This compared with an aggregate of nearly 2000 in 1971 and an average of over 40.

He fared little better in the other games also and it was not long before Alan Smith tried another opening pair, bringing in Amiss who had also begun the season so indifferently that with Kallicharran in such good form he could not command a place in the first team. He, however, snapped out of whatever it was that was afflicting him and he never looked back after his promotion, largely fulfilling the promise which Warwickshire members had always been confident he possessed.

These two transformations of fortune apart, and the début of Willis, who had made an immediate impact by nearly bowling the second team to victory against Worcestershire, taking six wickets for 8 runs in 12·2 overs and working up a rare pace, it was the Australians who provided most of the season's early talking points, especially the bowling of Lillee, the fastest seen in this country for a good many summers, and the recall of 'Mike' Smith to the England side.

The tourists' visit to Edgbaston in August for the third one-day match with England produced record receipts for one day of £13 322, but the attendance of 17 000 was generally regarded as disappointing and something of a reflection on cricket's supporters, so-called, in the

587

city. It was also variously blamed on TV, the weather and too high charges for admission, vigorously criticised by Alec Hastilow at the annual meeting, for none of which, of course, the Warwickshire Club was responsible.

The match with the county in June had provided a brilliant rescuing century by Walters, one of whose hits off Lewington over the Rea Bank Stand must rank among the biggest ever made on the ground. It evoked in Jack Fingleton, writing in *The Sunday Times*, remembrance of things past – Jack Parsons's onslaught on Scott, the West Indian slow bowler, in 1928. Fingleton also had some complimentary things to say about Rouse's bowling – 'he runs only fourteen paces and bowls faster than some who run thrice as far' – and about Edgbaston itself: 'This is a lovely ground, with superb appointments for the crowd and it is sad it hasn't a Test this coming series.'

'Mike' Smith's recall was obviously inspired by weaknesses in England's middle-order batting and by his unbeaten 78 against the tourists at Edgbaston, which was suddenly ended by a violent storm, with Warwickshire only 108 runs short of their target of 336 and with five wickets in hand, a situation pregnant with possibilities as they used to say. It was ironic that in this game Jameson played one of his best innings of the season, 44, marked by some typical driving, while Amiss made his bid with a 45, but only Smith got a place in the team for any of the full Tests. No England batsman particularly distinguished himself in the first Test at Old Trafford, a low scoring match in which Smith contributed 10 and 34. Was there any significance in the fact that he was out on both occasions to Lillee, once lbw and the second time caught at the wicket?

In mid-June Warwickshire wrote another piece of history – they had their first sponsored Championship match, the steel firm, Schoeller-Bleckmann Steels (Great Britain) Ltd, of Oldbury, taking over the game with Middlesex, and being so well pleased with the results that they repeated the experiment with the Essex game in 1973. Although the first day was rather spoiled by rain Warwickshire marked the occasion with their first win of the season and it also brought a turn of fortune to Amiss, who won the £100 the firm offered for the man-of-the-match. It was the first of several such awards.

During the three days the firm entertained no fewer than 180 of its customers and there remained little doubt that as more firms see the benefits to be obtained in image-making, sales promotion and publicity from sponsoring Championship games, other matches would be sponsored. This game marked the first appearance in the senior side of Murray, who had finished his examinations at Nottingham University.

It was 'Mike' Smith's turn to play a rescue innings in the second Test at Lord's, which will always be known as 'Massie's Match', for the

Australian took eight wickets in each innings – for 84 and 58. England would have been out for a good deal fewer than 272 in the first innings had it not been for the middle-order batsmen – Smith 34, D'Oliveira 32, Greig 54 and Knott 43 – and Smith was top scorer with 30 in an even worse second innings which closed for 116, Australia winning by eight wickets, a nice revenge for the defeat at Old Trafford.

Smith also took two splendid catches – at 39 his eye in the field was as uncannily good as ever. He had been on the point of using contact lenses while batting as well as when fielding when his recall to the England side made him defer the experiment, and when he returned to the county eleven their Championship prospects were so promising that he felt he owed it to the Club still further to delay using the lenses at least while batting.

While the Test was going on there was better news for Warwickshire, who won their second Championship match in succession by beating Hampshire at Portsmouth, thanks largely to a withering 121 not out by Kanhai, ably assisted by Jameson, though Amiss twice failed. At this stage Warwickshire and Gloucestershire had each played eight games, but the latter had won one more match and led by fourteen points.

The vagaries of the different fixture lists brought Warwickshire and Worcestershire into conflict five times during the season, and they were the occasions for a remarkable series of innings by Glenn Turner. It all began with a County Championship game at Worcester in which he made 156. On the Saturday of the return Championship match at Edgbaston he followed with 122; the next day in the John Player League game he got 108 and with Headley, 82, shared in an opening partnership of 182 off thirty-four overs which equalled the record for any wicket in the League. Even so, Worcestershire, the reigning champions, lost, Warwickshire hitting off 247 runs with three balls to spare.

Back in the Championship game on the Monday, Amiss, promoted to open, followed up his 59 in the John Player League game with his second century, and then Turner crowned his efforts with yet a fourth century, his third in four days. These innings apart, the match was best forgotten for its inordinately slow play with Worcestershire mostly to blame.

The Glamorgan match at Edgbaston was also notable for three outstanding individual performances, one from Alan Smith, who revived memories of his hat trick at Clacton in 1965 by taking three wickets in eight balls, completely transforming an innings which had begun comfortably with an opening stand of 49. When play ended prematurely for the day just before lunch five wickets had gone down for 9 runs and Smith's analysis was 7 overs, 0 maidens, 23 runs and 4 wickets.

Then it was Glamorgan's turn, Majid Khan hitting the fastest century of the season in 70 minutes, which clipped 32 minutes off the previous best time. He was missed off a hard chance when he was 48 and went on to make 113, including one six and twenty fours. His second 50 took only 23 minutes. Warwickshire were left to score at the rate of 91 an hour and with Kanhai in just as dazzling stroke-playing form as Majid – even though he was missed at 20 and his 123 took a little longer – and 'Mike' Smith aiding and abetting him in an unbroken stand of 162, they hit off the runs, with five overs to spare and eight wickets still outstanding, a notable victory.

With both Smiths away on Test duties, Kanhai took over the captaincy for the first time in the next Championship match at Edgbaston with Lancashire, who, for some unfathomable reason, asked Warwickshire to bat first, a decision Bond must have bitterly regretted. First Amiss and Whitehouse had a first-wicket stand of 84 and then when Whitehouse went for 54 Amiss and Kanhai took over the afternoon. First, they thoroughly mastered the bowling and then proceeded to take it apart. In the process Kanhai reached his 1000 runs for the season; Amiss hit his third century in six matches as an opening batsman and went on to make the highest score of his career to date, 192; and Kanhai finished with 165, his second hundred in two days, his second against Lancashire and his sixth of the season. Their partnership of 318 for the second wicket was only 26 runs short of the county record. And they took only three hours to do it, no fewer than 104 runs being scored in ten overs after tea, 34 of them off two overs, and this despite some splendid ground fielding.

Not surprisingly, Warwickshire won, but with only eight balls in hand when they took Lancashire's last wicket. Kanhai set them to get 262 in 188 minutes and just when a draw seemed certain he put Kallicharran on to bowl, and the last three wickets fell in two overs and two balls, and Warwickshire had won by 35 runs. Thus, with twelve matches played, Gloucestershire and Warwickshire were joint leaders of the table with 125 points each.

Warwickshire players and supporters sympathised with 'Mike' Smith when, after making only 17 and 15 in the third Test – and again he was out to Lillee in each innings – he was once more discarded after making 140 in the three games. But they were very glad to have him back in the county side, especially against Kent at Dartford where he and Kanhai plundered 143 runs in only 83 minutes from an attack admittedly minus Underwood, who was wrecking Australia's innings at Headingley.

Their haul of batting points – Kanhai made 115 and Smith was only 13 short of his century – took Warwickshire to the leadership of the Championship table by the narrow margin of four points, which were just as narrowly achieved off the last ball of the final over but one with four wickets to spare. This time the honours went to Amiss, who scored 121 not out of a Warwickshire total of 214 which had to be obtained in two hours.

Unfortunately because of the 20-match programme there was only one Championship encounter between Warwickshire and their closest rivals. This was at Edgbaston late in July, and it was a pity the game was washed out after Gloucestershire had scored 312 for seven declared, of which Shepherd made 106, and Warwickshire had scored almost half those runs, 149, for the loss of half their wickets, a good performance on a pitch affected by Sunday night rain, 'Mike' Smith getting a very useful 55 not out. The bonus points were divided five-three in favour of Gloucestershire, reducing Warwickshire's lead to two points, but they increased the margin to five following another washed-out match with Somerset for whom Cartwright – ultimately joint top wicket-taker in the country with Stead at 98 – had the pleasure of getting four for 32 against his former team-mates.

Then came the match which proved a turning point. With Amiss making his fifth century and Kallicharran his first for Warwickshire, a punishing 164, they took a record twenty-four points from Notts at Coventry – 10 for a win, five bowling bonus points and nine batting bonus points. Middlesex obligingly beat Gloucestershire while Warwickshire were otherwise engaged with Scotland, and then came an annihilating victory over the Champions, Surrey, which Alan Smith rated the side's best performance of the season. It was notable also for the fact that Kallicharran got a century before lunch – and he should have been stumped first ball.

Next, Close, of all people, was instrumental in doing Warwickshire a good turn. He had something to celebrate – his recall to the England captaincy in the one-day internationals following Illingworth's injury in the last Test – and he made a hundred against Gloucestershire, Somerset holding them to a draw. So the margin between the clubs widened until it became evident that, barring miracles, Warwickshire could not be caught.

Nevertheless, they had a narrow escape from what would have been their only Championship defeat of the season by what proved to be their 'bogey' side, Leicestershire, whom they also met five times, but the two Smiths and Kallicharran, on only the second bad wicket the last named had ever encountered, fought a tense but successful rearguard action to save the game by two wickets. Then it was Willis's turn, his eight for 44 against Derbyshire at Edgbaston, including the hat trick and a near-one as well, virtually clinching the title and bringing him his county cap as well as the ball suitably mounted and inscribed. Kanhai chipped in with yet another century, his eighth of the season, and David Brown with an innings of 79, his highest yet, which showed, not for the first time, that had he not chosen to be a fast bowler he could have been a very good batsman.

Alas, there were no more than 1500 or so spectators to see the title made safe, and rain on the third day put a damper on it all when otherwise no doubt there would have been more people present to salute the new Champions. One voice long familiar to the Edgbaston crowd would have been only too happy to add its plaudits, but unhappily it was silent. It was that of Mr Albert Sanderson, better known as 'Albert the Voice', who had died just before the season began. J. M. Solan, with his usual felicity of phrase, paid a poignant tribute to him in *The Birmingham Post*, and most would have agreed with his final comment: 'No one I have ever heard could exclaim "Oh, dear" with quite the same feeling of anguish.' This was one occasion on which Albert would not have needed to say it.

There was a kippers and champagne breakfast for the team when they went to Trent Bridge for the last match of the season, though that could hardly be blamed for five missed catches on one day. The feast was in fulfilment of a promise (of which he admits he had to be reminded) made very early in the season by Alan Smith. Saturday, the first day of the Notts match, was washed out. Notts batted on the Monday when the excess of fielding lapses allowed them eventually to total 294, but the celebratory breakfast was not held until the Tuesday morning. Report had it that eleven bottles and ninety kippers (which sounds fishily excessive) were disposed of before play began and another six or seven bottles before lunch. Warwickshire managed only 129 in reply, but thanks to a very sporting declaration by Notts, at 26 for one wicket, were left with only 152 to get. This they did with four wickets in hand and one over to spare.

The city's official recognition of Warwickshire's success came when the team returned home and were received by the Lord Mayor, Alderman Fred Hall, to whom Alan Smith presented an autographed bat. Not the least pleasing aspect of the function was the presence of three members of the 1951 County Championship winning side – Tom Pritchard, Bert Wolton and Ray Hitchcock.

Later the Club enjoyed its own celebrations, this time in its own premises, the Pavilion Suite. They took the form of a reception and cocktail party attended by 400 members. Speeches were made and toasts were drunk, and George Paine showed another facet of his art when he presented a statuette of the Bear and Ragged Staff he had carved in sycamore, mounted on a cricket ball on a walnut plinth. The dual honours of County Championship and Gillette Cup were listed with, of course, space left for more. He also designed and made the showcase in which it is displayed at the head of the Committee Room staircase.

Amiss's season had been crowned, not by selection for any of the Tests – though his form, one would have thought, would have warranted his being preferred to some batsmen more fortunate – but by a series of triumphs in the three one-day internationals at Old Trafford,

Lord's and Edgbaston. At Old Trafford after Australia had been dismissed for 222, Amiss and Boycott gave England a good start with an opening stand of 48 and then Amiss shared with Fletcher in a second wicket stand of 126 in 88 minutes. He went on to make 103 – and collected £200 as Cyril Washbrook's choice for the man-of-the-match award.

England won this game by six wickets, but at Lord's although England scored more runs, 236, of which Amiss contributed 25, Australia batted more consistently and they got home with five wickets in hand. This, of course, gave additional spice to the last match of the three at Edgbaston where a crowd of 18 000 saw Australia dismissed for only 179 and England, despite another opening stand, this time of 76, by Boycott and Amiss, who made 40, scraped home by only two wickets.

Barry Wood's electrifying fielding – two superb catches and a run out – as well as two other wickets from his own bowling, earned him the Man-of-the-Match award, but Amiss, deservedly in most opinions, was chosen as England's Man of the Series, along with Keith Stackpole, for Australia, each receiving a £200 cheque from Mr Kenneth Usherwood, chairman of the Prudential Assurance Company. Warwickshire's share of the sponsorship fee was £1900.

Just before this match Amiss had also learned that he had been chosen as Warwickshire's sole representative in the M.C.C. party to tour Pakistan and India during the winter, and in December, just before he left, he gave an interview to *The Birmingham Post* in which he reassured his admirers that there was nothing wrong with his temperament. 'It's experience that counts,' he was reported as saying, 'it's just been a struggle trying to work it all out.' He went on to make a point with which many cricketers would sympathise: 'There's no sort of security. If they could say to us, "Look, you've got three Test Matches – go out and play," I think it would be totally different.' He showed that it was.

Later there was some compensation for Jameson, who toured Rhodesia with an International Wanderers Side and was appointed coach for the Rhodesian district of Manicaland. Three other Warwickshire players also went out to South Africa with Derrick Robins's XI – David Brown as captain, Willis and Lewington – and a former Warwickshire player, Jack Bannister, was the manager.

Meanwhile Alan Smith's August had been enlivened by matters on another field, that of football, for after some turbulent upheavals in the Aston Villa boardroom, which are no part of this history, he was elected a director, thus maintaining an association between the two clubs which has lasted for many years.

There was no such thing as a cricket 'double' to be won in 1951 when Warwickshire last won the Championship, and though they had twice before won the Gillette Cup and reached the final four times they had never before been so close to a double success as they were in 1972. In the early rounds of the Cup they disposed of Yorkshire (and Boycott) at Headingley; Leicestershire, thus revenging three previous defeats, though they clinched it by only 3 runs with two balls left; Glamorgan, another close finish with a margin of 10 runs; and Worcestershire, crushingly by eight wickets in their fifth meeting of the season before an Edgbaston crowd of 11 000.

But attendances generally brought a pointed comment in the annual report on comparative gates at three-day and one-day games:

Whatever the cause may be, it has cost the three-day game its public support, with the result that in 1972 only 13 000 spectators paid to watch the thirty days' home cricket in Warwickshire in the County Championship, compared with the 204 000 who watched from the popular side when the title was last won in 1951.

Leslie Deakins later told the annual dinner of the Wolverhampton Cricket Club that the figures were 'engraved on his heart' as well they might be after all his efforts.

When they eventually went to Lord's to meet Lancashire in the final, Warwickshire were in a very favourable Championship position, for they had a nine points lead over Kent who had overhauled Gloucestershire. They took the field without their captain, Alan Smith deciding on the morning of the match that he could not rely on his injured leg standing the strain, but that handicap was balanced by the fact that Lancashire were without their regular opening bowlers, both Lever and Shuttleworth failing fitness tests.

Winning the toss, Warwickshire batted well enough to give Lancashire the task of making more runs to win, 235, than had been set in any previous final, but then they had the misfortune to encounter Clive Lloyd, who had been out of form, coming back on the crest of a wave which Warwickshire's bowlers could no more contain than could Canute the sea.

There will be argument for years whether, if Warwickshire's earlier batsmen had been a little more enterprising and had not allowed Lloyd, in his other role of bowler, to send down twelve accurate but by no means devastating overs for only 31 runs, and if no fewer than three later batsmen had not been seized by so overwhelming a desire for self-destruction as to run themselves out one after the other, they would have made so many additional runs that even Lloyd's innings would not have brought Lancashire victory. On the whole it would perhaps be true to say that Lancashire did not so much win as Warwickshire lose.

On the other hand, Lancashire might well have retorted that had they taken all their chances in the field – Whitehouse (twice), Amiss, 'Mike' Smith (twice) and Kallicharran were all let off at one time,

594

Engineer having a disastrous match, for he also injured himself –
Warwickshire would not have made as many as they did, 234 at an
average of 3·9 per over. Their score card had a peculiarly top-heavy
look, with the first six players all reaching double figures, Whitehouse
(68), Kallicharran (54) and 'Mike' Smith (48) heading the list, and the
rest all single figures.

When Lancashire batted, Willis bowled with the greatest possible
economy, conceding only 4 runs in his first four overs and, with eighteen overs bowled, Lancashire were behind Warwickshire's run rate.
Lloyd struggled and took a long look at the bowling, scoring only 6 runs
in the first eight overs he was at the wicket, but then he suddenly
exploded into life, off-driving Brown for four and then hooking the next
ball for six into the scorebox, a colossal blow. The first ball of the next
over he glanced for two and the second ball he drove so hard that one
felt that if it had hit Brown at mid-on it would have taken his foot off.
The third ball he tucked away to leg for a single – 17 off five successive
balls. And that was how he went on. He was particularly hard on Brown
to whom he must have brought memories of the hammering he had
given him in the World Cup series at Edgbaston. At one point
Brown had bowled four overs for only 5 runs, and then saw Lloyd hit
him for 19 off the next two.

Meanwhile Pilling plodded away at the other end and the partnership
had assumed such dangerous proportions that Smith might well have
brought back Willis earlier than he did if only to try to put the brake
on. As it happened, it was a misjudged run by Lloyd which brought
Warwickshire some relief, though unhappily for them it was Pilling
who went, sacrificing his wicket to save Lloyd. Willis again bowled
extremely well in his second spell and nearly caught and bowled Lloyd,
but Brown, pitching short, was hit first bounce into the crowd and the
next ball went for six to the same place.

Lloyd was nearly run out by a brilliant throw from Kanhai, but he
duly went to his century – only the second to be made in a Gillette Cup
final – out of 174 for three wickets. Both Compton and Benaud, who
were commenting on television at the time, described it as the best
hundred they had ever seen at Lord's which, splendid innings though it
was, seemed to be putting it a trifle high, even though one could agree
with Compton that when Lloyd was in this mood no bowler in the world
could keep him quiet.

Lancashire brought their run rate up to four an over and were coast-
ing home when at last Lloyd went. He hit Willis for six, then went
down the pitch to the next ball, missed and was leg before. He had made
126 out of 219 and Lancashire were able to get comfortably home with
three overs to spare and four wickets in hand. Lancashire thus won the
Cup for the third year in succession, a wonderful retiring present for

their popular captain, Jackie Bond, who well deserved the special award presented to him.

Warwickshire also got to the semi-final of the Benson and Hedges competition and had at least the consolation of knowing that they were beaten by the eventual winners, Leicestershire, whose first major cricket honour this was. There had been a cloudburst over the Grace Road ground on the Tuesday before the match and it had flooded the square, so that Illingworth, on winning the toss, sent Warwickshire in.

Not surprisingly in these conditions, the bowling of the England and Leicestershire captain was a decisive factor in the dismissal of Warwickshire for only 96 in 39·5 overs, Illingworth taking three of their wickets for 19 runs. Nevertheless, the wicket was not so difficult as to account for only three batsmen reaching double figures, McVicker 23, Amiss 20 and 'Mike' Smith 16. Leicestershire's innings, in which they hit off the runs for the loss of only three wickets, was largely a formality, and they went on to beat Yorkshire in the final.

Warwickshire could hardly have fared worse in the John Player League than they did in the previous season when they finished at the foot of the table. In fact, they did a good deal better, finishing eleventh and losing only one more match than they won. Among their more pleasurable recollections of this competition, which was won by Kent – who thus gained some compensation for being runners-up in the County Championship – will be putting Yorkshire out for 74 at Edgbaston, where the gate was £1118, the highest for a home Sunday League match; Willis's near hat trick in the first over of the match against Gloucestershire, even though Procter did go on to make 109 in just over an hour; and the remarkable finish at Lord's when Middlesex wanted 4 to win off the last ball and every fielder, including the wicket-keeper, was on the boundary. Middlesex could get only a two and thus lost the match by 1 run as well as the chance of winning the League.

Warwickshire, always leading the Midland Zone, also reached the semi-final of the other new competition of the season, the Under-25 Championship. The match was at Edgbaston against Glamorgan and even before it began, Glamorgan's secretary, Wilf Wooller, never averse to an argument, protested at the inclusion in the Warwickshire side of Kallicharran and Willis on the ground that they were capped players, not for Warwickshire but for the West Indies and for England respectively. He was promptly answered by Alan Oakman, Warwickshire's coach, selector of the Warwickshire team and secretary of the competition, who said that if Mr Wooller had wanted to protest he should have done so when Gloucestershire included Zahir Abbas, of Pakistan, against Glamorgan; and Worcestershire, Imran Khan, also capped by Pakistan.

As it happened, Kallicharran was top scorer for Warwickshire, with

54 out of 173, but neither Willis nor any other of the Warwickshire bowlers could prevent Glamorgan from hitting off the runs for the loss of six wickets. In his eight overs, in fact, Willis took only one wicket for 29. Glamorgan, however, lost the final by 8 runs to Middlesex, who had beaten Derbyshire in the other semi-final, also played at Edgbaston.

Unhappily for the organisers, one club withdrew from the competition, later re-named The Warwick Pool Under 25 County Cricket Competition, and it was feared that another would do so; short-sighted decisions. A similar comment might well have been made about the lukewarm response to a suggestion by M. J. K. Smith, who had been appointed chairman of the Club's Cricket Sub-Committee, that the two days set apart for second-eleven cricket should be devoted to a single innings match so that batsmen might have opportunities for learning how to build an innings, which the one-day game had been criticised for not providing.

At the end of the summer the Club said farewell to one of its longest-serving and most devoted players, 'Billy' Ibadulla, and the fact that he had answered so long to so English a first name was an indication of the respect and affection he enjoyed. He was never, perhaps, possessed of that genius which can take a match, or an innings, and shape it as he will, no matter what the bowlers or fielders do, but he was that supremely valuable asset to any side, a highly useful player, who was always doing something in the game, whether batting, bowling or fielding. His name will remain long in the county records for he shared in two of the Club's highest partnerships – 402 for the fourth wicket with Kanhai against Notts in 1968, and 377, unbroken, for the first wicket with Norman Horner against Surrey in 1960. He has the best record of any Warwickshire bowler in the Gillette Cup, and his catching of Graveney in the final in 1966 was the sort of match-winning marvel which those fortunate enough to have seen it talk about for years.

Ibadulla succeeded Laurie Fishlock as coach at St Dunstan's School, Catford, and he was a very good choice for he had the keenest of eyes for a promising young player. It was he was first saw the potentialities of Glenn Turner and it was not Ibadulla's fault that Turner joined Worcestershire instead of Warwickshire, who already had their quota of overseas players. In the spring of 1972 he also brought back from Tasmania, where he had been coaching, a boy of 14, David Robinson, so highly spoken of as a batsman that he may well play for Australia one day. He was reputed to be the youngest player ever to appear in top-class cricket in the island and was promoted to open the innings for the first eleven of the Devonport Club where Ibadulla coached. During the summer of 1972 he stayed with the Ibadullas in Birmingham, where he went to school and played several games with Warwickshire Young

Amateurs and the Club and Ground side with whom he created a favourable impression, before returning home to complete his education. Whether he will ever be able to play for Warwickshire is something that only the future can decide.

As one career closed, others began, for Warwickshire gave engagements to Keith Gardom, aged 19, an all-rounder from Sutton Coldfield, a Warwickshire colt and winner of the National Cricket Association's Young Cricketer of the Year Award, who is an opening bat and bowls leg spinners, an unusual combination; and to David Smith, a young Northumberland batsman; while another Oxford University captain, in A. K. C. Jones, of Solihull School, former Young Amateur, and member of the Colts' and Second Elevens, who had developed under the watchful eye of George Paine, also became available at the end of the university year in 1973.

During the winter Bernard Flack and his staff helped the Moseley Rugby Football Club to make their ground fit after days of heavy rain for the much anticipated visit of the All Blacks. Its condition was afterwards praised by the tourists' manager, Ernie Todd, and the Moseley Club showed its appreciation of Flack's work by making him an honorary life member.

Financially the season brought better fortune for the county clubs. The Test and County Cricket Board announced that it had a record figure of £600 000, most of it from Tests, TV and sponsorships, to share out among the counties and this was largely responsible for the fact that Warwickshire were able to reduce the loss on the season to £13 583, the lowest for some years. The season also brought the usual discussion of ambitious ground projects, including the perennial sports complex, especially on the North Side, and there were consultations with the Calthorpe Estates, but the Committee was at pains to express in the annual report that it was 'concerned at all times to retain complete sovereignty and control over every square yard of the Edgbaston ground as a bounden duty they feel they owe to the earlier pioneers of Warwickshire cricket who secured the freehold, laid out the playing area and, in effect, decreed it as an open space "in perpetuity".' At the same time, a sub-committee consisting of the Club chairman, a member of the General Committee and of the Ground and House sub-committee, Philip Gough, and Alan Smith, was appointed to investigate and report on the possibilities of development.

Meanwhile, the second phase of the Pavilion (centre) construction was completed and phase three was begun. This work included resiting the wooden premises of the Edgbaston Road frontage, formerly occupied by the Supporters Association, completing the boundary wall, with a niche in which the ashes of S. F. Barnes rest, and extension of the forecourt gardens.

The Supporters' Association was not without its worries during the year, one of them being the rumoured possibility that the Government might decide to give local councils the right to run their own lotteries with the possibility that they might affect the takings of the pool. Even so, as the annual report pointed out, the Association arranged for 'appreciable amounts' to be available to the Club on short-term loan – with the result that considerable sums came in on the credit side through interest – and for the Club to be assisted with its overdraft. The Association also formed a Promotions Sub-Committee under the chairmanship of Eric Walker, who succeeded Derek Salberg as the Association's vice-chairman.

Just how much the Club is indebted to the Association and the pool since its inception in 1953–54 is shown in the following table. In studying the figures it should be borne in mind that since many members send in more than one entry, the total number of members may be rather fewer than the total given in the table under 'Membership':

Year	Membership	Prize Money (£)	Turnover (£)
1953–54	39 000	30 000	46 000
1954–55	22 000	15 000	36 000
1955–56	42 000	25 000	55 000
1956–57	85 000	52 000	115 000
1957–58	149 000	96 000	218 000
1958–59	208 000	143 000	325 000
1959–60	272 000	187 000	426 000
1960–61	358 000	337 000	574 000
1961–62	542 000	317 000	864 000
1962–63	603 000	361 000	1 008 000
1963–64	640 000	362 000	1 060 000
1964–65	682 000	440 000	1 113 000
1965–66	700 000	471 000	1 192 000
1966–67	700 000	471 000	1 192 000
1967–68	730 000	425 000	1 237 000
1968–69	720 000	349 000	1 229 000
1969–70	680 000	300 000	1 054 000
1970–71	600 000	286 000	1 057 000
1971–72	435 000	412 000	1 420 000
1972–73	400 000	377 000	1 298 000

The slight decline in entries in recent years was due to increasing the stake from 5p to 10p, but, as anticipated, apart from seasonal fluctuations, this led to more prize money to be won and greater turnover.

Meanwhile, the Association's own social club in the Pavilion (east wing) was restructured and redecorated at a cost of £30 000, Peter West, the broadcaster, performing the opening ceremony. The Association had now given Club members the use of the premises, thus fulfilling a wish many of them had expressed that some part of the ground should be open all the year round. Edgar Hiley had made no secret of the fact that one day the Association would like to hand over the social club as 'a going concern' to the county Club and would be able to erect its own more commodious premises on the North Side.

Another Association, that of the cricketers themselves, of whom Jack Bannister was secretary, with Norman McVicker as treasurer, successfully staked a claim with the Test and County Cricket Board for a share of the fees paid by B.B.C. television for big cricket – £100 000 in 1972. They pointed out that their footballing colleagues received 10 per cent from the Football League and 12½ per cent from the Football Association, a total of £30 000, compared with the cricketers' yearly donation from the Board of £750 and £5000 a year from the John Player organisation. They were successful to the extent of a donation of £3 500 for the ensuing four years, subject to review after two years, the amount being recognised as the players' share of the game's income. Perhaps even more important from the point of view of their long-term wellbeing, the County Cricket Board approved the terms of a provident fund of £17 000 a year to be jointly administered.

The old problem of whether or not spectators should be allowed on the playing area cropped up again several times following complaints against the practice, and a petition signed by 250 members led to a special meeting of the Committee to consider the matter again. It was eventually agreed that, beginning with the 1973 season, no one would be allowed on the grass area before, or during, hours of play, irrespective of the position of the rope boundary, and that walking on the grass, but not on the square, would be allowed only during the lunch and tea intervals, weather permitting. This rule would be lifted for presentations in front of the pavilion and for any other special occasions.

The question of a Pop festival also popped up again, but once more the Committee showed caution, deferring a decision until there was more knowledge available of what might be involved. They must have felt on surer ground with the idea of a betting shop, however, for they agreed to give consent, provided there were no bets on the performances of individual players, which would obviously be most undesirable.

And in the spring of 1973 the Test and County Cricket Board decided on its own gamble. No one else having come forward to sponsor the County Championship as a whole, the Board announced its own scheme – a first prize of £3000 to the champions; £2000 to the runners-up; £1000 to the third team and £500 to the fourth. Moreover, there would be a prize of £500 to the side whose bowlers took most wickets in relation to the number of overs bowled. But the counties themselves had to finance it, £500 each from 17 of them.

So 'the cricket we have all grown up to love', as the President put it at the annual meeting, was given a fillip which the chairman also welcomed. Coupled with it, came the long-threatened imposition of fines for slowness – £500, to be paid by the players, for any side failing to maintain an average of 18·5 overs an hour throughout the season, with a similar amount to be paid out of the fine money to any team maintaining a rate of 19·5 overs an hour, plus some more carrots in the form of additional bonus points awards for faster scoring.

On their showing in 1972 of 18·05 overs an hour, Warwickshire would have had to pay a fine, but neither Hampshire (19·04) nor Leicestershire (18·86) who led the overs table would have benefited. Indeed, Warwickshire would have been one of no fewer than fifteen counties who would have had to pay up, so bad had the situation become. Naturally the players were not enthusiastic at the prospect of having to pay fines, but when one considered that the over rate had sometimes slumped to as low as thirteen an hour it was only too obvious that some of the slow coaches would get their just deserts if they did not improve.

On the other hand, had there been a premium for fast scoring, Warwickshire would have gained, for they led the table, averaging 55·75 runs per 100 balls bowled. Derbyshire had the lowest average, only 39·79.

It remained to be seen what effect, if any, these stimulants would have on the three-day game. Incentives have long been known in industry, but it was difficult not to reflect sadly on the need to use them to induce men to play in attractive fashion what began as a game devised to give simple enjoyment to those who played it and those who cared to watch.

Towards the Centenary

WHEN at the end of his Introduction to Santall's history, William Ansell asked what the future of Warwickshire cricket was to be, he answered himself by saying that it was difficult to forecast. It was not, he added, a natural cricketing county like Surrey or Kent, and Warwickshire lacked the village greens and commons of these counties (did it, even then?), as well as other suitable places where the game could be played.

He thought that both the climate – 'frequently June is half-way through before we get real summer' – and the encroachments of football were against the game; golf was alluring the middle-aged, lawn tennis the less robust, and cycling had its devotees. But he took heart from the fact that the population was large and he thought it needed only 'energetic action and enthusiasm on the part of the rulers of the game to make up the slight leeway recently lost and Warwickshire should again be in the forefront of the counties of England'.

Ansell was writing in the uncomplicated days of 1910, though doubt-less he found them troublesome enough, for he had his problems as we have seen. But if he felt it was difficult for him to forecast the future then – though, in fact, his hopes were realised the very next year with the Club gaining its first Championship – what would he have thought of the prospects today?

The meteorological climate has not changed much, the encroachments of football are even greater, golf and tennis and a good many other things Ansell had not heard of are luring people away from cricket, and though cycling still has its devotees the vehicle on four wheels is the one we have to contend with. As for the population, that is larger than Ansell could ever have imagined that it might become, but still not a large enough proportion of it supports Warwickshire cricket to permit the Club to stand firmly on its own financial feet. And the rulers of the game? Ansell had plenty to say about them in his day and he would hardly be any less critical now.

Indeed, when one takes into account, as this history has tried to do, all the factors which have affected cricket over, say, the last 100 years it is, perhaps, astonishing that there are still any county cricket clubs left with histories to record. In Warwickshire's case, of course, the supreme irony for the cricket purist is that the Club has been enabled to survive by transplants from an offshoot of its great rival for the title of England's national game – a football pool – a fact which, one imagines, would have brought amused smiles to the faces of the founders of the Warwick County Football Club, formed only five years after its cricket counterpart, but which itself soon went the way of so much sporting flesh.

That the Warwickshire Club has been sustained in this way and could, indeed, continue to play matches and pay its staff and players even if no spectator ever set foot inside the ground again – thanks to the Supporters' Association – is a striking indication of how the British public loves a gamble for itself alone, irrespective of the object the prize money goes to support.

It is probably safe to say that by far the majority of the 300 000 or so members of the pool belong to it, not so much because they love cricket (though there is a great affinity between them and the Warwickshire Club), or, for that matter, football, as because they enjoy a flutter in which the expenditure of a trifling sum may bring them thousands of pounds. This is true also of the national pools, or premium bonds – it is the appeal of a gamble and the lure of get-rich-quickly which keeps them all going, not the love of a great game, or even of country.

The development of pools and sponsorship as means of financial support has been the most potent of all the many changes of which the history of cricket in the last twenty years has been compounded, both being adopted in the hope of attracting back the crowds and keeping the county clubs alive; but even if both disappeared overnight the game would not die. These two factors, bringing regular financial blood transfusions, have been linked with the third most striking development in the lifetime of present-day cricket followers – the trend away from the three-day game (though that is getting a boost now) to the one-day and half-day competitions for which the public has shown such a profound preference.

He would be a foolish man indeed who said that cricket had now reached the end of the line in any of these directions, for a game that does not change stagnates, which was one of the prime causes for the decline of interest in first-class cricket in the first place. The whole tendency of the age, whether we like it or not, is towards instant-this and instant-that and it is not likely to stop now; indeed, it may well veer off in some at present totally unexpected direction.

How, then, do those responsible for the future of Warwickshire cricket regard what has happened and how do they see the future? What follows is the considered opinion of Edmund King, chairman of the Club during perhaps the most tumultuously changing years of its history:

During the years I was Chairman of Warwickshire County Cricket Club, I suppose county cricket has been in greater financial difficulties than at any other period of its existence. For some reason or other, gates at county grounds have steadily declined and many clubs have been approaching bankruptcy.

Thanks to the opportunity provided by my chairmanship of Warwickshire, I have been appointed to various committees at Lord's, from the County Advisory Committee to various sub-committees of the Test and County Cricket Board, including the Financial and General Purposes Committee. I mention this because it is of interest to recall the decisions made at Lord's, Warwickshire's reactions to them, and what they hold for Warwickshire in the future.

The County Advisory Committee, which represented all the first-class and minor counties, was a body advisory to M.C.C. on the administration of county cricket. In fact, M.C.C. held complete authority, but they used their power sparingly and they were not only wise and competent in their judgments, but also very generous. Great harmony always existed between M.C.C. and the counties.

In 1968 M.C.C. took an unprecedented step. It was clear to all that the finances of the counties and indeed M.C.C. were worsening year by year. At the same time other sporting bodies were receiving financial support from the Government, but M.C.C. being a private club, was in no position to receive such support. Accordingly, M.C.C. handed over the responsibility for administering all cricket in the United Kingdom to a newly formed Cricket Council with two operating bodies, The Test and County Cricket Board and the National Cricket Association, to represent first-class, minor county cricket and club and league cricket respectively.

This important change was welcomed by all the counties and Warwickshire has played its part in making the new structure work. Counties now play a much closer part in national cricket affairs.

The new administration for cricket clearly could not wave a wand and bring spectators and money through the turnstiles and, except for Test Matches, gates have continued, with isolated exceptions, to sink lower and lower.

In 1964 M.C.C. appointed a Committee under the chairmanship of David Clark to look into the structure of county cricket and advise on changes which might be made to make the game more appealing without a lowering of standards. I had the privilege of sitting on this Committee. Warwickshire have felt for a long time that the main reason for the poor support for county cricket is that there is too much of it to suit the pattern of this day and age. They have maintained that if the amount is cut down, people will be able to find time to come and watch and the players will play better. In fact, the structure proposed in the Clark Report was just this, but it was 'put into cold storage' – and it is still there!

There is no doubt that the emergence of one-day county cricket in the Gillette Cup in 1963 had a dramatic effect on people's attitude to county cricket, and instead of a reduction in the amount of cricket, as proposed in the Clark Report and supported by Warwickshire, we now have the John Player League on Sundays and the Benson and Hedges Cup as well. These new one-day competitions have been arranged after much thought and long negotiations with the sponsors and there is no doubt that, short term, they will bring in a lot of money and get a lot of support, so Warwickshire sees its call for less cricket finishing up with more!

I am sure I echo the feelings of my Committee when I say that we are not really getting down to the roots of the problem. We want cricket to have a scarcity value with expert, well-paid players playing 'all out' in a curtailed main championship. We would like the framework to be such that the best of our club cricketers can afford the time to play first-class cricket.

Referring to Warwickshire's own financial affairs, we have been wonder-fully lucky to have behind us The Warwickshire Supporters' Association. This remarkable organisation has virtually given us all the buildings on our great ground and provided an Endowment Fund, now standing at about £350 000, for investment to augment our income. Without this support we should not be in the forefront of county clubs, as I think we are, or indeed a Test Match ground at all. Like most other county clubs, our Club loses money year in and year out on its cricket activities; running a Test ground such as ours is a very expensive proposition.

The Committee has investigated various ways of augmenting its income from cricket activities with other sources of income, and although we have gone some way in this direction we still make substantial annual losses. We are secure for some time with our Endowment Fund behind us, but, long term, there is no doubt that something must be done to make us financially viable on our own.

I think that the sort of scheme most favoured by the Committee is a Multi-Sports Centre with the County Ground and Club secure as an integral part. Such things as squash racquets, indoor tennis, swimming, Badminton, hockey, archery, golf ranges, etc., all come to mind and there must be attractive club house facilities to go with them. Such developments would be far more desirable than building development, which we have also studied. It is not easy to make a sports complex pay its way, but it can be done, and we have an ideal site on which to do it.

Our members have been marvellous, but they have 'stomached' two increases in subscriptions in four years and it is not fair for them to carry more of the burden. The most recent adjustment of subscriptions included the creation of Shareholder Membership. This was carefully thought out to give members relatively a much better deal – I hope it will be popular.

To sum up – I, and I am sure my Committee, are concerned to see the Warwickshire Club completely secure, with pavilion facilities second to none for its cricket members. We would like to see other games introduced outside the perimeter of the playing area with very good club facilities for these. We want our cricketing public to be very well looked after.

Whatever type of sports complex may be designed we want it to fit gracefully into the Edgbaston picture. The further we can move away from 'concrete' the better, and much thought must go into landscaping the area.

We would like to see three-day county cricket continue as the main first-class cricket competition, with each county playing the other counties once only. We think the Gillette Cup should continue as at present. This restricted programme with first-class amenities at the ground might, in our view, bring about a revival of interest.

With the other competitions already arranged – and thank Heaven for them financially – it will be some time before our wishes could be considered, but I think they may one day come about for the betterment of the game and everyone who loves it.

Cyril Goodway, Edmund King's successor, concurred in these views and all he wished to add was: 'There will be changes in cricket, of course – I believe we have too many – but, come what may, I know that so long as players enjoy playing cricket, so long will cricket survive – and The Warwickshire County Cricket Club.'

Next, because even the most perfervid optimist can see only a struggle ahead for the Club to survive (even with the help of sponsored competitions and additional revenue from a future sports complex), unless the Supporters' Association is able to continue backing it, however scrupulously and precisely the officers of that organisation define the nature of their help, I went to their chairman, Edgar Hiley, for his views:

With increasing competition, the ageing of agents, the heavy load of taxation paid by pools – no less than $33\frac{1}{3}\%$ of all we take – and many other difficulties, we are at times inclined to be pessimistic, until we realise what a success story we are living with, and we have the feeling that, barring hostile legislation, we shall continue to play a vital role in keeping the first-class game alive, not only in Warwickshire but country-wide.

But what form will that legislation take? Having recently secured temporary legislation to keep us legal for up to five years, we have had a warning that, unless we diversify, we may find ourselves without protective legislation at the end of that period. As to diversification, it is idle for anyone to assume that we have not given immense thought to alternative means of raising funds, without coming up with any ideas which could be really productive. One always fears the coming of a Puritan wave since history has shown the alternatives of gaiety and Puritanism (the Stuarts, then Cromwell; the Regency, then Victoria; the Edwardians, then George V) and now we are having one of those gay spells. I wonder what follows.

Or there may be legislative sanction for national or municipal lotteries, probably without the restrictions, or taxation, under which we labour. Such proposals, which are raised fairly frequently, infer grossly unfair competition. After all, public statutory bodies have their own legally enforceable ways and means of raising their funds, which are denied to bodies such as ours who support sport or charities, and any intrusion into our fields by the authorities will not only ruin us but will lead to the necessity, if the causes such as ours are to survive, of their being a charge on public funds. Such provision would, judging from experience, be inadequate, capricious and liable to interference in the running of sports by people not qualified so to meddle.

No, this is a field in which one greatly prefers private enterprise, perhaps better put as self-help, to Government aid, Government competition, or Government interference. Given this freedom, there is no reason why we should not continue to do a great deal of good, without doing any harm at all, for many years to come.

On the strength of those statements alone, Edmund King, Cyril Goodway and Edgar Hiley can all be written down as optimists, as they very much need to be. I have left until last the most incorrigible optimist of them all – Leslie Deakins – whose views and influence have had much to do with the shaping of the events of the period covered by the third book of this narrative.

At the time of writing, his work is not yet done, but when eventually he carries his bat from Edgbaston there will not be any need to name a stand after him, as they did for William Ansell and perhaps ought to have done for R. V. Ryder. The ground itself will be his memorial, for while he would be the last to belittle the contributions which those who went before him have made and on whose foundations he was able to build, modern Edgbaston is largely his creation and of those who have given him their support.

It began long ago as a dream nurtured during the long night-watches of his naval service and he has been more fortunate than most men to see much of it realised. Not disappointments nor frustrations, still less derogatory comments such as 'Deakins's Folly', or 'concrete mauso-leums', have ever turned him even slightly away from his ultimate objective – that of providing for the Warwickshire Club the finest cricket ground and facilities in England, indeed in the world if there were the money available to make this possible.

But it has been even more than that. There are those less imaginative who, hearing Edgbaston, on some days, echoing hollowly to the sound of bat hitting ball and seeing only a few pairs of clapping hands, might think that Leslie Deakins's life has been a tragedy of unfulfilment – to have worked so hard and helped create so much in the hope, as the ground grew, of attracting and providing for ever-increasing numbers, only to see them drifting away and returning only on comparatively rare occasions.

But that is not as Leslie Deakins sees it. Cricket, of course, has always been his great love and it has been for cricket that he has primarily striven all his working life, but he has always conceived Edgbaston as something far greater than a ground for one game, however noble, to be played on it. In his eyes it should be the greatest sports and social centre in the land, with every conceivable facility for sports and pastimes,

607

every possible amenity for recreation and leisure, that money can supply. And perhaps one day that is what it will be. But let him sum up his Edgbaston credo for himself:

This Edgbaston ground is at once the home of those playing and administering at the moment and the happy memorial of those who have gone before. The work I may have put into the development of the ground has been materially helped and encouraged by a variety of people and, notably in the early stages, by the wonderful support of a great President in the person of Dr Harold Thwaite, who wanted to see both the ground and the Club successfully developed during his period in office, and who, I am always pleased to feel, was largely rewarded in this respect. His outstanding generosity in the immediate post-war years made all subsequent development possible, and his encouragement and refusal at all times to be frustrated, were salient factors in this period of high development where so much was achieved. In a quiet way he was an astonishing man of action.

In addition to the doctor, who showed the way, the Club has, since the Second World War, been particularly fortunate in a succession of able chairmen – Colin Langley, Alec Hastilow, Edmund King and now Cyril Goodway – and they have at all times been supported by sound Committee colleagues and excellent sub-committees who have done much of the sifting and sorting that is so essential.

It is readily understandable that, on occasions, the Committee, with whom I have always enjoyed the happiest relationship, and the Secretariat, have been at pleasant variance on questions of policy. As an example, over the years I have always favoured development of the ground and premises with the resources at the Club's disposal, leaving the premises thus created to earn their own income, whereas the Committee has, in recent years, preferred to invest those resources and to use the income derived in this way to reduce losses and in time to endow the Club in such a way that it would be safeguarded even if, by some mischance or change of circumstance, the Supporters' Association were to lose, or to have seriously curtailed, its sources of revenue. The one great advantage of such differences of opinion is that it ensures that both sides of any problem, or policy-making, are fully investigated and presented, without creating embarrassment, or difficulty, since the ultimate aim of both is always 'the best interest of the Club'.

As to the future, I can only sensibly base it on experience in the past and from this I would say that a truly great club is one that benefits from contributions from succeeding generations, and, despite the inevitable changes in officers that must take place, and, of course, in the conditions and way of life which always vary, continues to make progress.

It is certain that some generations may, through force of circumstances, be able to achieve more than others and it is, therefore, essential to ensure that when conditions are favourable no opportunity to develop is lost. Was it not a Warwickshire man who once said 'There is a tide in the affairs of men which taken at the flood leads on to fortune'? No such tide should be missed.

It is, of course, a fact that ground development of genuine worth can be made only if funds are available and, therefore, in speaking of the period covered by the past twenty years, the Club can count itself fortunate in that, following the great generosity and drive of men like Dr Thwaite, the Supporters' Association came into being at a most appropriate moment to enable the tempo of development to be maintained.

I should perhaps make it clear that the creation of Supporters' Associations, with their ability to generate funds, was, and is, open to all county clubs and to many other similarly constituted organisations, and the fact that Warwickshire has derived better advantage than most is entirely due to the human element, for whilst money in itself may be important the individuals with the energy and drive are even more important.

Thus in Warwickshire, on the foundation laid by Ray Hitchcock, David and Winifred Blakemore have developed the Supporters' Association to an outstanding measure of achievement. Their contribution has been the prime and all-important one in developing the ground and securing the future of Warwickshire cricket. They have at all times been admirably supported by an excellent Committee initially under the chairmanship of the late M. F. K. Fraser and, since 1959, under Edgar Hiley, and throughout the twenty years of the Association's existence the relationship with the County Club Committee and staff has always been perfect.

That the actual development has been to a degree halted in the past ten years is no doubt a matter of regret to many, but it is a clearly established fact that the ground's seating capacity for a single occasion can now more than cover the aggregate attendance for a full Championship season's cricket.

There are, of course, wide areas at Edgbaston in which development could be maintained to bring other sports within the orbit of the ground to the lasting benefit of both cricket and the public it seeks to serve in the great city of Birmingham. However, the funds generated by the Supporters' Association are for the time being held in an Endowment Fund, which provides investment income to bolster the Club's normal revenue, but while the Committee endorses this arrangement it cannot appeal to them as a happy way of running a cricket club, which should to a much greater degree be self-supporting by virtue of the product it offers – the game of cricket. Difficult situations call for special remedies and this is a case in point.

Looking back across the past forty-five years, the Club is infinitely stronger, the ground far more in keeping with modern demands, and it is undoubtedly a great asset to the city of Birmingham since it brings to it regularly the *only* international sporting occasion it can command.

The team in the field has been more successful in the past twenty-five years than at any time in its history, with two Championships and two Gillette Cup triumphs. The membership is soundly based on the shareholder system whereby every member can feel he owns a square yard or so of the lovely Edgbaston ground, and the general administration is second to none in the country.

Whilst William Ansell left the Club a great birthright in the freehold of the ground, it is true to say that succeeding generations have played their part in developing that tremendous asset, and I am sure that they will continue to make their contributions, particularly with funds available, so that 'The Bear and the Ragged Staff' will always be carried boldly but with honour and proud dignity wherever the game is played in this country, and its home at Edgbaston will be pre-eminent among the cricket grounds of the world.

It is, of course, always difficult to plan, indeed even to look, too far ahead, but may I conclude by expressing the hope that an impressive and successful future will always acknowledge the work of earlier generations. Perhaps the happiest manner of reflecting this would be in the words of Rudyard Kipling, who said everything for men of action and, indeed, for the dreamers, so much better, more concisely and more effectively than virtually anyone else who has handled the English language. He knew a generation was always coming with wider vision, broader scope, better capacity and knowledge, perhaps better opportunities, to fashion the things of tomorrow based on the experience of today, when he wrote:

When I was a King and a Mason – a Master proven and skilled –
I cleared me ground for a Palace such as a King should build.
I decreed and dug down to my levels. Presently, under the silt,
I came on the wreck of a Palace such as a King had built.

. . . .

Masonry, brute, mishandled, but carven on every stone:
'After me cometh a builder. Tell him I, too, have known.'

Yet in the long run the future of cricket will depend not upon what men in offices and the committee rooms do, whether at Edgbaston or Lord's, or on the sponsors, or even the poets, but on how thirteen men on the field play the game. Not a World Cricket Cup, when it materialises, not Test Matches, not the County Championship, the Gillette Cup, the John Player League, the Benson and Hedges League Cup, or any other form of competition which may be devised, not even if everyone stands on his head and defies the laws of gravity by playing cricket upside down, will attract the crowds without whom the sponsors will melt away like the snows of yesteryear, unless the men in the middle *hit* the ball with the bat. The future of cricket depends on something as basically simple as that.

The Warwickshire County Cricket Club's history began ninety-one years ago. In a very few years there will be a centenary to celebrate and then the second hundred years will begin. What they will bring no one can tell, but so long as successive players – I put them first – and administrators show themselves as enterprising and adaptable as the men who founded the Club and those who followed them, so long will its future be assured. They will have a great but immensely rewarding responsibility.

During the last three years I have spent many hours at Edgbaston, both above and below ground, for the Club's meticulously kept records are safely locked away in a strong room beneath the level of that carpet of turf on which many of us love to gaze and occasionally even to tread. Sometimes, looking at the great ground when all is deserted in the winter, strange thoughts, even possibly treasonable ones, creep in, such as whether all this elaborate grandeur is necessary to enable twenty-two men to play a game originally devised only for the enjoyment and diversion of those who played it and them alone. But, of course, the answer comes back from the echoing stands that we can no more go back to Hambledon and the time when

> *The youth at cricks did play*
> *Throughout the merry day*

than we can to the days of the hansom cabs which rattled the club men along to Lord's when 'W.G.' went in to bat.

I have many memories of those three years, but one abides. One mild May evening I emerged from the strong-room to stretch muscles and breathe fresh air after a long day's delving in musty minute books to find that a second-eleven match between Warwickshire and Lancashire was approaching its climax. I did not have a scorecard, so I had to rely on my few neighbours to put me in the picture.

With seven wickets down and three overs to go, it appeared, Lancashire needed 16 to win. Then another wicket fell and when the last over came 6 runs were wanted and someone, recalling a remark reputed to have been made by George Hirst to Wilfred Rhodes in a famous Test Match at The Oval long ago, said: 'Perhaps they'll get 'em in singles.'

They very nearly did. Off each of the first five balls of that final over a single was run – and the match was a tie. The last ball was thumped for four, a splendidly decisive way to settle it, and that was that.

But not quite. An elderly man got up from his seat, stretched his legs and remarked: 'Well, I wouldn't have missed that for anything.' He picked up his walking stick and added feelingly but to no one in particular: 'It's a great game still.' He spoke for cricketers and cricket-lovers the world over, who, in their time, have seen many changes, but for whom, in Harold Begbie's line

> '. . . the meadow game with the beautiful name, is king and
> lord of them all.'

Bibliography

The Warwickshire County Cricket Club Records 1882–1972.

G. W. EGDELL & M. F. K. FRASER, *The Warwickshire County Cricket Club: A History*, Cornish Bros.

S. SANTALL, *History of The Warwickshire County Cricket Club*, Cricket & Sports Pub.

Records in *The Birmingham Post* and *Mail* Library.

Wisden Cricketers' Almanac 1864–1972.

SIR DONALD BRADMAN, *Farewell to Cricket*, Hodder & Stoughton.

GERALD BRODRIBB, *Hit for Six*, Heinemann.

BRIAN CLOSE, *Close to Cricket*, Stanley Paul.

H. E. (TOM) DOLLERY, *Professional Captain*, Stanley Paul.

FRANK R. FOSTER, *Cricketing Memories*, The London Pub. Co.

ERIC HOLLIES, *I'll Spin You a Tale*, Museum Press.

A. A. LILLEY, *Twenty-Four Years of Cricket*, Mills & Boon.

SIDNEY ROGERSON, *Wilfred Rhodes*, Hollies & Carter.

A. A. THOMSON, *Cricketers of My Times*, Stanley Paul.

R. E. S. WYATT, *Three Straight Sticks*, Stanley Paul.

APPENDICES

APPENDICES

❖ ❖ ❖

1. Officers of the Club

APPENDIX 1

1902	H. W. Bainbridge and T. S. Fishwick
1903 – 1906	J. F. Byrne
1907	T. S. Fishwick and J. F. Byrne
1908 – 1909	A. C. S. Glover
1910	H. J. Goodwin
1911 – 1914	F. R. Foster
1919	G. W. Stephens
1920 – 1929	The Hon. F. S. G. Calthorpe
1930 – 1937	R. E. S. Wyatt
1938 – 1947	Peter Cranmer*
1948	H. E. Dollery and R. H. Maudsley
1949 – 1955	H. E. Dollery
1956	W. E. Hollies
1957 – 1967	M. J. K. Smith
1968 –	Alan C. Smith

* Between 1940 and 1945, when the Club did not play any official cricket, Peter Cranmer was serving in the Armed Forces.

2. Club Statistics

The following Club and individual statistics have been compiled by Philip Pike, Warwickshire's scorer until he retired in 1973, in consultation with Ted Hampton, the Club's honorary statistician, and are accepted by the Club as the official records. I am greatly indebted to both of them. The figures throughout relate to performances in first-class cricket for Warwickshire only, except where indicated, and are complete to the end of the 1972 season.

ALL FIRST CLASS MATCHES PLAYED BY WARWICKSHIRE

County	Played	Won	Lost	Drawn or Abandoned	Tied
Derbyshire	136	38	34	64	—
Essex	81	23	21	37	—
Glamorgan	70	28	14	28	—
Gloucestershire	115	42	31	42	—
Hampshire	112	35	30	47	—
Kent	90	23	37	30	—
Lancashire	132	20	49	63	—
Leicestershire	132	46	20	66	—
Middlesex	84	20	30	34	—
Northamptonshire	104	41	15	48	—
Nottinghamshire	76	19	25	32	—
Somerset	78	27	18	33	—
Surrey	123	20	43	60	—
Sussex	95	32	28	34	1
Worcestershire	127	34	27	66	—
Yorkshire	133	13	65	55	—
Cambridge Univ.	37	12	8	17	—
Oxford Univ.	28	10	6	12	—
Australians	20	1	8	11	—
South Africans	13	1	6	6	—
All India—Indians	7	1	1	5	—
New Zealanders	7	1	1	5	—
West Indies	9	2	3	4	—
Pakistanis	4	1	1	2	—
M.C.C. and Ground	3	1	1	1	—
Philadelphians	2	1	1	—	—
London County	8	2	—	6	—
Scotland	16	4	2	10	—
Combined Services	8	4	—	4	—
Rest of England	1	—	1	—	—
Canadians	1	—	—	1	—
	1852	502	526	823	1

APPENDIX 2

POSITION IN THE COUNTY CHAMPIONSHIP SINCE ENTRY IN 1895

Season	Position	Season	Position	Season	Position
1895	6th	1919	15th	1946	14th
1896	12th	1920	12th	1947	15th
1897	7th	1921	16th	1948	7th
1898	9th	1922	12th	1949	4th
1899	7th	1923	12th	1950	4th
1900	6th	1924	9th	1951	1st
1901	5th	1925	8th	1952	10th
1902	6th	1926	12th	1953	9th
1903	7th	1927	11th	1954	6th
1904	7th	1928	11th	1955	9th
1905	7th	1929	14th	1956	14th
1906	6th	1930	15th	1957	11th
1907	9th	1931	9th	1958	16th
1908	12th	1932	9th	1959	4th
1909	12th	1933	7th	1960	15th
1910	14th	1934	4th	1961	12th
1911	1st	1935	8th	1962	3rd
1912	9th	1936	13th	1963	4th
1913	11th	1937	11th	1964	2nd
1914	7th	1938	13th	1965	11th
1915–18 World War I		1939	11th	1966	6th
		1940–5 World War II		1967	10th
				1968	11th
				1969	4th
				1970	8th
				1971	2nd
				1972	1st

1911 CHAMPIONSHIP TABLE

				First Inns		Poss	Points	
	P	W	L	W	L	Points	Scored	Percentage
1. Warwickshire	20	13	4	3	0	100	74	74·00
2. Kent	26	17	4	3	2	130	96	73·84
3. Middlesex	22	14	5	3	0	110	79	71·81
4. Lancashire	30	15	7	5	3	150	93	62·00
5. Surrey	30	15	7	4	4	150	91	60·66
6. Essex	18	8	5	4	1	90	53	58·88
7. Yorkshire	27	14	8	1	4	135	77	57·03
8. Notts	20	9	5	3	3	100	57	57·00
9. Worcestershire	24	12	11	0	1	120	61	50·83
10. Northants	17	8	9	0	0	85	40	47·05
11. Hampshire	24	7	10	4	3	120	50	41·66
12. Gloucestershire	20	5	12	0	3	100	28	28·00
13. Sussex	24	4	16	2	2	120	28	23·33
14. Derbyshire	18	2	13	0	3	90	13	14·44
15. Leicestershire	22	1	16	2	3	110	14	12·72
16. Somerset	16	1	13	0	2	80	7	8·75

1951 CHAMPIONSHIP TABLE

	P	W	L	D	No Dec	1st inns lead in match L	D	Pts
Points Awarded		12				4	4	
Warwickshire	28	16	2	10	0	0	6	216
Yorkshire	28	12	3	11	2	0	10	184
Lancashire	28	8	2	14	4	1	9	136
Worcestershire	28	9	7	10	2	2	4	132
Glamorgan	28	8	4	13	3	1	7	128
Surrey	28	7	6	13	2	0	9	120
Middlesex	28	7	6	13	2	1	7	116
Essex	28	6	2	18	2	0	9	110
Hampshire	28	5	7	13	3	1	9	100
Sussex	28	6	6	15	1	0	5	94
Derbyshire	28	5	6	16	1	2	6	92
Gloucestershire	28	5	9	12	2	1	6	88
Northamptonshire	28	4	4	17	3	1	7	80
Somerset	28	5	15	6	2	3	1	76
Leicestershire	28	4	7	16	1	0	4	64
Kent	28	4	15	8	1	1	2	60
Nottinghamshire	28	1	11	13	3	0	7	40

Note: Essex and Sussex include two points for tie on first innings in drawn match.

1972 COUNTY CHAMPIONSHIP TABLE

	P	W	L	D	No Dec	Bttg Pts	Blg Pts	Pts
1. Warwickshire	20	9	0	11	0	68	69	227
2. Kent	20	7	4	9	0	69	52	191
3. Gloucestershire	20	7	4	9	0	38	77	185
4. Northants	20	7	3	10	0	34	77	181
5. Essex	20	6	4	10	0	50	63	173
6. Leicestershire	20	6	2	12	0	43	68	171
7. Worcestershire	20	4	4	12	0	59	68	167
8. Middlesex	20	5	5	10	0	48	61	159
9. Hampshire	20	4	6	10	0	50	64	154
10. Yorkshire	20	4	5	11	0	39	73	152
11. Somerset	20	4	2	14	0	34	71	145
12. Surrey	20	3	5	12	0	49	61	140
13. Glamorgan	20	1	7	12	0	55	61	126
14. Notts	20	1	6	13	0	38	73	121
15. Lancashire	20	2	3	14	1	42	56	118
16. Sussex	20	2	8	10	0	46	49	115
17. Derbyshire	20	1	5	13	1	27	60	97

HIGHEST AND LOWEST SCORES FOR WARWICKSHIRE

	Highest	Ground	Year	Lowest	Ground	Year
Derbyshire	635	Edgbaston	1900	28	Derby	1937
Essex	614/8	Edgbaston	1904	53	Edgbaston	1957
Glamorgan	543/8	Edgbaston	1927	61	Neath	1959
Gloucestershire	518	Gloucester	1937	62	Edgbaston	1900
Hampshire	657/6	Edgbaston	1899	36	Portsmouth	1927
Kent	513	Edgbaston	1928	16	Tonbridge	1913
Lancashire	532/4	Edgbaston	1901	49	Edgbaston	1896
Leicestershire	605	Leicester	1899	48	Coventry	1919
Middlesex	507/6	Lord's	1927	55	Lord's	1956
Northamptonshire	565/8	Northampton	1933	97	Northampton	1923
Nottinghamshire	520	Edgbaston	1930	71	Coventry	1929
Somerset	485/7	Taunton	1926	44	Taunton	1906
Surrey	585/7	The Oval	1905	45	The Oval	1953
Sussex	517/9	Leamington	1910	65	Edgbaston	1923
Worcestershire	645/7	Dudley	1914	66	Edgbaston	1950
Yorkshire	536/7	Edgbaston	1929	35	Edgbaston	1963
Australians	384	Edgbaston	1964	68	Edgbaston	1919
Cambridge University	460	Cambridge	1905	43	Cambridge	1936
Combined Services	368/9	Edgbaston	1949	112	Edgbaston	1953
Indians	375/9	Edgbaston	1946	181	Edgbaston	1936
New Zealanders	401	Edgbaston	1931	146	Edgbaston	1969
Oxford University	401/6	Edgbaston	1962	86	Stratford-on-Avon	1951
Pakistanis	439/6	Edgbaston	1967	170	Edgbaston	1954
Philadelphians	296	Edgbaston	1897	153	Coventry	1903
Scotland	401/4	Edgbaston	1966	157	Edgbaston	1959
South Africans	440	Edgbaston	1924	76	Edgbaston	1947
West Indies	384	Edgbaston	1928	104	Edgbaston	1923

	Highest	Ground	Year	Lowest	Ground	Year
Derbyshire	561	Derby	1902	39	Edgbaston	1894
Essex	522/8	Leyton	1930	47	Leyton	1968
Glamorgan	500	Swansea	1930	40	Cardiff	1929
Gloucestershire	504	Edgbaston	1898	56	Bristol	1953
Hampshire	616/7	Portsmouth	1920	15	Edgbaston	1922
Kent	571	Tonbridge	1898	42	Edgbaston	1925
Lancashire	526	Edgbaston	1920	76	Old Trafford	1906
Leicestershire	429	Leicester	1905	47	Edgbaston	1900
Middlesex	543/7	Lord's	1920	77	Edgbaston	1934
				77	Edgbaston	1958
Northamptonshire	413/9	Northampton	1967	53	Edgbaston	1912
Nottinghamshire	656/3	Coventry	1928	34	Nuneaton	1964
Somerset	427	Taunton	1926	50	Edgbaston	1951
Surrey	634	The Oval	1906	61	The Oval	1962
Sussex	546/5	Edgbaston	1937	23	Worthing	1964
Worcestershire	633	Worcester	1906	71	Edgbaston	1903
				71	Edgbaston	1949
Yorkshire	887	Edgbaston	1896	49	Huddersfield	1951
Australians	506	Edgbaston	1921	181	Edgbaston	1953
Cambridge University	446	Edgbaston	1921	36	Cambridge	1966
Combined Services	288/5	Edgbaston	1956	85	Edgbaston	1953
Indians	562	Edgbaston	1971	76	Edgbaston	1911
New Zealanders	492/6	Edgbaston	1927	159	Edgbaston	1931
Oxford University	349	Oxford	1950	53	Oxford	1905
Pakistanis	255/6	Edgbaston	1962	105	Edgbaston	1962
Philadelphians	269	Edgbaston	1897	112	Coventry	1903
Scotland	359	Edgbaston	1951	63	Edgbaston	1957
South Africans	520/7	Edgbaston	1947	74	Edgbaston	1901
West Indies	474	Edgbaston	1933	156	Edgbaston	1950

INNINGS TOTAL OF OVER 600 RUNS BY WARWICKSHIRE

657 for 6 wkts	v. Hampshire, Edgbaston	1899
605	v. Leicestershire, Leicester	1899
635	v. Derbyshire, Edgbaston	1900
614 for 8 wkts	v. Essex, Edgbaston	1904
645 for 7 wkts	v. Worcestershire, Dudley	1914
603 for 9 wkts	v. Worcestershire, Edgbaston	1920

INNINGS TOTAL OF UNDER 30 RUNS BY WARWICKSHIRE

| 16 | v. Kent, Tonbridge | 1913 |
| 28 | v. Derbyshire, Derby | 1937 |

INNINGS TOTAL OF OVER 600 RUNS AGAINST WARWICKSHIRE

887	by Yorkshire, Edgbaston	1896
602	by Surrey, The Oval	1897
609	by Surrey, The Oval	1898
634	by Surrey, The Oval	1906
633	by Worcestershire, Worcester	1906
631 for 5 wkts	by Rest of England, The Oval	1911
616 for 7 wkts	by Hampshire, Portsmouth	1920
656 for 3 wkts	by Nottinghamshire, Coventry	1928

INNINGS TOTAL OF UNDER 30 RUNS AGAINST WARWICKSHIRE

| 15 | by Hampshire, Edgbaston | 1922 |
| 23 | by Sussex, Worthing | 1964 |

TIE MATCHES

| | v. Sussex, Hove | 1952 |

RECORD WICKET PARTNERSHIPS FOR WARWICKSHIRE

1st Wkt	377*	N. F. Horner and K. Ibadulla v. Surrey, The Oval	1960
2nd ,,	344	J. Devey and S. P. Kinneir v. Derbyshire, Edgbaston	1900
3rd ,,	327	W. G. Quaife and S. P. Kinneir v. Lancashire, Edgbaston	1901
4th ,,	402	R. B. Kanhai and K. Ibadulla v. Nottinghamshire, Trent Bridge	1968
5th ,,	268	W. Quaife and W. G. Quaife v. Essex, Leyton	1900
6th ,,	220	H. E. Dollery and J. Buckingham v. Derbyshire, Derby	1938
7th ,,	250	H. E. Dollery and J. S. Ord v. Kent, Maidstone	1953
8th ,,	228	A. J. Croom and R. E. S. Wyatt v. Worcestershire, Dudley	1925
9th ,,	154	G. W. Stephens and A. J. Croom v. Derbyshire, Edgbaston	1925
10th ,,	128	F. R. Santall and W. Sanders v. Yorkshire, Edgbaston	1930

* Unbroken

RECORD WICKET PARTNERSHIPS AGAINST WARWICKSHIRE

1st Wkt	352	T. Hayward and J. B. Hobbs for Surrey, The Oval	1909
2nd „	333	P. Holmes and E. Oldroyd for Yorkshire, Edgbaston	1922
3rd „	292	Col. A. C. Johnson and C. P. Mead for Hampshire, Southampton	1911
4th „	250	H. H. I. H. Gibbons and M. Nichol for Worcestershire, Dudley	1929
5th „	393	E. G. Arnold and W. B. Burns for Worcestershire, Edgbaston	1909*
6th „	260	A. Wharton and K. Cranston for Lancashire, Edgbaston	1948
7th „	229	W. Timms and F. Walden for Northamptonshire, Northampton	1926
8th „	292	R. Peel and Lord Hawke for Yorkshire, Edgbaston	1896
9th „	283	J. Chapman and A. R. Warren for Derbyshire, Blackwell	1910†
10th „	131	E. Tyldesley and R. Whitehead for Lancashire, Edgbaston	1914

* English Record
† World Record

3. Individual Figures
for 1972

AVERAGES – ALL FIRST-CLASS MATCHES

Pld 23   *Won* 9   *Lost* 1   *Drawn* 13

Batting	Matches	Inns	Total	Highest Score	Not Out	Ave	100	50	Ct	St
R. B. Kanhai	21	30	1607	199	5	64·28	8	3	28	—
D. L. Amiss	18	29	1219	192	7	55·40	5	1	14	—
M. J. K. Smith	19	28	1107	119	6	50·31	2	8	4	—
A. Kallicharran	22	32	1153	164	5	42·70	2	5	14	—
D. L. Murray	14	21	412	54	6	27·46	—	1	40	4
J. Whitehouse	18	30	674	55	2	24·07	—	3	6	—
J. A. Jameson	17	28	543	78	2	20·88	—	3	4	1
A. C. Smith	17	17	227	28	5	18·91	—	—	12	1
N. M. McVicker	22	25	318	65*	6	16·73	—	2	2	—
R. N. Abberley	4	6	75	49	1	15·00	—	—	6	—
D. J. Brown	17	17	195	79	4	15·00	—	1	7	—
K. Ibadulla	7	9	69	41	1	8·62	—	—	3	—
R. G. D. Willis	10	7	42	12	2	8·40	—	—	5	—
L. R. Gibbs	21	14	64	24	7	9·14	—	—	17	—
B. J. Flick	2	2	7	6*	1	7·00	—	—	2	3
W. N. Tidy	3	3	12	12*	1	6·00	—	—	—	—
S. J. Rouse	13	8	33	9	2	5·50	—	—	9	—
P. J. Lewington	6	4	8	8*	2	4·00	—	—	3	—
W. Blenkiron	2	0	0	0	0	0·00	—	—	2	—

* Not Out

Bowling	Overs	Mdns	Runs	Wkts	Ave	5 Wkts
N. M. McVicker	580·1	159	1571	66	23·80	3
A. C. Smith	233·2	73	540	22	24·54	1
D. J. Brown	369·2	78	973	37	26·29	1
L. R. Gibbs	596·1	162	1428	52	27·46	2
S. J. Rouse	321·3	58	989	36	27·47	1
W. Blenkiron	56	10	199	7	28·42	—
R. G. D. Willis	273·1	65	803	28	28·67	1
W. N. Tidy	64	10	288	10	28·80	—

APPENDIX 3

Bowling contd.	Overs	Mdns	Runs	Wkts	Ave	5 Wkts
P. J. Lewington	139·1	31	471	16	29·43	—
R. N. Abberley	23	4	72	2	36·00	—
A. Kallicharran	64·4	7	258	7	36·85	—
K. Ibadulla	154·4	43	407	9	45·22	—
J. Whitehouse	55	9	170	3	56·66	—
J. A. Jameson	96	16	278	4	69·50	—
D. L. Amiss	3	0	25	0	—	—
R. B. Kanhai	8	1	23	0	—	—
M. J. K. Smith	2	1	4	0	—	—

Overall

Warwickshire		Opponents
7765	Batted Runs	8499
67	Byes	100
161	Leg-Byes	207
20	Wides	22
105	No Balls	76
8118	Total Runs	8904
245	Wickets	306
33·13	Ave runs per wkt	29·09

AVERAGES — COUNTY CHAMPIONSHIP MATCHES

	Points		
	Batt	Bowl	Total
Pld 20 *Won* 9 *Lost* 0 *Drawn* 11	68	69	227

Batting and Fielding

	Matches	Inns	Total	Highest Score	Not Out	Ave	100	50	Ct	St
D. L. Amiss	15	24	1129	192	7	66·41	5	1	13	—
R. B. Kanhai	20	28	1437	199	4	59·87	7	3	26	—
A. Kallicharran	20	28	994	164	4	41·41	2	3	11	—
M. J. K. Smith	16	23	743	102	5	41·27	1	6	4	—
D. L. Murray	14	21	412	54	6	27·46	—	1	40	4
J. Whitehouse	15	24	528	55	1	22·95	—	3	6	—
J. A. Jameson	15	24	469	78	2	21·31	—	3	4	1
A. C. Smith	14	13	161	26*	4	17·88	—	—	12	1
N. M. McVicker	20	23	297	65*	5	16·50	—	2	2	—
D. J. Brown	15	15	174	79	4	15·81	—	1	6	—
R. G. D. Willis	9	6	39	12	2	9·75	—	—	4	—
R. N. Abberley	3	4	26	25	1	8·66	—	—	3	—
P. J. Lewington	5	3	8	8*	2	8·00	—	—	1	—
L. R. Gibbs	19	13	54	24	6	7·71	—	—	16	—
K. Ibadulla	5	5	22	12	0	4·40	—	—	1	—
S. J. Rouse	12	7	26	9	1	4·33	—	—	8	—
W. Blenkiron	2	0	0	0	0	0·00	—	—	2	—
W. N. Tidy	1	1	0	0	0	0·00	—	—	0	—
'Substitute'									1	

* Not Out

Bowling	Overs	Mdns	Runs	Wkts	Ave	5 Wkts
A. C. Smith	202·3	66	449	20	22·45	1
N. M. McVicker	527·1	137	1496	63	23·74	3
L. R. Gibbs	551·1	148	1324	50	26·48	2
D. J. Brown	332·2	70	902	34	27·70	1
S. J. Rouse	288·2	52	894	32	27·93	1
W. Blenkiron	56	10	199	7	28·42	—
P. J. Lewington	106·1	26	322	11	29·27	—
R. G. D. Willis	246·1	57	732	25	29·28	1
A. Kallicharran	54·4	5	232	6	36·36	—
W. N. Tidy	17	0	119	3	39·66	—
K. Ibadulla	92	26	251	5	50·20	—
J. Whitehouse	46	9	123	2	61·50	—
J. A. Jameson	80	14	216	3	72·00	—
R. N. Abberley	6	1	12	0	—	—
R. B. Kanhai	8	1	23	0	—	—
M. J. K. Smith	2	1	4	0	—	—

Overall

Warwickshire		Opponents
6519	Batted Runs	7298
56	Byes	87
130	Leg-Byes	194
13	Wides	18
84	No Balls	63
6802	Total Runs	7660
207	Wickets	267
32·85	Ave runs per wkt	28·68

Centuries (15)

R. B. Kanhai (7)

199 v. Lancs at Old Trafford
165 v. Lancs at Edgbaston
124 v. Derbyshire at Edgbaston
123* v. Glamorgan at Edgbaston
121* v. Hampshire at Portsmouth
115 v. Kent at Dartford
121 v. Northants at Northampton

D. L. Amiss (5)

192 v. Lancs at Edgbaston
156 v. Worcs at Edgbaston
151* v. Middlesex at Edgbaston
121* v. Kent at Dartford
120 v. Notts at Coventry

A. Kallicharran (2)

164 v. Notts at Coventry
149 v. Surrey at Edgbaston

M. J. K. Smith (1)

102 v. Essex at Chelmsford

* Not Out

APPENDIX 3

Pld 16   *Won* 7   *Lost* 8   *Aban* 1   *Pts* 29

Batting	Matches	Inns	Total	Highest Score	Not Out	Ave	100	50	6s	Ct
R. B. Kanhai	16	15	444	120	1	31·71	1	2	8	6
K. Ibadulla	3	2	31	16*	1	31·00	—	—	—	—
A. Kallicharran	16	15	340	101*	4	30·90	1	1	7	3
D. L. Amiss	12	11	256	73	2	28·44	—	3	—	5
D. L. Murray	15	11	177	46*	4	25·28	—	—	1	18
D. J. Brown	11	4	43	38	2	21·50	—	—	—	—
M. J. K. Smith	13	12	253	50	0	21·08	—	1	4	4
J. Whitehouse	16	15	222	38	1	15·85	—	—	1	6
A. C. Smith	4	2	15	15*	1	15·00	—	—	—	2
N. M. McVicker	15	9	101	23	2	14·42	—	—	4	2
J. A. Jameson	13	12	167	28	0	13·91	—	—	3	1
S. J. Rouse	15	5	25	13	2	8·33	—	—	—	2
W. Blenkiron	9	5	20	8	1	5·00	—	—	—	2
R. N. Abberley	4	3	4	4*	1	2·00	—	—	—	—
E. E. Hemmings	4	1	31	31*	1	—	—	—	—	1
R. G. D. Willis	7	2	6	6*	2	—	—	—	—	—
L. R. Gibbs	3	1	0	0	0	—	—	—	—	—

Bowling	Overs	Mdns	Runs	Wkts	Ave	4 wkts
A. C. Smith	25	2	66	10	6·60	1
R. G. D. Willis	46·4	5	179	15	11·93	—
K. Ibadulla	22	2	80	5	16·00	1
W. Blenkiron	63	6	288	13	22·15	—
J. A. Jameson	23	1	139	5	27·80	—
N. M. McVicker	109	12	403	14	28·78	—
D. J. Brown	73	5	293	8	36·62	—
S. J. Rouse	113	6	462	9	51·33	—
R. N. Abberley	14·4	0	66	1	66·00	—
L. R. Gibbs	24	2	83	1	83·00	—
E. E. Hemmings	14	0	88	1	88·00	—

Also Bowled: D. L. Amiss 3-0-23-1; R. B. Kanhai 2-1-2-1; A. Kallicharran 0.1-0-2-0.

Overall

Warwickshire		Opponents
2135	Batted Runs	2174
18	Byes	18
78	Leg-Byes	85
7	Wides	7
14	No Balls	13
2252	Total Runs	2297
100	Wickets	93
22·52	Ave runs per wkt	24·69

Centuries (2)

R. Kanhai   120   v. Leicestershire at Edgbaston
A. Kallicharran 101* v. Derbyshire at Chesterfield
*Not Out

4. Representative Match Appearances

❖ ❖ ❖

TEST CRICKETERS

England	No of Tests	Aust.	S.A.	W.I.	N.Z.	Ind.	Pak.	R.O.W.
Amiss D. L.	10	1	—	1	—	3	4	1
Barber R. W.	28	7	8	2	3	5	3	—
Brown D. J.	28	8	2	8	5	—	3	2
Calthorpe Hon F. S. G.	4	—	—	4	—	—	—	—
Cartwright T. W.	5	2	2	—	1	—	—	—
Dollery H. E.	4	2	1	1	—	—	—	—
Foster F. R.	11	8	3	—	—	—	—	—
Hollies W. E.	13	1	3	5	4	—	—	—
Howell H.	5	4	1	—	—	—	—	—
Jameson J. A.	2	—	—	—	—	2	—	—
Kinneir S. P.	1	1	—	—	—	—	—	—
Lilley A. A.	35	32	3	—	—	—	—	—
Paine G. A. E.	4	—	—	4	—	—	—	—
Quaife W. G.	7	7	—	—	—	—	—	—
Smith A. C.	6	4	—	—	2	—	—	—
Smith E. J.	11	7	4	—	—	—	—	—
Smith M. J. K.	50	14	7	6	18	2	3	—
Spooner R. T.	7	—	6	1	—	—	—	—
Wyatt R. E. S.	40	12	17	9	2	—	—	—
	271	110	57	41	35	12	13	3

Captains of England

	Tests as Captain	Opponents						Results			Toss won
		Aust.	S.A.	W.I.	N.Z.	Ind.	Pak.	W	L	D	
Calthorpe Hon F. S. G.	4	—	—	4	—	—	—	1	1	2	2
Smith M. J. K.	25	5	8	1	6	5	—	5	3	17	11
Wyatt R. E. S.	16	5	5	5	1	—	—	3	5	8	7

West Indies

R. B. Kanhai	66 times plus 5 for Rest of World v. England 1970
L. R. Gibbs	56 „ „ 4 „ Rest of World v. England 1970
D. L. Murray	5 „
A. Kallicharran	2 „

New Zealand

M. P. Donnelly	7 times
Don Taylor	3 „

India and Pakistan

		Toss			
		W	*L*	*D*	*won*
Abdul Hafeez	3 times				
A. H. Kardar	23 „ all as Captain	6	6	11	10
K. Ibadulla	4 Tests for Pakistan 1964–7				

GENTLEMEN V PLAYERS
1865–1962

ALL GROUNDS

WARWICKSHIRE PLAYERS' APPEARANCES

Gentlemen

Allan J. M.	1	1956
Barber R. W.	4	1959–1962
Bainbridge H. W.	2	1894–1895
Byrne J. F.	1	1905
Calthorpe Hon. F. S. G.	12	1920–1933 (Captain 1932–1933)
Dempster C. S.	1	1937
Donnelly M. S.	4	1946–1948
Fiddian-Green C. A.	1	1922
Foster D. G.	3	1929–1932
Foster F. R.	8	1910–1914
Kardar A. H.	1	1949
Kemp-Welch G. D.	1	1931
Lewis E. B.	2	1954–1957
Parsons Rev. J. H.	4	1929–1931
Partridge N. E.	1	1936
Smith A. C.	4	1960–1962
Smith M. J. K.	13	1955–1962
Wheatley O. S.	6	1958–1962
Wyatt R. E. S.	23	1926–1947 (Captain 1931, 1934, 1935)

Note: D. Buchanan played in 1868–69–70–71–72–73–74; H. W. Bainbridge 1885–86; J. Cranston 1889–90; E. J. Aires 1884–85–86; F. R. Evans 1865; H. Rotherham 1880–82–83–84; and H. O. Whitby in 1884, all before Warwickshire became a first-class county.

Players

Barnes S. F.	8	1902–1914
Bates L. A.	1	1925
Cartwright T. W.	1	1959
Croom A. J. W.	2	1930–1931
Diver E. J.	1	1899
Dollery H. E.	5	1939–1955 (Captain 1950)
Field F. E.	1	1911
Gardner F. C.	1	1957
Hargreaves S.	3	1902–1904
Hollies W. E.	4	1946–1957
Howell H.	8	1920–1925
Jeeves P.	1	1914
Kinneir S. P.	2	1909–1911
Lilley A. A.	14	1895–1909 (Captain 1904, 05, 06, 08, 09)
Mayer J. H.	1	1931
Paine G. E. A.	1	1934
Parsons J. H.	3	1914–1927
Pritchard T. L.	2	1948–1951
Quaife W. G.	12	1897–1913
Quaife W.	1	1895
Smith E. J.	5	1911–1928

OXFORD AND CAMBRIDGE UNIVERSITY 'BLUES'
1864–1971

Oxford University

Allan J. M.	1953–6
Donnelly M. P.	1946–7 Captain 1947
Hewetson E. P.	1923–5
Holdsworth R. L.	1919–22
Jones A. K. C.	1971
Kardar A. H.	1947–9
Maudsley R. H.	1946–7
Sale R.	1939–46
Smith A. C.	1958–60 Captain 1959–60
Smith M. J. K.	1954–6 Captain 1956

Note: F. R. Evans also got his 'Blue' in 1864; E. M. Kenney 1866–8; G. P. Robertson, 1866; H. O. Whitby 1884 and A. R. Cobb 1866, before Warwickshire became a first-class county.

Cambridge University

Bainbridge H. W.	1884–6 Captain 1886
Barber R. W.	1956–7
Buchanan D.	1850
Calthorpe Hon. F. S. G.	1912–14; 1919
Fiddian-Green C. A.	1921–2
Goodwin H. J.	1907–8
Jameson T. E. N.	1970
Kemp-Welch G. D.	1929–31 Captain 1931
McDowall J. I.	1969
Mills J. M.	1946–8 Captain 1948
Partridge N. E.	1920
Rotherham G. A.	1919
Singh S.	1955–6
Thompson J. R.	1938–9
Wheatley O. S.	1957–8
White A. F. T.	1936

Note: C. W. Rock played 1884–6.

5.
Career Figures for all Warwickshire Players in First–Class Cricket (1894–1972)

❖ ❖ ❖

Player	Period of Service	Inns	Runs	Highest Score	Not Out	Ave	100s	1000 Runs	Test Matches	Overs	Mdns	Runs	Wkts	Ave	100 Wkts
Abberley R. N.	1964–72	266	6034	117*	18	24·31	2	3	—	43	5	149	2	74·50	—
Abell R.	1967	8	27	12	2	4·50	—	—	—	41	10	112	4	28·00	—
Adderley C. H.	1946	—	—	—	—	—	—	—	—	83·1	18	255	4	63·75	—
Allan J. M.	1966–8	58	744	76*	17	18·14	—	—	—	850·1	235	2274	58	39·48	—
Amiss D. L.	1960–72	388	12 287	192*	47	36·03	19	7	10	123·4	23	395	11	35·90	—
Austin H.	1919	6	45	13	2	11·25	—	—	—	72·4	9	234	2	117·00	—
Bainbridge H. W.	1894–1902	186	4973	162	16	29·25	6	2	—	11	—	36	1	36·00	—
Baker C. S.	1905–20	356	9269	155*	42	29·50	10	3	—	243·4	31	1009	22	45·86	—
Bannister J. D.	1950–68	446	3088	71	121	9·40	—	—	—	11 296	3269	25 918	1181	21·95	3
Barber E.	1936	3	31	13	0	10·33	—	—	—	—	—	—	—	—	—
Barber R. W.	1963–9	214	5978	138	11	29·44	5	2	28	1668·3	399	4854	197	24·63	—
Barber W. H.	1927–33	6	71	23	1	14·20	—	—	—	87	15	253	7	36·14	—
Barbery A.	1906–7	3	13	6	0	4·33	—	—	—	59·2	6	245	3	81·66	—
Barker M. P.	1946	9	55	17	2	7·85	—	—	—	136·3	24	378	16	23·62	—
Barnes S. F.	1895–6	6	38	13	2	9·50	—	—	—	78	23	199	3	66·33	—
Barnes T. P.	1956	1	7	7	0	7·00	—	—	—	—	—	—	—	—	—
Barton J.	1895–6	4	38	16	0	9·50	—	—	—	69	23	165	7	23·57	—
Bates L. A.	1913–35	745	19 326	211	53	27·92	21	12	—	89·4	7	429	8	53·62	—
Bates S. H.	1910–19	10	46	22	1	5·11	—	—	—	58	14	182	6	30·33	—
Bayley M. G.	1969	2	2	1*	1	2·00	—	—	—	53	22	125	3	41·66	—
Baynton R. G.	1921–3	19	212	36	1	11·77	—	—	—	168·1	29	479	14	34·21	—
Benjamin H.	1919	2	12	8	0	6·00	—	—	—	13	—	60	1	60·00	—
Benson G. L.	1959–61	5	102	46	2	34·00	—	—	—	17	7	32	2	16·00	—
Blenkiron W.	1964–72	116	1254	62	27	14·08	—	—	—	2770·2	655	7492	268	27·95	—
Bostock-Hill A. J.	1920	2	4	4	0	2·00	—	—	—	4	0	22	0	—	—
Breedon C. L.	1910	8	80	27	1	11·42	—	—	—	7	2	29	0	—	—
Brewster V.	1965	4	58	35*	1	19·33	—	—	—	71·3	29	175	10	17·50	—
Bridge W. B.	1955–68	130	1054	56*	34	10·97	—	—	—	2920·4	987	7363	281	26·31	1
Brindle R. G.	1949	2	74	42	0	37·00	—	—	—	—	—	—	—	—	—
Broberg F.	1920	1	4	4	0	4·00	—	—	—	5	2	16	0	—	—
Bromley P. H.	1947–56	66	1183	121*	11	22·30	1	—	—	486·1	145	1264	35	36·11	—
Brown A.	1932	1	1	1*	1	—	—	—	—	36	8	96	2	48·00	—
Brown D. J.	1961–72	229	2095	79	62	12·54	—	—	28	5306·5	1202	14 329	620	23·10	—

Brown E.	1932 – 3	25	99	19*	8	5·82	—	—	—	646·3	159	1629	52	31·32	—
Brown J.	1913 – 14	12	12	7	5	1·71	—	—	—	96	22	264	9	29·33	—
Buckingham J.	1933 – 9	142	2840	137*	23	23·86	3	1	—						
Busher H. A.	1908	2	15	15	1	15·00	—	—	—						
Byrne G. R.	1912	12	36	11	0	3·00	—	—	—	24·1	3	84	6	14·00	—
Byrne J. F.	1897 – 1912	215	4721	222	10	23·02	4	—	—	606·2	110	2123	70	30·32	—
Calthorpe Hon. F.S.G.	1919 – 30	362	8311	209	28	24·88	10	2	4	5815·5	1451	15 297	513	29·82	—
Cannings V. H. D.	1947 – 9	77	745	61	25	14·32	—	—	—	1228	332	2914	88	33·11	—
Carter R. G.	1951 – 61	109	599	37	19	6·65	—	—	—	2423·5	632	6699	241	27·79	—
Cartwright T. W.	1952 – 69	558	10 783	210	70	22·09	5	3	5	9364·3	3694	19 838	1058	18·75	7
Charlesworth C.	1898 – 1921	632	14 289	216	27	23·61	15	5	—	2880·1	603	8838	295	29·95	—
Clarkson W.	1922 – 3	4	59	41	0	14·75	—	—	—	17·4	1	52	2	26·00	—
Clugston D. L.	1928 – 46	9	64	17	0	7·11	—	—	—	110	5	475	4	118·75	—
Collin T.	1933 – 6	75	1399	105*	7	20·57	1	—	—	449·3	100	1302	26	50·07	—
Cook D. R.	1962 – 8	9	108	28*	5	27·00	—	—	—	261·5	80	534	23	23·21	—
Cook M. S.	1961 – 2	4	110	52	0	27·50	—	—	—						
Cooke R.	1925 – 6	21	66	14	4	3·88	—	—	—	209	59	507	16	31·68	—
Cordner J.	1952						—	—	—	19	6	36	0	—	—
Cotton R. H.	1947	3	0	0	1	—	—	—	—	44	9	128	2	64·00	—
Cowan C. F. R.	1909 – 21	47	759	78	2	16·86	—	—	—	3·4	1	9	0	—	—
Cranmer P.	1934 – 54	268	5595	113	13	21·94	4	3	—	275	35	1051	21	50·04	—
Crawford A. B.	1911	10	140	40	3	20·00	—	—	—	78·3	10	310	13	23·84	—
Cresswell J.	1895 – 9	23	149	16	10	11·46	—	—	—	593·4	187	1134	42	27·23	—
Crichton H. T.	1908	3	26	26	0	8·66	—	—	—	8	0	30	2	15·00	—
Crockford E. B.	1912 – 22	34	355	55	0	10·44	—	—	—	49	5	178	2	89·00	—
Croom A. J.	1922 – 39	622	17 662	211	65	31·70	24	12	—	1576	160	6062	138	43·92	—
Croom L.	1949	8	73	26	0	9·12	—	—	—						
Cross A. J.	1969	2	38	20	0	19·00	—	—	—						
Cross E. P.	1921 – 3	12	61	12*	3	6·77	—	—	—						
Curle A. C.	1920	4	60	40	1	16·66	—	—	—						
Curle G.	1913	9	54	34	0	6·00	—	—	—	1·4	0	3	1	3·00	—
Davies C. S.	1930 – 6	11	112	63	0	10·18	—	—	—	179	32	672	14	48·00	—
Dempster C. S.	1946	5	69	40	0	13·80	—	—	—						
Devey J.	1894 – 1907	250	6512	246	20	28·31	8	1	—	233·5	53	655	16	40·93	—
Dickins F.	1898 – 1903	32	172	35	6	6·61	—	—	—	841·5	289	1782	75	23·76	—
Diver E. J.	1894 – 1901	186	4280	184	10	24·05	4	1	—	65·3	18	187	6	37·17	—

Player	Period of Service	Inns	Runs	Highest Score	Not Out	Ave	100s	1000 Runs	Test Matches	Overs	Mdns	Runs	Wkts	Ave	100 Wkts
Dobson F.	1928	3	9	7	0	3·00	—	—	—	59	16	138	7	19·71	—
Dobson K. W. C.	1925	4	27	12*	1	9·00	—	—	—	6	1	24	0	—	—
Docker L. C.	1894–5	18	465	85*	2	29·06	—	—	—	—	—	—	—	—	—
Dollery H. E.	1934–55	679	23 457	212	63	38·07	49	15	4	9·2	2	32	0	—	—
Dollery K. R.	1951–6	94	927	41	21	12·69	—	—	—	2027	336	5549	215	25·80	—
Donnelly M. P.	1948–50	30	988	120	0	32·93	1	—	7	9	3	35	2	17·50	—
Dunkels P.	1971	1	0	0	0	—	—	—	—	25	2	91	0	—	—
Durnell T. W.	1921–30	11	21	5*	3	2·62	—	—	—	419·3	78	1143	41	27·87	—
Edmonds R. B.	1962–7	100	1006	102*	31	14·57	1	—	—	1709·3	582	3994	146	27·35	—
Elson G.	1946	2	7	4	1	7·00	—	—	—	52	14	116	1	116·00	—
Everitt R. S.	1909	5	57	38	0	11·40	—	—	—	—	—	—	—	—	—
Fabling A. H.	1921	2	8	7	0	4·00	—	—	—	—	—	—	—	—	—
Fantham W.	1935–48	103	1168	51	12	12·83	—	—	—	871	139	2907	64	45·52	—
Farren G.	1912	1	0	0	0	—	—	—	—	83·4	15	344	5	68·80	—
Fiddian-Green C. A.	1920–8	106	2309	95	24	28·15	—	—	—	—	—	—	—	—	—
Field F. E.	1897–1920	344	1865	39	102	7·70	—	—	—	7414·5	1670	22 862	978	23·37	2
Fishwick T. S.	1896–1909	342	8644	140*	13	26·28	12	2	—	5	0	35	0	—	—
Flaherty K. F.	1969	—	—	—	—	—	—	—	—	36	7	107	4	26·75	—
Fletcher B. E.	1956–61	79	1511	102*	13	22·89	1	—	—	3	1	13	0	—	—
Flick B. J.	1969–72	3	8	6*	1	4·00	—	—	—	—	—	—	—	—	—
Flint D.	1948–9	10	44	18*	3	6·28	—	—	—	185	45	465	12	38·75	—
Forester T.	1896–9	36	243	38	13	10·57	—	—	—	1001	325	2229	77	28·94	—
Foster A. W.	1914	2	1	1*	1	1·00	—	—	—	—	—	—	—	—	—
Foster D. G.	1929–34	72	726	70	5	10·83	—	—	—	1140·4	231	3415	138	24·74	—
Foster F. R.	1908–14	216	5436	305*	14	26·91	5	2	11	4471	1049	12 183	596	20·44	2
Fox J.	1922–8	50	469	27*	19	15·12	—	—	—	422·2	109	908	15	60·53	—
Fox J. G.	1959–61	54	515	52	6	10·72	—	—	—	0·3	0	0	0	—	—
Franklin R. C.	1900	1	0	0	0	—	—	—	—	—	—	—	—	—	—
Gardner F. C.	1947–61	593	17 826	215*	66	33·82	29	10	—	17·5	1	99	0	—	—
George W.	1901–6	18	342	71	2	21·25	—	—	—	—	—	—	—	—	—
Gibbs L. R.	1967–72	92	355	24	46	7·77	—	—	56	3500	1084	8019	333	24·08	1
Giddings A.	1919	20	147	32	1	7·73	—	—	—	20	3	67	4	16·75	—

Glassford J.	1969	1	0	0	0	—	—	—	58	11	161	5	32·20	—
Glover A. C. S.	1895 – 1909	226	5161	124	28	26·06	7	1	526	110	1578	49	32·20	—
Glynn B. T.	1959 – 61	3	13	7	0	4·33	—	—	17	7	32	2	16·00	—
Gobey S. C.	1946	3	2	2	0	0·66	—	—	2	0	9	0	—	—
Goodway C. C.	1937 – 47	66	484	37*	12	8·03	—	—	152·4	23	541	14	38·64	—
Goodwin H. J.	1907 – 12	36	728	101	1	20·80	1	—	0·4	0	1	0	—	—
Gordon A.	1966 – 71	59	891	65	4	16·20	—	—						—
Granville R. St. L.	1934	2	9	7	0	4·50	—	—						—
Gray J. D.	1968 – 9	6	34	18	3	11·33	—	1	199·1	48	534	21	25·42	—
Grayland A.	1922 – 30	6	15	6	1	3·00	—	—	55·5	6	204	2	102·00	—
Green J. H.	1927	1	0	0*	1	—	—	—	4	0	16	0	—	—
Greenings T. J.	1912	2	26	14	1	26·00	—	—	33	5	91	1	91·00	—
Griffiths S.	1956 – 8	26	76	17*	12	5·42	—	—	708·4	158	1827	74	24·68	—
Gross F. A.	1934	1	0	0*	1	—	—	—	25	4	76	1	76·00	—
Grove C. W.	1938 – 53	288	2973	104*	36	11·79	1	1	6529·3	1607	15484	697	22·21	2
Guy J. B.	1950	3	24	18	0	8·00	—	—						—
Hacking J. H.	1946	2	17	14	0	8·50	—	—	16	2	66	0	—	—
Hall W.	1905	3	11	8	0	3·66	—	—	3	0	13	0	—	—
Hampton W. M.	1922	1	34	34	0	34·00	—	—	44·5	7	137	4	34·25	—
Hands B. O.	1946 – 7	2	13	9	0	6·50	—	—						—
Hands W. C.	1909 – 20	91	856	63	23	12·58	—	—	1171·3	233	3435	137	25·21	—
Harris A. J.	1919	2	18	14	0	9·00	—	—						—
Harris D. F.	1946	1	2	2	0	2·00	—	—						—
Harris W. H.	1904 – 19	17	172	42	1	10·75	—	—						—
Hargreave S.	1899 – 1909	242	1803	45	60	9·90	—	5	8032	2382	18493	848	21·80	—
Harvey W. H.	1927	1	24	24	0	24·00	—	—						—
Hastilow C. A. F.	1919	2	12	12	0	6·00	—	—						—
Hawkins C.	1957	5	16	11*	2	5·33	—	—						—
Hayhurst A.	1934 – 5	8	98	42	0	12·25	—	—	138·5	31	457	12	38·08	—
Heath D. M. W.	1949 – 53	23	376	54	1	17·09	—	—						—
Hellawell M.	1962	2	59	30*	2	—	—	—	34·5	7	114	6	19·00	—
Hemmings E. E.	1966 – 71	82	1397	80	20	22·53	—	—	1124·3	293	3217	85	37·84	—
Hewetson E. P.	1919 – 27	34	312	37*	5	10·75	—	—	588·5	103	1681	66	25·46	—
Hewitt E. J.	1954	2	41	40	0	20·50	—	—	17	3	60	1	60·00	—
Hickman G.	1929	4	19	17	0	4·75	—	—						—
Hilditch T. A.	1907 – 13	11	42	17	1	4·20	—	—	85·1	9	319	9	35·44	—

Player	Period of Service	Inns	Runs	Highest Score	Not Out	Ave	100s	1000 Runs	Test Matches	Overs	Mdns	Runs	Wkts	Ave	100 Wkts
Hill G. H.	1958 – 60	47	247	23	6	6·02	—	—	—	1257·4	441	3178	107	29·70	—
Hill H. G.	1894 – 1900	7	41	13	1	6·83	—	—	—	84·3	19	248	5	49·60	—
Hill J. E.	1894 – 1900	34	665	139*	1	20·15	1	—	—	3	0	14	0	—	—
Hill W. A.	1929 – 48	279	6423	147*	22	24·99	6	2	—	12	1	27	1	27·00	—
Hitchcock R. E.	1949 – 64	511	12 269	153*	70	27·82	13	5	—	1985	563	5199	182	28·56	—
Holbeach W. H.	1910	2	0	0	0	—	—	—	—						
Holdsworth R. L.	1919 – 21	54	1222	141	1	23·05	1	—	—	3	0	17	1	17·00	—
Hollies W. E.	1932 – 57	570	1542	47	258	4·94	—	—	13	20 147	6451	45 019	2201	20·45	14
Horner N. F.	1951 – 65	647	18 217	203*	33	29·66	25	12	—	10·2	1	73	0	—	—
Hopkins F. J.	1898 – 1903	16	32	13	0	2·00	—	—	—	246	59	765	25	30·60	—
Hossell J. J.	1939 – 47	62	1217	83	5	21·35	—	—	—	116·2	18	370	7	52·85	—
Houghton W. E.	1946 – 7	11	165	41	0	15·00	—	—	—						
Howell A.	1919 – 22	56	249	26	16	6·22	—	—	—	557·5	74	1947	55	35·41	—
Howell H.	1913 – 28	261	1369	34	88	7·91	—	—	—	6415·2	1217	18 089	899	20·12	6
Hyde A.	1905 – 7	1	2	2*	1	—	—	—	—	26	0	121	2	60·50	—
Ibadulla K.	1954 – 72	630	14 766	171	70	26·36	17	6	3	5314·5	1637	12 548	418	30·01	—
Illingworth E. A.	1920	12	17	8*	3	1·88	—	—	—	83	9	312	8	39·00	—
Jackson A. K.	1928 – 31	3	5	3*	2	5·00	—	—	—	15	1	73	0	—	—
Jameson J. A.	1960 – 72	421	11 832	231	37	30·81	14	8	2	682	145	2114	60	35·28	—
Jameson T. E. N.	1970	2	63	32	0	31·50	—	—	—	20	7	75	0	—	—
Jarrett H.	1932 – 3	15	228	45	1	16·28	—	—	—	396·3	35	1615	47	34·36	—
Jeeves P.	1912 – 14	80	1193	86	6	16·12	—	—	—	1458·1	389	3919	194	20·20	1
Jennings G. A.	1923 – 5	27	243	41	5	11·04	—	—	—	318·4	60	916	23	39·82	—
Jones A. K. C.	1969	2	46	35	0	23·00	—	—	—						
Jones R. H.	1946	2	32	23	0	16·00	—	—	—	11	3	27	0	—	—
Kallicharran A.	1971 – 2	35	1192	164	6	41·10	2	1	2	71·4	7	290	7	41·42	—
Kanhai R. B.	1968 – 72	168	7528	253	24	52·27	24	5	66	24·2	2	107	0	—	—
Kardar A. H.	1948 – 50	69	1372	112	9	22·86	1	—	—	1451	503	3047	110	27·70	—
Kemp-Welch G. D.	1927 – 35	83	1419	123	7	18·67	1	—	—	118·5	17	429	5	85·80	—
Kendall J. T.	1948 – 9	4	26	18*	1	8·66	—	—	—						
Kennedy J. M.	1960 – 2	55	1188	94	9	25·82	—	—	—	1·3	0	1	2	0·50	—
Kent K. G.	1927 – 31	10	40	23*	1	4·44	—	—	—	192	33	689	10	63·90	—
Kilner N.	1924 – 37	539	16 075	228	35	31·89	23	12	—	34·2	7	150	2	75·00	—

Name	Seasons	I	Runs	HS	NO	Avge	100	0	O	M	R	W	Avge	5wi	10wm
King E. H.	1928–32	10	84	24	0	8·40	—	—	5	1	15	0	—	—	—
King I.	1952–5	60	345	29*	18	8·21	—	—	1448·4	637	2560	95	26·94	7	—
Kingston J. P.	1894	1	24	24	0	24·00	—	—	411·2	192	1420	47	30·38	—	—
Kinneir S. P.	1898–1914	507	15040	268*	46	32·62	25	—	—	—	—	—	—	—	—
Kirk E.	1898	1	0	0	0	—	—	—	—	—	—	—	—	—	—
Kirton H. O.	1925–9	3	80	52	0	26·66	—	—	26	9	61	0	—	—	—
Knutton H. J.	1894	1	4	4	0	4·00	—	—	224	48	674	23	29·30	—	—
Lane A. F.	1919–25	21	259	58	3	14·38	—	—	371·4	53	1391	54	25·75	—	—
Langley C. K.	1908–14	50	451	61	1	9·20	—	—	301·2	66	751	27	27·81	—	—
Latham H. J.	1955–9	13	129	26	2	11·72	—	—	—	—	—	—	—	—	—
Law A.	1894–9	81	1459	89	5	19·19	—	—	293·2	104	657	26	25·26	—	—
Leach C. W.	1955–8	64	1025	67	6	17·67	—	—	437	103	1250	50	25·00	—	—
Leadbeater E.	1957–8	35	458	116	5	15·26	1	—	425·1	114	1241	47	26·40	—	—
Legard E.	1962–8	24	144	21	11	11·07	—	—	369	43	1189	35	33·97	—	—
Lewington P. J.	1970–2	13	60	19	4	6·66	—	—	9·2	2	31	2	15·50	—	—
Lewis E. B.	1949–58	52	541	51	11	13·19	—	—	335·4	91	821	26	31·57	—	—
Lilley A. A.	1894–1911	497	12813	171	29	27·49	16	—	16	2	41	1	41·00	—	—
Lobb B.	1953	—	—	—	—	—	—	—	—	—	—	—	—	—	—
Lord W. A.	1897–9	18	69	10*	8	6·90	—	—	83·3	10	281	11	25·54	—	—
Loveitt F. R.	1898–1905	42	846	110	6	23·50	1	—	155·3	26	576	15	38·40	—	—
Lowe J. C. M.	1907	2	8	8	0	4·00	—	—	22	7	51	1	51·00	—	—
Lowe P. J.	1964	—	—	—	—	—	—	—	82	22	187	7	26·71	—	—
Luckin V. V.	1919	13	153	59*	6	21·85	—	—	—	—	—	—	—	—	—
Lynes J.	1897–1905	8	79	26	0	9·87	—	—	—	—	—	—	—	—	—
Manton J.	1898	2	5	5	0	2·50	—	—	—	—	—	—	—	—	—
Marshall A. G.	1961–2	3	18	18*	2	18·00	—	—	—	—	—	—	—	—	—
Marshall F. W.	1922	2	14	10	0	7·00	—	—	—	—	—	—	—	—	—
Marshall J. M. A.	1946–50	49	790	47	4	17·55	—	—	528·5	72	1581	47	33·63	—	—
Matheson E.	1899	2	14	9	0	7·00	—	—	—	—	—	—	—	—	—
Maudsley R. H.	1946–51	74	1706	107	3	24·04	2	—	414·5	102	1173	39	30·07	—	—
Mayer J. H.	1926–39	408	2831	74*	18	7·26	—	115	10052·1	2337	25360	1145	22·14	35	2
McDowall J. I.	1969	11	181	49*	3	22·62	—	—	—	—	—	—	—	—	—
McVicker N. M.	1969–72	101	1163	65*	29	16·15	—	—	2237	523	6456	248	26·03	—	—
Mead-Briggs R.	1946	2	46	44*	1	46·00	—	—	30	10	96	1	96·00	—	—
Meldon W. H.	1909–10	9	122	44	0	13·55	—	—	40·4	6	149	4	37·25	—	—
Melville J. H.	1946	3	14	13	0	4·66	—	—	35	8	84	5	16·80	—	—

TT

Player	Period of Service	Inns	Runs	Highest Score	Not Out	Ave	100s	1000 Runs	Test Matches	Overs	Mdns	Runs	Wkts	Ave	100 Wkts
Mence M. D.	1962 – 5	43	467	53	8	13·34	—	—	—	708·4	155	1983	61	32·50	—
Meunier J. B.	1920	3	12	9	0	4·00	—	—	—	9	0	38	0	—	—
Miller H. R.	1928	1	8	8	0	8·00	—	—	—	13	2	38	1	38·00	—
Miller R.	1961 – 8	166	1657	72	34	12·55	—	—	—	3028·5	1007	7289	241	30·24	—
Mills J. M.	1946	7	106	26	0	15·14	—	—	—	55	5	167	3	55·66	—
Mitchell F. R.	1946 – 8	29	224	43	2	8·29	—	—	—	332·4	71	856	22	28·90	—
Moorhouse F.	1900 – 8	154	1549	75	37	13·02	—	—	—	2391	574	6262	261	23·99	—
Morris L. J.	1925 – 6	11	262	76	0	23·81	—	—	—	15·1	1	70	3	23·33	—
Morter F. W.	1922	5	13	8	2	4·33	—	—	—	43	5	138	3	46·00	—
Morton J.	1929 – 30	14	162	38	0	11·57	—	—	—	—	—	—	—	—	—
Murray A. L.	1922	17	161	33	0	9·47	—	—	—	11	0	49	2	24·50	—
Murray D. L.	1972	21	412	54	6	27·46	—	—	5	—	—	—	—	—	—
Nelson A. J.	1895	2	0	0	0	—	—	—	—	—	—	—	—	—	—
Nelson G. M.	1920 – 2	21	97	23	8	7·46	—	—	—	198·4	23	746	22	33·90	—
Norton E. W.	1920	1	26	26*	1	—	—	—	—	5	0	19	0	—	—
Oakes D. R.	1965 – 6	8	81	33	1	11·57	—	—	—	1·1	0	1	0	—	—
Old A. G. B.	1969	1	34	34	0	34·00	—	—	—	30	5	93	1	93·00	—
Ord J. S.	1933 – 53	459	11 788	187*	35	27·80	16	6	—	60	9	244	2	122·00	—
O'Rourke C.	1968	1	23	23*	1	—	—	—	—	—	—	—	—	—	—
Paine G. E. A.	1929 – 38 – 49	323	3234	79	55	12·06	—	—	4	9289·5	2744	21 867	962	22·73	5
Pallett H. J.	1894 – 8	98	915	55*	21	11·88	—	—	—	3173·2	1034	6365	296	21·50	—
Palmer G. A.	1928	12	87	20	2	8·70	—	—	—	179	47	450	8	56·25	—
Parkes H. R.	1898	1	1	1	0	1·00	—	—	—	—	—	—	—	—	—
Parry M. C.	1908 – 10	3	26	10	0	8·66	—	—	—	3	0	16	0	—	—
Parsons J. H. Rev.	1910 – 19 } 1923 – 34	494	15 737	225	48	35·28	35	8	—	460·4	75	1464	47	31·14	—
Partridge N. E.	1921 – 37	144	2360	102	17	18·58	1	—	—	2982·4	655	7900	347	22·76	—
Paul N. A.	1954 – 5	4	75	40	0	18·75	—	—	—	35·5	11	65	2	32·50	—
Peare W. G.	1926	9	17	12*	7	8·50	—	—	—	40	9	75	2	37·50	—
Pell G. A.	1947	2	24	16*	1	24·00	—	—	—	12·2	2	31	4	7·75	—
Pereira E. Rev.	1895 – 6	8	117	34	1	16·71	—	—	—	2	0	13	0	—	—
Perkins H. G.	1926 – 7	5	10	6*	2	3·33	—	—	—	21	6	55	1	55·00	—
Phillips H. R.	1951	1	3	3*	0	3·00	—	—	—	—	—	—	—	—	—

Player	Years	I	Runs	HS	NO	Avg	100			O	M	R	W	Avg	5wi
Phillips J. H.	1904 – 11	7	35	16	0	5·00	—	—	—	42	3	159	1	159·00	—
Potter W.	1932	2	0	0	0	—	—	—	—	12	2	21	1	21·00	—
Pridmore R. G.	1902 – 12	26	315	49	1	12·60	—	—	—	—	—	—	—	—	—
Pritchard T. L.	1946 – 55	245	2827	81	29	13·08	—	—	—	6121·2	1270	16 211	695	23·32	3
Pugh J. G.	1922 – 27	9	82	41	0	9·11	—	—	—	5·8	11	206	6	34·33	—
Quaife B. W.	1920 – 6	81	1096	99*	7	14·81	—	—	1	14·2	0	65	4	16·25	—
Quaife W.	1894 – 1901	202	4928	144	10	25·66	7	—	—	93	25	204	6	34·00	—
Quaife W. G.	1894 – 1928	1112	33 862	255*	176	36·17	71	7	20	8581	1355	24 779	900	27·53	—
Ratcliffe D. P.	1957 – 62 – 68	33	603	79	2	19·45	—	—	—	—	—	—	—	—	—
Rhodes J.	1895	6	89	64	0	14·83	—	—	—	—	—	—	—	—	—
Rhodes T. B.	1899	7	105	55	1	17·50	—	—	—	—	—	—	—	—	—
Rice W. I. Rev.	1920	4	15	9	0	3·75	—	—	—	—	—	—	—	—	—
Richards W.	1895 – 6	11	112	61*	1	11·20	—	—	—	—	—	—	—	—	—
Richardson B. A.	1963 – 7	72	1323	126	4	19·45	2	—	—	40	6	153	1	153·00	—
Richardson S. H.	1920	4	18	8*	1	6·00	—	—	—	—	—	—	—	—	—
Riley T. M. N.	1961 – 4	23	440	84	2	20·95	—	—	—	2	0	15	0	—	—
Roberts H. E.	1949 – 50	8	52	30	0	6·50	—	—	—	—	—	—	—	—	—
Roberts H. J.	1932 – 7	27	348	61	4	15·13	—	—	—	123·1	20	407	9	45·22	—
Robins D. H.	1947	4	54	29*	1	18·00	—	—	—	—	—	—	—	—	—
Robinson M. S.	1951 – 2	13	234	57	1	19·50	—	—	—	3	2	5	0	—	—
Robinson T. L.	1946	7	27	13	0	3·85	—	—	—	92	15	277	6	46·16	—
Roll H. T.	1927	1	0	0	0	—	—	—	—	9	0	40	0	—	—
Rotherham G. A.	1919 – 21	75	1116	62	4	15·71	—	—	—	1130·5	203	3678	88	41·79	—
Rotherham H.	1903	1	33	33	0	33·00	—	—	—	—	—	—	—	—	—
Rouse S. J.	1970 – 2	31	260	38*	9	11·81	—	—	—	698·3	138	2144	69	31·07	—
Russell J. B.	1920	2	31	23	0	15·50	—	—	—	—	—	—	—	—	—
Sale R.	1939 – 47	33	929	157	3	30·96	2	—	—	—	—	—	—	—	—
Sanders W.	1927 – 34	100	706	64	18	8·40	—	—	—	1909	480	4663	119	39·18	—
Sanderson G. B.	1901	1	0	0	0	—	—	—	—	—	—	—	—	—	—
Santall F. R.	1919 – 39	787	17 503	201*	83	24·86	21	—	7	3780·2	569	12 139	277	43·22	—
Santall S.	1894 – 1914	535	6490	73	115	15·45	—	—	—	12 677·3	3764	28 924	1206	23·98	1
Scorer R. I.	1921 – 6	52	718	113	0	16·31	1	—	—	189·5	24	618	18	34·33	—
Sharp N.	1923	1	3	3	0	3·00	—	—	—	—	—	—	—	—	—
Shaw D. G.	1949	1	17	17	0	17·00	—	—	—	34	8	106	2	53·00	—
Shilton J. E.	1894 – 5	23	153	30	6	8·94	—	—	—	648·3	181	1300	56	23·21	—
Shortland N. A.	1938 – 50	40	487	51	5	13·91	—	—	—	—	—	—	—	—	—

Player	Period of Service	Inns	Runs	Highest Score	Not Out	Ave	100s	1000 Runs	Test Matches	Overs	Mdns	Runs	Wkts	Ave	100 Wkts
Shuckburgh C. G. S.	1930	1	0	0	0	—	—	—	—	—	—	—	—	—	—
Simms H. L.	1921–2	10	133	38	0	13·30	—	—	—	65·4	8	216	5	43·20	—
Smart C.	1920–2	81	922	59	10	12·98	—	—	—	103	3	508	9	56·44	—
Smart J.	1920–36	339	3421	68*	43	11·55	—	—	—	346·2	58	1190	20	59·50	—
Singh S.	1956–8	43	872	68*	10	26·42	—	—	—	575·5	212	1248	42	29·71	—
Smith A. C.	1958–72	458	7643	94	69	19·64	—	1	6	498·4	123	1310	52	25·19	—
Smith E. J.	1904–30	744	15911	177	48	22·86	20	6	11	12·5	2	40	1	40·00	—
Smith H. W.	1912	1	15	15	0	15·00	—	—	—	1	0	5	0	—	—
Smith I. W.	1905–6	2	1	1	—	00·50	—	—	—	32	6	106	2	53·00	—
Smith M. J. K.	1957–72	641	24562	200*	86	44·25	45	14	50	26·3	8	97	1	97·00	—
Speed A. W.	1927–8	7	29	11	3	7·25	—	—	—	196·1	44	538	29	18·44	—
Spencer H. N. E.	1930	2	4	3*	1	4·00	—	—	—	66	18	146	1	146·00	—
Spooner R. T.	1948–59	506	12037	168	58	26·86	11	6	7	1	0	4	0	—	—
Stephens F. G.	1907–12	50	1102	144*	1	22·48	1	—	—	52·2	0	205	3	68·33	—
Stephens G. W.	1907–25	203	3952	143	13	20·80	3	—	—	15·1	0	80	4	20·00	—
Stevenson J. F.	1919	2	16	16	0	8·00	—	—	—	—	—	—	—	—	—
Stewart W. J.	1955–69	471	14249	182*	53	34·08	25	6	—	3	0	15	2	7·50	—
Street L. C.	1946	7	17	8*	2	3·40	—	—	—	50	11	146	3	48·66	—
Street N. K.	1908	9	43	14	0	4·77	—	—	—	—	—	—	—	—	—
Suckling J.	1919	2	6	4	0	3·00	—	—	—	3	0	12	0	—	—
Tate C. F.	1931–3	8	34	17	2	5·66	—	—	—	115	36	297	6	49·50	—
Taylor A.	1913	11	83	17	2	9·22	—	—	—	40·2	3	137	4	34·25	—
Taylor A.	1927	1	0	—	0	—	—	—	—	5	1	7	0	—	—
Taylor C. J.	1908–9	4	6	5	0	1·50	—	—	—	72·2	12	257	9	28·55	—
Taylor C. R. V.	1970	1 match d.n.b.													
Taylor D. D. S.	1948–50	23	519	121	7	32·43	1	—	—	327	132	607	15	40·46	—
Taylor Don	1949–53	82	1624	90*	5	21·09	—	—	—	80·5	23	236	11	21·45	—
Taylor F.	1939	1	0	0	0	—	—	—	—	20	5	71	3	23·66	—
Taylor F. E.	1910	8	112	44	0	14·00	—	—	—	1	0	5	0	—	—
Taylor K. A.	1946–9	155	3145	102	10	21·67	1	—	—	8	0	33	2	33·00	—
Tennant P.	1964	1 match d.n.b.													
Thompson J. R.	1938–54	76	1922	103	3	26·32	2	—	—	2	0	13	0	—	—
Thompson R. G.	1949–62	184	655	25*	70	5·74	—	—	—	4639·1	1212	10824	470	23·0	—
Tidy W. N.	1970–2	32	70	12*	13	3·68	—	—	—	850	173	2778	82	33·5	—

Player	Career	I	R	HS	NO	Avge				O	M	R	W	Avge	
Timms B. S. V.	1969–71	33	421	61	7	16·19	6	—	—	3532·2	736	9238	323	28·60	—
Townsend A.	1948–60	549	11 978	154	69	24·70	—	5	—	4	0	17	0	—	—
Venn H.	1919–25	59	896	115	0	15·18	1	—	—	—	—	—	—	—	—
Waddy Rev. E. F.	1919–22	42	955	109*	2	23·87	1	—	—	8	2	29	1	29·00	—
Walker G.	1912	2	13	13	0	6·50	—	—	—	—	—	—	—	—	—
Ward L. M.	1930	1	5	5	0	5·00	—	—	—	—	—	—	—	—	—
Ward W.	1895–1900	16	79	26	5	7·18	—	—	—	381	102	966	30	32·16	—
Waring J. S.	1967	2	15	15	0	7·50	—	—	—	37	4	129	2	64·50	—
Warner G. S.	1966–71	48	965	118*	7	23·53	2	—	—	5·2	1	14	0	—	—
Wassell A.	1923	11	24	10	3	3·00	—	—	—	109	21	344	10	34·40	—
Watson T. H.	1904	3	18	12	0	6·00	—	—	—	55	12	137	0	—	—
Webster R. V.	1962–6	66	658	47	15	12·90	—	—	—	1750·1	482	4532	234	19·36	—
Weldrick G.	1906–7	11	53	12	1	5·30	—	—	—	—	—	—	—	—	—
Welford J. W.	1896	23	459	118	2	21·85	1	—	—	56	15	180	2	90·00	—
Wheatley O. S.	1957–60	76	209	17	34	4·97	—	—	—	2349·3	571	5934	237	25·03	—
White A. F. T.	1936–7	15	311	55*	2	23·92	—	—	—	—	—	—	—	—	—
White H. A.	1923	15	107	32	3	8·91	—	—	—	8	0	35	0	—	—
White M. F.	1946	2	0	0	0	—	—	—	—	—	—	—	—	—	—
Whitehead G.	1902	1	1	1	0	1·00	—	—	—	20	5	50	0	—	—
Whitehead S. J.	1894–1900	73	455	46*	25	9·47	2	—	—	1883·5	559	4008	170	23·57	—
Whitehouse J.	1971–2	66	1969	173	4	32·75	—	1	—	57·4	9	190	3	63·33	—
Whitehouse P. G.	1926	6	41	13	3	13·66	—	—	—	42·1	9	122	8	15·25	—
Whittle A. E.	1900–6	80	1685	104	10	24·07	1	—	—	514·1	153	2012	56	35·92	—
Williams O.	1967	2	6	6*	1	6·00	—	—	—	16	8	60	1	60·00	—
Williams R.	1897–8	8	80	38	1	11·42	—	—	—	3	0	14	0	—	—
Wilmot K.	1931–9	101	871	54	25	11·46	—	7	—	1679·5	287	5018	154	32·58	—
Windridge J. E.	1909–13	12	161	34*	1	14·63	—	—	—	2	0	13	1	13·00	—
Weeks R.	1950–7	139	1048	51	35	10·00	—	—	—	2835·2	1073	6004	228	26·33	—
Willis R. G. D.	1972	7	42	12	2	8·40	—	—	4	273·1	65	803	28	28·67	—
Wilson B. A.	1951	1	0	0	0	—	—	—	—	20	4	75	1	75·00	—
Woodroffe A.	1947–8	7	77	41	0	11·00	—	—	—	—	—	—	—	—	—
Wolton A. V.	1947–60	477	12 896	165	61	31·00	12	—	—	489	134	1227	37	33·16	—
Wright A.	1960–4	76	315	27	20	5·62	—	—	—	2421·5	618	5953	236	25·21	—
Wyatt R. E. S.	1923–39	627	21 687	232	105	41·54	51	12	—	7985·2	2087	21 687	662	32·54	—
Youll M.	1956–7	2	15	9	0	7·50	—	—	40	84·2	6	282	14	20·13	—

* Not Out

6. *All-Round Performances*

10 000 RUNS AND 500 WICKETS

T. W. Cartwright	10 783 runs and 1058 wickets	
W. G. Quaife	33 862 runs and 900 wickets	
R. E. S. Wyatt	21 687 runs and 662 wickets	

'THE DOUBLE'

F. R. Foster	1459 runs and 124 wickets	1911
F. R. Foster	1396 runs and 117 wickets	1914
T. W. Cartwright	1176 runs and 106 wickets	1962

7. Batting

❖ ❖ ❖

HIGHEST INDIVIDUAL SCORE AGAINST EACH OPPONENT

County Championship			Ground	
Derbyshire	J. Devey	246	Edgbaston	1900
Essex	W. G. Quaife	223*	Leyton	1900
Glamorgan	J. H. Parsons	225	Edgbaston	1927
Gloucestershire	L. A. Bates	211	Gloucester	1932
Hampshire	S. P. Kinneir	268*	Edgbaston	1911
Kent	E. J. Smith	173	Edgbaston	1928
Lancashire	J. F. Byrne	222	Edgbaston	1905
Leicestershire	H. E. Dollery	212	Edgbaston	1952
Middlesex	T. W. Cartwright	210	Nuneaton	1962
Northamptonshire	F. R. Santall	201*	Northampton	1933
Nottinghamshire	R. B. Kanhai	253	Trent Bridge	1968
Somerset	F. C. Gardner	215*	Taunton	1950
Surrey	W. G. Quaife	255*	The Oval	1905
Sussex	M. J. K. Smith	163	Hove	1962
Worcestershire	F. R. Foster	305*	Dudley	1914
Yorkshire	C. Charlesworth	206	Dewsbury	1914

Other Opponents			Ground	
Australians	R. W. Barber	138	Edgbaston	1964
Cambridge University	J. A. Jameson	194	Cambridge	1970
Combined Services	W. J. Stewart	151	Portland Road	1959
Indians	J. A. Jameson	231	Edgbaston	1971
London County	J. Devey	155	Crystal Palace	1901
New Zealanders	Rev. J. H. Parsons	190	Edgbaston	1931
Oxford University	J. Whitehouse	173	Oxford	1971
Pakistanis	M. J. K. Smith	173*	Edgbaston	1967
Philadelphians	A. Law	72	Edgbaston	1897
Scotland	D. L. Amiss	150*	Edgbaston	1966
South Africans	A. J. Croom	109	Edgbaston	1929
West Indies	J. H. Parsons	161	Edgbaston	1928

* Not Out

647

CENTURIES SEASON BY SEASON 1894–1971

1894	J. E. Hill (1)	139*	v. Nottinghamshire, Trent Bridge
1895	A. A. Lilley (3)	158*	v. Leicestershire, Leicester
		139	v. Derbyshire, Edgbaston
		135	v. Gloucestershire, Edgbaston
	H. W. Bainbridge (3)	142	v. Surrey, Edgbaston
		111	v. Essex, Edgbaston
		104*	v. Derbyshire, Edgbaston
	W. Quaife (1)	105	v. Hampshire, Southampton
1896	A. A. Lilley (2)	132	v. Derbyshire, Derby
		121	v. Gloucestershire, Edgbaston
	W. G. Quaife (2)	110	v. Hampshire, Edgbaston
		105	v. Leicestershire, Leicester
	H. W. Bainbridge (1)	118	v. Hampshire, Southampton
	E. J. Diver (1)	112*	v. Essex, Edgbaston
	J. W. Welford (1)	118	v. Leicestershire, Leicester
1897	W. G. Quaife (3)	178*	v. Hampshire, Southampton
		136*	v. Hampshire, Edgbaston
		120	v. Essex, Edgbaston
	H. W. Bainbridge (2)	162	v. Hampshire, Southampton
		101	v. Gloucestershire, Edgbaston
	E. J. Diver (2)	111	v. Leicestershire, Leicester
		110	v. Leicestershire, Edgbaston
	J. F. Byrne (1)	100	v. Leicestershire, Edgbaston
	A. C. S. Glover (1)	115	v. Leicestershire, Leicester
	W. Quaife (1)	101	v. Gloucestershire, Edgbaston
1898	W. G. Quaife (3)	157*	v. Yorkshire, Edgbaston
		130*	v. Gloucestershire, Edgbaston
		117*	v. Hampshire, Edgbaston
	A. A. Lilley (1)	112	v. Derbyshire, Edgbaston
	W. Quaife (1)	109	v. Derbyshire, Edgbaston
1899	W. G. Quaife (6)	207*	v. Hampshire, Edgbaston
		148	v. Lancashire, Edgbaston
		119*	v. Worcestershire, Worcester
		117	v. Leicestershire, Leicester
		115	v. Essex, Edgbaston
		100*	v. Kent, Catford
	W. Quaife (3)	144	v. Gloucestershire, Edgbaston
		123*	v. Hampshire, Bournemouth
		101	v. Leicestershire, Leicester
	J. Devey (2)	154	v. Hampshire, Bournemouth
		102	v. Yorkshire, Edgbaston
	A. S. C. Glover (2)	119*	v. Hampshire, Edgbaston
		108	v. Gloucestershire, Edgbaston
	E. J. Diver (1)	184	v. Leicestershire, Edgbaston
	T. S. Fishwick (1)	109	v. Hampshire, Edgbaston
	S. P. Kinneir (1)	111	v. Leicestershire, Leicester
1900	S. P. Kinneir (2)	156	v. Derbyshire, Edgbaston
		102*	v. Worcestershire, Edgbaston

	A. A. Lilley (2)	112	v. Surrey, The Oval
		111	v. Gloucestershire, Bristol
	W. G. Quaife (2)	223*	v. Essex, Leyton
		124*	v. Surrey, The Oval
	J. Devey (1)	246	v. Derbyshire, Edgbaston
	T. S. Fishwick (1)	131	v. Gloucestershire, Bristol
	W. Quaife (1)	115	v. Essex, Leyton
1901	W. G. Quaife (5)	177	v. Lancashire, Edgbaston
		118*	v. Yorkshire, Edgbaston
		117*	v. Derbyshire, Derby
		104*	v. Worcestershire, Edgbaston
		101*	v. London County, Edgbaston
	S. P. Kinneir (4)	215*	v. Lancashire, Edgbaston
		145	v. Surrey, The Oval
		132	v. Leicestershire, Edgbaston
		123	v. Yorkshire, Bradford
	J. Devey (2)	155	v. London County, Crystal Palace
		111	v. Essex, Leyton
	A. A. Lilley (2)	124	v. London County, Edgbaston
		121	v. Essex, Leyton
	J. F. Byrne (1)	110	v. Worcestershire, Edgbaston
	T. S. Fishwick (1)	140*	v. Derbyshire, Edgbaston
1902	W. G. Quaife (3)	153*	v. Leicestershire, Edgbaston
		144*	v. London County, Crystal Palace
		106	v. Lancashire, Old Trafford
	C. Charlesworth (1)	106	v. Hampshire, Edgbaston
1903	T. S. Fishwick (1)	106	v. Essex, Edgbaston
	F. R. Loveitt (1)	110	v. Gloucestershire, Edgbaston
	W. G. Quaife (1)	130	v. Leicestershire, Edgbaston
1904	W. G. Quaife (5)	200*	v. Essex, Edgbaston
		193	v. Hampshire, Edgbaston
		131*	v. Leicestershire, Leicester
		123	v. London County, Coventry
		110	v. Surrey, Edgbaston
	A. C. S. Glover (2)	124	v. Yorkshire, Edgbaston
		106	v. Surrey, The Oval
	T. S. Fishwick (2)	113	v. Leicestershire, Leicester
		103	v. Cambridge Univ., Edgbaston
	S. P. Kinneir (2)	152	v. Lancashire, Edgbaston
		105	v. Worcestershire, Edgbaston
	A. E. Whittle (1)	104	v. Essex, Edgbaston
1905	W. G. Quaife (6)	255*	v. Surrey, The Oval
		176*	v. Derbyshire, Edgbaston
		169	v. Hampshire, Leamington
		110	v. Essex, Leyton
		109*	v. Yorkshire, Edgbaston
		101*	v. Worcestershire, Edgbaston
	T. S. Fishwick (4)	137	v. Cambridge Univ., Edgbaston
		118	v. Hampshire, Southampton
		116	v. Essex, Edgbaston

1905	T. S. Fishwick (*cont.*)	106	v.	Northamptonshire, Northampton
	S. P. Kinneir (3)	158	v.	Lancashire, Edgbaston
		105	v.	Sussex, Edgbaston
		103	v.	Essex, Edgbaston
	C. S. Baker (1)	102	v.	Cambridge Univ., Cambridge
	J. F. Byrne (1)	222	v.	Lancashire, Edgbaston
	J. Devey (1)	125	v.	Yorkshire, Edgbaston
	A. A. Lilley (1)	121	v.	Worcestershire, Edgbaston
1906	S. P. Kinneir (3)	171	v.	Hampshire, Basingstoke
		136	v.	Hampshire, Edgbaston
		100	v.	Sussex, Edgbaston
	C. S. Baker (2)	144	v.	Surrey, The Oval
		106	v.	Surrey, Edgbaston
	J. Devey (2)	110*	v.	Worcestershire, Edgbaston
		106	v.	Surrey, Edgbaston
	T. S. Fishwick (2)	135	v.	Leicestershire, Leicester
		129	v.	Somerset, Edgbaston
	A. A. Lilley (2)	122	v.	Surrey, The Oval
		101	v.	Northamptonshire, Peterborough
	W. G. Quaife (2)	116*	v.	Hampshire, Edgbaston
		109	v.	Worcestershire, Worcester
	J. F. Byrne (1)	115	v.	Leicestershire, Edgbaston
1907	C. S. Baker (1)	105	v.	Worcestershire, Worcester
	C. Charlesworth (1)	103	v.	Hampshire, Southampton
	A. A. Lilley (1)	171	v.	Worcestershire, Worcester
1908	W. G. Quaife (3)	189*	v.	Worcestershire, Worcester
		131*	v.	Derbyshire, Edgbaston
		104	v.	Hampshire, Edgbaston
	C. S. Baker (2)	119	v.	Derbyshire, Derby
		101*	v.	Surrey, The Oval
	A. C. S. Glover (2)	117*	v.	Sussex, Hove
		109	v.	Worcestershire, Worcester
	C. Charlesworth (1)	105	v.	Northamptonshire, Edgbaston
	H. J. Goodwin (1)	101	v.	Sussex, Hove
1909	S. P. Kinneir (2)	133	v.	Surrey, The Oval
		123	v.	Worcestershire, Worcester
	W. G. Quaife (2)	147*	v.	Northamptonshire, Northampton
		100*	v.	Leicestershire, Edgbaston
1910	C. Charlesworth (3)	216	v.	Derbyshire, Blackwell
		133	v.	Worcestershire, Edgbaston
		105	v.	Gloucestershire, Edgbaston
	A. A. Lilley (2)	114	v.	Hampshire, Southampton
		104	v.	Sussex, Leamington
	W. G. Quaife (2)	124	v.	Yorkshire, Huddersfield
		109*	v.	Sussex, Leamington
	C. S. Baker (1)	155*	v.	Worcestershire, Worcester

1911	S. P. Kinneir (5)	268*	v. Hampshire, Edgbaston
		148	v. Hampshire, Southampton
		124 ⎱	v. Sussex, Chichester
		110 ⎰	
		102*	v. Leicestershire, Edgbaston
	C. Charlesworth (4)	142	v. Leicestershire, Hinckley
		130	v. Northamptonshire, Northampton
		116	v. Sussex, Coventry
		110	v. Lancashire, Old Trafford
	F. R. Foster (3)	200	v. Surrey, Edgbaston
		105	v. Yorkshire, Edgbaston
		101	v. Yorkshire, Harrogate
	W. G. Quaife (3)	144*	v. Derbyshire, Edgbaston
		113	v. Northamptonshire, Edgbaston
		104*	v. Gloucestershire, Edgbaston
	C. S. Baker (1)	101*	v. Worcestershire, Edgbaston
	E. J. Smith (1)	113	v. Surrey, Edgbaston
1912	E. J. Smith (1)	134	v. Hampshire, Coventry
	F. G. Stephens (1)	144*	v. Lancashire, Edgbaston
	W. G. Quaife (1)	134	v. Hampshire, Coventry
1913	W. G. Quaife (6)	129*	v. Leicestershire, Edgbaston
		127	v. Sussex, Coventry
		124 ⎱	v. Surrey, The Oval
		109 ⎰	
		107	v. Northamptonshire, Edgbaston
		105	v. Surrey, Edgbaston
	C. Charlesworth (2)	100 ⎱	v. Surrey, Edgbaston
		101* ⎰	
	J. H. Parsons (2)	161*	v. Gloucestershire, Nuneaton
		118	v. Derbyshire, Edgbaston
	C. S. Baker (1)	151	v. Sussex, Coventry
	F. R. Foster (1)	111	v. Hampshire, Southampton
	S. P. Kinneir (1)	152*	v. Surrey, The Oval
1914	C. Charlesworth (3)	206	v. Yorkshire, Dewsbury
		115	v. Gloucestershire, Coventry
		104	v. Leicestershire, Hinckley
	S. P. Kinneir (2)	102	v. Leicestershire, Hinckley
		100	v. Leicestershire, Edgbaston
	W. G. Quaife (2)	134	v. Gloucestershire, Coventry
		111*	v. Lancashire, Lancaster
	C. S. Baker (1)	103	v. Lancashire, Lancaster
	F. R. Foster (1)	305*	v. Worcestershire, Dudley
	J. H. Parsons (1)	102	v. Worcestershire, Dudley
1919	W. G. Quaife (3)	127	v. Gloucestershire, Edgbaston
		106	v. Leicestershire, Hinckley
		102*	v. Northamptonshire, Edgbaston
	L. A. Bates (2)	119	v. Derbyshire, Derby
		117	v. Leicestershire, Hinckley
	J. H. Parsons (2)	125	v. Northamptonshire, Northampton
		108	v. Northamptonshire, Edgbaston

1920	Hon. F. S. G. Calthorpe (1)	102	v. Gloucestershire, Edgbaston
	R. L. Holdsworth (1)	141	v. Worcestershire, Edgbaston
	G. W. Stephens (1)	111	v. Worcestershire, Edgbaston
	H. Venn (1)	115	v. Kent, Catford
	W. G. Quaife (1)	126*	v. Worcestershire, Worcester
1921	Hon. F. S. G. Calthorpe (3)	209	v. Hampshire, Edgbaston
		176	v. Somerset, Edgbaston
		120	v. Cambridge Univ., Edgbaston
	W. G. Quaife (3)	107*	v. Cambridge Univ., Edgbaston
		103	v. Leicestershire, Edgbaston
		100	v. Worcestershire, Edgbaston
	L. A. Bates (1)	157	v. Cambridge Univ., Edgbaston
	R. I. Scorer (1)	113	v. Hampshire, Edgbaston
	E. J. Smith (1)	100	v. Worcestershire, Worcester
	Rev. E. F. Waddy (1)	109*	v. Middlesex, Lord's
1922	L. A. Bates (2)	149	v. Middlesex, Edgbaston
		118	v. Middlesex, Lord's
	Hon. F. S. G. Calthorpe (1)	105	v. Nottinghamshire Trent Bridge
	E. J. Smith (2)	115	v. Worcestershire, Stourbridge
		114	v. Hampshire, Southampton
	W. G. Quaife (1)	107	v. Derbyshire, Derby
1923	J. H. Parsons (1)	131	v. Northamptonshire, Edgbaston
	G. W. Stephens (1)	143	v. Gloucestershire, Edgbaston
	W. G. Quaife (1)	121	v. Northamptonshire, Northampton
1924	Hon. F. S. G. Calthorpe (2)	108*	v. Sussex, Hove
		106	v. Hampshire, Edgbaston
	J. H. Parsons (2)	121	v. Kent, Dover
		106	v. Hampshire, Edgbaston
	E. J. Smith (1)	104	v. Hampshire, Edgbaston
	W. G. Quaife (1)	141	v. Glamorgan, Edgbaston
	F. R. Santall (1)	102	v. S. Africans, Edgbaston
1925	J. H. Parsons (3)	127	v. Surrey, Edgbaston
		124	v. Sussex, Edgbaston
		106	v. Middlesex, Edgbaston
	E. J. Smith (3)	149	v. Leicestershire, Coventry
		139*	v. Sussex, Edgbaston
		134	v. Leicestershire, Leicester
	Hon. F. S. G. Calthorpe (2)	174	v. Lancashire, Edgbaston
		109*	v. Sussex, Edgbaston
	F. R. Santall (2)	119*	v. Yorkshire, Dewsbury
		110	v. Middlesex, Edgbaston
	L. A. Bates (1)	104	v. Sussex, Eastbourne
	A. J. Croom (1)	125	v. Worcestershire, Dudley
	N. E. Partridge (1)	102	v. Somerset, Edgbaston
	W. G. Quaife (1)	136*	v. Northamptonshire, Edgbaston
	G. W. Stephens (1)	121	v. Derbyshire, Edgbaston
	R. E. S. Wyatt (1)	104	v. Worcestershire, Dudley

1926	J. H. Parsons (4)	171	v.	Hampshire, Edgbaston
		171	v.	Northamptonshire, Northampton
		125	v.	Kent, Tunbridge Wells
		104	v.	Leicestershire, Coventry
	L. A. Bates (3)	187	v.	Derbyshire, Derby
		141	v.	Middlesex, Edgbaston
		104	v.	Surrey, Edgbaston
	N. Kilner (2)	146	v.	Surrey, Edgbaston
		121	v.	Worcestershire, Edgbaston
	R. E. S. Wyatt (2)	102	v.	Somerset, Edgbaston
		101*	v.	Derbyshire, Derby
	Hon. F. S. G. Calthorpe (1)	103*	v.	Somerset, Taunton
	W. G. Quaife (1)	107	v.	Northamptonshire, Edgbaston
1927	J. H. Parsons (5)	225	v.	Glamorgan, Edgbaston
		141	v.	Sussex, Edgbaston
		136	v.	Yorkshire, Hull
		135	v.	Surrey, The Oval
		105	v.	Lancashire, Edgbaston
	L. A. Bates (4)	144 116	} v.	Kent, Coventry
		118*	v.	Somerset, Edgbaston
		106*	v.	Lancashire, Edgbaston
	E. J. Smith (4)	177	v.	Derbyshire, Edgbaston
		132	v.	Middlesex, Lord's
		132	v.	Kent, Coventry
		101*	v.	Nottinghamshire, Edgbaston
	N. Kilner (3)	167	v.	Middlesex, Lord's
		125	v.	Northamptonshire, Edgbaston
		120	v.	Sussex, Edgbaston
	W. G. Quaife (1)	155*	v.	Glamorgan, Edgbaston
	R. E. S. Wyatt (1)	117	v.	Hampshire, Portsmouth
1928	J. H. Parsons (6)	161	v.	West Indies, Edgbaston
		130	v.	Sussex, Edgbaston
		114	v.	Derbyshire, Edgbaston
		110	v.	Leicestershire, Edgbaston
		109	v.	Sussex, Hove
		101	v.	Middlesex, Edgbaston
	R. E. S. Wyatt (6)	177	v.	Somerset, Edgbaston
		159*	v.	Surrey, The Oval
		134*	v.	Nottinghamshire, Coventry
		112	v.	Nottinghamshire, Trent Bridge
		104	v.	Derbyshire, Derby
		102	v.	Leicestershire, Leicester
	A. J. Croom (2)	104*	v.	Sussex, Edgbaston
		102*	v.	Somerset, Edgbaston
	E. J. Smith (2)	173	v.	Kent, Edgbaston
		108	v.	Nottinghamshire, Coventry
	L. A. Bates (1)	200	v.	Worcestershire, Edgbaston
	N. Kilner (1)	137*	v.	Lancashire, Edgbaston
	W. G. Quaife (1)	115	v.	Derbyshire, Edgbaston

1929	R. E. S. Wyatt (7)	161*	v. Surrey, Edgbaston
		150	v. Glamorgan, Edgbaston
		146*	v. Kent, Edgbaston
		132	v. Worcestershire, Edgbaston
		129*	v. Worcestershire, Dudley
		125	v. Middlesex, Edgbaston
		104*	v. Derbyshire, Edgbaston
	A. J. Croom (2)	131*	v. Northamptonshire, Edgbaston
		109	v. South Africans, Edgbaston
	F. R. Santall (2)	111	v. Worcestershire, Dudley
		109	v. Yorkshire, Edgbaston
	E. J. Smith (2)	142	v. Yorkshire, Edgbaston
		109	v. Gloucestershire, Edgbaston
	N. Kilner (1)	121	v. Surrey, Edgbaston
1930	R. E. S. Wyatt (4)	174*	v. Leicestershire, Hinckley
		145	v. Derbyshire, Derby
		117	v. Kent, Edgbaston
		117	v. Leicestershire, Nuneaton
	E. J. Smith (3)	132	v. Gloucestershire, Edgbaston
		126	v. Glamorgan, Swansea
		124	v. Essex, Edgbaston
	L. A. Bates (2)	199	v. Worcestershire, Edgbaston
		110	v. Essex, Edgbaston
	Rev. J. H. Parsons (2)	114*	v. Worcestershire, Dudley
		114	v. Surrey, The Oval
	F. R. Santall (2)	105*	v. Yorkshire, Edgbaston
		105	v. Nottinghamshire, Edgbaston
	A. J. Croom (1)	110	v. Derbyshire, Derby
	N. Kilner (1)	150	v. Worcestershire, Edgbaston
1931	A. J. Croom (6)	159	v. Nottinghamshire, Edgbaston
		109	v. Kent, Edgbaston
		105	v. Northamptonshire, Peterborough
		103*	v. Glamorgan, Swansea
		103	v. Derbyshire, Edgbaston
		102	v. Lancashire, Old Trafford
	Rev. J. H. Parsons (4)	190	v. New Zealanders, Edgbaston
		119*	v. Lancashire, Edgbaston
		106	v. Somerset, Edgbaston
		108	v. Nottinghamshire, Trent Bridge
	R. E. S. Wyatt (3)	161*	v. Northamptonshire, Coventry
		124	v. Somerset, Taunton
		100	v. Surrey, The Oval
	L. A. Bates (2)	133	v. Somerset, Taunton
		105	v. Nottinghamshire, Edgbaston
1932	A. J. Croom (2)	115	v. Glamorgan, Edgbaston
		103	v. Leicestershire, Hinckley
	N. Kilner (2)	119	v. Yorkshire, Hull
		104*	v. Leicestershire, Hinckley
	R. E. S. Wyatt (2)	131	v. Leicestershire, Hinckley
		103*	v. Middlesex, Edgbaston

	L. A. Bates (1)	211	v.	Gloucestershire, Gloucester
	Rev. J. H. Parsons (1)	104	v.	Sussex, Eastbourne
	F. R. Santall (1)	127*	v.	Glamorgan, Edgbaston
1933	N. Kilner (6)	197	v.	Yorkshire, Edgbaston
		145	v.	Glamorgan, Cardiff
		114	v.	Northamptonshire, Northampton
		104	v.	Glamorgan, Edgbaston
		102	v.	Hampshire, Edgbaston
		102	v.	Worcestershire, Edgbaston
	R. E. S. Wyatt (5)	187*	v.	Worcestershire, Dudley
		166	v.	Derbyshire, Edgbaston
		150*	v.	West Indies, Edgbaston
		116	v.	Leicestershire, Edgbaston
		102*	v.	Derbyshire, Derby
	F. R. Santall (4)	201*	v.	Northamptonshire, Northampton
		142	v.	Surrey, Edgbaston
		131	v.	Kent, Tonbridge
		101	v.	Lancashire, Edgbaston
	A. J. Croom (2)	116	v.	Northamptonshire, Northampton
		115	v.	Worcestershire, Edgbaston
	L. A. Bates (2)	134	v.	Leicestershire, Hinckley
		124	v.	Gloucestershire, Bristol
	Rev. J. H. Parsons (1)	130	v.	Leicestershire, Hinckley
1934	F. R. Santall (3)	130	v.	Nottinghamshire, Edgbaston
		120	v.	Nottinghamshire, Trent Bridge
		102*	v.	Gloucestershire, Edgbaston
	A. J. Croom (2)	211	v.	Worcestershire, Edgbaston
		149*	v.	Middlesex, Edgbaston
	N. Kilner (2)	153*	v.	Sussex, Edgbaston
		120	v.	Worcestershire, Edgbaston
	R. E. S. Wyatt (2)	161*	v.	Leicestershire, Leicester
		101	v.	Northamptonshire, Edgbaston
	P. Cranmer (1)	113	v.	Northamptonshire, Edgbaston
	G. D. Kemp-Welch (1)	123*	v.	Glamorgan, Swansea
	Rev. J. H. Parsons (1)	101	v.	Middlesex, Lord's
1935	N. Kilner (3)	228	v.	Worcestershire, Worcester
		124	v.	Nottinghamshire, Trent Bridge
		102	v.	Kent, Folkestone
	F. R. Santall (3)	122	v.	Glamorgan, Edgbaston
		113	v.	Derbyshire, Derby
		101	v.	Worcestershire, Worcester
	H. E. Dollery (2)	101*	v.	Glamorgan, Edgbaston
		100	v.	Gloucestershire, Edgbaston
	R. E. S. Wyatt (2)	111*	v.	Surrey, The Oval
		103*	v.	Gloucestershire, Edgbaston
	A. J. Croom (1)	101	v.	Middlesex, Lord's
	T. Collin (1)	105*	v.	Gloucestershire, Edgbaston

1936	R. E. S. Wyatt (3)	109*	v. Nottinghamshire, Edgbaston
		107	v. Northamptonshire, Peterborough
		100*	v. Middlesex, Edgbaston
	H. E. Dollery (1)	140	v. Surrey, Edgbaston
	W. A. Hill (1)	147*	v. Northamptonshire, Edgbaston
	N. Kilner (1)	101	v. Kent, Edgbaston
	F. R. Santall (1)	104*	v. Sussex, Horsham
1937	R. E. S. Wyatt (8)	232	v. Derbyshire, Edgbaston
		201*	v. Lancashire, Edgbaston
		152	v. Yorkshire, Edgbaston
		128	v. Leicestershire, Oakham
		127	v. Glamorgan, Pontypridd
		112	v. Sussex, Edgbaston
		109	v. Leicestershire, Edgbaston
		107	v. Sussex, Hove
	H. E. Dollery (4)	165	v. Lancashire, Edgbaston
		152	v. Glamorgan, Edgbaston
		128	v. Derbyshire, Edgbaston
		110	v. Yorkshire, Edgbaston
	A. J. Croom (3)	177	v. Northamptonshire, Northampton
		118	v. Yorkshire, Edgbaston
		115	v. Worcestershire, Worcester
	W. A. Hill (2)	122*	v. Sussex, Edgbaston
		105	v. Derbyshire, Derby
	J. Buckingham (1)	109	v. Gloucestershire, Gloucester
	N. Kilner (1)	103	v. Sussex, Edgbaston
	F. R. Santall (1)	133	v. Leicestershire, Edgbaston
1938	H. E. Dollery (4)	134*	v. Derbyshire, Derby
		127*	v. Leicestershire, Leicester
		126*	v. Yorkshire, Leeds
		113	v. Derbyshire, Edgbaston
	R. E. S. Wyatt (2)	121*	v. Northamptonshire, Edgbaston
		107	v. Leicestershire, Edgbaston
	J. Buckingham (2)	137*	v. Northamptonshire, Northampton
		124	v. Derbyshire, Derby
	P. Cranmer (1)	104	v. Worcestershire, Dudley
1939	H. E. Dollery (4)	177	v. Derbyshire, Edgbaston
		170	v. Hampshire, Edgbaston
		117	v. Northamptonshire, Edgbaston
		108	v. Gloucestershire, Edgbaston
	R. E. S. Wyatt (3)	151	v. Northamptonshire, Northampton
		138	v. Yorkshire, Scarborough
		115	v. Lancashire, Edgbaston
	A. J. Croom (2)	145	v. Glamorgan, Edgbaston
		110*	v. Northamptonshire, Northampton

	W. A. Hill (1)	138	v. Northamptonshire, Northampton
	R. Sale (1)	101	v. Sussex, Edgbaston
	F. R. Santall (1)	156	v. Lancashire, Edgbaston
	J. S. Ord (1)	105*	v. Hampshire, Edgbaston
1946	H. E. Dollery (4)	144	v. Leicestershire, Edgbaston
		126	v. Kent, Edgbaston
		121	v. Essex, Edgbaston
		113	v. Derbyshire, Edgbaston
	J. S. Ord (1)	115	v. Nottinghamshire, Trent Bridge
	R. Sale (1)	157	v. Indians, Edgbaston
1947	J. S. Ord (3)	125	v. Surrey, Coventry
		114	v. Gloucestershire, Edgbaston
		111	v. Derbyshire, Derby
	P. Cranmer (2)	111	v. Worcestershire, Dudley
		101	v. South Africans, Edgbaston
	W. A. Hill (2)	120	v. Northamptonshire, Northampton
		104	v. Cambridge Univ., Edgbaston
	H. E. Dollery (1)	116	v. Middlesex, Edgbaston
	K. A. Taylor (1)	102	v. Gloucestershire, Edgbaston
1948	J. S. Ord (5)	134	v. Middlesex, Lord's
		126	v. Scotland, Edgbaston
		107* 101	}v. Nottinghamshire, Trent Bridge
		101	v. Glamorgan, Edgbaston
	H. E. Dollery (2)	167	v. Derbyshire, Derby
		102	v. Lancashire, Old Trafford
	F. C. Gardner (1)	126	v. Kent, Edgbaston
	C. W. Grove (1)	104*	v. Leicestershire, Leicester
1949	H. E. Dollery (6)	200	v. Gloucestershire, Gloucester
		121	v. Hampshire, Bournemouth
		118	v. Kent, Maidstone
		111	v. Leicestershire, Leicester
		107	v. Leicestershire, Edgbaston
		100	v. Derbyshire, Edgbaston
	F. C. Gardner (2)	140*	v. Worcestershire, Edgbaston
		108	v. Sussex, Coventry
	J. R. Thompson (2)	103	v. Somerset, Taunton
		102*	v. Combined Services, Edgbaston
	R. H. Maudsley (1)	107	v. Hampshire, Bournemouth
	J. S. Ord (1)	156*	v. Hampshire, Bournemouth
	D. D. S. Taylor (1)	121	v. Leicestershire, Edgbaston
	A. V. Wolton (1)	111*	v. Somerset, Edgbaston
1950	H. E. Dollery (4)	185	v. Middlesex, Edgbaston
		163	v. Derbyshire, Derby
		150	v. Somerset, Edgbaston
		100	v. Kent, Edgbaston

1950	F. C. Gardner (4)	215*	v. Somerset, Taunton
		126	v. Northamptonshire, Northampton
		113 101* }	v. Essex, Ilford
	M. P. Donnelly (1)	120	v. Yorkshire, Edgbaston
	A. H. Kardar (1)	112	v. Middlesex, Lord's
	J. S. Ord (1)	142*	v. Nottinghamshire, Trent Bridge
1951	R. T. Spooner (4)	158	v. Middlesex, Lord's
		122	v. Worcestershire, Edgbaston
		102	v. Glamorgan, Edgbaston
		101	v. Leicestershire, Leicester
	H. E. Dollery (3)	111	v. Yorkshire, Edgbaston
		108*	v. Lancashire, Edgbaston
		110*	v. Hampshire, Edgbaston
	F. C. Gardner (3)	144	v. Worcestershire, Dudley
		139	v. Northamptonshire, Coventry
		101	v. Leicestershire, Leicester
	R. H. Maudsley (1)	107	v. Oxford University, Stratford-on-Avon
	J. S. Ord (1)	123	v. Somerset, Wells
	A. Townsend (1)	112	v. Nottinghamshire, Trent Bridge
	A. V. Wolton (1)	157*	v. Gloucestershire, Coventry
1952	F. C. Gardner (5)	184*	v. Lancashire, Liverpool
		147*	v. Nottinghamshire, Edgbaston
		118	v. Cambridge Univ., Edgbaston
		114	v. Glamorgan, Edgbaston
		104*	v. Surrey, Coventry
	H. E. Dollery (4)	212	v. Leicestershire, Edgbaston
		159	v. Yorkshire, Edgbaston
		158*	v. Leicestershire, Leicester
		100	v. Derbyshire, Edgbaston
	J. S. Ord (2)	187*	v. Cambridge Univ., Edgbaston
		143*	v. Oxford Univ., Oxford
	P. H. Bromley (1)	121*	v. Essex, Edgbaston
	N. F. Horner (1)	140	v. Oxford Univ., Oxford
	R. T. Spooner (1)	117	v. Kent, Coventry
1953	H. E. Dollery (3)	173	v. Somerset, Coventry
		169	v. Kent, Maidstone
		131	v. Hampshire, Edgbaston
	F. C. Gardner (3)	143	v. Derbyshire, Derby
		137	v. Somerset, Coventry
		110	v. Australians, Edgbaston
	R. T. Spooner (3)	168	v. Lancashire, Old Trafford
		103	v. Yorkshire, Edgbaston
		101*	v. Worcestershire, Worcester
	N. F. Horner (2)	122	v. Essex, Clacton
		115	v. Yorkshire, Bradford
	J. S. Ord (1)	109	v. Kent, Maidstone
	A. Townsend (1)	124	v. Worcestershire, Worcester

1954	H. E. Dollery (3)	142	v. Leicestershire, Hinckley
		124*	v. Middlesex, Edgbaston
		109*	v. Essex, Edgbaston
	A. V. Wolton (3)	165	v. Worcestershire, Dudley
		120	v. Essex, Westcliff
		118	v. Northamptonshire, Edgbaston
	F. C. Gardner (2)	150	v. Essex, Westcliff
		148*	v. Cambridge Univ., Cambridge
	R. T. Spooner (1)	111	v. Gloucestershire, Edgbaston
	A. Townsend (1)	106	v. Scotland, Coventry
1955	H. E. Dollery (4)	156	v. Essex, Westcliff
		151	v. Nottinghamshire, Edgbaston
		106	v. Leicestershire, Hinckley
		105	v. Somerset, Edgbaston
	R. E. Hitchcock (4)	128	v. Essex, Edgbaston
		123*	v. Surrey, Coventry
		121	v. Leicestershire, Hinckley
		110	v. Derbyshire, Derby
	A. V. Wolton (3)	136	v. Combined Services, Edgbaston
		107	v. Yorkshire, Edgbaston
		105*	v. Oxford Univ., Oxford
	F. C. Gardner (1)	167	v. Somerset, Bath
	N. F. Horner (1)	119	v. Gloucestershire, Bristol
	R. T. Spooner (1)	125	v. Leicestershire, Edgbaston
1956	F. C. Gardner (2)	120	v. Gloucestershire, Bristol
		103	v. Sussex, Edgbaston
	R. E. Hitchcock (1)	113	v. Kent, Coventry
	N. F. Horner (1)	129*	v. Leicestershire, Edgbaston
	A. Townsend (1)	100*	v. Combined Services, Edgbaston
	A. V. Wolton (1)	101	v. Sussex, Edgbaston
1957	F. C. Gardner (3)	163	v. Gloucestershire, Edgbaston
		126	v. Sussex, Eastbourne
		110	v. Oxford Univ., Oxford
	M. J. K. Smith (3)	127	v. Yorkshire, Edgbaston
		110	v. Middlesex, Edgbaston
		104*	v. Derbyshire, Derby
	N. F. Horner (1)	152	v. Derbyshire, Derby
	R. T. Spooner (1)	118	v. Glamorgan, Cardiff
	W. J. Stewart (1)	104	v. Leicestershire, Edgbaston
	A. Townsend (1)	154	v. Worcestershire, Dudley
1958	N. F. Horner (3)	155	v. Middlesex, Lord's
		110	v. Northampton, Coventry
		104	v. Somerset, Edgbaston
	M. J. K. Smith (2)	131	v. Combined Services, Edgbaston
		103*	v. Yorkshire, Edgbaston
	F. C. Gardner (2)	122	v. Derbyshire, Derby
		120	v. Glamorgan, Coventry
	T. W. Cartwright (1)	128	v. Kent, Edgbaston
	E. Leadbeater (1)	116	v. Glamorgan, Coventry
	A. V. Wolton (1)	102	v. Worcestershire, Edgbaston

1959	M. J. K. Smith (6)	200*	v. Worcestershire, Edgbaston
		184*	v. Leicestershire, Edgbaston
		182*	v. Gloucestershire, Stroud
		142*	v. Northamptonshire, Edgbaston
		142	v. Derbyshire, Burton-on-Trent
		130*	v. Surrey, Edgbaston
	W. J. Stewart (5)	156	v. Essex, Coventry
		155 125 }	v. Lancashire, Blackpool
		155	v. Glamorgan, Neath
		151	v. Combined Services, Portland Road
	N. F. Horner (4)	173	v. Middlesex, Edgbaston
		126	v. Glamorgan, Neath
		107	v. Nottinghamshire, Edgbaston
		101	v. Middlesex, Lord's
	A. V. Wolton (2)	136	v. Oxford Univ., Oxford
		115	v. Hampshire, Edgbaston
	T. W. Cartwright (1)	101*	v. Somerset, Edgbaston
	K. Ibadulla (1)	134	v. Cambridge Univ., Edgbaston
	A. Townsend (1)	111	v. Northamptonshire, Northampton
1960	N. F. Horner (4)	203*	v. Surrey, The Oval
		132*	v. Hampshire, Edgbaston
		109	v. Gloucestershire, Bristol
		106	v. Leicestershire, Coventry
	M. J. K. Smith (4)	169*	v. Worcestershire, Dudley
		127*	v. Northamptonshire, Northampton
		116*	v. Somerset, Weston-super-Mare
		106	v. Middlesex, Lord's
	K. Ibadulla (3)	170*	v. Surrey, The Oval
		131	v. Middlesex, Lord's
		106*	v. Middlesex, Edgbaston
	R. E. Hitchcock (2)	108	v. Middlesex, Edgbaston
		104	v. Nottinghamshire, Coventry
	F. C. Gardner (1)	103	v. Northamptonshire, Northampton
	W. J. Stewart (1)	129	v. Northamptonshire, Northampton
1961	M. J. K. Smith (5)	145	v. Essex, Edgbaston
		117	v. Nottinghamshire, Coventry
		112*	v. Lancashire, Old Trafford
		103	v. Nottinghamshire, Trent Bridge
		102	v. Middlesex, Edgbaston
	R. E. Hitchcock (3)	145	v. Lancashire, Edgbaston
		128	v. Yorkshire, Edgbaston
		105*	v. Kent, Blackheath
	N. F. Horner (3)	140	v. Worcestershire, Edgbaston
		117*	v. Essex, Colchester
		102	v. Yorkshire, Edgbaston

	W. J. Stewart (3)	143	v.	Hampshire, Southampton
		135	v.	Derbyshire, Edgbaston
		104	v.	Somerset, Street
	T. W. Cartwright (1)	119*	v.	Lancashire, Edgbaston
	K. Ibadulla (1)	171	v.	Oxford Univ., Oxford
1962	W. J. Stewart (7)	182*	v.	Leicestershire, Hinckley
		136	v.	Sussex, Edgbaston
		133*	v.	Kent, Folkestone
		123	v.	Essex, Edgbaston
		110*	v.	Sussex, Hove
		109	v.	Scotland, Edgbaston
		105	v.	Northamptonshire, Edgbaston
	K. Ibadulla (6)	119	v.	Oxford Univ., Edgbaston
		106	v.	Northamptonshire, Edgbaston
		101	v.	Leicestershire, Hinckley
		100*	v.	Sussex, Hove
		100	v.	Leicestershire, Edgbaston
		100	v.	Sussex, Edgbaston
	M. J. K. Smith (5)	163	v.	Sussex, Hove
		148	v.	Derbyshire, Edgbaston
		124	v.	Kent, Folkestone
		105*	v.	Derbyshire, Chesterfield
		104	v.	Glamorgan, Swansea
	T. W. Cartwright (1)	210	v.	Middlesex, Nuneaton
	R. E. Hitchcock (1)	153*	v.	Derbyshire, Chesterfield
1963	N. F. Horner (3)	113	v.	Worcestershire, Edgbaston
		108	v.	Nottinghamshire, Trent Bridge
		102	v.	Derbyshire, Edgbaston
	M. J. K. Smith (3)	144*	v.	Derbyshire, Derby
		115	v.	Hampshire, Coventry
		112	v.	Glamorgan, Edgbaston
	R. W. Barber (1)	113	v.	West Indies, Edgbaston
	R. E. Hitchcock (1)	106	v.	Derbyshire, Edgbaston
	K. Ibadulla (1)	104*	v.	Nottinghamshire, Edgbaston
1964	K. Ibadulla (4)	169*	v.	Yorkshire, Harrogate
		137	v.	Essex, Ilford
		133	v.	Cambridge Univ., Cambridge
		100	v.	Hampshire, Southampton
	R. W. Barber (3)	138	v.	Australians, Edgbaston
		103*	v.	Nottinghamshire, Nuneaton
		101	v.	Yorkshire, Harrogate
	N. F. Horner (2)	119	v.	Leicestershire, Edgbaston
		102	v.	Lancashire, Old Trafford
	J. A. Jameson (2)	165	v.	Oxford Univ., Edgbaston
		133*	v.	Essex, Ilford
	D. L. Amiss (1)	114	v.	Oxford Univ., Edgbaston
	R. E. Hitchcock (1)	106*	v.	Northamptonshire, Northampton
	M. J. K. Smith (1)	132	v.	Surrey, Edgbaston
1965	J. A. Jameson (2)	137*	v.	New Zealanders, Edgbaston
		101	v.	Oxford Univ., Edgbaston
	T. W. Cartwright (1)	112*	v.	New Zealanders, Edgbaston

1965	W. J. Stewart (1)	102	v. Surrey, The Oval
1966	M. J. K. Smith (3)	117	v. Nottinghamshire, Trent Bridge
		113*	v. Hampshire, Edgbaston
		103*	v. Sussex, Hastings
	D. L. Amiss (2)	160*	v. West Indians, Edgbaston
		150*	v. Scotland, Edgbaston
	R. N. Abberley (1)	117*	v. Essex, Edgbaston
	R. B. Edmonds (1)	102*	v. Scotland, Edgbaston
	J. A. Jameson (1)	118*	v. Somerset, Taunton
	W. J. Stewart (1)	166	v. Oxford Univ., Edgbaston
1967	D. L. Amiss (5)	176*	v. Nottinghamshire, Coventry
		161*	v. Northamptonshire, Northampton
		151*	v. Leicestershire, Edgbaston
		146	v. Scotland, Edgbaston
		138*	v. Oxford Univ., Oxford
	M. J. K. Smith (3)	173*	v. Pakistanis, Edgbaston
		123	v. Oxford Univ., Oxford
		111	v. Nottinghamshire, Trent Bridge
	B. A. Richardson (2)	126 105	} v. Cambridge Univ., Edgbaston
1968	R. B. Kanhai (6)	253	v. Nottinghamshire, Trent Bridge
		193	v. Leicestershire, Leicester
		152	v. Lancashire, Liverpool
		119	v. Cambridge Univ., Cambridge
		111	v. Yorkshire, Edgbaston
		106	v. Glamorgan, Edgbaston
	W. J. Stewart (4)	143*	v. Cambridge Univ., Cambridge
		117	v. Leicestershire, Leicester
		111	v. Oxford Univ., Oxford
		101*	v. Yorkshire, Edgbaston
	D. L. Amiss (2)	128	v. Kent, Edgbaston
		126	v. Worcestershire, Edgbaston
	J. A. Jameson (2)	114	v. Scotland, Edgbaston
		107*	v. Essex, Edgbaston
	R. W. Barber (1)	125	v. Sussex, Hove
	K. Ibadulla (1)	147*	v. Nottinghamshire, Trent Bridge
	G. S. Warner (1)	118*	v. Scotland, Edgbaston
1969	W. J. Stewart (2)	134	v. Northamptonshire, Edgbaston
		119	v. Oxford Univ., Oxford
	D. L. Amiss (1)	120	v. Somerset, Edgbaston
	R. B. Kanhai (1)	173	v. Northamptonshire, Peterborough
1970	R. B. Kanhai (6)	187*	v. Derbyshire, Coventry
		165	v. Derbyshire, Derby
		162*	v. Sussex, Hove
		132*	v. Worcestershire, Worcester
		107	v. Kent, Gravesend
		105	v. Nottinghamshire, Trent Bridge
	J. A. Jameson (4)	194	v. Cambridge Univ., Cambridge
		158*	v. Lancashire, Old Trafford
		141*	v. Lancashire, Edgbaston
		101	v. Surrey, The Oval

	M. J. K. Smith (2)	153* v. Oxford Univ., Oxford	
		109 v. Lancashire, Edgbaston	
	R. N. Abberley (1)	108 v. Somerset, Edgbaston	
	D. L. Amiss (1)	110 v. Gloucestershire, Gloucester	
	G. S. Warner (1)	102 v. Cambridge Univ., Edgbaston	
1971	M. J. K. Smith (6)	127 v. Pakistanis, Edgbaston	
		122 v. Kent, Edgbaston	
		113* v. Northants, Edgbaston	
		113 v. Yorkshire, Middlesbrough	
		105 v. Surrey, The Oval	
		101* v. Lancashire, Edgbaston	
	R. B. Kanhai (3)	135* v. Lancashire, Old Trafford	
		135 v. Yorkshire, Edgbaston	
		103 v. Yorkshire, Middlesbrough	
	J. A. Jameson (3)	231 v. Indians, Edgbaston	
		155 v. Lancashire, Old Trafford	
		135 v. Sussex, Edgbaston	
	D. L. Amiss (2)	124 v. Hampshire, Bournemouth	
		112 v. Yorkshire, Middlesbrough	
	J. Whitehouse (2)	173 v. Oxford Univ., Oxford	
		122 v. Nottinghamshire, Trent Bridge	
1972	R. B. Kanhai (8)	167* v. Oxford Univ., Oxford	
		199 v. Lancashire, Old Trafford	
		121 v. Northamptonshire, Northampton	
		123* v. Glamorgan, Edgbaston	
		165 v. Lancashire, Edgbaston	
		121* v. Hampshire, Portsmouth	
		115 v. Kent, Dartford	
		124 v. Derbyshire, Edgbaston	
	D. L. Amiss (5)	156* v. Worcestershire, Edgbaston	
		151* v. Middlesex, Edgbaston	
		192 v. Lancashire, Edgbaston	
		121* v. Kent, Dartford	
		120 v. Nottinghamshire, Coventry	
	A. Kallicharran (2)	164 v. Nottinghamshire, Coventry	
		149 v. Surrey, Edgbaston	
	M. J. K. Smith (2)	119 v. Cambridge Univ., Cambridge	
		102 v. Essex, Chelmsford	

A CENTURY ON DEBUT IN FIRST-CLASS CRICKET FOR WARWICKSHIRE

J. E. Hill	139* v. Nottinghamshire, Trent Bridge	1894
J. F. Byrne	100 v. Leicestershire, Edgbaston	1897
J. Whitehouse	173 v. Oxford Univ., Oxford	1971

A CENTURY ON DEBUT IN FIRST-CLASS CRICKET AGAINST WARWICKSHIRE

1894	F. H. Bacon	114 for Hampshire, Edgbaston
1947	P. Hearn	124 for Kent, Gillingham

CENTURY IN EACH INNINGS OF A FIRST-CLASS MATCH FOR WARWICKSHIRE

S. P. Kinneir	v. Sussex, Chichester	124	110	1911
W. G. Quaife	v. Surrey, The Oval	124	109	1913
C. Charlesworth	v. Surrey, Edgbaston	100	101*	1913
L. A. Bates	v. Kent, Coventry	144	116	1927
J. S. Ord	v. Nottinghamshire, Trent Bridge	107*	101	1948
F. C. Gardner	v. Essex, Ilford	113	101*	1950
W. J. Stewart	v. Lancashire, Blackpool	155	125	1959
B. A. Richardson	v. Cambridge Univ., Edgbaston	126	105	1967

CENTURY IN EACH INNINGS OF A FIRST-CLASS MATCH AGAINST WARWICKSHIRE

J. T. Tyldesley	for Lancashire, Edgbaston	106	100*	1897
L. G. Wright	for Derbyshire, Edgbaston	176	122	1905
J. B. Hobbs	for Surrey, Edgbaston	160	100	1909
A. C. Johnston	for Hampshire, Coventry	175	100*	1912
G. Gunn	for Nottinghamshire, Trent Bridge	100	110	1927
C. Hallows	for Lancashire, Edgbaston	123	101	1928
E. Hendren	for Middlesex, Edgbaston	189	100*	1931
E. Paynter	for Lancashire, Edgbaston	125	113*	1938
T. W. Graveney	for Gloucestershire, Edgbaston	106	101*	1957
K. Barrington	for Surrey, Edgbaston	186	118*	1959
R. Virgin	for Somerset, Edgbaston	124	125*	1965
H. Pilling	for Lancashire, Old Trafford	119*	104*	1970
J. H. Edrich	for Surrey, The Oval	111	124	1971
G. M. Turner	for Worcestershire, Edgbaston	122	128*	1972

HIGHEST INDIVIDUAL SCORE FOR WARWICKSHIRE

305*   by F. R. Foster v. Worcestershire, Dudley   1914

HIGHEST INDIVIDUAL INNINGS AGAINST WARWICKSHIRE

316 by R. H. Moore for Hampshire, Bournemouth   1937

CENTURY BEFORE LUNCH FOR WARWICKSHIRE

E. J. Diver	v. Leicestershire, Edgbaston	1899
T. S. Fishwick	v. Gloucestershire, Bristol	1900
T. S. Fishwick	v. Leicestershire, Leicester	1904
E. J. Smith	v. Hampshire, Coventry	1912
F. R. Santall	v. Northamptonshire, Northampton	1933
(173 scored before lunch – *world record*)		
N. F. Horner	v. Leicestershire, Edgbaston	1956
W. J. Stewart	v. Lancashire, Blackpool	1959
W. J. Stewart	v. Combined Services, Portland Road	1959
M. J. K. Smith	v. Gloucestershire, Stroud	1959
M. J. K. Smith	v. Worcestershire, Edgbaston	1959
W. J. Stewart	v. Leicestershire, Hinckley	1962
R. W. Barber	v. Australians, Edgbaston	1964
R. N. Abberley	v. Essex, Edgbaston	1966
A. Kallicharran	v. Surrey, Edgbaston	1972
R. B. Kanhai	v. Oxford Univ., Oxford	1972

APPENDIX 7

BATTING THROUGH BOTH INNINGS FOR WARWICKSHIRE

S. P. Kinneir   v. Leicestershire, Leicester   1907
(70 and 69 not out)
(Only four players have done this in the whole game)

BATTING THROUGH ONE INNINGS FOR WARWICKSHIRE

H. W. Bainbridge	65 v. Kent, Edgbaston	1894
W. G. Quaife	178 v. Hampshire, Southampton	1897
T. S. Fishwick	85 v. Lancashire, Old Trafford	1907
S. P. Kinneir	65 v. Somerset, Taunton	1908
J. H. Parsons	161 v. Gloucestershire, Edgbaston	1913
L. A. Bates	96 v. Surrey, The Oval	1921
L. A. Bates	50 v. Yorkshire, Huddersfield	1922
C. A. Fiddian-Green	60 v. Hampshire, Southampton	1922
N. Kilner	40 v. Kent, Tunbridge Wells	1928
A. J. Croom	131 v. Northamptonshire, Edgbaston	1929
A. J. Croom	58 v. Gloucestershire, Cheltenham	1930
A. J. Croom	102 v. Lancashire, Old Trafford	1931
A. J. Croom	69 v. Leicestershire, Hinckley	1936
K. A. Taylor	81 v. Yorkshire, Edgbaston	1948
F. C. Gardner	140 v. Worcestershire, Edgbaston	1949
F. C. Gardner	73 v. Glamorgan, Swansea	1950
F. C. Gardner	184 v. Lancashire, Liverpool	1952
R. T. Spooner	98 v. Worcestershire, Worcester	1952
F. C. Gardner	62 v. Glamorgan, Edgbaston	1954
D. L. Amiss	160 v. West Indies, Edgbaston	1966

BATTING THROUGH ONE INNINGS AGAINST WARWICKSHIRE

J. B. Hobbs	60 for Surrey, Edgbaston	1907
C. P. Mead	88 for Hampshire, Leamington	1909
A. E. Knight	137 for Leicestershire, Edgbaston	1909
C. J. B. Wood	54 for Leicestershire, Hinckley	1911
L. Oliver	75 for Derbyshire, Edgbaston	1912
C. J. B. Wood	164 for Leicestershire, Hinckley	1913
A. E. Dipper	120 for Gloucestershire, Edgbaston	1920
F. Pearson	151 for Worcestershire, Worcester	1921
A. E. Dipper	87 for Gloucestershire, Bristol	1923
H. L. Wilson	108 for Sussex, Hove	1924
H. H. I. H. Gibbons	70 for Worcestershire, Kidderminster	1934
Dilawar Hussain	101 for Indians, Edgbaston	1936
V. M. Merchant	86 for Indians, Edgbaston	1946
W. Place	101 for Lancashire, Manchester	1950
E. Cooper	69 for Worcestershire, Dudley	1951
G. Boycott	53 for Yorkshire, Bradford	1969
G. Boycott	138 for Yorkshire, Edgbaston	1971

APPENDIX 7

DOUBLE CENTURIES FOR WARWICKSHIRE

L. A. Bates	200	v. Worcestershire, Edgbaston	1928
L. A. Bates	211	v. Gloucestershire, Gloucester	1932
J. F. Byrne	222	v. Lancashire, Edgbaston	1905
Hon. F. S. G. Calthorpe	209	v. Hampshire, Edgbaston	1921
T. W. Cartwright	210	v. Middlesex, Nuneaton	1962
C. Charlesworth	216	v. Derbyshire, Blackwell	1910
C. Charlesworth	206	v. Yorkshire, Dewsbury	1914
A. J. Croom	211	v. Worcestershire, Edgbaston	1934
J. Devey	246	v. Derbyshire, Edgbaston	1900
H. E. Dollery	200	v. Gloucestershire, Gloucester	1949
H. E. Dollery	212	v. Leicestershire, Edgbaston	1951
F. R. Foster	200	v. Surrey, Edgbaston	1911
F. R. Foster	305*	v. Worcestershire, Dudley	1914
F. C. Gardner	215*	v. Somerset, Taunton	1950
N. F. Horner	203*	v. Surrey, The Oval	1960
J. A. Jameson	231	v. Indians, Edgbaston	1971
R. B. Kanhai	253	v. Nottinghamshire, Trent Bridge	1968
N. Kilner	228	v. Worcestershire, Worcester	1935
S. P. Kinneir	215*	v. Lancashire, Edgbaston	1901
S. P. Kinneir	268*	v. Hampshire, Edgbaston	1911
Rev. J. H. Parsons	225	v. Glamorgan, Edgbaston	1927
W. G. Quaife	207*	v. Hampshire, Edgbaston	1899
W. G. Quaife	223*	v. Essex, Leyton	1900
W. G. Quaife	200*	v. Essex, Edgbaston	1904
W. G. Quaife	255*	v. Surrey, The Oval	1905
F. R. Santall	201*	v. Northamptonshire, Northampton	1933
M. J. K. Smith	200*	v. Worcestershire, Edgbaston	1959
R. E. S. Wyatt	232	v. Derbyshire, Edgbaston	1937
R. E. S. Wyatt	201*	v. Lancashire, Edgbaston	1937

DOUBLE CENTURIES AGAINST WARWICKSHIRE

W. E. Alley	221*	for Somerset, Nuneaton	1961
L. E. G. Ames	210	for Kent, Tonbridge	1933
E. G. Arnold	200*	for Worcestershire, Edgbaston	1909
I. M. Chappell	202*	for Australians, Edgbaston	1968
E. Cooper	216*	for Worcestershire, Dudley	1938
D. Denton	200*	for Yorkshire, Edgbaston	1912
W. J. Edrich	225	for Middlesex, Edgbaston	1947
H. K. Foster	215	for Worcestershire, Edgbaston	1908
C. Hallows	227	for Lancashire, Old Trafford	1921
W. R. Hammond	238*	for Gloucestershire, Edgbaston	1929
H. T. W. Hardinge	205	for Kent, Tunbridge Wells	1928
J. Hardstaff jnr.	221*	for Nottinghamshire, Trent Bridge	1947
T. Hayward	208	for Surrey, The Oval	1906
T. Hayward	204	for Surrey, The Oval	1909
J. W. Hearne	215*	for Middlesex, Edgbaston	1920
J. W. Hearne	202	for Middlesex, Edgbaston	1921
J. W. Hearne	221*	for Middlesex, Edgbaston	1922
E. Hendren	209*	for Middlesex, Edgbaston	1928
J. B. Hobbs	215	for Surrey, Edgbaston	1925

J. B. Hobbs	200* for Surrey, Edgbaston	1928
P. Holmes	220* for Yorkshire, Huddersfield	1922
P. Holmes	209 for Yorkshire, Edgbaston	1922
P. Holmes	275 for Yorkshire, Bradford	1928
P. Holmes	250 for Yorkshire, Edgbaston	1931
J. Iddon	204* for Lancashire, Edgbaston	1933
E. T. Killick	206 for Middlesex, Lord's	1931
C. H. Lloyd	217* for Lancashire, Old Trafford	1971
C. P. Mead	207* for Hampshire, Southampton	1911
C. P. Mead	211* for Hampshire, Southampton	1922
C. P. Mead	222 for Hampshire, Edgbaston	1923
R. H. Moore	316 for Hampshire, Bournemouth	1937
A. D. Nourse jnr	205* for South Africans, Edgbaston	1947
R. Peel	210* for Yorkshire, Edgbaston	1896
A. Sandham	204 for Surrey, Edgbaston	1930
R. T. Simpson	201 for Nottinghamshire, Trent Bridge	1946
R. T. Simpson	200 for Nottinghamshire, Trent Bridge	1952
H. Sutcliffe	206 for Yorkshire, Dewsbury	1925
H. Sutcliffe	205 for Yorkshire, Edgbaston	1933
K. Taylor	203* for Yorkshire, Edgbaston	1961
E. Tyldesley	244 for Lancashire, Edgbaston	1920
E. Tyldesley	256* for Lancashire, Old Trafford	1930
J. T. Tyldesley	209 for Lancashire, Edgbaston	1907
P. F. Warner	244 for The Rest of England, The Oval	1911
C. Washbrook	209* for Lancashire, Edgbaston	1951

TWO THOUSAND RUNS IN A SEASON FOR WARWICKSHIRE

2075 by R. E. S. Wyatt	in 43	innings	1928
2114 by N. Kilner	in 48	„	1933
2084 by H. E. Dollery	in 48	„	1949
2073 by H. E. Dollery	in 51	„	1952
2074 by M. J. K. Smith	in 59	„	1957
2417 by M. J. K. Smith	in 50	„	1959
2099 by M. J. K. Smith	in 53	„	1961
2090 by M. J. K. Smith	in 56	„	1962
2318 by W. J. Stewart	in 62	„	1962
2098 by K. Ibadulla	in 64	„	1962

THOUSAND RUNS FOR WARWICKSHIRE BY 30 JUNE

W. G. Quaife	29 June	1905	
R. E. S. Wyatt	26 June	1928	
N. Kilner	28 June	1933	
R. T. Spooner	27 June	1951	
A. V. Wolton	30 June	1954	
H. E. Dollery	30 June	1955	
M. J. K. Smith	27 June	1959	
W. J. Stewart	12 June	1962	(1st in the Country)
M. J. K. Smith	19 June	1962	
K. Ibadulla	29 June	1962	
D. L. Amiss	30 June	1967	
R. B. Kanhai	30 June	1968	(1st in the Country)
R. B. Kanhai	13 June	1970	(1st in the Country)
J. A. Jameson	21 June	1971	(1st Englishman in Country)

8. Bowling

	Year	Overs	Mdns	Runs	Wkts	Ave
S. Hargreave	1901	1003·2	295	2324	110	21·12
S. Hargreave	1902	902·4	287	1851	106	17·46
S. Hargreave	1903	816·1	252	1642	128	12·82
S. Hargreave	1905	1110·5	310	2649	110	24·08
S. Hargreave	1906	982	294	2318	101	22·95
S. Santall	1907	738	192	1679	100	16·79
F. E. Field	1908	710·3	136	2190	106	20·66
F. E. Field	1911	788·5	160	2627	128	20·46
F. R. Foster	1911	802·4	152	2441	124	19·67
P. Jeeves	1913	780·5	206	2214	106	20·88
F. R. Foster	1914	831·2	201	2135	117	18·24
H. Howell	1920	908·1	205	2378	136	17·48
H. Howell	1921	615·2	107	1756	104	16·88
H. Howell	1922	831·1	138	2450	120	20·41
H. Howell	1923	1067·4	193	3029	152	19·92
H. Howell	1924	803·5	159	2098	124	16·91
H. Howell	1925	808·4	127	2470	111	22·25
J. H. Mayer	1929	1053·4	240	2817	126	22·36
J. H. Mayer	1930	945·4	248	2197	108	20·34
G. E. A. Paine	1931	955·1	228	2439	127	19·20
G. E. A. Paine	1932	1103·2	320	2575	136	18·93
G. E. A. Paine	1933	1350·1	453	3010	123	24·47
G. E. A. Paine	1934	1269·5	459	2626	155	16·94
G. E. A. Paine	1935	1045·1	294	2511	110	22·83
W. E. Hollies	1935	996·1	309	2463	127	19·39
W. E. Hollies	1937	1018	282	2862	109	26·26
W. E. Hollies	1938	981·4	225	2503	100	25·03
W. E. Hollies	1939	725·1	101	2584	117	22·09
W. E. Hollies	1946	1470	426	2725	180	15·13
W. E. Hollies	1947	1042·4	231	2598	107	24·28
W. E. Hollies	1948	1214	343	2566	142	18·02
T. L. Pritchard	1948	1185·3	260	2978	166	17·93
W. E. Hollies	1949	1370·1	497	2858	144	19·84
T. L. Pritchard	1949	1043	189	2794	113	24·78
W. E. Hollies	1950	1144·3	423	2320	126	18·41
T. L. Pritchard	1950	937·4	191	2547	104	24·49
W. E. Hollies	1951	1393·2	500	2566	145	17·69

C. W. Grove	1951	979·4	271	2038	110	18·52
W. E. Hollies	1952	1146·4	438	2412	118	20·44
C. W. Grove	1952	945·3	240	2022	118	17·13
W. E. Hollies	1954	1274·2	510	2389	122	19·58
W. E. Hollies	1955	1053·1	400	2035	115	17·69
W. E. Hollies	1957	1200·4	402	2436	128	19·03
J. D. Bannister	1960	1025·3	295	2288	105	21·79
O. S. Wheatley	1960	1086·1	261	2733	110	24·84
J. D. Bannister	1961	1190·3	352	2779	131	21·21
W. B. Bridge	1961	1134·4	392	2753	121	22·75
T. W. Cartwright	1962	932·2	338	2126	106	20·05
A. Wright	1962	992·5	254	2472	116	21·31
J. D. Bannister	1962	1087	326	2323	108	21·50
T. W. Cartwright	1963	881·1	360	1786	100	17·86
T. W. Cartwright	1964	965·2	433	1765	128	13·78
T. W. Cartwright	1965	684·4	287	1385	100	13·85
T. W. Cartwright	1966	842·5	304	1795	100	17·95
T. W. Cartwright	1967	1194	488	2282	147	15·52
T. W. Cartwright	1969	880·5	373	1748	108	16·18
L. R. Gibbs	1971	1024·1	295	2475	131	18·89

SEVENTEEN WICKETS IN A MATCH AGAINST WARWICKSHIRE

G. R. Cox	17–106 for Sussex, Horsham	1926
A. P. Freeman	17– 92 for Kent, Folkestone	1932

FIFTEEN WICKETS IN A MATCH FOR WARWICKSHIRE

S. Hargreave	15– 76 v. Surrey, The Oval	1903
T. W. Cartwright	15– 89 v. Glamorgan, Swansea	1967

FIFTEEN WICKETS IN A MATCH AGAINST WARWICKSHIRE

T. Richardson	15– 83 for Surrey, The Oval	1898
C. L. Townsend	15–205 for Gloucestershire, Cheltenham	1898
H. Young	15–154 for Essex, Edgbaston	1899
F. Harry	15– 70 for Lancashire, Old Trafford	1906
J. B. Statham	15– 89 for Lancashire, Coventry	1957
N. I. Thompson	15– 75 for Sussex, Worthing	1964
R. E. East	15–115 for Essex, Leyton	1968

TEN WICKETS IN ONE INNINGS FOR WARWICKSHIRE

		O	M	R	W	
H. Howell	v. Yorkshire, Edgbaston	25·1	5	51	10	1923
W. E. Hollies	v. Nottinghamshire, Edgbaston	20·4	4	49	10	1946
J. D. Bannister	v. Combined Services, Portland Road	23·3	11	41	10	1959

TEN WICKETS IN ONE INNINGS AGAINST WARWICKSHIRE

		O	M	R	W	
H. Verity	for Yorkshire, Leeds	18·4	6	36	10	1931
E. A. Watts	for Surrey, Edgbaston	24·1	8	67	10	1939
N. I. Thomson	for Sussex, Worthing	34·2	19	49	10	1964

APPENDIX 8

NINE WICKETS IN AN INNINGS FOR WARWICKSHIRE

F. Field	9–104 v. Leicestershire, Leicester	1899
F. R. Foster	9–118 v. Yorkshire, Edgbaston	1911
S. Hargreave	9– 35 v. Surrey, The Oval	1903
W. E. Hollies	9– 93 v. Glamorgan, Edgbaston	1939
W. E. Hollies	9– 56 v. Northamptonshire, Northampton	1950
H. Howell	9– 35 v. Somerset, Taunton	1924
H. Howell	9– 32 v. Hampshire, Edgbaston	1925
H. J. Pallett	9– 55 v. Essex, Leyton	1894
C. W. Grove	9– 39 v. Sussex, Edgbaston	1952
R. G. Thompson	9– 65 v. Nottinghamshire, Edgbaston	1952
J. D. Bannister	9– 35 v. Yorkshire, Sheffield	1955

EIGHT WICKETS IN AN INNINGS FOR WARWICKSHIRE

J. Whitehead	8– 95 v. Nottinghamshire, Edgbaston	1894
J. Whitehead	8– 47 v. Nottinghamshire, Trent Bridge	1894
J. Whitehead	8– 49 v. Surrey, The Oval	1894
H. J. Pallett	8– 69 v. Derbyshire, Edgbaston	1895
J. Whitehead	8– 64 v. Lancashire, Liverpool	1895
F. Field	8–144 v. Gloucestershire, Edgbaston	1898
S. Santall	8– 32 v. Essex, Edgbaston	1898
S. Santall	8– 23 v. Leicestershire, Edgbaston	1900
S. Hargreave	8– 66 v. London County, Edgbaston	1901
S. Hargreave	8– 62 v. Gloucestershire, Edgbaston	1901
S. Hargreave	8– 52 v. Lancashire, Old Trafford	1902
S. Hargreave	8– 42 v. Essex, Leyton	1903
S. Santall	8– 72 v. Yorkshire, Sheffield	1907
S. Santall	8– 44 v. Somerset, Leamington	1908
S. Santall	8– 86 v. Hampshire, Leamington	1909
C. K. Langley	8– 29 v. Worcestershire, Edgbaston	1912
H. Howell	8– 69 v. Derbyshire, Edgbaston	1921
H. Howell	8– 31 v. Northamptonshire, Northampton	1922
H. Howell	8– 65 v. Leicestershire, Leicester	1925
J. H. Meyer	8– 62 v. Surrey, Edgbaston	1928
G. E. A. Paine	8– 44 v. Northamptonshire, Peterborough	1931
H. Jarrett	8–187 v. Leicestershire, Hinckley	1932
E. Brown	8– 35 v. Surrey, Edgbaston	1933
W. E. Hollies	8– 54 v. Gloucestershire, Edgbaston	1933
G. E. A. Paine	8– 43 v. Worcestershire, Edgbaston	1934
G. E. A. Paine	8– 62 v. Yorkshire, Scarborough	1934
G. E. A. Paine	8–121 v. Nottinghamshire, Edgbaston	1935
W. E. Hollies	8– 67 v. Nottinghamshire, Edgbaston	1935
W. E. Hollies	8– 61 v. Worcestershire, Worcester	1935
T. L. Pritchard	8– 43 v. Northamptonshire, Northampton	1948
W. E. Hollies	8–107 v. Australians, Edgbaston	1948
W. E. Hollies	8– 71 v. Worcestershire, Edgbaston	1949
W. E. Hollies	8– 54 v. Surrey, Edgbaston	1949
T. L. Pritchard	8– 20 v. Worcestershire, Dudley	1950
C. W. Grove	8– 38 v. West Indians, Edgbaston	1950
T. L. Pritchard	8– 55 v. Glamorgan, Edgbaston	1951
J. D. Bannister	8– 54 v. Yorkshire, Leeds	1954

K. R. Dollery	8– 42 v. Sussex, Edgbaston	1954
W. E. Hollies	8– 42 v. Essex, Westcliff	1955
G. H. Hill	8– 70 v. Gloucestershire, Cheltenham	1958
R. G. Carter	8– 82 v. Somerset, Edgbaston	1958
R. G. Thompson	8– 94 v. Hampshire, Edgbaston	1959
W. B. Bridge	8– 66 v. Gloucestershire, Stroud	1959
W. B. Bridge	8– 56 v. Cambridge University, Edgbaston	1959
R. G. Thompson	8– 40 v. Gloucestershire, Edgbaston	1959
T. W. Cartwright	8– 39 v. Somerset, Weston-super-Mare	1962
T. W. Cartwright	8– 45 v. Hampshire, Coventry	1963
D. J. Brown	8– 69 v. Sussex, Edgbaston	1964
R. Webster	9– 19 v. Cambridge University, Cambridge	1966
T. W. Cartwright	8– 50 v. Glamorgan, Swansea	1967
L. R. Gibbs	8– 37 v. Glamorgan, Edgbaston	1970
R. G. D. Willis	8– 44 v. Derbyshire, Edgbaston	1972

HAT TRICKS FOR WARWICKSHIRE

F. E. Field	v. Hampshire, Edgbaston	1911
R. Cooke	v. Kent, Tunbridge Wells	1925
D. G. Foster	v. Hampshire, Edgbaston	1929
G. E. A. Paine	v. Middlesex, Lord's	1932
G. E. A. Paine	v. Glamorgan, Cardiff	1933
C. W. Grove	v. Somerset, Taunton	1947
T. L. Pritchard	v. Leicestershire, Edgbaston	1948
T. L. Pritchard	v. Kent, Maidstone	1949
T. L. Pritchard	v. Glamorgan, Edgbaston	1951
K. R. Dollery	v. Gloucestershire, Bristol	1953
J. D. Bannister	v. Yorkshire, Sheffield	1955
K. R. Dollery	v. Kent, Coventry	1956
R. G. Thompson	v. Sussex, Horsham	1956
R. W. Barber	v. Glamorgan, Edgbaston	1963
A. C. Smith	v. Essex, Clacton-on-Sea	1965
J. A. Jameson	v. Gloucestershire, Edgbaston	1965
T. W. Cartwright	v. Somerset, Edgbaston	1969
R. G. D. Willis	v. Derbyshire, Edgbaston	1972

HAT TRICKS AGAINST WARWICKSHIRE

T. Richardson	for Surrey, The Oval	1898
J. W. Hitch	for Surrey, The Oval	1914
S. G. Smith	for Northamptonshire, Edgbaston	1914
G. G. Macaulay	for Yorkshire, Edgbaston	1923
C. A. Preece	for Worcestershire, Edgbaston	1924
C. Wright	for Kent, Edgbaston	1925
G. S. Boyes	for Hampshire, Edgbaston	1926
E. A. McDonald	for Lancashire, Edgbaston	1930
R. T. D. Perks	for Worcestershire, Edgbaston	1933
W. H. Copson	for Derbyshire, Derby	1937
H. E. Hammond	for Sussex, Hove	1946
R. Pollard	for Lancashire, Blackpool	1947
R. Howorth	for Worcestershire, Edgbaston	1950
J. Laker	for Surrey, The Oval	1953

BOWLERS BOWLING UNCHANGED THROUGH A COMPLETED MATCH FOR WARWICKSHIRE

S. Hargreave and S. Santall	v. Surrey, The Oval	1903
S. Hargreave and S. Santall	v. Leicestershire, Coventry	1907
S. Hargreave and S. Santall	v. Leicestershire, Leicester	1909

9. *Wicketkeeping*

❖ ❖ ❖

Wicketkeeper	Period of Service	Caught	Stumped	Total
Barnes T. P.	1956	1	—	1
Buckingham J.	1933 – 9	130	88	218
Cross E. P.	1921 – 3	6	—	6
Dollery H. E.	1947	37	12	49
Flick B. J.	1969 – 72	1	3	4
Fox J. G.	1959 – 61	97	13	110
Goodway C. C.	1937 – 47	43	21	64
Hawkins C.	1957	7	2	9
Jameson J. A.	1972	0	1	1
Kendall J. T.	1948 – 9	5	4	9
Legard E.	1962 – 8	33	9	42
Lewis E. B.	1949 – 58	82	23	105
Lilley A. A.	1894 – 1911	504	132	636
Lowe P. J.	1964	2	—	2
McDowall J. I.	1969	14	1	15
Murray D. L.	1972	40	4	44
O'Rourke C.	1968	3	—	3
Robins D. H.	1947	3	—	3
Smart J.	1930–36	221	93	314
Smith A. C.	1958 – 72	569	39	608
Smith E. J.	1904 – 30	643	139	782
Spooner R. T.	1948 – 59	529	157	686
Taylor C. R. V.	1970	2	—	2
Tennant P.	1964	3	1	4
Timms B. S. V.	1969 – 71	54	10	64
White M. F.	1946	3	1	4

MOST DISMISSALS IN A MATCH FOR WARWICKSHIRE

E. B. Lewis	(9) 8ct 1st	v. Oxford University, Edgbaston	1949
A. A. Lilley	(8) 8ct	v. M.C.C., Lord's	1896
A. A. Lilley	(8) 8ct	v. Kent, Edgbaston	1897
E. J. Smith	(8) 5ct 3st	v. Derbyshire, Edgbaston	1926
E. J. Smith	(8) 7ct 1st	v. Worcestershire, Edgbaston	1930

R. T. Spooner	(8)	8ct		v. Leicestershire, Edgbaston	1959
R. T. Spooner	(7)	6ct	1st	v. Nottinghamshire, Edgbaston	1957
A. C. Smith	(7)	7ct		v. Derbyshire, Derby	1970
B. S. V. Timms	(7)	6ct	1st	v. Northamptonshire, Northampton	1971

MOST DISMISSALS IN AN INNINGS FOR WARWICKSHIRE

E. J. Smith	(7)	4ct	3st	v. Derbyshire, Edgbaston	1926
J. Buckingham	(6)	5ct	1st	v. Sussex, Edgbaston	1939
E. B. Lewis	(6)	6ct		v. Cambridge University, Cambridge	1956
R. T. Spooner	(6)	6ct		v. Nottinghamshire, Edgbaston	1957
A. C. Smith	(6)	6ct		v. Derbyshire, Derby	1970

10. *Warwickshire Benefits*

❖ ❖ ❖

Year	Player	Amount
1895	Shilton	£500
1897	Pallett	£500
1899	Law	£380
1901	Lilley	£850
1904	Richards and Whitehead	£200
1906	Devey	£400
1908	Santall S.	£400
1910	Quaife W. G. (First)	£400
1912	Field	£620
1914	Kinneir	£467
1920	Charlesworth	£1050
1922	Smith E. J.	£700
1924	Howell	£804
1926	Parsons	£881
1927	Quaife W. G. (Second)	£917
1930	Bates	£792
1933	Mayer	£509
1935	Santall R.	£712
1936	Croom	£679
1937	Kilner N.	£778
1938	Paine	£876
1948	Hollies	£4896
1949	Dollery H. E.	£6362
1950	Ord	£4833
1951	Grove	£4469
1952	Pritchard	£3816
1957	Spooner	£3784
1958	Gardner	£3750
1959	Wolton	£3542
1960	Townsend	£4143
1962	Horner	£6465
1963	Hitchcock	£6410
1964	Bannister	£8846
1967	Stewart	£8346
1968	Cartwright	£9592
1969	Ibadulla	£7797
1973	Brown	£21 109 (Club record)

A testimonial to Hollies in 1954 realised £1796, and a joint testimonial to 'Tiger' Smith and George Austin in 1955 £1797—£898 each.

number of people per stand

A	564	G	401	M	1182	1	1500	6	12
B	1249	H	484	N	1176	2	1600	7	751
C	1027	J	1248	O	806	3	1200	8	100
D	1337	K	1372	P	735	4	1000		
E	1200	L	1152	Q	744	5	300		

EDGBASTON

1 The William Ansell stand
2 Pavilion (west wing)
3 Pavilion (centre)
4 Pavilion (east wing)
5 Stanley Barnes stand
6 Thwaite score board
7 Press box stand
8 Press box
9 Indoor cricket school
10 Memorial score board
11 St Johns Ambulance & Police
12 Invalid carriage enclosures
13 W.C.C.S.A. offices
14 Club offices
15 "The Pavilion Suite"
16 "The Calthorpe Suite"
17 The Warwick Social Club
18 Head Groundman's store
19 Maintenance stores
▨ Sight screen block
▶ turnstile entrances

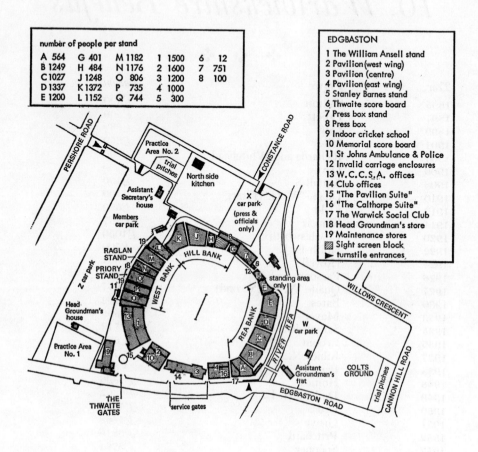

Index

Brookes, Denis, 255, 306
Brown, David, 379, 427, 435, 442,
    451, 457, 458, 460, 462, 463, 469,
    472, 476, 482, 484, 486, 487, 490
    ff., 503, 507 ff., 512, 520–1, 522,
    544, 547, 566, 571, 576, 582,
    591, 593, 595
Brown, F. R., 304, 306, 323, 324,
    395, 543, 582
Brown, George, 153–4
Brown, J. T., 61, 67
Brown, W. A., 288–90
Buchanan, David, 3, 7, 8, 11, 13,
    16, 18–19, 37, 76
Buckingham, Jack, 190, 211, 212,
    232, 233, 240–1, 247, 268
Buller, Syd, 550
Burns, Walter, 107
Byrne, J. F., 36, 90, 96–8, 104, 117,
    183, 225, 238, 303, 323, 345, 422

Caesar, Julius, 6–7
Caffyn, William, 7, 14
Caldicott, C. M., 7
Calthorpe, Lord, 18–19, 98
Calthorpe, Hon. F. S. G., 135, 144,
    146–7, 150, 152–4, 155, 156 ff.,
    160, 165, 166 ff., 170, 175, 179,
    182, 183, 185, 205, 221, 230, 388,
    459, 549
Calvert, C. P., 253
Cannings, Vic, 280, 390
Cardus, Sir Neville, 4, 57–8, 84,
    269, 274, 323, 324
Carr, A. W., 181
Carr, D. B., 457, 586
Carter, R. G., 354, 357, 397, 400
Cartland, G. H., 12, 16, 18, 20, 21,
    33, 39–40, 48, 51, 54, 60, 65, 71,
    74, 76, 77, 79–80, 81, 87, 96, 98,
    107, 110, 117, 120–1, 137, 140,
    157, 175, 177, 196
Cartland, J., 18
Cartwright, Tom, 326, 334, 389–90,
    399–400, 409, 410, 421, 426 ff.,
    430, 434, 436, 443, 445, 448, 449,
    451, 452, 457, 458, 460 ff., 475,
    476, 477, 482, 489–92, 496, 497,
    501, 506, 507, 511, 516, 518, 521,
    523–6, 527, 529, 549, 550, 567–8,
    582, 591; moves to Somerset
    C.C.C., 524–5
Catterall, Arthur, 163, 184

Chapman, A. P. F., 189, 301
Chapman (Derbyshire), 108
Charlesworth, Rev. A. A., 86
Charlesworth, Crowther, 53, 63, 72,
    78, 92, 98, 108, 112, 113, 116,
    117–20, 128, 130, 142, 150, 183,
    220, 351–2
Chester, Frank, 112, 303, 550
Chloe, mare 268–70
Chubb, G. W. A., 420–1
Clark, D. G., 449–50, 457, 466,
    548, 575, 603
Clark, E. A., 13
Clarke, C. B., 253
Clarke, William, 6
Clay, J. C., 286
Clements, Edward, 11
Close, Brian, 385, 474, 486, 491–3,
    567–8, 573
Clugston, D. L., 181, 424
Coaching scheme introduced, 336
Cobham, Viscount, 121, 225, 371
Collin, Tom, 211, 217
Collishaw, Fred, 22, 25, 28, 44, 45,
    230
Compton, Denis, 297–8, 313, 333,
    385, 386, 517, 595
Constatine, Sir Learie (later Lord),
    149, 180–1, 206, 253–4, 259, 260,
    468
Cook, E. Frank, 383
Cook, M. S., 428
Cooke, R., 167
Copson, W. H., 233, 244
Cotter, Albert, 97
Cotterill, C. W., 248
Cricketers' Association, 501, 560,
    576, 583–4, 599
County Cricket Council, 27, 33–4, 68
Coventry, Earl of, 8
Cowan, Captain C. F. R., RN, 110,
    231, 236, 246, 253, 273, 281, 285,
    295, 300, 372, 403
Cowdrey, M. C., 377, 385–6,
    398, 416, 436, 439–40, 474, 508,
    509, 512, 544
Cox, George, 168, 170, 392
Crane, E. D., 13
Cranmer, P., 203, 211–12, 233,
    235, 239, 240, 242, 244, 246,
    248, 267, 273, 275, 276, 278, 279,
    280, 281, 282, 331, 372, 407, 424,
    454, 483, 530; appointed captain,

Edgbaston—*continued*
opening of new Pavilion Suite,
382; new Indoor Cricket School,
382; success of Test at, 386–7,
398–9, 425–6; criticism of ground
by Australians, 431–2; criticism
of wicket, 456–7, 464–5, 486–9,
510; ground developments, 466–
467; first Sunday match at, 473;
proposed developing of North
Side, 532–3; pitch damaged by
anti-apartheid group, 538;
University tournament staged, 574
'Edgbaston mutiny' (1894), 45–6
Edmonds, R. B., 443, 449, 452, 463,
483
Edrich, John, 422, 450, 563, 567
Edrich, W. J., 245, 259, 260, 297–
298, 306, 313, 333
Egdell, George, 160, 180, 297
Egdell-Fraser history, 59–60, 104,
112
Elkington (pro), 8
Ellis, 58
Ellison, M. J., 34
Emmett, George, 305, 306, 314
Emmett, Tom, 24, 95
Engel, Tony, 541
Evans, Canon, F. R., 8
Evans, Godfrey, 386
Evans, Stanley, 139
Evans, William, 19
Everitt, Russell, 107

Fagg, A., 286, 298, 315
Fantham, W., 233, 248, 273, 274
Farnes, K., 211, 214
Farrimond, W., 214
Faulkner, Aubrey, 100
Fellows, Leslie F., 536
Fender, P. G. H., 164
Ferris, 30, 33
Fiddian-Green, C. A., 147
Field, Frank, 53–4, 61, 69–70, 72,
76, 78, 79, 92, 94, 103–4, 106–7,
111, 113 ff., 121, 126, 132, 133,
137, 142, 143, 213
Fielder, A., 108, 118
Findlay, W., 331
Fingleton, J. H., 564, 588
Fishlock, L., 277
Fishwick, H., 13

Fishwick, T. S., 63, 73, 97–8, 306,
327, 379
Flack, Bernard, 368–9, 382, 385,
398, 446, 447, 464–5, 476, 487,
488, 508, 563, 587, 598
Flavell, Jack, 361, 364, 389
Fletcher, B. E., 422–3, 428
Flowers, W., 22
Foster, A. W., 134
Foster, D. G., 183, 184, 188, 193,
194, 196
Foster, Frank, 60, 61, 102–4, 107 ff.,
132–4, 135, 142, 144, 205, 213,
220, 223, 276, 328, 371, 388,
403, 432; leg theory of, 125,
127–8, 205; tremendous feats of,
132–6
Foster, G. N., 134
Foster, Rev. H., 102
Foster, H. K., 105
Foster, N. J. A., 134
Foster, R. E., 76
Foster, W. H., 134
Fraser, M. F. K., 104, 261, 301,
341–3, 382, 403, 404, 415, 609
Freeman, A. P., 168, 181, 188, 202,
247
Fry, C. B., 35, 73, 76, 82, 105, 106,
120

Gardner, Fred, 268, 279, 286, 296,
304, 305, 308, 310, 312 ff., 317,
318, 329, 333, 334, 345–6, 349,
364, 365, 371, 379, 389, 390,
396, 397, 399, 400, 409, 422,
426, 429
Gardom, Keith, 598
Geary, George, 227
Gibbs, Lance, 444, 474, 482, 489,
499, 500, 503, 507, 510, 513, 521,
541, 543–4, 547 ff., 565 ff., 585–
586; named Cricketers' Cricketer
1971, 580; Cricketer of the Year
1971, 580
Gibson, A. Lummis, 382
Gibson, C. H., 151
Giffen, George, 41
Gill (Leicestershire), 96
Gilligan, A. E. R., 163–4, 166,
168, 172, 212, 223
Gimblett, Harold, 251, 252, 567
Gissane, Professor William, 171

Gladwin, Cliff, 393
Glover, A. C. S., 61, 70–1, 73–4,
104, 107, 108, 306, 349
Goddard, T. L., 420, 430–1
Goddard, Tom, 228, 259, 299
Godrich, John, 394
Godson, H., 13, 16
Goodway, Cyril, 242, 249, 259, 267,
268, 278, 339, 343, 404, 415, 438,
447, 461, 480, 487, 494, 505, 513,
531–3, 536, 540, 553 ff., 558,
580, 587, 606, 608
Goodwin, F. S., 175
Goodwin, H. J., 99, 108, 140, 142,
175
Goodwin, S. F., 242–3
Gordon, Sir Home, 260
Gover, Alf, 215
Grace, E. M., 15, 31
Grace, W. G., 9, 15, 24, 25, 31,
61, 67, 70, 85, 97, 99, 119, 135,
137, 249, 251, 345, 518
Graham, W. H., 13
Graveney, T. W., 314, 381, 390,
417, 430–1, 437, 443, 477, 500,
550, 597
Greenway, J., 7
Greenwood, F. E., 351–2
Gregory, D., 9
Gregory, S. E., 85, 106, 150, 154,
404
Greig, A., 544, 577, 589
Grice, L. Palmer, 238
Griffin, G. M., 417, 420–1
Griffith, Charles, 445, 478, 566
Griffith, 14
Griffith, S. C., 468, 586
Griffiths, A. C., 236, 242
Grigg, 58
Grimmett, Clarence, 189, 211, 392
Grove, C. W., 242, 243, 247, 259,
260, 268, 278, 279, 285, 286, 291,
297, 298, 302–3, 305, 309 ff.,
313 ff., 318, 325, 330, 332, 333,
337, 348, 349, 353–62, 393,
404, 516; not re-engaged, 353;
involved in 'Affair', 353–61; as
coach, 401
Grundy, J., 7, 8, 47
Gunn, George, 173, 174, 181, 193,
403
Gunn, G. V., 193
Gunn, William, 150

Hackett, Gilbert, 198
Haigh, Schofield, 79, 94, 108
Hain, Peter, 542–3
Hall, Fred, 592
Hall, Wes, 445, 566
Hall, W. E., 297, 311, 318, 319,
335, 362, 370
Hammond, W. R., 184, 195, 199–
200, 206, 211, 214, 255, 258, 259,
260, 301, 309, 386, 408, 430, 509
Hampton, Ted, 353–5, 366, 372,
381, 412
Handford, Peter, 294
Hands, W. C., 118, 134, 143, 303
Harbord, W. E., 214
Harborne, W. H., 22
Harding, Charles, 79
Hardinge, H. W., 167, 181
Hardstaff, Joe, 277, 306
Hardstaff, J. Sen., 108
Hargreave, Sam, 48, 50, 53, 75,
78, 79, 85, 90–1, 92, 94, 97, 99,
104–5, 186, 490
Harkness, Sydney S., 267, 277, 280,
356 n., 382
Harper, Harry, 277, 529, 551
Harris, Lord, 10, 33, 195, 205
Harvey, Neil, 289, 380, 425–6
Hassett, Lindsay, 288–90, 345–6,
493; barracking of, 346–7
Hastilow, B. W., 431
Hastilow, C. A. F., 60, 112, 136,
231, 234, 236, 268, 281, 284, 285,
294–5, 302, 320, 325, 341, 354,
356–7, 360, 365, 367, 371, 375,
381, 406–7, 419, 431, 432, 438–9,
441, 459, 483, 513, 552, 572, 588,
608
Hawke, Hon. M. B. (later Lord),
28, 32, 52, 63, 65, 66, 98, 120,
163, 164
Haycock, Anthony, 480, 536
Hayward, Simpson, 8, 87
Hayward, Tom, 7, 14, 41, 57, 76,
82, 104, 108, 111, 120, 134, 408
Hearne, J. T., 40
Hearne, J. W., 120, 156, 165
Heath, A. H., 13
Heaton, Guy, 236, 341
Heaton, J. P., 178, 186
Hemmings, E., 483, 521, 572
Hendren, E., 163, 168, 184, 214, 221
Hewetson, E. P., 172, 203

Ord, J. S., 190, 232, 233, 247, 268,
282, 285, 287, 296, 299, 304, 308,
312, 314, 316 ff., 323, 329, 333,
348, 350, 373, 404; as deputy
coach, 373
O'Reilly, W. J., 211, 241
Overy, Mrs Hilda, 551

Page (Warwick School), 45
Paine, George, 170, 173, 181, 183,
188, 193, 201, 202, 205, 207, 208,
211–12, 214, 217, 218, 226, 232,
241 ff., 247, 273, 279, 369, 423,
424, 592
Pallett, H. J. (pro), 16, 25, 26, 29,
30 ff., 35, 41, 44–5, 47, 49 ff.,
53, 56, 58, 64–5, 70, 111, 137
Pardon, S. H., 133
Parker, Charlie, 188, 571
Parker, G. W., 163
Parker, Jack, 392
Parkin, Cecil, 164, 569
Parnell, J., 13, 16
Parr, George, 6–7
Parsons, James, 424, 448
Parsons, Canon J. H., 112–13, 118,
119, 130, 132, 136, 139–40,
142 ff., 157–8, 161, 165, 167 ff.,
171 ff., 179 ff., 184, 193, 194,
205, 207, 210, 212–13, 248, 256–
257, 272, 287, 303, 311, 351, 371,
404, 419, 420, 424, 429, 588;
becomes ordained, 182
Parsons, Sir Leonard, 171, 236, 310
Parsons, Michael, 536
Partridge, N. E., 135, 147–9, 151,
156, 170, 172, 181, 185, 210, 236
Payne, A., 6
Payne, George, 250, 261
Paynter, Eddie, 259, 319
Pearson, 14
Peate, E., 24, 134
Peebles, I. A. R., 202
Peel, Bobby, 24, 28, 32, 41, 69
Pegler, S. J., 201
Pellew, C. E., 150
Pepper, Cecil, 258, 259
Pereira, Rev. Edward, 243
Perks, Reg, 207, 213, 247, 251,
318, 361
Peyton, G., 12, 16
Phillips, J. H., 108
Pike, Philip, 496

Pilch, Fuller, 6
Platts, John, 9
Poidevin, Dr L. S., 85–6
Pollock, Peter, 577
Ponsford, W. H., 189, 386
Pope, Fred, 251, 280, 295
Porter, Rev., 16
Porter, John, 456
Pougher, A. D., 56, 133–4
Poulton, W. E., 338–9, 344
Powis, Captain, 13
Preston, J., 13
Price, T. H., 9
Pritchard, Tom, 259, 268, 275, 278,
279, 284 ff., 291, 297, 298, 301,
305, 309 ff., 314, 315, 317, 325,
327, 330, 334, 348, 354, 357, 375,
379, 404, 592
Procter, M. J., 543–4, 596
Professors (professionals), 43–55:
alleged dissatisfaction among, 47;
pay of, 49; coaching by, 49–50;
complaints by, 50
Pugh, Miss Margaret, 281
Pullin, A. W., 94
Pythian-Adams, Henry, 21

Quaife, B. W., 156, 176, 180–1, 323
Quaife, Walter, 35, 38, 41, 44,
49 ff., 54, 57, 60, 61, 66, 68, 70–
71, 73 ff.; selected to play for
England, 73; not re-engaged by
county, 80
Quaife, Willie G., 34–5, 41, 50, 57–
58, 65, 68, 71 ff., 78, 91 ff., 96,
97, 99, 100, 105, 107, 114, 115,
117, 118, 120, 121, 126, 128, 130,
132–3, 142, 144, 145, 147, 151,
153–4, 156, 157, 161, 165, 167,
169, 172 ff., 176–7, 180, 181, 195,
196, 220, 221, 223, 249, 301,
323, 349, 358, 364, 395, 429,
496, 565, 581; ends career with
Warwickshire, 179

Rait Kerr, Colonel R. S., 387
Ramadhin, Sonny, 385 ff., 570
Ranjitsinhji, K. S., 32, 67, 70, 76,
82, 408
Ransford, Vernon, 106, 124, 403
Ratcliffe, D. P., 402
Read, Maurice, 57
Read, Walter, 25, 28, 57

Warwickshire County Cricket Club
—*continued*
   industrial sponsorship for, 558;
   shareholder membership proposed,
   558–9; County Champions, 579–
   581, 591–2; first sponsored
   Championship match played, 588;
   Warwickshire County Cricket
   Supporters' Association football
   pool organised by, 338–44;
   summonses against Supporters'
   Association running football pools,
   437–8; help given to W.C.C.C.
   by Supporters Association, 479–
   481, 497–8; change in Supporters'
   Association football pool, 577–8;
   Supporters' Association social
   club opened, 599
Warwickshire Cricket Association:
   formation of, 536–7; 'Cricket
   Occasion', 552
Warwickshire Old County
   Cricketers' Association: formation
   of, 404–5; match played by, 424
Warwickshire Young Amateurs, 551
Washbrook, Cyril, 209, 252, 260,
   316, 422, 593
Webster, R. V., 436, 441, 443, 452,
   460, 468, 475–6, 478
Weeks, Ray, 309, 312, 314, 315,
   317, 325, 327, 348, 379, 402, 422
Weigall, Gerry, 291
Weldrick, G., 53
Wellings, E. M., 392, 410, 469
Wensley, A. F., 168
Westell, Claude, 219, 261, 268
Weston, Harry, 324
Wheatley, O. S., 390, 400, 409, 410,
   421
Wheeler, E. C., 22, 175, 186
Whitby, H. O., 25
White, G. C. (South Africa), 100
White, J. C., 148, 170
Whitehead, Stephen James, 31, 41,
   44, 47, 50, 56, 58, 66, 93–4
Whitehouse, John, 528, 549, 551,
   565, 584, 590, 595; as Young
   Cricketer of 1971, 565
Whitehouse, P. G., 341
Whittle, A. E., 53, 77
Whysall, W. H., 181
Wilcox, D. M., 275
Wildsmith, J. A. C. D. B., 480, 554

Wilkinson, Col. Howard, 103
Wilkinson, Jack, 448, 496
Williams, J. E., 13, 14, 16
Williams, R., 20
Williams, T., 368
Willis, R. G. D., 576, 582, 584,
   587, 591, 593 ff.; controversy
   regarding registration of, 582–3
Wilmot, K., 190, 229, 243
Wilsher, E., 14
Wilson, J. V., 280, 312, 319, 370,
   371
Wisden, 5, 7, 25 ff., 32, 34, 37, 41,
   42, 44, 52, 53, 56, 65, 66, 69,
   71 ff., 76, 78, 81, 85, 87, 91, 93, 95,
   96, 97, 103, 105, 107, 118, 119 ff.,
   127, 128, 130, 132, 133, 135,
   137 ff., 143, 148, 153, 156, 164 ff.,
   169, 178–9, 186, 188, 190, 206,
   207, 210, 216, 217, 226, 231, 234,
   240, 244, 252, 260, 281, 295 ff.,
   301, 304, 307, 309, 322, 325, 329,
   334, 361, 365, 369, 380, 385, 392,
   395, 397, 400, 409, 416, 417, 418,
   421, 423, 426, 439, 440, 449, 450,
   453, 457, 461, 464, 468, 469, 471,
   474, 478, 485, 486, 495, 510, 511,
   514, 519, 520, 526, 546, 580
Wisden, John, 6–7
Wise, H. C., 7
Wolton, A. V., 296, 298, 308, 309,
   310, 314, 316, 318, 346, 370, 371,
   380, 400, 409, 410, 429–30, 592
Wood, C. J. B., 116
Wood, G. E. C., 149
Woodcock, John, 487
Woodfull, W. M., 189
Woods, S. M. J., 24
Wooller, Wilfred, 332, 365, 596
Woolley, Frank, 108, 118, 120, 124,
   130–1, 163, 164, 167–8, 181, 184,
   185, 193, 220, 254, 255, 426
Woodward, J., 13
Workman, 253
Worrell, Sir Frank, 302–4, 504
Wright, A., 435, 442
Wright, Douglas, 277, 304, 306, 332
Wright, L. G., 104
Wyatt, R. E. S., 60, 146–7, 159–60,
   165, 167, 168, 170, 171, 173, 174,
   179 ff., 187–95, 199, 201, 202,
   205–6, 208, 213 ff., 221, 225,
   226, 228, 229, 231 ff., 240,